Cover Illustration: Shutterstock.com

Interior Illustrations: Art Explosion, Jupiterimages, Shutterstock.com

The brand-name products mentioned in this book are trademarks or service marks of their respective companies. The mention of any product in this book does not constitute an endorsement by the respective proprietors of Publications International, Ltd., nor does it constitute an endorsement by any of these companies that their products should be used in the manner represented in this book.

Louis Weber, CEO
Publications International, Ltd.
8140 Lehigh Avenue
Morton Grove, Illinois 60053

Permission is never granted for commercial purposes.

ISBN-13: 978-1-4508-7145-7
ISBN-10: 1-4508-7145-3

Manufactured in China.

8 7 6 5 4 3 2 1

Library of Congress Control Number: 2013941220

The Book of

Weird and Unusual Trivia

Publications International, Ltd.

Contents

✳ ✳ ✳ ✳

Welcome to *The Book of Weird and Unusual Trivia*. Here you'll find accounts of remarkable people and inexplicable events, fascinating animals and strange coincidences. We'll introduce you to the quirky facts behind some historical events, untangle some myths from the truth behind them, and give you insight into topics that range from ancient Roman graffiti to very odd baseball owners to spooky lighthouses. Some stories will make you laugh, while others might scare you, but all of them will give you a small glimpse into something extraordinary.

Chapter 1

The Natural World

A Fungus Among Us

The world's largest living organism has been growing underground for thousands of years.

❋ ❋ ❋ ❋

State Celebrity

SURE, A BLUE whale can reach lengths of up to 80 feet and can weigh up to 110 tons, but that's small potatoes compared to the *Armillaria ostoyae*. Otherwise known as the Honey Mushroom, the fungus has the honor of being the world's largest living organism.

If you've never heard of this monstrous mushroom, it's probably because it has only recently been discovered. In 1992, researchers in Michigan used DNA techniques to study a fungus that was infecting the state's forests. While above ground one might see various collections of small, honey-colored mushrooms, underground there is a vast network of string-like tendrils, which would invade the tree's root systems. The researchers found that all of the samples they were collecting were actually genetic clones of each other: They had stumbled upon an enormous spreading fungus estimated to be at least 1,500 years old and weigh nearly 100 tons.

The discovery caused a media sensation. The *New York Times* ran a front-page story heralding "the largest and oldest living organism on Earth." The town of Crystal Springs, Michigan, near where the fungus was found, began hosting "Humongous Fungus" festivals. The fungus was even featured as a Michigan tourist attraction on U-Haul moving vans.

A Rival Appears

However, it didn't take long for researchers to find other *Armillaria* to rival Michigan's favorite fungus. In 2000, an *Armillaria* was identified in Oregon's Blue Mountains and is now officially considered the world's largest living thing. Covering an area of over 2,200 acres—an expanse larger than 1,600 football fields—it is estimated to be at least 2,400 years old. Oregon's most recently discovered attraction has a lot of scientists interested in its secrets, but as of yet, there's no festival in its honor.

A Lizard for the Ages

Horned toads may be the official state reptile of Texas, but one has gone well beyond its cold-blooded brethren to secure its own spot in Texas history.

✳ ✳ ✳ ✳

IN 1897, THE cornerstone of the County Courthouse in Eastland was being placed. Among the gathered crowd were County Clerk Ernest Wood and his son, Will, who had a fondness for capturing lizards.

Horned toads, by the way, are lizards, not frogs, and have a rounded body and protrusions around their heads. Some types of horned toads actually squirt blood from the corners of their eyes, something that discourages predators but thrills many young boys.

During the placement of the cornerstone, several items were placed in a hollow in the marble cornerstone. County Clerk Wood got a wild hair and added Will's horned toad.

Is It a Miracle?

Thirty-one years later, more than 3,000 people gathered to see the reopening of that cornerstone to check on the lizard. When the old cornerstone was opened and the dusty and apparently lifeless horned toad was held aloft, it began kicking a leg and looking for breakfast.

Dubbed Old Rip, the horned toad lived another year during which it toured the United States and received a formal audience with President Calvin Coolidge. It was also featured in "Ripley's Believe It or Not," and newsreels showed Rip's warty face across the land. Unfortunately, celebrity status proved to be too much. Old Rip returned home and died of pneumonia. But it was carefully preserved in a tiny velvet-lined coffin in a glass case, becoming a miniature tourist attraction.

Even in death, Old Rip continued its adventures. At one point Rip was kidnapped, and at another, its leg fell off due to rough handling by a visiting politician. Old Rip may have been the inspiration for the Warner Brothers cartoon character "Michigan J. Frog," the tap-dancing, singing frog that comes to life when a building is razed.

Weird Science

In more recent years, science has continued to lead the way in helping society understand its surroundings. Here are a few more examples of those who took giant leaps in logic.

✳ ✳ ✳ ✳

New Radioactive Elements Discovered by the Curie Duo

IN 1896, A physicist named Antoine Henri Becquerel accidentally discovered the phenomenon of radioactivity. No one quite knew what it meant. But two years later, Marie Curie and her husband, Pierre, discovered radium, an element so radioactive that it actually glows in the dark! That same year, they also discovered polonium, naming it after the country where Marie was born—Poland.

Through their experiments, Marie and Pierre Curie began to discover the properties of radiation and new elements. This was quite dangerous, even if they didn't know it. Radioactivity can be harmful, even fatal, after prolonged exposure without proper shielding from its rays. Back then, however, the discovery of radiation was so recent that no one knew it was dangerous, not even the Curies. Their laboratory conditions were considered primitive, even by the standards of the early 1900s. The scientists handled the radioactive substances without protective equipment, often carrying it in their pockets, keeping it next to their bed at night, and holding it with their bare hands! In fact, the original notebooks used by the Curies are so contaminated by radiation that they must be kept in a sealed lead vault at the Bibliothèque Nationale in Paris. They are so dangerous that anyone wishing to view them must sign a waiver releasing the authorities of any liability for exposure to radioactivity. The radium that infects them has a half-life of about 1,600 years, so in the 37th century, they'll be only half as radioactive as they are now. It will be quite some time before they are safe to handle without protective equipment.

In 1903, the Curies, along with Becquerel, won the Nobel Prize in Physics for their research on radiation. Sadly, weakened by his exposure to radiation, Pierre died three years later, at the age of 46, in a traffic accident—it was rumored that he was not strong enough to dodge the vehicle that hit him. Marie went on to receive a second Nobel Prize in Chemistry (for the discovery of radium and polonium) in 1911. She died in 1934 of leukemia—presumably caused by her prolonged exposure to radiation. She was 66.

The Atomic Structure According to Rutherford

You can feel this book in your hands, right? It's made of paper and ink, right? Well, not exactly.

It's made of millions and millions of atoms. Atoms are so tiny they can't be seen with the naked eye, but everything—and that means *everything*—is made up of atoms. The weird thing is that atoms are made up of mostly nothing but empty space. That was proved by a physicist named Ernest Rutherford.

Rutherford was born in New Zealand in 1871. Voracious for scientific knowledge and understanding, he studied and taught at a number of universities around the world, including Cambridge University in England and McGill University in Canada. In 1909, Rutherford discovered that atoms were similar to the solar system, in that they have a nucleus with various particles orbiting around it. With that discovery, however, Rutherford came to believe that most of an atom is just empty space. This disputed the ruling theory at the time, which was that atoms were like "plum pudding." Scientists presumed that an atom had the same consistency throughout except for the electrons positioned like plums within the atom.

When Rutherford bombarded a thin piece of gold foil with alpha particles (a weak type of radiation), a small percentage of the alpha particles scattered at extremely wide angles. The physicist described the result "as if you fired a fifteen-inch shell at a piece of tissue paper and it came back and hit you." The reflected alpha particles were colliding with the previously unknown, positively charged nucleus. His theory was that the atom consisted of a tightly packed nucleus, a lot of empty space, and a few negatively charged particles orbiting around it. Rutherford's theory became the foundation for understanding the nature of the atom and nuclear physics. He died at age 66 in 1937.

Nuclear Fission According to Hahn

They say curiosity killed the cat, but satisfaction brought him back. If you applied that principle to a physicist, what would you get? A Nobel Prize in Chemistry—just what physicist Otto Hahn received in 1944.

When Italian physicist Enrico Fermi created several radioactive elements by bombarding the heaviest natural element, uranium, with neutrons, Hahn paid attention. He wanted to understand how uranium could turn into two or more different elements.

Born in Germany in 1879, Hahn studied chemistry at the University of Marburg. After graduating, he conducted research at several universities before returning to Germany. He discovered several radioactive elements and made many discoveries. Prior to winning the Nobel Prize in 1944, Hahn was nominated in 1914 for discovering a radioactive element called mesothorium 1. His greatest discovery, however, came in 1938.

In collaboration with Lise Meitner and Fritz Strassman, Hahn successfully split the nucleus of a uranium atom and discovered that some of its mass was converted to energy. The rest was divided into two lighter nuclei. The physicists called this process fission. The implications astounded their fellow scientists, who believed that the energy created from splitting a uranium atom could cause a chain reaction that would, in turn, split other uranium atoms. They further theorized that this energy could be harnessed and put to use. This particularly interested the Nazi German government, which forced many scientists to research the theory in an attempt to create a new kind of weapon—an atomic bomb. Hahn is credited with being the "founder of the atomic age." He died in 1968.

Are Bookworms Worms?

Librarians hate these kinds of bookworms.

* * * *

LIBRARIANS WOULD LIKE to banish bookworms from the stacks forever. The literature lovers in question aren't people—they're tiny winged creatures known as book lice or barklice. They resemble flies, not worms, and they don't even like paper. They feed off mold, like in damp, mildewed tomes.

Other bugs, including silverfish and cockroaches, feast on organic substances such as the flour and cornstarch found in old library paste. Wood-boring beetles eat wood, naturally, but will consume paper made of wood pulp, too. Though beetles technically are not worms, they probably inspired the term "bookworm."

Nineteenth-century French book dealer and bibliophile Étienne-Gabriel Peignot reported finding a bookworm that had burrowed clear through a set of twenty-seven volumes, leaving a single hole, like the track of a bullet, in its wake. How far did it go? Given that many old tomes are at least three inches thick, the critter might have traveled nearly seven feet.

The best way to keep bugs out of books is to stop them before they get in. Contemporary librarians strive to maintain clean, dry buildings. Replacing wood shelving with metal discourages beetles. And those signs that say, "Please do not eat in the stacks"? Heed them. A few moldy crumbs can be a bonanza to hungry book lice. Once insects settle in, it's difficult to get rid of them. Sometimes the only effective method is professional fumigation.

Modern construction and bookbinding methods have done a lot to make libraries free of bookworms—free of the six-legged kind, that is. If you're a human bookworm, come right in. Just check your lunch at the door.

Going Batty!

Bats love Texas—and Texans love their bats.

✳   ✳   ✳   ✳

BATS HAVE NEVER been nature's most popular animals. In fact, they give most people the willies. But their reputation as creepy is undeserved: Bats benefit humans and the environment by helping to control pesky insects (especially mosquitos) and pollinating fruit trees.

In Texas, bats also provide entertainment. Several regions throughout the state have become popular tourist attractions where people congregate in the evenings to watch the mammals, which often number in the millions, fly en masse from their dark, dank homes to grab a quick bite of dinner.

A whopping 32 species of bats currently call Texas home, among them the Mexican long-tongued bat and the hairy-legged vampire bat. Fossil skeletal remains also suggest that four other species used to flit about the Texan night sky. Bats congregate in a variety of places, including caves, under bridges, and in abandoned buildings.

Where to Go

In Mason, the Nature Conservancy of Texas opened the Eckert James River Bat Cave Preserve so families could experience the wonder of evening bat emergences. Each summer and early fall, an estimated 4 million female Mexican free-tailed bats visit the cave to give birth and raise their young.

A similar spectacle can be witnessed outside the tiny town of Fredericksburg at the Old Tunnel Wildlife Management Area. The abandoned railroad tunnel there is home to an estimated two or three million bats, which exit the tunnel as a group every evening about an hour before sunset. (A word of advice to visitors: Wear a hat.)

Meanwhile, in the city of Austin, crowds gather nightly to watch nearly 1.5 million Mexican free-tailed bats emerge from under the Congress Avenue Bridge. Across the street, you'll find a sculpture titled *Nightwing*, which honors the bug-munching beasties. A smaller colony of bats can be found about 15 miles north of Austin, beneath the I-35 underpass at McNeil Road, Round Rock.

How Many People Does It Take to Clean Lake Erie?

Lake Erie is the shallowest, the warmest, and unfortunately the most polluted of the Great Lakes. Its illustrious past includes leagues of dead birds, deluges of phosphorus, and the sweet smell of dead fish everywhere.

* * * *

CONSIDERING THE MASSIVE industrial plants that sprung up along rivers throughout Ohio during the 20th century, it should be no surprise that Lake Erie became the polluted mess that it is today. The Detroit, Cuyahoga, Sandusky, and Huron rivers all feed this lake. Industrial waste was dumped into these water sources with abandon. On June 22, 1969, the Cuyahoga River caught fire due to the oil and other pollutants sullying its surface.

The Cesspool at the Center of Debate

In the 1960s and '70s, Lake Erie became the center of the nation's water pollution debate and was referred to as the "Dead Sea of North America." It was also the victim of extreme eutrophication (a process catalyzed by high phosphorus or nitrogen levels that cause increased sediments), decreased filtration of sunlight, and a rapid growth of algae and bacteria that killed off fish and other animal populations. The central basin of the lake was declared a "dead zone" during summer months. Vast amounts of algae grew on the surface (thanks to industrial phosphorus waste), sank to the bottom, and were eaten by bacteria and fungi. These, in turn, used up so much oxygen during this decomposition process that parts of the lake became depleted of oxygen—meaning no fish could survive.

In 1972, Congress passed the Clean Water Act, which set federal guidelines on pollution levels. The Great Lakes Water Quality Agreement of 1972 was struck between Canada and the United States to set guidelines specific to the Great Lakes system. Phosphorus levels were quickly reduced, and some areas of the lakes were reached by sunlight for the first time in decades. By 1995, walleye and bass had returned to once-dead zones. (The wisdom of actually eating these fish, however, remained uncertain.)

Best Efforts

From 1970 to 1989, oxygen in Lake Erie's central basin definitely improved. Yet thanks to relaxed pollution restrictions during the next two decades, the dead zones returned with a vengeance. It was clear the catastrophe was far from over when, in 1999, vast numbers of dead birds and fish glutted Lake Erie's shorelines. The cause: type E botulism, a potent toxin that prevents the transmission of neural impulses. The precise cause is unknown, but its emergence is linked to the various side effects of oxygen degradation in the ecosystem. More than one influx of dead wildlife hit the region, happening again in 2001, 2002, and 2006.

Local communities began cleanup work, and local and state oversight programs were put in place as well. The sheer obviousness of the Lake Erie waste—it can be seen *and* smelled—has inspired Herculean efforts. In its sixth year, the annual Pennsylvania–Lake Erie International Coastal Cleanup project attracted 1,305 volunteers and collected 55,300 items of trash, including 32,004 cigarette butts or cigar tips. But the region remains thoroughly polluted. As for how many Midwesterners it takes to clean up Lake Erie, the only certain answer is that, so far, there has not been enough.

✳ **Ohio is well equipped with rivers: specifically, 44,000 miles of rivers and streams. That's not quite enough to circle the earth twice, but it's close.**

You Say Uranus, I Say George

Its name has been the butt of countless bad jokes, but was the planet Uranus—the dimmest bulb in our solar system and nothing more than a celestial conglomeration of hydrogen, helium, and ice—first known as George?

✳ ✳ ✳ ✳

THERE'S ACTUALLY MORE truth than rumor in this story, but the lines of historical fact and fiction are blurred just enough to make the discovery and naming of the seventh planet fascinating. The heavenly globe that eventually was saddled with the name Uranus had been seen for years before it was given its just rewards. For decades, it was thought to be simply another star and was even cataloged as such under the name 34 Tauri (it was initially detected in the constellation Taurus). Astronomer William Herschel first determined that the circulating specimen was actually a planet. On the evening of March 13, 1791, while scanning the sky for the odd and unusual, Herschel spotted what he first assumed was a comet.

After months of scrutiny, Herschel announced his discovery to a higher power, in this case the Royal Society of London for the Improvement of Natural Knowledge, which agreed that the scientist had indeed plucked a planet out of the night sky. King George III was duly impressed and rewarded Herschel with a tidy bursary to continue his research. To honor his monarch, Herschel named his discovery Georgium Sidus, or George's Star, referred to simply as George. This caused some consternation among Herschel's contemporaries, who felt the planet should be given a more appropriate—and scientific—appellation. It was therefore decided to name the new planet for Uranus, the Greek god of the sky.

Let the mispronunciations begin!

A Question of Cleanliness

Smooch your pooch at your own risk. It's not man's best friend that could kiss and kill.

✳ ✳ ✳ ✳

MOST DOG OWNERS will tell you that their dog's mouth is much cleaner than a human's. In fact, this old wives' tale has been touted so loudly and for so long that most people assume it's true. Most veterinarians, however, disagree. They'll tell you it's a stalemate—both human and canine mouths are rife with bacteria.

One of the biggest reasons people believe the myth is the fact that dogs lick their wounds, and those wounds tend to heal very quickly. But it's not as though a dog's saliva has amazing antibacterial properties. Dogs' cuts and scrapes get better fast because their tongues help get rid of dead tissue and stimulate circulation, which in turn facilitates the healing process.

You Know Where It's Been

If you still think a dog's tongue is more antiseptic than your own, just take a look at what your pet's tongue touches over the course of a day. Dogs use their tongues for eating and drinking, as well as for activities such as bathing and exploring garbage cans and weird dead things in the yard.

A dog bite, like a human bite, can cause infection if it breaks the skin. But the bacteria transmitted in each are fairly species-specific. In other words, a bug that's harmful to humans likely won't be transmitted to your pooch if you give him a big, slobbery kiss on the mouth, and vice versa.

At least your dog's bite isn't as dangerous as that of a Komodo dragon. The mouth of this giant, carnivorous lizard, indigenous to Indonesia, is a veritable petri dish of disgusting bacteria, many of which can cause an agonizing, often fatal infection.

The Bear Truths

Although bearlike in appearance, with their rounded ears, plush fur, and black noses, koalas aren't actual bruins. Pandas, on the other hand, are true to form.

✳ ✳ ✳ ✳

Cute as an Opossum?

THERE ARE FEW animals on Earth cuter than the cuddly koala. They're sometimes called Australia's teddy bears, but koalas are in fact related more closely to the ratlike American opossum than the impressive American grizzly.

Koalas are marsupials, which means they raise their young in special pouches, just like kangaroos, wallabies, and wombats. Their young, called joeys, are about the size of a large jelly bean when born and must make their way through their mother's fur to the protection of the pouch if they are to survive. As a baby grows, it starts making trips outside the pouch, clinging to its mother's stomach or back but returning to the pouch when scared, sleepy, or hungry. When a koala reaches a year old, it's usually large enough to live on its own.

Unlike real bears, koalas spend almost their entire lives roosting in trees, traveling on the ground only to find a new tree to call home. Koalas dine on eucalyptus leaves, of which there are more than 600 varieties in Australia. Eucalyptus leaves are poisonous to most other animals, but koalas have special bacteria in their stomachs that break down dangerous oils.

The Case for Pandas

Until recently, the giant panda was also considered a non-bear. Some scientists believed pandas were more closely related to the raccoon, whereas others speculated that they were in a group all their own. However, when they studied the animals' DNA, scientists were able to confirm that the giant panda is a closer relative to Yogi Bear than it is to Rocky Raccoon.

If These Bones Could Talk

Early in the 20th century, archaeologists searched frantically for the "missing link"—a fossil that would bridge the gap between apes and man. What was found, however, made monkeys out of everyone involved.

✳ ✳ ✳ ✳

Fossil Facts or Fiction?

IN NOVEMBER 1912, a story appeared in the English newspaper *Manchester Guardian*: Skull fragments had been found that could be of the utmost significance. "There seems to be no doubt whatever of its genuineness," wrote the reporter, characterizing the bones as perhaps "the oldest remnant of a human frame yet discovered on this planet." The story generated feverish speculation. On the night of December 18, 1912, a crowd jammed into the meeting of the Geological Society of London to learn about this amazing discovery.

What they heard was that solicitor and amateur archeologist Charles Dawson had discovered two skull fragments and a jawbone from a gravel bed near Piltdown Common in East Sussex. He had been interested in this area ever since workmen, knowing of his archeological interest, had given him some interesting bone fragments from the pit several years before. Dawson had since been making his own excavations of the pit, aided by Arthur Smith Woodward, keeper of the Department of Geology at the British Museum.

The skull fragments were definitely human, but the jawbone was similar to an ape. If they came from the same creature, as Woodward and Dawson both hypothesized, then the two men had discovered the missing evolutionary link between ape and human. Woodward announced, "I therefore propose that the Piltdown specimen be regarded as a new type of genus of the family *Hominidae*."

A Deep Divide

Almost immediately, two distinct camps were formed: doubt-ers and supporters. In Woodward's favor were the facts that the remains were found close together, that they were similar in color and mineralization, and that the teeth were worn down in a flat, human way—unlike those of an ape. Doubters con-tended the jawbone and skull fragments were too dissimilar to be from the same creature. American and French scientists tended to be skeptical, while the British generally accepted the validity of the discovery.

Woodward's side scored valuable points when a canine tooth missing from the Piltdown jaw was discovered in 1913 close to where the jawbone originally had been found. Hard on the heels of that find came another—an elephant bone that had been rendered into some type of tool and supposed to have been used by Piltdown Man.

In 1915, there came perhaps the most conclusive evidence of all: Dawson found the remains of a similar creature a scant two miles away from the site of the first discovery.

Bone Betrayal

So Piltdown Man entered the archaeological record. After Dawson died on August 10, 1916, no significant new Piltdown discoveries were made, but no matter. Even when a few scien-tists identified the jaw as that from an ape, they were ignored.

However, as other fossil discoveries were made in subsequent years, it became evident that something wasn't quite right about Piltdown Man. Things began unraveling in 1949, when a new dating technique called the fluorine absorption test was used on Piltdown Man. The test revealed that both the skull fragments and the jawbone were relatively modern. Finally, in 1953 a group of scientists proved conclusively that Piltdown Man was a hoax. The jawbone had been stained to look old, the teeth filed down, and the bones placed at the site.

Although the identity of the Piltdown Man hoaxer has never been revealed—even Sir Arthur Conan Doyle, author of the Sherlock Holmes series of mysteries, is considered a suspect by some—most suspicion falls on Dawson, who was later found to have been involved in other archeological frauds. Ultimately, it seems that if seeing is believing, then Piltdown Man is proof that people will only see what they want to believe.

Rats! They're ... Everywhere?

Urban folklore would have us believe that we're never farther than a few feet from a rat. The thought is enough to make your skin crawl, but are there really that many rats around us?

✳ ✳ ✳ ✳

Why are rats so reviled? Not everyone hates rats. The Jainist religious sect of south Asia honors all life—even that of a rat. People love their pet rats. Your weird friend (you know which one) even likes wild rats. Of course, that might change when he contracts bubonic plague.

Beyond that, the only creatures that like rats are rat predators. The same animal lover who would feed and care for stray dogs would likely pay an exterminator good money to dispose of stray rats. Wild rats carry diseases and filth, eat unspeakable things, are very difficult to kill, can grow to an enormous size, and run in large packs that could overwhelm any human. To the majority of people, rats are the stuff of nightmares, as Winston Smith finds in George Orwell's *1984*.

So just how close to us are they? Do you spend a lot of time in the alleys of a large city's slums, cuddled up next to a garbage can, drinking in the smell of fermenting everything? Do you often seek shelter in the cool, tranquil comfort of your favorite sewer pipe? Do you spend idle afternoons sifting through that landfill you love so well in search of rare treasures?

If you answered yes to any of these questions, you've been in real close proximity to rats. Then again, if these are your preferred haunts, you know that already. For your safety, you might want to peruse the February 13, 1998, *Morbidity and Mortality Weekly Report*. In it you'll find an article that describes a couple of bona-fide cases of rat-bite fever.

Then we'll just avoid those places. Unfortunately, rats aren't picky about where they live. Some estimates say there is one rat per U.S. resident, which is hard to confirm because vermin don't answer the Census. But suppose there are that many. They'd be concentrated in big cities where there's also a lot of food and places to hide and scurry. Any poorly secured storage of food, either fresh or discarded, will attract them. People living in immaculate suburban mansions probably don't have a homey woodpile or trash heap in their backyards, but that's not to say rats don't roam idyllic family neighborhoods.

What do we do if we encounter a rat? The number of rats reported to health officials in the suburbs has been steadily increasing, and it's now common for municipalities to offer some sort of "rat patrol" to assist citizens in the fight against these critters. Have you heard the horror stories about rats that get into residential toilets after swimming up through sewer pipes? We'd like to say that those are also urban folklore—but they're not.

Is the Red Sea Blue?

How do intensely blue-green waters get identified as red? Read on to find out.

✳   ✳   ✳   ✳

STANDING ON THE shore of the Red Sea, you might wonder how its waters, clearly blue-green, could be so mislabeled with the moniker "Red." Did the person who named this 1,200-mile strip of sea, located between Africa and Asia, suffer from an acute case of colorblindness? No, it's more likely he or she saw the Red Sea while the *Trichodesmium erythraeum* was in full bloom. Before you get all excited, *Trichodesmium erythraeum* is not some kind of wildly exotic orchid indigenous to Egypt. It's simply a type of cyanobacteria, a.k.a. marine algae.

You've seen how an overgrowth of algae can turn your favorite pond or motel pool a murky shade of opaque green, right? In the case of the Red Sea, the alga is rich in a red-colored protein called phycoerythrin. During the occasional bloom, groups of red- and pink-hued *Trichodesmium erythraeum* blanket the surface of the sea. When they die off, they appear to transform the waters from a heavenly shade of blue to a rustier reddish-brown.

While this algae-induced color change is a widely accepted derivation for the Red Sea's name, there is another theory: Some say mariners of antiquity were inspired by the region's mineral-rich red mountain ranges and coral reefs, so they named the body of water *Mare Rostrum* (Latin for "Red Sea"). In 1923, English author E. M. Forster agreed, describing the Red Sea as an "exquisite corridor of tinted mountains and radiant water."

However you choose to color it, one fact still remains: Beneath its ruddy exterior, there lies a deep Red Sea that is true blue.

Freaky Facts: Animals

* Most fish have voices that get deeper with age.

* A cockroach can regrow its wings, legs, and antennae, and can live without a head for up to a week.

* A polar bear's fur is actually transparent rather than white; it merely appears white due to the way it reflects light.

* Mosquito Bay in Puerto Rico is filled with bioluminescent organisms that glow when the water is disturbed.

* Just as humans favor their right or left hand, elephants favor their right or left tusk.

Loud and Clear!

Animals send out messages for very specific reasons, such as to signal danger or for mating rituals. Some of these calls, like the ones that follow, are so loud they can travel through water or bounce off trees for miles to get to their recipient.

✳ ✳ ✳ ✳

1. **Blue Whale**—The call of the mighty blue whale is the loudest on Earth, registering a whopping 188 decibels. (The average rock concert only reaches about 100 decibels.) Male blue whales use their deafening, rumbling call to attract mates hundreds of miles away.

2. **Howler Monkey**—Found in the rain forests of the Americas, this monkey grows to about four feet tall and has a howl that can travel more than two miles.

3. **Elephant**—When an elephant stomps its feet, the vibrations created can travel 20 miles through the ground. They receive messages through their feet, too. Research on African and Indian elephants has identified a message for warning, another for greeting, and another for announcing, "Let's go." These sounds register from 80 to 90 decibels, which is louder than most humans can yell.

4. **North American Bullfrog**—The name comes from the loud, deep bellow that male frogs emit. This call can be heard up to a half mile away, making them seem bigger and more ferocious than they really are. To create this resonating sound used for his mating call, the male frog pumps air back and forth between his lungs and mouth, and across his vocal cords.

5. **Hyena**—If you happen to hear the call of a "laughing" or spotted hyena, we recommend you leave the building. Hyenas make the staccato, high-pitched series of hee-hee-hee sounds (called "giggles" by zoologists) when they're

being threatened, chased, or attacked. This disturbing "laugh" can be heard up to eight miles away.

6. **African Lion**—Perhaps the most recognizable animal call, the roar of a lion is used by males to chase off rivals and exhibit dominance. Female lions roar to protect their cubs and attract the attention of males. Lions have reportedly been heard roaring a whopping five miles away.

7. **Northern Elephant Seal Bull**—Along the coastline of California live strange-looking elephant seals, with huge snouts and big, floppy bodies. When it's time to mate, the males, or "bulls," let out a call similar to an elephant's trumpet. This call, which can be heard for several miles, lets other males—and all the females nearby—know who's in control of the area.

World's Weirdest Sea Creatures

From creatures that look like rocks to fish that make their own light, the sea is filled with things you definitely don't want to encounter while swimming!

✳   ✳   ✳   ✳

Sea Horse

SEA HORSES ARE weird in so many ways. For instance, they travel less than one foot per minute, are monogamous, and have prehensile tails. They do not have teeth or a stomach, and the males are the ones who become pregnant and give birth. Maybe sea horses should have their own reality show!

Deep Sea Anglerfish

Living more than 3,000 feet underwater, deep-sea anglerfish don't see much light. Instead, they create their own. The female grows a bioluminescent "fishing rod" to attract and distract prey. When some species of anglerfish mate, the male uses his mouth to attach himself permanently to the female's body; from that point forward, they share circulatory and reproductive systems.

Cone Shell

The cone shell is a sea snail that slowly and methodically hunts and tracks its prey. When the victim is within range, the cone shell fires a tiny poisonous harpoon at it. After the prey is paralyzed, the cone shell pulls it to its mouth by the thread that attaches the harpoon to its body.

Stonefish

The stonefish bears the dubious honor of being the most poisonous fish in the world. Although treatable if caught in time, its venom can kill a human within hours or at least require the amputation of a limb. Stonefish are found in shallow waters where waders can easily step on the fish's spiny, venomous dorsal fins. To make matters worse, they are nearly impossible to spot, as their camouflage renders them invisible against the ocean floor.

Fallacies & Facts: Snakes

There are any number of myths about these fascinating creatures. Let's find out some of the truths.

✳ ✳ ✳ ✳

Fallacy: You can identify poisonous snakes by their triangular heads.

Fact: Many non-poisonous snakes have triangular heads, and many poisonous snakes don't. You would not enjoy testing this theory on a coral snake, whose head is not triangular. It's not the kind of test you can retake if you flunk. Boa constrictors and some water snakes have triangular heads, but aren't poisonous.

Fallacy: A coral snake is too little to cause much harm.

Fact: Coral snakes are indeed small and lack long viper fangs, but their mouths can open wider than you might imagine—wide enough to grab an ankle or wrist. If they get ahold of you, they can inject an extremely potent venom.

Fallacy: A snake will not cross a hemp rope.

Fact: Snakes couldn't care less about a rope or the material from which it's formed, and they will readily cross not only a rope but a live electrical wire.

Fallacy: Some snakes, including the common garter snake, protect their young by swallowing them temporarily in the face of danger.

Fact: The maternal instinct just isn't that strong for a mother snake. If a snake has another snake in its mouth, the former is the diner and the latter is dinner.

Fallacy: When threatened, a hoop snake will grab its tail with its mouth, form a "hoop" with its body, and roll away. In another version of the myth, the snake forms a hoop in order to chase prey and people!

Fact: There's actually no such thing as a hoop snake. But even if there were, unless the supposed snake were rolling itself downhill, it wouldn't necessarily go any faster than it would with its usual slither.

Fallacy: A snake must be coiled in order to strike.

Fact: A snake can strike at half its length from any stable position. It can also swivel swiftly to bite anything that grabs it— even, on occasion, professional snake handlers. Anyone born with a "must grab snake" gene should consider the dangers.

Fallacy: Snakes do more harm than good.

Fact: How fond are you of rats and mice? Anyone who despises such varmints should love snakes, which dine on rodents and keep their numbers down.

Fallacy: Snakes travel in pairs to protect each other.

Fact: Most snakes are solitary except during breeding season, when (go figure) male snakes follow potential mates closely.

Otherwise, snakes aren't particularly social and are clueless about the buddy system.

Fallacy: The puff adder can kill you with its venom-laced breath.

Fact: "Puff adder" refers to a number of snakes, from a common and dangerous African variety to the less aggressive hog-nosed snakes of North America. You can't defeat any of them with a breath mint, because they aren't in the habit of breathing on people, nor is their breath poisonous.

Can You Grow Your Own Penicillin?

Mold. Ugh! The slimy stuff covering leftovers that have been sitting in the fridge for too long. Who needs it? Well, you do if you want to fend off the occasional invasion of deadly bacteria.

✻   ✻   ✻   ✻

PENICILLIN, ONE OF the world's most powerful antibiotics, is a common form of mold. You've no doubt seen it yourself on bread, potatoes, and other foods. Growing it certainly doesn't take much equipment or skill. Want to try? The British Pharmacological Society recommends the orange method: Pierce a medium-size orange thoroughly with a fork, squeeze it a little to make sure you've gone deep enough to draw out some juice, place it in a shallow dish, and leave it in a cool, dark place at room temperature. After seven to ten days, your orange should sport a fuzzy, bluish-green beard. Penicillin is identified mainly by its color: The blue is *Penicillium italicum*; the green is *Penicillium digitatum*.

Does this mean that applying a piece of moldy fruit to an open wound is a good idea? Could be. For centuries, folk healers employed mold to fight infections. The remedy didn't always work, however, because penicillin spores are elusive little critters. Under natural conditions, it's difficult to find concentrations dense enough to win a face-off with bacteria.

Antibiotic penicillin is derived from a strain called *Penicillium chrysogenum*, which was first isolated in 1943. During World War II, the search for rich sources of penicillin became desperate. Throughout Allied countries, scientists scoured grocery stores for moldy food. Peoria, Illinois, came up with the winner: a rotten cantaloupe that harbored one of the highest concentrations of penicillin ever seen. This "magic cantaloupe" helped the Allies cook up enough penicillin to save the lives of millions of soldiers. It is no exaggeration to say that penicillin did as much to defeat Germany and Japan as bombs.

How exactly does penicillin work its magic? Bacteria multiply via a process known as binary fission. Penicillin contains a substance called beta-lactam that prevents bacteria from reproducing by inhibiting the formation of cytoplasmic membranes, or new cell walls. If they are unable to successfully divide, the bacteria cannot conquer. Cell walls collapse, and the colony rapidly withers away.

Of course, a few individual bacteria will inevitably prove resistant to penicillin, which is why biochemists are always developing alternative antibiotics. If you have a condition that requires frequent antibiotic use, your doctor will probably try to vary the type just to keep those sneaky bacteria on their toes and out of your corpus. Despite this drawback, penicillin remains one of our mightiest medications, providing generations with longer and healthier lives.

Still wondering what to do with of those slimy leftovers? Throw them out. Please! Like your mom said, cleaning out the fridge is a good way to stay healthy, too.

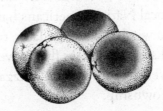

A Festival That's for the Birds

The residents of Hinckley don't know why the buzzards come, but they embrace their arrival every year with a festival.

✳   ✳   ✳   ✳

EVERY MARCH 15, the citizens of Hinckley Township celebrate the seasonal return of the buzzards with a huge festival. It's just like the return of the swallows to Capistrano in San Juan, California—only with more carrion. The event draws buzzard-loving crowds from around the world and includes events such as Buzzard Bingo, live music, crafts, and storytelling.

The buzzards—turkey vultures, to be specific—make their annual reappearance at the Buzzard Roost in Hinckley Reservation. An officially appointed buzzard spotter scans the skies and clocks the arrival of the first bird. A local radio station sometimes hosts a lottery, and the contestant with the closest time to the first buzzard's arrival wins a prize. Once the first one shows up, the fun starts.

Why Hinckley?

No one seems to know why the buzzards show up, though there are several theories. One story suggests that the birds were drawn to the region following the big Hinckley Hunt of 1818, in which a group of men and boys went hunting for food and vermin and returned with more dead critters than they knew what to do with. It was a big mess for the townsfolk, and a big buffet for the buzzards.

Another theory is that the buzzards were drawn to the region in 1808 when the local Native Americans hanged a woman suspected of being a witch. Two years later, trapper William Coggswell reported seeing vultures flying over where the gallows stood. Whatever the case may be, buzzards have been good to Hinckley Township.

Animal Cannibals

Cannibalism, the act of consuming one's own species, is more common in the natural world than you might think. Read on for examples of animals that take a bite out of their own kind.

✳ ✳ ✳ ✳

Rats and Mice—When populations of mice and rats rise rapidly, there's less food to go around. And when this happens, the hungry and stressed survivors sometimes kill and eat their young. What's particularly interesting about rat cannibalism is that a lot of the time, it's the mama rat that does the eating. When a baby rat is sick or deformed, the mother may eat it because she knows it won't survive, and it will give her strength after labor.

Lions—An adult lion that wants to take over a pride will often kill the group's lion cubs. Basically, it's a way to ensure that there's no rivalry between the preexisting cubs and any that he may father. Sometimes the lions will also eat the cubs. An odd side benefit (for the lion, anyway): If her cubs are dead, a lioness will usually go into heat after two or three weeks, allowing the lion to mate with her sooner. Nice way to woo a lady.

Chickens—Chickens will eat a lot of funky stuff—including their own kin. Cannibalism occurs in chickens most often when they are kept in close captivity and mistake pecking their brethren for typical food foraging. It's also been suggested that some laying hens crave more protein and, er, get by with a little help from their friends.

Caterpillars—Before monarch and queen butterflies become beautiful winged creatures, they're less-than-adorable caterpillars that often eat the eggs of their own species. Hey, it takes a lot of energy to turn from a wormy-looking grub into a lovely butterfly, and they need the calories.

Baboons—The males of several primate species practice infanticide. Baboons have been known to kill and eat their young.

Bands of male primates will attack a rival group and drive off any males. Like the lions, they then kill the offspring so they can mate with the females.

Seagulls—Perhaps a response to overcrowding and food scarcity, male gulls often make a lunch (or breakfast or dinner) of gull eggs and hatchlings.

Crows—It's not pretty, but it's effective: Sometimes a crow will eat the eggs and chicks of his rivals to ensure his own successful breeding.

Spiders—If you're going on any dates with a black widow spider in the near future, watch your back: These and other female arachnids are known to kill and eat their mates either before, during, or after intercourse. But why? There are many theories as to why the female does this, including for nourishment or as a biological habit. As to why the males continue to let it happen, that's a mystery.

Mantid—Perhaps the most well-known cannibal in nature is the Chinese mantid, or praying mantis. The female eats her mate immediately after mating. In fact, it has been studied that more than 63 percent of a female mantis's diet is made up of her paramours.

Hippos—Hippos are one of the largest mammals in the world, able to grow 11 feet long and almost 5 feet tall. These animals eat grass for the most part, but there have been cases when, faced with starvation, hippos have committed cannibalism. Considering the average male hippo weighs between 3,500 and 9,920 pounds, that's a big meal.

Sand Gobies—There are a lot of fish in the sea—and some of them eat their own species. The male sand goby tends the eggs, while the female goes off to mate again. If the eggs still haven't hatched after a long breeding season, sometimes the male goby will eat them.

Leave It to Beavers

They toil 365 days a year. If you knock down their work, they rebuild in a matter of hours. They use just about everything they can find to forge their structures. Read on to learn more about these mad builders.

✳ ✳ ✳ ✳

✳ Beavers are the largest rodents in the world after the South American capybara.

✳ Beavers can stay submerged in water for up to 15 minutes. Using their webbed feet for speed and their flat tail as a rudder, they can swim as fast as five mph.

✳ Beavers construct dams in order to deepen shallow waterways. This in turn creates ponds, which is where beavers like to build their lodges.

✳ Their instinct is to stop the movement of water, which is fine for the beavers but an unnatural state of affairs for a stream. Their obsessive focus is a potentially disastrous one in streams that function as part of a community's storm water drainage system.

✳ Beavers are seriously resourceful. Though the majority of dams are made of mud and sticks, beaver dams have been found made of cornstalks, leaves, soybean plants, sand, and gravel. There are even tales of dams built within city limits containing fence posts, lawn furniture, and hobbyhorses—even animal carcasses!

✳ One trapper found a dam made entirely of footwear. A shoe store had closed and the company apparently felt it would be a great idea to dump the leftover shoes into a nearby stream. Though this was clearly a bad idea, the beavers used the shoes to build their dam, which remained stable for years.

Why Aren't There Southern Lights?

There are! We just hear more about their northern counterparts.

✳ ✳ ✳ ✳

THE SOUTHERN LIGHTS are called the "aurora australis," and according to those who've seen them (including famed explorer Captain James Cook, who named the lights in 1773), they are just as bright and alluring as the aurora borealis in the north. We don't hear about them because the viewing area—around the geomagnetic South Pole—is mostly unpopulated.

Northern or southern, the lights are the result of solar storms that emit high-energy particles. These particles travel from the sun as a solar wind until they encounter and interact with the earth's magnetic field. They then energize oxygen atoms in the upper atmosphere, causing light emissions that can appear to us as an arc, a curtain, or a green glow. If these oxygen atoms get really excited, they turn red. There are other atoms in the ionosphere, and they produce different colors when they're titillated by those solar winds. Neutral nitrogen will produce pink lights, and nitrogen radicals glow blue and violet.

Usually, the lights are visible only in latitudes between ninety degrees (at the poles) and thirty degrees. In the north, that includes most of Europe, large parts of Asia, the United States, and Canada. In the south, though, only the southernmost tips of Australia and Africa and the countries of Chile, Argentina, and Uruguay in South America are within that zone.

Blind as a Bat?

Despite the phrase, bats can see. Some have pretty good vision.

✳ ✳ ✳ ✳

TAKE THE MEGACHIROPTERA bat (more commonly known as the Old World fruit bat or flying fox). Members of this

—

tropical suborder are known for their large eyes and excellent nighttime eyesight. Studies have shown that they're able to see things at lower light levels than even humans can. Most Megachiroptera bats rely completely on their vision to find the fruits and flower nectar they like to munch.

Smaller Microchiroptera bats count on their eyesight, too. These insect-eating bats can see obstacles and motion while navigating speedy, long-distance trips. However, like many bat species, mouselike Microchiroptera also receive some extra guidance from a remarkable physiological process known as echolocation. When flying in the dark, these bats emit high-frequency sounds and then use the echoes to determine distance and direction, as well as the size and movement of anything in front of them.

This "biological sonar system" is so refined that it can track the wing beats of a moth or something as fine as a human hair. Neuroethologists (people who study how nervous systems generate natural animal behavior) will tell you that our military doesn't even have sonar that sophisticated.

Bats have been the subject of myth, mystery, and misconception for centuries. Until recently, traditional thinking was that nocturnal bats could see at night but were blind by day. Now scientists at the Max Planck Institute for Brain Research in Frankfurt, Germany, and at The Field Museum of Natural History in Chicago have discovered that Megachiroptera bats have daylight vision, too. Apparently, this vision comes in handy for locating predators and even for socializing. Flying foxes don't sleep all day—they bounce from treetop to treetop for daytime confabs with their batty neighbors.

So there you have it: Bats can see, and they know where they are going. The next time you want to use a creative—though rather impolite—idiom to describe nearsightedness, you'd be more accurate to say "blind as a mole." That small, burrowing mammal has very small eyes and, indeed, very poor vision.

Nature's Nerds: The World's Brainiest Animals

It's notoriously difficult to gauge intelligence, both in humans and animals. Comparing animal IQs is especially tricky, since different species may be wired in completely different ways. But when you look broadly at problem-solving and learning ability, several animal brainiacs do stand out from the crowd.

✳ ✳ ✳ ✳

Great Apes—Scientists generally agree that after humans, the smartest animals are our closest relatives: chimpanzees, gorillas, orangutans, and bonobos (close cousins to the common chimpanzee). All of the great apes can solve puzzles, communicate using sign language and keyboards, and use tools. Chimpanzees even make their own sharpened spears for hunting bush babies, and orangutans can craft hats and roofs out of leaves. One bonobo named Kanzi has developed the language skills of a three-year-old child—and with very little training. Using a computer system, Kanzi can "speak" around 250 words and can understand 3,000 more.

Dolphins and Whales—Dolphins are right up there with apes on the intelligence scale. They come up with clever solutions to complex problems, follow detailed instructions, and learn new information quickly—even by watching television. They also seem to talk to each other, though we don't understand their language. Scientists believe some species use individual "names"—a unique whistle to represent an individual—and that they even refer to other dolphins in "conversation" with each other. Researchers have also observed dolphins using tools. Bottlenose dolphins off the coast of Australia will slip their snouts into sponges to protect themselves from stinging animals and abrasion while foraging for food on the ocean floor. Marine biologists believe whales exhibit similar intelligence levels as well as rich emotional lives.

Elephants—In addition to their famous long memories, elephants appear to establish deep relationships, form detailed mental maps of where their herd members are, and communicate extensively over long distances through low-frequency noises. They also make simple tools, fashioning fans from branches to shoo away flies. Researchers have observed that elephants in a Kenyan national park can even distinguish between local tribes based on smell and clothing. The elephants are fine with one tribe but wary of the other, and for good reason: That tribe sometimes spears elephants.

Parrots—People see intelligence in parrots more readily than in other smart animals because they have the ability to speak human words. But in addition to their famed verbal abilities, the birds really do seem to have significant brain power. The most famous brainy bird, an African gray parrot named Alex, who died in 2007, exhibited many of the intellectual capabilities of a five-year-old. He had only a 150-word vocabulary, but he knew basic addition, subtraction, spelling, and colors, and had mastered such concepts as "same," "different," and "none."

Monkeys—They're not as smart as apes, but monkeys are no intellectual slouches. For example, macaque monkeys can understand basic math and will come up with specific cooing noises to refer to individual objects. Scientists have also trained them to learn new skills by imitating human actions, including using tools to accomplish specific tasks. They have a knack for politics, too, expertly establishing and navigating complex monkey societies.

Dogs—If you're looking for animal brilliance, you might find it right next to you on the couch. Dogs are good at learning tricks, and they also demonstrate incredible problem-solving abilities, an understanding of basic arithmetic, and mastery of navigating complex social relationships. A 2009 study found that the average dog can learn 165 words, which is on par with a two-year-old child.

Lethal Lightning

There are about 25 million lightning strikes per year in the United States, and for every 83,000 flashes, there's one injury. For every 345,000 zaps, there's one death. Here are the states with the most lightning fatalities (between 1959 and 2011).

✳ ✳ ✳ ✳

Florida: 463

Texas: 212

North Carolina: 193

Ohio: 145

Colorado: 141

Tennessee: 140

Louisiana: 139

New York: 138

Pennsylvania: 130

Maryland: 126

✳ In any year in the United States, the odds of being struck by lightning are 1 in 700,000. The odds of being struck in your lifetime are 1 in 3,000.

✳ Ice in a cloud can contribute to the development of lightning. As ice particles swirl around, they collide and cause separation of electrical charges. Positively charged ice crystals rise to the top of the storm cloud, and negatively charged particles drop to the lower parts of the storm cloud. These enormous charge differences can cause lightning.

✳ If your hair stands on end during a storm, it could indicate that positive charges are rising through you toward the negatively charged part of the storm. Get indoors immediately.

* Every year, lightning-detection systems in the United States monitor some 25 million strikes of lightning from clouds to ground during approximately 100,000 thunderstorms. It is estimated that Earth is struck by an average of more than 100 lightning bolts every second.

There's More to Know About Tycho

A golden nose, a dwarf, a pet elk, drunken revelry, and… astronomy? Read about the wild life of this groundbreaking astronomer.

* * * *

Look to the Stars

TYCHO BRAHE WAS a Dutch nobleman who is best remembered for blazing a trail in astronomy in an era before the invention of the telescope. Through tireless observation and study, Brahe became one of the first astronomers to fully understand the exact motions of the planets, thereby laying the groundwork for future generations of star gazers.

In 1560, Brahe, then a 13-year-old law student, witnessed a partial eclipse of the sun. He reportedly was so moved by the event that he bought a set of astronomical tools and a copy of Ptolemy's legendary astronomical treatise, *Almagest,* and began a life-long career studying the stars. Where Brahe would differ from his forbears in this field of study was that he believed that new discoveries in the field of astronomy could be made, not by guesswork and conjecture, but rather by rigorous and repetitious studies. His work would include many publications and even the discovery of a supernova now known as SN 1572.

Hven, Sweet Hven

As his career as an astronomer blossomed, Brahe became one of the most widely renowned astronomers in all of Europe. In fact, he was so acclaimed that when King Frederick II of

Denmark heard of Brahe's plans to move to the Swiss city of Basle, the King offered him his own island, Hven, located in the Danish Sound.

Once there, Brahe built his own observatory known as Uraniborg and ruled the island as if it were his own personal kingdom. This meant that his tenants were often forced to supply their ruler (in this case Brahe) with goods and services or be locked up in the island's prison. At one point Brahe imprisoned an entire family—contrary to Danish law.

Did We Mention That He Was Completely Nutty?

While he is famous for his work in astronomy, Brahe is more infamous for his colorful lifestyle. At age 20, he lost part of his nose in an alcohol-fueled duel (reportedly using rapiers while in the dark) that ensued after a Christmas party. Portraits of Brahe show him wearing a replacement nose possibly made of gold and silver and held in place by an adhesive. Upon the exhumation of his body in 1901, green rings discovered around the nasal cavity of Brahe's skull have also led some scholars to speculate that the nose may actually have been made of copper.

While there was a considerable amount of groundbreaking astronomical research done on Hven, Brahe also spent his time hosting legendarily drunken parties. Such parties often featured a colorful cast of characters including a Little Person named Jepp who dwelled under Brahe's dining table and functioned as something of a court jester; it is speculated that Brahe believed that Jepp was clairvoyant. Brahe also kept a tame pet elk, which stumbled to its death after falling down a flight of stairs—the animal had gotten drunk on beer at the home of a nobleman.

Brahe also garnered additional notoriety for marrying a woman from the lower classes. Such a union was considered shameful for a nobleman such as Brahe, and he was ostracized because of the marriage. Thusly all of his eight children were considered illegitimate.

However, the most lurid story of all is the legend that Brahe died from a complication to his bladder caused by not urinating, out of politeness, at a friend's dinner party where prodigious amounts of wine were consumed.

The tale lives on, but it should be pointed out that recent research suggests this version of Brahe's demise could be apocryphal: He may have died of mercury poisoning from his own fake nose.

These Animals Are Wild!

Talk a walk on the wild side with these unpredictable creatures. These animals definitely don't want to fit in with the plans that humans might have for them!

✳ ✳ ✳ ✳

1. Mooo!—The lure of Nashua, New Hampshire, proved to be too much for two Massachusetts cows. In June 2009, the animals wandered away from their farm and walked five miles across the state line. One cow was captured after it got stuck up to its neck in mud. The other, it seems, made it to greener pastures.

2. Dolphin Dilemma—If there's one thing New Jersey is famous for, it's dolphins. Well, at least for a little while in 2009 when a few dolphins found their way into the Shrewsbury River, searching for food. After the water froze, the good people of New Jersey feared the worst, but witnesses at a seafood restaurant later claimed they saw our flippered friends headed into the open waters of Sandy Hook Bay, apparently none the worse for wear.

3. Grin and "Bear" It—The sedate atmosphere of a Denver suburb was broken in October 2009 when a bear cub found itself trapped inside a car. There was no word on how the bear made its way into the vehicle. Rather than eat his rescuers, the cub simply ran from the car once an officer (who presumably drew the short straw) opened the door.

4. Oh Deer!—A Winston-Salem deli must have some of the best sandwiches in town. Why else would a pet deer break free from its owner (who happened to be taking the animal for a walk), crash through the eatery's window, and run through the establishment? As for the question of why a person would have a deer for a pet in the first place, we don't have an answer.

5. Eat Me—An Angus steer was none too happy to learn that it was on the menu. When the 1,000-pound animal arrived at a suburban Cincinnati meat-packing business, it spotted an open gate and made a mad dash for freedom. A market spokesman was quoted as saying, "It's not a mean animal . . . it's running, not even knowing where it's headed."

6. What About the Butter?—When you're stuck in a tank at the supermarket, what else are you going to do but plot your escape? In 2007, a group of lobsters took advantage of a loose lid to depart their cages and exit the store via the front door, where they were later apprehended.

7. Last Call for Alcohol—Dogs just don't know when to say when. Case in point: In 2008, a pooch was taken to the vet reeking of booze and unable to stand. Seems the hound ate a pound of yeast dough, which then fermented in the animal's tummy.

8. Bad Dog—So what's a dog that's chasing a car going to do when it catches the vehicle? Why, rip off the bumper with its teeth, of course! That's what two pit bulls did in October 2009 in Arkansas, when a resident called police to report that the pups were attacking her parked car. Part of the vehicle's bumper and fender were torn off by the pooches before they fled the scene.

9. Gobble Gobble BITE—After years of being the main course, turkeys in Davis, California, seem to have mounted a counterattack. Sort of. A pack of wild turkeys—the kind of ne'er-do-wells who hang out in cemeteries—began attacks on residents in 2007. The three-foot-tall birds were especially fond of bicyclists.

Do You Hear Something?

People who lived just a few miles from Gettysburg did not hear the Civil War battle, but people 50 miles away heard it clearly— due to an unusual phenomenon called acoustic shadow.

✳ ✳ ✳ ✳

THE CIVIL WAR may have taken place in the 19th century, but Winston Churchill once referred to it as "the first 20th century war." Once the ironclad battleships began firing on each other, navies full of wooden ships became obsolete.

But the generals of the Civil War still lacked things like airplanes that 20th century generals would use for reconnaissance, and both generals and scouts had to rely instead on their eyes and ears to get a sense of where the other armies were and what was happening around them. Generals would sometimes send in reinforcements to areas where the sounds of battle seemed to be the "hottest," and wouldn't think to send troops into areas where they could see or hear no sign of battle.

But using your eyes and ears wasn't always totally reliable— wind could blow sound waves around causing all sorts of strange things to happen to the sounds as they echoed through the battlefield. As early as the 1600s, scientists and observers had noted that sounds of naval battles could be heard in some places, but not in others that were the same distance away—or, in some cases, even closer.

During the Battle of Gettysburg, for instance, many people who lived close enough to the battle to see the flash of the cannons couldn't hear a thing, but people in Pittsburgh, more than 150 miles away, could hear the sound of the battle clearly! This phenomonan is known as an "acoustic shadow," and the bizarre ways that sounds of battles can travel, or not travel, over large areas of terrain created some confusion for generals during the Civil War.

This strange quirk of acoustics is usually caused by high winds carrying sounds to distant areas, but lots of factors in the environment can affect the way sound travels. Trees, hills, and other features of the terrain can absorb sounds close to their source, but winds and changes in temperature, which can actually bend the very sound waves themselves, can carry the noises to places quite far from the source, away from the features that would absorb them.

There were times when these "shadows" contributed to battle-field decisions and influenced the outcome of the war. At the Battle of Luka in 1862, Union Brigadier General William Rosencrans's army was attacked and scarcely able to hold off the confederates. It was a narrow victory for the union, but it should have been an easy one; the southern army would have been crushed if union Major General Edward Ord had sent in reinforcements from his own army, which was only four miles away. Ord's men were close enough to see the smoke from the battle, but, being upwind, Ord heard no sounds, and assumed that the smoke was simply Rosencrans and his men's campfires, not the result of a major battle. People further away might have heard the sounds better than Ord himself did.

But the strange quirks of how sound travels would sometimes work in the Union's favor, as well. At the Battle of Five Forks in April, 1865, as the war was drawing to a close, Confederate Major Generals George Pickett and Fitzhugh Lee were away from their posts to attend a "shad bake" and couldn't hear a thing when their men were attacked by the Union Army barely a mile away. The pine trees between them and the army absorbed the sound, so that even though people further away were allegedly able to hear the sounds, they didn't realize what was happening. Since they didn't have any inkling that they needed to call for reinforcements or help, their armies were decimated, and the resounding defeat was a major factor leading to the collapse of General Lee's army only days later, which was effectively the end of the war.

Though modern technology has made it easier to tell when and where battles are happing, acoustic shadows continued to be observed during later wars, as well. During the course of World War I, English civilians noted that they could hear the sounds of battle in France during the summer months, while German civilians heard distant rumbles from France in the winter, due to the ways that the temperature bent the sound waves.

Sudden Impact

We've all seen movies where an Earth-bound mass of rock from space is set to cause some major havoc. Complete fiction, right? Maybe not. Earth has been invaded by asteroids and comets in the past.

✳   ✳   ✳   ✳

IMPACT CRATERS ARE found on most of the planets, satellites, and even asteroids in our solar system—at least those with a surface hard enough to bear a mark. Impact craters are most often caused by one of two culprits: asteroids, which are space bodies that usually reside between the orbits of Jupiter and Mars, or comets, which are masses of gas, dust, and debris. Asteroids and comets are not always well behaved, and wayward ones can—and have—struck Earth.

Time to Duck and Cover?

An impact on Earth isn't as likely as it may sound. For starters, the comet or asteroid has to come close enough to Earth—all the way from Jupiter—to be affected by our planet's gravitational pull. And the body has to be large enough to go through our atmosphere and not burn up before it strikes the surface.

However, in our planet's history, some very large impacting bodies *have* managed to get through. More than 150 impact craters have been identified on Earth, some on the surface and some hidden below the surface. The oldest—at around two billion years old—and largest is the approximately 186-mile-wide Vredefort Dome in South Africa; four other craterlike features on Earth may be older, but they are too eroded to verify dates. The 1.8-billion-year-old, 18-mile-wide Sudbury crater in Ontario, Canada, ranks as another biggie. It's also one of the most profitable—the metals from the 6- to 12-mile-wide asteroid that caused the crater brought a mother lode of nickel, copper, and platinum, making Sudbury a metal haven.

Where Have All the Dinos Gone?

One of the more interesting terrestrial impact craters is believed to have precipitated the demise of the dinosaurs some 65 million years ago. The 105-mile-wide Chicxulub crater in Yucatán Peninsula, Mexico—an impact crater identified by geologists in 1992—is thought to be associated, or at least partially associated, with the extinction of the dinosaurs. A 6- to 12-mile-wide asteroid fell approximately 64.98 million years ago, throwing enough material into the atmosphere to create climate changes around the world. It may not have been the only asteroid—but for now, Chicxulub is the only identified impact crater that is close enough in size and age to have created such chaos.

That Was a Close One!

More recently, we've had some near-misses. On June 30, 1908, a huge explosion was recorded in the northern Siberian region of Tunguska, with theories ranging from a crashing UFO to a mini-black hole. Eventually, scientists realized a stony asteroid had vaporized just above Earth's surface; the shock wave affected a 320-square-mile area. There was no crater, but trees were stripped of their branches and knocked down like toothpicks. More than half the area was incinerated from the blast.

Even more recently, after the U.S. government allowed some of their classified military satellite data to be released, many explosions were identified in the upper atmosphere. These bursts may have been smaller asteroids or comets that actually made it to Earth and burned up in the atmosphere. Either that, or they were larger ones that, luckily, dropped harmlessly into the oceans.

How Well Do You Understand Sharks?

They look frightening and strike fear into the hearts of nearly everyone who dips their toes into the ocean. Unfortunately, sharks are still one of the most misunderstood creatures on Earth. Do you know which rumors are true and which aren't?

✳   ✳   ✳   ✳

Sharks are vicious man-eaters. False! People are not even on their preferred-food list. Every hunt poses a risk of injury to sharks, so they need to make every meal count. That's why they go for animals with a lot of high-calorie fat and blubber—they get more energy for less effort. Humans are usually too lean and bony to be worth the risk.

Sharks are loners. That depends on the shark. Some species, such as the great white, are only rarely seen in the company of other sharks.

However, many other species aren't so antisocial. Blacktip reef sharks hunt in packs, working together to drive fish out of coral beds so every shark in the group gets a meal. Near Cocos Island off Costa Rica, hammerheads have been filmed cruising around in schools that consist of hundreds of sharks.

You have a greater chance of being killed by a falling coconut than by a shark. True! Falling coconuts kill close to 150 people every year. In comparison, sharks kill only five people per year on average. The International Shark Attack File estimates that the odds of a person being killed by a shark are approximately 1 in 264 million.

Sharks have poor vision, and most attacks are cases of mistaken identity. As popular as this belief is, it's wrong. Scientists have observed that sharks' behavior when they are hunting differs significantly from what most people report when a bite occurs. Sharks are extremely curious creatures and, since they don't have hands, they frequently explore their environment with the only things they have available—their mouths. Unfortunately for humans, a curious shark can do a lot of damage with a "test" nibble, especially if it's a big shark.

Most shark attacks are not fatal. True! There are about 60 shark attacks around the world each year, and, on average, just 1 percent of those are fatal. What we usually call "attacks" are only bites. Scientists report that an inquisitive shark that bites a surfboard (or an unlucky swimmer) shows far less agression than when it is on the hunt and attacks fiercely and repeatedly.

Most shark attacks occur in water less than six feet deep. True! And the reason is obvious—that's where the majority of people are. It makes sense that most of the interactions between humans and sharks happen where the concentration of people is at its greatest.

Shark cartilage is an effective treatment for cancer. False! Anyone toting the benefits of shark cartilage as a nutritional supplement to cure cancer is selling snake oil. Multiple studies by Johns Hopkins University and other institutions have shown that shark cartilage has no benefit. This myth got started with the popular but incorrect notion that sharks don't get cancer.

Sharks have to swim constantly or they drown. There are a few species that need to keep moving, but most sharks can still get oxygen when they're "motionless." They just open their mouths to draw water in and over their gills.

Most sharks present no threat to humans. True! There are more than 400 species of sharks, and approximately 80 percent of them are completely harmless to people. In fact, only four species are responsible for nearly 85 percent of unprovoked attacks: bull sharks, great white sharks, tiger sharks, and great hammerhead sharks.

Don't Let the Bedbug Bite

Good night, sleep tight. Don't let the bedbugs bite! For decades, bedbugs were all but extinct in many places. But recently, increased travel and less-toxic modern pesticides have allowed a resurgence of these creepy crawlies.

✳   ✳   ✳   ✳

✳ When full of blood, bedbugs can swell as large as three times their normal size.

✳ A female bedbug can lay up to five eggs per day and 200–500 eggs in her lifetime.

✳ When bedbugs bite, proteins in their saliva prevent the wound from closing.

✳ Bedbugs can consume as much as six times their weight in blood at one feeding.

✳ It takes a bedbug five minutes to drink its fill of blood.

✳ Normally, a bedbug is brown. After eating, however, its body appears dark red.

* Bedbugs are nocturnal—they become active when humans are sleeping.

* Bedbugs only eat once every seven to ten days.

* Bedbugs migrated from Europe to the United States during the 1600s.

* Contrary to popular belief, the presence of bedbugs does not indicate a dirty house.

Do Birds Get Tired in Flight?

Flying uses up a lot of energy. How do birds keep on truckin'?

✳   ✳   ✳   ✳

FLIGHT—ESPECIALLY MIGRATION—CAN BE an exhausting experience for any bird. Reducing the amount of energy that is spent in the air is the primary purpose of a bird's body structure and flight patterns. Even so, migrating thousands of miles twice a year takes its toll on a bird's body, causing some to lose up to 25 percent of their body weight. How do they do it?

Large birds cut energy costs by soaring on thermal air currents that serve to both propel them and keep them aloft, which minimizes the number of times the beasts have to flap their wings. The concept is similar to a moving walkway at an airport: The movement of the current aids birds in making a long voyage faster while expending less energy.

Smaller birds lack the wingspans to take advantage of these currents, but there are other ways for them to avoid fatigue. The thrush, for instance, has thin, pointed wings that are designed to take it great distances while cutting down on the energy expended by flapping. Such small birds also have light, hollow bone structures that keep their body weights low.

If you've ever seen a gaggle of migrating geese, you likely noticed the distinctive V-formation that they take in flight.

They do this to save energy. The foremost goose takes the brunt of the wind resistance, while the geese behind it in the lines travel in the comparatively calm air of the leader's wake. Over the course of a migration, these birds rotate in and out of the leader position, thereby dispersing the stress and exhaustion.

While large birds routinely migrate across oceans, smaller birds tend to keep their flight paths over land—they avoid large bodies of water, mountain ranges, and deserts. This enables them to make the occasional pit stop.

Perhaps the most amazing avian adaptation is the ability to take short in-flight naps. A bird accomplishes this by means of unilateral eye closure, which allows it to rest half of its brain while the other half remains conscious. In 2006, a study of Swainson's Thrush—a species native to Canada and some parts of the United States—showed that the birds took hundreds of in-flight naps a day. Each snooze lasted no more than a few seconds, but in total, they provided the necessary rest.

How sweet is that? After all, who among us wouldn't want to take naps at work while still appearing productive?

Beast of Burden

The amazingly adaptable camel can plod through the desert for a week without fluids—but don't attribute this water-conservation ability to that big hump.

✳   ✳   ✳   ✳

WITH AN UNWIELDY body that defies its life's mission and a disposition that often has it spitting at its owner, a camel's value as a "desert horse" seems questionable. Then there's that oversized hump, or humps in the case of the Bactrian camel. Hideous so far as aesthetics go, this natural canteen is the camel's true claim to fame. Because of it, the ungainly beast can travel with impunity in temperatures hot enough to fry an egg or kill a person. Or so many people believe.

In truth, this assertion is all wet. A camel does not store water in its hump. That bulge is composed primarily of fatty tissue that, when metabolized, serves as a source of energy. When this energy supply runs low because of a lack of nourishment, the hump shrinks considerably, sometimes to the point of flopping over to one side. On a healthy camel, however, the hump can weigh as much as 80 pounds.

A camel has a unique way of carrying and storing water—through its bloodstream. For this reason, it can go as many as eight days without a drink and can lose as much as 40 percent of its body weight before it feels ill effects. The amount it drinks when water is available—as much as 21 gallons in about ten minutes—would cause severe problems in most animals. What's more, a camel isn't too particular about the water it drinks. A muddy puddle that another animal might wrinkle its nose at would be slurped dry by a thirsty camel.

Who Lives at the North Pole Besides Santa and His Elves?

The population at the North Pole is as transient as the terrain itself, which is in a constant state of flux due to shifting and melting ice.

✳ ✳ ✳ ✳

HUMAN LIFE IN this frigid region consists of researchers floating on makeshift stations and tourists who aren't the sit-on-a-beach-in-the-Bahamas type. There are no permanent residents at the North Pole. When you're talking about the North Pole, you're referring to four different locales: geographic, magnetic, geomagnetic, and the pole of inaccessibility. The geographic North Pole, known as true north or ninety degrees north, is where all longitudinal lines converge. It sits roughly four hundred fifty miles north of Greenland, in the center of the Arctic Ocean. The magnetic pole—the point marker for compasses—is located about one hundred miles south of the geographic pole, northwest of the Queen Elizabeth Islands, which are part of northern Canada. Its position moves about twenty-five miles annually. In fact, the magnetic pole has drifted hundreds of miles from its point of discovery in 1831. Then there's the North Geomagnetic Pole, the northern end of the axis of the magnetosphere, the geomagnetic field that surrounds the earth and extends into space. Last is the Northern Pole of Inaccessibility, the point in the Arctic Ocean that is most distant from any landmass.

If the North Pole were more like its counterpart the South Pole, it would be a lot more accessible. Since the South Pole is located on a continent, Antarctica, permanent settlements can be established. In fact, research stations at the South Pole have been in place since 1956. These bases range in population size, but most average fifteen personnel in winter (April to November) and one hundred fifty in summer (December to March). Combined, the stations house a few thousand people in the summer. The U.S. McMurdo Station alone might exceed a thousand individuals at the peak time of year.

All of this helps explain why Santa chose to live at the North Pole rather than the South Pole. If you're S. Claus and you don't want to be found, there isn't a better place than the North Pole to set up shop, even if that shop is always in danger of floating away.

Pearls of Wisdom

Is it true that oysters produce pretty pearls? The answer isn't quite so black and white, round or smooth, say biologists.

✳ ✳ ✳ ✳

PEARLS DO COME from oysters, which are members of the mollusk family, but not all types of oysters produce pearls. This is especially true of the kind we eat, so don't expect a pretty white surprise the next time you're enjoying oysters on the half shell at your favorite raw bar. Nor are oysters the only mollusks that produce pearls. Clams and mussels are also known to generate the coveted orbs.

Oysters are bivalves, which means their shell is made of two parts held together by an elastic ligament. An organ called a mantle manufactures the oyster's shell, which is lined with a substance called nacre—a beautiful iridescent material made of minerals derived from the oyster's food. Pearls are produced when a foreign substance, such as a grain of sand, becomes embedded in the shell and irritates the mantle. To reduce the irritation, the mantle covers the substance with layer upon layer of nacre. Over time, this creates a pearl.

Natural pearls are most prized, but because of the way they're produced, they're not the most common variety. To meet consumer demand, most pearls used in jewelry are cultivated— which involves making a tiny cut in an oyster's mantle and inserting an irritant. The oyster does the rest of the work.

Another common myth about oysters is that it's safe to eat them only in months that contain the letter "r"—September through April. It is thought that oysters harvested in the remaining four months are more likely to carry harmful bacteria, which could cause food poisoning. According to the Centers for Disease Control and Prevention, however, oyster-related bacterial illnesses occur year round.

What Happens to an Astronaut's Body in Outer Space?

Cruising around on the surface of the moon may look like good, clean fun, but space travel is no picnic for the human body.

✳   ✳   ✳   ✳

ASTRONAUTS' BODIES ENDURE some crazy changes in the celestial firmament, and it takes awhile for them to recover once they're back on solid ground. What's the problem? In a word, weightlessness. And the most immediate consequence of the zero-G lifestyle is something that astronauts call space adaptation syndrome. It occurs because the structure of the inner ear that gives you your sense of balance is acclimated to the constant force of gravity; when that force disappears, your inner ear tells you that you're perpetually falling forward. This typically causes nausea, vomiting, dizziness, and disorientation.

There are other, more serious consequences from leaving Earth, and they have to do with gravity's effect on the rest of the body. Here on Earth, we spend our entire lives within the planet's gravitational field. Even when we're not trying to leap over a puddle or pull off a Superman dunk, the force of gravity is constantly compressing our bodies—and, importantly, our bodies are fighting back.

To understand how your body is forever fighting gravity, just think of your circulatory system. The force of gravity tries to pull your blood supply down into your lower extremities; your heart meanwhile works hard against gravity to keep the blood flowing into your upper body, too. If you were to leave Earth's gravitational field, your heart would be working too hard at forcing the blood upwards, causing your face to swell and leading to nasal congestion and bulging eyes. But eventually, your body would adjust to its new environment; your heart would pump less intensely and your blood pressure would lower.

And without the force of gravity, your muscles atrophy—they get smaller and weaker. Hardest hit are postural muscles like your hamstrings and back muscles, the ones that fight against gravity to keep you standing tall. But all of your muscles begin to wither, as it requires less effort to make any movement. Even your heart is affected, in part because of your lowered blood pressure. As a perk, your intervertebral discs—essentially shock absorbers for the spine—expand, making you two to three inches taller. But even this height enhancement can be painful.

The biggest problem is the effect of weightlessness on the bones. In order to stay strong enough to meet the demands of daily living, your bones constantly regenerate themselves in accordance with the level of strain that they experience. For example, if you lift weights regularly, your bones will grow stronger and more calcium-fortified.

In space, however, the reduced level of stress causes bones to weaken and lose their mass. Studies on astronauts working in Skylab in the 1970s showed a 0.3 percent loss of bone mass during each month of weightlessness.

Due to all of these physical changes, astronauts are in pretty bad shape when they get back home. Their lowered blood pressure can lead to fainting. (To alleviate this problem, they sometimes wear special suits that compress the legs and feet, forcing more blood to the torso and head.) Their sense of balance is out of whack for about a week, making it hard for them to remain steady on their feet. And they're very weak because of the muscle degeneration; it can take months to fully regain lost muscle mass. Bone regeneration can take years, and extended missions—like a three-year Mars trip—would cause permanent bone damage.

It's a lot of wear and tear for the opportunity to hit a golf ball on the moon. Rocketing into space doesn't sound quite as cool anymore, does it?

The Impossible 'Possum

Let's face it: Opossums are weird. But here are some interesting facts that might change your mind about the unique opossum.

✳ ✳ ✳ ✳

✳ Opossums are the only marsupial (i.e., a mammal that carries its young in a pouch) found in North America.

✳ The word "opossum" comes from the Algonquin word *apasum*, meaning "white animal." Captain John Smith used "opossum" around 1612, when he described it as a cross between a pig, a cat, and a rat.

✳ Although it is often colloquially called the " 'possum," the opossum is completely different from a possum, an Australian marsupial.

✳ The opossum's nickname is "the living fossil," as it dates back to the dinosaurs and the Cretaceous Period, 70 million years ago. It is the oldest surviving mammal family on Earth.

✳ When cornered, opossums vocalize ferociously and show all 50 of their teeth, which they have more of than any other mammal. But they are lovers, not fighters, and prefer to run from danger.

✳ If trapped, they will "play 'possum," an involuntary response in which their bodies go rigid, and they fall to the ground in a state of shock. Their breathing slows, they drool a bit, and they release smelly green liquid from their anal sacs. This is enough to convince most predators the opossum is already dead, leaving it alone.

✳ Despite their predilection for eating anything—including rotting flesh—opossums are fastidious about hygiene. They bathe themselves frequently, including several times during each meal.

* Opossums are extremely resistant to most forms of disease and toxins, including rabies and snake venom, the latter probably due to their low metabolism.

* The idea that opossums mate through the female's nostrils is a myth. Although the male opossum has a forked (bifid) penis, he mates with the female in the normal manner. Conveniently, she has two uteri, so he deposits sperm into both of them at once.

The Mysterious Blue Hole

State Route 269 hides a roadside attraction of dubious depth and mysterious origin, a supposedly bottomless pool of water that locals simply call the "Blue Hole."

* * * *

EVERY STATE HAS its tourist traps and bizarre little roadside attractions that are just intriguing enough to pull the car over to see. Back in the day, no roadside attraction brought in the Ohio travelers more than a bottomless pond filled with blue water: the mysterious Blue Hole of Castalia.

The Blue Hole's Origins

The Blue Hole is believed to have formed around 1820, when a dam burst and spilled water into a nearby hole. The ground surrounding Castalia is filled with limestone, which does not absorb groundwater well. The water quickly erodes the limestone, forming cave-ins and sinkholes. It wouldn't be until the late 1870s, however, that most people were made aware of the Blue Hole's existence; the hole was in a very isolated location in the woods. Once the Cold Creek Trout Club opened up nearby, however, its members began taking boat trips out to see the hole, and people all over the area were talking about the mysterious Blue Hole hiding out in Castalia. In 1914, a cave-in resulted in the Blue Hole growing to its current size of almost 75 feet in diameter.

Stop and See the Mystery

The owners of the property where the Blue Hole is situated began promoting it as a tourist stop beginning in the 1920s. It didn't hurt that the entrance to the Blue Hole property was along State Route 269, the same road that people took to get to Cedar Point amusement park. It is estimated that, at the height of its popularity, close to 165,000 people a year came out to take a peek at the Blue Hole.

The Blue Hole was promoted as being bottomless. Other strange stories were often played up as well, including the fact that the water temperature remained at 48 degrees Fahrenheit year-round. Tour guides would point out that regardless of periods of extreme rainfall or even droughtlike conditions, the Blue Hole's water level remained the same throughout.

So What's Up with This Hole, Anyway?

Despite the outlandish claims and theories surrounding the Blue Hole and its origins, the facts themselves are rather mundane. The Blue Hole is really nothing more than a freshwater pond. It isn't even bottomless. Sure, the bright blue surface of the water does indeed make the hole appear infinitely deep, but in fact, it's really only about 45 feet to the bottom even at its deepest parts.

The blue color of the water is from an extremely high concentration of several elements, including lime, iron, and magnesium. That's the main reason there are no fish in the Blue Hole; they just can't survive with all that stuff in the water.

One Hole or Two?

During the 1990s, the owners of the Blue Hole fell on hard times, forcing them to close the attraction. Families who would show up at the front entrance were forced to stare sadly through a locked gate at the small trail into the woods. That is until several years ago, when the nearby Castalia State Fish Hatchery began clearing land to expand its hatchery. Lo and behold, workers uncovered a second Blue Hole.

Just how this second Blue Hole came to be is still unknown, although the popular belief is that both holes are fed by the same underground water supply. None of that seems to matter to the Blue Hole faithful—they're just thankful to be able to take a gander at a Blue Hole again.

Freaky Facts: Crazy Critters

✳ Through balloonlike air sacs in its mouth, the African bullfrog can make a bellowing sound that can be heard as far as a half mile away.

✳ The 6.5-inch-long, deep-sea creature known as the dragonfish has long, fanglike upper and lower teeth. It also swims with its own attached fishing line, known as a "barbel," hanging from its chin to catch small fish and haul them straight up to its gaping mouth.

✳ The male Australian lyrebird is such a skilled mimic that he can reproduce mechanical sounds, such as automobile horns, and is famous for his 24-inch tail feathers that assume the shape of a lyre when fanned.

✳ Oysters must hitchhike on fish if they want to grow up. Oyster larvae catch a ride on a passing fin and hang on for several months, feeding on their benefactor's body until they grow large enough to let go and settle into a spot of their own on the river bottom.

✳ The monkeylike common potto is the only mammal that keeps part of its backbone on the outside, with a row of bare bones protruding slightly from its back. The potto has a defensive pose where it clamps down its feet and hands and lowers its head to bring forth the exposed vertebrae.

Shark Attack!

Both beautiful and fear-invoking, sharks fascinate us like no other animal. People pay money to go shark diving and set their TiVos to record Shark Week on TV. The movie Jaws made $470 million way back in 1974. Humans are not usually the shark food of choice, but cases of mistaken identity, the smell of blood from an injury or a very very hungry shark can lead to terrifying – and often deadly — encounters.

✳   ✳   ✳   ✳

California's First—In the first recorded shark attack in California, Barry Wilson, a 17-year-old swimmer, was about 30 feet off the shore near Pacific Grove in 1952 when a shark attacked him. Hearing his screams, several bystanders swam to his rescue. His injuries were severe, however, and by the time they got him to shore, he was dead.

The Swim Fin—Nineteen-year-old Robert Pamperin was diving for abalone near La Jolla when a 22-foot great white attacked him. His friend tried to scare off the shark, but it was too late for Pamperin, who was already waist-deep in the shark's mouth. Coast Guard divers searching for his remains found only a single swim fin.

Soul Surfer—This story has a happier ending. Competitive surfer Bethany Hamilton was attacked by a 14-foor tiger shark but managed to get away. Unfortunately, her arm was badly injured, and it had to be amputated at the shoulder. The 13-year-old inspired millions of people with her faith and resilience. Her return to surfing—with only one arm—was documented in the 2010 movie *Soul Surfer*.

Savage Shadows—When amateur underwater photographer and filmmaker Henri Bounce was attacked by a shark near Lady Julia Percy Island in Australia, he not only got away, he recreated enough footage to make the documentary *Savage Shadows*.

The shark snuck up on Bounce and bit off his leg. Bounce broke free by poking the shark's eyes. Fellow divers got Bounce on the boat and radioed ahead for medical help.

Worse than the *Titanic* —When a Japanese submarine fired torpedoes at the USS *Indianapolis* during WWII, 900 men jumped ship. Hundreds of sharks attracted by the commotio, and later, the blood, circled the men, killing 583 of them.

Survivor—Rodney Fox is widely known as one of the most famous shark attack victims ever—mostly because he survived. Fox was spear fishing in Australia when a great white attacked and swam off with the fisherman firmly clasped in his mouth. Fox gouged at the shark's eyes and got away, only to be attacked again and have the flesh torn from his arm. Fox was released, attacked a third time, and released yet again. Fox was rescued and taken to the closest hospital. The fact that his rescuers left his wetsuit intact is credited with saving his life. His wounds were so deep and severe that the suit was all that held his body together in some places. Fortunately no arteries were severed and 360 stitches and four hours of surgery later, he survived.

Rarest Animals in the World

The following are the rarest animals in the world listed in ascending order, with those with the smallest population estimates first.

✳ ✳ ✳ ✳

1. Vancouver Island marmot

2. Seychelles sheath-tailed bat

3. Javan rhino

4. Hispid hare (Assam rabbit)

5. Northern hairy-nosed wombat

6. Tamaraw (dwarf water buffalo)

7. Iberian lynx

8. Red wolf

9. Dwarf blue sheep

10. Yellow-tailed woolly monkey

11. Kouprey (Cambodian forest ox)

12. Riverine rabbit

13. Malabar large spotted civet

14. Saola (Vu Quang ox)

15. Tonkin snub-nosed monkey

16. Sumatran rhino

17. Northern muriqui (woolly spider monkey)

18. Visayan spotted deer

19. Hirola (Hunter's hartebeest)

20. Addax (Sahara antelope)

21. North Atlantic right whale

22. Black-faced lion tamarin

23. Ethiopian wolf

24. Black-footed ferret

25. African wild ass

26. Vaquita (Gulf of California porpoise)

27. Arabian oryx

28. Mediterranean monk seal

29. Bactrian camel

30. Hairy-eared dwarf lemur

Portrait of a Killer

Though some argue that humans are the most dangerous creatures on Earth, the distinction actually belongs to a tiny, common insect.

✳   ✳   ✳   ✳

DISEASES TRANSMITTED VIA mosquito bites have caused more death and misery than the total number of casualties and deaths suffered in all of history's wars. The Roman Empire crumbled in the 3rd and 4th centuries when the Legions, decimated by malaria, were unable to repel barbarian invaders. American planners took control of the Panama Canal construction project when French interests withdrew after losing more than 22,000 workers to mosquito-borne illnesses over an eight-year period.

More than 2,500 species of mosquito spread disease throughout the world. The killers begin life as larvae, hatched in almost any kind of water. Within one week, adults emerge to ply their deadly trade.

As with other species, the female is the deadlier of the two sexes, while the male concerns himself with nothing more than fertilizing eggs. Females need blood to nourish their eggs; unfortunately, the process of collecting this food supply can wreak havoc on humans.

Mosquitoes can fly more than 20 miles from the water source in which they were born. Sensory glands allow the insects to detect carbon monoxide exhaled by their victims and lactic acid found in perspiration. When a female mosquito dips her proboscis into an unwilling victim, she transfers microorganisms through her saliva into her donor. These are responsible for some of the world's most deadly and debilitating diseases, which include malaria; Yellow, Dengue, and Rift Valley fevers; West Nile virus; and at least six different forms of encephalitis.

According to the U.S. Department of Health and Human Sciences, more than 500 million cases of malaria are reported throughout the world each year, resulting in an average of one million deaths.

Positively Platypus

What would you get if you could cross a duck with a beaver, a venomous snake, a chicken, and an otter? Well, it might look something like the duck-billed platypus.

✳ ✳ ✳ ✳

What on Earth . . . ?

THE OLDEST PLATYPUS fossil (of the platypus in its current form) dates back more than 100,000 years. Indigenous to the southeastern coast of Australia and Tasmania, the platypus is a *monotreme,* or egg-laying mammal. In fact, it is one of only two mammals that reproduce by laying eggs (the other is the echidna). In 1798, Captain John Hunter sent sketches and the skin of a platypus back to England that described a small, egg-laying animal with a pelt and a flat bill. They thought he was joking. British scientist Dr. George Shaw, thinking it was a hoax, tried to cut the pelt with scissors, expecting to find stitches attaching the bill to the body.

It's no wonder: The platypus is one strange-looking animal. With its fur and body shape, it resembles an otter. The tail looks like that of a beaver, but while beavers use their broad tails for propulsion, the platypus uses its tail for fat storage. It has four webbed feet, but only the front two are used for swimming. The rear feet are used for steering in water and aid in walking when on dry land.

Then there's the "duck bill." The platypus's rubbery snout is actually decidedly different than a duck's The bill of a duck is hinged. The platypus's bill is a single piece of leathery skin with two nostrils on the top and a small mouth on the bottom.

High Tech Meets Monotreme

Platypuses have a unique sense of perception called *electro-reception*. Located inside the platypus's bill, electroreceptors can detect electrical fields that are generated by muscular contractions of other animals in the vicinity. Since the platypus swims with its eyes closed, the electroreceptors enable it to detect even the smallest movement of its prey. If it senses an oncoming attack from a predator, the male platypus can sting with an ankle spur that is loaded with poisonous venom. While it is not lethal to humans, the venom is powerful enough to kill dogs and other animals.

Dining and Breeding

The platypus is a semiaquatic mammal and spends up to 12 hours a day searching for food under water. In order to survive, it must eat up to 25 percent of its body weight every day. And because it thrives on insects, worms, larvae, freshwater shrimp, and other small organisms, the platypus has to be an accomplished diver and stay submerged for up to 40 seconds at a time. A bottom feeder, the platypus normally forages shallow river bottoms, rooting around for things to eat. While underwater, the platypus fills its cheeks with prey until it reaches the surface, where it takes time to enjoy its meal. At the end of the day, the platypus retires to a nest dug out of a riverbank and furnished with leaves, grass, and twigs. While the platypus is admittedly more awkward out of water, it's still agile enough to run along the ground.

When it comes to the birds and the bees, the platypus is definitely one of the more interesting critters out there. Many are confounded by the fact that the platypus lays eggs, but yet is not a bird. The female usually lays two eggs two weeks after mating, and the eggs are incubated for 10 to 14 days, as the mother holds the eggs to her body. Even more baffling, instead of feeding from its mother's teats like other mammals, the baby platypus gets its milk by lapping it up from the hairs and grooves in the mother's skin.

You'd be hard pressed to think of an animal that has more unusual characteristics than the duck-billed platypus. But hey, after 100,000 years spent plodding around on the planet, it must be doing something right!

A Quicksand Sham

If you happen to get trapped in one of nature's suction pits, hang loose. Your moves are the only things that can drag you down.

❊   ❊   ❊   ❊

Lᴇᴛ's sᴀʏ ʏᴏᴜ'ʀᴇ running through the woods and you trip and fall. As you attempt to right yourself, you realize that the earth below you isn't really earth at all, and you find it impossible to find purchase. You are wet and covered in a granular grime, but it's not a body of water or sand pit that you've fallen into. This substance seems more like a combination of the two. In fact, it is—you have fallen into a quicksand pit. What you do from this point forth will determine whether this will be a momentary inconvenience or just a slightly longer inconvenience.

A Quicksand Primer

Quicksand is a sand, silt, or clay pit that has become hydrated, which reduces its viscosity. Therefore, when a person is "sucked" down, they are in reality simply sinking as they would in any body of water.

So why does quicksand make people so nervous? It's probably due to the fact that it can present resistance to the person who steps in it. This is particularly true of someone who is wearing heavy boots or is laden with a backpack or other load. Obviously, the additional weight will reduce buoyancy and drag one down.

It's All in the Legs

In the human thirst for drama, quicksand has a reputation as a deadly substance. The facts show something different. Because quicksand is denser than water, it allows for easy floating. If you stumble into a pit, you will sink only up to your chest or shoulders. If you want to escape, all you need to do is move your legs slowly. This action will create a space through which water will flow, thereby loosening the sand's grip. You should then be able to float on your back until help arrives.

Flying Fish

Find out the facts about these fascinating fish!

* * * *

* To escape predators such as swordfish, tuna, and dolphins, flying fish extend their freakishly large pectoral fins as they approach the surface of the water; their velocity then launches them into the air.

* A flying fish can glide through the air for 10 to 20 feet— farther if it has a decent tailwind. It holds its outstretched pectoral fins steady and "sails" through the air, using much the same action as a flying squirrel.

* If you'd like to catch sight of a member of the Exocoetidae family, you'll have to travel to the Atlantic, Indian, or Pacific oceans, where there are more than 50 species of flying fish.

* Whiskers are not an indication that a flying fish is up there in years; it's the opposite. Young flying fish have long whiskers that sprout from the bottom jaw. These whiskers are often longer than the fish itself and disappear by adulthood.

* Attached to the eggs of the Atlantic flying fish are long, adhesive filaments that enable the eggs to affix to clumps of floating seaweed or debris for the gestation period. Without these filaments, the eggs (which are more dense than water) would sink.

* Flying fish can soar high enough that sailors often find them on the decks of their ships.

Cocky Cockroaches

Would the cockroach be the sole survivor of a nuclear war?
No, but the mightiest of the mighty still looks up to this creepiest
of crawlers.

※　※　※　※

WE'VE ALL HEARD the scenario: A swarm of nuclear missiles is launched in unison, aimed at strategic targets throughout the world. The end of humankind is assured. In the span of a few minutes, entire civilizations are obliterated and the vital peoples and creatures that once roamed the planet are left dead or dying. Soon all life forms will succumb to the insidious effects of radiation. All except one, that is.

Blattodea, better known as the common cockroach, is the tough-guy holdout in this nightmarish scene. But would it be?

The pesky insect might be forgiven for flaring its chest with pride. It has the ability to withstand doses of radiation that would easily kill a human, It is generally accepted that a human will perish after receiving a 400- to 1,000-rad dose of radiation. In contrast, the hardy cockroach can withstand a 6,400-rad hit and continue crawling, which suggests that this bothersome bug is champ.

But the cockroach shouldn't gloat too much. It may outlast a human, but the insect kingdom boasts tougher players still in the form of tiny fruit flies. Fruit flies may be small, but they sure are resilient. It takes 64,000 rads to deck the average specimen. The Caribbean fruit fly, the "mighty mite" among these little fellows, takes a 180,000-rad dose like it's nothing. This figure beats the roach by a factor of ten.

The Fate of the Passenger Pigeon

When Europeans first visited North America, the passenger pigeon was easily the most numerous bird on the continent. But by the early 1900s, it was extinct. What led to this incredible change in fortune?

❋   ❋   ❋   ❋

Pigeons on the Wing

FROM THE FIRST written description of the passenger pigeon in 1534, eyewitnesses struggled with how to describe what they saw. Flights of the 16-inch-long birds were staggeringly, almost mind-numbingly big; flocks were measured in the millions, if not billions, and could be heard coming for miles. When passing overhead, a flight could block out the sun to the point that chickens would come in to roost. Passenger pigeons flew at around 60 miles an hour—one nickname dubbed the bird the "blue meteor"—but even so, a group sighted by Cotton Mather was a mile long and took hours to pass overhead. At least one explorer hesitated to detail what he had seen, for fear that the entirety of his report would be dismissed as mere exaggeration.

Settlers viewed the pigeons with trepidation. A passing flock could wreak havoc on crops, stripping fields bare and leading to famine. A flight passing overhead or roosting on your land would leave everything covered with bird droppings—a situation that would lead to more fertile soil in following years but did little to endear the creatures to farmers at that moment.

Pigeons on the Table

With such vast numbers, what could possibly have led to the extinction of the passenger pigeon? There are a number of theories, but the most likely answer seems to be the most obvious: People hunted them out of existence. Native Americans had long used the pigeons as a food source, and the Europeans followed suit, developing a systematic approach to harvesting the birds that simply outstripped their ability to reproduce. At first, the practice was an exercise in survival—a case of explorers feeding themselves on the frontier or settlers eating pigeon meat in place of the crops the birds had destroyed. However, necessity soon evolved into a matter of convenience and simple economy—the birds were cheap to put on the table.

Killing the birds in bulk was almost a trivial exercise. Initially, settlers could walk up under trees of nesting birds and simply knock them down using oars. As the birds became more wary, firearms were a natural choice for hunters; flocks were so dense, one report gives a count of 132 birds blasted out of the sky with a single shot. Nets were strung across fields, easily yanking the birds from the air as they flew. Perhaps most infamously, a captive bird would be tied to a platform that was raised and then suddenly dropped; as the pigeon fluttered to the ground, other pigeons would think the decoy was alighting to feed and would fly down to join him—a practice that became the origin for the English term "stool pigeon." Hunters would catch the birds in nets, then kill them by crushing their heads between thumb and forefinger.

Pigeons on Display

By 1860, flocks had declined noticeably. By the 1890s calls went out for a moratorium on hunting the animals, but to no avail. Conservation experts tried breeding the birds in captivity to little effect; it seemed the pigeons longed for their enormous flocks and could not reproduce reliably without them.

Sightings of passenger pigeons in the wild stopped by the early 1900s. A few survivors remained in captivity, dying one by one as ornithologists looked on helplessly. The last surviving pigeon, a female named Martha, died at the Cincinnati Zoological Garden on September 1, 1914. Her body was frozen in ice and shipped to the Smithsonian Institution, a testament to the downfall of a species.

The Buoyant Pachyderm

In an "only in New York" manner, an imprisoned elephant flees her Coney Island keepers. The catch? She makes her escape by water, not land. It gets better: She makes it as far as Staten Island by swimming six miles. Or does she?

✳ ✳ ✳ ✳

To call Coney Island's escaped elephant "determined" would be like calling Babe Ruth a good hitter, at least in the most famous telling of this offbeat tale. On June 4, 1904, the hulking animal named Fanny took flight from her captors at Coney Island's Luna Park. Inexplicably, Fanny launched her bid in a westerly direction, across water, ignoring a far easier land path to the north. Five miles of open bay lay between the elephant and Staten Island's New Dorp Beach. Could the gray beast make it to the other side, where the Savannah-like grass might offer a life similar to that of her African home?

The Scheme

The above telling of the tale may or may not be true. An alternative holds that the elephant's Coney Island handler was angry that his enormous charge was no longer generating profits. Hatching a scheme to float Fanny by barge to a point just off New Dorp Beach, he allegedly pushed the beast into the drink during a deep fog and crossed his fingers. Certainly the publicity elicited by "the elephant who swam five miles!" would restore Fanny's earning power.

One fact is beyond dispute. The elephant *did* swim completely unaided to New Dorp Beach for at least half a mile. Fishers who sighted this unlikely swimmer were dumbfounded. Police "apprehended" Fanny when she reached shore. Charged with vagrancy, the elephant was lassoed and whisked off to a police stable, where she'd remain until her handler retrieved her. Crowds rejoiced when the now-famous Fanny was returned to Coney Island via boat and trolley car. Published reports suggest that business at Coney was especially good that season. And why not? The "New Dorp Elephant" was holding court beside the amusements and sideshows. *Ka-ching, ka-ching.*

That Ain't Corn!

A farmer's field gives birth to a volcano

✳   ✳   ✳   ✳

A S FARMER DIONISIO Pulido moved about his cornfield in Paricutin, Mexico in February 1943, he observed a phenomenon that left him dumbfounded. Just before him, amongst countless rows of corn, the ground had cracked wide open. The putrid smell of rotten eggs was wafting from the new fissure.

With nothing to draw on as a possible explanation for this sudden six-foot-wide, 150-foot-long gash in the earth, Pulido and his farmhands believed that they might be witnessing an earthquake. They were wrong. What they were observing was an earthly event so extraordinarily rare few have ever seen it. A sleeping giant had awoken—a volcano had been born.

Mountain from a Molehill

Shortly after Pulido's encounter, he sensed urgency in the situation. The one-foot-deep depression that he first observed was now a prominent conical mound more than six feet tall. Fine gray ashes were blowing out of the opening, accompanied by thunder-like vibrations that rocked the landscape and the nerves of the men watching. The newborn volcano was clearly erupting. Pulido and his hands retreated to safety.

Perhaps the most startling component of the Paricutin volcano was the speed in which it developed. From its inception, molten material spouted continuously from the newly formed opening. When the projectiles fell back to the ground, they created a cinder cone or scoria. In just over 24 hours, the Paricutin volcano had grown to the astonishing height of a sixteen-story building. In six more days, it would measure double that height.

How tall the mound would grow or how long the eruption would last was anyone's guess. But one thing was certain: The site had now grown into a dangerous no-man's-land of scorching lava and ash—a far sight from the innocuous cornfield that had preceded it.

No Safe Place

By the second day of the eruption Pulido's cornfield had been completely consumed by the pyroclastic invader. Even worse, hot ash and scorching lava were beginning to overrun the village of Paricutin, as well as nearby San Juan Parangaricutiro. Eventually, inhabitants from both villages would relocate to lands just out of harm's way. From this relatively safe vantage they watched in sheer awe as the volcano grew into a monster that strained the limits of human comprehension.

On the one-year anniversary of the eruption—with lava and volcanic materials regularly belching from its lofty summit vent —the volcano at Paricutin had grown to 1,102 feet tall. Its fury would continue on and off for the next eight years. Before it expelled its last plume of smoke in 1952 and became dormant, the volcano had grown to the dizzying height of 1,391 feet—a figure that put the Paricutin volcano on a par with the Empire State Building, then ranked as the world's tallest skyscraper.

Epilogue

The Paricutin volcano caused no direct deaths. It did however kill three people as a result of lightning generated by its pyroclastic eruptions. The event presented volcanologists the rare opportunity to witness the birth, growth, and death of a volcano and much was learned during its long life span. Before the volcano had finished erupting, lava flows and ejected matter blanketed an area of ten square miles, completely obliterating the towns of Paricutin and San Juan Parangaricutiro in the process. The Paricutin volcano stands as a long dormant reminder of the natural forces that lay just beneath earth's surface.

22 Peculiar Names for Groups of Animals

1. A shrewdness of apes

2. A battery of barracudas

3. A kaleidoscope of butterflies

4. A quiver of cobras

5. A murder of crows

6. A convocation of eagles

7. A charm of finches

8. A skulk of foxes

9. A troubling of goldfish

10. A smack of jellyfish

11. A mob of kangaroos

12. An exaltation of larks

13. A troop of monkeys

14. A parliament of owls

15. An ostentation of peacocks

16. A rookery of penguins

17. A prickle of porcupines

18. An unkindness of ravens

19. A shiver of sharks

20. A pod of whales

21. A descent of woodpeckers

22. A zeal of zebras

Snake Milker

Talk to the expert! If you've ever wanted to know how venom is extracted from snakes, read this interview with a snake milker.

✳ ✳ ✳ ✳

Q: So where are the udders on a snake?

A: Funny! But I admit that the process does look a lot like milking. I extract venom from some of the most dangerous reptiles in the world. Snakes here in Australia are much worse than most North American vipers, including the copperhead. In any event, there's a constant need for snake venom, so I don't expect to be out of work anytime soon.

Q: What use is the venom?

A: The primary value is in creating antivenin to help a victim recover from a snakebite. These work the same way vaccines work—if you inject a living being with something harmful, its body will generally produce the antigens to fight the invasion. Sheep are most commonly used to produce antivenin. An antivenin can't put right what has already been damaged by a toxin, but it can help the victim's body halt further damage. Time is of the essence.

Q: How do you milk the snakes?

A: Much of it lies in being good at wrangling snakes. Here at the Australian Reptile Park, we have quite a few captive snakes and spiders. They don't produce a lot of venom, so we have to get every drop; we usually let them go a couple of weeks between milkings. Please don't try this at home: First I stretch some latex rubber over a glass beaker. I hold the snake carefully, as close behind the head as possible so it can't backlash. The snake doesn't care for this, and I let it strike at the beaker. If I do it right, the snake's fangs go through the latex and inject venom into the beaker.

Q: How many times have you been bitten?

A: Just two nicks. You see, most snakes husband their venom with care. They don't like to waste it. If the snake can't get its fangs out of its victim, it annoys and scares the snake; it knows that while its fangs are stuck in something, it's utterly vulnerable. In that case the snake pumps in more poison. The nicks were unpleasant but not severe—nothing like what I'd have received had I stepped on the creature in the bush.

Q: What are some of the most dangerous snakes?

A: The coastal taipan, inland taipan, and Australian brown snake are all bad news. But other regions in the world have some very dangerous snakes as well. I'd avoid a bite from an Indian king cobra if I were you, and the same goes for Central America's bushmaster.

Q: On to the commercial side of snake milking: Are there companies that deal in snake venom?

A: There are in Australia, with careful government oversight. Some snake species are threatened—we can't afford to lose a single broad-headed snake, for example, so we take great care not to damage the population.

Q: How much is the venom worth?

A: Some of it sells for a few hundred U.S. dollars per gram. If you want a gram of death adder venom, expect to pay $4,000. It all depends on supply and demand; some venom can be used to produce broad-spectrum antivenin, while others are useful against only one kind of bite. Some reptiles are harder to milk, or produce less venom, and that affects the price as well.

Bird on a Wire

Few names call to mind a love of birds more than that of John Audubon, but any bird with a brain would have done well to steer clear of him!

✳ ✳ ✳ ✳

THERE IS NO doubt that 19th-century wildlife illustrator John James Audubon cared about his feathered friends. He devoted his life to their study, observing and drawing them from the time he was a child. However, Audubon's shotgun was as important a tool as his paintbrush. He may have loved birds, but he had no qualms about killing them.

In the era before photography, most wildlife illustrators used stuffed animal carcasses as their models. That's how Audubon, a self-taught artist, began drawing birds. Frustrated by the lack of vibrancy in his illustrations, he set out to find new ways to draw the birds he had shot. His ultimate goal was to "represent nature...alive and moving!" It was at this time that he began piercing freshly killed birds, securing them to boards and using wires to pose them into "lifelike" positions. Eventually, Audubon mastered the technique of manipulating fresh carcasses and was able to draw birds as they had never been rendered before. His paintings showed animals in lifelike situations—nesting, hunting, and even feeding one another.

Burn, Baby, Burn

For the last few decades, late-night comedians have joked that Cleveland is the only city in the world where both the mayor's hair and the river have caught fire.

✳ ✳ ✳ ✳

AROUND NOON ON a sleepy Sunday in June 1969, a train car was making its way across the Cuyahoga River in downtown Cleveland. A spark from a broken wheel touched off an explosion in a pool of volatile sludge in the water below. The river, which moved slowly through the city center, tended to collect logs, railroad ties, and other debris around the foot of the trestles. These provided additional fuel, while the water itself was full of petroleum and other industrial runoff from steel plants upstream.

In Flagrante Delicto

The blaze quickly reached heights of five stories and consumed the Norfolk & Western Railway Company trestle. Three fire departments sent teams to battle the flames from shore, while a fireboat worked from the water. The fire was out within 20 minutes, before any members of the press could even make it to the site to snap a picture. The Norfolk & Western trestle incurred $45,000 worth of damage and had to be closed and rebuilt. A nearby trestle used by the Newburgh & South Shore Railway only needed $5,000 worth of repairs. There were no deaths attributed to the fire.

The next day, the newspapers published photos from the aftermath of the blaze, merely smoldering embers and trestle rails bent from the heat. As river fires went—even in Cleveland's history—the damage wasn't bad, but the fallout from the fire is still felt today.

The Crooked River's Crooked Past

The Cuyahoga River—which means "Crooked River" in the Iroquois language—has been an important waterway since European fur traders moved into the area in the 1700s. As Ohio's population increased and the state became a center for the steel and coal industries, the river assumed a vital role in Ohio's industrial landscape. Factories popped up along its length, especially in the stretch between Akron and Cleveland.

From the start of the Industrial Revolution through the mid-1900s, the river's pollution (which was notable even then) wasn't necessarily viewed as problematic. Instead, the river's filth was a sign of industrial progress, success, and wealth.

The infamous fire of 1969 was not the first—or even the most destructive—river fire in Cleveland's history. The first recorded Cuyahoga River fire was in 1868 and was followed by successive fires in 1883, 1887, 1912, 1922, 1936, 1941, 1948, and 1952. The 1912 blaze was responsible for five deaths, as the fire spread through the shipyards before being contained. The 1952 fire caused $1.5 million worth of damage and yielded dramatic photographs that, even now, erroneously accompany any discussion of the unphotographed 1969 fire.

The Right Fire at the Right Time

Perhaps the fire of 1969 is still discussed because of two key factors: *Time* magazine and the shifting attitudes of the public. Two months after the fire, *Time* published a major article about it—giving it more column inches (and more eyeballs) than the local newspapers had. Aside from the lurid descriptions of the putrid Cuyahoga ("Some River! Chocolate-brown, oily, bubbling with subsurface gases, it oozes rather than flows"), the article was accompanied by dramatic photographs of the destructive 1952 fire.

No matter how persuasive the article was, it would not have made a difference if people hadn't been ready to hear its message. By 1969, there was a growing ecology movement, and the general public was becoming concerned about lasting damage being done to the country's waterways. The *Time* article encapsulated these fears, complete with horrifying photographs, and Cleveland—specifically the Cuyahoga—became the symbol for industrial pollution.

Thus, the fire of 1969 became a turning point for the environmental movement. In 1972, Congress passed the Federal Water Pollution Control Amendments, also known as the Clean Water Act. This began to regulate the disposal of industrial waste and by-products, and it required cities to improve sewage treatment plants and processes and monitor the storm water and overflow.

Despite all this, the state of the river did not immediately improve. In a study conducted on the length of river between Akron and Cleveland in 1972, marine biologists could not find a single living fish or even any samples of species known to thrive in polluted water. By 1994, however, fish-eating birds such as the great blue heron and bald eagle began returning to the region, and in 2000, the Ohio Environmental Protection Agency reported finding 62 species of fish, including clean-water species such as steelhead trout.

After Burn

More than 40 years after the fire-heard-'round-the-world, the Cuyahoga could be considered a "clean" river. Even the much-maligned stretch between Cleveland and Akron meets or exceeds most of the requirements set forth in the Clean Water Act. But the Cuyahoga's filthy reputation lives on, in standard fodder for comedy club routines, in Randy Newman's song "Burn On," even in the Great Lakes Brewing Company's tasty Burning River Pale Ale—and certainly in Cleveland's collective memory.

A local ribbon-cutting mishap turned to embarrassment on a national level when Cleveland mayor Ralph Perk accidentally set his hair on fire on October 16, 1972. The ceremony was for a welding convention, the ribbon was a strip of metal, and Perk was doing the cutting with an acetylene torch.

Life on the Moon?

When Neil Armstrong landed on the moon on July 21, 1969, and uttered his famous phrase, "That's one small step for man; one giant leap for mankind," millions of people asked, "Can shopping malls be far behind?" Suddenly, living on the moon seemed a very real possibility. Yet as of 2009, only 12 people have ever set foot on the moon. What happened to lunar colonies?

✳ ✳ ✳ ✳

BACK IN 1954, science-fiction author Arthur C. Clarke predicted future moon dwellers would inhabit inflatable igloos heated by nuclear power. During the early '60s, several aerospace engineers proposed building underground bases beneath the moon's inhospitable surface. Robert Wilson and Jack LaPatra combined these two approaches with their 1968 design for Moonlab, a multilevel structure that would feature an astronomical observatory and a lunar farming community. They believed their colony could be fully functional and capable of supporting 24 residents by 1984.

University of Utah plant science professor Frank Salisbury went even further. His 1991 article *Lunar Farming* took readers on an imaginary tour of "Lunar City" in the year 2019. This thriving colony had over 100 residents engaged in growing dozens of crops, among them peanuts, sugarcane, wheat, rice, potatoes, and spinach.

Unfortunately, it doesn't look like we're going to catch up to Salisbury's vision within the next decade. The sheer cost of establishing a moon colony has proven daunting, and new problems keep cropping up. In addition to extreme temperatures and the general lack of elements such as carbon and nitrogen that are essential to life, colonists would also have to contend with falling meteorites and gritty moon dust gumming up the workings of all their machines.

However, those still eager to become lunar pioneers may have reason for hope. In September 2009, scientists working on a joint venture between NASA's Moon Mineralogy Mapper and India's Chandrayaan-1 announced that they had discovered water on the moon. Details are still forthcoming, but it is at least possible that humankind may yet make that leap to living on the moon.

Leaping Lemmings

A bit of fraudulent filmmaking and a popular video game have done much to uphold the long-standing misconception that lemmings commit mass suicide.

✳ ✳ ✳ ✳

THE IMAGE OF lemmings hurtling over cliffs to certain doom is entrenched in our culture to the point where "lemming" has become a metaphor for any sort of collective form of self-destruction. But, come on: Lemmings don't commit suicide. No animal does, with the exception of human beings. Unlike people, lemmings do not mindlessly follow crowds at their own peril. They do engage in one behavior en masse: mating.

Numbers Are Up, Numbers Are Down

These fuzzy Arctic rodents mate only a few weeks after being born and birth litters of as many as 13 pups three weeks after mating. Lemmings can give birth multiple times in one summer, leading to an exponential boom in population.

Every four years, there is what is known as a "lemming year," when the critters' numbers reach a critical mass that can no longer be sustained by their surroundings. Violence among the animals increases, and they begin to disperse over large distances in search of food. Contrary to popular belief, they do not move together as one single pack but instead go in all directions, following one another in randomly formed lines. They often end up at riverbanks or cliffs and will enter the water and swim as far as they can in an attempt to reach land or an ice patch. Of course, some end up drowning—but that's purely accidental.

Curiously, "lemming years" are followed by a crash in population numbers, with the next year's crowd dwindling to practically nothing. What happens to all of the lemmings after a boom year? Scientists have settled on increased predation as the explanation. When the lemming population surges, owls, foxes, and seabirds gorge themselves on the rodents, which in turn gives rise to a boom in their own populations. The next summer there are so many more predators that they bring the lemming population down to near extinction. That's where the furious mating comes in handy—in no time, the cycle starts all over again.

Another Disney-Made Myth

So how did the popular theory about lemming mass suicides come to be? Most sources point to the 1958 Disney movie *White Wilderness*. This film depicts a collection of lemmings scurrying across a cliff until they reach the edge of a precipice overlooking the Arctic Ocean. The lemmings then leap over the cliff to sad and certain oblivion. But a bit of creative license was taken to create this shot—it was filmed in Alberta, Canada, which is landlocked. (Lemmings aren't even native to Canada. All of the creatures used in the film were imported.) In order to give the illusion that the lemmings were migrating in large groups, the filmmakers covered a turntable with snow and put a few lemmings on it, filming as the animals went around and around. To show the lemmings landing in the water, the filmmakers herded a group over a riverbank. Once in the water, the little guys had just a short, safe swim to shore.

Those who missed the Disney nature film can witness (and manipulate) a version of a lemming mass suicide in a video game released in 1991. *Lemmings*, one of the most popular video games of all time, has players rescuing lemmings as they follow one another aimlessly off ledges and into a host of treacherous death traps, many involving lava or acid. Suddenly, a plunge into a cool pool of water doesn't look so bad.

How to Avoid a Mountain Lion Attack

Mountain lions, also known as cougars, pumas, and panthers, are the largest cats in North America and live in a vast area from the Yukon Territory in Canada to the Pacific Coast, the Rocky Mountains, and even Florida. Mountain lions are more plentiful than most people realize, and, though they generally avoid people, attacks do occur. These tips may help you avoid one, although no approach is guaranteed.

✳ ✳ ✳ ✳

* Hike in groups. Mountain lions avoid crowds and noise, and the more people on the lookout, the better. If there are children in the group, make sure they are supervised.

* Be aware of your surroundings, paying attention to what's behind and above you in trees and on rocks and cliffs.

* Don't back the animal into a corner—give it a way out. It would much rather run off and survive to hunt again.

* If you encounter a mountain lion, stand still rather than try to run away. Running may cause the animal to chase you, and it's much faster than you are. Stand still while facing the mountain lion, but avoid looking it in the eye, which it takes as a sign of aggression. Watch its feet instead.

* Do things that make you appear larger and bigger than the cat, such as raising your arms over your head or holding up a jacket, a backpack, or even your mountain bike.

* Make loud noises. Growling can make you sound like something the cat would prefer not to mess with.

* Don't crouch down or bend. This makes you appear smaller and, therefore, an easy target. Don't move a lot but don't play dead. To a mountain lion, a perfectly still human looks like an entrée.

* Remain calm and don't act afraid. Like many animals, mountain lions can detect fear.

Hummingbirds

When early Spanish explorers first encountered hummingbirds in the New World, they called them joyas voladoras—or "flying jewels." But the hummingbird is more than just beautiful: Its physical capabilities put the toughest human being to shame.

✳ ✳ ✳ ✳

* The ruby-throated hummingbird—the only hummingbird species east of Mississippi—migrates at least 2,000 miles from its breeding grounds to its wintering grounds. On the way, it crosses the Gulf of Mexico—that's 500 miles without rest. Not bad for a creature that weighs just an eighth of an ounce and is barely three inches long.

* A hovering hummingbird has an energy output per unit weight about ten times that of a person running nine miles per hour. If a person were to do the same amount of work per unit weight, he or she would expend 40 horsepower.

* A man's daily energy output is about 3,500 calories. If one were to recalculate the daily energy output of a hummingbird—eating, hovering, flying, perching, and sleeping—for a 170-pound man, it would total about 155,000 calories.

* An average man consumes about two and a half pounds of food per day. If his energy output were the same as that of a hummingbird, he would have to eat and burn off, in a single day, the equivalent of 285 pounds of hamburger, 370 pounds of potatoes, or 130 pounds of bread.

* The ruby-throated hummingbird can increase its weight by 50 percent—all of it fat—just before its winter migration. This provides extra fuel for the long, nonstop flight across the Gulf of Mexico. In comparison, a 170-pound man would have to pack on enough fat to increase his weight to 255 pounds in just a few weeks.

* The wing muscles of a hummingbird account for 25 to 30 percent of its total body weight, making it well adapted to flight. However, the hummingbird has poorly developed feet and cannot walk.

* Due to their small body size and lack of insulation, hummingbirds lose body heat rapidly. To meet their energy demands, they enter torpor (a state similar to hibernation), during which they lower their metabolic rate by about 95 percent. During torpor, the hummingbird drops its body temperature by 30° F to 40° F, and it lowers its heart rate from more than 1,200 beats per minute to as few as 50.

* Hummingbirds have the highest metabolic rate of any animal on Earth. To provide energy for flying, they must consume up to three times their body weight in food each day.

* Unlike other birds, a hummingbird can rotate its wings in a circle. It can also hover in one spot; fly up, down, sideways, and even upside down (for short distances); and is the only bird that can fly backward.

* The smallest bird on Earth is the bee hummingbird (Calypte helenae), native to Cuba. With a length of only two inches, the bee hummingbird can comfortably perch on the eraser of a pencil.

* The most common types of hummingbirds include the Allen's, Anna's, berylline, black-chinned, blue-throated, broad-billed, broad-tailed, buff-bellied, Costa's, Lucifer, Magnificent, ruby-throated, Rufous, violet-crowned, and white-eared.

* Like bees, hummingbirds carry pollen from one plant to another while they are feeding, thus playing an important role in plant pollination. Each bird can visit between 1,000 and 2,000 blossoms every day.

* There are about 330 different species of hummingbirds. Most of them live and remain in Central and South America, never venturing any farther north. Only 16 species of hummingbirds actually breed in North America.

Simple Twist of Fate

Is it possible that screenwriters scripted the special effects that accompanied the movie Twister when it made the rounds on the drive-in-movie circuit in Ontario, Canada?

✳ ✳ ✳ ✳

IN 1974, HOLLYWOOD introduced the innovative but ultimately ineffective concept of Sensurround to promote the movie *Earthquake*. Featuring a sonic sound explosion that actually shook the seats to create the sensation of an earthquake, the gimmick was dismissed by both cinematic critics and finicky fans. Tinseltown championed other innovations, such as THX sound and IMAX, to get couch potatoes out of the house and into theaters. In 1996, Sensurround made a dramatic return to the screens, scripted with not-so-subtle substance by nature itself.

All myths worth their weight in mystery must be built on a basic foundation of truth, and in the case of the movie *Twister*, the facts are as fascinating as fiction. On May 20, 1996, a tornado tore through the community of Thorold, Ontario, a sleepy little hamlet in the Niagara region of southern Ontario. Most of the city escaped major damage, but the same could not be said of the local drive-in theater, which saw all of its four screens ripped and ravaged by the tempest. Like the whirling winds, rumors were soon flying that the tornado had touched down just as spectators at the drive-in were fueling themselves with popcorn and watching the blockbuster movie *Twister*. The cars-only cinema was indeed showing the disaster flick, but the tornado actually hit during the day, not at night when the movie was being played.

Teleportation: Not Just the Stuff of Science Fiction

Scientists say that it's only a matter of time before we're teleporting just like everyone does on Star Trek.

✳   ✳   ✳   ✳

Beam Us Up

WE'RE CLOSER THAN you might think to being able to teleport, but don't squander those frequent-flyer miles just yet. There's a reason why Captain Kirk is on TV late at night shilling for a cheap-airfare Web site and not hawking BeamMeToHawaiiScotty.com. For the foreseeable future, jet travel is still the way to go.

If, however, you're a photon and need to travel a few feet in a big hurry, teleportation is a viable option. Photons are subatomic particles that make up beams of light. In 2002, physicists at the Australian National University were able to disassemble a beam of laser light at the subatomic level and make it reappear about three feet away. There have been advances since, including an experiment in which Austrian researchers teleported a beam of light across the Danube River in Vienna via a fiber-optic cable—the first instance of teleportation taking place outside of a laboratory.

These experiments are a far cry from dematerializing on your spaceship and materializing on the surface of a strange planet to make out with an alien who, despite her blue skin, is still pretty hot. But this research demonstrates that it is possible to transport matter in a way that bypasses space—just don't expect teleportation of significant amounts of matter to happen until scientists clear a long list of hurdles, which will take many more years.

Here, Gone, There

Teleportation essentially scans and dematerializes an object, turning its subatomic particles into data. The data is transferred to another location and used to recreate the object. This is not unlike the way your computer downloads a file from another computer miles away. But your body consists of trillions upon trillions of atoms, and no computer today could be relied on to crunch numbers powerfully enough to transport and precisely recreate you elsewhere.

As is the case with many technological advances, the most vexing and long-lasting obstacle probably won't involve creation of the technology, but rather the moral and ethical issues surrounding its use. Teleportation destroys an object and recreates a facsimile somewhere else. If that object is a person, does the destruction constitute murder? And if you believe that a person has a soul, is teleportation capable of recreating a person's soul within the physical body it recreates? These are questions with no easy answers.

Freaky Friends

Some people are drawn to cute and cuddly puppies or furry little kittens while others like the idea of owning a unique one-of-a-kind pet. It's perfectly legal to keep some very unusual animals as pets (double-check before you buy one). But would you want to?

✳ ✳ ✳ ✳

Serval—If you're a cat-lover, this might be the pet for you. Servals are larger than the average house cat, measuring three feet from head to tail and weighing anywhere between 15 and 40 pounds. They're regal animals but beware—they don't take to litter box training as well as most house cats.

Stick—No, we're not promoting a new Pet Rock fad here. A stick is a three- to four-inch-long insect that resembles, well, a stick. With proper care they can live for several years. Like the popular hermit crabs, their needs are simple and they're inexpensive to own. Sticks like company, so you if you've got the space, you might want to buy two.

Chinchilla—Chinchillas look like a cross between a rabbit and a squirrel and are known for their thick luxurious gray fur. Their coats are so thick and water-resistant that they clean themselves by rolling in dirt. While it may be legal to own a chinchilla, it is not legal to kill it to make its coat your own.

Wallaroo—Even the name is cute. If you want a pet the size of a 5th grader this may be the one for you. A cross between a kangaroo and a wallaby (in size and appearance) this Australian marsupial's typically lifespan is 15 to 20 years.

Kinkajou—At first glance, you might think this animal was a primate, but it's really a part of the raccoon family. Weighing in at a mere three to seven pounds, kinkajous love to hang by their tails. They have long and skinny tongues—which help them dine on honey and termites in the wild. And for a good parlor trick, kinkajous take the "moon walk" dance to a new level—they can turn their feet backwards to run in either direction.

Capybara—One look at this adorable animal (in a photo) and you'd probably be hooked. But would you feel differently if we told you the capybara is the world's largest rodent at four feet tall and 100+ pounds? Think twice before you get one, though—they prefer a home with a swimming pool, can be territorial and have very large teeth. And did we mention that it's a rodent?

Pygmy Goat—Social, and good-natured animals, pygmy goats are the goat family's answer to the popular potbellied pig. Sort of. Ranging from 50 to 85 pounds, these pets are best housed outside. The good news? When you own your own goat, you never run out of milk!

✳ **Chapter 2**

History and Civilization

Who Are the Aborigines?

Why are some Australians called Aborigines?

✳ ✳ ✳ ✳

IN COMMON USAGE, *aborigine* can be used to refer to a member of the indigenous population of any country. When the word *aborigine* begins with a capital *A*, however, it refers to a member of the indigenous population of Australia. Why do indigenous Australians have a monopoly on the term?

Human populations are believed to have first existed in Africa and from there walked north to the sprawling Eurasian continent. Indigenous Australians separated from these populations fairly early. Evidence suggests that humans arrived in Australia 50,000 years ago, probably by boat from southern Asia.

From that time onward until colonization, the population of Australia was isolated from the rest of the world. When Europeans first met the indigenous Australians in the 17th century, they had stumbled upon a population that had existed in its own geographic bubble for 50,000 years. The colonizers immediately used the term *aborigine*, (meaning "there from the beginning") to describe these Australians.

What's Older Than the Pyramids?

Ask most people what they consider the oldest architecture in the world, and the pyramids of Egypt are sure to be part of the answer. They are magnificent, but they are not the oldest.

✳ ✳ ✳ ✳

THE PYRAMIDS OF Giza are the most famous monuments of ancient Egypt and the only structures remaining of the original Seven Wonders of the Ancient World. Originally about 480 feet high, they are also the largest stone structures constructed by humans. They are not, however, the oldest. That glory goes to the prehistoric temples of Malta, a small island nation south of Sicily. The temples date from 4000 to 2500 B.C. At approximately 6,000 years old, they are a thousand years older than the pyramids. Not much is known about the people who built these magnificent structures, but they were likely farmers who constructed the temples as public places of worship.

Because the Maltese temples were covered with soil from early times and not discovered until the 19th century, these megalithic structures have been well preserved. Extensive archaeological and restorative work was carried out in the early 20th century by European and Maltese archaeologists to further ensure the temples' longevity. The major temple complexes are now designated as UNESCO World Heritage Sites.

The Oldest Egyptian Pyramid

The Step Pyramid at Saqqara is the oldest Egyptian pyramid. It was built during the third dynasty of Egypt's Old Kingdom to protect the body of King Djoser, who died around 2649 B.C. It was this architectural feat that propelled the construction of the gigantic stone pyramids of ancient Egypt on a rocky desert plateau close to the Nile. These pyramids, known as the Great Pyramids, were built around 2493 B.C. The largest structure served as the tomb for Pharaoh Khufu.

The Anasazi

There is a prevalent belief that the prehistoric Native American culture referred to as the Anasazi mysteriously disappeared from the southwestern United States. Here are the facts.

✳ ✳ ✳ ✳

ACROSS THE DESERTS and mesas of the region known as the Four Corners (where Arizona, New Mexico, Colorado, and Utah meet), backcountry hikers and motoring tourists can easily spot evidence of an ancient people. The towering stone structures at Chaco Culture National Historical Park and the cliff dwellings at Mesa Verde National Park tell the story of a culture that spread out across the arid Southwest during ancient times.

The Anasazi are believed to have lived in the region from about A.D. 1 through A.D. 1300 (the exact beginning of the culture is difficult to determine because there is no particular defining event). They created black-on-white pottery styles that distinguish subregions within the culture, traded with neighboring cultures (including those to the south in Central America), and built ceremonial structures called kivas, which were used for religious or communal purposes.

Spanish conquistadors exploring the Southwest noted the abandoned cliff dwellings and ruined plazas, and archaeologists today still try to understand what might have caused the Anasazi to move from their homes and villages throughout the region. Over time, researchers have posed a number of theories, including the idea that the Anasazi were driven from their villages by hostile nomads, such as those from the Apache or Ute tribes. Others believe that the Anasazi fought among themselves, causing a drastic reduction in their populations. A few extraterrestrial-minded theorists have suggested that the Anasazi civilization was destroyed by aliens.

Today, the prevalent hypothesis among scientists is that a long-term drought affected the area, destroying agricultural fields and forcing people to abandon their largest villages. Scientists and archaeologists have worked together to reconstruct the region's climate data and compare it with material that has been excavated. Based on their findings, many agree that some combination of environmental and cultural factors caused the dispersal of the Anasazi from the large-scale ruins seen throughout the landscape today.

Their Journey

Although many writers—of fiction and nonfiction alike—romanticize the Anasazi as a people who mysteriously disappeared from the region, they did not actually disappear. Those living in large ancient villages and cultural centers did indeed disperse, but the people themselves did not simply disappear. Today, descendents of the Anasazi can be found living throughout New Mexico and Arizona. The Hopi tribe in northern Arizona, as well as those living in approximately 20 pueblos in New Mexico, are the modern-day descendants of the Anasazi. The Pueblos in New Mexico whose modern inhabitants consider the Anasazi their ancestors include: Acoma, Cochiti, Isleta, Jemez, Laguna, Nambe, Picuris, Pojoaque, San Felipe, San Ildefonso, Ohkay Owingeh (formerly referred to as San Juan), Sandia, Santa Ana, Santa Clara, Santo Domingo, Taos, Tesuque, Zia, and Zuni.

The History of Indoor Plumbing

A "civilized" life would not be possible without water pipes.

❋ ❋ ❋ ❋

HUMBLE HOLLOW TUBES have been improving our quality of life for thousands of years. The piping of water in and out of living spaces originated in many different ancient civilizations. Plumbing technology was often developed only to be lost until it was reinvented from scratch.

Lead pipes have been found in Mesopotamian ruins, and clay knee joint piping has been traced to Babylonia. The Egyptians used copper piping. But the most sophisticated ancient water-works flourished at the hands of the Harappan Civilization (circa 3300–1600 B.C.) in the areas of present-day India and Pakistan.

The Harappans boasted of a network of earthenware pipes that would carry water from people's homes into municipal drains and cesspools. Archeological excavation in the 1920s uncovered highly planned cities with living quarters featuring indoor baths and even toilets. Thanks to the Harappans' advanced ceramic techniques, they were able to build ritual baths up to 29 feet long and 10 feet deep—as big as modern-day swimming pools.

While the Romans can't be credited with the invention of water pipes, their mastery of pipe-making influenced plumbing up to the 20th century. (The word *plumbing* comes from the Latin word for lead, *plumbum*.) Pipes were made by shaping sheets of the easily malleable (and highly toxic) molten lead around a wooden core. Plumbers then soldered the joints together with hot lead. It could be said that they were largely responsible for "civilizing" Rome, making it a place where homes had bathtubs as well as indoor toilets that flushed into underground sewage systems. Fresh water was piped directly into kitchens, and there were even ways of "metering" how much water was being used by the width of the pipe installed. (Even then, convenience had its price!)

Ancient Roman Graffiti

Be careful what you write on a bathroom wall. It may stick around for a while.

✳   ✳   ✳   ✳

IN THE YEAR A.D. 79, Mount Vesuvius erupted without warning, instantly burying the nearby Roman city of Pompeii under 20 feet of ash. Within only 36 hours of the eruption, the city was so thoroughly buried that it would not be discovered again until 1748.

When the ashes were finally cleared away, the ruined city beneath provided an unprecedented glimpse of what life in an ancient Roman city was really like. Most of what we know about the everyday life of the Romans has come only from guesses, since most of the classical literature on the subject is more concerned with the lives of politicians and military men. Other ruins have been ransacked by barbarians. The ruins of Pompeii, however, showed how the Romans really lived—and how they talked.

The best indication of how the average Romans talked—and how their language differed from the "classical" Latin found in books—was the graffiti that was found all over the city. The people of Pompeii were really, really fond of writing and carving words and phrases into walls. Sometimes replies would be posted, and whole conversations wound up being recorded in a manner not unlike what one sees today on Facebook or message boards. More than 10,000 individual pieces of graffiti have been found in Pompeii, on surfaces ranging from the good old reliable bathroom walls to the outer walls of private mansions. Sometimes drawings were added, including some showing phenomenally well endowed men that were plastered over by Victorian excavators and have only recently come to light after the plaster wore away.

This all seems to have been sanctioned by the city. Sometimes artists would be hired to paint slogans on walls during political campaigns. No one seems to have gotten in big trouble for writing on the outer walls of the homes of the rich; indeed, such residences seem to have been regarded as prime territory, particularly for political slogans (for which the homeowners presumably gave permission).

Some of the graffiti takes the form of reviews of businesses. Other examples are simply notes wishing others well. But, like modern graffiti, much of it is about sex and bodily functions. And then there are some scribbles that simply sound like things you'd find on a corny poster on an office wall.

Here are some examples:

"To the person who is pooping here: beware of the curse!" (outside of a water distribution tower)

"Atimetus got me pregnant." (outside of a merchant's house)

"A small problem gets larger if you ignore it." (in the basilica)

"He who has sex with a fire will burn his privates." (sage advice in the basilica)

"Dear host of this inn: We have wet the bed. We know we shouldn't have, but there were no chamber pots." (at an inn)

"Secundus defecated here" (this one showed up three times on one wall)

Writing on walls was probably just as common in other Roman cities of the day, but the evidence has generally been worn away over the centuries. Nor were the Romans the only ones to mark their territory in this way—ancient cathedrals throughout Europe are full of graffiti and drawings from centuries past.

Dirty Doings

Sanitation ain't what it used to be…and let us all rejoice, because it used to be pretty disgusting.

✳   ✳   ✳   ✳

✳ The ancient Greeks liked baths, but the purpose was often medicinal rather than hygienic; bathing was prescribed for many ailments. After sports, the typical Greek athlete bathed after scraping all the dust and oil off with a strigil, which resembled a dull carpet knife.

* In the ancient world, personal cleanliness was just part of sanitation. More importantly: When thousands of people live in a town, where does all their waste go? In many places, the answer was 'where the individual deposited it,' which contributed heavily to death by disease (blamed on spirits or divine disfavor). Worse: It was often thrown out a window. Look out below!

* Baths were Rome's social centers, much resembling a modern resort with brothel. Roman men though nothing of stopping in for a haircut, a meal, sex, a bath and a political debate with friends—though perhaps not always in that exact order.

* As far as Arab Muslims were concerned, the Vikings had deplorable hygienic standards. Ibn Fadlan said "They are as stray donkeys," and called them "the filthiest of God's creatures." In particular, Ibn Fadlan found the communal spitting-bowl revolting, because the Vikings also washed their hair in it.

* Numerous early Christian saints considered non-bathing a form of mortification, punishing the body to uplift the soul. This worked very well for the lice of Europe.

* Because ritual bathing was required by Jewish law, a European city's Jews were often its cleanliest people. Often forbidden to bathe in the local river or use public baths, the Jewish community would build its own facility for the *mikveh* (ritual bath).

* The Dutch religious scholar Erasmus (1466–1536) records that the Spaniards brushed their teeth with urine. He also suggested that kids not fidget in their seats, lest someone assume they were passing gas.

* If nearly all medieval Europe stank, why do we have accounts complaining that some individual smelled bad? Simple answer: The person had to out-reek the ambient reek, which was no mean feat.

* Rome's great sewer system was called the Cloaca Maxima. Today, *cloaca* is the veterinary/anatomical term for a bird or reptile's combined anal and genital area. Every egg you've ever eaten rode down a cloaca.

* The much-despised pubic louse (crabs) may die out in North America. With more Americans shaving 'down there,' the little pests are losing their habitat. We aren't holding our breaths waiting for a 'save the crabs' movement...

* Some Native Americans had more lice than others. At the Little Bighorn National Monument's national cemetery lie the remains of numerous soldiers, Native American scouts and warriors, civilians, and family members. One stone marks the resting place of an Oglala Lakota warrior named Many Lice, who died fighting Custer.

* The height of frontier sanitary luxury can be seen at the Z-Bar Ranch in Strong City, Kansas, a formidable limestone mansion built in 1881 by a cattle baron. The three-hole outhouse includes a lower one for small children!

Suetonius's 12 Caesars

Suetonius was one of the most interesting Roman writers. Here are his 12 biographical subjects, along with a quirk about each.

✳   ✳   ✳   ✳

Julius Caesar was dictator, never emperor.

Oddity: Caesar was not a heavy drinker—almost a perversion among Roman politicians.

Augustus was actually titled "first citizen"; special powers gained over his lifetime worked out to the equivalent of emperorship.

Oddity: Augustus had only a few small, rotten teeth. He also had a unibrow.

Tiberius sent the "first citizen" concept out to sea, preferring to goof off on the Isle of Capri and have underlings run the empire.

Oddity: Tiberius served leftovers at formal dinners.

"Caligula" was a nickname ("Little Army Boots") that stuck, though no one would call him that when he was emperor.

Oddity: Caligula was exceptionally hairy—and thin-skinned about it. He executed anyone who mentioned goats.

Claudius drooled and had some sort of twitch, likely from a nervous condition. What most people don't realize is how well he ran the empire (though Caligula was an easy act to follow).

Oddity: Claudius was a gambler and wrote a book on dice games.

Nero sang while Rome burned, but he didn't play his lyre, much less a not-yet-invented fiddle. Suetonius says Nero started the fire himself as inspiration for a song.

Oddity: Nero was pot-bellied, thin-legged, and acne-prone.

Galba ushered in the Year of Four Emperors, an era when the new guy barely had new drapes measured before dying. Galba ruled for just six greedy months before the army butchered him.

Oddity: Galba was nearly crippled with arthritis, perhaps brought on by gout.

Otho stuck around for three months, which is about how long it took the next guy's legions to reach Italy. He might have made a decent emperor had he not stabbed himself.

Oddity: Otho had all his body hair removed and put wet bread on his face to inhibit beard growth.

Vitellius was vulgar and loutish. Always eating, he'd gobble sacrificial food right off the gods' altar. He lasted eight months.

Oddity: Vitellius invited himself to people's houses for impromptu banquets, gorging himself at the expense of his hosts.

Popular with the military and the bane of the senatorial staff, **Vespasian** straightened Rome out. If you admire the Colosseum, thank Vespasian for having it built.

Oddity: When Vespasian instituted the infamous Public Urinal Tax, Titus complained about the sickening nature of the rule. Vespasian then produced a coin and asked his son, "Does this smell bad?" (indicating that the source of money is irrelevant).

Titus wasn't around long, but he did a good job. When Mt. Vesuvius destroyed Pompeii (near modern Naples), Titus had a disaster plan. No one is sure if Titus then fell ill or was poisoned by younger brother Domitian, but you'll soon see that Domitian was clearly capable of fratricide.

Oddity: Titus believed in a daily good deed. If at dinner he realized he hadn't done his usual favor, he called that a wasted day.

Domitian debased not merely Roman coinage but Rome itself, executing people in fits of paranoia, signing his name "Dominus et Deus" (Lord and God), interrogating victims by burning them on the genitals, and running a morality campaign while engaging in carnal misdeeds. His assassination was met with the army's sorrow, the Senate's glee, and the public's apathy.

Oddity: Domitian would have a slave stick his hand out with fingers spread—then shoot arrows between the fingers without harming the slave.

The Vikings in North America

According to Norse sagas, Leif Eriksson set foot in North America. Why didn't a Viking settlement survive?

✳ ✳ ✳ ✳

AFTER WINTERING AT the place we now call Newfoundland in the year 1000, Leif Eriksson went home. In 1004, Leif's brother Thorvald led another expedition to North America. This group ran into Native Americans. The Vikings killed eight of the nine natives they encountered. A greater force retaliated, and Thorvald was killed. His men then returned home.

Six years later, a larger expedition of Vikings set up shop in North America. This group lasted two years. The Vikings traded with the locals initially, but they soon started fighting with them and were driven off. There may have been one further attempt at a Newfoundland settlement by Leif and Thorvald's sister, Freydis.

In 1960, Norse ruins were found in L'Anse aux Meadows, Newfoundland. The Vikings had been there, all right. Excavations over the next seven years uncovered houses and ironworks, as well as woodworking areas. Also found were spindlewhorls, weights that were used when spinning thread; this implies that women were present.

The sagas say that the Viking settlers fought with the local *Skraelings* (a Norse word meaning "natives") until the *Skraelings* came at them in large enough numbers to force the Vikings out. This sounds plausible, given the reputation of the Vikings— they'd been raiding Europe for centuries—and the Eriksson family's history of violence. Erik the Red, Leif's father, founded a Greenland colony because he'd been thrown out of Iceland for murder, and Erik's father had been expelled from Norway for the same reason. Would you want neighbors like them?

An Archaeological Puzzle

A millennium ago, the land of Wisconsin was teeming with activity.

✳   ✳   ✳   ✳

ZTALAN WAS A fortified settlement of mysterious people who worshiped the sun. The Middle Mississippian culture erected stepped pyramids, may have practiced cannibalism, and enjoyed coast-to-coast trade. Some have linked the Mississippians to the Aztecs and even to the legendary city of Atlantis. All that is truly certain is that they lived in Wisconsin for 150 years. Then they disappeared.

Aztalan, near present-day Lake Mills, Wisconsin, is now a state park and a National Historic Landmark. Still, what happened at Aztalan and the truth about the people who lived there are among the greatest archaeological puzzles in the world.

Aztalan is centuries old. During the period when it was settled, sometime between A.D. 1050 and 1100, gunpowder was invented in China. Macbeth ruled Scotland. The Orthodox and Roman Catholic churches split. In America, across the Mississippi from St. Louis in what is now Illinois, there was a strange, 2,000-acre city of earthen pyramids later dubbed "Cahokia." Its population was roughly 20,000—more than London at that time.

Aztalan appears to be the northern outpost of the Cahokia peoples. Because of location, archaeologists call their civilization Middle Mississippian. They are distinct from the Woodland peoples, who were there first and remained afterward. The Mississippians were quite enamored with the sun. At Cahokia, residents erected wooden solar observatories, similar to Britain's Stonehenge.

Like Cahokia, Aztalan was a truly weird place: 22 acres were surrounded by a stockade with 32 watch towers, all made from heavy timbers and then covered with hard clay. Inside, pyramidal mounds stood as high as 16 feet. Outside the fortifications, crops were planted. According to Cahokia experts, the Mississippians are the ones who introduced corn to North America.

Aztalan Today

Today, Aztalan looks much different than it did at its peak. The mounds remain, and part of the stockade has been rebuilt. Also, the Friends of Aztalan group is trying to recreate antique agriculture with a small garden of gourds, squash, sunflowers, and an early type of corn, all planted just as the Mississippians would have done.

In addition to vegetables, the Mississippian diet may have included some more interesting dishes—namely human flesh. At Cahokia there's evidence of human sacrifice, and since the time of Aztalan's discovery by whites in 1836, it has been thought that its residents practiced at least some sort of cannibalism. But science and interpretations change with time. There is speculation that the so-called "cannibalism" could have simply been a ceremonial or funerary practice that had nothing to do with eating human flesh.

The City Beneath the City

It's not obvious today, but the San Antonio River Walk got its start as drainage and irrigation ditches built before the Alamo.

✳ ✳ ✳ ✳

THE SAN ANTONIO River flows through San Antonio to join the Guadalupe River. Early in the 1700s, settlement began with a fortified presidio, villa, and mission being built at the location of today's city. The settlers called it San Antonio de los Llanos. As the settlement grew, so did its need for water. Early settlers depended on the San Antonio River for drinking water and crop irrigation, but they soon realized that the river had a destructive side: annual flooding destroyed any settlements along its banks. Settlers built bypass channels to prevent these regular floods. In 1900, the San Juan Ditch Corporation was founded, and a series of dams and locks was built to control the flow of water.

In the 1920s, as the city continued to grow, the San Antonio Conservation Society organized and began discussing the construction of shops along the bypass channel. The Depression put a halt to these plans, which were revisited in 1939. Throughout the early 1940s, walkways, stairways to street level, footbridges, and rock walls were built. In 1946, the first restaurant, Casa Rio, opened.

During the 1950s, the area was turned over to the Department of Parks and Recreation, which placed park rangers along the walkways for visitor safety and set up a small botanical garden. At the close of the decade, a Tourist Attraction Committee was formed to explore expansion and attract economic development. Committee members listened to ideas from the Disney Corporation and took junkets to New Orleans to garner ideas.

In 1963, a full-scale development plan was unveiled that included a convention center, major hotels, a mall, and more restaurants, in addition to parks and gardens. Construction and renovation continued through the 1980s.

A Burgeoning River Culture

Today major hotels, a three-story shopping mall, the Henry B. Gonzales Convention Center, and a wide variety of restaurants and shops flank the River Walk. Visitors can traverse the 2.5-mile stretch on foot or by water taxi, or they can take a guided tour on a boat.

Restaurants are plentiful and suit every taste and pocketbook. History buffs can dine in one of several restaurants that have been in San Antonio or on the River Walk since its early days, such as Schilos (1917) and Casa Rio (1946). For the gourmet, there is Boudro's, rated one of the top 50 restaurants in the United States.

Shopping for souvenirs, handicrafts, or clothing is easy at any one of the many specialty stores and street vendors scattered along the waterway. Special festivals and events throughout the year bring in vendors specializing in unique items.

Dining and shopping are not the only options on the River Walk; there are many botanical gardens, nature parks, and alcoves for photos, leisure activities, or just sitting and enjoying the scenery. One such popular spot is Marriage Island, located across from the CPS Energy building. For a nominal fee, couples can arrange a brief wedding ceremony on the island, which can hold as many as 30 people.

The River Walk is also a scenic way to connect to other landmarks and attractions in San Antonio. Stairways to street level bring visitors close to the Alamo, museums, the Tower of the Americas, and downtown.

Keeping It All Together

Maintaining the River Walk is an annual affair. Every January, the water is drained from the canals during the Mud Festival, named for the muddy residue that remains at the bottom of the waterways. While Department of Operations employees remove debris, repair the brick walls, and perform minor renovations, citizens and tourists can enjoy an arts and crafts fair, musical performances, and mud-related activities, and they can join in the crowning of the Mud King and Queen.

Debris cleanup has yielded some interesting finds. The most common items found include sunglasses, cameras, cell phones, strollers, deck chairs, and silverware from the restaurants that line the waterway. Historical items occasionally surface from the mud and have included glass inkwells, medicine bottles, and even a casket handle. The more unique items are on display at the Department of Operations office. The largest item ever recovered was a small foreign car that had been submerged in the deeper North canal.

San Antonio's River Walk continues to expand, with current plans to upgrade the electrical lighting and landscaping along the entire 2.5 miles and refurbish and attract new business to the North canal region. The city continues to attract thousands of convention-goers and other visitors each year because of the River Walk. This unique "city beneath the city" will remain a popular vacation spot for years to come.

Notable Fraternal Organizations

Fraternal organizations have been in operation—under varying degrees of secrecy—for hundreds of years.

✳ ✳ ✳ ✳

Freemasons

WHILE THE FREEMASONS' symbols of the square and the compass may be derived from the building of King Solomon's Temple in the tenth century B.C., the origins of the society itself are somewhat more modern. The organization developed among the guilds of stonemasons that were created during the construction of the great cathedrals of Europe in the Middle Ages. From these original professional associations came today's Masons, committed to philanthropy and ethics. Although Freemasonry includes reverence of the "Great Architect of the Universe," it is not a religion. Most lodges serve the communities in which they reside, and many are involved in charity. While they don't consider themselves a secret society, Freemasons argue that they are an esoteric society with certain signs, tokens, and words that are private.

Order of DeMolay

A civic organization dedicated to helping young men grow into the responsible leaders of tomorrow, the Order of DeMolay was started by Frank Land in Kansas City, Missouri, in

1919. Membership is open to men ages 12–21, and through mentoring relationships with adults, the young men of the society focus on character and leadership skills. While it is not officially affiliated with the Freemasons, the Order developed much of its philosophy and many of its rituals from the Masonic tradition. The name of the group was chosen to honor Jacques DeMolay, the last Grand Master of the Knights Templar. Today, the Order of DeMolay has more than 1,000 chapters located around the world.

Rosicrucians

The Rosicrucians are an order that attempts to understand the connection between the soul, the body, and the higher consciousness. Many legends, both oral and written, explain aspects of Rosicrucian thought. The group seems to have roots in the mysticism of ancient Egypt and can trace its evolution through the development of Western philosophy until the group's eventual incorporation in 1915. Alchemy, specifically as applied to the transmutation of people rather than matter, has played a key role in Rosicrucian thought. Today, Rosicrucians focus on history, spirituality, and the humanities as tools for understanding the challenges confronting the people of the modern world.

Knights of Columbus

The Knights of Columbus was established in Connecticut in 1882 by Father Michael McGivney; he brought together the men of his parish to create a brotherhood of the faithful to mutually support each other and fellow Catholics. The group selected its name to honor Christopher Columbus, who had brought Christianity to the Americas. Originally envisioned as a network of social assistance in prewelfare days, the K of C, as it is known, sought to provide for widows and orphans. Since that time, the organization's ideals of charity, civic duty, and evangelism have expanded into a much broader mission. Regardless, providing insurance to the families of members still remains one of its objectives today.

P.E.O. Sisterhood

The P.E.O. (or Philanthropic Educational Organization) started as an on-campus group at Iowa Wesleyan College in 1869. The original seven members founded their association on the ideals of friendship and philanthropy. Since that time, the group has evolved into an all-female society dedicated to furthering educational opportunities for women. The organization has several scholarship and loan funds designed to advance that purpose.

Fallacies & Facts: Pilgrims

When it comes to the Pilgrims, sorting fact from fiction can be a confusing task.

✳   ✳   ✳   ✳

Fallacy: Pilgrims left England for America because of religious persecution.

Fact: Then called Separatists, the Pilgrims did indeed leave England to escape religious persecution. The catch: They first went to the college town of Leiden in the Netherlands, not the wilderness of America. After some peaceful years in Leiden, the Separatists grew discontented at the bottom of the commerce-driven Dutch society. Worse still, their children were learning liberal Dutch ideas, including religious tolerance. To keep Satan from gaining an ugly victory through the children, and to preserve their English identity, the Separatists decided to leave.

Fallacy: They sought religious freedom in America.

Fact: Not as most Americans understand it today. By "religious freedom," Pilgrims meant freedom to be a Pilgrim, not something other than a Pilgrim. Native Americans and Quakers would discover that the fine print didn't include a cheerful embrace of pluralistic religious beliefs.

Fallacy: Most of the *Mayflower* passengers were Pilgrims.

Fact: Not quite half were. It's easy to forget now that the *Mayflower* voyage was in essence a commercial venture, with the Separatists/Pilgrims as homesteaders and cheap labor. The backers jacked the Separatists around, bending or breaking various promises. The secular passengers—who would cause some trouble in the New World—were mostly fortune-seekers completely uninterested in a devout lifestyle.

Fallacy: The Pilgrims first landed at Plymouth.

Fact: Actually, they made their first landfall at Provincetown on Cape Cod after a perilous approach. It didn't take them long to see that Provincetown made a crummy site for a colony.

Fallacy: Pilgrims were essentially Puritans.

Fact: Not at first. The key theological difference between them was their relationship to the Anglican Church. Puritans wanted to reform the Church; Pilgrims abandoned it. However, when the Puritans began to follow the Pilgrims to New England, Puritanism essentially absorbed its Separatist brethren.

Fallacy: The Pilgrims immediately began stealing Indian land.

Fact: This isn't even possible. The tribes of the region had already been depleted by a staggering 90 percent because of disease, yet even that hardy, tragic remnant vastly outnumbered the initial colonists from the *Mayflower*. Most Pilgrim leaders made successful efforts to get along with their Indian neighbors. Any other course would have been self-destructive.

Flags a' Flyin'

Ask true Texans about "Six Flags over Texas," and they won't talk about any amusement parks. Instead, they'll share some history.

✳ ✳ ✳ ✳

THE SIX NATIONAL flags that have flown over Texas belong to Spain, France, Mexico, the Republic of Texas, the Confederate States of America, and the United States. Each of these has waved over a specific era and provides a glimpse into the history of the state.

Texas Under Spain, 1519–1821

The Spanish flag depicts the lions of León and the castles of Castile. Spain was the first European nation with a presence in what is now Texas, beginning in 1519 when Hernán Cortés established a Spanish foothold in Mexico. Alonso Álvarez de Piñeda mapped the Texas coastline, and soon after came explorers Francisco Vasquez de Coronado and Juan De Oñate. Despite this early presence, it was nearly 160 years before Spain established its first settlement, Ysleta Mission, near present-day El Paso. Other Spanish missions, forts, and settlements were established for nearly a century, until Mexico threw off the European rule and became an independent country in 1821.

Texas Under France, 1685–90

The French flag features a host of golden fleur-de-lis emblazoned on a field of white. Planning to expand its base from French Louisiana, France took a bold move in 1685, planting its flag in eastern Texas near the Gulf Coast. Although the territory had already been claimed by Spain, the Spanish had very little presence in the area, and the nearest Spanish settlements were hundreds of miles away. French explorer René-Robert Cavelier, Sieur de LaSalle established Fort St. Louis on Matagorda Bay, between modern-day Houston and Corpus Christi, but the tiny town of 150 was doomed from the start.

Many settlers suffered from disease and famine, while the remaining were plagued by hostile Native American attacks. By 1690, France's bold claim to Texas had evaporated.

Texas Under Mexico, 1821–36

The Mexican flag pictures an eagle, a snake, and a cactus on bars of brilliant red, green, and white. Texas was a frontier for Hispanics from the south and Anglos from the north and east who settled the land and became Mexican citizens. The divergent cultures had conflicting beliefs, and skirmishes broke out between the settlers. The final blow was dealt by General Santa Anna, who discarded the Mexican constitution and declared himself dictator of Texas. Texans revolted and won their independence from Mexico on April 21, 1836.

Republic of Texas, 1836–45

After gaining independence from Mexico, the new republic elected Sam Houston as president and established a capital in the small town of Waterloo. During the ten years Texas existed as an independent republic, Texans endured epidemics and financial crises. But this decade also saw the birth of the American cowboy and the use of the Colt six-shooter.

In 1845, Texans voted to join the United States. The state flag featuring the lone star on a red, blue, and white background seen today is the same flag that flew over the proud republic.

Texas in the Confederacy, 1861–65

The original flag of the Confederate States of America featured a circle of stars on a blue background with two red stripes and one white stripe (the cross-barred banner most people associate today with the Confederacy was actually a battle flag). Sixteen years after Texas declared statehood, the Civil War erupted. Texans joined their Confederate brothers in the epic battle and suffered the devastation and economic collapse shared by all the Southern states. Texas was re-admitted to the Union as a state on March 30, 1870.

Texas in the United States, 1845–1861, 1865–present

Struggling through Reconstruction after the Civil War, Texans marshaled their strength to rebuild their economy and guide the future of this proud state. The Texas Longhorn provided beef for the nation; the vast farmlands yielded crops; and the discovery of oil pushed Texas into the spotlight.

But That's Not All

In addition to the formally recognized national flags, Texas has rallied around other standards. In the mid-1830s when the idea of gaining independence from Mexico was gaining support, Captain William Scott had a flag made to rally the cause. It featured a lone star and the word *independence* in capital letters.

Another revolutionary flag was an alteration of the Mexican flag, which replaced the center emblem with the number 1824 (in reference to the Mexican constitution of that year). Although no one knows for certain, many believe that this flag flew over the Alamo during the infamous battle.

The First Flag of the Republic, created after the first Constitutional Convention declared Texas an independent republic, featured a lone star surrounded by the word *Texas*. The most defiant flag created during this period was the Republic of Texas Gonzales Flag, which featured a lone star and a cannon with the words *Come and Take It* emblazoned beneath.

In November 1835, the Republic of Texas Navy was commissioned. The flag of the Navy was created by Charles Hawkins, the first commodore, and featured a lone star on a blue background and thirteen stripes, alternating red and white.

No matter which flag has flown over Texas, its people have vigorously defended their culture and heritage. Texans are proud of their history and the six flags that have officially flown over their state.

Benedict Arnold

Here's the story: On his deathbed in 1801, Benedict Arnold donned his old Continental Army togs and repented his treason with the words "Let me die in this old uniform in which I fought my battles. May God forgive me for ever having put on another." And here's the truth.

* * * *

WHILE SERVING AS a general in the Continental Army during the Revolutionary War, Benedict Arnold switched sides when he attempted to surrender the American fort at West Point to the British. Twenty years later, as Arnold lay dying of dropsy at home in England, his wife, Margaret, could do little to relieve his terminal suffering and delirium. When she broke the sad news to his sons in America, she described him as barely able to breathe, suffering from "a very dreadful nervous symptom." The same letter says nothing about a uniform or a dying wish.

Another weakness in the story: It sounds exactly like what later generations of patriotic Americans would like to hear. It also sounds far too noble for Arnold, who had turned his coat seeking opportunity and ended up finding little. If people want a feel-good story about Arnold, they should note that this brave, energetic officer did the colonial cause far more good than harm. By the time he betrayed the colonies, much had gone wrong for the British (thanks in part to Benedict himself). Arnold was in heavy debt and felt slighted in favor of mediocre officers. Most good officers rise above such frustrations, but the temperamental Arnold chose high treason instead.

His unsavory reputation had followed him from Canada to England, making him a tolerated but unpopular figure. His postwar businesses hadn't thrived, and with Napoleon running amok, Arnold's death and burial were relatively insignificant.

The Burr Conspiracy

Forget Hollywood: One of America's most dramatic plotlines comes straight from the Buckeye State. The scene involves a deadly duel, an island-based militia, and a plot to take over multiple states—all at the hands of a former vice president.

✳ ✳ ✳ ✳

A ARON BURR GAINED fame as vice president under Thomas Jefferson from 1801 to 1805. It was toward the end of that term, though, that Burr's name really became notorious.

In July 1804, Burr decided he'd heard enough slandering from his political opponent, Alexander Hamilton. Burr and Hamilton, who was once the secretary of the Treasury, faced off in a historic duel at Weehawken, New Jersey. Burr won, shooting and killing Hamilton.

Needless to say, the whole idea of murdering a political opponent didn't go over so well in Washington. Burr still finished his term as VP but soon headed west to carry out some more sinister plans. In those days, the West was, well, wild, with sparse settlements and limited control. Burr had his sights set on the newly acquired Louisiana Purchase along with the future great state of Texas, which was still colonized by Spain. Burr figured he might as well build his own military, dominate the land, and establish his own empire.

Burr's first brainstorm was to turn to Britain. The inspired conspirator met with the nation's U.S. minister and threw out the idea of leading a revolt in the West in exchange for his country's money and ships. The boys from Britain, however, weren't too keen on the concept, and the plan never came together.

Still, Burr was determined. In 1806, he secured the support of the wealthy Harman Blennerhassett. Blennerhassett owned his own island, a small spread in the Ohio River now known as Blennerhassett Island. Burr and Blennerhassett teamed up to take over the world—or at least part of America. The two started training a militia on the private island. A U.S. Army commander named James Wilkinson was kind enough to provide them with heavy artillery.

Just when Burr's conspiracy seemed to be taking shape, his plans fell apart. Newspapers started picking up word of the army he was creating. It wasn't until the governor of Ohio stepped in, though, that the joyride came to a definitive end.

The short story: Ohio's state militia raided Blennerhassett Island. The troops took boats and supplies, but Burr, Blennerhassett, and most of their army were already long gone.

The Fallout

Burr could only hide for so long. By early 1807, Burr was captured and put on trial. The case, heard by the Supreme Court, would become one of history's most famous. The evidence made it clear that Burr had toyed with the idea of building his own military in the West. Burr, though, argued that the Constitution defined true treason as an overt—not merely planned—military act. What's more, he said the act had to take place in the same district where the case was being tried.

All that legal gobbledygook ended up meaning a lot: Burr, his crew admitted, did deal with a militia and enough weapons to weigh down a herd of elephants while in Ohio. But no one could prove that any of it was actually intended to be used for treason—and no one could definitively connect the material items with the bad guy pep talks Burr had given to his followers. Given all that, the judge ended up ruling in Burr's favor.

It probably goes without saying that the case brought a lot of attention to the state. Ohioans took great pride in their governor's fast action in invading Blennerhassett Island. Still, sometimes it's best to leave a tainted past behind. Ohio ended up saying so long to Blennerhassett Island, giving it to West Virginia and cutting its ties with the troubling land.

Presidential Nicknames

Nicknames can be a measure of a president's place in history.

✳   ✳   ✳   ✳

Theodore Roosevelt had quite a few memorable nicknames. He was known as "The Trustbuster," who broke up giant corporations, and "The Rough Rider," whose wartime heroics in Cuba made him "The Hero of San Juan Hill." Yet Roosevelt was also dubbed "The Meddler" for his intervention in many sectors of society.

Abraham Lincoln was best known as "Honest Abe," but the 16th president had other monikers as well. His supporters hailed Father Abraham as "The Rail Splitter" and "The Great Emancipator." His detractors, playing on his long limbs, tagged him "The Illinois Ape."

Two recent presidents, Bill Clinton and Ronald Reagan, had numerous nicknames. Clinton has been called "The Comeback Kid," "Bubba," and "Slick Willie." Reagan was dubbed "The Great Communicator" and "The Gipper." Reagan also had a nickname any politician would crave: "The Teflon President"— meaning that few criticisms stuck to him.

It seems odd that the longest-serving president, Franklin Delano Roosevelt, had no lasting nicknames except for his initials, FDR. Shortening Roosevelt's name to initials set a precedent for some future chief executives, namely JFK (John Fitzgerald Kennedy), and LBJ (Lyndon Baines Johnson).

Some nicknames fit the character like a well-measured shoe. A nickname may never have fit better than the one for tight-lipped Calvin Coolidge: "Silent Cal." At one state dinner, a guest told Coolidge she had wagered friends that she could get at least three words out of the Sphinx of the Potomac. Coolidge coolly replied: "You lose."

Many nicknames were hard to live down. The guileful Richard Nixon was known as "Tricky Dick." Chester A. Arthur was called "Prince Arthur" because of his weakness for fine clothes. Grover Cleveland, who holds the record for most presidential vetoes, was dubbed "His Obstinacy." Worse, Cleveland was called "The Hangman of Buffalo" (while sheriff in Buffalo, New York, Cleveland personally slipped the noose around two felons). And the grandly named Rutherford B. Hayes was tagged "RutherFraud" after his disputed 1876 election.

Nicknames can be used for political advantage. Dwight Eisenhower used his for a catchy campaign slogan: "I Like Ike." George W. Bush used his mildly derisive nickname, "Dubya," to tweak opponent Al Gore's supposed invention of the Internet, noting that he himself was referred to as "Dubya, Dubya, Dubya" (as in the World Wide Web).

Some nicknames are stirring, especially those gained in the military. Zachary Taylor was called "Old Rough and Ready" for his spartan style of fighting. Andrew Jackson was named "Old Hickory" for leading a campaign while recovering from a dueling wound. William Henry Harrison was dubbed "Tippecanoe" to commemorate the name of his victorious battle.

Some nicknames are deflating. John Tyler was called "His Accidency" when he took office after the untimely death of William Henry Harrison. Franklin Pierce was dubbed "The Fainting General" for having been knocked unconscious during a battle. James Madison, best known as "The Father of the Constitution," was vilified as "The Fugitive President" for fleeing Washington, D.C., during the British invasion of 1814.

And when then-Vice President John Adams suggested that George Washington be referred to as "His Majesty," Adams's foes were so irked by the regal, undemocratic-sounding title that they responded by sticking the stout VP with his own honorific: "His Rotundity."

Counting On You Since 1790: The U.S. Census

The U.S. Census builds on a governmental question dating back to ancient Mesopotamia: "How many people do we have?" Of course, the original U.S. Census had a few... well, inequities.

✳   ✳   ✳   ✳

EVER SINCE ANCIENT Sumer, governments have desired to estimate military-capable manpower, facilitate urban and transportation planning, provide some idea of economic status, and (most importantly) aid taxation.

After full independence (1783), it took the young United States some years to do the things real nations did: mint coins, lean on bootleggers, build a real navy, enact shortsighted public policy, storm out of diplomatic summits over petty slights, oppress minorities, and tell the citizenry "no" once in awhile. Real nations had censuses; plus, the Constitution mandated one to determine congressional representation. Congress decreed August 2, 1790, Census Day.

The First Census

Remember that time when you didn't answer the door for the Census people? Good luck with that; U.S. Marshals took the first census. If you lied or didn't cooperate, the fine was $200 ($4,680 in 2007 dollars, following the Consumer Price Index). The cops wanted to enumerate (census-ese for "count") everyone living in each dwelling, specifically:

* Who's the head of household?

* How many free white males age 16+ live here? Under 16?

* Free white females (age irrelevant)?

* Nonwhite free persons (specify gender and color; age irrelevant)?

* Slaves (gender and age irrelevant)?

Sexist, surely; racist, terribly—but it revealed the country's military and industrial potential. In a pattern Native Americans would soon recognize, the census didn't count them. For tax and legislative purposes, a slave counted as three-fifths of a person, thus clarifying where they stood in the Land of Liberty's pecking order.

The first census revealed 3.93 million people, including nearly 700,000 slaves (actual number before the three-fifths coefficient was applied). Thomas Jefferson and George Washington figured the police had botched it somehow, that the numbers should have been higher.

The First Century

Congress decided to take a decennial census (census-ese for "once a decade"). Here are some of the ongoing changes:

1800: More age categories, and women's ages now mattered. Native Americans now counted.

1810: First attempt to gather economic data. Data reveals that marshals are lousy at collecting economic data.

1820: First occupational questions. Results indicate that marshals are also inconsistent at collecting occupational data.

1830: First use of standard questionnaires; age data now collected by decade of life. Government gives up on economic data for the time being, since cops keep bungling that one. First questions about blindness, deaf/muteness.

1840: Nosiest census yet with questions about education, literacy, occupation, and resources.

1850: The Census begins taking its modern shape. Every free person is listed by name (even women!). Slaves are assigned numbers. "Mulatto" is now an official racial category. In addition to deaf, blind, and "dumb," a person of any race can be described as "insane," "idiotic," "pauper," or "convict." Slaves cannot be described as paupers or convicts (which makes a certain tragic sense) but can still be "insane" or "idiotic." The number of escaped slaves must be described, as must the number manumitted (released from slavery) in the past year. Clearly, equality is on the march.

1860: Marshals are out of the census business. Much rejoicing among marshals.

1870: With slavery abolished, slave questionnaire no longer necessary. First census to include racial categories "Chinese" (all east Asians) and "Indian" (Native American).

1880: Enumerators first ask about crippling disabilities (other than blindness, deafness, idiocy, or insanity).

1890: First use of an electric tabulating system. No one realizes it at the time, but this system is an ancestor of later computing monolith IBM.

1903: U.S. Government celebrates Census's 113rd anniversary by finally establishing the U.S. Census Bureau.

From the Grave

A former U.S. congressman and Virginia plantation owner was buried in a curious manner—in order to keep a watchful eye on his slaves even in death.

✳   ✳   ✳   ✳

IN A DAY and age when slavery was the norm, Colonel George Hancock (1754–1820) was a decided cut below. When dealing with the slaves on his estate, Hancock took special pleasure in their toil and torment. In his sadistic view, he had every right. After all, weren't these the same liars that shunned their duties whenever he turned his back? Driven by such relentless suspicion, Hancock was forever on the lookout for better ways to keep his slaves in line—during and *after* his natural life.

Ambitious and Malicious

On paper, one would hardly find reason to suspect that Hancock was anything but a refined southern gentleman. A colonel during the Revolutionary War, Hancock became a lawyer at the war's end and eventually entered politics. He was elected as a U.S. congressman and served from 1793 to 1797.

When his congressional term came to a close, Hancock acquired the southern Virginia estate of Fotheringay—named for the English castle where Mary, Queen of Scots was beheaded in 1587. There, like most prosperous southern men of his day, he kept slaves.

Whenever political duties took Hancock away from his mansion, he would return with a large and bitter chip on his shoulder. So certain was he that his slaves had been misbehaving and slacking off in his absence, Hancock would dole out punishment without any proof that they had in fact done anything wrong. Completely overlooking his own sadistic ways, Hancock openly questioned the loyalty of his slaves—then punished them whether or not he had cause.

Heartbreak and Burial

In 1820, Hancock's 29-year-old daughter Julia died unexpectedly. It was more than the colonel could bear. Crushed by her sudden demise, Hancock himself took ill and passed away shortly thereafter. A double funeral service was held for father and daughter at Fotheringay. At the colonel's request, he was placed beside his daughter in a vault overlooking his acreage.

But from there, according to reports, his request got a bit strange. Apparently, it was the wish of the colonel to be buried sitting up. What was the colonel's rationale for requesting burial in an upright position? It would enable him to watch over his slaves in the fields below "and keep them from loafing on the job," he reportedly said. In death—as in life—Hancock apparently had no intention of easing up on his slaves.

Cruel Man of His Word

For years the legend of Hancock's upright burial was just that—a legend. But then a newcomer decided to delve deeper and learn the truth. In 1886, the new owner of Fotheringay, Anne Beale Edmundsun, took action. Hancock's mausoleum had begun to crumble, and she decided to enter it to learn the full extent of the damage. Of course, this would also enable her to investigate the account of his burial and separate fact from fiction.

Once inside, Edmundsun and her family members discovered a mass of bones. At the top of the heap they found a skull. They assumed the skull could only belong to Colonel Hancock, since all other family members were accounted for. Just beneath the heap were bones that appeared to be from the colonel's legs and trunk. A cruel overseer to the very end, Hancock had indeed been buried sitting up.

The Myth of the Big Easy

After Hurricane Katrina, lawmakers and media commentators questioned the wisdom of reconstructing New Orleans, a city that they claimed was "built ten feet below sea level."

✳　✳　✳　✳

ACCORDING TO RECENT geographical surveys, about 50 percent of New Orleans rests at or above sea level, and the other half rarely drops lower than minus six feet. Of the few points that lay ten feet below sea level—approximately 50 acres of the 181 total square miles of the city—none have been developed for commercial use or habitation, serving instead as culverts, canals, and highway underpasses.

A Precarious Edge of Disaster

Geography, nature, and economics have conspired over the centuries to make New Orleans particularly vulnerable to floods. The location that became "the inevitable city on an impossible site" was chosen by French settlers in 1718 because it offered an easy portage between the Mississippi River—the main water artery for the interior of North America—and Lake Ponchartrain, an outlet into the Gulf of Mexico for trading ships. (It was well into the 19th century before the mouth of the Mississippi became readily navigable for oceangoing ships.)

Isle d'Orleans

Although that land consisted mostly of cypress swamps, silt deposits left by seasonal floods over thousands of years created high ground along the banks of the river. The famous French Quarter—the original core of the city—was laid out on part of this elevated ground, some 15 feet above sea level. Over decades, the higher ground along the bending curve of the Mississippi was also settled, as the Crescent City grew behind an expanding system of levees. Because it was surrounded by a river, a lake, and swamps, the French referred to New Orleans as *Isle d'Orleans*, and for a century the city was a physical and cultural island, an outpost of the Caribbean on U.S. soil.

Developing the Land

The jewel of Jefferson's Louisiana Purchase, New Orleans grew faster than any other American city between 1810 and 1840, becoming the country's third largest after New York and Baltimore. But New Orleans's improbable geography limited its growth. The lower-lying land remained undeveloped until the early 1900s, when engineer A. Baldwin Wood invented an industrial-size screw pump for an ambitious drainage system that was built to protect the city from floods.

It's Sinking...

With nature seemingly under control, New Orleans expanded greatly during the 20th century. The shores of Lake Pontchartrain, which represent some of the lowest-lying land, were filled in and new levees were built. But the levee system also stopped the seasonal deposits of silt that created most of the land in southern Louisiana. As a result, the city and much of its surrounding landscape is sinking as the loose soil settles without replenishment. Scientists estimate that the current rate of subsidence ranges from one-third to one and a half inches per year, with the possibility that 15,000 square miles will fall at or below sea level within 70 years.

Although the flooding of New Orleans after Hurricane Katrina was definitely a manmade disaster—the levee system designed by the U.S. Army Corps of Engineers failed to perform to its design specifications—the leveed "bowl" in which the city rests is inevitably subject to flooding.

Penance for Your Sins

It started out as a unique way to help reform prisoners. It ended up being a literal torture chamber where men often died agonizing deaths. Sadly, many of those tortured souls have been unable to leave the Eastern State Penitentiary—even in death.

✳   ✳   ✳   ✳

The Road to Penance

THE REMAINS OF the Eastern State Penitentiary, the location of a truly unique experiment in the history of law enforcement, stand on what is now Fairmount Avenue in Philadelphia. Designed by John Haviland, the facility was different from other prisons in that it was meant to stress reform rather than punishment. It was thought that by giving a prisoner plenty of time to reflect on his wrongdoing, the prisoner would eventually reform himself by turning to God to make penance— hence the word *penitentiary*.

In October 1829, when the Eastern State Penitentiary officially opened for business, it was one of the largest public buildings of its kind in the United States. The entire complex resembled a giant wagon wheel, with seven wings of cells emerging from the center like spokes. The hallways themselves looked like the vestibules of a church.

Isolation and Madness

Individual cells were designed to house only one inmate each. The idea was that prisoners needed time to reflect on what they had done wrong, and giving them cell mates would only distract them from doing that.

The only people with whom inmates were allowed to interact on a regular basis were the warden—who visited every prisoner once a day—and the guards, who served meals and brought inmates to and from their cells. Inmates were permitted to go outside for exercise, but they could only do that alone. When an inmate was removed from his cell for any reason, he was required to wear a hood. Prisoners were to remain silent at all times unless asked a direct question by prison personnel; failure to adhere to this rule meant swift, sadistic punishment.

Torturous Behavior

The facility's initial intent may have been to get inmates to understand that they needed to follow the rules in order to be reformed, but that idea quickly broke down and became a practice of brutality by the guards and officials. Minor offenses, including making even the smallest noise, were often enough for authorities to subject inmates to a series of hellish punishments. Restraint devices such as straitjackets and the "mad chair"—a chair equipped with so many restraints that it made even the slightest movement impossible—were often employed. If an inmate was caught talking, he might be forced to wear the "iron gag"—a piece of metal that was clamped to his tongue while the other end was attached to leather gloves that he was forced to wear; movement resulted in excruciating pain. Legend has it that several prisoners accidentally severed their own tongues while wearing the iron gag, and at least one died while wearing the device.

Another method of torture utilized at the Eastern State Pen was the water bath. Inmates were tied to the penitentiary walls and doused with freezing water, even in the middle of winter;

under the most extreme conditions, the water would freeze on the inmates' bodies.

Perhaps one of the most heinous means of punishing an inmate was to place him in the "Klondike." While other prisons have "The Hole"—which is essentially solitary confinement—the Klondike at the Eastern State Pen was a group of four subterranean cells without windows or plumbing; inmates were made to live down there—often for several weeks at a time.

Swift Decline and Abandonment

The Eastern State Penitentiary was designed to change the world of incarceration in a positive way, but it failed miserably. In fact, when British author Charles Dickens visited the United States in 1842, one of the places that he wanted to see was the Eastern State Pen. From across the Atlantic, Dickens had heard about the marvelous and unique penitentiary and wanted to see it for himself. He was shocked by what he witnessed there, calling it "hopeless . . . cruel, and wrong."

Over the years, changes were enacted in an attempt to remedy the situation, but they didn't help. Finally, in 1971, the penitentiary was officially closed. In the mid-1990s, after sitting abandoned for years, the building was reopened for tours.

"Not All Who Walk These Blocks Are Among the Living . . ."

Looking back at the tortuous history of the Eastern State Pen, it should come as no surprise that more than a few ghosts can be found there. In fact, records indicate that inmates reported paranormal activity on the premises as early as the 1940s, so it seems that ghosts were in residence there long before the prison closed. Perhaps that explains what happened to locksmith Gary Johnson while he was working on a lock during a restoration of the prison in the early 1990s. After Johnson popped the door open, he saw shadowy shapes moving all around him. It was as if he'd allowed all the ghosts to once again roam free.

If there's one area of the penitentiary where visitors are most likely to experience paranormal activity, it is Cellblock 12. Many people have reported hearing voices echoing throughout the cellblock and even laughter coming from the cells themselves. Shadow figures are also seen in abundance there.

Another location at the Eastern State Penitentiary that is said to be haunted is the guard tower that sits high atop the main wall. People standing outside the prison have seen a shadowy figure walking along the wall; it calmly looks down at them from time to time.

"Dude, Run!"

Over the years, various ghost-hunting television shows have visited the Eastern State Penitentiary and submitted paranormal evidence to their viewers. The facility was featured in a 2001 episode of MTV's *Fear*. In 2007, *Most Haunted* investigated the place, and *Ghost Adventures* filmed an episode there in 2009. But if the Eastern State Penitentiary is forever linked to a paranormal research show, it would be *Ghost Hunters*, due to its team's 2004 investigation and the actions of one of its members.

At approximately 3 A.M., investigator Brian Harnois of The Atlantic Paranormal Society (TAPS) entered Cellblock 4 with Dave Hobbs, a member of the show's production crew. As Hobbs snapped a photograph, he and Harnois thought they saw a huge black shape rise up and move in front of them. They both panicked, and Harnois yelled out the now-famous line, "Dude, run!" after which the pair bolted down the hallway, much to the chagrin of their fellow investigators (who quickly deduced that the shape had been caused by the camera flash). The incident overshadowed an intriguing piece of evidence that was captured later that night, when one of the team's video cameras recorded a dark shape—almost human in form— that appeared to be moving quickly along a cellblock. Try as they might, TAPS was unable to come up with a scientific explanation for the shape, leaving who or what it was open to interpretation.

Get Out of Jail Free

If you would like to potentially encounter a ghost and have a firsthand look inside one of the unique architectural structures in the United States, the Eastern State Penitentiary is open for tours. You can also take part in a nighttime ghost tour there. Should you choose to embark on one of these adventures, be careful: A lot of the ghosts there are "lifers," and they just might jump at the chance to escape by following you home!

The Cincinnati Observatory

In 1842, Ormsby M. Mitchel started a series of public astronomy lectures that fascinated the Ohio River city. He asked people to donate money—as shareholders—to establish the Cincinnati Astronomical Society. Its mission: to buy a well-crafted telescope and build an observatory to house it. To Mitchel's surprise, 300 people pledged money.

✳   ✳   ✳   ✳

IT WAS IN 1842 that Ormsby M. Mitchel traveled to Munich to inspect a 12-inch objective lens manufactured by a German optical factory. He ordered one and returned home to start constructing the Cincinnati Observatory on four acres donated by wealthy businessman Nicholas Longworth. It stood atop Mount Ida, 400 feet above the growing city.

On November 9, 1843, former President John Quincy Adams participated in laying the observatory's cornerstone. He delivered his last public speech that day. A believer in the sciences, Adams had tried, unsuccessfully, to persuade Congress to build a national observatory. When he left town, the appreciative city renamed the hill in his honor—Mount Adams.

By the time the telescope arrived from Germany in January 1845, the nation had slipped into an economic depression.

Because most of the pledged money had been spent to buy the telescope, Mitchel had to use his own money and raise more from the public to start constructing the building. Many workers agreed to help at no charge.

On April 14 of that year, Cincinnati's telescope started operating. Mitchel discovered a companion to the bright star Antares. He also founded *The Sidereal Messenger*, the first astronomical publication in the United States. Just as the observatory seemed ready for great work, the Cincinnati College burned, leaving Mitchel without an employer and the observatory with no source of funds. He agreed to serve as director without pay while the society limped along on donations.

Enduring and Reopening

Still without a paycheck by the early 1850s, Mitchel moved to Albany, New York, to help develop a new observatory. When the Civil War started in 1861, Mitchel returned to Ohio to become a Union general. After helping Cincinnati build defensive positions, he moved on to other missions. He died of yellow fever while serving in South Carolina in 1862.

The Cincinnati Observatory, meanwhile, was closed during the war. In 1868 it reopened, and a new director, Cleveland Abbe, moved it to neighboring Mount Lookout to avoid the city's heat, dust, and smoke. The new observatory opened in 1873, using the old telescope. But Abbe accomplished more than scanning the skies: He established regular weather reports and storm predictions, for which he was nicknamed "Old Probabilities." Impressed by his predictions, the federal government hired him to come to Washington, D.C., to establish the United States Weather Bureau.

Again, the Cincinnati Observatory closed temporarily. But in time, it hired new directors and expanded. In 1904, a 16-inch refractor telescope was installed in the old building, and a new building was constructed to house the original reflector telescope, with a shortened tube.

In 1997, preservation became a priority when local astronomy enthusiasts formed the Cincinnati Observatory Center as a volunteer committee that was dedicated to saving the observatory in its historical surroundings. Late that same year, the group won designation for the observatory as a National Historic Landmark from the U.S. Department of the Interior.

Today, the nation's oldest observatory serves more than 6,000 people annually, both youths and adults. "There are a lot of closet astronomers out there," said Dean Regas, staff outreach astronomer. "We appeal to them and to a lot of other people who just want to look at the stars."

Faces of Death

In today's modern world taking casts of a dead person's face might seem a bit macabre, but the practice offered family and loved ones a tangible connection to the deceased.

✳ ✳ ✳ ✳

DEATH MASKS DATE back to an era before photography or voice recording. While death masks made of wax or plaster can be traced back to the Middle Ages, those made in more recent times tend to capture the imagination. Some of these castings also prove that the practice remained popular even after photography became possible. Here are a few notable and interesting casts:

* The death mask of Mary Queen of Scots looks downright fetching, despite the fact that it was taken *after* her beheading by Queen Elizabeth in 1587. Apparently royals know how to keep up appearances—even in the afterlife.

* Composer Ludwig van Beethoven (1770-1827) had his death mask taken only after his friend Stephen Von Breuning labored over the decision. In the end, Von Breuning felt that denying the process might be "regarded as an insult to the public."

* The genius who gave us alternating current, Nicola Tesla, was immortalized with a death mask when he died nearly forgotten and penniless in 1943. Not surprisingly, his final expression isn't one of great joy.

* Bank robber John Dillinger will live through the ages via a death mask taken by the Cook County Morgue just after he was gunned down in 1934. Crime might not pay but it can produce some interesting souvenirs.

* Proving that all of us, no matter how powerful, will succumb, the death mask of George Reeves, the star of television's *The Adventures of Superman*, was taken after his mysterious shooting death in 1959.

Utopian Societies

In 1516, Sir Thomas More coined the term utopia in a book of the same name. In it he refers to an ideal, imaginary island where everything is lovely all the time. For centuries since then, groups of people have broken off from society to develop their own communities intended to bring peace, harmony, and spiritual enlightenment to their citizens—and ultimately the whole world. Unfortunately, utopian societies seldom work out as planned.

✳ ✳ ✳ ✳

Founder: Charles Fourier

Plan: In the mid-19th century, Fourier contacted out-of-work New Englanders with the proposition that they would join communal-living groups he called *phalanxes*. These groups would be arranged according to members' trades or skills. Children are good at digging in the dirt, for example, so they would be in charge of maintaining the garbage dumps. Group members would be compensated for their contributions to the community.

Outcome: Fourier died in Paris before he saw the development of any phalanxes. In the early 1840s, a group of devotees, or

Fourierists, founded the North American Phalanx on farmland in New Jersey and kept it going until disputes over women's rights and abolition drove many away. A fire destroyed buildings on the site in 1854, and operations ceased completely in 1856.

Founder: Robert Owen

Plan: Owen called his version of utopia New Harmony and hoped his "empire of goodwill" would eventually take over the world. His attempt at communal bliss started in Indiana in 1825.

Outcome: Hundreds of devoted followers lived according to Owen's ideals, with individual members plying their crafts and contributing to the community (even if that meant there was no one with the ability to spin the wool shorn by an abundance of sheepshearers). With no sound economic plan, New Harmony was in chaos from the start. There were five constitutions drafted in the first year alone. New Harmony failed within two years.

Founder: The Spiritualists

Plan: The Mountain Cove Community was the Spiritualists' attempt to create their own idea of harmony. They founded their group in Virginia in 1851 on a spot once considered to be the Garden of Eden. The group insisted that no one individual would be allowed to dictate to others; all the direction anyone needed would come from "the spirits."

Outcome: As part of their introduction into the community, members were required to give up all their possessions, again leaving issues such as finances to the spirit world. Not surprisingly, the experiment lasted less than two years.

Founder: Etienne Cabet

Plan: Cabet's *Voyage en Icarie*, written in 1840, depicted an ideal society, the Icarians, in which an elected government controlled all economic activity as well as social affairs. Cabet decided to make his dream a reality and set sail for America.

Outcome: In 1848, the group landed outside New Orleans on swampland not fit for settlement. Malaria and starvation took many of this group, and the rest deserted around 1856.

Founder: The Shakers

Plan: The Shakers were an 18th-century religious denomination of Protestants who decided to leave the immoral world behind and create a pious place in which to live and serve God.

Outcome: By the mid-1800s, the Shakers had built 19 communal settlements in New England, Kentucky, and Ohio that attracted some 200,000 followers. Their numbers gradually dwindled, but their simple way of life continues to attract widespread interest. The Shakers are generally considered to be one of the few successful utopian societies.

The Tomb in Washington Square Park

What lies beneath the surface of a popular New York City park?

✳   ✳   ✳   ✳

WHEN YOU WALK through an old public park in a large city, there's always a chance you're walking over an old graveyard. Many cities had to use parks to bury the dead during times of plague, and some major parks, like Chicago's Lincoln Park, actually served as the town's official burial ground before being converted into a normal public park as the city grew up around it.

Graveyard is only one of many functions that New York City's Washington Square Park has served over the years. It's been a friendly public gathering place for generations, but in earlier times it served as the town's site for public executions. A common urban legend states that the large elm tree at the northwest corner once served as the "hangman's elm," from which convicts were hanged by the neck until dead.

Only one actual hanging is known to have taken place in the park, and eyewitness descriptions vary as to where, exactly, that hanging took place. But at more than 300 years old, the tree was certainly standing at the time when the execution occurred. It's the oldest tree in Manhattan.

Lost Plot(s)

In the early days of the 19th century, the park served not only as a place of execution, but also as the city's "potter's field," a patch of ground where unmarked bodies were buried. But as New York grew from a market town into a modern metropolis, the city outgrew the small space, and it was closed for use as a cemetery in 1825. Records vary, but sources indicate that between 2,000 and 20,000 bodies were interred there. A 2005 archaeological survey suggested that 20,000 was a fairly low estimate, and found no evidence that any effort at all had been made to move the bodies when the space was converted into a "military parade ground" and park.

But apparently it wasn't only the poor and friendless who were buried in the park, and not all of the graves were anonymous or unmarked. As recently as 2009, an intact tombstone was found buried two feet under the ground, featuring an inscription stating, "Here lies the body of James Jackson who departed this life the 22nd Day of September 1799 aged 28 years native of the county of Kildare Ireland."

A Tomb of One's Own

Mr. Jackson's body itself was not found, but perhaps his was among the many that had already been dug up inadvertently over the years. Since most people known to be interred in the old park were buried in unmarked graves, finding a tombstone was unexpected—but not as big a shock as the one that came in 1965. In that year, workers from the Consolidated Edison company were digging in the park to install a new electrical transformer when they came across something unexpected, a concrete dome buried four or five feet under the surface.

Workers assumed it to be one of the countless abandoned tunnels that lie beneath the ground in Manhattan, but upon breaking through the concrete, they found another dome made of brick and mortar. Breaking through that dome led them to a staircase, one that led downward to a wooden door.

And when they opened the wooden door, they found that it led to a brick-walled underground room full of skeletons.

A spokesman for Consolidated Edison said that "The room was whitewashed, dry, and odorless....There were the outlines of coffins—the wood had disintegrated—and one of the skeletons lying in or near the outline of a coffin. Other skeletons were piled in a corner." Another spokesman said that he personally had never uncovered so much as a thigh bone before, but couldn't resist making a crack about the hippies who populated the park in those days: "I have," he told *The New York Times* with a wink, "seen some skeletons walking around that park with sandals on."

Finding skeletons in the park was hardly unusual for workers in the area—in fact, students of the nearby New York University once lined a fence with skulls that had ben dug up by workers digging out underground pipes and mains. Still, finding a full tomb in the park was completely unexpected. No one had any record of such a thing being built, and archaeologists could only guess about when it was constructed—and why.

The prevailing opinion was that the tomb had been hastily built to house victims who had been killed off by one of the many "plagues" that swept through the city in the late 1700s, such as a yellow fever epidemic from 1798. However, some records indicate that the "northeast quadrant" had once been a church cemetery, and that the vault was built for members of a Scottish Presbyterian church.

Even as late as 2005, when archaeologists released a study on the park, they were not entirely sure what the vault was, or how long it had been there, or even whether it was the only underground vault in the northeast quadrant. Workers in 1965 simply covered it back up, so the mysterious tomb is still lying beneath a seating plaza and a playground today. Those particular skeletons seem to be there to stay—but others continue to be found in the park regularly.

Tales From Central Park: At the Center of It All

A stroll through New York City's Central Park might lead you to believe that it is the one remaining slice of nature amid the towering skyscrapers of steel and glass that flank it. But, in fact, this urban park was almost entirely human-made. Even though Manhattan's northern half was laid out in the early 19th century, the park was not part of the Commissioners' Plan of 1811.

Between 1821 and 1855, the population of New York nearly quadrupled. This growth convinced city planners that a large, open-air space was required. Initial plans mimicked the large public grounds of London and Paris, but it was eventually decided that the space should evoke feelings of nature—complete with running water, dense wooded areas, and even rolling hills.

❋ ❋ ❋ ❋

Planning the Park

THE ORIGINAL PARK layout included the area stretching from 59th to 106th streets and also included land between 5th and 8th avenues. The land itself cost about $5 million. This part of Manhattan featured an irregular terrain of swamps and bluffs and included rocky outcrops left from the last Ice Age 10,000 years earlier; it was deemed unsuitable for private development but was ideal for creating the park that leaders envisioned. However, the area was not uninhabited. It was home to about 1,600 poor residents, most of them Irish and German immigrants, though there was a thriving African American community there as well. Ultimately, these groups were resettled, and the park's boundaries were extended to 110th Street.

In the 1850s, the state of New York appointed a Central Park Commission to oversee the development of the green space. A landscape design contest was held in 1857, and writer and landscape architect Frederick Law Olmsted and architect Calvert Vaux won with their "Greensward Plan."

Olmsted and Vaux envisioned a park that would include "separate circulation systems" for its assorted users, including pedestrians and horseback riders. To accommodate crosstown traffic while still maintaining the sense of a continuous single park, the roads that traversed Central Park from east to west were sunken and screened with planted shrub belts. Likewise, the Greensward Plan called for three dozen bridges, all designed by Vaux, with no two alike. These included simple granite bridges as well as ornate neogothic conceptions made of cast iron. The southern portion of the park was designed to include the mall walk to Bethesda Terrace and Bethesda Fountain, which provided a view of the lake and woodland to the north.

Construction Begins

Central Park was one of the largest public works projects in New York during the 19th century, with some 20,000 workers on hand to reshape the topography of nearly 850 acres. Massive amounts of gunpowder (more, in fact, than was used in the Battle of Gettysburg) were used to blast the rocky ridges, and nearly three million cubic yards of soil were moved. At the same time, some 270,000 trees and shrubs were planted to replicate the feeling of nature.

Despite the massive scale of work involved, the park first opened for public use in 1858; by 1865, it was receiving more than seven million visitors a year. Strict rules on group picnics and certain activities kept some New York residents away, but by the 1880s, the park was as welcoming to the working class as it was to the wealthy.

Over time, the park took on a number of additions, including the famous carousel and zoo, and activities such as tennis and bike riding became part of the landscape. Today, Central Park plays host to concerts, Shakespeare plays, swimming, and ice-skating. It also features a bird sanctuary for watchers and their feathered friends alike and is a pleasant urban retreat for millions of New Yorkers.

California Divided Against Itself

Although admitted into the Union as a free state, California spent the next few years in the heated battle over slavery.

✳   ✳   ✳   ✳

BECAUSE MOST OF the Civil War was concentrated in the eastern portion of the United States, it is often forgotten that at the outbreak of the conflict, California had been a state for more than a decade. It had been admitted into the Union as a free state, but California had spent much of its time as a state searching for its place in the slavery debate. The fact that the state elected an abolitionist and a slave owner as its first two senators didn't help matters.

A Strange Proposition

Shortly after becoming a state in 1850, California was presented with an unusual offer. The California Assembly received a petition signed by more than 1,200 South Carolinians requesting that they be allowed to immigrate to the Golden State with their slaves. They argued that the full potential of the rich California soil could only be reached if slaves were used to till the land. The California Assembly denied the request, but many slave owners moved west anyway.

This migration of slave holders and slaves soon became an issue that could not be ignored. In 1852, the state assembly passed a controversial fugitive slave law. Although California was a free state, this law required that if slaves escaped from their masters within California were found, they had to be returned to their masters. In 1855, the state legislature failed to renew the law, allowing it to lapse.

California continued to wrestle with the treatment of non-whites, passing more laws that removed the rights of free blacks and other minorities. "Black and mulatto persons are rendered incompetent as witnesses to give evidence against white persons," one law read. Another piece of legislation outlawed mixed marriages, an act that would not be repealed until 1948.

A Land Without Laws

During this period of California's history, San Francisco was considered the cultural center of the state. The state's southern portion was considered by many to be almost lawless. Law enforcement was inadequate at best in that area, and escaped criminals used the region to hide out and launch attacks on travelers and ranchers. The region also became a safe zone from prosecution where slave owners and military deserters could live their lives as they wished.

Slavery sympathizers continued to make inroads into the free state's political system, especially in southern California. The California territory had debated the idea of creating two separate states even before its admittance to the Union, although the idea had not come from the desire to create a slave state. Instead, it was a protest against unequal taxation and the lack of law enforcement and infrastructure in the southern region. But slave owners and their political cronies identified this as a perfect opportunity to turn the turmoil to their advantage.

Laws of Division

Bills were introduced almost every year during the 1850s asking for the state to be split in two around the town of San Luis Obispo. Over and over again, the proposals were defeated until a referendum finally passed during the administration of Governor John B. Weller in 1859. Although the legality of the referendum was openly questioned, the people voted to split California into two distinct units, and all that was needed to put it into effect was the approval of the U.S. Congress. Congress, however, was tied up with a small problem of its own—keeping the entire nation together. The issue of some squabbling ranchers and gold seekers was not as important as the possible secession of the South and the dissolution of the Union. Congress let the movement to divide California die as it moved on to other items on the agenda.

No Speed to Secede

Not every state that ultimately joined the Confederacy was in a rush to leave the Union.

✳   ✳   ✳   ✳

THE VARIOUS STATES of the Confederacy didn't all secede from the Union at the same time, of course. A number of them even had considerable debate over whether to secede at all. So while seven Southern states—South Carolina, Mississippi, Florida, Alabama, Georgia, Louisiana, and Texas—opted to leave the Union within a period of less than a month and a half, four others—Virginia, Arkansas, North Carolina, and Tennessee—held out for longer than that.

To be truthful, support for secession was not unanimous in any of the Southern states, and significant numbers of Southern men fought for the federal cause. Much of the dissent within individual states was between the residents of different geographical regions that, like the North and South in general, differed from each other economically and culturally.

The Stragglers Secede

Virginia was the first of the second wave of states to secede, doing so on April 17, 1861. This was in reaction to President Lincoln ordering the state to deploy its militia against the rebels who had attacked Fort Sumter in South Carolina. Soon after Virginia joined the Confederacy, Richmond replaced

Montgomery, Alabama, as the capital of the Confederate States of America. Despite this honor, however, Virginia was so divided between pro- and anti-Union tendencies that its westernmost regions counter-seceded from the state. They were admitted to the United States as a brand new state, West Virginia, in 1863. So in addition to being ravaged by the war—more major battles were fought on its soil than on that of any other state—Virginia also lost some of its territory and about 400,000 of its citizens before the fighting had finished.

Arkansas was also strongly divided between those loyal to the Union and those favoring secession. The eastern and southern parts of the state were controlled by cotton planters—whose plantations were farmed by the state's 111,000 slaves—and they opted for secession, while the northern and western portions were dominated by small farmers who opposed it. In March 1861, the state legislature voted to remain within the Union, a decision that was reversed amid much dissension on May 6, 1861, when the legislature voted to secede. Some 13,000 of the state's residents, many black, subsequently served in the Union forces.

North Carolina was a relatively progressive, prosperous state that by 1861 was making advances in education, tax reform, transportation, and women's rights, but its economy was based largely on agriculture and slave-supported tobacco plantations. Pro-Union sentiment stalled secession, but on May 20, 1861, North Carolina became the tenth state to leave the Union.

The Last State to Go

Tennessee also had its regional differences. It was torn by almost unanimous support for the Confederacy in its slave-holding middle and western areas but equally fervent support for the Union in its east. The Tennessee legislature ultimately voted to secede on June 8, 1861. More than 31,000 of its residents showed their loyalty to the Union, however, by fighting for it, and Tennessee was wrecked by the conflict, seeing more battles fought on its soil than any state other than Virginia. Even though the state seceded, one of its senators, Andrew Johnson, refused to withdraw from the Senate. He continued to represent the people of his state, even though they had abandoned him, until Lincoln made him military governor of occupied Tennessee in 1862.

Helping Children to "See the Truth"

The power of the written word is nothing new, so it's not surprising that both the North and South used publications to try to influence children during the Civil War.

✳ ✳ ✳ ✳

IN ANY WAR, winning the hearts and minds of those on the home front is often as important as winning battles in the heat of the conflict. During the Civil War, written propaganda was widely used on both sides to achieve this aim. And the propaganda was aimed not only at adults but at children, as well.

Northern Influence

In the North, with its industrial centers as resources, countless magazines and books containing factual and fictional war tales were aimed directly at children. One of the most popular Northern children's magazines of the day, *The Little Corporal*, used a banner across the cover to proclaim: "Fighting against wrong and for the good, the true and the beautiful." This magazine told stories of how children could help their Republic through love of God and country. It also offered toys and games with a military theme.

Older children who enjoyed reading had their choice of limitless titles and "dime novels." Adventure books with such titles as *The Spy of Atlanta, Vicksburg Spy,* and *War Trails* spun yarns of brave Northern heroes who gave their lives to defeat what was portrayed as a Godless South and its treacherous soldiers.

Teaching children to support the war even entered the educational system, as can be seen in a simple ABC book of the time: "A is for America, land of the free, B is a battle our soldiers did see." This primer sought to influence students and was illustrated with engravings of dead and dying Confederate soldiers. Other books taught the alphabet using letter examples such as A for "Abolitionist" and B for "Brother with a skin of somewhat darker hue."

The glorification of children in combat also began at this time, leading to a new literary style called the "dead drummer boy poem." Dramatic poems that glorified the lost lives of innocent boys became immensely popular and are still emotionally gripping today. Northern writers were even accused of encouraging young boys to run away from home to join up under a false ideal of war.

Southern Views

The South also produced literature for its youth, but due to the shortage of ink, paper, and printing facilities, the number of books was limited, and the writings focused mostly on religion and learning. In fact, of all the children's books published in the South during the war, three-quarters were schoolbooks. The textbooks worked to create a sense of Southern nationalism in the next generation of Confederates and included such books as *The Dixie Primer, The Confederate Spelling Book,* and *A New Southern Grammar.*

Southern children had their literary heroes as well, but they were limited. Protagonists were usually faceless and nameless men and boys or the great generals of the South. In contrast to the Northern themes of heroism and winning for the glory of God, family, and country, however, the stories printed in the South leaned more toward teaching young people how to deal with the horrors of war. Southern children's magazines showed the young that they should accept loss and death as part of the greater good. "We are fighting . . . to drive wicked invaders from our land," one source told Southern kids. Stories such as "The Young Confederate Soldier" and "Story of a Refugee" implanted images of horrid treatment of brave Confederate soldiers and civilians at the hands of Yankees.

Educators and social scientists continue to debate the effectiveness of such children's propaganda. While most agree with the importance of involving children in an ongoing conflict such as the Civil War, some have speculated that the information and attitudes presented on both sides may have laid the groundwork for belief systems that permeate the North and the South to this day.

Confederate Cash

Printing nearly $1.7 billion in Confederate money during the Civil War wasn't as easy as it seemed.

✳ ✳ ✳ ✳

WHEN THE CONFEDERACY declared its independence from the Union in 1861, the fledgling government knew it had to establish the institutions that all functioning and legitimate governments must have. Within its first two months, the Confederacy introduced its first run of currency—a big gamble, riding on whether or not its independence would be successful and whether the money would actually be worth anything in the long run. This decision ultimately devastated the South, flooding it with useless, valueless currency. But there were still more problems ahead before matters got to that point.

Lack of Skill

Perhaps the first indication that the South should have held off on printing its own currency was the fact that the currency had to be printed in the North. The agriculturally based economy of the South had previously had no need for skilled industrial tradespeople available to engrave and print money. In the first year of the war, the Confederate government contracted the National Bank Note Company of New York to produce one million dollars in paper currency and transport it secretly across the battle lines.

When the mint in New Orleans discovered that the South lacked sufficient metals to produce its own coinage, mint officials again reached out, this time to a Philadelphian, Robert Lovett, Jr. The Northern minter decided against trying to create and smuggle thousands of pounds of enemy coins into the Confederacy, and he quickly abandoned the project. As a result, the South was never able to establish its own coinage. Over time, the South took control of printing its own paper currency, but its quality would never match the Northern product. In fact, Southern currency had several crucial shortcomings that would plague the Confederacy throughout the war.

Please Sign Here

One of the more troubling features of Southern banknotes was the official signatures they bore. Each note had the signatures of the Confederate registrar and treasurer, which were placed there to thwart counterfeiters. Unfortunately, Confederate printers couldn't figure out how to turn the signatures into printer's dies. This meant that each official had to sign the millions of notes by hand—an impossible task. Ultimately, the job fell to hundreds of clerks who copied the signatures with varying degrees of success, making them useless as a tool for identifying counterfeit money.

Worthless Wealth

Backed by the rebellious spirit that fueled the war effort, Confederate money was initially a hot property. Over time, however, the unrestrained printing of money and a lack of oversight that allowed individual states and banks to develop their own notes resulted in mass confusion and hyperinflation. During the five years of the war, nearly $1.7 billion in Confederate currency was printed, far more than the Confederate economy was really worth.

Outside of the South, the only place where these bills were desired was the Union, where curious Northerners purchased them as souvenirs—$2,000 worth of Confederate money could be bought for 50 U.S. cents.

Some Still Journey Along the Underground Railroad

In the first half of the 19th century, some landowners staged a concerted effort to help slaves escape bondage in the South and find freedom in the North. These strangers in hostile territory enabled slaves to escape their torment via the Underground Railroad. This, of course, was not an actual mode of transportation but rather a series of tunnels and hidden rooms in which escaped slaves were able to hide for a day or two, get a good meal, and travel onward toward freedom. Their journeys were fraught with fear, stress, and sometimes illness or injury. And if caught, the slaves were not only returned to their owners, they were also punished severely, and some were killed on the spot. So it goes without saying that many of the houses, farms, forests, and passageways of the Underground Railroad are still haunted by slaves who didn't succeed in their quest for freedom.

✳ ✳ ✳ ✳

Deadman's Hill (Willmar, Minnesota)

LOCATED IN WILLMAR, Minnesota, Deadman's Hill is far north of areas that are typically associated with slavery, but for many of the escapees of the mid-1800s, the state was a stop on the way to Canada. Considered a free state, Minnesota outlawed slave ownership, but unfortunately, it was legal at the time for slave traders and bounty hunters to catch escaped slaves anywhere in the country and return them to their "owners." That was the case of one slave who was captured by a bounty hunter and chained to a fence post. The resourceful slave managed to escape by pulling the post out of the ground. A fence post makes for some pretty cumbersome luggage, however, and the bounty hunter caught up with the slave again. A fight ensued, and the slave killed his captor with the man's own sword. But the slave was injured in the fight, and his body was later found on a farmer's doorstep amidst a pool of blood and the uprooted fence post. Both men were buried on the property: The bounty hunter rests atop Deadman's Hill, and the slave is buried next to the farmhouse. Although the runaway slave's ghost has never been seen, plenty of people have heard his moans, the rattle of chains, and the distinct sound of something heavy being dragged.

Hannah House (Indianapolis, Indiana)

It was indeed a sad situation when slaves who tried to escape to better lives died in the process. That's what happened at Hannah House, which was a well-known stop on the Underground Railroad. Slaves waiting in the cellar of the mansion were taken by surprise when someone accidentally tipped over a lantern. Flames engulfed them and trapped them in the basement; they all died within a few minutes.

Since then, visitors have heard voices, moans, and the rattling of chains coming from both the basement and the attic. People have also detected the smell of burning bodies, which has burdened Hannah House with the unpleasant moniker "the house that reeks of death."

While no full-bodied apparitions have been spotted there, plenty of unexplained phenomena have been experienced: Doors open and close by themselves, people report feeling cold breezes even when the windows are closed, and objects move to new locations with no human assistance.

In 2006 and 2007, Indy Ghost Hunters—a local paranormal investigation team—visited Hannah House and recorded numerous EVPs (electronic voice phenomena), including mysterious voices imploring them for help and warning them to "Get out!" Cameras also captured a shadow moving across the attic, even though all living beings were well out of their range.

Hanson Home (Alton, Illinois)

As if having the Underground Railroad stop at the Hanson Home wasn't enough, the site on which it stood is where the Enos Sanitarium was built for tuberculosis patients in the early 1900s. In 1857, when Nathaniel Hanson built his home on a bluff just above the Mississippi River, he created underground rooms and tunnels out of limestone, specifically for the purpose of assisting slaves to reach their freedom. Unfortunately, many slaves lost their lives on this journey, and some of their spirits may have remained at the Hanson Home.

The structure is now used as an apartment building, and many residents have had their belongings—keys, books, jewelry, and even a bottle of wine—disappear; they almost always reappear a day or so later in an entirely different spot. Like most ghosts, these spirits like to open and close doors and turn the lights on and off, and people often report hearing footsteps when no one else is around.

Much of this activity seems to take place on the building's upper floors (where the sanitarium was located), but the basement has its own set of ghosts—spirits of slaves that cry out in despair.

Hickory Hill (Equality, Illinois)

Hickory Hill—which is also known as "The Old Slave House"—is one of the most haunted places in the state of Illinois. Its first owner, John Hart Crenshaw, amassed a fortune during the abolition years by operating what is known as a "reverse underground station": Slave catchers and bounty hunters captured escaped slaves and took them to Hickory Hill, where Crenshaw then sold them back into bondage or put them to work in his salt mines.

Visitors to this place have felt cold drafts and the soft brushes of spirits passing by; they've also claimed to hear crying and moaning mixed with the rattling of chains.

Wedgwood Inn (New Hope, Pennsylvania)

If you're a 12-year-old girl, you may just be in luck if you're hoping to meet a ghost in this small Pennsylvania town. On her way to freedom in the mid-1800s, a 12-year-old slave girl named Sara stayed at the house that is now the Wedgwood Inn. No one knows the cause of her death, but the building's owners uncovered her remains while renovating the place in 2000. Sara's spirit seems to have remained at the hotel in order to tell her story to other girls her age—many young girls have reported meeting her at the inn, and when they recount the details of her life as a slave and how she escaped by using the Underground Railroad, their stories are eerily similar.

Prospect Place (Trinway, Ohio)

A prime stop for slaves heading to Canada, the basement of Prospect Place was a temporary safe house for hundreds of escapees. Built by George W. Adams—a prominent mill owner and abolitionist—this 1856 mansion has 29 rooms, not counting the secret ones located below ground. Today, it is thought to be haunted by both slaves and the generous souls who lived on the property.

One story about the ghosts of Prospect Place centers on a girl who fell to her death from an upstairs balcony one winter during the early 1860s; her body was kept in the basement until the ground thawed in the spring. Her ghost is thought to wander the house and has been heard crying in the basement. The girl's mother died of pneumonia soon after the girl passed, and her spirit roams the house as well. The girl's ghost has been seen on the balcony, in the old servants' quarters, and in the basement, and another slave who died at the house has been seen standing in the basement, as if guarding the girl's body. Also, a husband and wife who were separated while escaping seem to search various areas of the property trying to find each other. And in true poetic justice, in the barn, farmhands hung a bounty hunter who searched for escaped slaves; his ghost still haunts the place where he met his death.

Riverview Farm (Drexel Hills, Pennsylvania)

The land on which Arlington Cemetery stands today was once part of Riverview Farm—the home of Thomas Garrett Jr., an abolitionist who reportedly helped as many as 2,700 slaves on the road to freedom. While no specific incident would have caused spirits to remain there, evidence suggests that they did. When taking pictures at a nearby home, a photographer captured the aura of something ghostly hovering in the background of an image. Could it be the spirit of one of these brave men and women who were searching for a better life?

Rolling on the River

A city's cleanup attempt turns into a less-than-fantastic voyage.

✳ ✳ ✳ ✳

THE CIVIL WAR was a breeding ground for disease. Horrific battlefield conditions and a lack of sanitation let sickness run wild. For every soldier lost to wounds, two died of illness. And for those who survived those perils, another snare was waiting: venereal disease.

It wasn't enough to warn soldiers not to gratify their lusts, so officers tried to make the means of gratification unavailable. Nashville, Tennessee, for example, had been taken over by the Union army in February 1862, and though the city was a win for the cause, assuming control also meant taking on its problems—specifically, prostitution.

An Immodest Proposal

By July 1863, prostitution was such a problem in Nashville that the authorities decided to solve it once and for all. Lieutenant Colonel George Spalding was ordered to seize all of Nashville's prostitutes and ship them to Louisville, Kentucky. Spalding sought suitable transportation and found the steamship *Idahoe*, whose captain and owner, John Newcomb, wanted a military contract. He agreed to transport Spalding's mysterious "cargo."

Newcomb, unsurprisingly, got more than he bargained for. Spalding's soldiers marched more than 100 "ladies of the night" onto the *Idahoe*, handing Newcomb orders not to let the women "leave the boat before reaching Louisville." Many of the women were ill, and Newcomb had neither food nor medicine. He was told that he was on his own and that he should sail immediately.

Hard-to-Handle Cargo

On July 9, the *Idahoe* set sail, with 111 angry women aboard. They destroyed furniture and vandalized the boat. The Nashville Dispatch reported the ladies' deportation, smugly noting, "Where they are consigned to, we are not advised, but suspect the authorities of the city to which they are landed will feel proud of such an acquisition to their population."

Throughout their journey, the women plied their trade to both crew and civilians who would swim out to the boat. Newcomb tried to land several times, but he was turned away by each river town where he attempted to dock. He had to buy food, medicine, and ice from other boats with his own funds.

Turned Away

Finally, on July 15, the battered *Idahoe* arrived at Louisville and was refused permission to land, Spalding's orders notwithstanding. The military commander in Louisville placed a guard aboard the steamboat and sent it to Cincinnati. Meanwhile, a few women escaped, only to be sent back to Nashville by train. At Cincinnati, the *Idahoe* was quarantined for 13 days before it was sent back to Nashville with its cargo intact. General Robert S. Granger, Union military commander for the area of Middle Tennessee, dealt with the prostitution problem in an unlikely— but effective—way: He legalized it. Nashville's prostitutes were examined and treated by doctors for various venereal diseases, and if deemed free of disease, they were granted an official license. Taking "clients" without a license could result in a sentence to the workhouse for up to 30 days.

Never the Same

Meanwhile, the *Idahoe* was in shambles. Newcomb presented a damage claim for $5,000, but it took more than a year for him to be compensated. Eventually, he received two bank drafts: $1,000 "for damage to the staterooms, furniture, bedding, cabin furniture, tableware, etc.," and $4,316 for "subsistence and medicines furnished 111 prostitutes on board the steamer *Idahoe* . . . at the rate of $1.50 a day for each." By the time he received the money, Newcomb had sold his interest in the *Idahoe*, which sank in 1869 near Columbia, Louisiana. One can only imagine the stories the boat's sailors told when reminiscing about their tumultuous tour with the ladies, or indeed, what the ladies' side of the story might have been.

White Man Sees Red

When Apache kidnapped Adolph Korn from his Texas farm, his life seemed all but over. But then something strange happened: Rather than curse his captors, he decided to join them. The unlikely alliance stands as one of Texas's more improbable tales.

✳ ✳ ✳ ✳

WHILE TENDING SHEEP on New Year's Day, 1870, 10-year-old Adolph Korn's life took a sudden twist when he was attacked by three Apache. Knocked unconscious, he was taken captive and forcibly thrust into Apache life. At first Korn resisted his captors, but over time, he adjusted to his new setting. Korn eventually found peace among his new family. Against all odds, he became one with his captors.

Rebirth

Korn wasn't the first white boy to be abducted by Native Americans. The practice had been used to increase the ranks of native cultures, giving them a fighting chance against a flood of hostile Europeans. And with Korn, they hit pay dirt. Not only was the youth willing to stand beside his new "brothers" in solidarity, he was willing to fight.

Traded to the Comanche during his first year of captivity, Korn fearlessly squared off against those white settlers and U.S. soldiers who threatened his new culture. But in 1872, nearly three years after he was first taken, Korn was "captured" by the U.S. Army and returned to his parents. To call the reunion less than joyous would be an understatement. Things had changed drastically since the day that Adolph Korn had been abducted. The boy was no longer the son they remembered.

Aftermath

Holding fast to his Native American ways, Korn completely turned his back on white society. With no luck in turning their son around, his family eventually let him go. Korn ultimately moved into a cave, where he lived his odd life as a man white in complexion, but Native American in spirit. He died in 1900, a castoff from both cultures.

The Ultimate Reversal

Chicago is known for its engineering marvels. The City of the Big Shoulders has been flexing its industrial muscle since the 1870s, when rapid growth—and a famous fire—forced the city upward and outward. But the city's greatest engineering feat was forcing the Chicago River to reverse its flow.

✳   ✳   ✳   ✳

WHEN THE CITY was founded in the 1830s, the Chicago River—then called "Chicagou," a Native American word for "bitter onions"—flowed directly into Lake Michigan, bringing with it both industrial pollution and bodily waste. By the 1860s and '70s, population and industry had grown so rapidly that pollution in the river and along Lake Michigan, the city's source of drinking water, was beginning to reach dangerous levels. When a major storm flushed thousands of gallons of waste into the lake in 1885, contaminating the city's water with bacteria, thousands of people died of typhoid and cholera. City officials were forced to act.

The city dredged and deepened the river and extended it inland. Combined with a series of enormous canal locks finished in 1900, the river's extension forced the water in the river to run backward from the lake and south through a network of waterways before spilling into the Mississippi.

At the beginning of the 20th century, with the lake and river sparkling clean, the city saw a boom in commercial and residential building that helped turn it from a gritty, industrial port into the business, travel, and cultural hub its residents enjoy today. Apartments and office buildings line the river, which, running under the world's largest network of drawbridges and splashing sidewalks and pavilions as it flows, remains one of the city's most treasured gems.

It's the only river in the world to run away from its mouth, and a little Chicago ingenuity has kept the city's greatest recreational spot—and its source of water—clean ever since.

What Nellie Bly Found on Blackwell's Island

If you visit Roosevelt Island, you'll notice a building called the Octagon. These days, it's a posh condominium, but it was once the site of human injustice and chaos, 19th-century-style. Crackerjack reporter—and beloved New Yorker—Nellie Bly uncovered the story.

✳   ✳   ✳   ✳

A LITTLE SLIP OF land in the East River, Roosevelt Island was called Blackwell's Island during the 18th and 19th centuries. It was just farmland and hunting ground initially, but a prison was built in 1832, and several years later it was joined by the New York Lunatic Asylum, which was dominated by the Octagon Tower. The structure was beautiful, with an enormous spiral staircase and a domed, octagonal roof, but from the start, the asylum was grossly mismanaged. More than 1,700 mentally ill inmates were crammed inside (twice as many as should have been there), and although nurses were on duty, inmates from the nearby prison handled most of the supervision.

Over the next few decades, more prisons, asylums, and workhouses were built on Blackwell's, inspiring the island's new nickname: Welfare Island. Mortality was high because the care was so poor. Infants born there rarely lived to see adolescence. Any time spent on Blackwell's Island was too long for most.

The Girl's Got Sass

Help was on the way. Born in Pennsylvania in 1864, Elizabeth Jane Cochrane was a spitfire from the start. As a teen, she wrote an angry editorial to the *Pittsburgh Dispatch* about an article she found insulting to women. The editor was so impressed he hired her. Elizabeth assumed the pen name "Nellie Bly" (after a popular song) and lobbied hard for juicy stories. Although she landed a few, newspaperwomen at that time were relegated to the fashion and arts beats, a fate Bly fought against. Yearning for more substantive work, she left the *Dispatch* for New York City in 1887. She had bigger fish to fry.

Bly got a job at Joseph Pulitzer's *New York World* in hopes of significant stories. She already had one to pitch: She would feign insanity and get into the Women's Lunatic Asylum on Blackwell's Island. Everyone had heard about the conditions there, but no one had dared check it out. Bly's editors were duly impressed and gave their new employee the green light.

That night, Nellie checked into a Manhattan boardinghouse and commenced to freak everyone out. She acted bizarrely, dirtied her face, and feigned amnesia. Before long, the police came and took her away—straight into the heart of Blackwell's insane asylum.

From Bad to Worse

What the 23-year-old reporter found when she got there was worse than she had feared. For the next ten days, she endured the terrors and neglect that long-term inmates knew all too well. Life in the asylum was reduced to the animal level. Rotten meat and thin broth, along with lumps of nearly inedible dough, were all inmates were given to eat. And to wash it all down? Unclean drinking water.

Everyone was dirty, surrounded by their own filth and excrement from the rats that had free reign over the place. Baths consisted of buckets of ice water poured over the inmate's head, and the residents passed their days on cold, hard benches in stultifying boredom.

Bly's editors rescued her after ten days, and Nellie wrote her exposé, a series of articles that eventually became a book called *Ten Days in a Mad-House.* The story blew up in the faces of the tin gods who controlled the prison and the asylum. Physicians and staff members tried to do damage control, but it was no use. A grand jury investigation commenced, and before long, new standards—many of which were suggested by Nellie herself—were implemented in institutions statewide. Moneys were allocated, and the asylum on Blackwell's received long overdue repair and rehabilitation.

As for the young reporter, she would never have to go back to the fashion pages again. Bly continued to seek out adventure and remained a respected investigative reporter until she retired in 1895.

Pullman: A Lesson for Control Freaks

Railroad magnate George Pullman thought he was doing his workers a favor by building them a brand-new town with all the amenities. Instead, he helped bring about the country's first nationwide strike and nearly brought the country to its knees.

✳   ✳   ✳   ✳

IN THE YEARS following the Civil War, American companies were focused on one key facet of business: increased worker productivity. Through the use of such new methods as the assembly line and such new technologies as the Bessemer converter to make steel or the mechanical thresher to increase agricultural production, American workers and businesses enjoyed a period of industrial production like the world had never seen. At the same time, progressives and liberals of the day sought better conditions for workers. These conflicting goals led to a violent 1893 uprising in Pullman, a company town 13 miles south of Chicago.

If Something Seems Too Good to Be True...

George Pullman built the town to house the thousands of workers who helped manufacture his company's luxurious sleeper cars. It was the fruition of Pullman's idea of a model community, built to replace the rundown tenements that often housed workers. The town consisted of strips of neat, tidy rowhouses. By providing such living quarters, Pullman hoped to better the health, environment, and spirit of his employees and thereby attract skilled workers, increase productivity, and avoid strikes. The town was, for the most part, built by Pullman factory workers and was completed in 1884.

The houses had all the most modern amenities, and Pullman made sure the town had everything the workers could ever want or need (a school, a bank, a post office, a library, a theater, shops, and restaurants); this way, workers would never feel the need to leave, and the days and weeks would progress exactly as Pullman planned.

For a while, everything went smoothly. Workers bristled at certain policies in the company town (alcohol was forbidden, there were inspectors on the payroll to make sure workers were "behaving," and homes were only leased, never sold), but for the most part, the workers were happy.

Frugality's a Cinch When You Have No Money

Tempers flared during a financial panic in 1893, however. As demands for the company's train cars plummeted, Pullman laid off workers. He cut the wages of the workers who remained by 30 percent, even though more work would likely be required of them. To make matters even worse, Pullman continued to deduct the same rent from workers' paychecks to ensure investors would continue to get the 6 percent return he had promised them. Pullman preached frugality from his Prairie Avenue mansion as his workers' families went hungry.

The Strike

Soon, matters came to a head. The American Railway Union (ARU), led by Eugene Debs, a fiery speaker who later ran for president on the Socialist ticket, called for a strike. Railroad workers across the nation refused to handle Pullman cars, and within four days, 125,000 workers on 29 railroads had quit work rather than handle the company's products.

The strike became a national issue. Many workers were left without jobs as the company hired scabs. The strikers appealed to Illinois Governor John P. Altgeld, who wrote George Pullman three times, asking him to do something about the "great distress" among his former workers. Pullman blamed the workers for their problems, arguing that if they had not gone on strike, they would not be suffering.

The Larger Battle

Beyond the plight of the workers, a debate rose up across the country over the role of workers, their rights, and the rights of businesses and managers to set wages and working conditions. Since the strike had halted the transportation of goods across the country, business owners and some newspaper editors began painting the union as a lawless, violent gang and called for the strike to be broken up—and by force, if necessary.

President Grover Cleveland, faced with nervous railroad executives and interrupted mail trains, declared the strike a federal crime. He deployed 12,000 troops, many of whom set up camp in Grant Park. By the end, 13 strikers were killed and 57 were wounded, with railroad workers also causing millions of dollars in property damage.

On August 3, 1894, the strike ended. Many workers and their supporters around the country were devastated as the Pullman employees were forced back to work. Debs went to prison, the ARU was disbanded, and the power of industrial workers' unions was effectively diminished until the Great Depression. Many did lay the blame at Pullman's feet, however; a presidential commission chastised him for ignoring his workers' plight.

An Ongoing Legacy

From a worker's perspective, not all was lost. For one, while serving his time in jail, Debs decided that labor needed to win political power to balance that of their employers. He became the Socialist Party's presidential candidate and received nearly a million votes in 1912. For another, the strike helped set in motion the Progressive Era in U.S. history, a period when President Theodore Roosevelt and others began to question the unchecked power of major industries.

In the years following the strike, railcars began losing ground to automobiles, and the company and the town gradually shut down. The state filed suit against the company's ownership of a town, and today, Pullman is an historic district of narrow streets and tidy row houses on Chicago's Southwest Side. Visitors come from around the world to recall a critical period in American history and an industrial tycoon who thought he had it all figured out.

What Are the Requirements to Be a Country?

You'd think that we could all agree on some basic facts about the world—like the number of existing countries. Not so fast...

✳ ✳ ✳ ✳

DEPENDING ON WHO you ask, there are as few as 192 or as many as 260 countries. Part of the problem is that there's no official rulebook that explains exactly what it takes to be a country. And we can't just take any would-be country's word for it—otherwise those gun-toting survivalists in northern Idaho might have a point about seceding from the Union. In fact, if you think about it, it's kind of hard to define what exactly a country is. The word "country" can evoke a landscape, the people who live on it, or the laws that govern them there—and often it conjures all of these things. The concept of country-hood is one of those ideas that we take for granted but struggle to articulate.

Fortunately, the lawyers of the world have got our backs. International laws can work only if the requirements of countryhood are well defined. One influential legal definition of a country is spelled out in the Montevideo Convention on the Rights and Duties of States, a treaty that was signed by North and South American nations in Montevideo, Uruguay, in 1933. In Article I, it says: "The state as a person of international law should possess the following qualifications: (a) a permanent population; (b) a defined territory; (c) government; and (d) capacity to enter into relations with the other states."

Article III of the treaty makes it clear that any group that meets these four requirements has the right to become a country, even if other countries refuse to recognize it as such. This was an innovation. In earlier times, becoming a country was more like joining an exclusive club: You had to impress the most popular members—namely, the nations that dominated the world with their wealth and military power—and convince them to let you in. Their opinions were the only things that mattered.

But even under the newer egalitarian rules, there's a loophole that keeps the global "country club" more exclusive than it might seem. According to the Montevideo definition, you need to have "the capacity to enter into relations with other states," which effectively means that other states have to agree to enter into relations with you. In other words, you still have to get at least one country to recognize you, even if you fulfill the other requirements for statehood.

So how do established countries decide which hopefuls they choose to recognize? In practice, it often comes down to political expediency. Taiwan, for example, looks like it fulfills all of the requirements of statehood that are laid out by the Montevideo Convention. But many countries—the United States included—haven't recognized Taiwan as an independent state, because the Chinese, who think of Taiwan as part of their own territory, would be angry.

The Brief Life of the German-American Bund

Hitler's feeble attempt to launch Nazism in the United States was a dud that did more harm than good for Germany's cause.

✳   ✳   ✳   ✳

WHEN ADOLF HITLER became Chancellor of the German Reich in 1933, he wanted to remain on friendly, or at least neutral, terms with the United States, lest it become a major obstacle to his plans for conquest. To further that cause, Hitler's deputy Rudolf Hess directed a Nazi operative named Fritz Spanknöbel to consolidate various U.S.-based Nazi splinter groups into the Friends of New Germany (FNG).

Its membership reached about 10,000 people at its peak, mainly German nationals and recently naturalized German-Americans. Its primary base was in New York City, and it had outposts in other large cities.

The FNG spent the next several years railing against Jews and Communists. New York's Jewish community responded with boycotts of nearby German-owned shops, and a Jewish congressman began investigating this new organization. Even in the established German-American community, the FNG gained few followers and scrambled to make ends meet during the Depression. In March 1936, hoping to reach a broader base, Berlin installed Fritz Kuhn, a naturalized U.S. citizen, as head of the renamed German-American Bund. Kuhn learned where he stood in the Nazi hierarchy when he attended the 1936 Berlin Olympics and barely managed to meet Hitler. Undaunted, Kuhn promptly returned home and announced that Hitler had named him "America's Führer."

As war clouds darkened over Europe, Kuhn's Bund raised its profile with events and inflated assertions. Rumors circulated that the Bund had hundred of thousands of fanatical members, when in fact it hadn't grown much since the FNG days. During the summers of 1936–39, Bundists and sympathizers gathered at Camp Siegfried on Long Island to camp, drink beer, sing Nazi anthems, and raise money for Germany.

Yet all was not well with the Bund. Hans Dieckhoff, the German Ambassador to the United States, complained to Berlin that Kuhn was "stupid, noisy and absurd"—and doing more harm than good.

The ambassador's complaints were grounded in his understanding of Americans. In American culture, immigrants were expected to shut up, learn English, fly the Stars and Stripes, work hard, and adopt American moral standards. Kuhn was loud, spoke terrible English, flew the Nazi flag, spent his days preaching racial antipathy, drank a lot, and openly consorted with a variety of single and married women. Berlin ordered Kuhn to cease using Nazi symbols and accepting non-U.S. citizens; Kuhn ignored the mandates.

The Bund's most visible moment came in February 1939 when it held a massive rally in Madison Square Garden. Nazi and U.S. flags hung from the walls along with a huge portrait of George Washington. At one point during Kuhn's oration, an enraged Jewish plumber tried to storm the stage and was wrestled down by Bund security men, but most attendees had come to "Heil" rather than heckle. Newsreel footage of the event shocked America. Many Americans had seen films of huge Nazi rallies set in Germany—but never before in New York.

Far from sparking a surge of American Fascism, the Garden rally ignited legal troubles that would soon destroy the German-American Bund. Manhattan District Attorney Thomas Dewey began investigating Kuhn and his Bund, and by May 1939 had sufficient evidence to indict Kuhn for grand larceny and forgery. In the meantime, the state government unleashed another devastating weapon by revoking Camp Siegfried's liquor license. By the time Kuhn entered New York's Sing Sing prison in December 1939, war had broken out in Europe and Camp Siegfried was an empty memory.

When the military draft began in 1940, the remnant Bund encouraged its members to evade conscription. The FBI had watched the Bund all throughout the thirties, and now had clear evidence of illegal activity. After August 1940, alien residents had to register at the nearest U.S. Post Office, including 315,000 German nationals from whose ranks most Bundists had come. With Germany's declaration of war on the United States shortly after Pearl Harbor, the U.S. government outlawed the Bund and locked up most of its current and former members, 10,905 in all. Kuhn's naturalization was revoked in prison. After the war he was deported to the new Federal Republic of Germany to stand trial for wartime Nazi activities.

What did the Bund accomplish? For the Nazis, it mostly caused setbacks. It did prompt loyal German-Americans and resident German nationals to demonstrate their loyalty and raise money for the German war effort. But it also helped convince the FBI to arrest and intern every Nazi sympathizer who might work against Allied interests. Its vocal presence in New York City helped raise awareness of the Nazis' true feelings toward Jews. And its final decline lowered Nazi prestige in American eyes. The Nazi seed in the United States, sown on the New York City pavement, bore no fruit worth harvesting.

The Zoot Suit Riots

A volatile mix of hot summer nights, angry sailors, and ethnic tension in Southern California during World War II could only lead to an explosion.

✳   ✳   ✳   ✳

THE COUNTRY WAS abuzz with wartime pressure and a fresh surge of racial tension in 1943. World War II was in full swing, and Los Angeles was flooded with sailors. They spilled out of local naval bases into a city already filled to the brim. Added to the heap of an overpopulated city came the self-described *pachucos* (a word that has its origins in a slang term for residents of El Paso, Texas). Pachucos, decked out in distinctive full zoot-suit garb and ducktail 'dos, had been seen around town for years and had fostered a reputation for stirring up trouble. It didn't seem to matter that this "trouble" was often the product of an anti-Latino bias that circulated through the streets of LA among residents and law enforcement officials alike. With the addition of so many military personnel to the city, the blend of diversity and testosterone proved to be violent.

An Unfamiliar Culture

Prior to their Los Angeles experience with Mexican Americans, the era's military personnel typically possessed little experience with the flamboyantly represented Latino culture they now found in their midst. The hue of pachucos' skin differentiated them from the white masses, but their telltale garb really jabbed at the restless forces. The ostentatious jewelry, prominently wide-brimmed hats, and elaborately tapered pants earmarked the pachucos as the "troublemaking" Zoot Suiters.

Despite the pachucos' cartoonish costumes, many Los Angelinos believed that there were good reasons for the masses to fear their presence. With their infiltration of Los Angeles came a rash of gang activity, and a mysterious but much-publicized gang-related death made headlines in 1942. These events served to perpetuate the public cries of the zoot-suit-menace mania that was already striking the area. All this racially laced trepidation came to a head in the summer of 1943.

The Mob Attacks

Based on claims of a pachuco-prompted altercation, a group of sailors initiated retaliation on a grand and vindictive scale. On June 3, 1943, a group of sailors embarked on an incursion into the barrios of East LA. Armed with belts, clubs, and chains, the assemblage was out for blood.

Although pachucos were typically clad in zoot suits, not all zoot-suit-adorned Mexican Americans were part of the pachuco group. That made no difference to the sailors, however. No Latino male was safe. Zoot-suit wearers were the initial targets, but soon the sailors found any East LA resident fair game. Zoot suit or not, any Mexican American man who crossed the mob's path was made victim of the angry onslaught. Women were raped. Even the occasional African American and Filipino American to happen onto the scene was attacked by the mob.

But Who's Responsible?

To add insult to injury, at the end of the days-long attack, a collective of mostly Mexican Americans was charged with the illegalities. While hundreds of Mexican Americans were arrested, a mere nine sailors were taken into custody. Of those nine, only one was deemed guilty—and just of a small-time crime.

The *Los Angeles Times* marked its approval of this discrimination with a headline that declared "Zoot Suiters Learn Lesson in Fight with Servicemen." The implication of the article was that the menacing Mexicans were simply out of control. The national press picked up the story and reported a similar version of the tale in other cities. In outrage, or perhaps in a frenzy of the racially tense excitement overtaking the nation, copycat riots emerged across the United States. In response to the fracas, the U.S. military ordered all personnel to keep away from the streets of Los Angeles in an effort to settle the unrest. Of course, in one last jab at the pachucos, an ordinance was passed in Los Angeles that declared the wearing of zoot suits illegal.

12 WPA Projects That Still Exist

In the darkest days of the Great Depression, the U.S. government stepped in to assist the needy and get the economy started again. Perhaps the widest-ranging and most productive New Deal measure was the Works Progress Administration. This group provided more than $10 billion in federal funds, employing millions of people in hundreds of thousands of jobs.

✳   ✳   ✳   ✳

1. **Doubleday Field in Cooperstown, New York**—This minor league stadium—which has hosted the annual major league Hall of Fame game every active baseball season since 1939—sits on the lot where Abner Doubleday supposedly invented baseball in 1839. A century later, the WPA refurbished the site's existing field, adding a grandstand, drainage system, wooden bleachers, and new fencing.

2. **Camp David, Maryland**—In 1936, the WPA began work on a recreational area in western Maryland's Catoctin Mountains, completing Camp Hi-Catoctin by 1939. For three years, it was used as a family camp for federal employees until President Franklin Delano Roosevelt visited in April 1942 and selected it as the location for presidential

retreats. In the early 1950s, President Eisenhower renamed the camp for his grandson. Camp David has hosted dozens of visiting foreign dignitaries for casual meetings with U.S. presidents, but it remains closed to the general public.

3. **Dealey Plaza, Texas**—In 1940, WPA workers completed this park in the heart of Dallas. Named for an early publisher of the *Dallas Morning News*, the plaza lives in infamy as the location of President John F. Kennedy's assassination on November 22, 1963. There may be other "grassy knolls" in American parks, but none have gone down in history like the one in Dealey Plaza.

4. **LaGuardia Airport, New York**—The Big Apple's desire for a city airport was only a dream until September 1937, when the WPA joined with the city to build one. Soon after opening in 1939, it was named New York Municipal Airport-LaGuardia Field to honor mayor Fiorello LaGuardia. The name was shortened to LaGuardia Airport in 1947.

5. **John Augustus Walker's Murals, Mobile, Alabama**—The WPA commissioned John Augustus Walker of Mobile, Alabama, to create a series of oil on canvas murals in the city's Old City Hall/Southern Market complex. They memorialize a range of Mobile's historic events, from the ship that brought the last payload of African slaves into the United States in 1859 to the importance of education and science to the city. Hurricane Katrina, which slammed into the city in August 2005, damaged the Museum of Mobile, where the murals are now located. The murals were not harmed, and the museum reopened in March 2006.

6. **The American Guide Series**—The Federal Writers Project was a WPA program that employed authors, playwrights, and poets between 1935 and 1943. The project used more than 6,000 writers—including future award-winning authors like Saul Bellow and Ralph Ellison—to

produce travel guides for each of the (then) 48 states as well as the District of Columbia. Each book in the series described the state's geography, history, and culture and was filled with maps, drawings, and pictures. Today, collectors seek many of the original volumes, which can fetch hundreds of dollars. Not bad for a series that supposedly started after a casual conversation between the WPA administrator and a writer at a cocktail party!

7. **Jackson Pollock, Male and Female, Pennsylvania**— Before he developed his famous drip method of painting— a technique in which the canvas is placed on the floor and splashed with paint—Pollock worked for the WPA's Federal Art Project from 1938 to 1942. He created Male and Female, one of his earliest paintings, in 1942. Now in the Philadelphia Museum of Art, the painting is an excellent example of Pollock's early abstract expressionism, characterized by vibrant color and texture.

8. **The Mathematical Tables Project**—Before the advent of computers, people created mathematical tables to compute complex calculations and formulas. The WPA's groundbreaking Mathematical Tables Project, which began in 1938 in New York City, employed hundreds of workers to mass-calculate the tables. Twenty-eight volumes of mathematical information were published, including navigation tables used by the Navy in World War II. The work was so valuable that the program was absorbed into the National Bureau of Standards in 1948.

9. **Donal Hord, Aztec Statue, California**—In 1936, San Diego sculptor Donal Hord was commissioned to carve a statue for the campus of San Diego State University. He completed the work, which he named Aztec, in 1937, and it soon became the inspiration for the school's mascot. Nicknamed "Montezuma," the statue makes its home in the university's Prospective Student Center. The funding for

the project was twofold—student groups raised $130 to purchase the one-ton chunk of black diorite for Hord to work with and the WPA Federal Arts Project supplied $6,000 to Hord and his assistants for their labor.

10. **Outer Bridge Drive, Illinois**—In the heart of the Windy City, this bridge, which crosses the Chicago River near Lake Michigan, was started in 1929, but the Great Depression prevented its completion until the WPA delivered funds in the mid-1930s. When completed in 1937, the bridge was 356 feet long and 100 feet wide, making it the world's longest and widest bascule bridge. Also known as the Lake Shore Drive Bridge, it still stands today, forming part of the scenic Chicago waterfront.

11. **Alton Tobey, The Founders of Hartford, Connecticut**—By age nine, Alton Tobey was a well-regarded artist who had won a scholarship to a class at New York's Metropolitan Museum of Art. In 1940, while studying at Yale's University School of Fine Arts, he accepted a commission from the WPA for a mural to adorn the East Hartford post office. Thus, The Founders of Hartford was born. His full-color preparatory painting for the mural is in the Smithsonian American Art Museum's collection in Washington, D.C.

12. **George Stanley's Muse Statues, California**—One of the world's largest and most famous natural amphitheaters—with a capacity of nearly 18,000—has a WPA link as well. The Hollywood Bowl's entrance, a massive fountain structure designed by sculptor George Stanley, contains three granite art deco statues representing the muses of music, dance, and drama. From 1938 to 1940, the statue project cost the WPA $100,000 and was the largest of hundreds of WPA sculpture projects in southern California. Stanley is also known for designing the "Oscar" statuette that goes to Academy Award winners.

Poison For Young Minds: Nazi Educational Literature

The methods and materials used to instill Nazi virtues of strength and purity in German children led to cultural disaster.

✳ ✳ ✳ ✳

THOUGH IT LASTED only 12 years, the German Reich was supposed to last a thousand. Early in his political career Hitler argued that in order to survive and prosper, future generations of Nazis would need to maintain a single-minded dedication to purity and strength. As such, the Nazis imbued all areas of public education with their party's ideology. These lessons took several forms:

Children's Stories

One of the more widespread lessons taught to young children was a story called "The Poison Mushroom." A mother and her son are picking mushrooms in the forest, and the boy finds some poisonous mushrooms. The mother compares the dangerous mushrooms to the dangers of a certain kind of people. The boy rightly concludes that she is speaking of the Jews. The mother is proud of her son and exhorts him to learn to identify Jews in all their dangerous guises. The story was part of a collection published by Julius Streicher, who was executed as a war criminal in 1946.

Primers

Nazi elementary books used simple illustrations and stories of children. Many of the stories include veneration for military parades and weapons. They also portray Hitler as a great man who is kind to children who bring him gifts. In one story, a boy named Karl attends a Hitler Youth rally. He wants to march with his older brother, but is too young. After the march, a race for young children takes place. Karl wins and receives a sausage and a pretzel, which he promptly eats.

Geography

Geography lessons stressed the concept of Lebensraum ("living space"), which Nazis proclaimed would provide the German people with land and resources that had been stolen from them after the Great War. Texts emphasize not only the need for this territory, but also the Germans' historical right to it. They mention Germany's cultural and historical influence on the countries surrounding it, as well as its geographic disadvantages, such as the ease with which the country was blockaded during World War I.

Biology

In German textbooks, biology was synonymous with racial purity and strength. Girls were given rigorous instruction in the selection of a suitable mate and the proper method of nurturing the next generation of Germans. Women's magazines often ran articles advising mothers to raise strong, physically active children who eschewed the classroom for the playing field. The articles advised parents to be stern with their children since "only he who has learned to obey can lead."

Nasty Nietzsche's Nazi Neighborhood: Nueva Germania in Paraguay

The husband was stern, commanding, and persuasive. The wife was the sister of a world-famous philosopher. Together, they sought to colonize a remote area of Paraguay as the starting point for their vision of utopia.

✳   ✳   ✳   ✳

CONTRARY TO POPULAR belief, the dream of a pure Aryan race was not the invention of Adolf Hitler. Four decades prior to Hitler's rise, a prominent couple envisioned a perfect world of Germanic people.

Bernhard Förster and Elisabeth Nietzsche

Herr Förster was a Berlin schoolteacher who was fired in 1883 for preaching racial hatred. He blamed the Jewish people in Europe for trying to destroy Germany and its culture through capitalistic business activities. At one point, Förster was able to collect more than 250,000 signatures on a petition demanding that Jewish immigration be halted and Jews be removed from the German stock market. It was ignored when delivered to German leader Otto von Bismarck, so Förster fostered a plan to build a superior race of Germans, traveling to South America after his dismissal from teaching. He chose Paraguay for its isolation and complete lack of Jewish people.

Fräulein Nietzsche was two years younger than her philosophizing brother, Friedrich. Before her marriage to Förster in 1885, Elisabeth was sheltered, living the good life with her mother. While she was not necessarily given to anti-Semitic beliefs before meeting Förster, she seemed to quickly embrace the vile practice.

Bringing Hatred to the New World

In March 1886, the Försters somehow convinced 14 families to pack up all they owned and travel more than 6,500 miles to where hatred could run as rampant as the jungle that surrounded them. After enduring a month-long sea voyage, the troop traveled for five days up the Parana River in a clunking steamer. Arriving in the city of Asunción, the Försters slept in its only hotel, while the other travelers bunked in drafty huts nearby. Their trek continued for another week by boat, then by horse and oxcart to the 40,000 acres of forest and farmland that Förster had purchased for a small down payment.

The Colony Collapses

Förster was convinced that fellow German anti-Semites would flock to the new fatherland he had created. He was wrong. While the Paraguayan land was fertile, it was foreign soil for German cultivation methods—they failed as farmers. Most were unable to weather such difficult travel to a land they knew nothing about. Lack of sanitation led to massive disease, and snakes were a constant concern.

Forty families made the trip to Nueva Germania in the first two years (minus the ten families who were smart enough to return to Germany). They could hardly fill the 40,000 acres that Förster owned. Heavily in debt, Förster left his wife at the colony in May 1889, moving back to an area near Asunción in search of more financing. Knowing that his vision had failed, Förster chose to take his own life.

What of Elisabeth?

Förster's widow inherited another crisis immediately, as her brother Friedrich became mentally ill. Returning to Europe to care for him, she took over the publishing of his writings and began to alter many of his views to embrace anti-Semitism. Following Friedrich's death in 1900, his sister released a highly edited and embellished work called *The Will to Power*, furthering her expressions of racial hatred.

Eventually, Förster-Nietzsche became a pen pal to Benito Mussolini, who dreamt of returning Rome to its ancient greatness. When Hitler took control of Germany in 1933, he embraced Elisabeth Förster-Nietzsche as a matriarchal figure. She died in 1935, and a sorrowful führer sat at the head of the casket during her funeral.

What of Nueva Germania?

After the end of World War II, many Nazis fled Germany and re-located to Nueva Germania, including Josef Mengele, the infamous concentration camp doctor. Remnants of the Förster colony remain in Paraguay, and several hundred people— including descendants of the original 14 German families—live there today. Generations of isolation, poverty, and inbreeding have left the people of Nueva Germania a mere curiosity in the world, instead of its masters.

Welcome to Hell Town

Looking for a scary adventure in Ohio? Dare to travel to Hell Town in Summit County. According to local legend, it's a sinister place where a host of nefarious characters partner with the U.S. government to protect dark secrets.

✳ ✳ ✳ ✳

STANFORD ROAD, THE only road into the once prosperous town of Boston Mills, is chained off at both ends. Throughout the town, conspicuous "U.S. PROPERTY—NO TRESPASSING" signs are affixed on abandoned houses. At night, local law enforcement officials curtly order loiterers to move on during regular patrols.

This is a place known throughout Ohio as Hell Town. According to local legend, it's an evil and foreboding place that holds dark secrets—and though it may seem quiet, danger is all around. From all the signs posted, conspiracy theorists have jumped to the conclusion that the U.S. government doesn't want people hanging around Boston Mills. Supposedly, it's all part of an elaborate scheme to cover up a disastrous chemical spill that turned town residents into disfigured mutants. The urban myth goes on to say that most were evacuated and never seen again, but some still lurk about, snatching those who unwittingly wander into the town.

Cults, Ghosts, and Lunatics

The legend maintains that the government cover-up is only part of the story. A lot of weird stuff is said to happen in Hell Town, all of which is perpetrated by a host of dark, sinister characters. In short, it's not just chemically altered mutants out to get you in Hell Town.

A Satanic cult now calls Boston Mills home! Satanists have chained Stanford Road to keep people out and their devilish activities a secret. Devil-worshipping congregations hold black masses at the old Mother of Sorrows church, which is marked by Satanic symbols of upside-down crosses, and practice other nefarious rituals in the abandoned funeral home (also called the old slaughterhouse) near the Boston Cemetery.

The Highway to Hell! An evil paranormal force compels cars to crash or veer off of Stanford Road, dubbed the "Highway to Hell." Passengers then fall prey to swarms of cult members who suddenly emerge from the woods—or to the ruthless axe murderer who lives in the woods and continues to elude capture by the police.

The marauding hearse! If they somehow manage to dodge the cult members and axe murderer on Stanford Road, visitors who reach town should beware a creepy man driving an old funeral hearse with one working headlight. If they try chasing him down, he and his ghoulish wheels will simply vanish.

The haunted cemetery! The grounds of the old Boston Cemetery are haunted by a specter that sits on a bench and stares off into the distance.

Get on the bus . . . of death! An old abandoned school bus sits in the town, a reminder of a grisly incident in which the last children to ride on it were slaughtered in the woods by an escaped mental patient (or a serial killer or the Satanists again) after the bus ran out of gas on a secluded road. There are no seats in the bus, but at night, the kids can be seen sitting on the bus in their spots—sometimes they're calm, other times they're crying and screaming. Sitting in the back of the bus is an eerie ghostlike man smoking a cigarette. All attempts to remove the bus have ended in tragic misfortune, so now it's left to sit.

The church cellar dweller! An evil old man dwells in the basement of the Boston Community Church. Once a respected member of the community, he now hides his face when spotted through the basement windows, ashamed of his secretive past as the leader of a clandestine Satanic cult.

And Now, the Real Story:

The federal government did force residents to leave Boston Mills, but not because of a disfiguring chemical spill. In the mid-1970s, the National Park Service appropriated hundreds of properties in the area to create national parkland—and most homeowners were compelled to sell and move from the area. It was all done rather quickly, thus making it seem as if the locals had vanished overnight. The government slapped its signs on the houses; some were demolished, some were boarded up and left untouched, and a few were used for firefighting training.

Abandoned houses, closed roads, government signs, police patrols—and not a soul for miles. It's all given rise to rumors of sinister happenings at Boston Mills. For the record, there never was a chemical spill at Boston Mills; the local municipality closed Stanford Road because it's in a state of disrepair. The cops on patrol are merely there to ward off the increased numbers of vandals and trespassers as the town grows in infamy.

Innovative Uses for Abandoned Structures

After these sites and structures fulfilled their original purpose, they moved into their second act.

✳ ✳ ✳ ✳

Piling It High in Old Virginny

IN 1974, A 165-acre city park was opened in Virginia Beach, Virginia. Nothing out of the ordinary, right? But it's what the park was built upon that makes it so unusual: The aptly named Mount Trashmore was built on top of a sanitary landfill. The play space has the usual park features, such as swing-sets and basketball courts, but the developers didn't stop there. Two lakes were also added to the complex, Lake Windsor and Lake Trashmore. Ironically, Lake Trashmore is a freshwater pond that is regularly stocked for fishing. A staircase leads to the top of the former dump some 60 feet above the surrounding terrain. We hear the view is breathtaking—in more ways than one.

Subterranean Soiree

A unique nightclub once existed *under* the sidewalks of New York City. Known as "The Tunnel," the Chelsea-based operation, which opened in the late 1980s, took its name from its main dance floor, a subway tunnel in use until the early 1900s. Partiers were often packed like sardines into the elongated club. In addition to its namesake room, The Tunnel sported a darkened lounge replete with peeling paint and exposed pipes.

Dealing in dancing and debauchery, the ultra-hip hotspot often found Canadian owner Peter Gatien at odds with the law. Still, this didn't dampen the spirits of thousands of partiers on any given weekend. But, alas, all parties must come to an end, and with charges of tax evasion and the threat of deportation looming over Gatien's head, he was forced to close the club. The space sold in 2001.

High Life on the High Line

If you're in the machine-made canyons of New York City and suddenly hear the sounds of children playing, people jogging, and other forms of recreation, just look up—you're probably standing beneath the city's funkiest new park.

The High Line is an elevated rail line-turned-verdant patch that stands 30 feet above the streets of Manhattan and stretches for nearly a mile and a half. The rail line was constructed in the 1930s to lift freight trains off the streets. Within its seven-acre spread, overstressed city workers can escape the rat race, if only during their lunch break. Future additions may include a swimming pool, a sundeck, and a vegetal balcony. So, why build a park along an elevated railroad right-of-way? Why not? In New York City, where open space is at a premium, residents must work with what is available. The sky's the limit, as they say.

Bridge of Flowers

At one time, picturesque Shelburne Falls, Massachusetts, was an endpoint along the Shelburne Falls & Colrain Street Railway, a trolley line built to haul freight and passengers. But in 1928, a decision was made to abandon the line in favor of trucking, a cheaper and more modern shipping alternative. Did this mean that Shelburne Falls would lose a portion of its heritage? Certainly. But what replaced it was arguably better. In 1929, the good townspeople decided to turn the abandoned Deerfield River Bridge—a span leftover from the trolley days—into a "Bridge of Flowers."

These days a walking path forms the right-of-way over the 400-foot-long span, and wisteria, tulips, roses, mums, and other beautiful flowers bloom beside it. Gardeners and volunteers tend this aromatic space that has now become the defining feature of Shelburne Falls. Each year, more than 20,000 people take the time to stop and smell the roses and other wistful blooms as they cross this unusual bridge.

Terminal Stillness

Since 9/11 airport security has grown exponentially. Such diligence presents major delays for most travelers. But no one ever stalled out at an airport longer than Mehran Nasseri. Before moving on he spent 17 years beneath a French aero dome.

❋   ❋   ❋   ❋

MODERN AMERICAN AIRPORTS are wholly different places than they were in the late Twentieth Century. Super stringent security measures have thrown the boarding process into a tailspin—a fact that finds a great many harried travelers cussing over inordinate delays. But what can be said about a man who spent 17 years waiting at an airport?

When Mehran Karimi Nasseri flew from Belgium to Paris in 1988 it was with high hopes for the future. A political refugee,

Nasseri had been living in Belgium for six years after being ousted from his native Iran for protests against the Shah. His ultimate goal was to settle in London, where he claimed to have relatives, but fate had other things in store for Nasseri. While in Paris his briefcase including his travel papers was stolen. Despite this, he boarded a plane for London but was sent back to France when he failed to produce a passport to British immigration.

Nasseri was arrested by French officials at Charles de Gaulle Airport for attempting to enter the country illegally, but the authorities dropped the charges and Nasseri was returned to the terminal. Nasseri had effectively become persona non grata—a man without a country—so far as French and British authorities were concerned and there was no solution in sight. Thus began his enduring odyssey at Terminal One.

Man in Waiting

Like any delayed traveler Nasseri hunkered down inside the terminal and prepared himself for a long wait. Surely the situation would be ironed out in a few days and he would be on his way to London. But Nasseri had become trapped in a bureaucratic no-man's land; one where a simple paperwork solution wasn't in the offing. Days turned into weeks, weeks turned into months, and months turned into years. Somehow, through it all, Nasseri maintained his sanity and did his best to make the most out of his new existence.

Over time Nasseri's plight became known to airport staff and shopkeepers. Not one to beg, Nasseri relied on small handouts received from his understanding new friends and bartered with them whenever possible. Airport restaurants became his source for food. Despite the implied irony, French fries became one of his favorite staples. For water he turned to the airport's water fountains. He learned to sleep sideways across the terminal's uncomfortable seats and used the men's washrooms to freshen up during off hours. He even managed to do his laundry in bathroom sinks. Thusly emboldened, he figured he could out-wait the bureaucracy.

Spielberg to the Rescue

Fifteen years into his wait nothing had changed. The bureaucratic snafu was as persistent as ever but luck came Nasseri's way when American director Steven Spielberg contacted him in 2003. He offered him $250,000 for the rights to his story as well as a percentage of the profits.

In 2004, *The Terminal* starring Tom Hanks was released. Based on Nasseri's odyssey, the film returned nearly four times its investment—a sum that assured Nasseri a comfortable life if only he could find a country that would accept him. In 2006 the long-awaited breakthrough came when Mehran took ill. After Nasseri spent six months in a French hospital, the stopped-up wheels of bureaucracy finally turned and Nasseri was granted permission to live in France. His ordeal had ended and a new life had begun.

The Road to Nowhere

A dark, abandoned portion of the Pennsylvania Turnpike has become a curious destination for thrill-seekers.

✳   ✳   ✳   ✳

IN OCTOBER 1940, a toll road unlike any other in America was opened to the public. Connecting the expanse between Harrisburg and Pittsburgh, the 160-mile-long Pennsylvania Turnpike made history when it became America's first bona fide superhighway. Seven long tunnels were built to sidestep the pesky mountains that stood in the way of the highway, offering drivers super-fast passage across the state. "The Tunnel Highway," as the turnpike was dubbed, was a success and became the prototype for America's Interstate Highway system.

Everything moved swiftly until the 1960s, when increased usage placed a greater demand on the turnpike. Backups became commonplace, particularly at those points where the roadway narrowed to pass through tunnels. After a 1968 decision was made to bypass the Ray's Hill and Sideling Hill tubes, the 12 total miles of roadway were abandoned in favor of a new "cut" through the mountains.

Forty-odd years is a long time to neglect a highway. Yet aside from overgrowth, the abandoned portion of the Pennsylvania Turnpike, including its tunnels, appears eerily intact. The abandoned section of turnpike still sees its share of visitors, mostly hikers, bicyclists, and urban explorers, despite the risk of a trespassing violation. Since nothing can be seen for miles except the pockmarked roadway, walking along its path, one feels like the only person left on Earth.

The abandoned tunnels have been the scenes of some odd happenings, from an ambush training session for the U.S. Army to a church choir that enjoyed a tunnel's acoustics. Plans are currently afoot to turn an eight and a half-mile portion of the roadway (including both tunnels, which will be brightly lit) into a bicycle trail. If this happens, some of the roadway's mystique and scariness will be lost. On the other hand, it's not every day that people can gleefully ride their Schwinns down the middle of our nation's first super-highway and come back in one piece.

To the Moon!

Television and film star Jackie Gleason was fascinated with the paranormal and UFOs. But he had no idea that an innocent game played with an influential friend would lead him face-to-face with his obsession.

✳   ✳   ✳   ✳

JACKIE GLEASON WAS a star of the highest order. The rotund actor kept television audiences in stitches with his portrayal of hardheaded but ultimately lovable family man Ralph Kramden in the 1955 sitcom *The Honeymooners*. He made history with his regularly aimed, but never delivered, threats to TV wife Alice, played by Audrey Meadows: "One of these days Alice, one of these days, pow, right in the kisser," and "Bang, zoom! To the moon, Alice!"

But many fans didn't know that Gleason was obsessed with the supernatural, and he owned a massive collection of memorabilia on the subject. It was so large and impressive that the University of Miami, Florida, put it on permanent exhibit after his death in 1987. He even had a house built in the shape of a UFO, which he christened, "The Mothership." The obsession was legendary, and it climaxed in an unimaginable way.

A High Stakes Game

An avid golfer, Gleason also kept a home close to Inverrary Golf and Country Club in Lauderhill, Florida. A famous golfing buddy lived nearby—U.S. President Richard M. Nixon, who had a compound on nearby Biscayne Bay. The Hollywood star and the controversial politician shared a love of the links, politics, and much more.

The odyssey began when Gleason and Nixon met for a golf tournament at Inverrary in February 1973. Late in the day their conversation turned to a topic close to Gleason's heart— UFOs. To the funnyman's surprise, the president revealed his own fascination with the subject, touting a large collection of books that rivaled Gleason's. They talked shop through the rest of the game, but Gleason noticed reservation in Nixon's tone, as if the aides and security within earshot kept the president from speaking his mind. He would soon learn why.

The story goes that later that evening around midnight, an unexpected guest visited the Gleason home. It was Nixon, alone. The customary secret service detail assigned to him was nowhere to be seen. Confused, Gleason asked Nixon the reason for such a late call. He replied only that he had to show Gleason something. They climbed into Nixon's private car and sped off. The drive brought them to Homestead Air Force Base in South Miami-Dade County. Nixon took them to a large, heavily guarded building. Guards parted as the pair headed inside the structure, Gleason following Nixon past labs before arriving at a series of large cases. The cases held wreckage from a downed UFO, Nixon told his friend. Seeing all of this, Gleason had his doubts and imagined himself the target of an elaborated staged hoax.

Leaving the wreckage, the pair entered a chamber holding six (some reports say eight) freezers topped with thick glass. Peering into the hulls, Gleason later said he saw dead bodies—but not of the human variety. The remains were small, almost childlike in stature, but withered in appearance and possessing only three or four digits per hand. They were also severely mangled, as if they had been in a devastating accident.

Returning home, Gleason was giddy. His obsession had come full circle. The enthusiasm changed in the weeks that followed, however, shifting to intense fear and worry. A patriotic American, Gleason couldn't reconcile his government's secrecy about the UFO wreckage. Traumatized, he began drinking heavily and suffered from severe insomnia.

The "Truth" Comes Out

Gleason kept details of his wild night with Nixon under wraps. Unfortunately, his soon-to-be-ex-wife didn't follow his lead. Beverly Gleason spilled the beans in *Esquire* magazine and again in an unpublished memoir on her marriage to Gleason. Supermarket tabloids ate the story up.

Gleason only opened up about his night with Nixon in the last weeks of his life. Speaking to Larry Warren, a former Air Force pilot with his own UFO close encounter, a slightly boozy Gleason let his secret loose with a phrase reminiscent of his *Honeymooners* days: "We've got 'em... Aliens!"

Top-Secret Locations

There are plenty of stories of secret government facilities hidden in plain sight. Places where all sorts of strange tests take place, far away from the general public. Many of the North American top-secret government places have been (at least partially) declassified, allowing the average person to visit. Others can be visited only in the imagination.

✳ ✳ ✳ ✳

Titan Missile Silo

JUST A LITTLE south of Tucson, Arizona, lies the Sonoran Desert, a barren, desolate area where nothing seems to be happening. That's exactly why, during the Cold War, the U.S. government hid an underground Titan Missile silo there.

Inside the missile silo, one of dozens that once littered the area, a Titan 2 Missile could be armed and launched in just under 90 seconds. Until it was finally abandoned in the 1990s, the government manned the silo 24 hours a day, with every member being trained to "turn the key" and launch the missile at a moment's notice. Today, the silo is open to the public as the Titan Missile Museum. Visitors can take a look at one of the few remaining Titan 2 missiles in existence, still sitting on the launch pad (relax, it's been disarmed). Folks with extra dough can also spend the night inside the silo and play the role of one of the crew members assigned to prepare to launch the missile at a moment's notice.

Wright-Patterson Air Force Base

If you believe that aliens crash-landed in Roswell, New Mexico, in the summer of 1947, then you need to make a trip out to Ohio's Wright-Patterson Air Force Base. That's because, according to legend, the UFO crash debris and possibly the aliens (both alive and dead) were shipped to the base as part of a government cover-up. Some say all that debris is still there, hidden away in an underground bunker beneath Hanger 18.

While most of the Air Force Base is off-limits to the general public, you can go on a portion of the base to visit the National Museum of the U.S. Air Force, filled with amazing artifacts tracing the history of flight. But don't bother to ask any of the museum personnel how to get to the mysterious Hanger 18— the official word is that the hanger does not exist.

Area 51

Located in the middle of the desert in southern Nevada lies possibly the world's best-known top-secret location: Area 51. If you've read a story about high-tech flying machines, chances are Area 51 was mentioned. That's because the government has spent years denying the base's existence, despite satellite photos showing otherwise. In fact, it was not until a lawsuit filed by government employees against the base that the government finally admitted the base did in fact exist.

If you want to find out what's going on inside Area 51, you're out of luck. While the dirt roads leading up to the base are technically public property, the base itself is very firmly not open for tours—if an unauthorized visitor so much as sets one toe over the boundary line, he or she is subject to arrest or worse. Let's just say that the sign stating the "use of deadly force is authorized" is not to be taken lightly.

Los Alamos National Laboratory

Until recently, the U.S. government refused to acknowledge the Los Alamos National Laboratory's existence. But in the early 1940s, the lab was created near Los Alamos, New Mexico, to develop the first nuclear weapons in what would become known as the Manhattan Project. Back then, the facility was so top secret it didn't even have a name. It was simply referred to as Site Y. No matter what it was called, the lab produced two nuclear bombs, nicknamed Little Boy and Fat Man—bombs that would be dropped on Hiroshima and Nagasaki, effectively ending World War II. Today, tours of portions of the facility can be arranged through the Lab's Public Affairs Department.

Fort Knox

It is the stuff that legends are made of: A mythical building filled with over 4,700 tons of gold, stacked up and piled high to the ceiling. But this is no fairytale—the gold really does exist, and it resides inside Fort Knox.

Since 1937, the U.S. Department of the Treasury's Bullion Depository has been storing the gold inside Fort Knox on a massive military campus that stretches across three counties in north-central Kentucky. Parts of the campus are open for tours, including the General George Patton Museum. But don't think you're going to catch a glimpse of that shiny stuff—visitors are not permitted to go through the gate or enter the building.

Nevada Test Site

If you've ever seen one of those old black-and-white educational films of nuclear bombs being tested, chances are it was filmed at the Nevada Test Site, often referred to as the Most Bombed Place in the World.

Located about an hour north of Las Vegas, the Nevada Test Site was created in 1951 as a secret place for the government to conduct nuclear experiments and tests in an outdoor laboratory that is actually larger than Rhode Island. Out there, scientists blew everything up from mannequins to entire buildings. Those curious to take a peek inside the facility can sign up for a daylong tour. Of course, before they let you set foot on the base, visitors must submit to a background check and sign paperwork promising not to attempt to photograph, videotape, or take soil samples from the site.

All Aboard the Cincinnati Subway

A plan to modernize the city that began at the turn of the century was abandoned and forgotten to history.

Attentive readers are probably scratching their heads, thinking, "Cincinnati doesn't have a subway." They're partially right: The city does indeed have a subway, albeit an incomplete and abandoned one. It was designed to modernize the city but ended up as a symbol of how even the best-laid plans can go astray.

✳ ✳ ✳ ✳

Cincinnati Needs a Facelift

WITH THE DAWNING of the 20th century, Cincinnatians were looking for ways to modernize. When it came to transportation, the mode of choice was the Miami-Erie Canal, which made its way alongside the city. The waterway had been an efficient means of transporting people and goods, but that was back in Cincinnati's infancy. As the population grew, the canal became a literal cesspool filled with debris and disease-carrying insects. But rather than clean the canal, city officials decided to resurrect a plan that had been discussed since the 1870s instead: turn the canal into a subway line. It seemed like a massive undertaking, but as officials started talking about the logistics, the idea began making sense. The canal bed already existed, and once drained, it would provide a perfect foundation for a subway. Workers could simply follow the canal's path to lay the tracks down. Once they encased the whole thing in concrete and steel and added a couple of stations, voilà—instant subway! Because the canal was roughly 40 feet wide, workers could get right inside the bed to work, thereby keeping construction congestion to a minimum.

Planning the Subway

In 1905, the first official plans saw the light of day. The plans called for running four parallel tracks for two miles between Walnut and Race streets up to near the Western Hills Viaduct.

From there, one set of tracks would connect with the existing Cincinnati and Westwood Interurban train line, while the second set connected with another train line to the north. But when it was discovered that all three tracks were different sizes and gauges, the idea was put on hold, and planners were sent back to the drawing board.

In December 1914, developers presented a revised plan calling for a two-track, 16-mile loop around the city, referred to as the Rapid Transit Loop, as well as almost 20 stations. The report listed four different configurations, or "schemes," by which to lay out the tracks. A very excited Rapid Transit Commission immediately took steps to get a bond issue on an upcoming ballot and ensure the funds would be available to begin construction.

"Is This Thing Ever Gonna Get Built?"

A $6 million bond issue for the construction of the subway was approved in 1916. The commission eventually chose Scheme IV, which called for a four-mile stretch of track to be placed underground from Ludlow Avenue to 3rd Street in downtown.

It seemed as though the wheels of progress were finally turning—that is, until April 1917, when the United States entered World War I. Because bonds were not allowed to be issued during times of war, Cincinnati was unable to get any of the expected $6 million, and breaking ground on the subway had to be postponed.

It wasn't until 1919 that workers began draining the canal and another year before actual construction began. But a $6 million bond from before the war did not hold the same value afterward. As a result, Scheme IV couldn't be completed as originally intended. Adjustments were made, and some stations were eliminated on the route. For a while, the construction could proceed, full steam ahead.

The Bottom Drops Out

By 1925, a two-mile-long tunnel running from Walnut Street to just north of the Western Hills Viaduct had been constructed. Three underground stations had also been completed along the route—one at Brighton's Corner, another at Liberty, and one at Race Street—with a fourth station just beginning construction. Plans were also underway for an offshoot of the tracks on Walnut Street to go through downtown to a station at Fountain Square. Then it happened: The $6 million ran out.

With no money left and an estimated $10 million still needed to complete the subway, plans were once again put on hold. The project was still delayed in 1929 when the stock market crashed, paving the way for the Great Depression. Years later, it was decided that the existing subway would be too costly to finish, and officials would instead modernize Cincinnati by creating a new motorway, Central Parkway, right over the existing subway. The Cincinnati Subway project was abandoned for good in 1948.

What Lies Beneath

Since the last digging tool was quieted within the subway more than 60 years ago, visitors can tour the abandoned tunnel, but city officials remain at a loss for what to do with it. It was furnished as a fallout shelter in 1962, but the need for it had ended by the 1980s. Proposals to turn the subway into everything from an underground shopping mall to a massive wine cellar have been floated, but none have yet come to fruition. City officials are in a bind, because even filling in the tunnels is a costly proposition.

Too expensive to demolish and too archaic to resurrect, the Cincinnati subway sits quietly below ground, with only the dull rumble of cars on the Central Parkway overhead to keep it company.

Welcome to the Kalakuta Republic

Fela Kuti is an internationally known Afropop musician. He was also the leader of a Nigerian anti-government movement. Read on to discover one man's trials and tribulations, as seen from his compound, otherwise known as the "Kalakuta Republic."

✳ ✳ ✳ ✳

A Corrupt Country

IN THE MID-1970S, Nigeria, with more than 100 million citizens, was the most populous country in Africa; as a new member of the Organization of Petroleum Exporting Countries (OPEC), it was also one of the world's leading oil exporters. Although enormous amounts of foreign money flowed into the government's coffers, it quickly flowed into the hands of the ruling class. But life for the vast majority of Nigerians was as hard as ever. Crime was rampant, poverty widespread, and all forms of dissention were violently suppressed. Yet one man in Lagos continued to publicly criticize the rulers and their backers: the musician, Fela Kuti.

From Lagos to London to Los Angeles

Afropop is a hypnotic, compelling blend of American funk arrangements, European classical compositional technique, jazz, and African tribal rhythms. Kuti, the genre's originator, was the son of a decidedly left-wing, middle-class family from Lagos. His jazz highlife band, Koola Lobitos, attracted sufficient attention to justify a 1969 tour of the United States. Kuti would later say that the ten months he spent in America galvanized all of his later political thinking.

In the United States, Kuti was exposed to the black power movement. A Black Panther friend gave him a copy of Malcolm X's autobiography; Kuti was an instant convert. He returned to Nigeria and formed Africa 70, a huge ensemble complete with horns, saxophonists, guitarists, dancers, and singers. Kuti and his band established themselves at the local club Shrine.

Although his songs frequently attacked the status quo, the country's leaders were generally content to leave the "crazy" musician alone.

An Independent Republic

Kuti established the area around his Lagos home as a commune, complete with medical facilities, farm animals, and a recording studio. Kuti went a step further and had the compound fenced with electrified barbed wire and proclaimed it a sovereign nation—the Kalakuta Republic. With Africa 70 selling millions of albums, Kuti's political and social diatribes became increasingly brazen. Military leaders hated him for his flagrant criticism, and the bourgeoisie hated him because of his free lifestyle.

Tensions between Kuti and the military reached a breaking point in 1976, following the second World Black and African Festival of the Arts and Culture. Kuti withdrew Africa 70 from the official lineup and staged a counter festival at Shrine, where he debuted "Zombie," a song mocking government soldiers. "Zombie" became an overnight sensation, but for the military, it was the last straw.

The Raid and Its Aftermath

On February 18, 1977, more than 1,000 soldiers amassed outside the Kalakuta Republic compound. They barricaded the building, set fire to the generator, and attacked the building with savage ferocity. Soldiers beat people, raped women, and smashed equipment. Kuti's aging mother, herself a renowned political activist, was thrown through a window and later died from her injuries. Kuti was dragged from the building and severely beaten, suffering a fractured skull and broken bones. The rest of the residents were carted to jail or the hospital. A government-sponsored committee later found no wrongdoing on the part of the soldiers.

Kuti and his music survived the raid. He established a new Kalakuta Republic and one year later married 27 women in a Yoruba ceremony. Though he was often jailed and beaten, he continued to reside in Lagos where he performed and preached against the ruling power. Kuti's persistence earned him the name *Abami Eda,* or "Chief Priest," among his fans. He remained a vibrant force in Nigeria and in world music until his death from AIDS in 1997. More than one million people attended his funeral procession.

Getting Back to the Basics in Luckenbach, Texas

Take two beers, listen to a country fiddle, smile and laugh, strum a guitar, kick your boots up, and don't call until morning. "Luckenbach," said the doctor, "is a habit-forming antidote for modern life."

✳ ✳ ✳ ✳

THE SMALL COMMUNITY of Luckenbach is tucked away among the rolling hills and prickly pear cacti of the Texas Hill Country, 75 miles west of Austin. Oil wasn't discovered here; neither was gold, silver, or diamonds. Nobody especially famous was born and raised here, either. It's off the beaten path, difficult to find, and far from modern conveniences

But that's the whole point. The late Hondo Crouch, celebrated Texas folklorist, writer, humorist, and self-styled "Clown Prince" of Luckenbach, orchestrated it to be that way. With a couple of buddies, in 1970 he purchased the ten-acre town for $30,000. At the time, only three residents remained, which meant that it was on the brink of becoming a ghost town.

Starting from Scratch

"Downtown" Luckenbach consisted of nothing more than a combination general store and tavern, an old-time dance hall, and a blacksmith shop. Nothing much had changed here since the German pioneers first arrived during the mid-1800s. In fact, the last time something newsworthy had happened was in

1849 when Minna Engel, the daughter of an itinerant preacher, opened the general store. She also named the town after her fiancé, Carl Albert Luckenbach.

After Crouch bought the town, he maintained the status quo by keeping growth to a minimum. He wasn't thinking of putting in a master-planned community, a strip mall, or even a theme park. He merely kicked back, began whittling, and invited some friends over to play some music. His most extravagant ambition was to greet visitors with a hearty welcome and to make them smile.

Building a Reputation

Single-handedly, Hondo Crouch invented Luckenbach and styled it as if it were the living room of his imagination. In fact, he referred to the town as a "free state . . . of mind."

As the town "mayor," he had a duty to act as both irreverent thinker and ringmaster. He liked to poke fun at politicians and often lampooned the "Texas White House," President Lyndon Johnson's ranch on the nearby Pedernales River. He also staged crazy festivals such as a women-only chili cook-off and the Luckenbach Great World's Fair. "Hug-ins" were a regular event, as was Mud Daubers' Day. "Everybody's Somebody in Luckenbach," decreed Crouch.

Then, one summer night in 1973, musician Jerry Jeff Walker and the Lost Gonzo Band recorded a live album there called *Viva Terlingua*. The antithesis of the Nashville scene, the record became a classic of the country-rock "outlaw" genre. More notoriety came in 1977 after Waylon Jennings and Willie Nelson released their hit "Luckenbach, Texas (Back to the Basics of Love)." Suddenly, the town's reputation as a venue to relax and strum a guitar transformed it into a cult destination.

Modern Times

Today, Luckenbach is still all about the music. On any night of the week, you can find musicians dressed in boots and faded jeans, wearing cowboy hats, sitting around pickin', grinnin', and singin'. Eager to be inspired by Luckenbach's muse, hopeful artists travel from across America just to play their new song at the dance hall. Somehow, they hope that a small amount of Luckenbach's legend will rub off on their tune and bless it with good fortune.

Around these parts, they like to say that "you can't find a place more laid-back without being unconscious," and they're right. In an age when people are obsessed with money, social status, and the so-called trappings of success, Luckenbach exists as a virtual tranquilizer—an antidote to life that has to be experienced rather than swallowed.

Bad MOVE in Philly

Looking more like a war zone than the City of Brotherly Love, Philadelphia, Pennsylvania, was ignited under a police-induced firestorm in 1985.

✳ ✳ ✳ ✳

Tensions Begin

THEY CALLED THEMSELVES MOVE, short for the word "movement." Formed around 1972 by Donald and John "Africa" Glassey, the radical organization was comprised predominantly of African Americans who believed that a back-to-nature approach was central to living a full life. MOVE preached vigorously against the ills of technology and strongly embraced the idea of a society without government or police. Not surprisingly, their actions drew the suspicion and ire of the Philadelphia police. Eventually, tensions between the two groups would climax in the police bombing of MOVE's headquarters in 1985. To this day the incident is still vigorously criticized.

Hostilities started in 1978, when MOVE members were living communally in a house owned by Donald Glassey. Philadelphia police were wary of the group's actions there, and they released a court order demanding that MOVE, well, move. The radical group refused to relocate, however, and the ensuing confrontation claimed the life of Officer James Ramp and also injured several people. Nine MOVE members were subsequently tried, convicted of third-degree murder, and sentenced to 30 years in prison for their part in the shooting.

The Situation Escalates

By 1985, the remaining MOVE members were living in a row house at 6221 Osage Avenue. But they weren't quiet about their new residence—group members were heard shouting obscenities over bullhorns during the early hours of the morning. MOVE was suspected of hoarding weapons, and from what the police could see, they had even built a wooden bunker on their roof. Additionally, every window and door of their house was barricaded with plywood. Their actions not only made the police nervous, but they also frightened the group's neighbors, who turned to city officials for help.

Devastating Destruction

Many Philadelphians will never forget May 13, 1985. On that morning, an organized force of police, firefighters, and city officials converged on the residence in an attempt to force MOVE members from their antisocial haven. In short order, a standoff ensued; MOVE exchanged gunfire with the police. Possibly fearing a repeat of the 1978 incident, Philadelphia police planned a proactive, though ultimately fateful, strategy. At 5:30 that evening, they maneuvered a police helicopter over the house and released a bomb containing C-4 explosive. Although police claimed the bomb was only intended to destroy the bunker, it did far more than that.

Within minutes, the house was engulfed in a firestorm so powerful it would leapfrog streets and spread to adjacent homes. The only survivors to come out of the MOVE house were Ramona Africa (most MOVE members had taken the surname Africa) and a 13-year-old boy. In all, within four hours 11 people were dead (including five children) and 61 residences were decimated.

The Aftermath

Almost immediately, public opinion turned against the police. Questions soon arose: Why had the police dropped a bomb when they knew innocent women and children were inside the residence? Why had the fire department neglected to put out the fire? And other than noisemaking and unruliness, what had the MOVE group done at the Osage residence to merit such an attack? To this day, these questions remain largely unanswered.

Ramona Africa was charged with conspiracy, riot, and multiple counts of assault and served seven years in prison. In 1996, she was awarded $500,000 in a civil suit against the city. When asked her opinion of the bombing during a 2003 interview, Africa was blunt: "If the government is saying that their solution to a neighborhood dispute is to bomb the neighborhood and burn it down, then there wouldn't be a single neighborhood standing."

Town for Sale

The Grove, in Coryell County, is one of dozens of ghost towns that dot the Texas landscape—but it went up for sale.

✳ ✳ ✳ ✳

Located north of Fort Hood and Killeen, between the cities of Temple and Gatesville, The Grove is actually a "Historical Museum Town," with about 60 residents. Founded around 1860, The Grove was named for its large stand of live oak trees. The town's first well was dug by hand through solid rock in 1872 and has supposedly never run dry, even during severe droughts. By 1900, The Grove was one of the most prosperous towns in the county, with nearly 500 residents, a school with two teachers and 60 students, and a number of businesses.

The Beginning of the End

In 1936, however, the Texas Highway Department told residents they would have to place a cover on their town well if they wanted Highway 36 to run through The Grove. Residents refused, and the highway bypassed the area, cutting businesses off from considerable traffic that would have flowed through town. Expansion of the nearby Fort Hood army base in the 1940s and the completion of Belton Dam a few years later took hundreds of thousands of acres of land away from many of the area's farmers, accelerating the town's steady decline into obscurity. The hamlet continued as home to a few dozen families while filling its new role as a historic museum town, thanks to Austin antiques dealer and collector Moody Anderson.

Anderson, who has been collecting antiques for nearly 50 years, discovered The Grove in 1972 and tried to buy several antique items in the W. J. Dube general store. Proprietor John Graham refused the sale. When Anderson offered to buy the whole store, though, Graham agreed. Anderson had already amassed a huge collection of artifacts from the state's frontier past, stored at a warehouse outside Austin. For more than 20 years he's rented many of his treasures to nearly 100 film and television productions, including the *Lonesome Dove* miniseries and movies such as *The Newton Boys* and *The Alamo*.

A New Niche

With The Grove, Moody Anderson saw another opportunity and began buying more buildings near the general store. The hamlet's other historic museum buildings included a blacksmith shop and the sheriff's office next door to the store. The Cocklebur Saloon was a short block away and opened every weekend with local bands playing dance music for crowds that often numbered in the hundreds. A doctor's office was found in another nearby building.

Dube's, which Anderson turned into the Country Life Museum, remained the center of town. The old store was jam-packed with all things old fashioned, including household goods and groceries, patent medicines, hardware, hand-crank washing machines, and even a coffin or two, all dating to the 19th and early 20th centuries. The Planters State Bank, established in the early 1900s, occupied one corner of the store, its original fixtures—including a walk-in safe—just as they were when the bank was robbed in 1927. The Grove U.S. Post Office, established in 1874, was on the opposite side of the general store. Anderson rented a number of the store's antiques to movie companies, including a bathtub used by Farrah Fawcett in the movie *The Substitute Wife*.

On the third Saturday of each month, musicians from around the state came to play and sing at The Grove. Tours were held on Saturdays and Sundays.

Eventually, however, preserving a town became too much for Anderson, then over 80 years old. He listed The Grove for sale with an Austin real estate company, hoping to find a buyer who would preserve the historical museum town and keep it open to the public for years to come. Instead, the town continued as a family affair. A woman named Fran Moyer bought the town for $200,000 at auction. Moyer was the granddaughter of W.J. Dube, once the owner of the general store.

Don't Mind the Mess!

Most people throw their garbage away. Jay and Annie Warmke of Gaysport used theirs to build their dream home.

✳ ✳ ✳ ✳

JAY AND ANNIE Warmke wanted their new home to be as ecofriendly as possible, so they built it from materials most people would consider trash, including old tires, bottles, and cans. Originally conceived by Michael Reynolds of Taos, New Mexico, Earthship homes like the Warmkes' are designed to be as environmentally friendly and sustainable as possible.

Ecofriendly and Cheap

The walls of the Warmkes' 1,650-square-foot abode were made from more than 1,000 old tires, for example, which were filled with compacted earth and stabilized with steel rods. They got the tires for free from area contractors who were cleaning up illegal dumps.

The Warmkes' was the first Earthship home built in Ohio, and it became quite an attraction. In fact, when the house was under construction, the Warmkes couldn't get any work done. People kept dropping by to see the "trash house." When crowds started visiting by the busload, the couple began charging gawkers admission.

Jay and Annie have taken their crusade to the people, selling custom-made tools and instructional pamphlets on how to build recycled buildings. They also host seminars on how to construct well-insulated buildings using bales of straw. The roof and siding were made of recycled slate, while the walls of the loafing station intended to shelter their five llamas were constructed of 21 straw bales sewn to a wood frame and then covered with mud.

The cost of those walls: $250. And brother, that ain't hay.

Make Way for Technocracy!

Humankind is overstaying its welcome on the planet. But don't worry—all our problems can be solved by the right technology.

✳   ✳   ✳   ✳

A Proposed Utopia: Techtopia

THE SOCIOPOLITICAL MOVEMENT called technocracy claims to have the medicine for our societal ills. Global warming, failed monetary policy—it can all be remedied. The movement began in the 1930s with the formation of the Technical Alliance, founded by technocracy pioneer Howard Scott. The basic idea is that society should not be run by politicians but according to scientific rigor and the strategic application of technology. Technocrats propose that after the inevitable collapse of the current world order, a new world order called a Technate will arise.

So how will the Technate be different from the world we know now? For one thing, there will be no money. Coupons called energy certificates will be handed out instead. The total number of certificates will depend upon total productive capacity of the Technate, and all citizens will receive the same number. Cities will be destroyed and replaced by urbanates, which will be just like modern cities, only meticulously planned in an ecologically sound manner. Under this system, all citizens will enjoy the highest standard of living.

Meanwhile, in the Here and Now

Until recently, technocracy has remained a predominantly American phenomenon. Its headquarters, called Technocracy, Inc., are in Washington state. In 2006, countries on the other side of the Atlantic established the Network of European Technocrats. However, technocracy is often used as a generalized term to refer to those who believe specialists should run society. In this sense of the word, technocracy is a worldwide but unorganized movement.

The Fate of the Freedom Ship

The Freedom Ship was conceived as a new kind of boundary-free community—a luxurious neighborhood that would constantly circumnavigate the globe. But a decade after its inception, construction has yet to begin.

✳ ✳ ✳ ✳

A Grand Idea

IMAGINE A LUXURY-FILLED community that offers the best in business, entertainment, and education. Now imagine it slowly floating around the world. According to its Web site, the

Freedom Ship is pitched as a 4,500-foot-long barge that would consist of individual neighborhoods. Each 'hood would house a number of different living units ranging from $9,136,600 (plus a $14,716 monthly maintenance fee) to an economy unit at $153,000 (plus a $492 monthly maintenance fee—and no kitchen). There would also be space for shops, restaurants, and businesses, and an onboard hotel for high-end guest lodging.

The Freedom Ship's plans also call for plenty of entertainment. The ship would feature a "world-class" casino, along with a convention center large enough to accommodate concerts and sporting events. Museums, aquariums, and nature preserves round out the entertainment options. Designs include plans for a flight deck for turboprop aircraft and a marina to let residents come and go at their leisure. But this isn't just a cruise ship. Not leaving anything out, the Freedom Ship's planners made sure that education and healthcare are key parts of the plans— a school system and state-of-the-art medical facility are also included in the budget.

A Docked Dream

It's all impressive, but in reality, the estimated $11 billion project hasn't amounted to anything more than an idea; and so far, this idea is showing no signs of sailing off any time soon.

A Man's Bedroom Can Be His Kingdom

The micronation of Talossa began with a 14-year-old kid in Milwaukee, long before the Internet. Now its global membership produces its own heraldry.

✳   ✳   ✳   ✳

ON DECEMBER 26, 1979, Talossa was born when Robert Ben Madison, a boy of 14, held a ceremony in his family home. Crowning himself with an old fire department dress uniform cap, he announced his bedroom's secession from the

United States. Madison had made a flag for the occasion and even chosen a national anthem (Fleetwood Mac's "Tusk"). With most people at the helm, Talossa would have lasted about a week. Ben Madison wasn't most people.

His family humored the eccentric young monarch. A linguistic prodigy, Madison borrowed Talossa (rhymes with mimosa) from the Finnish for "in the house." A selected motto translated to "A Man's Room is His Kingdom" from rough Finnish. The Kingdom of Talossa had become a micronation of one. Since the U.S. government offered no comment, Madison inferred that Uncle Sam didn't mind.

Madison began publishing newsletters, adopting and changing political alignments, switching the national language, rebelling against Talossa's (his own) "oppressive" regime, and living an active "national" fantasy life. He soon began involving his friends. Talossa's first "war" involved another teenage micronationalist vandalizing the Madison family's garage and tripping the king's sister after church.

Madison dissolved Talossa in July 1981, having encountered insurmountable difficulty in explaining his "kingdom" to girls. However, when ending Talossa didn't end his dating problem, Madison decided to reactivate his micronation. In large part due to his charisma, will, and abundant spare time, Talossa struggled along. For the next 15 years, it normally consisted of a dozen or so Milwaukeean "citizens," some active and others simply humoring Madison (who lived at home into adulthood). Talossa claimed a chunk of Milwaukee's East Side as its territory, as well as a slice of Antarctica and a French island. The political system became a parliamentary monarchy.

Talossa's political development peaked and valleyed, featuring parties like PUNK (People United for No King), the Bob Fights Ticket, and STOMP (Schneider's Talossan Marxist Party). Madison designed Talossan as a Romance language, authoring a dictionary and rules of grammar. El Glhe ("the tongue") used every accent mark, circumflex, and other foreign character Madison could locate. Talossa adopted Gloria Estefan as National Entertainer (whether she realized this or not) and Taco Bell as its ethnic cuisine. Its citizens gathered for meals, political events, and board-gaming sessions. Talossans published newsletters, ranging from the mature to the angry to the bizarre; in one infamous episode, a dissident citizen began publishing detailed records of his bathroom visits.

The pre-Internet Regipäts Talossan ("Kingdom of Talossa") eventually grew to about 30 citizens, mostly Milwaukeeans. Madison remained its primary sustaining force.

Going Online—and Worldwide

In January 1996, Madison published Talossa's first web page. Its whimsical, inviting tone attracted notice. Few "bathtub kingdoms" had their own languages, let alone 16 years of history and personality. Madison was bombarded with online inquiries, and a few people were even willing to jump through all the naturalization hoops.

Thereafter, the diversifying citizenry would increasingly define Talossa in terms beyond face-to-face friendship with Ben Madison. Some "Old Growth" Talossans spurned the Internet entirely; most "cybercits" were unlikely to make pilgrimages to Milwaukee. Madison bridged the space between the two groups. By this time, numerous online micronations had sprung up, but Talossa remained the most successful and mature (at least, in a cultural development sense). Talossa denied citizenship to citizens of "bug nations"—Madison's scornful term for other micronations.

From 1996 to 2004, Madison's control over the Regipäts gradually declined. Various groups continued the long-term political role-playing game begun in 1979: ranting, resigning ministries, starting and disbanding parties, renouncing and regaining citizenship, amending its 1997 constitution, developing the language, and growing to roughly 75 citizens located in over half a dozen countries. The Milwaukee core was anything but unified, and had become a decided minority to boot.

A Crumbling Kingdom

On June 1, 2004, while Madison was touring Africa, his brainchild kingdom schismed out of his grasp. Citing grave exception to Madison's mistreatment of some citizens, 11 of the more active Talossans seceded to form the "Republic of Talossa," taking with them administration rights to the "Wittenberg" discussion group where most of Talossa happened. Madison and his loyalists fought back by relaxing citizenship requirements, quickly growing the Regipäts back to its former size. After an early burst of activity, and some new faces in the form of former kingdom citizens and rejected hopefuls, the republic stagnated.

The kingdom thrived—but away from Madison. Barely a year later, the new influx of Talossa citizens had his loyalist faction politically outgunned. On August 15, 2005, Madison renounced his Talossan citizenship. Except for a short-lived rump kingdom, which gathered no steam, Ben Madison was done with Talossa.

Post-Madisonian Talossa

The loss of its longtime king, which might have killed Talossa in 1985, barely dented it in 2005. The citizenry chose a Coloradoan as its new king, and the kingdom continued to grow. Relations with the republic remained chilly for years, until its citizenry rejoined the royal fold in 2012. In true Talossan fashion, the ex-republicans promptly formed an anti-monarchical political party.

At this writing, the Kingdom of Talossa boasts about 200 citizens, a busy discussion board, noisy politics in eight "provinces," a comprehensive website, and translations of various literary works into Talossan (for some ten fluent speakers). It issues peerages, knighthoods, and coats of arms, maintaining its constitutional monarchy to this day.

Travel Guide: By the Numbers

Of course there's more to a city than its crime rate, air pollution levels, and water quality. But when you're planning a trip or considering a move, these measures are sure to be high on your list. As this look at each end of the scale demonstrates, there's an astounding gap between the top and the bottom.

✳ ✳ ✳ ✳

Cleanest

IN 2007, FORBES published a list of the 25 cleanest cities (which included 26 cities because there was a tie for 25th place). The editors based the list on how well cities handled problems such as sanitation, energy production, recycling, and transportation—data they gathered from consulting firm Mercer's in-depth studies of 300 cities. Here's a summary:

✳ Canada dominated the list, claiming top honors with Calgary and nabbing four other spots (Ottawa, Montreal, Vancouver, Toronto).

✳ The United States ranked second overall. Honolulu nabbed the #2 spot, and Minneapolis, Boston, Lexington, and Pittsburgh also made the list.

✳ Overall, ten European cities made the list, and Switzerland took three spots (Zurich, Bern, and Geneva).

✳ Japan grabbed three spots (Katsuyama, Kobe, and Omuta), but no other Asian countries made the list.

✳ Only two cities below the equator made the list—Auckland and Wellington, both in New Zealand.

Dirtiest

Forbes has also published a less flattering list, ranking the 25 dirtiest cities. The 2008 list was based on Mercer's profiles of how 215 cities handled waste management, air pollution, disease, water cleanliness, and hospital care.

As you might expect, the list was dominated by cities in impoverished third-world countries: Baku, in the former Soviet Republic of Azerbaijan, claimed the top spot, thanks to extreme air pollution from many years of oil drilling. Almaty, in the former Soviet Republic of Kazakhstan, also made the list, as did Moscow, which has severe air pollution.

* African countries dominated the list, taking 16 spots. In most of these cities, the biggest problems are poor waste management in high population areas, which leads to severely polluted water supplies.

* Water pollution also put two Indian cities on the list (Mumbai and New Delhi), as well as Dhaka in neighboring Bangladesh.

* The only cities in the Americas that made the list were Port au Prince, Haiti, and Mexico City, Mexico.

* In a 2007 article, *Forbes* named smoggy Los Angeles the dirtiest U.S. city.

Safest and Deadliest

As part of their 2008 "Quality of Living" report, Mercer identified the cities with the highest and lowest "personal safety rankings." Their criteria included crime rate, law enforcement effectiveness, stability, and quality of relationships with other countries. Here's a look at the two extremes on their list:

* The tiny European country Luxembourg's capital city, Luxembourg, scored the highest on personal safety.

* Helsinki, Finland, tied for second place with three Swiss cities (Bern, Zurich, and Geneva).

* The report ranked Baghdad, Iraq, as the most dangerous city, followed by Kinshasa in the Democratic Republic of Congo; Karachi, Pakistan; Nairobi, Kenya; and Bangui, in the Central African Republic.

And what about the United States? Every year, CQ Press ranks the safety of U.S. cities with populations greater than 75,000, based on crime statistics gathered by the FBI (specifically, per-capita rates of murder, rape, aggravated assault, robbery, burglary, and car theft). Here's a summary of the 2008–2009 report's conclusions:

* Ramapo, New York, made the top of the safe list, with only 688 reported crimes and no murders reported in 2007.

* Second place went to Mission Viejo, California, which had taken first place in the previous year's report.

* The report ranked New Orleans as the most dangerous city, with 19,034 reported crimes and 209 murders.

* After New Orleans, the report listed Camden, New Jersey; Detroit, Michigan; St. Louis, Missouri; and Oakland, California, as the most dangerous U.S. cities.

Don't Mess With Her

Universal gender equality may be a relatively new social concept, but history records plenty of women who went out and got respect anyway—by force, if necessary.

✳ ✳ ✳ ✳

Then-CPT Kim Campbell—Born in 1975, this Air Force Academy graduate became an A-10 Warthog (ground support) pilot. On April 7, 2003, Iraqi ground fire shot her Hog to Swiss cheese, knocking out her hydraulics. Refusing to eject over Baghdad, she managed to land the plane safely without hydraulics—an amazing feat that won her the Distinguished Flying Cross (Valor).

Phoolan Devi—Born into a low–ranking Indian caste in 1963, she became a *dacoit* (bandit) in her teens. After being captured and gang-raped by a rival gang from the Thakur (landowner) caste, she led an attack that massacred 21 of their number, including some of her rapists. She eventually surrendered, did prison time, and became a parliamentary champion of the Dalit ('untouchable') caste until her assassination in 2001.

Dahomey's *Mino*—From the early 1700s to the late 1800s, these women formed a fearsome regiment in the Dahomeyan king's military. Executing prisoners was part of their desensitization training. Superbly conditioned, and dedicated to winning or dying, they rarely met defeat until the French Foreign Legion arrived with machine guns in the 1890s.

'Stagecoach' Mary Fields—Born around 1832 into slavery in Tennessee, she went west some years after the Civil War. Fields wound up supervising construction work in Cascade, Montana. One roughneck resented taking orders from an African American woman, and hit her; Fields shot him dead. She drove the local mailcoach for years, and died a local legend in 1914.

Fredegund—Born a slave attendant around 550, she was a Merovingian Frankish queen with a ruthless rep. She seduced her way into the affections of King Chilperic I, arranging oft-sadistic assassinations to clear the way for his ambitions (which were often more hers than his). When Chilperic died, Fredegund maneuvered similarly to advance her son Chlothar's prospects. Many Frankish nobles breathed easier after her death in 597.

Tomoe Gozen—Born in 1157 in Japan, this samurai warrior was an expert rider, swordswoman, archer, and wielder of the naginata (a sort of halberd). In a culture and caste where honor and bravery were all, Tomoe was Lord Minamoto's preferred first captain in battle. Stories conflict; some say she retired from arms and died peacefully in 1247. Others say she sought and found death in battle grieving her liege's slaying.

Violette Morris—Born in 1893 in France, she believed she could do anything a man could do—and proved it as a boxer, wrestler, Olympic medalist, and race car driver. Morris actually had a double mastectomy just to better fit into cars! Sadly, during

World War II, she went to work for the Gestapo occupiers. The Resistance gunned her down during an ambush in 1944.

Jennifer Musa—Born into a large County Kerry Irish Catholic family in 1917, she fell in love with a young Afghan Baluchistani prince in college. Moving to his rugged homeland, then going into Pakistani exile with him, she defied gender restrictions and got away with it. After her husband's 1956 death, she became her adopted people's foremost advocate. Called 'The Irish Queen of Balochistan,' Musa passed away in 2008.

Sr. Lt. Anna Yegorova—Born in 1916, this Soviet pilot started out flying harassment bombing against the Nazi invaders, but unlike most Soviet female pilots, she flew with the men. She survived wartime captivity after her Il-2 Sturmovik was shot down, then survived the NKVD persecution common to all captured Soviet personnel. Named a Heroine of the Soviet Union, Yegorova died in 2009.

Chapter 3

Business and Commerce

Who Put the PB in PB&J?

What goes equally well with jelly, bacon, marshmallow fluff, chocolate, and banana? Peanut butter, of course. And most schoolkids think that George Washington Carver is the man behind that magic.

✳   ✳   ✳   ✳

The Well-traveled Peanut

THE MYTH THAT George Washington Carver invented peanut butter has spread as easily as this spreadable favorite. But by the time Carver was born in 1864, peanuts were being crushed into a paste on five continents. Peanuts have been grown for consumption in South America since 950 B.C., and the Incas used peanut paste in much of their cooking. Fifteenth-century trade ships took peanuts to Africa and Asia, where they were assimilated into local cuisines, often as a paste used for thickening stews. In the 18th century, peanuts traveled back across the Atlantic Ocean to be traded to North American colonists. In 1818, the first commercial peanut crop was produced in North Carolina. Today, there are approximately 50,000 peanut farms in the United States, and half of the peanuts produced on these farms are turned into peanut butter.

A Popular Nut Paste

So the Incas, not Carver, must be credited with first grinding of peanuts into a paste. But the forefather of modern-day peanut butter was an anonymous doctor who, in 1890, put peanuts through a meat grinder to provide a protein source for people with teeth so bad they couldn't chew meat. A food-processing company saw the potential in the doctor's product and started selling the nut paste for $0.06 per pound. Dr. John Harvey Kellogg (the inventor of corn flakes) had been feeding a similar paste made from steamed, ground peanuts to the patients at his sanatorium in Michigan. In 1895, he patented his "process of preparing nut meal" and began selling it to the general public.

The nut paste caught on, and peanut-grinding gadgets became readily available, along with cookbooks full of recipes for nut meals, pastes, and spreads. In 1904, visitors at the St. Louis World's Fair bought more than $700 worth of peanut butter. In 1908, the Krema Nut Company in Columbus, Ohio, began selling peanut butter—but only within the state because of problems with spoilage.

Carver's Contributions

So how did George Washington Carver get in the middle of this peanutty story? Carver was an agricultural chemist, inventor, and innovator who had a strong interest in peanut production and a firm belief that it could benefit American agriculture. Although born to slaves, Carver worked and studied hard. He earned master's degrees in botany and agriculture from Iowa Agricultural College (now Iowa State University), and he became the director of agriculture at the Tuskegee Normal and Industrial Institute for Negroes in 1897.

At the Tuskegee Institute, Carver researched and developed approximately 290 practical and esoteric uses for peanuts, incorporating them into foods, cosmetics, ink, paper, and lubricants. He didn't patent any of these products, believing that the earth's crops and their by-products were gifts from God. Although he published several works about the benefits of peanuts in agriculture, industry, and cuisine, he became nationally associated with the crop only late in his career.

Influential Nonetheless

The story of Carver's humble beginnings, talents, and professional success took on mythic proportions. A number of articles and biographies generously (and erroneously) credit him with everything from inventing dehydrated foods to rescuing the South from crushing poverty by promoting peanut products. At some point, the invention of peanut butter was attributed to him.

Schoolchildren everywhere are entranced by Carver's personal success story and his contributions to American agriculture. He is a role model despite the fact that he didn't invent peanut butter. Giving credit where it's due—to the Incas—does not diminish the value of Carver's accomplishments.

Thomas Crapper: Wizard or Washout?

There are many myths about Englishman Thomas Crapper swirling around like so much…conjecture. Some claim he invented the toilet, and others credit his last name with creating a crude colloquialism. It's time to flush away the guesswork.

✳   ✳   ✳   ✳

THOMAS CRAPPER WAS an actual person, a 19th-century London plumber who held several patents in systems for waste-handling. But the concept of the flush toilet dates back to the late 1500s, when England and France used a "closet" full of water to wash waste out of the toilet bowl and into a sewer line. Even before that—in the 26th century B.C.—flushlike toilets were used by members of the Indus civilization in what is now Pakistan. By the late 1700s, the practice of keeping water in the bowl served to eliminate odors by sealing off the drain line. Crapper ran a London plumbing business and installed many "water closets" in the late 1800s. And though this was certainly a noble effort to keep the city smelling fresh and clean, Crapper was never knighted by royalty, quelling the rumor that he was given the title "Sir."

Regarding the word attributed to Crapper's last name: The 15th-century Middle English word *crappe* referred to husks of grain on a barn floor (similar to *chaff*). Other meanings of the word *crap* date back to the 1500s, when it referred to anything cast off, or a useless residue. It is reported that U.S. soldiers returning from World War I had encountered toilets overseas sold by Thomas Crapper's company. Seeing the brand name on the side of the tank led them to associate the maker with the device they used, and as often happens, noun becomes verb.

Mansa Musa's Reverse Gold Rush

History's epic gold rushes were generally characterized by masses of people trekking to the gold. But in 1324, the legendary Mansa Musa bucked the trend by trekking masses of gold to the people—which had the result of severely depressing the Egyptian gold market.

✳   ✳   ✳   ✳

I F YOU COULD talk to a gold trader from 14th-century Cairo, he might say that the worst time of his life occurred the day Mansa Musa came to town.

Musa, king of the powerful Mali Empire, stopped over in Cairo during his pilgrimage to Mecca. Arriving in the Egyptian metropolis in 1324, Musa and his entourage of about 60,000 hangers-on were anything but inconspicuous. Even more conspicuous was the 4,000-pound hoard of gold that Musa hauled with him.

While in Cairo, Musa embarked on a spending and gift-giving spree unseen since the pharaohs. By the time he was finished, Musa had distributed so much gold around Cairo that its value plummeted in Egypt. It would be more than a decade before the price of gold recovered from the Mali king's extravagance.

A Fool and His Money?—Not Musa

Musa's story conjures the old adage about fools and their money soon parting—especially when you consider he had to borrow money for the trip home. But Musa was no fool.

Musa ruled Mali from 1312 until 1337, and ushered in the empire's golden age. He extended Mali's power across sub-Saharan Africa from the Atlantic coast to western Sudan. Mali gained tremendous wealth by controlling the trans-Sahara trade routes, which passed through Timbuktu and made the ancient city the nexus of northwest African commerce. During Musa's reign, Mali exploited the Taghaza salt deposits to the north and the rich Wangara gold mines to the south, producing half the world's gold.

Musa's crowning achievement was the transformation of Timbuktu into one of Islam's great centers of culture and education. A patron of the arts and learning, Musa brought Arab scholars from Mecca to help build libraries, mosques, and universities throughout Mali. Timbuktu became a gathering place for Muslim writers, artists, and scholars from Africa and the Middle East. The great Sankore mosque and university built by Musa remain the city's focal point today.

Musa's *Hajj* Puts Mali on the Map

Musa's story is seldom told without mention of his legendary pilgrimage, or *hajj*, to Mecca.

The *hajj* is an obligation every Muslim is required to undertake at least once in their life. For the devout Musa, his *hajj* would be more than just a fulfillment of that obligation. It would also be a great coming-out party for the Mali king.

Accompanying Musa was a flamboyant caravan of courtiers and subjects dressed in fine Persian silk, including 12,000 personal servants. And then there was all that gold. A train of 80 camels carried 300 pounds of gold each. Five hundred servants carried four-pound solid-gold staffs.

Along the way, Musa handed out golden alms to the needy in deference to one of the pillars of Islam. Wherever the caravan halted on a Friday, Musa left gold to pay for the construction of a mosque. And don't forget his Cairo stopover. By the time he left Mecca, the gold was all gone.

But one doesn't dish out two tons of gold without being noticed. Word of Musa's wealth and generosity spread like wildfire. He became a revered figure in the Muslim world and inspired Europeans to seek golden kingdoms on the Dark Continent.

Musa's journey put the Mali Empire on the map—literally. European cartographers began placing it on maps in 1339. A 1375 map pinpointed Mali with a depiction of a black African king wearing a gold crown and holding a golden scepter in his left hand and a large gold nugget aloft in his right.

Extra Cheddar, Please: Facts About Cheese

* Archaeological surveys show that cheese was being made from the milk of cows and goats in Mesopotamia before 6000 B.C.

* Travelers from Asia are thought to have brought the art of cheese making to Europe, where the process was adapted and improved in monasteries.

* The Pilgrims had a supply of cheese onboard the *Mayflower* in 1620.

* The world's largest consumers of cheese include Greece (63 pounds per person each year), France (54 pounds), Iceland (53 pounds), Germany (48 pounds), Italy (44 pounds), the Netherlands (40 pounds), the United States (31 pounds), Australia (27 pounds), and Canada (26 pounds).

* The United States produces more than 25 percent of the world's supply of cheese, approximately 9 billion pounds per year.

* The only cheeses native to the United States are American, jack, brick, and colby. All other types are modeled after cheeses brought to the country by European settlers.

* Processed American cheese was developed in 1915 by J. L. Kraft (founder of Kraft Foods) as an alternative to the traditional cheeses that had a short shelf life.

* Pizza Hut uses about 300 million pounds of cheese per year.

* In 1886, the University of Wisconsin introduced one of the country's first cheese-making education programs. Today, you can take cheese-making courses through a variety of university agricultural programs, dairy farms, and cheese factories.

* Because they can produce large volumes of milk, butterfat, and protein, black-and-white (sometimes red-and-white) Holsteins are the most popular dairy cows in the U.S., making up 90 percent of the total herd.

* The Cheese Days celebration in Monroe has been held every other year since 1914. Highlights include a 400-pound wheel of Swiss cheese and the world's largest cheese fondue.

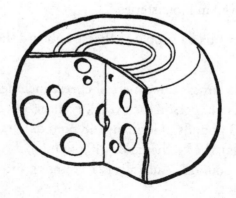

Curious Classifieds

* This is the model home for your future. It was panned by Better Homes and Gardens.

* The hotel has bowling alleys, tennis courts, comfortable beds, and other athletic facilities.

* For a successful affair, it's the Empire Hotel.

* Tickle Me Elmo. New in box. Hardly tickled. $700.

* Free dinner with any pest control job.

* Tired of cleaning yourself? Let me do it.

* For sale—Diamonds, $20; microscopes, $15.

* Girl wanted to assist magician in cutting-off-head illusion. Blue Cross and salary.

* Wanted: chambermaid in rectory. Love in, $200 a month. References required.

* Will swap white satin wedding gown (worn once) for 50 pounds fresh Gravy Train.

* Used tombstone, perfect for someone named Homer HendelBergenHeinzel. One only.

* Save regularly in our bank. You'll never reget it.

* Springmaid sheets are known as America's favorite playground.

* Valentine's Day Sale: Ty-D-Bol blue toss-ins.

* Wanted: Unmarried girls to pick fruit and produce at night.

* Illiterate? Write today for free help.

Satisfaction Guaranteed

After a rough round of ropin', ridin', and ranchin', red-blooded rowdies in need of a little romancin' often headed for the Chicken Ranch in La Grange, Texas, where the beer was cold, the food was hot, and the women were legal.

❋ ❋ ❋ ❋

A T ONE TIME, the Chicken Ranch was possibly the oldest continually operating brothel in the United States. It fulfilled the appetites of Texas students, politicians, soldiers, cowboys, and farmers for almost 130 years. Located on the outskirts of La Grange, a small community in Fayette County, Texas, near the Colorado River, the operation was originally founded in 1844 by a widow known only as Mrs. Swine. She imported three young ladies of questionable repute but unquestionable beauty from New Orleans and set them up in the world's oldest profession. Business was brisk and the profits were lucrative, at least until she was accused of holding "Yankee sympathies" during the Civil War. The operation quickly took on a lower profile.

The business was eventually taken over by a woman named Jessie Williams, who relocated the establishment near the highway just outside of town. Jessie and her girls stayed on the proper side of the law, indulging politicians and other community officials and discouraging drunken and rowdy behavior.

Widespread Attention

The ranch continued to service its customers until 1973, when a consumer-affairs reporter named Marvin Zindler from Houston's KTRK-TV decided to do a week-long exposé on the real "food" being sold at the Chicken Ranch and its possible connections to organized crime. Zindler's disclosure was front-page news around the country, causing panic rather than profit. Within days, the best-known secret in Texas was shut down, obliged to live on in song, memory, and movies. The

Broadway musical and subsequent motion picture *The Best Little Whorehouse in Texas* was based on the infamous Chicken Ranch, as was the boisterous blues bender "La Grange" by ZZ Top, the biggest little band in Texas.

The Rise of the Rubber Duckie

America's favorite bath toy dates back centuries. He makes bath time lots of fun, but your tub buddy has a lot of history under his belt, er, beak.

✳ ✳ ✳ ✳

The Early Birds

THIS YELLOW BATH bird is believed to have made his first appearance sometime in the 1800s, when rubber became common in toy production. Historians say the first ducks were actually made of a hard rubber and were far less squeaky than the modern variety.

Duckie's Debut

You can credit *Sesame Street's* Ernie with bringing rubber duckies into the spotlight. The Muppet's ode to his bathtime buddy catapulted the duck into mainstream culture. The song, first performed on *Sesame Street* in 1970, idolizes the "cute and yellow and chubby" friend who's always waiting in the "tubby." Doo-doo-be-doo, indeed!

The Modern Duck

These days, most rubber ducks are not rubber at all. Instead, they're created from a vinyl plastic made to mimic the original product's appearance.

A Worldly Traveler

Once in a while, a rubber duckie likes to take a dip outside the tub. In 1992, storms sent cargo from a ship into the ocean. One of the boxes happened to hold 29,000 rubber toys, including thousands of duckies, all of which broke free and swam the open sea.

The ducks drifted all the way from the International Date Line to Alaska, where they washed up 10 months later.

Duck Love

To some, the ducks are more than just toys. Hundreds of devoted collectors spend their days scouring for every possible model. The Guinness World Record holder currently owns more than 2,600 different ducks—and, we assume, not too many dates.

Running The Blockade

When President Lincoln set out to put an end to Southern trade, blockade running kept the Confederate economy alive.

✳   ✳   ✳   ✳

AFTER THE ATTACK on Fort Sumter, President Lincoln moved quickly to choke off Southern trade in the Atlantic and the Gulf of Mexico. He believed that if he could blockade Confederate ports and shut down the Southern economy, he could put a speedy end to the rebellion. The catch was that this plan required a navy, and the Union had only a few ships at its disposal: just 27 steam ships and 44 sailing vessels to guard 3,350 miles of Confederate coastline.

While the North borrowed, built, or bought any ship it could, the South, realizing trade meant survival, did what it could to slip through the noose. It wasn't long before mariners stepped forward to take up the challenge of sneaking in and out of ports such as Galveston, Texas; Mobile, Alabama; and Wilmington, North Carolina.

The Business of Running

While a few blockade runners were commissioned by the Confederate government, most of the ships were owned by their captains or by syndicates of rich merchants. The most successful captains were often former officers of the U.S. Navy.

Because the South didn't have a manufacturing base, many of the runners were built in England. Their specifications combined the perfect mix of characteristics for a fast ship, sacrificing seaworthiness for speed and mobility. The *Banshee* was a prime example of this: A length of 214 feet and a width of only 20 feet allowed the ship to slice through the water. Burning hard Welsh anthracite coal so it wouldn't make smoke (most Southern mines brought up soft bituminous coal that left a telltale cloud behind the ship), the *Banshee* could move at speeds as fast as 18 knots, or 20.7 miles per hour. The ship had telescoping stacks to lower its silhouette and was painted a dull gray, one of the first instances of naval camouflage.

Cotton Currency

The Southern economy relied on supplying Europe with cotton. Blockade runners would be piled high with baled cotton for a dash to Bermuda or the Bahamas. There the cargo would be traded for Southern necessities, and the runner would speed back to any open Confederate port on the railroad, where those goods would be sold for a huge profit. As long as the system worked, everyone got rich. A captain could make $5,000 for one voyage, and even common sailors were paid $250, a fortune in the 1860s. But due to inflation, prices for goods shot up higher and higher as the blockade tightened. By 1864, it cost $300 Confederate for a barrel of flour and $40 Confederate for a pound of coffee.

While blockade-runner captains such as John Maffitt of the *Cecile* or John Wilkinson of the *R. E. Lee* were patriots who carried only goods the Confederacy needed, others brought in luxury items such as European liquors and linens. Maffitt went on to captain the commerce raider CSS *Florida*, which captured 23 Union merchant ships, or "prizes," as they were called. Wilkinson captained the CSS *Chickamauga*, another raider of Union commerce.

Northern Incentives

Union sailors on the blockade line made only $16 per month, but they could also receive prize money for captured blockade runners and their cargoes, which were auctioned off at prize courts. As the Union navy grew from 264 ships by the end of 1861 to 588 ships by the end of 1863, more and more Southern runners were being captured. Not only were there more Union ships, but they were faster, with more experienced crews. As the Union armies worked their way through the South, fewer and fewer ports were left open to the Confederacy.

By early 1865, the Union took control of the last Confederate port, the one where it had all started—Charleston, South Carolina—and the days of blockade running were over. The *Banshee* was already long gone, captured on her ninth trip in 1863 and added to the Union blockade fleet.

The Downside to Collecting Coins

Faced with a frustrating coin shortage, a New York barkeep took matters into his own hands.

✳   ✳   ✳   ✳

BY THE SECOND year of the Civil War, Northern merchants were finding it more and more difficult to make change for their customers. Americans, set on edge by the war and worried that financial catastrophe was just around the corner, started to hang onto their coins. At that time, coins were cast from actual gold and silver, commodities that would remain valuable even if the government that had stamped its name on the coins were to crumble. This paranoia led to a coin shortage, which made everyday life difficult. The machinery of the American economy threatened to grind to a halt.

Lindenmueller Coins

In 1863, frustrated with the lack of coins, New York bartender Gustavus Lindenmueller took matters into his own hands.

In order to make change for his patrons, he literally made change—about one million cents' worth—and began to distribute it. The coins were simple, featuring his bearded face on the front and a frothy mug of ale on the back. The large volume of coins Lindenmueller dumped into circulation in the city made them popular with a public equally annoyed by the lack of coins. Many businesses accepted them, despite the facts that they had absolutely no true value and that there was no indication they would be honored if ever put to the test. Streetcars began to accept them, for instance, because exact change made traveling easier than using cumbersome paper money.

Filling a Void

Lindenmueller coins were just one of several tokens privately created in the war's early years. It's believed nearly 25 million such tokens were minted across the North. They filled a void that the government had not been able to account for and reflected American ingenuity and patriotism. Many were adorned with spirited slogans and pro-Union sentiments. It may seem strange that so many people and even companies accepted these dubious tokens and private currencies, but in the midst of the Civil War, they had little choice. As long as everyone agreed to treat the tokens as though they had real worth, the needs of daily life could be met.

Put to the Test

The situation could not remain like this forever. The Third Avenue Railroad served the city of New York with streetcar service, and rather than go bankrupt due to the lack of coins for train fare, they decided to play along with the Lindenmueller tokens, accepting them from riders in lieu of actual U.S. currency. Lindenmueller had given them out as change instead of real U.S. coins, so the rail-road apparently assumed that, as a reputable and honorable tavern keeper, he would honor them himself. When the company presented him with a large number of his tokens in an attempt to redeem them for actual money, however, Lindenmueller laughed in their faces.

Although he was happy to give them out, he had no intention of accepting them himself—at least not in bulk. Because the railroad had participated in the scheme willingly, and because Lindenmueller had never made explicit promises to honor the coins, there was absolutely nothing the railroad could do. Problems such as this finally stirred the government to take action against these illegal currencies.

Two-Cents Worth

The U.S. Congress undertook a two-pronged attack on the Civil War tokens, rendering them both unnecessary and illegal. Anyone caught using or creating such currency would be subject to the same treatment as counterfeiters or forgers—a significant fine and possibly five years in jail. Congress also decided to beat those tokenmakers at their own game by introducing the two-cent coin. In many ways, it was modeled after the very tokens it was created to eliminate. But it also added a new feature that had never before appeared on U.S currency, a motto that stuck: "In God We Trust."

Bad Ad Grab Bag

"Advanced Products Inc., 10% Satisfaction Guaranteed."

"Wanted: Looking for someone to do yard work. Must have hoolahoop."

"1 man, 7 woman hot tub—$850/offer."

"Amana washer $100. Owned by clean bachelor who seldom washed."

"Snow blower for sale...only used on snowy days."

"Free puppies...part German shepherd, part dog."

"2 wire mesh butchering gloves, 1 5-finger, 1 3-finger, pair: $15."

"'83 Toyota hunchback—$2,000."

"Tickle me Elmo, still in box, comes with its own 1988 mustang, auto, excellent condition $6,800."

"Free puppies: ½ cocker spaniel ½ sneaky neighbor's dog."

"Full sized mattress. 20 yr warranty. like new. slight urine smell."

"Free 1 can of pork & beans with purchase of 3 br 2 bth home."

"German shepherd. 85 lbs. neutered. speaks German. free."

Bill's Septic Cleaning: "We haul American made products."

"24 Hour Service Animal Control…Removal of Nuisance Wild Animals, Chimney Caps, Rats & Bats." In an ad with images of "nuisance wild animals," including raccoons, bats, skunks—and a baby boy.

"If you had no idea what to get her for Valentine's Day… Imagine how overwhelming arranging her funeral would be. Give her the perfect gift, make pre-arrangements as a couple with the affordable funeral home. By the way did we tell you we were affordable?"

"Tough Glass Cutting Board—Easily Cleaned, Hygienic— Warning: Not Suitable for Chopping Food On."

Chain Puller

Talk to the expert! No, we're not pulling your chain: This guy has pulled the chain in lumber mills for 40 years.

Q: Most people probably don't understand your work. What is this chain you pull?

A: First of all, lumber mills turn logs into lumber. At a couple of points in that process, the wood has to be stacked or unstacked. Someone, or a machine, breaks the lumber load down and sends it through a series of chains about waist-high, all going the same speed, like big parallel conveyer belts. That lumber needs to be sorted, and workers, called "graders," decide how it should be sorted. Chain pullers pull lumber off the chain and stack it by grade and length.

Q: What are the different chains?

A: Coming out of the sawmill, green chain—to divide the lumber so it'll dry right. After drying, dry chain—the dried loads are stored until the boss is ready to run them through the planer. Next is where I pull the planer chain, which sorts the boards into the stacks that will go onto trucks or train cars and eventually to your hardware store. Many mills have done away with pullers on some of the chains, replacing them with a machine, or one sorry worker pitching every board that comes down one of about 20 sorting chutes.

Q: So there's more than one chain puller on a shift?

A: One person can't do it all. Think about the different grades of lumber we could get, all out of the same drying load. We have lengths from 6 feet to 16 feet. Because you can't pile different grades or lengths together, there are a lot of lumber piles. Each puller is responsible for certain piles. The most common length and grade go to a stacking machine. In the end, it takes about three pullers to do the work of one machine.

Q: Your crew grabs boards and throws them on stacks? Sounds exhausting.

A: In fact, it's all technique. The load is below you and there are steel rollers all along the chain. Usually, the person in front of you pulls out your boards for you, to help you notice. As those come, you pull the board out farther and bear down. It whistles down the roller pretty fast, and you catch it at the end and drop it. Only at the very top of the load do you have to heave a board upward a little.

Q: How do you know when the load is full?

A: That's second-grade math. You calculate however many rows high for that thickness of lumber, and that's when it's full. You have to know when you can't pile on any more boards. No one will stop production while you count on your fingers either. If the carrier doesn't pick up your load, you get to put the extra boards somewhere until it does.

Q: Don't you get tons of splinters from the boards?

A: Not too often, because we wear quarter-inch-thick leather aprons that get a shiny surface from all the sappy boards sliding down them, and we also wear big leather mittens. Regular work gloves don't last an hour. But you still have to watch out for hazards, such as falling off the platform or, worst of all, the lumber carrier catching the edge of the load and ramming the boards in under the chain. If you were standing in the way of that, you just lost your leg at the hip.

The Shipwrecks of Lake Erie

Incredibly, it is estimated that close to 2,000 ships have found their way to the bottom of Lake Erie.

✳   ✳   ✳   ✳

THERE ARE MANY reasons that Lake Erie can be dangerous and the number of past shipwrecks is high: For one, the lake is quite shallow—only a little more than 200 feet at its deepest point. That means it wouldn't take much for rough weather to quickly churn the waters up. On top of that, Lake Erie runs east to west, which allows storms to pick up intensity as they move across the entire lake. The following is a list of some of the most infamous shipwrecks in the history of Lake Erie, including the four ships that all went down during a violent storm on Friday, October 20, 1916—Black Friday.

Cortland and *Morning Star*

Even though the evening of June 20, 1868, was a rainy, foggy affair, ships were still successfully passing in the night—until the steamer *Morning Star* crashed into the *Cortland*. The *Morning Star* sank almost immediately, while the *Cortland* managed to stay afloat for another 90 minutes before sinking.

Atlantic

One of the worst disasters in the history of Lake Erie occurred on August 20, 1852, when the *Atlantic* collided with another ship, the *Argo*. The *Argo* remained afloat and aided in the rescue attempts as the *Atlantic* sank. It is estimated that 150–300 individuals died that fateful night.

Marquette & Bessimer #2

The *Marquette & Bessimer #2* is considered the Holy Grail of Lake Erie shipwrecks, as the reasons why the massive steamer sank, as well as the exact location of its remains, are a mystery. The last known contact with the ship happened sometime between 3:00 and 5:00 A.M. on December 8, 1909, when people in the town of Port Stanley, Ontario, reported hearing the *M&B2*'s distress whistle. It is believed that the blizzardlike conditions on the lake that night contributed to the sinking of the ship.

D. L. Filer

Although the boat was anchored off Bar Point when the 1916 Black Friday storm hit, the weather dragged the *D. L. Filer* out into open water, and the ship began to sink. Captain John Mattison ordered his crew of six to head for higher ground and climb the ship's masts with him. One by one, the men either lost their grips on the rigging, or the masts broke. Captain Mattison was the only one rescued from the *Filer* before it sank.

James Colgate

As the heavy winds of the 1916 Black Friday storm poured gigantic waves over the sides of the *Colgate*, the ship began to list terribly. As the ship took on more and more water, Captain Walter Grashaw and his crew of 20 were forced into the icy water. Almost 30 hours passed before help arrived. Miraculously, rescuers found Captain Grashaw alive, floating on a makeshift raft.

Merida

It is unknown exactly when the 1916 Black Friday storm claimed the *Merida,* as Captain Harry Jones and his crew of 22 offered up no distress signal. While the ship was listed as "missing" on Saturday, October 21, 1916, it would be another two days before the bodies of three *Merida* crew members, still wearing life jackets, were found. No other bodies were ever recovered, and it would be another 60 years before the wreckage of the *Merida* would be located.

Marshall Butters

The final shipwreckees of the 1916 Black Friday storm, the crew of the *Marshall Butters* tried throwing their cargo of lumber over the side in an attempt to lighten their load and keep from sinking. The plan didn't work, but daring rescue attempts by other ships in the area prevented any casualties when the *Butters* finally sank.

There's a Maze Under Your Feet

Years ago, there were nearly as many tunnels as streets in Chicago—and many of them are still there!

✳   ✳   ✳   ✳

CABLE TV DOCUMENTARIES make it seem as though Al Capone personally dug out an entire network of escape tunnels. Capone wasn't anywhere near that industrious—the tunnels were already there! By the time of Prohibition, the city was full of tunnels that had been made for horse and pedestrian traffic and freight delivery years before. (During the late 19th century, intense shipping traffic on the river meant that the Chicago River bridges were raised much of the time; this in turn led to problems for pedestrian traffic, and the solution the city came up with was to construct pedestrian tunnels.) Many buildings were connected by tunnels, and the bootleggers of the Prohibition era found them awfully convenient. While few will ever see them, most of them are still there today!

One of the oldest tunnels went underneath the river at La Salle Street—this tunnel was dug out in 1871, just in time for it to become an escape route during the Great Fire. That tunnel was then used by cable cars, and eventually by streetcars, before being closed in the 1930s. It's still there—the entrance ramp to the parking garage in the middle of La Salle at Kinzie is the old tunnel entrance—but it was walled off and filled with damp sand in the 1950s.

Some of the old city tunnels have even been tourist attractions at times. A tunnel beneath Congress Street once connected the Congress Hotel to the Auditorium Theatre. The marble-lined tunnel was known as Peacock Alley and was one of the crown jewels of the city in the early 20th century. It's still there too—marble and all—but the entrances have been bricked off for many years.

The most extensive of the Chicago tunnels were the freight tunnels 40 feet below the Loop. These narrow tunnels were originally used to deliver coal and mail. The earth dug out for them was placed along the shore and eventually became Grant Park. At one point, nearly every major building in the Loop had an entrance to these freight tunnels.

As companies switched from coal to gas heating, the tunnels became less useful. Those companies that kept using coal for heat began to have it delivered via truck. The tunnels officially stopped being used during the '50s, and the entrances were mostly bricked off. But the tunnels remain, far below the city streets. All told, there are nearly 60 miles of freight tunnels still in existence under the Loop. For many years, breaking into the tunnels to go exploring was a popular pastime, but the city always frowned on the practice—even when they were in operation, the tunnels weren't exactly safe. Security concerns about how much trouble could be caused by people breaking into the tunnels became prominent after September 11, 2001, and today all entrances have been closed off.

At least, as far as anyone knows. Many old buildings had an entrance to the tunnels, and it's quite possible that some of them are still there in the basements of the city's oldest buildings, just waiting to be discovered.

✳ **In 1992, the city paid dearly for neglecting the freight tunnels. A private contractor accidentally drilled into the tunnel under Kinzie Street, and Chicago River water began filling the freight tunnels. Months later, the tunnels were full, and the water had only one place to go—into the basements of the buildings that had utilized the tunnels years before. The flood was invisible to all above ground, but it paralyzed and embarrassed the city. Subway service had to be rerouted and businesses shut down. It was weeks before the Loop returned to normal. Damages resulting from the flood were estimated at around $1 billion.**

Butter Battles in the Dairy State

Wisconsin has a reputation as a friendly place to visit, with hospitality as sweet as whipped cream. But a portion of Wisconsin's history is not so sweet. In fact, the "Oleo Wars" could be downright sour!

✳   ✳   ✳   ✳

THE "OLEO WARS" between butter and the butterlike substitute oleomargarine are a little-known footnote to our nation's intrepid history. This is puzzling because skirmishes in this war are *still* being fought to this very day, some 40 years after the combatants officially laid down their "sticks."

A Likely Battleground

In a way, the Wisconsin Oleo Wars were predestined. Really, what can you expect from a dairy region that is currently ranked second in the nation in butter production?

In the early 1870s, wives on dairy farms made butter, and variations in equipment, churning skills, and cleanliness resulted in a finished product of widely varying quality. During this time, oleomargarine arrived on the scene with little fanfare. The French product was cheaper than butter, far more consistent in quality, and it kept for longer periods. Slowly but surely, oleomargarine tempted the taste buds of quality-conscious consumers, even if many hid their fondness from fellow citizens. An oleo–butter battle loomed large.

The Battle's Beginnings

In 1872, Wisconsin dairy producers banded together to form the Wisconsin Dairymen's Association (WDA). This protectionist organization eventually zeroed in on oleomargarine and the alarming headway it had made into the butter market. In 1880, former WDA president Hiram Smith warned farmers that "oleomargarine is giving better satisfaction than most dairy butter as now made." To protect their industry, Wisconsin dairy leaders decided to improve their own product and to launch a preemptive strike against oleomargarine for added insurance.

In 1881, Wisconsin passed its first anti-margarine law, which required that butter and oleomargarine be marked as such to avoid confusion between the two. In 1886, the state passed even more stringent legislation, which added a stiff tax and imposed labeling and packaging restrictions upon oleomargarine. In 1895, Wisconsin brought forth yet another law. It required restaurants and hotels to display signs announcing that margarine was sold on the premises. It also prohibited the manufacture and sale of oleomargarine—whitish in its normal state—that had been colored yellow to mimic butter.

Fighting Words

To turn consumers against oleomargarine, butter proponents drew wretched pictures of farmers being economically driven off their farms by the evil spread. The "Three-Headed Hydra," drawn by A. Berghaus in 1890 for *The Rural New Yorker*, depicted a hideous serpent poised to attack an alarmed but at-the-ready farmer holding a rifle. The words *oleomargarine* and *fraud* were drawn prominently on its body.

By this time, margarine backers weary of taking it on the chin went on the offensive. They noted that their product was as "wholesome as butter" and reminded the state assembly of documented cases where spoiled butter had been reprocessed and sold as fresh. They also reminded consumers that creameries routinely colored their butter to make it more yellow. In answer to unsavory drawings depicting oleomargarine as a three-headed monster, "oleophiles" reportedly fired back with artwork that portrayed diseased and dirty dairy cows being milked in mucky barnyards.

In 1915, a new wave of anti-margarine propaganda featured illustrations of sickened rats that had ingested vegetable oils—a prime ingredient in oleomargarine. This opportunity to further demean oleomargarine presented itself after a University of Wisconsin research study of vitamins went public. It suggested that laboratory rats fed milk fat were healthier than those that had ingested vegetable oils. A margarine supporter said of the incident: "Some [anti-margarine propaganda] is put out by persons who actually think that any industry, domestic or foreign, that is at all in competition with dairy farming, has no rights in our economic system and ought to be outlawed."

Oleo Makes Headway

World War II saw a changing tide in the Oleo Wars. Due to stronger food rationing penalties against fats than those against vegetable oil, oleomargarine made substantial inroads into the butter market. By war's end, oleomargarine was commonly found on tables throughout Wisconsin.

A growing resentment against unfair taxation on oleomargarine was also gathering steam. More than a few consumers were irked that an economical food source was being effectively denied to them due to petty, protectionist policies. Plainly, the war had battles left to fight.

In the mid-1950s, oleomargarine was still being heavily taxed in Wisconsin. The uncolored oleomargarine tax rate of 15 cents per pound was significant in a day and age when the minimum wage was just 75 cents per hour. This caused oleomargarine-loving Wisconsinites to smuggle the product in from out-of-state sources. Newspaper photos from the period show value-minded people cramming their cars with Illinois-bought oleomargarine to take back into Wisconsin. A state official estimated that a ton of colored margarine came across the Illinois–Wisconsin border each week. Butter may have looked like it was winning the present battle, but if such underground trends continued, many felt it would eventually lose the war.

Concessions

By 1967, opinions among Wisconsin state legislators were starting to change. Aware of oleomargarine's popularity, lawmakers brought forth a bill that would eliminate the ban on the sale of colored margarine but still retain a tax of 5 $3/4$ cents per pound through 1972 (the tax was ultimately extended to December 31, 1973). After that, oleomargarine would be tax-free. The bill passed in the state assembly on April 6, 1967, and went into law on July 1, 1967. For the first time in 72 tumultuous years, colored oleomargarine was legal in Wisconsin. But was it?

Despite the repealed ban, dairy protectionism continued well beyond the 1960s. In fact, butter's parting shot has survived right up to this day. As proof, an obscure law officially designated Wisconsin Statute 97.18(4) states: "The serving of colored oleomargarine or margarine at a public eating place as a substitute for table butter is prohibited unless it is ordered by the customer." The law is used as a sort of trump card by dairy-backers and is applied sporadically, usually coming into play only after a butter-loving patron turns in an offending restaurant.

Such a violation occurred in 2004. Wisconsin citizen Nels Harvey ordered a baked potato at a Ponderosa Steakhouse in Menomonee Falls and was horrified to see that it was dripping with margarine. When he asked for butter in its place, the server replied, "We don't have any butter." Treating this admission like a shot fired across the bow, Harvey sprang into action.

The 71-year-old, who had lived half his life under the rules set by the Oleo Wars, filed a complaint with the Waukesha County Department of Health and Human Services. Within hours an inspector was dispatched to the offending restaurant. When she arrived, she demanded that butter be made available to customers. Despite the steeper price of the dairy product and the fact that no one other than Harvey seemed to care, the owner complied with the request.

Perhaps supporters on either side of the stick shouldn't behave so indignantly, particularly this late into the Oleo Wars. Wisconsin is dairy country, after all.

Lucy the Beached Elephant

Imagine this exchange between a ship's lookout and his captain as the vessel closed in on the New Jersey coastline near Atlantic City during the 1880s:

Captain: "Tell me, what do you see?"

Lookout: "Elephant!"

Captain: "Elephant? I told you to stay out of the rum!"

But it was true. From the coast rose a six-story, white wooden elephant standing serenely on the beach in South Atlantic City.

✳ ✳ ✳ ✳

Real Estate Agent

THE ICONIC ELEPHANT (later named Lucy) was built as a real estate gimmick in the early 1880s by James Lafferty Jr. Now, Lafferty had acquired overgrown, bramble-filled beachfront lots in South Atlantic City, and he needed to sell them. He figured a 65-foot-high wooden elephant standing on the beach near the lots was just the thing to attract attention. Sure enough, the people came. Tourists were suitably impressed by the elephant, climbed the stairs inside her leg to her hollow center, stood on top of her to enjoy the gorgeous ocean view— and then went home, money in hand. As it turned out, Lucy was a dismal failure as a real estate agent, and Lafferty was forced to sell her to Anton Gertzen.

Extraordinary Attraction

Gertzen didn't put Lucy to work. He didn't have to, because enough people (including U.S. President Woodrow Wilson and inventor Henry Ford) came to see the wooden pachyderm that she did just fine for decades as an oddity attraction. Occasionally, Lucy pursued other careers, serving as a rooming house and tavern.

But by 1963, Lucy was aging, and she was rapidly falling apart. Margate (formerly South Atlantic City) officials wanted to demolish the elderly elephant. For several years the fight raged between preservationists and officials, but in the eleventh hour, the elephant was restored. In 1976, Lucy was named a National Historic Landmark. More than 100 years later, Lucy is still Queen of the Beach.

Taste of Wisconsin

Set to the collegiate anthem "On, Wisconsin!" the Sundae Fight Song represents the continued fight by the town of Two Rivers, Wisconsin, to herald its claim as the true birthplace of the ice cream sundae.

✳ ✳ ✳ ✳

A Sweet Tradition

MAKE NO CONES about it. Driving through Two Rivers, a city of nearly 13,000 on Lake Michigan, one can't miss the 28-square-foot state historical sign, a brown beacon recalling the magical event that gave birth to the ice cream sundae.

It was the summer of 1881, and George Hallauer, a Two Rivers native who had defected to Illinois, stopped by Edward Berners' soda fountain at 1404 15th Street while vacationing in town. Hallauer spotted a bottle of chocolate syrup normally used for ice cream sodas and asked Berners to put some atop his vanilla ice cream. Initially, Berners protested, saying it would ruin the flavor of the ice cream. But Hallauer was adamant, and thus the ice cream sundae was born.

Selling for five cents each, sundaes were an instant hit. Berners went on to explore ice cream and topping pairings, giving his creations names like Flora Dora, Mudscow, and Jennie Flip. Word of his new concoction spread to the neighboring town, and Berners credited his ice cream counterpart in Manitowoc, George Giffy, with creating the term "sundae." Giffy only sold his ice cream treats on Sundays, until a sugar-sweet 10-year-old girl begged to have one . . . on a day other than Sunday. The story holds that in an effort to avoid blaspheming the Sabbath, the Sunday was renamed "sundae."

Even with a fight song and strong oral history of the invention, Two Rivers' claim comes with contention. Several other cities, including Evanston, Illinois; Buffalo, New York; even Baltimore, Maryland; have made weak claims to being home of the sundae. But Ithaca, New York, is the top threat to this coveted spot in American food history, unwilling to melt away from the heated competition.

Sundae Wars

City executives continue to banter, asking the other to back off from its claim. In 2006, the battle rose to a new level when Ithaca began promoting itself as the rightful birthplace. Two Rivers' representatives called on Ithaca to cease and desist. Then they started trading licks.

Ithaca placed an ad in Two Rivers' newspaper calling on the community to prove it. Two Rivers' city manager Greg Buckley countered, telling Ithaca to do the work.

And they did. The director of Ithaca's visitors' bureau combed through old newspapers and found an ad in *The Ithaca Journal* advertising a "Cherry Sunday," a new ten-cent "ice cream specialty" served at a little joint called Platt and Colt's. That ad ran in the April 5, 1892, issue, making Ithaca's claim to sundae dominance a full 11 years later than Hallauer's gustatory pursuit.

The road between Two Rivers and Ithaca was already a rocky one, but the barbs continued. Two Rivers introduced its Sundae Fight Song. Ithaca officials placed an ad in Two Rivers' local paper with a copy of Platt's 1892 ad, chiding: "Got proof? We do. Love, Ithaca."

Two Rivers bit back and placed a coupon in *The Ithaca Journal*, redeemable for a free sundae, but only in Two Rivers, and handed out preprinted postcards addressed to Ithaca's mayor at the city's annual Sundae Thursday, encouraging residents to embark on a birthright-claiming blitz.

Despite continued efforts by Ithacans to slurp, er, rather, usurp, Wisconsin's claim, Two Rivers maintains that it is the rightful Birthplace of the Ice Cream Sundae. In any case, the reward remains just as sweet.

Bad Ad Grab Bag

"If it's in stock, we have it!"

"Nice parachute never opened, used once slightly stained."

"Joining nudist colony, must sell washer & dryer—$300."

"Stops that irritating whine." Found in an ad for wedding rings.

"Lambskin Leather Gloves Offer Unsurpassed Warmth and Softness…Be assured, no lambs are killed in order to make these gloves."

"Light Up Ghost…Not A Real Ghost, $12.99."

"Valentine's Day Sweetheart Special—Free Handgun, Today Thru Valentine's Day!"

"Fresh, Locally Grown ICE."

"Your Trade Is Worth $4,000."* (*If your trade-in is worth $4,000)

Sportcraft Roller Dice: "Teach your kids the elements of dice before sending them to the casino."

"Check Out Our Huge Selection of Newly & Gently Used Goods! Toilet Tissue just 25¢/roll."

"1 bag of boys 18–24 months, $25, takes it all!"

"Polly Miller works in the kitchen of St. Stephen School preparing for the school's annual soup festival....Those attending are asked to bring their own soup and bowl."

"City Market Food & Pharmacy, Career Opportunity—$9.70/hr., with wages possible after just 12 weeks."

"Cows, calves never bred...also 1 gay bull for sale."

"Management Positions Available—Contact Tony—Vacation, uniforms, meals and possible salary."

Degrees of Funny

For those who've dreamed of donning a red foam nose and tripping over a banana peel, Akron is the place to be. That's the location of the Ohio College of Clowning Arts, a school that teaches everything about the serious art of clowning around.

✳ ✳ ✳ ✳

I N 1989, A group of individuals at Ohio's North Canton Playhouse, led by Bob Kreidler, launched an outreach program that would teach clowning techniques. The program was popular and graduated its first class the following year. Seeing opportunity, the group formed a separate organization in 1991, conducting classes at Walsh University, a community college in northern Ohio. Within a few years, the burgeoning school found a place within the University of Akron, and the Ohio Clown School (as they called themselves) went about teaching clowning to interested students for the next five years.

Several more moves followed—and a name dispute between the school and Ringling Bros. and Barnum & Bailey circus was settled—but by 2008, the officially titled, Akron-based Ohio College of Clowning Arts was accepting students for its 20th year of operation and also offering online classes. The course of instruction is 30 weeks from September to April and prepares graduates for professional clowning at fairs, festivals, store openings, hoedowns, trade shows, and conventions.

Becoming a Clown

Clowning really is an art form—there are dozens of different types of clowns and clown styles, from the classic "whiteface" clown to the character clown, from the circus or rodeo clown to clowns that specialize in the Italian *commedia dell'arte* style.

At the OCCA, various styles are taught, but emphasis is largely placed on clowning as a mode of intensely physical, comedic performance that is more than a rainbow-colored wig and a goofy voice. Instructors help students develop involved characterization and movement, as well as the art of makeup application and costume construction. Since the goal of the program is to prepare grads for entrance into a professional environment, several courses offer instruction regarding how clowns go about marketing themselves and managing their own businesses.

Though the school recognizes that making balloon animals, performing basic magic tricks, and doing face-painting is often part of a clown's oeuvre, the administrators consider these skills to be tangential to the work of a clown and don't prioritize them for beginning students. Instead, students learn the basics of clowning and become well versed in broad physical comedy before they start making balloon hats.

What to Expect, Funny Face

Students can enroll in the college's 30-week program and learn to hit, trip, fall, tumble, and use their bodies to create a routine. The students may also work with the school to tailor a class or intensive training session for their organization, office, or church group. Since the OCCA is one of the only schools in the country offering this particular style of performance, it helps if students live in Ohio. However, the OCCA prides itself on striving to meet the needs of anyone interested in clowning, whatever their schedule or situation.

But prospective students, be warned: Even after completing the program, one shouldn't expect to reach fame and fortune with one's newfound clowning skills. The school can teach clowning techniques and give insight into the business, but it doesn't promise fame and fortune—after all, how many famous clowns are out there? Fortunately, for most people interested in learning the art of the clown, riches aren't what they're after. Founder Kreidler says that while it may not be the most profitable way to earn a living, clowning is "a million dollar experience."

Hearst at His Worst

Media mogul William Randolph Hearst built an empire out of sensationalism and dishonesty. Owning a large percentage of America's newspapers in the first half of the 20th century, he exemplified the notion of yellow journalism.

✳ ✳ ✳ ✳

IN THE 1890s, long before the advent of broadcast television, cable, and the Internet, even before radio, America relied on the daily newspaper to deliver the news. Propped up at the breakfast table, opened and folded on the trolley car, or perused from a park bench, newspapers became the trusted source for "what's what" across the country. Publishers such as Horace Greeley and James Gordon Bennett, taking advantage of their influential powers, forged a path of biased, politically and monetarily swayed reporting that would soon be undertaken by other newspaper publishers such as Joseph Pulitzer and, especially, famed magnate William Randolph Hearst.

Wee Willie

Hearst was born in 1863 in San Francisco, the son of a successful mining entrepreneur. Even as a young lad, he knew how to stir up trouble. For example, he set off some fireworks in his bedroom one night, yelled, "Fire!" down the hallway, locked the door, and waited as the fire department came crashing through it. While attending Harvard University, he was expelled—possibly for a combination of pranks and poor grades. Inheriting his father's Comstock mining fortune in 1887, Hearst decided that publishing would be a lucrative, secure venture and took over a number of faltering newspapers, including the *San Francisco Examiner*.

All the News That's (Un)Fit to Print

In efforts to up his numbers, Hearst became something of a champion of the people. He focused on revealing corruption in the San Francisco Police Department, city hall, and at Folsom Prison. He relished reporting on lurid crimes and blazing fires, and he filled the *Examiner* with political cartoons of all sorts. One writer for the paper masqueraded as a homeless person and was admitted to the city's hospital. When her story revealed the rampant cruelty and neglect she found there, the entire hospital staff was fired.

The number of publications under the Hearst banner grew, and he eventually built an unprecedented empire. At its height, he owned a whopping 28 newspapers and a variety of magazines; during the course of his career, he owned a total of 36 newspapers and multiple magazines. Among these were some of the most influential and widely read publications in the country, including the *Washington Herald*, the *Seattle Post-Intelligencer*, and the *Baltimore Post*.

Hearst's chief rival, Joseph Pulitzer, ran the *New York World*, another newspaper deeply rooted in aggressive reporting. In 1895, a strange cartoon character began appearing in Pulitzer's paper. A bald boy with a toothy smile, he was called the "Yellow Kid" (the Kid appeared in a color cartoon and sported a nightshirt of this shade). After a fierce bidding war, the popular "Yellow Kid" was moved to Hearst's *New York Journal* in 1896 and, with both papers' reputation for using their pages to stir up trouble, the concept behind their nature became known as "yellow journalism." As the years went on, so did the stories peppered with increasingly exaggerated and biased claims. Hearst often published articles colored with shades of his own prejudices and agendas—the opposite of fair news reporting.

A War, Made to Order

Hearst and Pulitzer received a lot of credit for getting America into the Spanish-American War in 1898. The accusations may be exaggerated, although their publications did keep Spain's occupation of Cuba on the front pages. An oft-told story (with questionable accuracy) has Hearst rebuffing a photographer's claim that there was no war in Cuba, stating, "You furnish the pictures—I'll furnish the war." For example, one week after America declared war on Spain, Hearst ran a front-page headline asking, "How Do You Like the Journal's War?" The devastating explosion that destroyed the U.S. battleship *Maine* while it was docked in the Havana harbor was immediately blamed on Spanish terrorists, yet it is more likely that an internal fire ignited the ammunition stored onboard. The *World* and the *Journal* led the way in exacerbating patriotic sentiment before and during the five-month conflict, with Hearst actually traveling to Cuba as a reporter and filing stories of the carnage.

Fanning the Flames

With the war behind them, the journalistic holdings of Pulitzer and Hearst took separate paths. Pulitzer, feeling somewhat guilty about the direction his paper had taken, righted his *New York World*. It became a respected and prestigious daily before closing in 1931. But Hearst hitched the *Journal* to the 1900 political campaign of William Jennings Bryan, a progressive Democrat who was running for president against Republican incumbent William McKinley. Hearst painted McKinley as a puppet of wealthy industrialists, with Bryan as a hero who would come to the country's rescue. Hearst papers also took shots at McKinley's running mate, Theodore Roosevelt. He was portrayed in political cartoons as an ugly, young boy in a Rough Rider hat who bullied McKinley.

Despite Hearst's efforts to defeat McKinley, the president returned to office. Prior to the inauguration in March 1900, Hearst editorials stooped to suggest shockingly that McKinley be assassinated. When fiction became fact in September of the next year, Hearst was accused of being somewhat responsible for McKinley's death through his papers' editorials. The backlash was so bad that he changed the name of the *Journal* to the more patriotic-sounding *American*.

Hearst did not limit his sensationalist provocations to American affairs. When the Japanese were victorious in the Russo-Japanese War in 1905, Hearst's papers warned their readers to beware of "the yellow menace." During the early years of World War I, Hearst's editorials had a pro-German slant, painting an anti-British picture. Between 1928 and the mid-1930s, he featured syndicated editorials by Benito Mussolini, dictator of fascist Italy. In 1930, Hearst asked a newly elected leader in Germany to write articles for him. The new columnist—Adolf Hitler—took advantage of the forum and wrote of his plans to bring Germany out of its economic woes. He also wrote of Germany's innocence in World War I and the unfair conditions of the Versailles Treaty. Hitler was ultimately fired from Hearst's stable for, among other reasons, missing too many deadlines.

At one point, Hearst's empire became a little too big for its own britches. In addition to the dozens of newspapers and magazines he owned, he added two news services, several radio stations, and a film company. Overextension and the Great Depression forced the liquidation of many of his holdings in the late 1920s.

What About Citizen Kane?

In 1941, a 26-year-old first-time filmmaker named Orson Welles cowrote, produced, starred in, and directed a film called *Citizen Kane*. The similarities between the title character, Charles Foster Kane, and William Randolph Hearst were hardly coincidental. The movie told of the life of a newspaper publisher famous for printing sensational stories, rampant artwork collecting, having an affair with a famous performer, and failed political aspirations—all factual occurrences from Hearst's life. Hearst was so outraged at first mention of the film's impending release, he offered RKO Pictures $800,000 to burn all prints and the master negative. When the studio refused, he barred every member of his media empire from even mentioning the film. Despite all Hearst's efforts to quell the movie, it came to be regarded as one of the greatest of all time by hordes or critics and filmgoers.

Beef Boner

Talk to the expert! Surviving employment in the meatpacking industry is no joking matter. When people realize how dangerous this job is, the laughter usually dies down.

Q: Most people would call you a butcher. In any event, you make a living cutting meat away from bones, and yet you still have all your fingers.

A: Many beef boners lose fingers—or worse. There is a reason many people who grow up around meatpacking plants are not interested in this line of work. I make a daily, concerted effort to be extremely attentive and careful. You have to watch for other people's knives as much as your own.

Q: Describe your boning knife.

A: It's similar to the steak knives you use at your dinner table. The blade is not very broad, it's smooth rather than serrated, and it has a very sharp tip. It's surprisingly small, considering how much animal flesh it slices up in a day. Some people imagine me waving a big meat cleaver all over the place, but that just happens in the movies.

Q: Do you cut up the whole cow?

A: Beef boners tend to specialize in one part of the animal—which is not usually a cow, but rather a steer. Whether I am working as a chuck boner, loin boner, ham boner, round boner, or blade boner, the basic work is the same: Cut out defects, bones, fat, and anything else people don't want to eat. You probably don't want me to go into too much detail here.

Q: What's the best way to avoid injury?

A: Stay alert and keep your boning knife sharp. It's true that a dull knife is more dangerous than a sharp one. Dull knives slip, and they make you work harder. The last thing I can be is fatigued.

The Mystery of the Concrete Ship

That's right—a concrete ship. What, you've never seen a floating cinder block?

❋ ❋ ❋ ❋

Are You Dense?

A FLOATING CINDER BLOCK seemingly goes against all logic, but that didn't stop a Norwegian named N. K. Fougner from launching the first oceangoing concrete ship on August 2, 1917, an 84-foot-long boat named *Namsenfjord*.

If a piece of concrete shaped like a ship contains enough air, its density will be less than the water it displaces, allowing it to float. When Fougner's ship didn't sink like, well, a concrete block, governments around the world took notice.

With steel in short supply because of World War I, the U.S. government decided to build a fleet of 38 concrete ships, though in the end, only 12 were built. Sailors took to calling the ships "floating tombstones." Mercifully, before the United States had moved on to ships made out of newspaper, the war had ended and steel was again available.

S.S. Atlantus

One notable concrete ship was the S.S. *Atlantus*, which weighed 2,500 tons and was 250 feet long. It was launched on December 5, 1918, at Brunswick, Georgia, and it operated as a coal steamer in New England. At war's end, however, the *Atlantus* was sent to Norfolk, Virginia, to rot—or flake—away.

Enter Colonel Jesse Rosenfeld, who wanted to start a ferry service between Cape May, New Jersey, and Cape Henlopen, Delaware. He thought that the *Atlantus* would be great as part of a ferry dock, so he towed the ship to Cape May in 1926 and moored it there.

Bad idea. On June 8, a storm hit and broke the ship free. It drifted 150 feet and lodged into the sandy bottom off Sunset Beach. It remains there to this day, a curious tourist attraction. It was even used as a billboard space during the 1950s, advertising boat insurance. Alas, the *Atlantus* continues to sink into the sand a little more each year; today it's barely visible above the surface.

Lotto Trouble!

Everyone fantasizes about winning the lottery and living the good life. But for every lucky winner who achieves the dream, there's another whose life is turned upside down. These true-life lottery horror stories may make you think twice about buying that scratch-off ticket.

✳   ✳   ✳   ✳

1. In 1988, **William Post** won $16.2 million in the Pennsylvania Lottery. Unfortunately, Post's good luck brought out the worst in his friends and family, including his brother, who tried to have Post killed for the inheritance. Post survived his brother's murderous intent only to be successfully sued by a former girlfriend for a share of his winnings. Post spent his money like a drunken sailor until he was $1 million in debt and forced to declare bankruptcy. When he died in 2006, Post had been living on his Social Security for several years.

2. Everyone believes that winning the lottery will bring an end to their problems, but for **Billie Bob Harrell Jr.**, that wasn't the case. After scoring $31 million in the Texas Lottery, Harrell spent big on cars, real estate, and gifts for family and friends. But wealth apparently couldn't buy the happiness Harrell was seeking, so he took his own life just two years after cashing that winning ticket.

3. **Evelyn Adams** was a two-time winner, hitting it big in the New Jersey Lottery in 1985 and 1986 for a total of more than $5 million. But Adams couldn't control her gambling habit and quickly frittered her winnings away on the slots. (She also gave away large sums to family and friends.) By 2001, the former multimillionaire was living in a trailer.

4. **Willie Hurt** won $3.1 million in the Michigan Lottery in 1989. Two years later, he was penniless and facing a murder

charge after squandering his fortune on a costly divorce and crack cocaine.

5. **Jeffrey Dampier** won a whopping $20 million in the Illinois Lottery and spent lavishly on friends and family—including his sister-in-law, Victoria Jackson. Hungry for a bigger chunk of Dampier's fortune, Jackson and her boyfriend lured Dampier to Jackson's apartment, then kidnapped and murdered him. Jackson was sentenced to life in prison without parole.

6. In December 2002, West Virginian **Jack Whittaker** won $314 million in the largest undivided Powerball jackpot in lottery history. He had nothing but good intentions for his money and gave generously to his church, his friends, and various civic organizations. But trouble seemed to follow Whittaker after he won the big one. Strangers hounded him for money, and some even threatened his family when he refused. He was hit with a variety of lawsuits and once was robbed of $500,000 in cash. But the greatest tragedy was when Whittaker's teenage granddaughter died of a drug overdose, her habit funded by the generous allowance she received from her grandfather.

7. **Wanda Rickerson** won more than half a million dollars in the Georgia Lottery in 2003. Three years later, the former sheriff's office administrative clerk was ordered to pay $84,000 to Columbia County after pleading no contest to theft and insurance charges. Rickerson's crime? Embezzling $56,000 from an inmate trust account she supervised at the Columbia County Detention Center.

8. An **anonymous British man** who won a sizable fortune in the national lottery was the victim of a home invasion following his windfall. Masked thugs wielding machetes burst into the man's home and held him, his wife, and his young son at knifepoint while they ransacked the place. The thieves escaped with jewelry and numerous personal items.

9. In 2001, **Victoria Zell and her husband** won an $11 million jackpot in the Minnesota Lottery. But Zell's good fortune didn't last long. In 2005, she was sent to prison for an alcohol-related car crash that killed one motorist and paralyzed another.

10. **Michael Carroll's** $17 million fortune couldn't keep him out of prison either. In 2006, the British lottery winner was sentenced to nine months in the hoosegow for going berserk in a disco.

Unhappy Birthday

Many people believe that the most sung song in the English language is a traditional folk melody that rests comfortably in the public domain. In fact, "Happy Birthday to You" is protected by strict copyright laws.

✳   ✳   ✳   ✳

THAT FOUR-LINE DITTY is as synonymous with birthday celebrations as a cake full of candles. According to the *Guinness Book of World Records*, the most popular song in the English language is "Happy Birthday to You." What is less well known, however, is that it is not a simple tune in the public domain, free for the singing by anyone who chooses. It's actually protected by a stringent copyright that is owned and actively enforced by the media conglomerate AOL Time Warner. You are legally safe singing the song at home, but doing so in public is technically a breach of copyright, unless you have obtained a license from the copyright holder or the American Society of Composers, Authors, and Publishers.

The popular seven-note melody was penned in 1893 by two sisters, Mildred J. Hill and Patty Smith Hill, as a song titled "Good Morning to All." It remains unclear who revised the words, but a third Hill sister, Jessica, secured copyright to the song in 1935. This copyright should have expired in 1991, but through a number of revisions to copyright law, it has been extended until at least 2030 and now lies in the hands of AOL Time Warner. The company earns more than $2 million a year from the song, primarily for its use in movies and TV shows. Because licensing the rights to the song is a costly endeavor, low-budget movies have to cut around birthday scenes, and many popular chain restaurants insist that their employees sing alternate songs to celebrate their customers' birthdays. Unless you license the rights, singing the song in public could result in something decidedly unhappy.

The Reich Stuff

Fanta sodas were first produced by the Coca-Cola Company at its plant in Germany at the start of World War II. Despite widespread rumors, however, the popular soft drink was not invented by the Nazis, nor was it produced under the direction of the Third Reich.

✳   ✳   ✳   ✳

COCA-COLA WAS HUGELY popular in Germany in the 1930s, more so than anywhere else in Europe. When the American-born director of the company's plant in Germany died in 1938, the German-born Max Keith took over. With the outbreak of World War II, Keith was unable to obtain the ingredients to continue producing the drink, but instead of halting production he created a new beverage, christened Fanta by one of his salesmen. To create the beverage, Keith originally used whey, a by-product of cheese, and apple fiber, a by-product of cider. He also used whatever fruits he could obtain at the time, which likely accounts for the number of fruit-flavored Fanta varieties still on the market today.

Plenty of Nazis undoubtedly enjoyed the new drink, but Keith created Fanta for the German market as a whole. He personally refused to join the Nazi party, and instead of making himself or the Third Reich rich from the production of Fanta, he handed the profits back to the Coca-Cola Company at the end of the war. The rumor that the Nazis invented Fanta probably started before the war when, as an international company, Coca-Cola advertised its product in the popular media of the day. In Germany, that would have inevitably included newspapers and magazines sympathetic to the Nazi cause. In 1960, the company bought the recipe for Fanta and began producing the drink in the United States, and people of all political persuasions have been enjoying it ever since.

Drink Up!

Impress your friends with some knowledge-quenching trivia the next time you grab one of these favorite beverages.

✳ ✳ ✳ ✳

7UP

THIRSTY? HERE, HAVE a Bib-Label Lithiated Lemon-Lime Soda. Not quite as catchy, eh? Believe it or not, though, that's what 7UP was originally called. Charles Leiper Grigg came up with the not-so-memorable moniker when he first branded the drink back in 1929. Luckily, he realized the drink would likely fizzle under the 12-syllable name. He changed it to 7UP Lithiated Lemon Soda, and then to plain ol' 7UP.

The reason for the "seven" is a bit of a mystery. Some theories say there were initially only seven ingredients in the drink, while others say that the original bottle held seven ounces. One thing that's considered fact, though: The 7UP formula did once contain lithium citrate. The mood-altering drug was a common ingredient in lemon-lime sodas at the time, though it's long since been removed.

Dr Pepper

It may be just what the doctor ordered, but an MD didn't invent Dr Pepper; rather, it was the brainchild of a pharmacist named Charles Alderton. He came up with the concoction while working at a corner drugstore in Waco, Texas, in the late

1800s. Legend has it his customers took to calling the drink "the Waco." So where's the good doc come in? Alderton's boss decided to dub the fizzy drink after a friend named Dr. Charles Pepper.

Coca-Cola

Coke's inventor, however, *was* a doctor. Dr. John Pemberton, a pharmacist from Atlanta, is credited with coming up with the original Coca-Cola formula. He created the first Coke inside a kettle he kept in his backyard. And yes, the rumors are true: The drink did contain cocaine until 1905.

The Coca-Cola name itself doesn't have much of a backstory: Pemberton's bookkeeper simply thought it'd work well in a logo, supposedly saying: "The two Cs would look well in advertising." The man wrote out "Coca-Cola" in his now-famous cursive handwriting, and the rest is history.

Pepsi Cola

Pepsi Cola's first sip also came courtesy of a pharmacist—Caleb Bradham of New Bern, North Carolina. Bradham brewed up the beverage at his drugstore's soda fountain, mixing carbonated water with sugar, vanilla, oil, and reportedly an enzyme called pepsin and some cola nuts. The last two ingredients, as you may have guessed, supposedly gave Pepsi Cola its name.

Mountain Dew

The man behind Mountain Dew was a fruit-flavoring salesman named William "Bill" H. Jones, who bought his way into a drink company called Tip in the 1920s. Folklore has it that one of the company's investors handed him the rights to an inactive trademark for the name Mountain Dew—the drink had been made as a lemon-lime mixer for some time, but it never caught on. Jones decided to develop the product, however, and the Dew was reborn. Later, Jones, on the verge of bankruptcy, added orange flavoring to his soda, as well as more caffeine and sugar, and less carbonation.

A&W Root Beer

Ever wonder who the "A" and "W" in A&W were? Here's your answer: Roy Allen and Frank Wright. The business partners bought a root beer formula from (no surprise) a pharmacist in June 1919. They named the drink A&W in 1922.

Kool-Aid

Kool-Aid came out of some guy's kitchen. No really: A young man named Edwin Perkins experimented with mixes in his mother's home until he stumbled upon a combination that would become the fruity drink. Perkins first sold the drink under the name "Fruit Smack." After figuring out how to break the beverage down into powder form, he changed the name to Kool-Aid.

Amway's Humble Origins

When a couple of Michiganders started selling vitamins in the 1940s, they didn't know they were onto something big.

✳ ✳ ✳ ✳

Take These . . . They're Good for You! Seriously!

IN THE BEGINNING, there was Carl Rehnborg, an American businessman. Rehnborg went to China in the 1920s, where he saw many undernourished persons. When he returned from China in 1927, he started mixing up vitamins. By 1934, Rehnborg was trying to get his friends to take them. People seemed to be a little skeptical about this new concept, and Rehnborg would return to find the supplements untouched.

Rehnborg decided: no more freebies. He founded the California Vitamin Corporation (CVC) to market his vitamins. When people paid for them, they found they liked them—and bought more. The multilevel marketing (MLM) business model began when Rehnborg's friends wanted him to sell to their friends. Instead, he invited them to do the selling themselves, on commission.

In 1939, CVC became Nutrilite. Other than a rough patch, where some of its salespeople went overboard with outlandish health benefit claims, the company did well. In 1945, Nutrilite signed Mytinger & Casselberry (M&C) to distribute its products. M&C formalized and refined Nutrilite's MLM process.

Ja-Ri! Ja-Ri! Ja-Ri!

Jay Van Andel and Rich DeVos were friends and young entrepreneurs from Michigan who came to maturity near the end of World War II. Their best business was their Nutrilite vitamin business, which they incorporated in 1949 as the Ja-Ri ("jah-ree") Corporation. (Interestingly, numerous sources credit a Michael Pacetti as a cofounder of Ja-Ri. Amway's own official history doesn't). DeVos and Van Andel worked hard and built Ja-Ri into a thriving business, but change was on the horizon.

Business Divorce

By the 1950s, increasing government regulations on the industry began hurting sales. In 1958, Nutrilite fell out with M&C over business direction: Nutrilite wanted to branch into cosmetics, but M&C felt that such a move would hurt vitamin sales. When Nutrilite and M&C brought out competing cosmetics lines, Nutrilite saw the obvious: The marriage was over. Remembering Van Andel's skillful efforts at mediation, Nutrilite asked him to run its distribution network. Van Andel thought carefully. Why couldn't Ja-Ri run its own distribution network? In effect, it was already doing so.

Going Direct

In 1959, Van Andel and DeVos powwowed with several important Ja-Ri distributors. The group agreed to branch out into cleaning products. Why those? Because the government wasn't regulating soap success claims as stringently as it was monitoring health benefit claims for vitamins. Van Andel and DeVos believed, with reason, that enthusiasm sold products. If salespeople have to watch their claims, selling is tougher. Van Andel, DeVos, and seven key distributors became Amway's first directors. Van Andel's original confidence proved well founded as the company grew. In 1972, Amway bought a controlling interest in Nutrilite, which it now owns outright. Today, Amway is a subsidiary of Alticor, a privately held corporation run by the Van Andel and DeVos families, with more than 10,000 employees and even more distributors.

Controversy

Amway's multilevel marketing method has been as widely attacked as it has been imitated. Those hostile to Amway accuse it of using rah-rah indoctrination seminars to hook people with the hope of a dream lifestyle few truly achieve. Its partisans deride the critics as negativist losers who didn't follow proven methods.

One fact is undebatable: Alticor is big. For fiscal year 2012, it reported global sales of $11.3 billion. That's a lot of vitamins and soap—plus hundreds of other products.

Fresh Kills Landfill

The world's largest, stinkiest dumping ground is being turned into a public park and ecologically friendly beauty spot.

✳ ✳ ✳ ✳

IN ITS PRIME it was, arguably, the biggest human-made structure on earth, larger in volume than the Great Wall of China, taller by 25 meters than the Statue of Liberty, capable of being seen with the naked eye from outer space. However, this was no wonder of nature, no miracle of human endeavor or ingenuity. Instead, it was just a pile of garbage; rotting, stinking, and overrun by feral dogs and cat-size rats that rummaged for their next meal in a veritable mountain of human waste.

The Fresh Kills Landfill, named because of its location alongside the Fresh Kills estuary on the western shore of Staten Island, was New York City's—and the world's—largest refuse heap during the second half of the 20th century. That wasn't the intention when the place began operations on the rural parcel of land back in 1948. Rather, the landfill was the result of city planner Robert Moses's scheme to use garbage as a foundation beneath the approach system to the double-decker Verrazano-Narrows Bridge that he intended to build between Staten Island and Brooklyn. (Constructed between 1959 and 1969, the suspension bridge would encourage a large increase in Staten Island's population . . . and its trash.)

At the time of the plan's inception, the "temporary landfill" was to last no longer than 20 years, after which the site would be converted into residential, recreational, and industrial areas. As things turned out, the dreck-dumping continued long past 1968, all the way to 2001. Years later the place is *still* in transition.

Toxic, Not Pretty

Just picture it: four 225-foot-high mounds of 50-plus years of decomposing trash—once transported there by a daily con-voy of up to 20 barges, each carrying 650 tons of rubbish that 400-ton cranes deposited into trucks—emitting noxious odors and toxic chemicals into the air and nearby waterways. Yuck. However, this hasn't deterred a wide assortment of birds from flying overhead as they migrate north and south each spring and fall, and it also hasn't prevented various birds of prey from populating the scenic surrounding region to keep the rodent community in check.

Future archaeologists who poke their way around mountains of cigarette butts, diapers, and empty food containers will get plenty of good info about New Yorkers' tastes and habits. However, Fresh Kills had certainly outlasted its own shelf life when, in 1992, a year after other landfill closures had turned it into the sole lucky recipient of the city's garbage, pressure from the United States Environmental Protection Agency (EPA), and local stench-assaulted residents, finally prompted city offi-cials to instigate plans to close the oversized dump.

In 1996 Mayor Rudy Giuliani and Governor George Pataki set a December 31, 2001, deadline for Fresh Kills' closure, aware that it would cost the city around $1 billion to do what needed to be done: Cover and seal the rotting refuse; construct a network of pipes, wells, underground walls, and treatment stations to protect people from the daily emission of about 30 million cubic feet of foul gases and one million gallons of poisonous liquids; and adhere to federal law by administering and maintaining the site for the next 30 years. Furthermore, to export trash from the five boroughs to landfills in other cities would at least double the roughly $100 million a year that was already being spent to bury it at Fresh Kills.

Tragedy, and New Purpose

In the end, the dump closed nine months ahead of schedule, on March 22, 2001—only to temporarily reopen after the 9/11 attacks on the World Trade Center so that debris could be buried there on a restricted 40-acre site.

The 9/11 landfill comprised nearly 45 percent of the 2,200-acre site, which now also includes lowlands, wetlands, and open waterways. All of it is being converted into Freshkills Park, a five-section recreation/education/wildlife area that is nearly triple the size of Central Park. For what used to be garbage, that's not bad.

Bad Ad Grab Bag

"Lost Cat—Last Seen: On Sunday April 27 at the Park County Rod & Gun Club Shooting Range."

"Artificial Christmas Tree For Sale. Like New. Needs stand, ornaments, lights and branches. $99.00 firm."

"Misc For Sale: $600."

"Due to the lack of interest by friends & relatives, the birthday party for Becky Pritchard has been cancelled."

"Perfection in Mountain Park Ranch—Pride of Ownership—3 BR, 2 Ba—Open and Spacious. Ceiling in Every Room."

"Found: Wedding dress. Kwik Car Wash, 2016 South Otsego."

"1989 Thunderbird, V6, AT, brn, great cond, speaks spanish, $4,550."

"Wanted: Somebody to go back in time with me. This is not a joke. You'll get paid after we get back. Must bring your own weapons. Safety not guaranteed. I have only done this once before."

"Youth Programs: Skydiving for Tots (ages 10 mos.-2 years). Introduce your toddler to the fun and thrill of skydiving before he or she develops unwarranted fears of freefalling."

"Turkey—FOR SALE. Partially eaten. Only eight days old. Both drumsticks still intact. $23.00 obo."

"Hariobért—If we can't make you look good…you ugly!"

"Baby Items: HUGGIES used diapers for sale, $4."

"Imitation Crap Meat lb. $2.99"

"Bar-S Franks, 16 Oz., Tasty Dog Chicken or All Meat, 2 for 88¢"

"Four poster bed, 101 years old. Perfect for antique lover."

"Wanted. Man to take care of cow that does not smoke or drink."

Stadium Mustard

Some may ask for Grey Poupon, but in Cleveland they'll give out something even better: a mustard you won't find on store shelves anywhere else.

✳ ✳ ✳ ✳

FOR SIX DECADES, the city's famous Stadium Mustard was slathered on hot dogs at the old Cleveland Municipal Stadium, where Cleveland's professional baseball and football teams played before its demolition in 1996. The stadium became a place of great nostalgia for generations of Clevelanders, representing not just its mid-century grandeur but home to an underdog spirit that has kept the city afloat through good times and bad. (As home of the famously lackluster Cleveland Indians and sometimes-defunct Browns, it'd have to be.)

A Taste of Nostalgia

The mustard somehow catches that ineffable underground spirit and tastes so much of Cleveland that, in 1969, its manufacturer made it available on the supermarket shelves and gave it an official moniker: The Authentic Stadium Mustard. Since then, the mustard has gained wide acclaim as a gourmet alternative to the yellow slop found at many ball parks; without fat, sugar, and preservatives, it might be the healthiest mustard you can put on a bun.

It's been called "the world's best" by *Fortune* magazine and "superb" by *Esquire*, yet outside of Cleveland, most people have never even heard of Stadium Mustard. While its rustbelt brethren have churned out world-famous condiments of other stripes and flavors, from Buffalo's Cool Whip to Pittsburgh's Heinz ketchup empire, Cleveland has kept a low profile with Stadium Mustard. Though it's available at more than 150 stadiums throughout the United States, it is sold by the bottle only in Cleveland supermarkets and through an online distributor.

But for real Clevelanders, the condiment is best served on top of a juicy beef frank in Browns Stadium and Progressive Field, where Stadium Mustard has been keeping the fans full even when the seats were not.

Nine Really Odd Things Insured by Lloyd's of London

Average people insure average things such as cars, houses, and maybe even a boat. Celebrities insure legs, voices, and some things you might not want to examine if you're a claims adjuster. Here are a few unusual things insured by the famous Lloyd's of London over the years.

✳ ✳ ✳ ✳

1. In 1957, world-famous food critic Egon Ronay wrote and published the first edition of the *Egon Ronay Guide to British Eateries*. Because his endorsement could make or break a restaurant, Ronay insured his taste buds for $400,000.

2. In the 1940s, executives at 20th Century Fox had the legs of actress Betty Grable insured for $1 million each. After taking out the policies, Grable probably wished she had added a rider to protect her from injury while the insurance agents fought over who would inspect her when making a claim.

3. While playing on Australia's national cricket team from 1985 to 1994, Merv Hughes took out an estimated $370,000 policy on his trademark walrus mustache, which, combined with his 6'4" physique and outstanding playing ability, made him one of the most recognized cricketers in the world.

4. Representing the Cheerio Yo-Yo Company of Canada, 13-year-old Harvey Lowe won the 1932 World Yo-Yo

Championships in London and toured Europe from 1932 to 1935. He even taught Edward VIII, then Prince of Wales, how to yo-yo. Lowe was so valuable to Cheerio that the company insured his hands for $150,000!

5. From 1967 to 1992, British comedian and singer Ken Dodd was in the *Guinness World Records* for the world's longest joke-telling session—1,500 jokes in three and a half hours. Dodd has sold more than 100 million comedy records and is famous for his frizzy hair, ever-present feather duster, and extremely large buckteeth. His teeth are so important to his act that Dodd had them insured for $7.4 million, surely making his insurance agent grin.

6. During the height of his career, Michael Flatley—star of *Riverdance* and *Lord of the Dance*—insured his legs for an unbelievable $47 million. Before becoming the world's most famous Irish step dancer, the Chicago native trained as a boxer and won the Golden Gloves Championship in 1975, undoubtedly dazzling his opponents with some extremely fast and fancy footwork.

7. The famous comedy team of Bud Abbott and Lou Costello seemed to work extremely well together, especially in their famous "Who's on First?" routine. But to protect against a career-ending argument, they took out a $250,000 insurance policy over a five-year period. After more than 20 years together, the team split up in 1957—not due to a disagreement, but because the Internal Revenue Service got them for back taxes, which forced them to sell many of their assets, including the rights to their many films.

8. Rock and Roll Hall of Famer Bruce Springsteen is known to his fans as The Boss, but Springsteen knows that he could be demoted to part-time status with one case of laryngitis. That's why in the 1980s he insured his famous gravelly voice for $6 million. Rod Stewart has also insured his throat, and Bob Dylan has a similar policy to protect his

vocal cords for that inevitable day when they stop blowin' in the wind.

9. Before rock 'n' roll, a popular type of music in England in the 1950s was skiffle, a type of folk music with a jazz and blues influence played on washboards, jugs, kazoos, and cigar-box fiddles. It was so big at the time that a washboard player named Chas McDevitt tried to protect his career by insuring his fingers for $9,300. It didn't do him much good because skiffle was replaced by rock 'n' roll, washboards by washing machines, and McDevitt by McCartney

An Indispensable Machine

Vending machines are a part of modern living, but they've been around much longer than you think.

✳ ✳ ✳ ✳

VENDING MACHINES SEEM to be distinctly modern contraptions—steel automatons with complex inner workings that give up brightly packaged goods. The first modern versions were used in London in the 1880s to dispense postcards and books. A few years later, they were adopted in America by the Thomas Adams Gum Company for dispensing Tutti-Frutti-flavored gum on subway platforms in New York City. The idea of an automated sales force caught on quickly, and vending machines were soon found almost everywhere. The idea perhaps reached its peak in Philadelphia with the Automat in 1902. These "waiterless" restaurants allowed patrons to buy a wide variety of foods by plunking a few coins into a box.

Today, we think of vending machines as an everyday part of our lives. Americans drop more than $30 billion a year into them, and Japan has one vending machine for every 23 of its citizens. All kinds of products—from skin care items, pajamas, and umbrellas to DVDs, iPods, and digital cameras—can be bought without ever interacting with a salesperson.

As high-tech as all that may be, the most remarkable thing about vending machines lies not in the modern era but in the distant past. A Greek mathematician and engineer named Hero of Alexander built the very first vending machine in 215 B.C.! Patrons at a temple in Egypt would drop a coin into his device. Landing on one end of a lever, the heavy coin would tilt the lever upward and open a stopper that released a set quantity of holy water. When the coin slid off, the lever would return to its original position, shutting off the flow of water.

The (Relatively) Harmless Truth About Those Packets That Say "Do Not Eat"

It's better to add fruits and veggies to your diet than to take up a weird new culinary habit. But if you consider "do not eat" merely to be a friendly suggestion, you're in luck.

✳   ✳   ✳   ✳

THE STUFF IN those little packages is silica gel, which is a desiccant—a substance that absorbs and holds water vapor. Silica absorbs 40 percent of its weight in water and prevents moisture from ruining things.

Silica gel protects leather jackets from being damaged by moisture, prevents condensation from harming electronic equipment, and aids in retarding mold in foods such as pepperoni. The packets are especially useful during shipment, when a product starts in one climate (say, chilly Canada) and crosses several different locales before reaching its destination (say, balmy Florida).

But just how dangerous is it to eat? What would happen if you popped a silica packet into your mouth? The silica would instantly absorb as much of the moisture from your mouth as it could hold, which would make you very thirsty. If you were to swallow it, your throat would probably become parched, and then you would get a tummyache. It might also make your eyes and nasal cavity feel dry. But it wouldn't be deadly—silica gel is nontoxic. In fact, the packets are more of a choking hazard than a toxin.

Now, if you decided to chow down on a bunch of silica packets, you would do some damage. But you probably couldn't afford all the pepperoni, leather jackets, and stereos it would take to make this a possibility.

Wisconsin Dells Has Ducks in a Row

Is it a boat? Is it a tank? Well, actually it's a little of both.

✳　✳　✳　✳

Fitting the (Duck) Bill

IF YOU LIVE or vacation in Wisconsin, you've probably heard of the Original Wisconsin Ducks. After all, they've been around for almost 60 years. One of the top attractions at the Wisconsin Dells, the amphibious Ducks transport more than 300,000 passengers a year through 8.5 miles of wooded terrain and scenic waterways. This one-hour excursion through the Lower Dells is calm until you hit one of the two featured splashdowns—when your vehicle suddenly hits the water and becomes a boat. Now that's something to quack about!

✳ A Duck is a combination land and water vehicle with a steel hull and six wheels.

✳ General Motors developed the first Ducks during World War II to transport troops and cargo by land and sea to hard-to-reach areas.

✳ While they are affectionately known as Ducks, their real name is DUKW, which was a combination of military code letters for the various aspects of the vehicle: D stands for 1942, the year they were designed; U is for utility or amphibious; K means it is front-wheel drive; and the W means it has two rear driving wheels.

* Ducks were used in Europe, North Africa, and the Pacific during World War II. They played a large role in the invasion of Normandy—2,000 Ducks transported troops and supplies to the shores of France.

* More than 21,200 Ducks were manufactured from 1942 through 1945, at a cost of $10,000 each. If that sounds cheap, compare it to the cost of a three-bedroom house, which cost less at that time.

* Each one of the Original Wisconsin Ducks is named after a military leader or WWII battle.

* The Duck's land motor is located in the front, and while in the water, the Duck operates by a rear propeller.

* Ducks are not small. They are 31 feet long and 8 feet wide, weighing in at 7.5 tons. They can reach speeds of 55 mph on land and 6 mph in the water.

* The Original Wisconsin Ducks attraction has more than 90 Ducks in its fleet, the largest in the nation. All told, there are about 300 Ducks still operating in the United States.

* More than 100 applicants each year apply for the position of Duck Driver. Only 60 get the call. Drivers must be at least 18 years old and have a commercial driver's license. Drivers must also have sufficient arm strength—there's no power steering.

* Duck Drivers go through an intensive six-week training— one week more than the soldiers who drove them in World War II. Drivers learn to work the double clutch in empty parking lots before venturing out on trails. All new drivers must also take the general manager on a tour before they get the nod to go it alone.

Great Moments in Kitsch History

"Kitsch" is a term used to describe objects of bad taste and poor quality. But despite its bad rap, plenty of people go to great lengths to collect kitsch and keep its "charms" alive.

✳ ✳ ✳ ✳

Pink flamingos: In 1957, Union Products of Leominster, Massachusetts, introduced the ultimate in tacky lawn ornaments: the plastic pink flamingo. Designed by artist Don Featherstone, they were sold in the Sears mail-order catalog for $2.76 a pair with the instructions, "Place in garden, lawn, to beautify landscape." Authentic pink flamingos—which are sold only in pairs and bear Featherstone's signature under their tails—are no longer on the market (Union Products shuttered its factory in 2006), but knockoffs ensure the bird's survival.

Troll dolls: Danish sculptor Thomas Damm created the popular troll doll as a handmade wooden gift for his daughter. After it caught the eye of the owner of a toy shop, Dammit Dolls were born, and plastic versions with trademark oversize hairdos hit the mass market. The dolls swept the United States in the early 1960s and were lugged around as good-luck charms by people of all ages and walks of life—including Lady Bird Johnson.

Lava Lites: In the early 1960s, Englishman Edward Craven-Walker invented the Lava Lite, and Chicago entrepreneur Adolf Wertheimer bought the American distribution rights after seeing it at a trade show. Within five years, 2 million Lava Lites had been sold in the United States.

Polyester leisure suits: Brightly colored leisure suits are actually an early 1970s interpretation of a style that took Europe by storm in the 1700s: the three-piece wool suit. Worn not to the office but on weekend outings, wool suits inspired leisure suits, which likewise never caught on as business attire but were the rage on Saturday nights at the disco.

The United Fruit Company

A tale of dramatic leaps, octopuses, railroads, corruption, contrition, and… bananas.

✳ ✳ ✳ ✳

O N MONDAY, FEBRUARY 3, 1975, corporate raider Eli M. Black stood before the glass window of his office on the 44th floor of the Pan American Building in New York City. As Black stood looking at the Manhattan skyline, it is possible he thought of the Honduran banana plantations that had recently been wiped out by Hurricane Fifi. Or perhaps he thought of the devalued United Fruit Company shares that were dragging down the market viability of his newly created United Brands Company.

Unfortunately, nobody will ever know exactly what Eli M. Black's thoughts were the moment he sent his briefcase sailing through Pan American's glass wall and dove after it, plunging to his death on the Park Avenue pavement far below.

Before the Fall

Seven years prior, Black had purchased enough shares to become the majority stockholder of the United Fruit Company—a powerful corporation that had molded Central and South American politics for nearly a century. Eli M. Black had the distinction of presiding over the final days of the United Fruit Company. The corporation, which ended so dismally, had an equally rough beginning. In 1871, railroad speculator Henry Mieggs secured a contract with the government of Costa Rica to develop the young country's railroad system. Unfortunately, the Costa Ricans ran out of money, and the railroad remained unfinished upon Mieggs's death. His nephew, Minor C. Keith, realized that the true value of the railroad lay not in its ability to transport people, but in its ability to transport the bananas that grew plentifully along its tracks. Keith borrowed money from London banks and private investors to finish the railroad. He then acquired tax-free rights to the land adjacent to the rails and earned exclusive trading status at the country's seaports. His banana empire thus secured, Keith joined his operation with Boston Fruit's Lorenzo Dow Baker and Andrew W. Preston. This merger brought substantial financial backing as well as one of the world's largest private holdings of transport ships, known as "The Great White Fleet." With control of the railroads and shipping, the new United Fruit Company soon came to dominate the region's trade.

Banana Republic

In 1901, the Guatemalan government hired the United Fruit Company to handle the country's postal service. Keith realized that Guatemala, with its right-wing dictator and ample supply of cheap labor, represented the "ideal investment climate." United Fruit soon lorded over every aspect of the Guatemalan economy. It established a base of operations in its own town, Bananera, and was able to procure extremely favorable terms from a succession of pliant governments. And with that, the "banana republic" was born.

As a key tactic, United Fruit extracted rights for vast tracts of property under the premise that the region's unpredictable weather necessitated backup plantations. The result: Large amounts of land lay fallow. Unable to farm, the majority of the populace, mostly Indian, struggled to subsist on the company's meager wages or simply had no work at all. Apologists for United Fruit cited the growth of infrastructure as well as the relatively high wages for its permanent employees, but for the average citizen, United Fruit's regional monopoly meant curtailed opportunity. Beginning in the 1920s, the company dominated life in the region so completely that locals began calling it El Pulpo—The Octopus.

The first real test of the company's power came in 1944 when Guatemalans overthrew their oppressive dictator, Jorge Ubico, and elected reformer Dr. Juan Jose Arevalo Bermej, who was peacefully and democratically succeeded by Jacobo Arbenz. Besides building schools and improving the circumstances of the average citizen, these men (Arbenz in particular) promised to break up the vast tracks of land held by private firms and redistribute it to the populace. As it was, 90 percent of the people had access to only 10 percent of the land. United Fruit Company, the primary land-holder in the region, appealed to the United States to overthrow the democratic Guatemalan government, claiming that Arbenz was allied with the Soviet Union. In 1954, a CIA-backed coup ousted Arbenz and installed a repressive right-wing dictatorial government, sparking a civil war that lasted 36 years and resulted in the deaths of hundreds of thousands of people. Many died as a result of being on a list of "dissidents" compiled by the CIA at the behest of the United Fruit Company.

In 1968, Eli M. Black bought his ill-fated shares in United Fruit. He later merged the company with his own—a move that created the United Brands Company. Financial problems, coupled with Black's mismanagement of the company, led to serious debt for the United Brands. A 1974 hurricane, which destroyed huge crops of bananas, was perhaps the final straw for Eli Black and may have been a factor in his 1975 suicide.

In 1999, three years after the end of the Guatemalan civil war, U.S. President Bill Clinton visited the region, and during a brief stop in Guatemala City, delivered a speech in which he expressed regret for the United States' role in the country's civil war, stating that Washington "was wrong" to have supported Guatemalan security forces during its "dark and painful" period. By the time President Clinton made these comments, the United Fruit Company had undergone its own "dark and painful" period but currently survives as Chiquita Brands International Corporation, which acquired the deceased Eli M. Black's United Brands in 1984.

Worth a Fortune: Very Rare U.S. Coins

Why are certain coins so valuable? Some simply have very low mintages, and some are error coins. In some cases (with gold, in particular), most of the pieces were confiscated and melted. Better condition always adds value.

❋ ❋ ❋ ❋

THE CURRENT MINTS and marks are Philadelphia (P, or no mark), Denver (D), and San Francisco (S). Mints in Carson City, Nevada (CC); Dahlonega, Georgia (D); and New Orleans (O) shut down long ago, which adds appeal to their surviving coinage. Here are the most prized and/or interesting U.S. coins, along with an idea of what they're worth:

1787 Brasher gold doubloon: It was privately minted by goldsmith Ephraim Brasher before the U.S. Mint's founding in 1793. The coin was slightly lighter than a $5 gold piece, and at one point in the 1970s it was the most expensive U.S. coin ever sold. Seven known; last sold for $625,000.

1792 half-disme (5¢ piece): Disme was the old terminology for "dime," so half a disme was five cents. George Washington supposedly provided the silver for this mintage. Was Martha the model for Liberty's image? If so, her hairdo suggests she'd been helping Ben Franklin with electricity experiments. Perhaps 1,500 minted; sells for up to $1.3 million.

1804 silver dollar: Though actually minted in 1834 and later, the official mint delivery figure of 19,570 refers to the 1804 issue. Watch out—counterfeits abound. Only 15 known; worth up to $4.1 million.

1849 Coronet $20 gold piece: How do you assess a unique coin's value? The Smithsonian owns the only authenticated example, the very first gold "double eagle." Why mint only one?

It was a trial strike of the new series. Rumors persist of a second trial strike that ended up in private hands; if true, it hasn't surfaced in more than 150 years. Never sold; literally priceless.

1870-S $3 gold piece: Apparently, only one (currently in private hands) was struck, though there are tales of a second one placed in the cornerstone of the then-new San Francisco Mint building (now being renovated as a museum). If the building is ever demolished, don't expect to see it imploded. One known; estimated at $1.2 million.

1876-CC 20-cent piece: Remember when everyone confused the new Susan B. Anthony dollars with quarters? That's what comes of ignoring history. A century before, this 20-cent coin's resemblance to the quarter caused similar frustration. Some 18 known; up to $175,000.

1894-S Barber dime: The Barber designs tended to wear quickly, so any Barber coin in great condition is scarce enough. According to his daughter Hallie, San Francisco Mint director John Daggett struck two dozen 1894-S coins, mostly as gifts for his rich banker pals. Dad gave little Hallie three of the dimes, and she used one to buy herself the costliest ice cream in history. Twenty-four minted, ten known; as high as $1.3 million.

1907 MCMVII St. Gaudens $20 gold piece: This is often considered the loveliest U.S. coin series ever. Its debut featured the year in Roman numerals, unique in U.S. coinage. The first, ultra-high-relief version was stunning in its clarity and beauty, but it proved too time-consuming to mint, so a less striking (but still impressive) version became the standard. About 11,000 minted, but very few in ultra-high relief; those have sold for $1.5 million.

1909-S VDB Lincoln cent: It's a collectors' favorite, though not vanishingly rare. Only about a fourth of Lincoln pennies from the series' kickoff year featured designer Victor D. Brenner's initials on the reverse; even now, an occasional "SVDB" will show up in change. There were 484,000 minted; worth up to $7,500.

1913 Liberty Head nickel: This coin wasn't supposed to be minted. The Mint manufactured the dies as a contingency before the Buffalo design was selected for 1913. Apparently, Mint employee Samuel W. Brown may have known that the Liberty dies were slated for destruction and therefore minted five of these for his personal gain. One of the most prized U.S. coins—and priced accordingly at $1.8 million.

1913-S Barber quarter: Forty thousand of these were made—the lowest regular-issue mintage of the 20th century. Some Barbers wore so flat that the head on the obverse was reduced to a simple outline. Quite rare in good condition; can bring up to $24,000.

1915 Panama-Pacific $50 gold piece: This large commemorative piece was offered in both octagonal and round designs. Approximately 1,100 were minted; prices range from $40,000 to $155,000.

1916 Liberty Standing quarter: This coin depicts a wardrobe malfunction... except by design! Many were shocked when the new coin displayed Lady Liberty's bared breast. By mid-1917, she was donning chain mail. Like the Barber quarter before it, the Liberty Standing wore out rapidly. With only 52,000 minted in 1916, the series' inaugural year, a nice specimen will set you back nearly $40,000.

1933 St. Gaudens $20 gold piece: This coin is an outlaw. All of the Saint's final mintage were to be melted down—and most were. Only one specific example is legal to own; other surviving 1933 Saints remain hidden from the threat of Treasury confiscation. The legal one sold in 2002 for an incredible $7.6 million.

1937-D "three-legged" Buffalo nickel: A new employee at the Denver Mint tried polishing some damage off a die with an emery stick. He accidentally ground the bison's foreleg off, leaving a disembodied hoof. No telling exactly how many were struck, but they sure look funny. Up to $30,000.

Snake Farm—Exit Soon

Since 1967, billboards for the Snake Farm in New Braunfels has been enticing tourists and local residents off Interstate 35 and into its environs.

✳ ✳ ✳ ✳

PEOPLE RUN HOT or cold on snakes. Some come to the Snake Farm and rave about the variety of snakes and the petting zoo. Others describe the attraction as "creepy" and recommend it only for people who love reptiles and crawly things.

The Snake Farm—officially known as Animal World & Snake Farm—is a modern-day legend and roadside attraction between Austin and San Antonio. But the farm is more than just a tourist site; it's dedicated to raising some of the biggest and most dangerous snakes in the world.

Making a Name

The origins of the Snake Farm are murky. Several stories point to a man named Mack—with no last name—who'd previously lived in LaPlace, Louisiana. There, his Snake Farm was widely known as a tourist attraction... with a brothel rumored to be in the back.

Moving to Texas, Mack started a new business with a chimpanzee. He put a sign by the side of the road that invited travelers to stop and buy a ticket to see his "gorilla." In the years that followed, Mack's carnival-style attraction evolved with several snakes in display pits. (A few old-timers, however, insist that the snakes were just a front for a "bawdy house," the same as Mack had built in Louisiana.)

The attraction was made famous by billboards along the highways of Texas, each showing a huge snake and directing people to the New Braunfels site. In fact, far more people likely know the notorious Snake Farm from the ubiquitous billboards than by ever actually darkening its door.

The Snake Farm changed hands several times after Mack moved on to other projects. Gradually, the attraction became what the signs said: a genuine snake farm.

A Variety of Reptilian Delights

Texas is home to more species of snakes than any other state. It was only natural, then, to build a farm to display them and educate the public about snakes. Today, all 15 varieties of Texas's venomous snakes are featured at the Snake Farm, along with a wide range of other reptiles, amphibians, and exotic animals.

John Mellyn and his wife, Susan, owned and ran the Snake Farm for about 13 years, starting in 1994. They transformed it into a more upscale attraction while still retaining its 1950s-style charm. Mellyn had a habit of freezing his deceased snakes, rather than disposing of the bodies. This once inspired Dorothy Cross, an artist from Dublin, Ireland, to create a cathedrallike exhibit of frozen snakes in a San Antonio art museum.

In December 2007, the Snake Farm was purchased by Eric and Dara Trager. Today, this husband-and-wife team is dedicated to the more than 500 animals in their care.

Moving into the Future

Despite a tragic fire that damaged part of the farm in late 2008, the Tragers and their staff have rebuilt and steadily expanded the facilities and the range of animals kept there. They're proud of what they've accomplished, and their hard work has produced great results. Parents and travel experts list the Snake Farm as a "must-see" on any road trip across Texas.

Most visitors to Animal World & Snake Farm give it a thumbs up. From time to time, however, someone comes in expecting a full-scale, traditional zoo and is disappointed. Herpetologists—people who study reptiles and amphibians—and children who love the "ick" factor may be the most enthusiastic Snake Farm guests.

The site has been especially popular since it was featured on the TV show *Dirty Jobs* in 2007. In the episode "Snake Wrangler," star Mike Rowe carried huge pythons, moved western diamondback snakes from their pit, and then, shirtless, helped clean the alligator and crocodile tank with the Snake Farm crew.

10 Most Dangerous Jobs in America

Before you complain about punching the time clock, read this list for some perspective. Maybe the coffee stinks and you don't like your boss, but at least the threat of death or injury isn't perpetually hanging over your head. The order may change from year to year, but these are typically the most dangerous jobs in America.

1. Logger

2. Pilot

3. Fisher

4. Iron/Steel Worker

5. Garbage Collector

6. Farmer/Rancher

7. Roofer

8. Electrical Power Installer/Repairer

9. Sales, Delivery, and Other Truck Driver

10. Taxi Driver/Chauffeur

More Curious Classifieds

* Job Wanted—Man, honest. Will take anything.

* Sale—Stock up and save. Limit one.

* Used Cars—Why go elsewhere to be cheated? Come here first!

* Explosives Worker—Man wanted to work in dynamite factory. Must be willing to travel.

* Christmas Tag Sale—Handmade gifts for the hard-to-find person.

* Furniture—Sofas. Only $299! For rest or fore play.

* Teacher—Three-year-old teacher needed for pre-school. Experience preferred.

* For Sale—Antique desk suitable for lady with thick legs and large drawers.

* Grand Opening—The Superstore—unequaled in size, unmatched in variety, unrivaled inconvenience.

* For Sale—Mixing bowl set designed to please a cook with round bottom for efficient beating.

* Expertise—We do not tear your clothing with machinery. We do it carefully by hand.

* Helper—Tired of cleaning yourself? Let me do it.

* Auto Repair Service—Free pick-up and delivery. Try us once, you'll never go anywhere again.

* For Sale—Amana washer $100. Owned by clean bachelor who seldom washed.

The Beta Wars

When videotape recorders entered the consumer market, formatting differences between Betamax and VHS didn't exactly spark a shooting war, but in some quarters they could have.

✳   ✳   ✳   ✳

ON FIRST HEARING about high-definition television, comedian Paula Poundstone said that she wasn't buying into another system until she was certain that it was the *last* system. It was a complaint that most Americans understood.

The question of media formatting goes back at least to the days when the printing press replaced hand-lettered manuscripts, but it became a matter of open, partisan warfare in 1975 when videotape was introduced as a mass medium. Sony introduced the Betamax video system, which was followed a year later by JVC's totally incompatible VHS.

Quality Versus Price and Convenience

There is little disagreement that Sony's Betamax was a technically superior system, but JVC's VHS (which stood for Video Helical Scan) was marketed intensively. Its players were cheaper and easier to make, and other manufacturers started to adopt the VHS format. Additionally, Beta featured only one-hour tapes—not long enough to record a movie—while VHS had two-hour tapes. By the time Beta developed two-hour and three-hour formats, VHS had a four-hour format. Eventually, Beta achieved five hours, and VHS reached 10.6 hours.

In 1985, Sony introduced SuperBeta; JVC countered with Super-VHS. As the systems tried to outdo each other, Beta was never quite able to catch up. Major studios released fewer movies on Beta. Then, in a 1989 episode of *Married . . . with Children*, the Bundys were described as "the last family on earth with Beta." That offhand comment was the kiss of death. VHS ruled the roost. At least, that is, until DVDs came along.

McDonald's Food Items That Didn't Make the Cut

If you remember "Two all-beef patties, special sauce, lettuce, cheese, pickles, onions on a sesame seed bun," you're familiar with McDonald's Big Mac—by far the chain's biggest hit. Standing in stark contrast to this celebrated sandwich are some wacky McDonald's offerings that even Ronald McDonald couldn't save.

✳ ✳ ✳ ✳

Hulaburger: Although veggie burgers and other meat replacements have gained ground over the years, people still prefer beef patties. Perhaps this explains why the Hulaburger dropped the hoop. In a move that's best described as fast-food folly, McDonald's targeted Catholic consumers (who couldn't eat meat on Fridays during Lent) with a sandwich featuring a sliver of *pineapple* instead of a meat patty. Rather than "hang loose" with this bizarre Hulaburger, consumers turned up their noses and hula-danced away.

McDLT: Okay, you *think* you know where this is headed, but do you really? Yes, the McDLT featured lettuce and tomato, just like its BLT namesake, but that's where the resemblance ended. In McDonald's wacky version, the hot and cold portions were completely separated in a rather unwieldy box. Hungry consumers were then expected to combine the two before mastication commenced. The public balked, the McDLT walked, and the rest is history.

McPizza: In a world that already featured Pizza Hut, Domino's, and a gazillion other local pizzerias, did McDonald's really believe it could sell pizza and prosper? You bet your pepperoni! But in the end, this McDonald's experiment failed for two key reasons: People preferred to dine at actual pizza parlors, and they craved the higher quality that such outlets promised. Say *ciao*, McPizza.

McLean Deluxe: First rule of contemporary food marketing: A healthful product should also taste good. This burger, which reduced fat by combining water with *seaweed* of all distasteful things, tasted awful. A savvy public allowed it to "sink."

McPasta: Try though they did, McDonald's could not find an audience for its pasta-based menu. Even with popular dishes like lasagna, spaghetti, and Fettuccini Alfredo fronting for the red, white, and green, the fare never caught on. *Molto triste.*

McHotdog: Wieners being hawked at a burger joint? Isn't this akin to sacrilege? Available at select outlets throughout the world, the venerable hot dog never found an audience under Ray Kroc's golden arches. Perhaps potential customers were too busy wolfing them down at ballparks?

McLobster: Most can see why this one failed, but if you haven't a clue, try this on for size: Lobster is generally found at more expensive dining establishments. Translation: People with a shellfish craving would likely *never* visit McDonald's. Toss in a relatively steep price, and the McLobster's fate was sealed. Even so, the sandwich maintains a claw-hold in Maine and in certain parts of Canada.

McGratin Croquette: This Japanese-market sandwich featured fried macaroni, shrimp, and mashed potatoes. Sound pretty awful? Many diners agreed. This effectively doomed the sandwich to bit-player status. It remains a seasonal offering.

Arch Deluxe: Billed as a sophisticated burger, the Arch Deluxe (featuring Spanish onions and a fancy bun) was aimed squarely at discriminating adults. But discrimination can cut two ways, as McDonald's soon found out. Despite a $100 million ad campaign, the burger for grown-ups flamed out. Many McHeads rolled after the giant misstep.

A Tangy Tourist Attraction: The Mustard Museum

In a world of idiosyncratic people and places, Barry Levenson and the Mustard Museum just may be the spice of your life.

✳ ✳ ✳ ✳

Triumph in the Face of Defeat

THEIR STORY BEGINS on the early morning of October 28, 1986. The Boston Red Sox had just lost the World Series to the New York Mets, and just hours after the devastating undoing, despondent Red Sox fan Barry Levenson traipsed through an all-night grocery soul-searching for a clearer understanding of life. Crushed by his team's seventh game squander, Barry sought comfort in the condiment corridor. He waltzed by the pickles, the ketchups, the relishes, the horseradishes, and the mayos. When he hovered over the mustards, he heard a powerful voice: "If you collect us, they will come."

At the time of this zestfully zany epiphany, the Massachusetts native served as Assistant Attorney General for the State of Wisconsin. Five years later, his mustard collection had grown so large that it warranted a bigger spotlight. So Levenson fully heeded that voice and devoted his attention full-time to the great golden hue, quitting law to start a museum with room enough to display the 1,000 jars he had already amassed.

Since then, tens of thousands of faithful minions and curiosity hounds have come to the Mount Horeb Mustard Museum, which opened April 6, 1992. Even after years of talking mustard, Levenson has not lost his interest in discussing the pungent paste's history, origins, varieties, and virtues, jawing at a pace approaching the speed of light.

The Wide World of Condiments

The Mount Horeb Mustard Museum represents the whole world of mustard powders and plants, from Azerbaijan to

Zimbabwe, and quite a few places in between. Slovenian, South African, Italian, Scottish, Welsh, Russian, and Japanese mustards receive special attention, and Wisconsin mustards are spotlighted as well.

The museum houses more than 5,000 mustards and hundreds of items of mustard memorabilia, including mustard and hot dog art, literature, apparel, toys, coffee mugs, billboards, gift boxes, dispensers, model trucks, and souvenir buses and railroad cars. Mustard gift boxes are available to suit any occasion, and the tasting area allows visitors to sample local, regional, and exotic mustard sources.

Gourmet mustard patrons learn just how versatile, practical, and diverse mustard is—the museum teaches that there are more savory mustards than just the standard yellow variety. Thousands of hot pepper, garlic, herb, maple walnut, spicy apricot, black truffle, champagne, organic, dill, Dijon, and fruit variations await discovery.

Cutting the Mustard

About 35,000 visitors a year from across the globe come to the museum in search of insight. It has been featured on *The Oprah Winfrey Show*, HGTV's *The Good Life*, and the Food Network. Nevertheless, for Levenson, who has even authored a children's book entitled *Mustard on a Pickle*, no praise is too lavish for one of the world's most ancient spices and oldest known condiments, dating back to at least 3000 B.C. when it was harvested in India. Today, Levenson says that about 700 million pounds of mustard are consumed worldwide each year, and that the U.S. uses more mustard than any other country.

But what if his beloved Red Sox hadn't lost the World Series to the Mets in October 1986? Would he have started collecting mustards that night—or ever? Would he have been so depressed as to wander the aisles of an all-night supermarket,? Would the mustards sometime after have cried out so resonantly? The world may never know.

Sea-Monkey See, Sea-Monkey Do

In the past 50 years, millions of people have ordered Sea-Monkeys. Alas, these people were disappointed to find their microscopic pets don't wear tiaras or even live very long. Here's a look at the PR machine that turned a homely crustacean into a generation-spanning fad.

✳ ✳ ✳ ✳

IN 1957, MAIL-ORDER marketer Harold von Braunhut had already given the world Invisible Goldfish and X-Ray Spex. Upon encountering brine shrimp, he saw potential for his next great venture, which he called "Instant Life."

Brine shrimp, or *artemia salina*, are the perfect pet for someone who doesn't have a lot of space and doesn't mind if their pet has zero personality. Fully grown, they are only ³/₄ inch long. The official Web site says the name stems from their monkey-like "funny behavior and long tail," but any simian resemblance is questionable. What appealed to von Braunhut was their cost-effectiveness: Brine shrimp eggs can exist out of water for years, dormant and seemingly lifeless. But just add water and the eggs hatch, making them perfect for warehouse storage and mail-order shipping.

A Shrimp by Any Other Name...

Initial sales were lackluster. In 1962, von Braunhut renamed his product "Sea-Monkeys," marketing them through colorful ads in comic books that depicted them as a family of smiling, playful merfolk. Despite fine-print warnings that these were not accurate representations, people were smitten. Von Braunhut began selling other products that people could buy to show their Sea-Monkeys affection, such as special desserts. Soon, competing toy companies began carrying Sea-Monkey accessories such as racetracks, ski lodges, and elaborately themed aquariums. Sea-Monkey ads are still ubiquitous. Each year another generation begs to order them.

Subterranean Secrets

Wisconsin is famous for its well-tended roads and highways, but hidden from public view lies a less visible web: the labyrinth of underground passages built by businesses, the military, and bootleggers throughout the state's colorful history.

❋　❋　❋　❋

Historic Hideaways

ONE OF WISCONSIN's oldest tunnels still in existence was built by abolitionist Joseph Goodrich. He constructed a unique, hexagonal inn in Milton in 1844. In addition, he added a tunnel that led from the Milton House's grout basement to a small log cabin in the backyard. It became a regular stop on the Underground Railroad, which was the route followed by escaped slaves that secretly helped them travel to safe locations.

In Fond du Lac, Mayor Isaac Brown had an eight-sided, grout and stucco place built in 1856. Like the Milton House, the Octagon House also hid a tunnel. The 14-foot passage led to a shed, which may also have served passengers from the Underground Railroad.

Oshkosh's Secret City

Some Wisconsin tunnels were built as a bow to the state's climate, allowing shoppers to move easily from store to store during winter months in the days before modern snow removal equipment was available. The city of Oshkosh boasts a very well-documented underground downtown, which was at one time a kind of subterranean shopping mall.

Many businesses operated in basements that were accessed by outside stairways and were connected to other merchants by passageways under the street-level sidewalks. These "hollow sidewalks" dating from the 1860s are now closed, but evidence of them still exists in the prismatic glass "windows" and iron trapdoors set into the upper sidewalks.

The most famous tunnel in Oshkosh led across downtown's Monument Square from the Athearn Hotel (now demolished) to the magnificent Grand Opera House. The tunnel was probably built in the early 1900s, and local legend says actors, showgirls, and whiskey-toting gangsters all made use of it. Oshkosh historian Julie Krysiak Johnson even wrote a book about it, called *Oshkosh Down Under*.

Tunnel Trespassers of Madison

In the days when institutions were heated by large steam plants, gigantic tunnel systems often housed the pipes and furnaces. Today, hundreds of students still tread over an array of steam tunnels under the University of Wisconsin-Madison's historic Bascom Hill. The tunnels splay outward to the Memorial Library and other buildings.

These tunnels are perhaps best known for their legendary resident, Tunnel Bob, a tall, haggard man who walked their maze-like length for many years. Some who saw Tunnel Bob reported he had ghastly scars from burns caused by the steam vents. Although the tunnels are strictly closed to visitors, Tunnel Bob proved impossible to oust, and the maintenance staff eventually began to tolerate his presence. Reputedly, they even paid him for changing lightbulbs in hard-to-reach places.

Oddly enough, Madison claims another Tunnel Bob. The second Bob belongs to Madison East High School. The school's newspaper has printed stories about a homeless man or drifter who was seen in the school's subterranean steam tunnels. Others say he still lives there—as some students claim to have glimpsed his ghost in the school's shadowy corners.

The Bong Boondoggle

The Richard Bong State Recreation Area in Kenosha County is a marshy, 4,515-acre tract of land originally developed in the mid-1950s as a base for the U.S. Air Force. It is named for World War II flying ace Major Richard Ira Bong. It was intended as a strategic point of defense against air attacks aimed at Milwaukee and Chicago. But construction stopped in 1959, before the base ever came into full use, leaving a partially graded 12,900-foot runway and a maze of underground tunnels and sewers.

The tunnels were a spot for partying area teenagers as late as the 1970s, and still exist, although they are now sealed. They gained a local reputation as a center of criminal, ghostly, and cult activity, and one Burlington paranormal group has also reported numerous UFO and ghostly light sightings in the skies above them.

Gangsters Underground

Famed Chicago gangster Al Capone kept hideouts in almost every corner of Wisconsin, if all such rumors are to be believed. A good example is Burlington, on the western edge of Racine County. The city became a hotbed of illicit taverns, during the Prohibition era of the 1920s and early '30s. Many residents believe underground tunnels connected these businesses so that liquor could be transported without being seen by the authorities, and so the criminals could move easily between them.

One speakeasy, located on Milwaukee Avenue where Coach's Sports Bar and Grill now stands, had no fewer than three tunnels leading from its basement. Other Burlington locations served by bootleg liquor tunnels include the First Banking Center on Highway 11 and what is now a parking lot on Milwaukee Avenue. That tunnel was reportedly large enough to hold its own bowling lanes!

Capone may have also crisscrossed his property, which covered more than 400 acres at Couderay, near Hurley. His Wisconsin retreat sported 18-inch-thick walls, gun turrets, an eight-car garage with gun portals, and secret underground passages. Still known by its gangster-era name, "The Hideout," the two-story stone lodge may have had tunnels leading from the home's basement to other buildings on the grounds, though the truth about such tunnels has not been verified.

Chilly Accommodations

Want to spend some vacation time at an ice hotel? Better make reservations before spring comes, or you'll risk a melting room.

✳ ✳ ✳ ✳

AN ICE HOTEL is a temporary hotel made entirely of ice and snow. Such hotels are open, logically enough, only during winter months; then they melt and are reconstructed the following year. Ice hotels are white-hot destination spots whose construction is based on some of the same theories used to build igloos: Blocks of ice and compacted snow from deep drifts are cut and arranged to build a structure that can protect and house the people using it. Two of the best-known hotels can be found in Sweden and Quebec.

ICEHOTEL, Sweden

ICEHOTEL in Sweden, located in the village of Jukkasjarvi, is 200 kilometers, or 125 miles, north of the Arctic Circle. It's the first-ever hotel built entirely of ice. Because the hotel—or, hotels, one should say, as there is a new one every year—rests near the River Torne, there's an endless supply of clear water for construction each year.

The hotel uses 2,000 tons of ice in its construction. It covers more than 30,000 square feet. It is all ice, no kidding. The registration desk, tables, beds, chapel, art exhibition hall—all are made of ice.

So, what do you need to know before scheduling some sleep time in a hotel made of ice? First, you need to know that the temperature is kept between 15 and 24 degrees Fahrenheit. Concerned about keeping your extremities warm while spending an entire night in freezing temps? No worries—the hotel provides guests with thermal sleeping bags, and each ice bed is covered with reindeer skins. As long as you don't kick off the covers in your sleep, you should be able to stay free of frostbite for the night. A visit to the sauna in the morning is included in the price, along with a hot cup of lingonberry juice at your bedside.

Ice Hotel, Quebec

Inspired by the Swedish ICEHOTEL, designer Jacques Desbois built a similar hotel in 1996 in Sainte-Catherine-de-la-Jacques-Cartier, about 30 minutes outside of Quebec City. Quebec is a natural location for an ice hotel—the city hosts the annual Bonhomme Winter Carnival. The debut of the Ice Palace at the 1955 Winter Carnival was an early attempt at merging the pragmatic construction of igloos with the fantastical dreaminess of larger-scale ice buildings.

The Ice Hotel, Quebec, is usually made with 500 tons of ice and 15,000 tons of snow. It has 18-foot-high ceilings and theme suites, which are more numerous with each annual reconstruction. The Ice Hotel also has an Ice Bar sponsored by Absolut Vodka—a frosty delight. Guests of the Ice Hotel, Quebec, can expect ice beds similar to those at the ICEHOTEL, Sweden, but the Quebec version offers a thick foam mattress, as well as deer pelts, in addition to the requisite thermal sleeping bags. The Canadian version of the ice hotel houses two art galleries and a movie theater, which shows only "cool" movies.

Around the World

Sweden and Canada aren't the only countries to have ice hotels, of course. They can be built anywhere that's cold enough. Similar structures have been constructed in Norway, Romania, and Finland.

The Town That Disappeared

Cheshire was a small town along the banks of the Ohio River, where many of the townsfolk worked for the nearby James M. Gavin Power Plant owned by American Electric Power. With Cheshire's population only 221 in 2000, American Electric had no trouble relocating the whole town when the plant polluted it beyond habitability in 2001. It only cost them $20 million to do it.

* * * *

THE SEEDS OF Cheshire's demise sprouted in 2000, when the Environmental Protection Agency (EPA) accused American Electric of violating the Clean Air Act. The company responded by installing two massive filters to reduce the plant's nitrogen-oxide emissions. But while American Electric may have appeased the EPA, the residents of nearby Cheshire weren't so lucky. The filters released sulfur trioxide, which, when mixed with the steam coming from the plant's scrubbers, created a blue mist of sulfuric acid that descended upon the town and lingered in the air.

The townspeople started suffering the consequences. There were complaints of burning eyes, headaches, breathing problems, and white sores that covered the lips and tongue. Chunks of grime settled on cars and buildings. A growing number of studies had linked power-plant emissions to lung and heart disease, and the people of Cheshire did not want to be test subjects. When American Electric offered to buy the town for $20 million, most of the townspeople agreed, and the deal was put forth on April 16, 2002.

An Unprecedented Move

It's not surprising that this historic buyout should occur along the Ohio River Valley. The area is one of the greatest producers of power-plant pollution in the United States and hosts 18 coal-burning power plants that supply the Midwest with electricity. In 1999, the Justice Department tried seven of the country's largest power companies in federal court, alleging that they released massive amounts of air pollutants for years.

American Electric would have likely faced heavy litigation as a result of the blue smog. Relocating Cheshire made good business sense—they had the option of switching to low-sulfur, cleaner coal, but that coal is far more costly than the going rate of $20 million for an entire town. Not to mention the fact that Cheshire had become a nuisance to the factory: After burning through the local coal mines, the company needed more space for the daily mass transport of coal brought in from other locations.

In the end, American Electric paid the 90 homeowners of Cheshire three times the value of their houses. Despite the cloud of pollution, most of them moved to nearby towns. Old homes were bulldozed, and what was once a residential neighborhood is now a field of grass surrounded by a handful of unpurchased houses. There has been a smattering of similar cases to Cheshire's, but it's more often the government, not a private company, buying up the town. Cheshire was the first time in national history that a company purchased a town to evade pollution standards.

The Ohio River's Unfortunate Legacy

American Electric Power continues to reduce its pollution output as a result of costly court settlements. Under duress from the Justice Department, the company spent $4.6 billion on antipollution equipment in its coal-powered plants in 2007. The company even had an unexpected showdown with the former residents of Cheshire, who had kept the spirit of their town afloat by expanding Cheshire's boundaries into the nearby towns they had moved to. In 2004, the local group Citizens Against Pollution filed suit against the company demanding cleaner air. The result: An out-of-court settlement requires American Electric to notify nearby residents when the Gavin plant emits more sulfuric acid than normal.

Naturally, residents of the new, expanded Cheshire aren't sure what they should consider "normal." The blue clouds have left, but the smog remains. As American Electric faces increasing antipollution standards, the residents who had their town bought and moved can only hope that when they look out the window, they keep seeing more sunshine than smog.

Slipstreaming for Savings

When the price of gasoline is sky high, everyone looks for ways to save money at the pump. But will opening a truck's tailgate really save fuel? The penny-wise want to know.

✳   ✳   ✳   ✳

WHILE TALKING WITH his pal Phil at the local service station, frugal Frank suggests a way to save money on gas. "When driving our pickup trucks, we should always keep our tailgates down," proclaims the thrifty man. "That way, drag will be reduced and we'll get more miles to the gallon."

Phil glances at his own truck, scratches his head, and says, "Maybe so, but how will I keep my dog from sliding out?"

On paper, opening one's tailgate to save fuel certainly looks plausible. Even a rudimentary understanding of aerodynamics suggests that swirling air trapped in an open box (the truck bed) will introduce drag, thereby increasing fuel consumption. Yet this notion doesn't quite jibe with the facts.

Kind of a Drag

Car companies put a lot of effort into designing their trucks so that air flows just above the tailgate, which will decrease drag. Other efficiency-boosting innovations include "skirts" on the sides of truck trailers and smaller gaps between the truck and trailer. Researcher Kevin Cooper has spent more than 35 years exploring vehicle aerodynamics for Canada's National Research Council, and his studies have shown that an open tailgate often *increases* drag. Here's why:

Backward-facing surfaces create much of a vehicle's drag. When a tailgate is left open or is removed completely, it increases the drag on the back of the truck's cab. The cab has a greater surface area than the tailgate, which erases any potential gains. Furthermore, "gate-droppers" can also experience increased rearward lift at higher speeds. A truly effective way to reduce fuel consumption is to install a tonneau or hard bed cover, which will increase aerodynamics and result in better gas mileage.

Unfortunate Product Names

Ever take a slurp of Pee Cola? Ever wash your clothes with Barf detergent? You can. These two products are just two of the many unfortunately named consumer goods that you can find as you travel around the world.

✳ ✳ ✳ ✳

Sars soda by 2003, the SARS respiratory disease, short for Severe Acute Respiratory Syndrome, had infected more than 8,000 people and caused 774 deaths. The SARS soft drink manufactured by Australian food company Golden Circle has done nothing similar. That doesn't change the fact that SARS is an unfortunate name for a soft drink.

There's a method behind Golden Circle's naming madness. SARS is short for sarsaparilla, a vine plant found mostly in Central America, Mexico, and South America. The soft drink has been around longer than the syndrome. Hopefully, it will outlast it, too.

Ayds If you were trying to lose weight in the late 1970s or early 1980s, you might have given Ayds diet candies a try. Unfortunately, the candy's name sounds exactly like AIDS. As the public became more aware of this disease in the early to mid-1980s, sales of the candies dropped. In 1988, the chairman of Dep Corporation, which was then distributing the dietary candies, announced that the product's name was changing to Diet Ayds. This didn't help, and the product soon disappeared.

You can still find the commercials for the candy scattered about the Internet. Some of the now regrettable taglines include "Thank goodness for Ayds" and "Ayds helps you lose weight."

Pee Cola If you're ever traveling in Ghana, you can take a swig of ice-cold Pee Cola. Of course, it's not what it sounds like; Pee, it turns out, is a rather common last name in the West African country of Ghana.

Maybe you can use Pee Cola to wash down some Shitto, also available in Ghana. Shitto is canned gravy that includes as its ingredients dried pepper, dried shrimp powder, garlic, tomatoes, and dried fish. Nothing goes with a Shitto quite as well as a Pee Cola.

Bad Ad Grab Bag

"Cuisine of India—Nashville's BEST Italian Restaurant."

"Toaster: A gift that every member of the family appreciates. Automatically burns toast."

"Now is your chance to have your ears pierced. Get an extra pair to take home."

"Lost: small apricot poodle. Reward. Neutered. Like one of the family."

"Dog for sale: eats anything and is fond of children."

"Dinner Special—Turkey $2.35; Chicken or Beef $2.25; Children $2.00."

"Human Skull, Used once only. Not plastic. $200 OBO Dr. Scott Tyler."

"Thanks to my DENTIST…I'm wearing my favorite jeans again!"

"1995 Nissan Maxima, green, leather, loaded, CD, auto start, sunroof, 4-door, good condition, $4500. Not for sale."

"China Cabinet, buffet, hutch solid pine, 6.5-foot tall by 4.5-foot wide, lighted windows, few cat scratches but cat has been killed. $700."

"For Sale—collection of old people."

"AS ADVERTISED—Shurfresh Whole Peeled Baby—2LB $1.69."

"Oscar Mayer Bilingual Turkey Franks 3 for $4."

"Amazing Smashing Wig Sale. A Beautiful Blend of Human & European Hair."

"Family Pride Cleaner—Tailoring—Mammograms—Shoe Repair"

"One of the greatest gifts you'll ever give your family may be your funeral."

Professional Nose

Talk to the expert! Not too many jobs are named for a body part. But if you're a professional nose, your schnoz could make a bloodhound envious.

Q: So, take a sniff.

A: You needn't ask, because it's what I do naturally. You are wearing Lancôme's dependable Poême, which features poppy and datur, along with notes of vanilla and rose. It's a totally reliable and affordable fragrance. It complements your body chemistry, and, thankfully, the pasta alfredo you had for lunch

doesn't ruin it. Oh, and pardon my unsolicited advice, but, on you, the fragrance isn't really appropriate for everyday wear. It would be much better as an accompaniment or would work a lot better with evening wear.

Q: How in the world do you know what scent I have on?

A: I'm a nose. I create perfumes, colognes, and fragrances of every kind. If I were unable tell you what you were wearing, it would be like a carpenter who can't pound a nail straight, or a chef with a dull sense of taste.

Q: Do you have a background in chemistry?

A: I attended the Sorbonne, just like Madame Curie. But that was only the beginning. I am gifted, or sometimes afflicted, with an outstanding sense of smell. I can identify nearly any scent while blindfolded, and if you mix scents, I can sort them out and tell you how much of each there is.

Q: How long did it take you to become a full perfumière?

A: After college, I worked for six years as an apprentice. In that time, I learned the essential ideas and procedures of fragrance design from the experts. My professional advancement now depends entirely on the commercial success of my fragrances.

From Addiction to Art

With a little creativity, a North Carolina-based artist turned a machine designed for feeding nicotine addictions into a high-tech dispenser of art: The Art-o-mat.

✳   ✳   ✳   ✳

Crinkling Inspiration

I T WAS THE sound of cellophane that first struck artist Clark Whittington with inspiration. Watching a friend's reaction and interest upon hearing the crinkling material, Whittington realized that a simple wrapper could grab attention. With that in mind, Whittington prepared for a 1997 art show at a local café by wrapping his black-and-white photographs in cellophane. As an added kick, he sold them at a dollar each out of a recently banned cigarette vending machine.

The gimmick was such a hit that the café owner decided to keep the machine permanently. Whittington recruited other artists to help stock its slots, and from there, a cultural phenomenon was born.

Widespread Sensation

There are currently more than 80 Art-o-mat machines scattered across 25 U.S. states, and others in Quebec, Canada, and Vienna, Austria. Whittington oversees each one, making sure every Art-o-mat vending machine is functional and well stocked. And what stock! Hundreds of artists from around the world contribute their small creations to be sold in the Art-o-mat. Pieces range from photos and earrings to screen prints and miniature watercolor paintings.

Micro Economics

Some of the machines sell thousands of items each year, which is no surprise when the price is kept low: With the pull of a knob, most of the works are available for as little as $5 to $7. The proceeds are split between Art-o-mat, the artist, and sometimes the venue.

It's not every day you see a deadly habit turn into a culture-maven creation, but the Art-o-mat has accomplished the unlikely transformation—no small task, indeed.

SkyMall: The United States' Oddest Shopping Mall

Need a butler robot? (Who doesn't?!) How about an indoor doggie bathroom or a singing Christmas tree? Everything you ever wanted but totally don't need can be found in the SkyMall catalog. Here's a sampling of what you've been missing.

✳ ✳ ✳ ✳

Interior Dog Restroom: This rather disturbing product looks like a rectangular patch of grass. But when you lift the grass covering, you realize that this green isn't for putting: There's a collecting tray underneath. Dogs "use" the grass indoors when their owners just can't get them outside.

Kitty Washroom Cabinet: The people at *SkyMall* don't discriminate against cats, either. The washroom cabinet resembles a big white box covered in wainscoting. This rather pleasant-looking piece of furniture, though, hides a stinky secret: Inside, owners can discretely hide their kitty's litter box.

Branding Irons: Want to make sure that everyone knows it was you who barbecued that steak or charbroiled that burger? Purchase your own set of personalized branding irons to scorch your initials in the chicken thigh you just burned.

Richard the Lionhearted Throne: The folks at *SkyMall* seem to be obsessed with the bathroom. If your plain toilet seat just isn't exciting enough, you can order the Richard the Lionhearted toilet seat. This commode capper comes inlaid with three regal lions against a rich blue background.

Unfortunately, once you buy this throne, you're stuck with it. *SkyMall* won't accept returns "due to the nature of this product."

Testing the Waters

Future visitors to Poseidon Resorts will dive into a whole new vacation experience.

✳ ✳ ✳ ✳

Living Underwater

WHETHER WALKING ON the moon or summiting Himalayan peaks, humans have a history of wanting to visit places largely inaccessible to them. Now there's a wave of interest in underwater living.

In the 1960s, Jacques Cousteau conducted research into this sort of living by building various Conshelf (Continental Shelf Station) habitats under the sea.

Conshelf II was the first habitat on the sea floor, inhabited for 30 days by a group of "oceanauts." They breathed a combination of oxygen and helium, and their research provided useful information about human physiology underwater.

A Bubble with a View

So where do people go if they just want to eat fine meals and admire undersea coral gardens? Well, in the 21st century, they take a trip to Poseidon Resorts, the world's first seafloor resort off Poseidon Mystery Island, a private island in Fiji. Accessible by yacht or the resort's twin-engine aircraft, the projected getaway is located within a coral atoll (a ring-shape coral reef) 40 feet underwater.

Visitors will take an elevator down to the futuristic-looking hotel. The resort will feature the world's largest undersea restaurant and lounge and a series of undersea suites. Besides the usual hotel features—bed, bath, TV—each suite will be surrounded in thick transparent acrylic plastic, so as to provide stunning views of the ocean life surrounding them. The hotel is situated near a reef teeming with life because, according to the resort's official Web site, "No one wants to look out on open ocean and peer into water with poor visibility." (So true.) Poseidon Resorts even advertises that guests will be able to push a button from their "control console" to feed the fish outside.

Sound fishy? Only time will tell if Poseidon Resorts will make a splash as a new sort of luxury destination.

Still More Curious Classifieds

* Fur coats made for ladies from their own skin.

* Sheer stockings. Designed for fancy dress, but so serviceable that lots of women wear nothing else.

* We will oil your sewing machine and adjust tension in your home for $1.00.

* Don't stand there and be hungry… come in and get fed up.

* GE Automatic Blanket—insure sound sleep with an Authorized GE Dealer.

* Open house—Body Shapers Toning Salon—free coffee & donuts

* Rabbit fur coat, size medium, $45. Small hutch, $55.

* Golden, ripe, boneless bananas, 39 cents a pound.

* Get rid of aunts: Zap does the job in 24 hours.

* Semi-Annual after-Christmas Sale

* Mother's helper—peasant working conditions.

* Found: dirty white dog… looks like a rat… been out awhile… Better be a reward.

Taste the Magic

Whether the real magic of Voodoo Doughnuts is in the doughnuts, the decor or the delightful marketing strategy really doesn't matter. Voodoo Doughnuts is wildly successful—and magically delicious.

* * * *

BEST-FRIENDS-FOREVER, TRES SHANNON and Kenneth "Cat Daddy" Pogson always knew they wanted to start a business together. And the fact that neither of them had ever made a doughnut in their life didn't stop them from setting up a doughnut shop in Portland, Oregon's Old Town in 2003. The rest is history.

Originally the duo worked all day baking the doughnuts and were open for business from 10:00 P.M. until 10:00 A.M.—just when hungry bar patrons were looking for a cheap treat. Soon people were lined up for an hour and a half to get a bite.

What's more, Voodoo Doughnuts was getting airtime on the likes of Jay Leno and the Travel Channel.

Wanting to offer something out of the ordinary, the pair created deliciously edible novelty items. The signature doughnut is a chocolate doughnut shaped like a voodoo doll, complete with a head, two arms, two eyes and an open mouth. A pretzel serves as the voodoo "pin" and when customers take a bite, red jelly "blood" oozes out.

In another nod to the magical, mystical nature of the business, Voodoo Doughnuts is proud to serve the "official" doughnut of Portland—the Portland Cream. It's a cream-filled doughnut with two eyeballs, symbolizing the vision of the city.

At Voodoo, you'll find doughnuts with cereal on top and doughnuts that are "R" rated. But the customer favorite? It's still the maple and bacon bar.

And for doughnut-loving lovers, why not book the Voodoo for your wedding? Both owners are ordained ministers and they offer a wedding package complete with a doughnut and coffee reception. It's magical.

The World's Most Expensive Foods

Food is one of the basic needs that all living things have in common. But all foods are not created equal, especially in terms of price, as the following list illustrates.

✳   ✳   ✳   ✳

1. **Hamburger:** At $99, the Double Truffle Hamburger at DB Bistro Moderne in Manhattan gives new meaning to the term whopper. The burger contains three ounces of rib meat mixed with truffles and foie gras stuffed inside seven ounces of sirloin steak and served on a Parmesan and poppy seed bun, with salad and truffle shavings. For penny-pinchers, the Single Truffle version is a mere $59.

2. **Caviar:** The world's most expensive caviar is a type of Iranian beluga called Almas. Pale amber in color, it comes from sturgeons that are between 60 and 100 years old, and a 3.9-pound container will set you back $48,750.

3. **Pie:** In 2006, a chef in northwestern England created the world's most expensive pie. Based on a traditional steak and mushroom pie, the dish includes $1,000 worth of Wagyu beef fillet, $3,330 in Chinese matsutake mushrooms (which are so rare that they are grown under the watchful eyes of armed guards), two bottles of 1982 Chateau Mouton Rothschild at a cost of about $4,200 each, as well as black truffles and gold leaf. The pie serves eight with a total cost around $15,900, or $1,990 per slice, which includes a glass of champagne.

4. **Bread:** Forget Poilâne's famous French sourdough at $19.50 a loaf. In 1994, Diane Duyser of Florida noticed that the toasted sandwich she was eating appeared to contain an image of the Virgin Mary. She kept it for ten years (it never went moldy), before selling it to Canadian casino Goldenpalace.com for $28,000 in 2004.

5. **Ice Cream Sundae:** At $1,000, the Grand Opulence Sundae at New York's Serendipity 3 certainly lives up to its name. Made from Tahitian vanilla bean ice cream covered in 23-karat edible gold leaf and drizzled with Amedei Porcelana, the world's most expensive chocolate, this indulgence is studded with gold dragées and truffles and topped with dessert caviar.

6. **Pizza:** At $1,000 a pie (or $125 a slice), the Luxury Pizza, a 12-inch thin crust, is the creation of Nino Selimaj, owner of Nino's Bellissima in Manhattan. To order this extravagant pizza, call 24 hours in advance because it is covered with six different types of caviar that need to be specially ordered. The pie is also topped with lobster, crème fraîche, and chives.

7. **Boxed Chocolates:** At $2,600 per pound, Chocopologie by Knipschildt Chocolatier of Connecticut, is the world's most expensive box of chocolates. The Chocolatier, opened in 1999 by Danish chef Fritz Knipschildt, also sells a decadent dark chocolate truffle with a French black truffle inside for a mere $250.

8. **Sandwich:** Since the 19th century, the club sandwich has been a restaurant staple. But thanks to English chef James Parkinson, the von Essen Platinum club sandwich at the Cliveden House Hotel near London is also the world's most expensive sandwich at $197. Weighing just over a pound, the sandwich is made of the finest ingredients, including Iberico ham cured for 30 months, quail eggs, white truffles, and 24-hour fermented sourdough bread.

9. **Omelette:** For $1,000, this gigantic concoction comes stacked with caviar and an entire lobster encased within its eggy folds. Still, one might expect a seafood fork made of platinum and a few precious stones within to justify the price of a few eggs (albeit with a few added trappings). Nicknamed "The Zillion Dollar Lobster Frittata," the world's most "egg-spensive" omelette is the objet d'art of chef Emilio Castillo of Norma's restaurant in New York's Le Parker Meridien Hotel. A smaller version is also available for $100.

10. **Spice:** Saffron, the most expensive spice in the world, has sold in recent years for as much as $2,700 per pound! The price tag is so high because saffron must be harvested by hand and it takes more than 75,000 threads or filaments of the crocus flower to equal one pound of the spice! Most saffron comes from Iran, Turkey, India, Morocco, Spain, and Greece. Prices vary depending on the quality and the amount, but high quality saffron has been known to go for as much as $15 per gram (0.035 ounces).

Haunting Up Cash

Every October, thousands of haunted attractions spring up across North America. For the price of admission, you get thrilled, chilled, and utterly spooked—and the organizers rake in the profits.

❋ ❋ ❋ ❋

Will Scare for Donations

A ROUND 2,000 HAUNTED attractions are produced in the United States every year. Ticket sales, vendors, construction costs, decorations, and other supplies make this approximately a $500 million industry, which isn't bad for a business model that offers its product for just one month a year. The scope of the haunted attraction industry has become extremely impressive as well: Haunted houses today look very different than they used to.

Many haunted attractions were originally staged for charitable causes. Decades ago, nonprofit groups often organized "haunted houses" to raise money for sick kids or needy folks in the community. (One Jaycees chapter in Durham, North Carolina, celebrated its 38th haunted house in 2010; in recent years, it has annually raised more than $10,000 for charity.)

Many groups that create haunted attractions still give at least a portion of their proceeds to charity, but over time, "scare houses" have become actual businesses run by companies that focus solely on entertainment value . . . and profits. To get people in the door, haunted houses have gotten scarier and more complex; staging them takes a lot of creativity, time, and money.

Freak-You-Out Economics

The initial investment needed to launch a successful haunted attraction can be around $250,000. This may sound like a lot, but the designers, carpenters, performers, safety teams, cleaning crews, and Web and marketing professionals needed to create a blockbuster haunted attraction all cost money. Many of the necessary props and costumes are specialty items that far exceed most people's budgets, which is why those who wish to run a successful haunted house typically pursue loans and capital investments.

The good news is that at around $15 (or more) per head, several hundred people lining up to move through your haunted house each night during the month of October makes it likely that you'll turn a hefty profit. To attract enough people, some proprietors enlist the help of metal bands and freak-show-style performers on opening night. For example, Marilyn Manson was once booked by a fright house in New Orleans that wanted to bring in its biggest crowd ever.

Cashing In on the Ghosts

If you're interested in the business of scaring people silly, plenty of Web resources are available. You can also attend the Midwest Haunters Convention, which is held each June. Annually, around 2,000 people attend this event to gather industry information, stay abreast of the latest trends, and make contact with vendors that sell everything from fake bloody limbs to dead-bride costumes.

Consumers are increasingly critical of those who try to earn their spending money, so proprietors of haunted attractions have their work cut out for them. Competition can be fierce: Haunts such as the Haunted Hoochie in Pataskala, Ohio, spans some 40 acres, and in 2010, the Lewisburg Haunted Cave in Lewisburg, Ohio, set a Guinness World Record for "Longest Walk-Through Horror House," boasting 3,564 linear feet of fright.

These days, it's typical for haunted attractions to reach 40,000 square feet or more—Canton, Ohio's Factory of Terror spans some 55,000 square feet—so make sure that you've got plenty of space. Those who love the haunted attraction experience are willing to travel to find the cream of the crop, so the scarier and more realistic, the better.

Unless, of course, it's *too* scary: In 2000, a woman filed a lawsuit against Universal Studios in Orlando, Florida, claiming that its annual Halloween Horror Nights attraction was so terrifying that she suffered emotional damage as a result; the outcome of her suit is unknown.

One Last Round of Classified Fun

* Teeth extracted by the latest Methodists.

* It takes many ingredients to make our burgers great but..."The secret ingredient is our people."

* Widows made to order. Send us your specifications.

* Tattoos...While you wait

* For you alone! The bridal bed set...

* Braille dictionary for sale. Must see to appreciate!

* Attorney at law; 10% off free consultation

* For rent: 6-room hated apartment

* The fact that those we have served return once again, and recommend us to their friends, is a high endorsement of the service we render. Village Funeral Home.

* LOST DIAPER BAG: With very sentimental items. In Taco Bell parking lot.

* "I love you only" Valentine cards: Now available in packs.

Weird Coffins

Over the years, people have gone to strange lengths to care for their buried bodies after death. Perhaps you're interested in being six feet under alongside your favorite band?

❋ ❋ ❋ ❋

Morbid Merchandise

OVER THEIR FOUR-DECADE career, the rock band Kiss has marketed thousands of products bearing their logo and faces. Since their first wave of popularity in the 1970s, they've marketed T-shirts, toys, makeup, costumes, books, and many other items, up to and including comic books that were printed using the band members' actual blood in 1977. (Each member of the band donated a vial of blood to add to the red ink.)

The "blood" comic held the mantle of "most morbid Kiss product" for nearly a quarter century, but in 2001, that particular title was usurped by a new product: the Kiss Kaske, an actual coffin emblazoned with a mural depicting the band's iconic logo and painted faces. For those fans who bought the coffin without plans to die anytime soon, it was waterproof and could double as an oversized cooler. Standard models went for $4,500, and autographed versions cost an extra $500.

But Kiss wasn't the first party to market a unique coffin. The last couple of centuries have seen countless models that go well beyond the simple "pine box."

Designed for Life After Death

In the 19th century, many people were terrified of being buried alive. Stories of it happening abounded, and they weren't all myths. In one cemetery that was moved to a new location, workers on the scene estimated that about 1% of the bodies showed signs of having tried to escape. Who can imagine anything more grim that waking up from a coma and finding oneself buried alive?

Such fears were far more common in the days before embalming made it a reasonably sure thing that everyone was dead before they left the funeral home—and nothing sells a product like fear. Many different coffins with escape mechanisms were patented in the 19th century. The most famous of these was probably Franz Vester's "security coffin." Introduced in 1868, this coffin was fitted with a large hollow cylinder and ladder, so that people buried alive could climb back out if necessary. The cylinder was removable, so that after an appropriate amount of time, it could be removed and reused. The original coffin could then be buried completely.

In the event that the not-quite-dead person woke up in the Vester coffin but didn't have the strength to climb out, there was also a bell attached to a string tied to the corpse's finger; if a person woke from a coma and started to move, the bell would begin to ring. Urban legends claim that this is where the phrases "dead ringer" and "saved by the bell" came from. No one is known to have been saved from premature burial by Vester's coffin, or by any of the similar models patented at the time, but one has to wonder if any bodies jerking from the escape of decomposition gasses caused any panics in the graveyard!

Invasion of the Body Snatchers

Even more pressing than the fear of being buried alive was the fear of having one's body stolen—a situation far more common than premature interment. Grave robbing was a very common problem in the 19th century, when every medical school had determined that it was impossible to train new doctors properly without giving them dead bodies from which they could learn the finer points of anatomy, and on which they could practice surgery without disastrous consequences in the event of a mistake.

Almost no one donated their body to science at the time, so schools had to rely on the services of "Resurrection Men" who stole bodies from graveyards for a fee. At times of peak demand, a grave robber could get as much money for a single fresh corpse as he or she would earn in a month of working in the coal mines.

Fear of having one's own body stolen led to an eager market for "burglar-proof" coffins and tombs. In 1818 a London candle maker named Edward Bridgman began to market a device simply known as the Patent Coffin. It was made of iron—too heavy to drag out of the grave and harder to saw through than a wooden coffin—and loaded with spring catches that made the lid impossible to open. The coffins were a big hit with the public. However, churches were resistant to them, as burials were still generally done in small churchyards at the time, and the churches depended on coffins to rot away quickly in order to make room for new bodies!

The threat of the "Resurrection Man" remained a constant fear for the rest of the century, and products continued to be marketed in later years, especially when more spacious "garden" cemeteries (in which everyone got their own plot) became common and the need for space in churchyards was less of a concern. In 1878, an Ohio watchmaker named Thomas Howell patented the "Grave Torpedo," a small bomb that would blow any would-be grave robbers to bits if the coffin was disturbed. (Of course, this would probably blow up your remains, as well, but at least you'd take the grave robber with you.) A newspaper ad for the device read, "SLEEP WELL, SWEET ANGEL! Let no fears of ghouls disturb thy rest, for above thy shrouded form lies a torpedo ready to make mincemeat of anyone who attempts to convey you to the pickling vat."

The most successful of these fancy coffins was designed not to protect bodies from robbers, but to protect them from decay. First sold in the 1850s, the Fisk Metallic Burial Case was designed mainly to cash in on the Ancient Egypt craze that was sweeping the United States at the time. The Fisk coffins were as ornate as a pharaoh's sarcophagus, made of elaborately carved metal, and featured a viewing window over the face. They were hugely popular, and the company received a letter of endorsement signed by several United States senators, including Jefferson Davis, the future president of the Confederate States of America.

Buyers of these caskets—which cost $100, a fortune at the time—surely believed that their remains would be preserved forever. And some of them got what they paid for. A Fisk coffin exhumed from an abandoned graveyard in Chicago in 1998 contained a man who was almost perfectly preserved—until the excavating machine chopped through his feet. But another, exhumed from a tomb in Milledgeville, Georgia, contained a body found to be in an advanced state of decay.

Let the buyer beware!

Quotables

"That the automobile has practically reached the limit of its development is suggested by the fact that during the past year no improvements of a radical nature have been introduced."

—SCIENTIFIC AMERICAN, JANUARY 1909

"So we went to Atari and said, 'Hey, we've got this amazing thing, even built with some of your parts, and what do you think about funding us? Or we'll give it to you. We just want to do it. Pay our salary, we'll come work for you.' And they said, 'No.' So then we went to Hewlett-Packard, and they said, 'Hey, we don't need you. You haven't got through college yet.'"

—APPLE FOUNDER STEVE JOBS, ON TRYING TO PITCH HIS IDEA OF A PERSONAL COMPUTER

Chapter 4

Arts, Entertainment, and Culture

Three Men, a Baby, and a Ghost

Pause your copy of the comedy hit Three Men and a Baby *in just the right spot, and you'll spot the ghost of a boy who committed suicide in the apartment where the movie was filmed. A scary, story but is it true?*

※ ※ ※ ※

ALTHOUGH THERE IS nothing supernatural about the movie *Three Men and a Baby*—beyond, perhaps, how it managed to gross more than any other movie in 1987—rumors persist that it was the first to capture a bonafide ghost on film. As with similar movie myths, the rumor about *Three Men and a Baby* began when the film was released on home video. In one scene, Ted Danson's character, Jack, paces around the apartment he shares with his two roommates, played by Tom Selleck and Steve Guttenberg. Pause at the right moment, and in the background of the shot you'll see the ghostly image of a boy in a window. Pause at a later point in the scene, and the boy has been replaced by the image of what looks like a rifle. According to rumors, a nine-year-old boy committed suicide with a shotgun in the apartment before it was used as a set in the movie.

Fortunately, the real explanation is far more mundane. There was no haunted apartment. The interior scenes of the movie were shot on a set that was built on a soundstage. In the movie, the Jack character is an actor, and an earlier scene features a cardboard-cutout prop of him from a film in which he had recently starred. If you look carefully at the "ghost boy" and the alleged rifle, you'll see that they are simply different shots of that cutout.

Behind the Films of Our Time

* John Wayne died in seven movies: *Reap the Wild Wind, The Fighting Seabees, Wake of the Red Witch, Sands of Iwo Jima, The Alamo, The Cowboys,* and *The Shootist.*

* *King Kong,* filmed in 1933, has a handful of scenes never seen by most. One features the gorilla taking off actress Fay Wray's clothes. Another involves Kong shaking a group of sailors off a bridge and into a spider-infested valley. The producer said the scene was so disturbing to the preview audience that he decided to remove it the next day.

* A chariot scene in the historical epic *Ben-Hur* has a small red car moving through the background.

* Film execs removed one song from the final cut of *The Wizard of Oz:* "The Jitterbug." In the sequence, Dorothy and her friends were attacked by "jitterbugs" on their way to the witch's castle. Even though the song took five weeks and $80,000 worth of effects to create, MGM worried the reference could make the movie seem dated because of the similarly named "jitterbug" dance that was popular that year.

* Liza Minelli, daughter of Judy Garland *(The Wizard of Oz's* Dorothy), ended up marrying Jack Haley Jr., whose father played the film's Tin Man.

* The movie *Clue* was created with three endings; viewers saw different ones depending on where they saw the film. The endings were randomly selected for movie theaters across America. The DVD, however, features all three.

Watt an Accomplishment: Obsessive Art in Los Angeles

What is nearly 100 feet tall, is comprised of 17 pieces, was decorated mostly from recycled materials, can withstand a force equivalent to nearly 80 mile-per-hour winds, and lives in Los Angeles? No, it's not some computer-generated monster starring in the latest summer blockbuster: It's Watts Towers, the strange but oddly attractive creation of an Italian immigrant who became a bit obsessed with an extracurricular art project.

✳   ✳   ✳   ✳

Buon Giorno, Signor Rodia

BORN IN SOUTHERN Italy in 1879, Simon Rodia immigrated to the United States with his older brother in the mid-1890s. The boys settled on the East Coast, where they worked various jobs in coalfields, rock quarries, and railroad camps. When his brother was killed in a jobsite accident, Rodia relocated to Seattle, where he met his wife and started a family before moving to Watts, a section of Los Angeles. Soon after, Rodia began an art project in his backyard to pay tribute to his adopted country. It would take him 33 years to complete.

The Towers

Rodia had been trained as a tile-layer, not as a carpenter or an engineer, so when he decided to build super tall towers on his modest one-tenth of an acre plot, he had to get creative. By tying beams together with chicken wire and scaling the sides of the towers (which were glued together with cement) as he built them, he got the job done. The steel pipes and rods, wire mesh, and crude mortar used for support might have been primitive and rather unorthodox, but they worked for Rodia.

As he built the structure, he decorated it. Way before "going green" was cool, Rodia chose to recycle old materials to adorn his edifice. By pressing broken dishes, glass, ceramic bits, and other shiny stuff into the concrete, he created a mosaic over every inch of Watts Towers—he even inlaid the floor. The multicolored chips form hearts, Rodia's initials, the dates 1921 and 1923 (the years his children were born), and flowers, but most of the tiles create swirls of random, free-form designs.

When he stepped off the final tower and declared he was finished, Rodia was 75 years old. Unfortunately, a general lack of understanding had plagued the structures for some time. During the 1930s and 1940s, rumors had spread that the towers were transmitting signals to the Communists and the Japanese. Annoyed by government officials and disheartened by a steady stream of vandals, Rodia signed the property over to his neighbor and friend, Louis H. Saucedo, and left town in the mid-1950s.

Trouble in Cement Paradise

Though the Watts Towers had survived numerous earthquakes throughout the years, in 1959, the city of Los Angeles threatened to raze the structures on account of them being an "unauthorized public hazard." Public outcry demanded that the towers be tested before being demolished, and the city agreed. More than a thousand people watched as 10,000 pounds of force were applied to the tallest tower. Ironically, the testing apparatus itself bent from the force, but the tower withstood the pressure just fine. The towers were reopened a year later and soon the Los Angeles community felt a sense of pride toward their unique landmark.

In 1978, the land on which the Watts Towers stood was deeded to the state of California, and the structures underwent extensive repair for seven years. After that, the towers were named a national historic landmark and were later named an official California State Park. Today, the towers are visited by thousands of people every year who enjoy the bizarre but fascinating work of the Italian-American folk artist.

The Multimillion-Dollar Manhattan Mystery

When a family hired an architect to design their new 4,200-square-foot apartment, they had no idea what they'd gotten themselves into.

✳ ✳ ✳ ✳

IN 2003, THE Klinsky family decided they wanted their recently purchased Manhattan home to be unique. It was an understandable request; after all, they paid $8.5 million for the place. So when the family found architect Eric Clough and heard his impressive vision, they immediately hired him.

Of course, what they didn't know then was that they'd heard only half of Clough's plan for their home—and that the other half wouldn't be discovered until months after they'd moved in.

The Conception

Clough says it all started when Mr. Klinsky handed him a poem he'd written and asked to have it put into a bottle and hidden behind a wall as a sort of time capsule for his family. The concept gave Clough the idea that would eventually make national news: He would set out to create a complex mystery built into the apartment, complete with clues that would take the family on a fictional journey through time. He laboriously researched ciphers and codes, secret compartments, and contraptions and spent years creating his most majestic design.

The Discovery

Fast forward to May 2006. The Klinsky family (including mom, dad, four children, and a dog) moved into their apartment. They were pleased with the results; everything looked great and seemed normal. Well, it did for about four months.

The first mystery was discovered when one of the sons and a friend were playing in his bedroom. The boy was looking intently at the room's radiator when he noticed letters carved into the grille. Somehow, the child realized they were in a code. Decoded, the words spelled the son's name.

Several more unusual events unfolded, all with Clough refusing to give any explanation. Finally, the family received a cryptic letter with a poem directing them to a hidden panel. That's when the true scavenger hunt began.

The First Clue

Inside the panel, the family found a book that Clough had custom-written and bound. Clue by clue, the story took them through trap doors and hidden compartments within their own home, producing a complex web that took weeks to unravel.

Eighteen difficult clues later, the mystery led them to a set of hallway panels. The Klinskys had to take off two decorative doorknockers and form them together to make a crank. In turn, that crank opened hidden panels in a dining room cabinet that contained another series of keys and keyholes. Once the family figured out what keys matched with what holes, they discovered a set of drawers with a crossword puzzle. The puzzle led to more hidden panels in another room, which led to a magnet, which opened more hidden panels, which contained—at long last—the original poem the father had asked Clough to hide.

The Process

This intense mystery spared no expense. Clough's fee for the renovation was more than $1.2 million—a number he says didn't even begin to cover the project's cost. While the renovation itself took about a year and a half, the creation of the unusual scavenger hunt took a full four years. Clough says he ate most of the overhead, and he had a few dozen friends who volunteered their time.

Paramount Pictures bought the rights to the story of the Klinsky mystery apartment. They, in collaboration with J.J. Abrams, are working o develop a film based on the story.

Behind the Music of Our Time

✳ Bruce Springsteen's 1984 album *Born in the U.S.A.* was, rather fittingly, the first compact disc ever made in the United States.

✳ The name Mony in the song "Mony Mony"—first recorded by Tommy James and the Shondells in 1968 and made famous again by Billy Idol in 1987—actually comes from the name of a New York bank. James was staying in a hotel across from the Mutual of New York (MONY) bank and says he saw the acronym flashing on and off from his window.

✳ Janet Jackson apparently has a tattoo said to show Mickey and Minnie Mouse having sex—though you'd have to view Ms. Jackson in the buff to be able to see it.

✳ Buddy Holly's real name was Charles "Buddy" Holley. Decca Records misspelled his last name on his original recording contract, and he decided just to stick with the e-free version.

✳ A printing mistake also led to Dionne Warwick's last name: The diva was Dionne Warrick until her first single, "Don't Make Me Over," came out with a typo. She also opted to stick with the altered alias.

✳ Singer and pianist Tori Amos was expelled from the prestigious Peabody Conservatory music school in Baltimore when she was 11 years old. Apparently she hated to read sheet music.

✳ The beach hit "Wipe Out" was written on a lark. The Surfaris needed a quick ditty to fill the b-side of their "Surfer Joe" single. "Joe" didn't make much of a dent, but "Wipe Out" became a surfer standard.

✳ Depeche Mode was originally named Composition of Sound.

✳ The band Chicago was first called Big Thing.

✳ The Beach Boys' original band name was Carl and the Passions.

✳ Simon and Garfunkel first formed under the name Tom and Jerry, after the cartoon characters.

✳ Lynyrd Skynyrd initially called themselves My Backyard before settling on their now-famous moniker.

Memorable Sales of Movie Memorabilia

Hollywood is full of history, and plenty of people want to own a piece of it. So how much would you pay for a famous prop from your favorite film? Here are some of the most noteworthy sales of movie memorabilia.

✳ ✳ ✳ ✳

Costly Cane—The bamboo cane Charlie Chaplin used in his 1936 flick *Modern Times* managed to hook in $91,800 at a 2004 memorabilia auction.

A Piece of Charlie—Chaplin's cane wasn't the only thing on the auction block. Two fake mustaches Chaplin wore in *The Great Dictator* (1940) drew $23,000 and $34,300 at the same sale.

Pricey Piano—The piano played in the Paris scenes of *Casablanca* sold to the tune of $154,000 in 1988. Donald Trump tried to get the instrument, but was outbid.

Bond Book—In 2008, an autographed edition of Ian Fleming's *You Only Live Twice* sold for $84,000 at auction. The book was inscribed by Fleming to the real James Bond, the American bird expert after whom the character was supposedly named.

Bond Buggy—James Bond is known for his cool cars, so it's no surprise that Planet Hollywood was willing to shell out $45,900 in 2004 for a moon buggy used in *Diamonds Are Forever* (1971).

Bigger Bond Purchase—The 1965 Aston Martin DB5 driven by Sean Connery in *Goldfinger* (1964) sold for just over $2 million in 2006. The word is rich. Very rich.

Snazzy Sled—The famous sled from Orson Welles's *Citizen Kane* (1941) is now in the hands of Steven Spielberg, who bought the prop for $60,500 back in 1982.

Conceptual Kane—Some papers described as "concept art" for the mansion in *Citizen Kane* (1941) sold for $16,100 at a 2003 auction.

Spinner Sale—The flying "Spinner" vehicle from *Blade Runner* (1982) spun its way up to the price of $63,250 when it was on the auction block in 2003.

Expensive Leather—In 2008, Hugh Jackman's black leather Wolverine battle suit from *X-Men* (2000) proved worthy of his "sexiest man alive" title. The get-up grabbed $90,000 from a fan.

Raiders Ride—An imitation German car used in the *Indiana Jones* film *Raiders of the Lost Ark* (1981) fetched an impressive $72,000 in 2008.

Whoa, Wilson—The friendly volleyball that kept Tom Hanks company in *Cast Away* (2000) cost quite a bit. One of the three balls used in the film scored a whopping $18,400 in a 2001 online auction, and it now sits in the office of Ken May, CEO of Fed Ex/Kinko's.

Invisible Suit—The "invisible suit" worn by Claude Rains in the 1933 horror film *The Invisible Man* went for a very visible $34,000 when it sold in 2003.

Fancy Hat—An original helmet worn by C-3PO in *Return of the Jedi* (1983) capped off a 2008 memorabilia auction with a price tag of $120,000.

Light Saber Liquidation—Luke Skywalker slashed his way past C-3PO's mark with the light saber he used in the original *Star Wars* (1977) and in *The Empire Strikes Back* (1980). In 2005, the prop sold for $240,000.

Darth Vader Disappointment—Turns out the bad guy couldn't top the Jedi at auction. In 2003, Darth Vader's original Lord of the Sith helmet sold for $80,500—merely a third of the final bid for Skywalker's light saber.

Small Sub—In 2003, a miniature of the *Seaview* submarine from *Voyage to the Bottom of the Sea* (1961) went for $54,625.

Flash Merchandise—A rare poster from the 1936 film *Flash Gordon* brought in $43,125 at auction in 2003.

Loud Outfit—In 2001, the flashy yellow suit worn by Jim Carrey in *The Mask* (1994) went for $16,001 in an online auction by New Line Cinema.

Classy Tie—A tie of Cary Grant's—which was reportedly quite worn and moth-eaten—still managed to sell for $700 in a 2001 Sotheby's auction.

Sandler's Socks—It seems Adam Sandler's socks from *Little Nicky* (2000) didn't share the smell of success. They sold for a mere $250 on eBay in 2001.

Pistol Purchase—The pistol used by Bruce Willis in *The Fifth Element* (1997) pulled in $12,650 at an auction in 2003.

Governator's Goods—In 2003, the shotgun used by Arnold Schwarzenegger in *Terminator 2: Judgment Day* (1991) brought in a final selling price of $10,350. However, the jacket he wore in the first *Terminator* (1984) film sold for $41,300.

Forbidden Costume—In 2003, a costume worn by a crew member of the spaceship in the 1956 film *Forbidden Planet* went for the not-so-modest price of $10,925.

Godfather Garb—The famous hat worn by Al Pacino in *The Godfather* (1972) sold for $16,100. An original copy of the script, which was annotated by Marlon Brando, went for $312,800 in 2003—a record-breaking amount for a single movie script.

Humphrey's Hat—A hat described as Humphrey Bogart's "signature fedora" sold for a mere $6,325 in 2003.

A Director's Sweater—Actor-turned-director Ron Howard saw his *Happy Days* sweater sell for $8,050 at a 2003 auction.

Disco Suit—The white polyester suit that John Travolta made famous in *Saturday Night Fever* (1977) sold for $2,000 in 1978. The buyer? Movie critic Gene Siskel. In 1994, the suit was resold for $145,000 at a Christie's auction.

Special Slippers—A rare pair of Dorothy's ruby slippers from *The Wizard of Oz* (1939) were snatched up at a Christie's auction in 2000 for $666,000. The slippers are one of only four pairs known to exist. Another pair is on display at the Smithsonian.

Hollywood Versus History

You may not be surprised to learn that Hollywood doesn't always get history right.

❋　❋　❋　❋

Don't ask us how we know this

AMERICAN PSYCHO (2000)—THOUGH the action takes place in 1992, the porn film glimpsed on Christian Bale's TV set while he chats on the phone with his fiancée is *Red Vibe Diaries: Object of Desire*, which was released in 1997.

The Millard Fillmore monument is so much more camera friendly

The Color of Friendship (2000)—In this story set in 1977, scaffolding used during the 2000 renovation of the Washington Monument is seen.

Say, man, check out that Mathew Brady dude

Glory (1989)—In this Civil War drama about black Union troops, the soldiers speak in the idiom of the 1980s.

But you had to crank it

O Brother, Where Art Thou? (2000)—This film, set in the 1930s, includes the song "You Are My Sunshine," which was not released until 1940.

On his feet and his hands

Tarzan (1999)—One of the apes wears sneakers.

Boy, somebody deserves to be executed for this one

Factory Girl (2006)—Andy Warhol watches an episode of *I Dream of Jeannie* a month before the show's premiere.

Dead silence might have been nice

Dirty Dancing (1987)—Sound track music alternates between period-appropriate pop tunes from the early 1960s and synth-rock.

Göring noticed that, too

They Saved Hitler's Brain (1963)—When Hitler speaks in German, the words are actually gibberish.

Thou shalt not covet thy neighbor's Bulova

The Ten Commandments (1956)—An old man who holds up a "graven image" is wearing a wristwatch.

Mention it and he'll punch your lights out

The Big Brawl (1980)—Although set in the 1930s, the film includes a character wearing a disco-style suit.

No, I'm not wearing earrings, those are my eyeballs

The Aviator (2004)—Howard Hughes flies his 1935 open-cockpit H-1 at 350 mph without goggles.

I guess that means the air bags have to go, too

Driving Miss Daisy (1989)—Styrofoam shows up in more than one scene, years before it was marketed commercially.

And a Wonderbra

Geronimo (1962)—Geronimo's Indian wife wears false eyelashes and eyeshadow.

Don't miss the Elvis mummy

The Mummy (1999)—An early shot of the ancient city of Thebes includes the Pyramids of Giza and the Great Sphinx, which are actually at the old city of Memphis, near Cairo.

We kid because we love you

Kelly's Heroes (1970)—Don Rickles has a box full of Almond Joy candy bars—which weren't introduced until after the war, in 1946.

When you're a pirate, every day is casual Friday

Pirates of the Caribbean: Curse of the Black Pearl (2003)—When Jack yells, "On deck, you scabrous dogs!" a member of the film crew—wearing a cowboy hat and sunglasses—is visible in the background.

Who's That Lady?

The Mona Lisa *has long been the subject of speculation, admiration, and controversy. The portrait has been adored by millions and is possibly worth billions, but who exactly was da Vinci's subject?*

＊　＊　＊　＊

The Mysterious Florentine

FOR CENTURIES, THE identity of the model who posed for Leonardo da Vinci's masterpiece prompted heated debate. There were no records among da Vinci's papers pertaining to the painting, and the artwork itself was unnamed, unsigned, and undated. What's more, the finished portrait was never delivered to the man who commissioned it. Da Vinci started work on his seminal piece in 1503 and kept it in his possession until his death in 1519. For decades, the image was known simply as "a certain Florentine lady," and it wasn't until the historian Giorgio Vasari published a biography of da Vinci's life and work in 1550 that the painting became known as *Mona Lisa*. Vasari claimed the lady in question was Madam Lisa Gherardini del Giocondo, the 24-year-old wife of a wealthy Florentine. But Vasari had acquired a reputation for inaccurate claims in his writings, and so skeptical historians discounted many of his claims.

In the Running

Over the years, half a dozen names were mentioned as possible sitters for da Vinci's greatest work. Some scholars suggested that the muse was Cecilia Gallerani, one of the many mistresses of Ludovico Sforza, Duke of Milan. Gallerani was the subject of da Vinci's *The Lady with an Ermine*, which he completed in 1490. But because her image had already been committed to canvas, most researchers discounted her. Other art analysts believed that the person in the portrait was Isabella of Naples, the granddaughter of King Ferdinand I and daughter of King Alphonse II and his wife, Ippolita Sforza. The rumor mill even generated a story that Isabella and da Vinci were a contracted couple, inked and linked together to produce outstanding offspring. The most vocal supporter of Isabella as da Vinci's subject was historian Maike Vogt-Luerssen, who wrote a book titled *Who Is Mona Lisa? In Search of her Identity*. Vogt-Luerssen's theory was dismissed, primarily because she claimed that the portrait was painted as early as 1489.

Other pretenders to the Mona Lisa throne included Costanza d'Avalos, Duchess of Amalfi and a noted poet, and da Vinci's own mother, Caterina.

And the Winner Is...

Despite such speculation, the truth was right there all along. In 2005, it was ascertained that Vasari's information was accurate. Armin Schlechter, a manuscript expert at the University of Heidelberg, discovered a margin note in a text that was once owned by Agostino Vespucci, a friend and confidante of da Vinci's. The note explains that while da Vinci was working on *The Battle of Anghiari* in the Great Council Hall of the Palazzo Vecchio in Florence, Italy, in 1503, he was also working on a pet project—a portrait of Lisa Gherardini, the wife of a local merchant, Franceso del Giocondo.

Today, we call her Mona Lisa.

Sculptor Jeff Koons

Koons rose to fame and fortune in the 1980s with his use of kitsch imagery and what some believe to be a dark sense of humor. His work is usually classified into either the "Neo-Pop" or "Post-Pop" categories of modern art.

✳ ✳ ✳ ✳

✳ Koons's most famous exhibit comes from his collection of "ready-made" sculptures. *Equilibrium* consists of a collection of basketballs floating at varying levels in several aquariums, accompanied by a set of Nike advertisements painted in oil.

✳ *Puppy* is Koons's 43-foot topiary structure in the shape of a West Highland terrier, erected over a steel frame and covered in multi-colored flowers. *Puppy* was originally exhibited in Germany in 1992 and then went on a well-received world tour. The structure now guards the Guggenheim museum in Bilbao, Spain, where it has come to be a mascot for the city.

✳ Just before the dedication of *Puppy* to the Bilbao Guggenheim, three people attempted to plant explosives-filled flowerpots near the sculpture. They were apprehended by police before any damage was done.

✳ Koons's *Popeye* painting and sculptures were priced from $500,000 to $650,000 in 2004. Prices for sculptures in Koons's epic *Celebration* series started at $1.5 million, and bids went up to $5 million for his massive steel *Balloon Dog*.

✳ As part of a series of works called *Banality*, Koons created a ceramic sculpture in 1988 titled *Michael Jackson and Bubbles*. Painted mostly in metallic gold and white, the sculpture depicts Jackson and his pet chimpanzee in matching outfits.

✳ These days, Koons seldom produces any work himself. He is the self-proclaimed "idea man" and allows his foundry and assistants to create pieces for him.

The "Tenth Muse"

In a literary canon that is almost exclusively male, Sappho, the captivating poet from the Greek island of Lesbos (modern Lesvos) stands out as a female author whose works achieved popular acclaim in antiquity.

✳   ✳   ✳   ✳

ORN AROUND 630 B.C., Sappho belonged to an aristocratic Lesbian family at a time when colonization, the creation of pan-Hellenic festivals (such as the Olympic Games), and the works of Homer (the *Iliad* and *Odyssey*) fueled the growth of a common aristocratic Greek culture. Within this culture, Greek aristocrats used lyric poetry to reflect on politics, values, and personal experience. Sappho's poetry addresses all these issues, but it is most famous for capturing the powerful, poignant—yet playful—sincerity of desire, longing, and affection.

An intriguing and sometimes controversial element of Sappho's poetry is that many poems are directed toward other women. It is, in fact, from these poems that the term "lesbian" was coined in the 19th century to mean "homosexual." However, though Sappho's world fostered intense and even erotic relationships among social peers, the relationships she wrote about would not have neatly corresponded to modern terms.

Despite these ambiguities, and the fact that only one complete Sappho poem survives today, the continued popularity of her poetry remains a testament to its universality and to her talent and insight. Sappho's language and unique meter (which came to be known as "Sapphic stanza") have influenced many other poets and authors since her time. Plato, writing nearly 200 years after her death, called Sappho the "tenth Muse," and writers from the Roman poets Catullus and Horace, to contemporary authors such as Erica Jong and Guy Davenport, have been inspired to evoke her character or poetry in their own work.

Paganini: 19th-Century Rock Star

Centuries before legendary bluesman Robert Johnson allegedly "stood at the crossroads" to sell his soul to the devil in return for uncanny abilities on the guitar, there was classical Genovese violinist Niccolo Paganini. Yet "classical" doesn't quite describe the mass hysteria his prowess provoked.

✳   ✳   ✳   ✳

A CHILD PRODIGY WHO played the mandolin with skill by age 5, Niccolo Paganini (1782–1840) took up the violin at 7 and gave his first public concert at 12. It wasn't long before he outpaced all of his potential teachers, so he began a regimen of his own construction that often ran more than 15 hours a day. Paganini's star soon rose at the royal court of Lucca on the Italian peninsula, with successively impressive appointments by Napoleon's sister, Elisa Baciocchi, Princess of Lucca. The violinist broke with the court soon enough, however, no doubt feeling stifled. By 1813, he had become a national sensation through a series of Milanese shows.

Calling All Groupies...

In 1828, Paganini embarked on a lengthy European tour, making him the first violinist to do so without backup musicians. He also memorized lengthy programs, never referring to sheet music onstage. He would cut the strings of his violin with scissors and perform complicated pieces on the single string that remained. He could tune a string so that it produced supernatural-sounding harmonies. People flocked to his shows, women fainted, and Paganini became a very wealthy man—the 19th-century equivalent of a modern-day rock star.

It was then, as his reputation grew, that some dubbed the master Hexensohn, which means "witch's brat." Whispers speculated that he must have cut a deal with Lucifer, or perhaps was even the son of Satan himself. How else to explain such Pagamania? The artist reveled in the rumors, sometimes inviting his mother to sit onstage, as if daring audience members to challenge his paternity. He took to wearing all black, often hiring a black carriage with four black horses to deliver him to theaters. But even before taking measures to accentuate it, he already presented an otherworldly appearance: Paganini was thin and pale with long black hair, a cadaverous face (major tooth loss) and eyes that rolled up inside his head as he played and swayed. He even had rock-star addictions—alcohol, women, and gambling. In fact, although he commanded the highest fees of any similar performer, he reportedly went bankrupt trying to open his own casino.

Playing to His Strengths

Research shows that Paganini may have had a genetic defect in collagen production now known as Ehlers-Danlos, resulting in joint hypermobility. He is also thought to have had Marfan's syndrome, a disorder of the connective tissue; symptoms include elongated facial features, limbs, and fingers. These disabilities were turned to his advantage: Paganini could play up to three octaves across the fret board without ever having to shift his hand.

Shunned in Death

On May 27, 1840, Paganini died in Nice, in present-day France, from larynx cancer. During his lifetime, he composed 24 caprices, a series of sonatas, and 6 violin concertos. Ironically, the reputation Paganini had so carefully cultivated literally followed him beyond death, with negative consequences. Not receiving final absolution—some say he even refused a priest who could have administered it—he was initially refused a Christian burial by the Catholic Church. Paganini's body was not buried in consecrated ground until five years after his death. One story claims his remains were stored in the family basement; a darker version has his son (by a mistress) traveling around Europe with the corpse until it was granted a decent resting place.

Whatever the case and however snubbed he was in death, the fame and intrigue of mythical proportions surrounding Paganini's life can be summed up in his quote, "I am not handsome, but when women hear me play, they come crawling to my feet."

Hey, it's not boasting if it's true.

Ed Wood: Made in Hollywood, USA

Only in Hollywood, the land of make-believe, could Ed Wood realize his dream of making movies; only in Hollywood could his enthusiasm, drive, and perseverance overcome his lack of cinematic skill. His gift was not in making movies but in persuading people that he could make movies.

✳   ✳   ✳   ✳

EDWARD D. WOOD, Jr., wrote, directed, and produced some of the worst sci-fi and horror films of the 1950s—or any decade. Wood had the uncanny ability to convince people to sink money into his pictures, which often involved writing a new part in the film for the prospective investor.

Background

Born in Poughkeepsie, New York, in 1924, young Wood quickly found his passion. As a boy, he sat enthralled in darkened movie theaters from open to close. Wood's mother, who wanted a daughter rather than a son, often dressed Ed in girls' clothing, which was the genesis of his lifelong habit of crossdressing. He joined the Marines at 17, later claiming to have often worn a bra and panties under his uniform during his World War II tour of duty. After the war, Wood settled in Hollywood to tilt at his own personal windmill.

Movies

Most notable of Wood's films was the 1953 autobiographical fantasy of cross-dressing, *Glen or Glenda?* Wood starred in it himself but used the pseudonym Daniel Davis.

His 1955 *Bride of the Monster* was a typical "mad scientist" flick, complete with laboratory (including, literally rather than proverbially, the kitchen sink) and a giant killer octopus. The octopus had been stolen from a prop warehouse—the only catch was that Wood forgot to pilfer the motor that moved the rubber tentacles, as well. *Night of the Ghouls*, shot in 1958, was a sequel of sorts to *Bride of the Monster*.

Wood's masterpiece, however, was the 1959 epic *Plan 9 from Outer Space*. Starting with a few minutes of silent footage, Wood made a very silly, yet very watchable, sci-fi film. Tagged by many as "the worst movie ever made," the film's appeal stemmed from its intense sincerity. *Plan 9* never *intentionally* winked at the camera—never mind the cardboard tombstones that fell over, the shower curtain that passed for the cockpit of an airplane, or the tiny cemetery crypt that seemed to hold more people than a taxi full of clowns.

An Oddball Acting Troupe

Each of Wood's films featured a unique cast of characters, both on- and off-screen. John "Bunny" Breckenridge was a proud homosexual who dreamed of undergoing permanent gender reassignment. Blonde, beautiful Dolores Fuller was Wood's girlfriend and confidant. White-haired eccentric The Amazing Criswell had startled TV audiences with his incredible (and usually inaccurate) predictions. Kenne Duncan was known in Hollywood as the "meanest man in the movies," and many believed him to be the most lecherous, as well. Buxom, wasp-waisted Maila Nurmi made her mark on LA television by hosting a horror movie show as the gaunt and dark-haired Vampira. Hulking Tor Johnson was a professional wrestler called the "Super Swedish Angel"—his nearly unintelligible Swedish accent (and total lack of acting talent) didn't seem to bother Wood at all.

Most amazing of Wood's troupe, however, was the aging, frail Bela Lugosi. A huge theater star in Europe and a hit on

Broadway in the late 1920s in the stage play *Dracula*, Lugosi naturally went on to portray the undead count in Universal's 1931 film of the same name. It was a high point that he would never again reach. He worked steadily through the 1930s and '40s, appearing (but seldom starring) in roles as gangsters, doctors (mad and sane), butlers, and servants. He eventually became a comedic foil for the Bowery Boys in several films. By the 1950s, Lugosi was in his 70s, ravaged by an addiction to painkillers.

Wood greatly admired Lugosi and gave the elderly actor friendship and a sense of being wanted once again. Too old to play the romantic leads that he once coveted, Lugosi was cast instead as a godlike character in *Glen or Glenda?* Wood continued to keep his Hungarian friend active in other films and shot footage in 1956 for a new film called *The Vampire's Tomb* in which, once again, Lugosi would rise as a blood-thirsty vampire. But Bela passed away after shooting only a few minutes of footage, some of it in his revered Count Dracula cape.

Wood Had a Plan

While Wood lost a great friend in Lugosi, his resolve was firm, and he wrote a brand-new script to incorporate the footage that Lugosi had already shot. *Grave Robbers from Outer Space* would be for Ed Wood what Citizen Kane was for Orson Welles: a masterpiece. Wood shot additional scenes, using local chiropractor Dr. Tom Mason as Bela's double. The fact that Mason looked nothing like Lugosi seemed to make no difference to Wood. Money problems led Wood to affiliate himself with a local Baptist church, which agreed to finance the film. As usual, parts were written into the film to accommodate the desires of the parish's would-be thespians. The church elders found the title reference to grave robbing to be in poor taste, so the film was renamed *Plan 9 from Outer Space* (though Criswell introduced the film with the original title). With a small, unpromising premiere, Wood had accomplished what he set out to do—he finished the movie as a tribute to his fallen friend.

Legacy

Consider that some people like fast-food restaurants while others prefer haute cuisine. But as long as one doesn't expect four-star fare from a fast-food hamburger, the flavor can be very palatable. Wood's work was never very good cinema, but his films are entertaining. They seem to improve with age—not in quality but in watchability. The more viewers get to know this eccentric film writer, producer, director, and sometimes actor, the more they can accept his work for what it is—no more, no less. Wood's films were born not from talent but from a deep passion for the movies.

Music's Wackiest Families

Some musicians claim that their rock band is like a family. But what happens when the family is a rock band?

✳ ✳ ✳ ✳

The Jacksons

ONCE UPON A time in Gary, Indiana, there lived a couple named Joseph and Katherine Jackson. He worked in a steel mill, and she was a salesclerk. The couple had nine children, six boys and three girls. The boys showed an unusual talent for music from an early age, and in the 1960s the five oldest brothers—Jackie, Tito, Jermaine, Marlon, and Michael—began touring together as the Jackson 5.

The Jackson 5 was one of the biggest musical acts of the early 1970s. As they grew older, the siblings began to pursue solo careers. Michael and Jermaine, along with their sisters Rebbie and Janet, achieved success as solo artists. Michael and Janet Jackson have 23 number-one singles between them.

It wasn't until the early '90s that whispers about the Jackson family turned into shouts of media scrutiny. In 1991, La Toya released her book *La Toya: Growing Up in the Jackson Family*, in which she portrays her father as a physically and sexually abusive monster who controlled his children and their careers. In 1993, Michael was accused of sexual molestation, and during the ensuing media circus, more Jackson family secrets began to leak out.

The Osmonds

While the Jackson family takes the cake in both controversy and reconstructive surgery, the Osmond clan wins in the less exciting—but more amusing—category of pure cheesiness. The nine Osmond children grew up in Utah and were raised in the Church of Jesus Christ of Latter-day Saints. Five of the Osmond brothers—Alan, Wayne, Merrill, Jay, and Donny— toured the country throughout the '60s and '70s as the Osmond Brothers. The two oldest brothers, Virl and Tom, are deaf and did not perform.

The most famous Osmond siblings are Donny and Marie. There is no entertainment medium unknown to the Osmonds, who have released records; written books; and appeared in television shows, movies, and even Broadway plays. Keeping true to her Mormon faith, Marie once turned down the role of Sandy in *Grease* because she felt that the movie was immoral.

Through all the hoopla, the Osmond family has mostly managed to steer clear of Jackson-esque controversy. This is not to say there are no skeletons in this family's closet: A 2001 TV movie, *Inside the Osmonds*, revealed that there was high tension, jealousy, and artistic conflict throughout the Osmonds' careers. Yet there is no real scandal to be found here—all Osmond siblings approved of the movie (youngest brother Jimmy was a producer!), and they were happy for their family to be portrayed in this complex light.

The Osmonds rounded out their square image in 2007, when they staged a 50th anniversary reunion tour in Las Vegas. In November 2007, the family patriarch passed away—George Osmond was survived by 9 children, 55 grandchildren, and 48 great-grandchildren.

The Osbournes

This is an "Os" of a different kind. In the realm of demons, goblins, and ghouls, people may find the scariest of America's musician families: the Osbournes. Ozzy Osbourne married wife Sharon in 1981 after he was kicked out of the heavy-metal band Black Sabbath because of his heavy drug and alcohol use. Sharon proceeded to clean Ozzy up and single-handedly launch his solo career, despite the fact that the couple was known for their drunken antics throughout the 1980s.

Ozzy often spoke of demonic voices in his head that told him to do bad things, and in 1989, he finally took heed. Responding to the voices' insistence that Sharon "had to die," Ozzy tried to strangle his wife. He later claimed to have no memory of the incident, while Sharon explained that "he was totally insane from all the drink and drugs he was doing, and well, these things happen." Ozzy is also known for biting the heads off of various animals, and one hazy day he shot all of his cats.

Someone at MTV had a feeling that this family could be ratings gold. The first season of the reality show *The Osbournes* debuted in 2002, featuring Ozzy, Sharon, and two of their three teenage children, Kelly and Jack. Ozzy and Sharon's eldest child, Aimee, refused to participate. The show ran for three years and enjoyed the highest ratings in MTV history. In 2002, it won an Emmy for Outstanding Reality Program. When Sharon signed the contract for the show's second season, she stipulated that MTV supply a lifetime of therapy for the family's pets.

A Whole New Dimension

Not until The Osbournes premiered was the world so thoroughly exposed to the skewed family life of famed musicians. Previously, fans had to read memoirs to reveal the hidden secrets of their favorite singers; now they simply have to tune in. A recent batch of reality television series capitalize on people's interest in the lives of their idols.

* From 2003 to 2005, MTV aired *Newlyweds: Nick and Jessica*, which focused on the marriage of young pop singers Jessica Simpson and Nick Lachey. The couple divorced in 2006.

* From 2005 to 2006, MTV aired *Meet the Barkers*, featuring ex-Blink 182 drummer Travis Barker and his wife, Shanna Moakler. The couple filed for divorce in 2006.

* In 2005, UPN aired *Britney and Kevin: Chaotic*, which chronicled the relationship of singer Britney Spears and aspiring rapper Kevin Federline. They divorced in 2007.

Strange Theme Restaurants

Eating at a restaurant is so boring. You sit down, you order, you eat, blah, blah, blah. Why not eat from a toilet-shape bowl or watch medieval knights joust each other while you dine?

✳ ✳ ✳ ✳

Banana Restaurant, Taiwan

OH, IF ONLY it was actually a banana-themed restaurant. Nope, this Taiwanese restaurant has a condom theme that just cloaks the concept with a euphemism. Condom-inspired art decorates the place, the dishes are visually suggestive and named with sexual innuendos, and every guest receives a free condom with their meal. The proprietors say the restaurant is condom-themed to promote safe sex and AIDS awareness.

O. Noir, Montreal, Quebec, Canada

Don't bother getting dressed up for dinner at O. Noir—no one will be able to see your outfit. Everything happens in the dark at this restaurant. Customers eat, converse, and order in pitch darkness. We're not sure how it all works in the kitchen, but the owners say that diners have a heightened sense of the food's flavors because one of their five senses is taken away. Five percent of the restaurant's profits are donated to local organizations that serve the blind and visually impaired.

Medieval Times, Numerous Locations

One of the most famous theme restaurants is also one of the strangest. Started in Spain in 1973, the Medieval Times Dinner & Tournament is now a nationwide chain in the United States. Diners enter a huge arena, receive paper crowns, and eat stew and bread with their bare hands while armored knights joust each other on horseback. Fair maidens are saved and villains are vanquished—all in a suburb near you!

The Toilet Bowl Restaurant, Taiwan

Matong means "toilet" in Chinese, and toilets are what you get at this restaurant, which opened in 2004. Patrons sit on converted toilet seats and dine from toilet-shaped bowls. Neon-lit faucets and urinals line the walls, and favorite dishes include chunky soups and soft-serve chocolate ice cream. We don't need to point out why those items are on the menu, do we?

Fortezza Medicea, Italy

For some, getting into this restaurant is easier than getting out. Located inside a maximum-security prison outside of Pisa, Fortezza Medicea is a restaurant staffed by criminals. Convicts pour wine and serve tasty Italian dishes to diners who line up for a seat at the simple wooden tables. But be prepared to eat with plastic forks and knives—the real stuff is contraband.

X-Rated Sushi

It's nothing new in Japan, but in the past few years, the time-honored tradition of eating sushi off a naked woman is gaining ground in the United States. Known as nyotaimori or "body sushi," this dining experience is generally offered by regular sushi joints hoping to bring in new customers for a meal and an eyeful. The women aren't totally naked: They commonly wear plastic wrap and enough lingerie to cover their private parts. Sushi is placed on their abdomens only and patrons use chopsticks to select their food. While some women's rights groups are enraged by the idea, eating raw fish off a warm body doesn't disgust enough people to keep them from doing it.

Griping in Tune: Complaint Choirs

People spend a whole lot of time and energy complaining about almost everything. Whether it's work, relationships, family, or the weather, a good percentage of our days are spent complaining or listening to someone else complain. Look out, disgruntled world—complaint choirs are popping up across the globe and are giving complaints a sonic facelift.

✳ ✳ ✳ ✳

A Disgruntled Dream

IN 2005, FINNISH artist Oliver Kochta-Kalleinen and his wife became interested in the Finnish expression *valituskuoro*, which, literally translated, means "complaints choir." The couple wanted to take a positive approach to complaining, so they took the literal meaning of *valituskuoro* to heart and set out to create the world's first complaint choir.

They approached several different venues with their idea and got some interest, but it wasn't until the Springhill Institute— an international artist-in-residence program in Birmingham, England—expressed interest that the first complaint choir was officially formed.

Birmingham residents had a lot to complain about—the economy wasn't very good, the public transit system left a lot to be desired, and the social scene was less than robust—so the idea of airing grievances in song was met with enthusiasm. Local composer Mike Hurley turned the complaints that had been gathered into lyrics for a chamber choir type of song, and participants gathered to rehearse.

Lights, Camera, Complain!

The Birmingham singers practiced for a few weeks before their first performance, which they filmed and posted on YouTube. Word started to spread, and soon the interest in complaint choirs snowballed. Before long, the Kalleinens were helping form a choir in their hometown of Helsinki. This large group of Finnish singers performed in public places such as train stations and parks. Crowds cheered when they heard the dulcet tones of the choir sing lines like, "Old forests are cut down and turned into toilet paper, and still the toilets are always out of paper," and truly bleak lines such as, "My dreams are boring."

In fact, one of the most distinguishing characteristics of the work of every complaint choir is the nature of the complaints. There is rarely any profanity, and most of the complaints have a decidedly humorous tone. One complaint from a Norwegian choir bemoans: "There's never enough time to polish all my nails—today I just polished my thumb."

Complaint choirs formed in Hamburg, St. Petersburg, Pennsylvania, Alaska, and Jerusalem. The Budapest choir is an especially active group, performing in huge numbers on rooftops, on trams, and in the middle of the street. Most of these choirs have videotaped their "concerts," which can then be viewed online.

Hey, I Have Complaints, Too!

If you'd like to get something off your chest, you can join a complaint choir or start your own. Instructions can be found online for those with a desire to sing their grievances to the world and use their griping to create a piece of music.

Rebel With a Curse: James Dean and "Little Bastard"

From the moment James Dean first walked onto a Hollywood set, countless people have emulated his cool style and attitude. When Dean died in a car crash in 1955 at age 24, his iconic status was immortalized. Perhaps this is partly due to the strange details that surrounded his death. Did a cursed car take the rising star away before his time?

✳ ✳ ✳ ✳

How Much Is that Porsche in the Window?

IN 1955, HEARTTHROB James Dean purchased a silver Porsche 550 Spyder, which he nicknamed "Little Bastard." Dean painted the number "130" on the hood and the car's saucy name on the back.

On the morning of September 30, Dean drove the Porsche to his mechanic for a quick tune-up before heading to a race he was planning to enter. The car checked out, and Dean left, making plans to meet up with a few friends and a *Life* magazine photographer later that day.

Everyone who knew Dean knew he liked to drive fast. The movie star set out on the highway, driving at top speeds in his beloved Porsche. He actually got stopped for speeding at one point but got back on the road after getting a ticket.

But when the sun got in his eyes and another car made a quick left turn, Dean couldn't stop in time. Screeching brakes, twisted metal, and an ambulance that couldn't make it to the hospital in time signaled the end of James Dean's short life.

You Need Brake Pads, a New Alternator, and a Priest

Within a year or so of Dean's fatal car crash, his Porsche was involved in a number of unusual—and sometimes deadly—

incidents. Were they all coincidental, or was the car actually cursed? Consider the following:

Two doctors claimed several of Little Bastard's parts. One of the docs was killed and the other seriously injured in separate accidents. Someone else purchased the tires, which blew simultaneously, sending their new owner to the hospital.

The Fresno garage where the car was kept for a while after Dean's death was the site of a major fire. The California State Highway Patrol removed the car from Fresno, figuring they could show the charred remains of Dean's car to warn teenagers about the dangers of careless driving. When the vehicle transporting the remains of the car crashed en route to the site, the driver was thrown from his vehicle and died.

The display the Highway Patrol produced was incredibly popular, of course, but it also turned out to be dangerous. The legs of a young boy looking at the car were crushed when three of the cables holding the vehicle upright suddenly broke, bringing the heavy metal down onto the boy's body. When the car left the exhibit, it broke in half on the truck used to haul it away and killed a worker involved in the loading process.

In 1959, there was another attempt to display the car. Legend says that though it was welded together, the car suddenly broke into 11 pieces.

The following year, the owner had finally had enough and decided to have the Porsche shipped from Miami back to California. Little Bastard was loaded onto a sealed boxcar, but when the train arrived in L.A., the car was gone. Thieves may have taken the car, sure, but there were reports that the boxcar hadn't been disturbed. Whether or not the car was cursed, with all the trouble it caused, perhaps it was for the best that it finally disappeared.

Twin Peaks and Seinfeld: A Connection About Nothing?

Some TV shows attract fans like flies to honey. The eerie, often-bizarre murder mystery Twin Peaks *is one of those shows; the smart comedy "about nothing,"* Seinfeld, *is another. While the shows couldn't be more different, content- and tone-wise, it turns out they do have a few odd similarities.*

✳ ✳ ✳ ✳

SURE, TELEVISION ACTORS tend to move around shows— you may see one actor as a bum on a cop drama, and the same actor as a businessman in a comedy. But *Twin Peaks* and *Seinfeld* have shared far more than just a couple actors. Was it insider actor-trading by opportunistic agents? A freaky coincidence? A conspiracy? It's like, what's the *deal* with that? Here are some examples of the oddball connection:

✳ Warren Frost played the father of George's fiancé on *Seinfeld*. He showed up on *Twin Peaks* as Doc Hayward, who performed the autopsy on the show's dead star, Laura Palmer.

✳ Grace Zabriskie played the tipsy mother of George's fiancé on *Seinfeld*. She also had a major part on *Twin Peaks* as Laura's mother.

✳ Brenda Strong played an assassin on *Twin Peaks*. In addition, she played "the braless wonder," Sue Ellen Mischke, on *Seinfeld*.

✳ Most know comedic actress Molly Shannon from *Saturday Night Live* fame. But Shannon also played an adoption agency worker on *Twin Peaks* and Elaine Benes's co-worker on *Seinfeld*.

✳ The actor who portrayed Elaine's boss, Mr. Pitt, in *Seinfeld* is Ian Abercrombie—who played the insurance adjuster in *Twin Peaks*.

* During an episode of *Seinfeld*, Kramer tries to avoid the cable guy. That cable guy is played by Walter Olkewicz, a.k.a. the evil smuggler on *Twin Peaks*.

* Remember the *Seinfeld* episode when Jerry steals the marble rye from the old lady? That old lady is actress Frances Bay, whom Laura Palmer and her pal Donna Hayward delivered meals to in *Twin Peaks*.

Behind the Films of Our Time

* One of the asteroids seen flying in *The Empire Strikes Back* is actually just a potato.

* The infamous light saber sound from the *Star Wars* films was created by moving a microphone near a television and recording the interference noise.

* *Return of the Jedi* was originally titled *Revenge of the Jedi*. George Lucas says he changed it because the idea of revenge didn't fit in with the Jedi concept.

* *Star Wars'* Chewbacca is named after the Tunisian town of Chebika City. Some of the movies' scenes were shot close to that location.

* The role of *Star Wars'* Princess Leia would have been offered to Jodie Foster if Carrie Fisher turned it down.

* Movie star Tom Hanks isn't only famous for his films—he's also related to President Abraham Lincoln (his third cousin four times removed).

* The first film shown in the White House was 1915's *Birth of a Nation*, during the Woodrow Wilson presidency.

* *Back to the Future* may have made Michael J. Fox a household name, but the actor's screen name wasn't given by his parents: Fox's middle name is actually Andrew.

* The first motion picture to feature Sylvester Stallone, *The Lords of Flatbush*, paid its star in T-shirts. Stallone received 25 T-shirts for his work on the film.

- *Snow White's* seven dwarfs almost had different names. Filmmakers considered various names, including Snoopy, Dippy, Blabby, Woeful, and Flabby.

- The only Civil War flick without a single battle scene is *Gone with the Wind.*

- The stars of *Gone with the Wind* didn't make much money by modern Hollywood standards. Clark Gable is said to have worked 71 days for a total of $120,000, while Vivien Leigh was on the project for 125 days and received only $25,000.

The Great Ghoulardi

Long before Howard Stern, a different type of shock jock stirred up America's airwaves. Ghoulardi, a character created by actor and announcer Ernie Anderson, ruffled plenty of feathers during his days on Cleveland's WJW-TV. His unique antics still live on in memories and pop culture tributes today.

✳ ✳ ✳ ✳

TO MANY, IT may sound like a kind of gourmet chocolate, but for families in Cleveland, the name Ghoulardi is anything but sweet. Ghoulardi was the brainchild of WJW-TV announcer Ernie Anderson, who created the character in 1963 as part of his hosting role on WJW's *Shock Theater* program—and shock is definitely what he did.

Meet Ghoulardi

Ghoulardi likely had a tough time blending into a crowd. The character was known for his outlandish outfits, which featured zany wigs, a long lab coat covered in colorful buttons, and his trademark sunglasses with only one lens intact. Ghoulardi also had a stylish fake goatee. The name was said to be inspired by the word "ghoul" and the last name of a local make-up artist, Ralph Gulko.

The greatest memories of Ghoulardi, however, may be the things he said: The unusual fellow flung catchphrase after catchphrase into his chatter. One minute, he might be saying "turn blue," while the next, he'd be talking about "knifs" (a "knif" being "fink" spelled backwards).

Ghoulardi would appear during breaks in various horror films shown during the *Shock Theater* show. He was known for telling the audience how terrible a particular flick was, or suggesting they might be better off going to bed rather than staying up for the show. (The program aired late on Friday nights.) He even went so far as to pop random, non sequitur clips in the middle of the movies, often featuring either himself or just irrelevant stock footage. The bits regularly featured memorable music, too: Anderson often worked little-known "hip" tunes into the background during his various segments.

Successes and Stresses

Ghoulardi was without question a hit. The TV station sold merchandise based on the character, and a charity sports team was even founded under the name. Still, tensions existed between Anderson and the station. Then-extreme tactics such as setting off firecrackers in the studio were said to have made executives nervous. It didn't help that the character constantly ridiculed Cleveland's suburbs, most notably the area of Parma. Skits branded as "Parma Place" mocked the working-class neighborhood to no end.

Ghoulardi stayed on the air until the end of 1966, when Anderson decided to retire the character to pursue an acting career in Los Angeles.

After Ghoulardi

Anderson's acting career never materialized, but that doesn't mean he didn't succeed in Hollywood: After leaving Ghoulardi behind, Anderson landed a gig as the main voice-over talent for ABC. He held the role for about two decades.

In 1997, Anderson died following a battle with cancer. His legacy went on, though: One of his former cohorts, an intern named Ron Sweed, started a program called *The Ghoulardi*

Show that was based on the Ghoulardi character. It went on to receive nationwide syndication. Comedian and Cleveland native Drew Carey honored the Ghoulardi reputation by wearing a Ghoulardi shirt in episodes of *The Drew Carey Show* and offering a quote in a book about the character. What might be the most touching tribute, though, comes from right within Anderson's own family: His son, film director Paul Thomas Anderson (*Boogie Nights, There Will Be Blood*) named his production unit "The Ghoulardi Film Company."

John Lennon Sees a UFO

Lucy in the sky with warp drive.

✳ ✳ ✳ ✳

IN MAY 1974, former Beatle John Lennon and his assistant/mistress May Pang returned to New York City after almost a year's stay in Los Angeles, a period to which Lennon would later refer as his "Lost Weekend." The pair moved into Penthouse Tower B at 434 East 52nd Street. As Lennon watched television on a hot summer night, he noticed flashing lights reflected in the glass of an open door that led onto a patio. At first dismissing it as a neon sign, Lennon suddenly realized that since the apartment was on the roof, the glass *couldn't* be reflecting light from the street. So—sans clothing—he ventured onto the terrace to investigate. What he witnessed has never been satisfactorily explained.

Speechless

As Pang recollected, Lennon excitedly called for her to come outside. "I looked up and stopped mid-sentence," she said later. "I couldn't even speak because I saw this thing up there...it was silvery, and it was flying very slowly. There was a white light shining around the rim and a red light on the top...[it] was silent. We started to watch it drift down, tilt slightly, and it was flying below rooftops. It was the most amazing sight." She quickly grabbed her camera and began clicking away.

Lennon's friend and rock photography legend Bob Gruen picked up the story: "In those days, you didn't have answering machines, but a service [staffed by people], and I had received a call from 'Dr. Winston.'" (Lennon's original middle name was Winston, and he often used the alias "Dr. Winston O'Boogie.") When Gruen returned the call, Lennon explained his incredible sighting and insisted that the photographer come round to pick up and develop the film personally. "He was serious," Gruen said. "He wouldn't call me in the middle of the night to joke around." Gruen noted that although Lennon had been known to partake in mind-altering substances in the past, during this period he was totally straight. So was Pang, a non-drinker who never took drugs and whom Gruen characterized as "a clear-headed young woman."

The film in Pang's camera was a unique type supplied by Gruen, "four times as fast as the highest speed then [commercially] available." Gruen had been using this specialty film, usually employed for military reconnaissance, in low-light situations such as recording studios. The same roll already had photos of Lennon and former bandmate Ringo Starr, taken by Pang in Las Vegas during a recording session.

Gruen asked Lennon if he'd reported his sighting to the authorities. "Yeah, like I'm going to call the police and say I'm John Lennon and I've seen a flying saucer," the musician scoffed. Gruen picked up the couple's phone and contacted the police, *The Daily News*, and the *New York Times*. The photographer claims that the cops and the *News* admitted that they'd heard similar reports, while the *Times* just hung up on him.

It Would Have Been the Ultimate Trip

Gruen's most amusing recollection of Lennon, who had been hollering "UFO!" and "Take me with you," was that none of his NYC neighbors saw the naked, ex-Beatle screaming from his penthouse terrace. And disappointingly, no one who might have piloted the craft responded to Lennon's pleas.

Gruen took the film home to process, "sandwiching" it between two rolls of his own. Gruen's negatives came out perfectly, but the film Pang shot was "like a clear plastic strip," Gruen says. "We were all baffled ... that it was completely blank."

Lennon remained convinced of what he'd seen. In several shots from a subsequent photo session with Gruen that produced the iconic shot of the musician wearing a New York City T-shirt (a gift from the photographer), John points to where he'd spotted the craft. And on his *Walls and Bridges* album, Lennon wrote in the liner notes: "On the 23rd Aug. 1974 at 9 o'clock I saw a U.F.O.—J.L."

Who's to say he and May Pang didn't? Certainly not Gruen, who still declares—more than 35 years after the fact—"I believed them." And so the mystery remains.

Hot Doug

Interested in sampling some scrumptious variations on the classic Chicago hot dog? Look no further that Hot Doug's.

✳   ✳   ✳   ✳

CHICAGO HAS ALWAYS been known as a great town for hot dogs. Once called "the Depression sandwich" because it provided nourishment from multiple food groups in one cheap meal, the classic "Chicago-style" dog consists of a bright red dog on a poppy-seed bun topped with yellow mustard, neon green relish, grilled onions, tomato slices, sport peppers, a pickle spear, and celery salt—and hold the ketchup.

Doug Sohn, proprietor of Hot Doug's, an eatery on the North Side of Chicago, has taken things to the next level, creating a variety of high-end hog dogs using game meats and wildly inventive ingredients.

As of this writing, the "Game of the Week" dog available at Hot Doug's is a ginger-spiked rabbit sausage topped with apple cream, ricotta salata, and cherry preserves. Meanwhile, this week's "Celebrity Sausage" is "The Barry Mann," a veal saltimbocca hot dog served with sage mustard, smoked Gouda cheese, and fried prosciutto.

Other specials on the constantly-changing menu include a hot dog made from smoked yak sausage with white cheddar cheese curds and fried onions, and a corned beef dog topped with Russian dressing, smoked Swiss cheese, and sauerkraut.

Delicious Dogs, Hot Press

Unlike some hot dog purveyors in Chicago, who refuse to add ketchup for customers over the age of five, Sohn is happy to add the noncanonical condiment if the customer requests it. After all, he doesn't care much for "food rules." This attitude has helped his business greatly: In 2007, his foie gras–topped dogs landed him the city's only citation for violating a short-lived foie gras ban, and brought him publicity worth exponentially more than the small fine he had to pay.

Doug Sohn and his establishment have been featured on countless television programs—some customers remark that it seems like there's a film crew there every time they stop in for a bite. Doug himself works the counter and personally greets every customer. Even on cold Chicago winter days, lines to get inside can stretch around the block. Sohn is the greatest hot dog genius in Chicago—and therefore, quite possibly the world!

As Good as It Gets

Jack Nicholson's sister was actually his mother. Who knew? Certainly not Jack.

✳   ✳   ✳   ✳

IT HAPPENED WHEN the soon-to-be smash movie *Chinatown* was opening in theaters. The film's star, Hollywood powerhouse Jack Nicholson, was being interviewed for a cover story for *Time* magazine. Amidst a battery of standard questions, an offbeat query was tossed Nicholson's way. The *Time* reporter asked if his sister was really his mother. Befuddled by the bizarre question, Nicholson denied it emphatically—but his curiosity was piqued.

When the actor was born, his 16-year-old biological mother June made a pivotal decision. Rather than derail a promising dancing career by admitting that she had become pregnant out of wedlock, she decided with her mother Ethel May to disguise the truth. The ploy was simple. June would pose as Nicholson's sister while Ethel May would pretend that both June and Jack were her children. The plan worked. Many years passed with Jack and most everyone else believing the ruse.

When the *Time* interview concluded, however, a suspicious Nicholson contacted his brother-in-law, Shorty, the husband of his sister Lorraine. At first Shorty told him that the rumor wasn't true, but later that day Lorraine tearfully confirmed the story. In one fell swoop Nicholson came to learn that his presumed sister June was his biological mother; his sister Lorraine was his aunt; and the woman that he had believed to be his mother was his biological grandmother.

Nicholson took the shocking news in stride. During a 2006 interview with director Peter Bogdanovich, the actor weighed in on the well-orchestrated story. "I understood it; I know exactly what my initial reaction was: gratitude... I've often said about them: Show me any women today who could keep a secret, confidence, or an intimacy to that degree, you got my kind of gal."

Bring the Tomatoes!

Now and then, Hollywood gets it spectacularly wrong. Be it bad taste, bad artistry, or bad revenues, these bombs sullied many people who helped make them.

✳ ✳ ✳ ✳

Intolerance (Wark Producing Co.; produced by D.W. Griffith, 1916, silent).

FLUSH WITH SUCCESS from the racist 1915 blockbuster *Birth of a Nation*, Griffith proposed a big-budget pacifist tale…that debuted shortly before the war ardor boom associated with U.S. entry into World War I. Today *Intolerance* is considered a classic, but Griffith's career died in the bomb blast.

Noah's Ark (Warner Bros./Darryl F. Zanuck, 1929, semi-silent)

This transition film was mostly silent with some sound sequences. The flooding scene killed three extras, cost one a leg, and sent six to the hospital. *Noah's Ark* bombed at the gate in such Biblical proportions that it almost took Warner Brothers down with it. Zanuck's career somehow survived.

Scipione l'Africano (ENIC/Vittorio Mussolini, 1937)

Italian *Duce* Benito Mussolini sought a winner in this nationalistic tale of Roman victory in Africa. Appointing his film novice 21-year-old brother as producer was *un errore*. In the climactic battle scene, telephone poles are visible; some toga-clad actors are wearing wristwatches. Il Duce ordered Italian theatres to show it, but couldn't pay an audience to endure it.

Underwater! (RKO/Howard Hughes, 1955)

During the filming of *The Outlaw*, Hughes once complained that the film wasn't getting enough production value out of Jane Russell's voluptuous figure. *Underwater!* sought to make up for that with a sunken-treasure story and plenty of Ms. Russell's chest. This red-ink bath was the last and worst of seven flicks she did with Hughes.

The Greatest Story Ever Told (United Artists/ George Stevens, 1965)

At 260 minutes, this was one of the longer single-film dullfests in cinema history. Designed to wow the faithful with Jesus' life story, *Greatest Story* was disliked even when cut down to 127 minutes.

Boom! (Universal/John Heyman and Norman Priggen, 1968)

Hollywood decided to adapt to film a Tennessee Williams play, but chose one of his flops: *The Milk Train Doesn't Stop Here Anymore*. Most of the film is comprised of dreary, pretentious dialogue between Elizabeth Taylor and Richard Burton. One critic called it, "An ordeal in tedium." Filmgoers wallet-voted *Boom!* a great bust.

Can't Stop The Music (Associated Film Distribution/ Allen Carr, 1980)

This not-so-fabulous musical comedy features the Village People and plenty of homoerotic overtones. It's now a gay camp classic, but it generated little revenue at the box office and got reviews like "It's true...you really can't stop the music, no matter how much you want to, and at times you'll want to very, very much..."

Steampunk: Why Some Science Fiction Fans Run Around in Corsets and Goggles

"Steampunk is what happens when Goths discover the color brown," goes the joke. If so, they have discovered it with a passion. In the science fiction community, steampunk costuming and events rival the popularity of zombies and vampires in much of today's pop culture.

❋ ❋ ❋ ❋

What Is Steampunk?

STEAMPUNK IS A fiction genre based on the Victorian era (1837–1901), from the Industrial Revolution to the development of electricity. Steampunk art, music, and fiction reimagine that era in light of modern views on social equality, and with special emphasis on pre-electric technology (such as steam engines, airships, etc.). In the late 1800s, Jules Verne's adventure stories were science fiction; steampunk today embraces them as heart and soul.

But steampunk doesn't merely remain on the printed page. Afficianados are known to don the dress of their favorite imagined worlds and characters. While the style of much steampunk costuming is derived from Victorian English formal wear and adventuring gear—usually decorative, often remarkably practical—its devotees are an embracing lot. Steampunk oftentimes envisions high development of airship technology—thus the oft-sported goggles. Some costumes are quite elaborate, with lots of leather and pouches; others merely involve gluing some gears to a derby hat and strapping on that ubiquitous pair of goggles. Half the fun is in the creation, and half is in the admiration that follows.

Steampunk sometimes involves role-play, with events and manners that would have fit into Victorian England. People tend to adopt a persona to match their costume. A steampunk picnic (say *that* five times fast) could feature several people sitting around conversing over lemonade, watching a pith-helmeted female Egyptologist play a friendly game of badminton with a heavily bearded airship captain.

Beyond the Goggles: the Arts

Several prominent steampunk bands are active at this writing, with music reflecting an industrial/goth influence. The lyrics can be dark, but without being depressing, focused on stories of strange evolutions of technology, dashing adventure, mad scientists, and imaginary robotics or cybernetics.

In addition to original inspirations such as Verne and H. G. Wells, there is a growing body of print and online steampunk writing. The 1990 release of the novel *The Difference Engine* (William Gibson, Bruce Sterling) marked a major forward stride in steampunk's popularity. Major science fiction writers such as Michael Moorcock and S. M. Stirling have written steampunk-themed stories. Online comics like Phil and Kaja Foglio's *Girl Genius* entertain and stimulate the imagination. Lots of artists and artisans enrich the genre with paintings, steampunk-themed props, and anything else they can imagine. There are also role-playing games similar to *Dungeons & Dragons* that immerse players in a steampunk adventure story. .

Facing History

Those who find steampunk tiresome might call it an excuse for women to dress up in corsets and hold parasols. Others remark that this emulated era spawned the extractive cultural devastation of colonialism; they thus question the value of nostalgia for this period in history. Persons of color in particular may fairly ask: "And how do I fit into this?"

The answer—for everyone—is simple: "However you want." Steampunk enthusiasts aren't interested in re-enacting King Leopold's Congo atrocities, nor anything else related to racism, sexism, or cruelty. An African American woman dressed as a cybernetically enhanced Zulu warrior would be a costumed rockstar. However, she could just as easily choose a more conventional steampunk persona without regard to what her forebears could have done. As for gender, while some female steampunk fans might dress like suffragette protesters, none would desire to fight anew the battle for votes for women.

When creativity and imagination are used to reimagine our world into new ones, the results are invigorating. Not to mention fun—and covered in goggles.

Fast Facts: *The Godfather*

✳ Marlon Brando wasn't the only guy up for the role of Don Vito Corleone. Paramount Pictures wanted Ernest Borgnine. Trade magazines also claimed at the time that George C. Scott and Laurence Olivier were considered for the role.

✳ During a screen test, Brando actually stuffed his cheeks with cotton or tissues to make his character look "like a bulldog."

* To achieve the look of an older, jowly man, Brando wore a dental device during his scenes. The piece is now displayed at the American Museum of the Moving Image in Queens, New York.

* Producer Robert Evans wasn't pleased with director Francis Ford Coppola's preliminary work, and from the beginning, he and Coppola had butted heads. Evans talked about having Elia Kazan on standby in case he decided to fire Coppola. Kazan was considered because he had worked previously with Brando on *A Streetcar Named Desire* (1951) and *On the Waterfront* (1954), and, therefore, might have been able to handle the actor's temperament better than Coppola.

* Pacino has said that studio execs weren't impressed with his early scenes and that they considered firing him. But the scene in which his character shoots Sollozzo and McCluskey in the restaurant convinced the studio to keep him onboard.

* Actors Martin Sheen, Warren Beatty, Jack Nicholson, Dustin Hoffman, Ryan O'Neal, and James Caan all read for the role of Michael Corleone.

* Brando never learned the majority of his lines. Instead, he read from cue cards while filming. This is typical of the way Brando worked as an actor because he liked to improvise the exact wording of his lines as a way of internalizing his characters.

* Sylvester Stallone tried out for the part of Paulie, which went to John Martino.

* Did you know that *The Godfather* spawned a board game? It hit store shelves in the early 1970s.

* *TV Guide*'s "50 Greatest Movies on TV and Video" ranked *The Godfather: Part II* at No. 1 and the original at No. 7.

* The cat Brando holds in the opening scene of *The Godfather* wasn't part of the script. Coppola found the stray wandering around the Paramount lot and, knowing the actor's talent with props, he plopped it in Brando's lap just before shooting.

* The score for *The Godfather* created a minor scandal in Hollywood. Composer Nino Rota was nominated for an Oscar, but then someone realized that he had simply taken his music from *Fortunella* (1958) and changed it around a bit. Subsequently, Rota's Oscar nomination was withdrawn.

* Paramount considered shooting *The Godfather* in Kansas City, Missouri, because executives had experienced problems with the unions on previous occasions when shooting in New York City.

* You won't find his name in the credits, but George Lucas worked on a montage of crime scene photos and newspaper headlines for *The Godfather*.

* The actors playing Brando's sons in the movie ranged from 6 to 16 years younger than him in real life.

The Mysterious Death of Christopher Marlowe

Who exactly is responsible for the death of Christopher Marlowe?

※　※　※　※

IN 1593, CHRISTOPHER Marlowe, the most famous playwright in London, was killed when he accidentally stabbed himself during a tavern brawl. His premature death is one of the greatest tragedies in English literature, snuffing out a career that may have still been in its infancy—Shakespeare, who was Marlowe's same age, was just coming into his own as a writer at the time. But some people continue to doubt the official story (i.e., that Marlowe accidentally stabbed himself while fighting over the bill). After all, Marlowe and some of the others in the room with him had ties to the Elizabethan underworld. Was his really an accidental death—or could it have been murder?

Rise of a Shoemaker's Son

Born to a shoemaker the same year that Shakespeare was born to a glove maker, Marlowe attended Cambridge University, where he posed for a portrait that showed him in a black velvet shirt, smirking beside his Latin motto, *Quod met nutrit me destruit* ("What nourishes me destroys me.") He was a distinguished enough scholar that he seems to have been recruited, as many Cambridge scholars of the day were, to work as an undercover agent. Letters from the government excusing him from missing classes seem to back up the widely held theory that he went on spy missions in Spain. When he returned to London, he found fame as a playwright, churning out "blood and thunder" shockers such as *Doctor Faustus* that helped pioneer the use of blank verse, and were some of the first great pieces of secular theatrical entertainment produced in the English language.

To say that Marlowe had a wild side is to put things mildly. He was imprisoned twice, once for his role in a fight that left a tavern keeper dead (he was acquitted when a jury determined that he'd acted in self-defense), and ran with an underground group of atheists who called themselves "The School of Night." They hung around in graveyards, reading poetry and having the sort of blasphemous debates that were illegal in Elizabethan England, where everyone was required to be a member of the Church of England. Breaking somewhat from her predecessors, Queen Elizabeth generally didn't care too much if people doubted religion in their minds, as long as they kept their mouths shut and kept attending church services. But for someone as famous as Marlowe to be a heretic was dangerous.

Richard Baines, a professional snitch, wrote a letter to the government containing a bunch of blasphemous things that he claimed to have heard Marlowe say, such as that Moses was really just a juggler, that people in the New World had stories and histories dating back 10,000 years (which went against the "official" view that the Adam and Eve had lived "within six thousand years,"), and that the Virgin Mary was "dishonest." Around the same time, the government arrested Thomas Kyd, Marlowe's former roommate, for possessing atheist literature, and Kyd said under torture that it was Marlowe who had led him to atheism in the first place.

And so, at the height of his fame, Marlowe was arrested for blasphemy. He was released on parole and ordered to check in every day until he was brought to trial, at which he faced a possible sentence of death. If lucky, he would just get his nose chopped off.

Marlowe never once checked in with authorities, so far as is known, and he was killed in Deptford only a couple of weeks later, while awaiting trial.

An Accident, or...?

The exact circumstances of his death are still not quite agreed upon, though a detailed coroner's report exists. Official documents state that Marlowe and a few other men had spent the day in an establishment owned by "The Widow Bull," but what sort of business this was is a matter of some mystery—it's been variously described as a tavern, a brothel, or a sort of bed and breakfast. The fact that the investigations into what happened that day mention a "reckoning" (bill) is about the only evidence we have that it was any sort of business at all, not just a house owned by Ms. Eleanor Bull.

According to official reports, a bill of some sort was presented to Marlowe and his friends. A fight broke out over who should pay it, and in the scuffle, Marlowe accidentally stabbed himself just below the eye and "then and there instantly died."

Now, most fights over bills don't end in knife fights, but this explanation seems sensible enough on the surface: The theatres were closed at the time due to a plague outbreak, and Marlowe was probably hard up for money. Perhaps he had taken up an offer of going to dinner thinking that his meal was being paid for, and when he was asked to kick in for the bill, his hot temper got the best of him. He reached for the dagger of one of the other men present—one Ingram Frizer—and stabbed himself while the other men tried to stop him from attacking.

The death was officially determined to be the result of an accidental, self-inflicted wound, but more and more scholars now believe that Marlowe was murdered to make sure he didn't reveal sensitive information at his upcoming trial. It does seem that a lot of people may have had a reason to want Marlowe to be killed before he could go to trial. Frizer, for example, had been working for Thomas Walsingham, a relative of Queen Elizabeth's secretary of state, and had Marlowe been convicted of atheism, Walsingham himself would have been disgraced, and financially ruined, for having once been Marlowe's patron. Perhaps Frizer was acting on his boss's orders and killed Marlowe to ensure his own future.

But others believe that the "political murder" theory doesn't go far enough, and that the body on the coroner's slab wasn't Marlowe at all, but the body of a man named John Penry who had been hastily hanged. According to this theory, Marlowe escaped to the continent, where he kept on writing. Some theories in this vein hold that he was the true author of Shakespeare's plays.

It seems far-fetched, but if anyone could have pulled off faking his own death, it was Christopher Marlowe.

Would You Like Fried Worms With That?

Granted, to some people a Twinkie probably looks pretty weird. But at least Twinkies don't slither or smell like poo. Here's a sampling of some of the weirdest foods in the world.

✳   ✳   ✳   ✳

Nutria

THE NUTRIA IS a semi-aquatic rodent about the size of a cat with bright orange teeth. After World War II, they were sold in the United States as "Hoover Hogs." Since the animals chew up crops and cause erosion, in 2002 Louisiana officials offered $4 for every nutria killed. Still, their meat is rumored to be lean and tasty.

Uok

The coconut: Without it, the piña colada and macaroons wouldn't exist. Neither would the Uok, a golf ball-size, coconut-dwelling, bitter-tasting worm enjoyed by some Filipinos. Just pull one down from a mangrove tree, salt, and sauté!

Balut

If you're craving a midnight snack, skip the cheesecake and enjoy a boiled duck embryo. Folks in Cambodia will let eggs develop until the bird inside is close to hatching, and then they boil it and enjoy the egg with a cold beer.

Frog Smoothies

In Bolivia and Peru, Lake Titicaca frogs are harvested for a beverage affectionately referred to as "Peruvian Viagra." The frogs go into a blender with some spices and the resulting brown goo is served up in a tall glass. Turn on the Barry White...

Duck Blood Soup

Bright red goose blood is the main ingredient in this Vietnamese soup. A few veggies and spices round out the frothy meal.

7 Stars Who Died During the Filming of a Movie

Long after their time is up, movie stars live on through DVDs and cable reruns. But the stars on this list died before completing a project, leaving directors in an emotional and logistical bind, and forever attaching a dark footnote to a movie's history. In some cases the movie was canceled, in others the star was recast, while in others production moved forward with some creative editing.

✳ ✳ ✳ ✳

1. **John Candy:** Funnyman John Candy, known for portraying portly, lovable losers in movies such as *Stripes*, *Uncle Buck*, and *Planes, Trains & Automobiles*, died of a massive heart

attack on March 4, 1994, during the filming of *Wagons East*. A body double was used to replace Candy, and the film—a comedy set in the Wild West—was released later that summer. The movie was widely panned by critics as an unworthy farewell to Candy, who was just 43 when he died.

2. **Marilyn Monroe:** Blonde bombshell Marilyn Monroe, famous for her film roles, multiple marriages, and memorable serenading of President Kennedy, died on August 5, 1962, before she could finish filming *Something's Got to Give*. The comedy, directed by George Cukor and also starring Cyd Charisse and Dean Martin, had been plagued with conflict from the start. At one point, Monroe was even fired. But Martin refused to work with any actress other than Monroe, so the famous beauty was rehired. Before Monroe could resume her role, however, she was found dead in her Brentwood, California, home, the result of an overdose of barbiturates. *Something's Got to Give* was scrapped, but parts of the unfinished film were included in a 2001 documentary titled *Marilyn: The Final Days*.

3. **Paul Mantz:** To Paul Mantz, stunt flying was a natural calling, and the legendary aviator even lost his spot at the U.S. Army flight school when he buzzed a train filled with high-ranking officers. Mantz landed a role in 1932's *Air Mail*, in which he flew a biplane through a hangar not much bigger than the aircraft itself. He appeared in numerous films through the years, including *For Whom the Bell Tolls*, *Twelve O'Clock High*, and *The Wings of Eagles*. On July 8, 1965, Mantz was killed while performing a stunt for *The Flight of the Phoenix*. Flying over an Arizona desert site, Mantz's plane struck a hill and broke into pieces, killing the famous aviator immediately. Because the majority of the movie had already been shot, filmmakers were able to substitute another plane for some remaining close-ups and *The Flight of the Phoenix* was released later that year.

4. **Vic Morrow:** Vic Morrow, a tough-talking actor known for his role in the TV series *Combat!* as well as a string of B-movies, was killed in July 1982, in a tragic accident on the set of *Twilight Zone: The Movie*. The script called for the use of both a helicopter and pyrotechnics—a combination that would prove lethal. When the pyrotechnics exploded, the helicopter's tail was severed, causing it to crash. The blades decapitated Morrow and a child actor, and another child actor was crushed to death. Although the filmmakers faced legal action from the accident, the project was completed and the movie was released in June 1983. It performed poorly at the box office, based partially on the controversy surrounding the accident.

5. **Oliver Reed:** Oliver Reed, as famous for drinking and partying as he was for acting, died in a pub on May 2, 1999, before he could finish filming Ridley Scott's epic *Gladiator*. Reed, 61, collapsed on the floor of a bar in Malta and died of a heart attack. Most of his scenes in *Gladiator* had already been shot when he died, but Scott had to digitally re-create Reed's face for a few remaining segments. The Internet Movie Database estimated the cost of the digital touch-ups at $3 million. When *Gladiator* was released in 2000, it grossed more than $187 million in the United States alone and snared five Oscars, including Best Picture.

6. **Steve Irwin:** Steve Irwin, aka "The Crocodile Hunter," was in the Great Barrier Reef to film a documentary titled *The Ocean's Deadliest* when he was struck by a stingray on September 4, 2006. Irwin, a 44-year-old Australian wildlife expert, was known for his daredevil stunts involving animals and could frequently be seen handling poisonous snakes and wrestling crocodiles on his Animal Planet TV show. Because of bad weather, Irwin was taking a break from filming his documentary at the time of the stingray attack, instead taping some snorkeling segments for a children's show. *The Ocean's Deadliest* aired in January 2007.

7. **Brandon Lee:** Brandon Lee, an aspiring actor and the son of martial arts star Bruce Lee, was killed in a freak accident on the set of *The Crow* on March 31, 1993. Lee, who was 28 at the time, was playing a character who gets shot by thugs upon entering his apartment. Tragically, the handgun used in the scene had a fragment of a real bullet lodged in its barrel, which was propelled out by the force of the blank being shot. Lee was hit in the abdomen and died later that day. The movie was nearly complete at the time of the shooting, but a stunt double was needed to complete a few remaining scenes, and Lee's face was digitally superimposed onto the stunt double's body.

The Mondo Movie Craze

This movie trend in the 1960s was all about celebrating excess for its own sake. How far would they go?

✳ ✳ ✳ ✳

WITH A WARNING that reads in part: "The duty of the chronicler is not to sweeten the truth but to report it objectively," *Mondo Cane (A Dog's World)*, the first mainstream "shockumentary," unspooled before thrill-seeking American audiences in 1963. The film promised to "enter a hundred incredible worlds where the camera has never gone before" and presented a loosely strung travelogue of outrageous rites, repulsive rituals, and downright bizarre behavior.

More, More, More

A combination of archival footage and staged sequences shot in grainy documentary style to appear authentic, *Mondo Cane* featured a wide range of shocking footage—including mass animal slaughter, a group of religious women tongue-bathing parish steps, a visit to a pet cemetery, diners feasting on cooked insects, a match in which two natives conk each other on the head with logs, and plenty of topless African women. The 108-minute film, underscored by sardonic narration, weaves back and forth between the "primitive" and the "civilized" world. The outrageousness is further accentuated by the inclusion of a perky song titled "More" that is endlessly repeated (the song garnered an Oscar nomination for Best Song in 1963).

Mondo Cane was cowritten and directed by Paolo Cavara and Gualtiero Jacopeti. The word *mondo* quickly became a euphemism for "extreme." The movie was so popular around the world that it started a trend of similar films throughout the 1960s. Each subsequent mondo release attempted to top the previous one. Titles included *Mondo Macabro, Mondo Mod, Mondo Exotica,* and *Mondo Topless.* By the time *Mondo Bizarro* was released in 1966, the footage in the films was almost all staged. The genre petered out by the end of the decade, but a resurgence of the genre occurred in the late 1970s with the *Faces of Death* series, whose hallmark was explicit and gory sequences. The influence of the mondo films can be seen in recent reality TV shows such as *Fear Factor* and *Survivor.*

Sister Aimee, Radio Sensation

Did an early 20th century evangelist stage her own death?

✳ ✳ ✳ ✳

SISTER AIMEE SEMPLE McPherson (1890–1944) was a woman far ahead of her time. In a male-driven society, McPherson founded a religious movement known as the Foursquare Church. Using her natural flamboyance and utilizing modern technologies such as radio, McPherson reached thousands with her Pentecostal message of hope, deliverance, and salvation. But turbulent waters awaited McPherson. Before the evangelist could grow her church to its fullest potential, she'd first have to survive her own "death."

The Seed Is Planted

McPherson was something of a firebrand right from the get-go. Born Aimee Elizabeth Kennedy in Salford, Ontario, the future evangelist was daughter to James Kennedy, a farmer, and Mildred "Minnie" Kennedy, a Salvation Army worker. As a teenager, the inquisitive Aimee often came to loggerheads with pastors over such weighty issues as faith and science—even as she questioned the teaching of evolution in public schools.

In 1908, Aimee married Robert James Semple, a Pentecostal missionary from Ireland. The marriage was short-lived. Semple died from malaria in 1910, but their union produced a daughter, Roberta Star Semple, born that same year.

Working as a Salvation Army employee alongside her mother, Aimee married accountant Harold Stewart McPherson in 1912. One year later they had a son, Rolf Potter Kennedy McPherson. But this marriage would also dissolve. Citing desertion as the cause for their rift, Harold McPherson divorced his wife in 1921.

By this point McPherson was well on her way as an evangelist. In 1924 she began to broadcast her sermons over the radio. This new electronic "reach"—coupled with McPherson's flair for drama—drew hordes into her fold. From an evangelistic standpoint, it was the best of times. But as Dickens said in the opening line of *A Tale of Two Cities*, such heady times rarely come without strings attached. McPherson would soon experience this directly—ostensibly from the afterworld.

Gone with the Tide?

On May 18, 1926, the shocking news broke like a wave crashing against a beach: Nationally famous evangelist Aimee Semple McPherson had gone missing while swimming in the Pacific Ocean near Venice Beach, California. She was presumed to be drowned.

Adding to the tragedy, two of her congregants perished while searching for her in the ocean. Despite continued efforts, no trace of McPherson—or her body—could be found.

From Death Comes Life

Oddly, police received hundreds of tips and leads that suggested that McPherson hadn't drowned at all. One letter—signed "The Avengers"—said that Aimee had been kidnapped and demanded $500,000 for her safe return. One month later, a very alive McPherson emerged near Douglas, Arizona. She claimed she had been kidnapped and held in a shack in Mexico. No such shack, however, could be found.

Even stranger, radio operator and church employee Kenneth G. Ormiston vanished at precisely the same time as McPherson. Gossip spread like wildfire that the married Ormiston and McPherson had in fact shacked up for a month of tawdry romance. Charges of perjury and manufacturing evidence were brought against Mcpherson and Ormiston but were inexplicably dropped months later.

Scandal Sells

Despite the scandal, McPherson's church continued to grow by leaps and bounds. McPherson married a third time in 1931, divorcing by 1934. In 1944, Aimee Semple McPherson died from an overdose of sedatives. Her death was ruled accidental, but many believed that McPherson had in fact committed suicide. Whatever the cause of her death, she left behind a strong legacy. By the end of the 20th century, the church she founded boasted more than two million members worldwide.

When Poe Scooped Dickens

Edgar Allan Poe wrote many classic tales of the macabre. As it turns out, he also proved himself adept at completing the work of another famous writer of his day.

✳   ✳   ✳   ✳

IN MARCH OF 1841, the first part of Charles Dickens's new novel, *Barnaby Rudge*, was published in the United States. A few years before, The *Pickwick Papers* had made him one of the most famous authors in the world; something like 80% of all people who could read owned a copy of it, and for a good century it would be considered the funniest book ever written.

Barnaby Rudge, though, was not a particularly funny book. It was a grim tale of the anti-Catholic riots that swept through England in 1780, and it is probably the least-read of all Dickens novels today. But *Barnaby* was fairly popular in its day, and the murder mystery introduced in the first chapter kept readers all over the world guessing as the book was published, one part at a time, over the course of a year.

One Early Fan: Edgar Allan Poe

Poe was then an up-and-coming writer in Baltimore, and he began writing reviews of *Barnaby Rudge* after the very first chapters were published. In a review that appeared in the May, 1841, edition of *The Saturday Evening Post*, he described the murder mystery that had been laid out: A few years before the opening of the story, a local man who lived near the Maypole Inn, a tavern, was found murdered, and his gardener and steward had vanished. A body was later found and identified by clothes and jewelry as being that of the steward, but the gardener had escaped.

Having described the mystery, Poe then proceeded to solve it. He laid out, in great detail, the identity of the murderer, the true identity of the body that had been found, and the precise method in which the crime had been carried out.

Poe was *almost* exactly right in his solution. Indeed, many believe that Poe's solution was a bit more elegant than the one Dickens ended up using. Some scholars have speculated that Poe's solution may have been precisely what Dickens had in mind when he started writing the book, but he changed it just a bit when he heard about Poe's review. Scholars have tried to gather evidence proving—or disproving—the theory that Poe had seen more chapters than he let on when he wrote his review. They are still fairly divided.

Pet Peeve

After the whole book had been published, Poe criticized Dickens for not making better use of Grip the raven, Barnaby Rudge's pet (who was named after a pet raven Dickens himself owned). Dickens had only really written the raven in because his children had asked him to, but Poe believed it could have been used to great symbolic effect; some say it was a determination to show how this could be done that inspired him to write "The Raven," Poe's most famous poem.

Poe never came right out and *said* that Grip inspired his famous poem, but it's hard not to notice a line in the fifth chapter of *Barnaby Rudge*, when Grip is first heard to make noise, and someone asks: "What was that — him tapping at the door?" And the reply is, "'Tis someone knocking softly at the shutter." The similarity to the opening stanza of Poe's classic poem is hard to miss:

While I nodded, nearly napping, suddenly there came a tapping
As of someone gently rapping, rapping at my chamber door.
"'Tis some visitor,' I muttered, "tapping at my chamber door—
Only this, and nothing more."

The stuffed body of the real Grip is now a part of the Edgar Allan Poe collection at the Free Library of Philadelphia, where it sits: voiceless there, forevermore.

Fast Facts: Disney

* Everyone's favorite rodent, Mickey Mouse was introduced in the cartoon short *Steamboat Willie* (1928), which was released just after the sync-sound revolution. The cartoon's use of synchronized music and sound effects helped to make it into a critical success.

* Disney's *Snow White and the Seven Dwarfs* (1937) was the first full-length animated feature produced in the United States. The movie debuted two decades after Argentina created the first-ever full-length animated movie, *El Apóstol*.

* Walt Disney called his nine animators the "Nine Old Men," though many were quite young when they started working for Disney Studios. All nine remained with Disney from *Snow White and the Seven Dwarfs* through *The Rescuers* (1977). The influence of the Nine Old Men—Ollie Johnston, Milt Kahl, Les Clark, Frank Thomas, Wolfgang Reitherman, John Lounsbery, Eric Larson, Ward Kimball, and Mark Davis—on commercial Hollywood animation cannot be underestimated.

* Singer Ricky Martin voiced the main character in the Spanish version of Disney's *Hercules* (1997). Tate Donovan did the voice in the original English flick.

* *Alice in Wonderland* (1951) was based on two of Lewis Carroll's books: *Alice's Adventures in Wonderland* and *Through the Looking Glass*. But the animated adaptation had one character that Carroll didn't create: the doorknob.

* *Beauty and the Beast* (1991) holds the honor of being the first full-length animated feature to receive a Best Picture Oscar nomination. It ended up losing to *The Silence of the Lambs,* but it still made history: The movie took home the Golden Globe for Best Picture, becoming the first animated movie to do so.

* The last film that bore the personal stamp of Walt Disney himself was *The Jungle Book* (1967).

* Although Kathleen Turner voiced all of Jessica Rabbit's speaking parts in *Who Framed Roger Rabbit* (1988), she was never credited. Actress Amy Irving did the character's singing.

* Dan Castellaneta—best known as the voice of Homer Simpson—stepped in to voice the genie in *The Return of Jafar* (1994), the sequel to *Aladdin* (1992), after Robin Williams turned down the chance to reprise his role. Williams later came back for a third film, the direct-to-video *Aladdin and the King of Thieves* (1995). Castellaneta had already voiced the film, but Disney discarded his voice track when Williams agreed to take the role. Castellaneta did not lose out entirely, however, because he voiced the genie for Disney's *Aladdin* cartoon television series.

* *The Little Mermaid* (1989) was the last animated Disney film to use hand-painted cels shot on analog film. Artists created more than a million drawings for the movie.

Krypton, U.S.A.!

According to the story, Superman came to Earth from the planet Krypton. But in reality, the Man of Steel is a native of Cleveland.

✳ ✳ ✳ ✳

JERRY SIEGEL AND Joe Shuster were pals at Glenville High School who shared a fondness for comics, adventure movies, and pulp magazines. Their dream was to make it big in the burgeoning field of comics, and in their early 20s, they managed to sell a few detective and adventure stories to Malcolm Wheeler-Nicholson, one of the first comic book publishers to use original material. Their greatest success, however, would come years later in the form of a man with a big red *S* on his chest.

A Superhero Is Born

Superman was an amalgam of concepts and images that had burned themselves into Siegel's young brain, including body-building ads in the backs of magazines, the popular pulp hero Doc Savage, and Philip Wylie's influential science fiction novel, *Gladiator*. Siegel distilled it all into a costumed superhero like no other, an almost indestructible figure who used his remarkable strength to fight for truth and justice.

Siegel and Shuster initially tried to sell Superman as a newspaper strip but were rejected by every syndicate they approached. They fared no better with various comic book publishers until Superman landed in the hands of Sheldon Mayer, an editor at what later became DC Comics, who sensed a potential appeal to teenage boys in the primitive strip. Superman was picked for the lead feature for the company's newest title, *Action Comics*, and the two were paid $130 for all rights to the character.

Supermania Sets In

Action Comics #1 hit the stands in the summer of 1938 and was an immediate success. Kids couldn't get enough of the Man of Steel, and he was quickly given his own title. The first issue sold

900,000 copies. Supermania swept the nation as the character appeared on everything from lunch boxes to decoder rings

Siegel and Shuster were making pretty good money writing and illustrating Superman's adventures, but because they had sold all rights to their creation, they shared none of the merchandising profits. They took DC Comics to court in 1947 in an attempt to get a percentage of the revenues being generated by their character. The courts ruled in the publisher's favor, and the two soon found themselves out of a job. Over the years, they found piecemeal work for DC and other publishers, but Shuster eventually developed vision problems that prevented him from drawing, and Siegel was forced to take a $7,000-a-year civil service job for the health benefits. By the 1970s, both men were practically destitute.

Righting Wrongs

In 1975, the press became aware of how shabbily the creators of Superman had been treated. The National Cartoonists Society took up their cause, enlisting the support of influential writers to force DC Comics to reward the men who had made the company so much money. After months of hard-fought negotiations, DC Comics agreed to a settlement that included $20,000 a year for each creator with built-in cost-of-living increases, provisions for their heirs, and, most importantly, creator credit on almost everything on which Superman appears.

The Man of Steel Today

Since his debut in 1938, Superman has become one of the most recognizable fictional characters in the world. He's saved Earth countless times, fought outrageous villains and monsters, and even come back from the dead. Outside of comic books, he has been featured in serials, television series, motion pictures, animated cartoon series, and video games. Per their deal with DC Comics, all of the above are noted as "created by Jerry Siegel and Joe Shuster." Not bad for two Cleveland kids with a supersize dream.

Fast Facts: *Star Wars*

✳ Released in 1977, the first *Star Wars* movie cost just over $11 million to make, compared to $113 million for *Star Wars: Episode III—Revenge of the Sith* (2005), which was produced nearly 30 years later.

✳ In the late 1990s, remastering and reediting *Star Wars* for its 20th anniversary edition cost nearly as much as it did to make the original movie.

✳ The first U.S. theater run for the original *Star Wars* pulled in $215 million.

✳ The first-ever *Star Wars* trailer began showing a full six months before the movie came out. Vague taglines such as "the story of a boy, a girl, and a universe" and "a billion years in the making" were meant to build up buzz before the film's debut.

✳ The first *Star Wars* film was originally going to be titled *The Star Wars*, but George Lucas decided to drop the introductory article. The movie's full title, *Star Wars: Episode IV: A New Hope*, was not used on posters, promotions, or publicity until the film was rereleased in 1981.

✳ George Lucas was initially set to receive about $165,000 for the making of *Star Wars*. But when production costs rose, he waived his fee in exchange for 40 percent of the box-office returns. That, combined with a lucrative merchandising deal and his foresight into snagging creative control and full merchandising rights for the sequels, made him millions.

✳ The filmmaker who directed *Scarface* (1983) cowrote the opening crawl text at the beginning of *Star Wars*. Brian De Palma helped pen the words: "It is a period of civil war. Rebel spaceships, striking from a hidden base, have won their first victory against the evil Galactic Empire..."

✳ The actors who played C-3PO and R2-D2—Anthony Daniels and Kenny Baker, respectively—are the only two people credited with appearing in all six of the *Star Wars* movies.

✳ Daniels' C-3PO costume was precision engineered and fit very tightly. If he moved too much, the pieces of the suit cut into him. Walking in the costume resulted in a great many scrapes, cuts, and abrasions—a problem throughout the shoot.

* After Harrison Ford tested for the part of Han Solo, he had the edge for the role, though early in the project, Lucas had decided he didn't want to use anyone he had directed in the past. The potential candidate list included Kurt Russell and Christopher Walken, among others.

* Jodie Foster and Cindy Williams auditioned for the role of Princess Leia, along with Linda Purl, Terry Nunn, and many others. Foster and Nunn were rejected because they were under 18 at the time.

* The character of Luke Skywalker went through many incarnations during script development. In the original treatment for the *Star Wars* script, which was written in 1973, Luke Skywalker was a general assigned to protect a rebel princess. In a later version, his name was Kane Starkiller, and he was a half-man, half-machine character who is friends with Han Solo. Later, he evolved into the young man closer to the character we are familiar with, but his name was Luke Starkiller. Just before shooting began, Lucas decided that the name might remind people of murderers like Charles Manson, so the name was changed to Luke Skywalker.

Boo-Boos on the Big Screen

It doesn't matter how big the budget or how many star names appear in a movie, just about every feature contains some kind of goof or continuity error

✳ ✳ ✳ ✳

WHETHER IT'S A camera reflected in a window or a change in an actor's clothing from one take to the next, few movies are perfect. Few, if any, members of the audience are likely to notice such minor slipups. But thanks to rabid fans and a DVD player's pause button, no mistake goes unnoticed for long. Here are some goofs from a few popular movies.

I Am Legend (2007)

This film focuses on the story of a lone human (Will Smith) left on Earth after a widespread plague. However, in the film's establishing scenes—which were meant to show a desolate and deserted New York City—people are clearly visible walking near buildings in one panning shot.

The Dark Knight (2008)

In the opening scene of the popular sequel to *Batman Begins* (2005), as the Joker and his gang are robbing the Gotham City bank, the shadow of the Steadicam operator can be seen as he passes the vault door. Later in the same sequence, as the bus leaves the bank, the camera is visible in the window's reflection.

During a couple of scenes in the movie, a sign that reads "Sweet Home Chicago" is clearly visible. Much of the film was shot in the Windy City.

Another error occurs later in the movie. After the chase scene through the streets of Gotham, Jim Gordon, wearing a distinctive pair of glasses, puts a shotgun to the Joker's head. A few seconds later, Gordon opens the armored car door to let out Harvey Dent. He is still wearing glasses but clearly a different pair this time.

Mamma Mia! (2008)

During the scene in which Meryl Streep's character sings "Mamma Mia," the amount of dirt on the knees of her dungarees changes with each shot. During the dancing scene on the beach, the decanter and ice bucket sitting on the bar also appear to move as the camera angles change.

Slumdog Millionaire (2008)

Even this Academy Award-winning Best Picture isn't free of errors. Early in the movie, when Salim and Jamal are hustling tourists at the Taj Mahal, Jamal is given a new $10 bill. Eagle-eyed viewers will note that this scene is supposed to be set in 2002, even though the new bill shown wasn't issued until 2006.

Another factual mistake involves the cricket match being played on a TV in the background of one scene. It would take a real enthusiast of the sport to pick this one up, but the match shown between India and South Africa was actually played in

Belfast, Ireland, although the commentator says that it is being played in the Wankhede Stadium in Mumbai.

Here's an easier mistake to spot: When Jamal stands at the front gate of Javed's house and tells the guard that he is the new dishwasher, his shirt changes from a dark, long-sleeved button-up to a light blue, short-sleeved button-up. When the guard lets him in and Jamal enters the house, he is back to wearing the long-sleeved shirt.

WALL-E (2008)

Continuity errors are not limited to live-action movies. In the animated feature *WALL-E*, when the title character adds the Zippo lighter to his collection, he carefully places it facing out. When he rotates the shelf unit after he meets EVE, the lighter is no longer there. Later, though, when EVE reaches for it, the lighter has returned.

Another error occurs in the scene in which WALL-E first meets the cleaner robot. The tread marks WALL-E leaves on the floor are pointing in the wrong direction.

Lulu: Idol of Germany

From Hollywood "It Girl" to heyday has-been in less than five years—this was the fate cast by Hollywood studio bosses, who were unable to reel in the rebellious and outspoken Louise Brooks. But the "girl in the black helmet," whose trademark shiny black bob has since been copied by every woman and starlet alike, didn't prove so easy to throw aside.

✳ ✳ ✳ ✳

LOUISE BROOKS, BORN Mary Louise Brooks to an attorney father and artistically eccentric mother in Kansas in 1906, picked up her contentious temperament early. The philosophy, if that's not too formal a term for it, of the Brooks household was every child for herself. Mother Myra Brooks was known to sit back and laugh as her "squalling brats" took to fisticuffs to settle their disputes. Fighting, it seemed, was in Louise's blood. She started her serious performing career at age 15 as a dancer in the prestigious Denishawn troupe but was later released because of her truculent tendencies. This dismissal marked an early indication of the turbulent path her Hollywood career would take.

A Hit in Hollywood

Despite her belligerent reputation, or perhaps partly because of it, the burgeoning movie industry took note of the young and talented Brooks, casting her in a slew of silent films. She was popular with the public and quickly became the premiere on-screen darling of Paramount. Offscreen, though, her bosses might have described her as anything but darling.

Only a couple of years into her film career, Louise was already at the top of the silent film heap; but, like F. Scott Fitzgerald's description of his wife, Zelda, Louise, too, thought of herself as a failed social creature. This weakness was her undoing. Unable—or at least unwilling—to comply with societal niceties, Louise was revered for her beauty, as well as for a charisma that translated effervescently to the big screen, but her talents were overshadowed by her unabashed honesty. Although Paramount capitalized on her acting aptitude (and Hollywood men on her sexual liberty), Louise irrecoverably cut ties with Paramount when executives reneged on one too many offers.

Europe Beckons

While on leave from Hollywood, Louise was quickly snatched up by German Expressionist filmmaker G. W. Pabst and was cast as Lulu in *Pandora's Box*. This now-infamous character was a sexually charged vaudevillian whose amorous exploits included the first-ever on-screen depiction of lesbian relations. Finally, a genre that seemed fitting to Louise's sexually charged and controversial nature! On the heels of *Pandora's Box* came *Diary of a Lost Girl*, another Pabst-directed exposé on society's sexual underbelly and social conduct. In this film, Louise's character, Thymiane, suffers through rape, the birth of her illegitimate child, the death of said child, and eventually, prostitution.

No Chance for a Comeback

Upon her return to Hollywood in 1930, Louise fell victim to the cold-hearted punishment of blacklisting. Unhappy with Paramount, she had refused to participate in sound editing for *The Canary Murder Case*. Thus, the film showcased Louise's role as "The Canary" with another songbird, Margaret Livingston, on vocals. Because her prior films had all been silent, Paramount was able to claim that Louise's melodious voice was inept for singing in talkies, a low blow that solidified her downhill reputation. From then on, Louise moved from roles in which she was critically ignored to low-budget films to an embarrassing final role in a John Wayne Western.

Louise never made it back to her short-lived Hollywood high point. She did, however, make a blaring reappearance late in life through a writing career in which she brutally dissected the world of cinema. In Louise's own words, the character of Lulu "dropped dead in an acute attack of indigestion" after devouring her "sex victims." It appears that fickle Hollywood had chewed up and spit out young Louise in much the same fashion.

Howard Hughes: The Paragon of Paranoia

The sad condition of reclusive mogul Howard Hughes in his last years is well known—he became a bearded, emaciated, germophobe hiding in his Las Vegas hotel room. But the actual details of Hughes's strange life are even more shocking.

❋　❋　❋　❋

A Golden Youth

BORN IN HOUSTON, Texas, in 1905, to an overprotective mother and an entrepreneur father who made a fortune from inventing a special drill bit, Howard Hughes moved to

California shortly after his mother died when he was 17. There he was exposed to the Hollywood film industry through his screenwriter uncle, Rupert Hughes. When his father died two years later, Howard inherited nearly a million dollars while still in his teens. Through shrewd investments he managed to parlay that into a serious fortune, which gave him the means to pursue his interest in films that had been ignited by Uncle Rupert.

Hughes became the darling of Hollywood beauty queens. He produced several successful films, including *Scarface* and *Hell's Angels* (which cost him nearly $4 million of his own money). Next, he turned his imaginative talents to aviation. He formed his own aircraft company, built many planes himself, and broke a variety of world records. He even won a Congressional Gold Medal in 1939 for his achievements in aviation. But his life took a drastic turn in 1946, when he suffered injuries in a plane crash that led to a lifelong addiction to painkillers. He also downed several seaplanes and was involved in a few auto accidents—and perhaps these mishaps helped give him the idea that the world was out to get him.

Evolving into a Hermit

Hughes married movie starlet Jean Peters in 1957, but they spent little time together and later divorced. He eventually moved to Las Vegas and bought the Desert Inn so he could turn its penthouse into his personal safe house.

In 1968, *Fortune* magazine named Howard Hughes the richest man in America, with an estimated wealth of $1 billion. But his personal eccentricities mounted almost as quickly as his fortune. Hughes was afraid of outside contamination of all sorts, from unseen bacteria to city water systems to entire ethnic groups. He was even afraid of children. He also burned his clothes if he found out that someone he knew had an illness.

Dangerously Decrepit

Biographer Michael Drosnin provided shocking details about Hughes's lifestyle: He spent most of his time naked, his matted hair hanging shoulder-length and his nails so long they curled over. Hughes even stored his own urine in glass jars. His home was choked with old newspapers and used tissues, and he sometimes wore empty tissue boxes as shoes. Hughes was obsessive, however, about organizing the memos that he scribbled on hundreds of yellow pads.

Hughes usually ate just one meal per day, and he sometimes subsisted on dessert alone. His dental hygiene was abysmal—his teeth literally rotted in his mouth. When he finally died from heart failure in 1976, the formerly robust man weighed only 90 pounds. He had grown too weak to handle his codeine syringe and had turned himself into a human pincushion, with five broken hypodermic needles embedded in his arms.

He Couldn't Take It with Him

Howard Hughes died without a will, although he had kept his aides in line for nearly two decades by dangling the promise of a fat windfall upon his death. In the end, his giant estate was inherited by some cousins.

Hughes left another legacy—his long list of achievements. He built the first communication satellite—the kind used today to link the far corners of the world. His Hughes Aircraft Company greatly advanced modern aviation. And he produced award-winning movies. However, the full extent of his influence on the world will probably never be known.

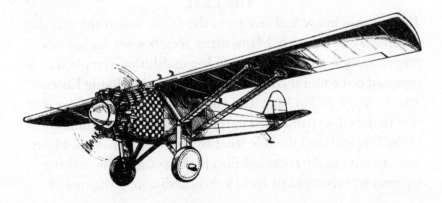

The Weird, Wacky, and Wonderful *Wizard of Oz*

The stories behind the 1939 classic are almost as entertaining as the movie itself.

✳ ✳ ✳ ✳

The Story

When L. Frank Baum wrote the book *The Wonderful Wizard of Oz* back in 1900, he had no idea what he was starting. The story follows the adventures of Dorothy Gale, a young girl from Kansas, who, along with her dog, Toto, gets caught up in a tornado and is magically transported to the land of Oz. The book sold tens of thousands of copies to a public who ate up the strange and wonderful tale.

In 1938, MGM bought the rights to the novel and adapted it for film. Many details were changed, including the famous shoes Dorothy wears: in the book, they were silver, not red. But the major difference between the movie and the book is that Baum's Dorothy really does go to a place named Oz; MGM felt that making Oz a place Dorothy visits in a dream would better explain the psychological motivations of her desire for love and acceptance. So after countless revisions, the script was finalized and production began.

The Cast

The cast you know and love from the movie wasn't the cast that producers started with. Many, many recasts were made from preproduction until after filming began. Shirley Temple was rumored to be up for the part of Dorothy, and Buddy Ebsen was the original Tin Man. But after suffering an allergic reaction to the silver paint used in the makeup, he was admitted to the hospital, and the role went to Jack Haley instead. Haley was unaware of what caused Ebsen's illness, and the makeup formula was changed to avoid a second disaster. The role of the Wicked Witch originally belonged to Gale Sondergaard, but she quit after execs changed the character from a haughty, glamorous witch to a green-faced old hag. Margaret Hamilton replaced her. And W. C. Fields was asked to play the Wizard, but he reportedly had a scheduling conflict with *You Can't Cheat an Honest Man*, a vehicle designed especially for his talents and thus a better opportunity for him. He was replaced by Frank Morgan.

Once the casting had settled down, the studio likely thought the snags in production were over. Not quite.

The Trouble

Only a few weeks into filming, director Richard Thorpe was fired by MGM. He was replaced by George Cukor, who would soon take on directing *Gone with the Wind* (1939). Cukor never actually filmed any scenes for *Oz* however; he was replaced by Victor Fleming, who was later joined by director King Vidor, who shot the black-and-white scenes. (And you thought the casting was complicated.)

In addition to personnel issues, physical injuries also ran rampant on the set. There was the incident with Ebsen and the makeup, and his replacement, Jack Haley, also endured a serious eye infection because of the makeup. Then, one day while filming, Margaret Hamilton was severely burned during a pyrotechnics accident. When she wasn't recuperating from burns, she was trying not to ingest any of the toxic makeup used to create her witch persona.

And then there were accounts from Judy Garland later in life about the pills administered to her by the studio to keep her weight down. Apparently, the studio plied her with amphetamines to control her weight and increase her productivity. As a result, she battled an addiction to pills the rest of her life, only to have MGM drop her contract during the 1950s because the addiction made her unreliable. In 1969, Garland died of an accidental overdose.

Moreover, the directors, producers, studio heads, songwriters, and scriptwriters all had opinions about the direction of the story, which slowed production and fired up more than a few tempers. Originally, there was a singing contest number in Oz in which Dorothy's "hip" vocal style won the hearts of the Munchkins. A group number known as "The Jitterbug" was taken out of the movie after five weeks and thousands of dollars were spent filming it, and, astonishingly, "Over the Rainbow," Dorothy's sweet, sad song (ranked No. 1 on the American Film Institute's list of 100 Greatest Songs in American Films), was also cut from the picture because the studio thought the film was running too long. Producer Arthur Freed and lyricist Harold Arlen, convinced of the song's power, lobbied hard for MGM founder Louis B. Mayer to put it back in. He begrudgingly agreed, which was a smart move because it won the Academy Award for Best Song. The movie itself won an Oscar for Best Original Score and was nominated for Best Picture as well as three technical awards.

The Reception

The film that cost MGM $2.8 million to produce was released in 1939 and made $3 million in its first theatrical run. Because of advertising and distribution costs, that wasn't enough of a profit for the studio to consider it a success, so ten years later, the film was rereleased and earned an additional $1.5 million, which made the producers happy.

But The Wizard of Oz is often considered "the movie that television made." In 1956, CBS broadcast the movie to an audience of 45 million viewers—even though most people at the time didn't have color TV sets and therefore never saw the movie's sequences in Technicolor. Three years later, the movie was broadcast again as a two-hour Christmas special and the response was overwhelming. People loved The Wizard of Oz so much that the movie was broadcast every year for decades, traditionally around special holidays, first by CBS, then by NBC. You can still catch it on cable channels or just reach into your video or DVD library. *The Wizard of Oz* has enjoyed some of the highest home video/DVD sales in history—millions of people own a copy of one of the many editions available for home viewing.

The Strange World of Joe Meek

The music business has produced more than its fair share of eccentric characters, but very few have been stranger than Joe Meek, the independent British pop-record producer of the 1950s and '60s.

A Complicated Man

PERHAPS YOU HAVE never heard of Joe Meek, but you've probably heard the musical recordings he produced and inspired: Meek was the first to develop the electronic effect reverb and sampling techniques. In 1962, he produced "Telstar," an electronics-soaked single by the Tornados that became a worldwide sensation. It was the first record by a British group to top the charts in the United States, more than a year before the arrival of The Beatles. "Telstar" sold more than five million copies around the world, making it one of the most successful instrumental records ever. Meek also recorded with then-unknown singer Tom Jones, although it was another two years (and with a different producer) before the singer made it big.

But that wasn't all there was to Meek. As well as being an innovative music producer, he was also an occultist, a paranoid eccentric, and, illegally at the time, a homosexual. Despite Meek's successes and influence on modern music, it's his strangeness that people remember.

304 Holloway Road

Joe Meek created his legendary home studio in a three-story apartment above a leather goods store in London. Meek's landlady operated the store below and frequently complained about the noise her tenant made. In the days before eight-track recording, records were recorded live with dubs added later. To obtain just the sound he was looking for, Meek would often have performers playing on the stairs or in the bathroom. When his long-suffering landlady complained by banging on the ceiling, Meek would simply turn up the volume to drown her out.

Meek's Downward Spiral

An obsessive Buddy Holly fan, Meek believed that the late rocker communicated with him from beyond the grave. He developed a similar obsession with the still-living bass player from the Tornados, Heinz Burt. When Meek confiscated a shotgun that Burt had brought to the studio one day, the components for violence were all in place.

In 1963, Meek was arrested in a men's public restroom after allegedly "smiling at an old man," which made the national press. Meek spiraled into depression, and his paranoia and outbursts worsened. On February 3, 1967, after yet another quarrel with his landlady, Meek blasted her with the shotgun that he had confiscated from Burt. He then turned the gun on himself. Coincidentally, it was also the eighth anniversary of Buddy Holly's death.

* Like many musicians at the time, Meek was known to pop plenty of pills and experiment with LSD. The drugs may have accounted for much of his strange behavior.

* Meek was once seen running alone late at night along London's Holloway Road, dressed in pajamas and screaming that he was being chased by someone with a knife.

* When Phil Spector, a legendary (and legendarily whacked-out) producer in his own right called Meek to tell him how much he loved his music, Meek accused Spector of stealing his ideas and hung up on him.

* Buddy Holly wasn't the only dead guy talking to Meek—he also believed he was in spiritual contact with the ancient Egyptian Emperor Rameses the Great.

Chapter 5

Sports, Games, and Adventure

Fast Facts

✳ The Olympics were first recorded in 776 B.C. Until the early 8th century B.C., there was only one event—the 200-yard dash.

✳ The ancient Egyptians loved playing a checkerboard game called senets. Players moved pieces around a board determined by tossing numbered throwing sticks.

✳ Mary Queen of Scots, an avid golfer, was reportedly seen playing a round on the links just two days after the murder of her second husband, Lord Darnley.

✳ Chess originated in India, where it was first played with four players. The Persians, then Arabs, modified this fine board game before passing the practice down to Europe.

✳ Chinese acrobatics were performed at least as far back as the Han Dynasty, around 200 B.C.

✳ Central American Mayans developed their own team sports similar to lacrosse, football, and soccer.

✳ Ancient Egypt had its own version of the Olympics, featuring gymnastics, javelin, running, swimming, and other events.

✳ In 1457, the Scottish parliament outlawed golf and football (soccer) because these sports were considered dangerous, time-wasting nuisances that detracted from more important pursuits—like archery.

* Native American tribes had many versions of, and names for, the modern sport of lacrosse. The Cherokee called it "Little Brother of War," because it was good training for combat.

* The Roman game of quoits, where a ring is tossed at a stake in the ground, is the forerunner of modern horseshoes.

Everybody Loves the Circus!

Can you imagine life in the 19th century with no TV, no computers, and no MP3 players? What did people do for entertainment? Well, if you were lucky, maybe once a year a circus came to town. The citizens of Baraboo were lucky all year round.

✳ ✳ ✳ ✳

They Called It Ringlingville

WISCONSIN GOT THE nickname "The Mother of Circuses" thanks to five young men by the name of Ringling. Even as boys, the brothers—Al, Otto, Charles, John, and Alf T.— had a love for the circus. They put on small shows complete with juggling, dancing, and animal acts. Little did they know what their passion had in store for them in the years to come.

The Ringling Brothers Circus began in Baraboo, Wisconsin, in 1884. It started out fairly small and traveled around the region just like other circuses of the time. By the end of the decade, however, the Ringling Brothers Circus had grown to be one of the largest circuses in the country. More importantly, the brothers were known for their honesty and integrity in a business that, well, wasn't always associated with those qualities. The brothers outlawed shell games and the three-card monte acts popular with other carnivals. They also didn't allow their customers to be shortchanged by ticket sellers. As their reputation for fair play grew, so did their circus and their profits.

The circus grew even more in 1889 when the Ringling Brothers bought some railroad cars. That may not sound like a big deal, but its impact was huge in the days when the primary mode of transportation was horse-pulled wagons—a slow and laborious way to travel. With the rails in front of it, the circus had no limits. The circus could travel farther away to larger cities where the demand for a circus—and the pay—was greater. It became the largest traveling circus of the day. Trains played an integral part in later years, as well, when the circus traveled across Wisconsin on a two-day trip from Baraboo to Milwaukee, as part of the Great Circus Parade.

The Greatest Show on Earth

When the Ringling Brothers started their circus, they set up winter quarters in Baraboo. Buildings were erected along the north bank of the Baraboo River, and many of them still stand today—the largest group of original circus buildings still around. The Ringling Brothers wintered there until 1918. In 1919, they merged with the Barnum & Bailey Circus and moved the winter quarters to Bridgeport, Connecticut.

In the 1930s, the Ringling Brothers and Barnum & Bailey Circus saw business suffer due to the Depression. While prosperity grew after World War II, the circus never regained its previous status. Suddenly, the country was bursting with a new love of technology—radio shows, movie theaters, and eventually television won American hearts. The circus lost its luster.

The Ringling Brothers and Barnum & Bailey Circus still exists today, and it travels the country with two circus trains, representing two different shows. They bring the traditional three-ring circus to life in large cities along the way.

And the Rest Is History

Back in Baraboo, the circus—and its storied history—is alive and well all year round. Circus World Museum spans 64 acres of land and features 30 buildings—as well as the original train complex. A National Historic Landmark, Circus World Museum houses one of the largest collections of circus artifacts in the world—from photos to wagons to posters. Everything is there—except the peanuts.

The Real Babe

The greatest female athlete to ever tear down the track, lope across the links, compete on the court, or dash round the diamond may have been born Mildred Ella Didrikson, but throughout her acclaimed and admired sporting life, she was known simply as Babe.

✳ ✳ ✳ ✳

MILDRED ELLA DIDRIKSEN (she later changed the spelling) was born in Port Arthur, Texas, in 1914 or 1911, depending on which source one believes. In her autobiography, Babe claimed to have been delivered onto this mortal coil in 1914, yet her tombstone and baptismal certificate assert she was born in 1911. While there may be a dispute over that date, there is no argument over the accomplishments she achieved on the playing field.

Skills on the Diamond

A natural at every pursuit she attempted, Didrikson excelled at basketball, diving, swimming, tennis, bowling, and lacrosse as a youngster. As talented as she was at this wide array of athletic aspirations, she made her first headlines and acquired her moniker playing the male-dominated sport of baseball. She could throw a baseball with alarming accuracy from astonishing distances, snare hotshot ground balls, and snag line drives with dexterity and grace.

It was her ability with the bat, however, that opened eyes and slackened jaws. She was so adept at hammering the horsehide that she drew instant comparisons to George Herman Ruth of the New York Yankees, known worldwide as the Babe. Didrikson's success with the stick earned her the same nickname, and she adopted the appellation with pride.

Although her greatest athletic achievements would come on the track and golf course, she continued to play baseball whenever and wherever the opportunity presented itself. In 1934, she spent the summer with the esteemed House of David baseball team, an amateur group with tremendous ability that toured the country playing—and often defeating—some of the best professional teams in the land.

Athletic Diversity

As adept as she was on the diamond, Babe was also a stand-out on the basketball court at Beaumont High School. The Employers Casualty Insurance Company of Dallas noticed her star status and enlisted her to play for the company's industrial league team, the Golden Cyclones. Between 1930 and 1932, she guided the team to the Amateur Athletic Union (AAU) national championship and was voted All-American each season. Her exceptional athletic versatility prompted the company to expand its women's sports program into track and field. The company sponsored Babe's involvement in the 1932 AAU championships, which served as an Olympic-qualifying tournament for the upcoming games. Babe competed in eight of ten events, winning five gold medals while setting world records in the javelin, 80-meter hurdles, high jump, and baseball throw.

That performance earned her a berth on the U.S. Olympic team, and she represented her country with distinction at the 1932 summer games in Los Angeles. Though technically a novice—she had never even seen a track and field meet until 1930—her competitive desire and prodigious prowess allowed her to overcome her inexperience with astounding results. Didrikson won Olympic gold in both the javelin and the 80-meter hurdles, breaking her own world records in the process. She also set a world record in the high jump, but her effort was downgraded from gold to silver-medal status because of a technicality: She cleared the record height by diving headfirst over the bar—a method so revolutionary that Olympic officials refused to award her a gold medal.

Hitting the Links

Following her unprecedented Olympic success, Didrikson didn't exactly settle into civilian life. She continued to barnstorm around the country, speaking on the rubber chicken circuit, appearing as a vaudeville novelty act playing harmonica while running on a treadmill, and playing basketball and baseball. She also pursued a new passion, the game of golf. After only a few months of practice, Babe deemed herself competent for competitive play and won the second tournament she entered in April 1935, the Texas Women's Amateur Championship.

Didrikson went on to record 82 career amateur and professional victories—including 10 major titles. She captured a trio of U.S. Open crowns in 1948, 1950, and 1954 and strung together a remarkable and unprecedented 17 consecutive wins from April 1946 to August 1947, a feat no other duffer of either gender has been able to equal.

Didrikson was a founding member of the Ladies Professional Golf Association (LPGA) and continued to win tournaments with uncanny ease until 1954, when she was diagnosed with colon cancer. Fourteen weeks later, she returned to the links and won the U.S. Women's Open. Though noticeably slowed by her illness, she captured another pair of titles before succumbing to the disease in September 1956.

She has definitely not been forgotten. In 1950, the Associated Press named her the female athlete of the first half of the century and, in 2000, *Sports Illustrated* magazine anointed her as the second-best female athlete of all time, behind heptathlete Jackie Joyner-Kersee. ESPN named her the 10th Greatest North American Athlete of the 20th century. And Beaumont, Texas, is home to a museum dedicated to her life and accomplishments.

Balls in the Air

A major mix-up puts two baseballs in play simultaneously.

✳ ✳ ✳ ✳

ONE OF THE most bizarre bits of baseball history occurred at Chicago's Wrigley Field on June 30, 1959, as the Chicago Cubs were playing the St. Louis Cardinals. The strange play got underway after a missed strike three got away from Cubs catcher Sammy Taylor. Thinking incorrectly that it was a foul ball, the catcher didn't pursue it. A bat boy who also thought it had fouled retrieved it and threw it to Pat Pieper, the field announcer. When Pieper saw that the play was continuing with the batter now running to first base, his heart sank. In an instant he realized that it was a live ball. Rather than catch it, he let it drop at his feet. Then third baseman Alvin Dark grabbed the ball. While this was occurring, the umpire, out of sheer habit, gave Taylor a new ball.

Amidst the confusion the first base runner, Stan Musial, made a beeline for second base. Cubs' pitcher Bob Anderson snatched the ball from Taylor's mitt and fired it to second base at precisely the same instant that third baseman Alvin Dark threw his ball to second base.

Ernie Banks was covering second at that fateful moment. He caught one of the balls that had been thrown towards him while the other ball rolled off into center field. He tagged Musial out with the ball while center fielder Bobby Thomson threw the other ball into the dugout. Musial, thinking that the latter was in fact the live ball, ran toward home and scored.

A heated discussion commenced between the umpires after the play. When the dust settled, an official ruling was made: Musial was out after being tagged by Banks.

Despite the ruling, the Cardinals won the game 4–1.

What Goes Up…

Popular during the 17th and 18th centuries in Europe, fox tossing (or Fuchsprellen *in German) was a competitive sport that is akin to hunting. Today, of course, such a game simply wouldn't fly.*

✳ ✳ ✳ ✳

IN THIS "SPORT" of yore, men and women (hunters, servants, and people of the court) would hold a blanket or net and put a fox (or other animal of choice) in the middle. The group (or a particularly strong solo person) would then toss the animal into the air. The ground was covered with sand or sawdust to provide a softer landing for the animal and prolong the play for the participants—after all, they didn't want the animal to die on the first toss. The higher the toss, the better. Skilled tossers could reach heights of 24 feet.

Popular with spectators, the sport often took place in a court-yard with fans looking on from the palace windows. And the sport wasn't just for strapping young lads looking to offload a little testosterone—it was common for couples to play against each other, and for the event to be turned into a sort of party featuring masks and costumes for players and animals alike. The players would dress up as sprites, nymphs, sphinxes, and other mythological creatures, and the animals would play the part of unpopular enemies and political figures.

Beware of Falling Animals

Today, PETA would undoubtedly cry foul on the sport, since it was nearly always fatal to the participating animal. In fact (animal lovers, close your eyes), in a 1648 match that took place in Dresden,Germany, an outstanding number of animals were thrown and killed, including 647 foxes, 533 hares, 31 badgers, and 21 wildcats. And the sport wasn't only dangerous for the critters. A tossed animal isn't a particularly happy or friendly animal, and it wasn't unusual for them to turn on the players and attack. And frankly, we can't say we blame 'em.

The Necessities of Survival

When rock climber Aron Ralston's arm was pinned by a boulder while he was out on a climbing trip, he did the unthinkable in order to survive.

✳ ✳ ✳ ✳

IN 2003, ARON Ralston went on a hiking trip in Utah's Blue John Canyon. Feeling confident and adventurous, Ralston, an experienced mountain climber, set out on the solo trip, neglecting to tell anyone he was leaving. The trip began perfectly: nice hike, beautiful day. Then, as Ralston tried to negotiate a narrow opening in the canyon, an 800-pound boulder fell and pinned his right forearm, completely crushing it.

It looked like there would be no escape. Ralston was completely trapped under the boulder, and his hand and arm were deadened due to the pressure of the blow. For the next five days, Ralston concentrated on staying alive, warding off exhaustion, hypothermia, and dehydration. He knew no one would be looking for him, since no one knew of his trip. Assuming the worst, he carved his name into the rock that held him down, along with what he thought would be his death date. Using a video camera he had packed with his supplies, he taped his goodbyes to his friends and family.

On the sixth day of being trapped, delirious and starving, Ralston made a hellish decision: He would cut off his own arm to escape. Bracing his arm against a climbing tool called a chockstone, Ralston snapped both his radius and ulna bones and applied a tourniquet with some rags he had on hand. Using the knife blade of his multi-tool, he then cut through the soft tissue around the broken bones and tore through tendons with the tool's pliers. The makeshift operation took about an hour.

After he was loose, Ralston still had to rappel down a 65-foot-tall cliff, then hike eight miles to his parked truck. Dehydrated and badly injured, he walked to the nearest trail and was finally discovered. A helicopter team flew Ralston to the nearest hospital where he was stabilized and sent immediately into surgery to clean up and protect what was left of his arm. He later received a prosthetic limb.

Once the press caught wind of his story, Ralston became a celebrity. These days, Ralston works as a motivational speaker, and he still goes on climbing trips, regularly setting new records. In 2010, his story was made in a movie, *127 Hours*.

Tennis Tantrums

Despite its genteel history and emphasis on decorum, a good game of tennis can provoke on-court behaviors that are tyrannical or simply tiresome. Here are a few professional players who lost more than their composure.

✳   ✳   ✳   ✳

John McEnroe vs. Tom Gullikson—Wimbledon, 1981: The *New York Times* once dubbed McEnroe "the worst advertisement for our system of values since Al Capone," so it's only fitting his name should appear (twice) on this list. In addition to his usual repertoire of ranting, raving, and racquet launching, McEnroe immortalized his rebellious reputation by continuously shouting, "You cannot be serious!" at umpires and line judges. This behavior continued throughout the duration of the tournament, and despite winning the prestigious prize for the first time, McEnroe was not offered a membership to the All-England club, an honor usually afforded to every first-time victor.

John McEnroe vs. Mikael Pernfors—Australian Open, 1990: Johnny Mac should have boned up on the rulebook before unleashing one of his patented temper tantrums. In his fourth-round match against Pernfors, McEnroe was issued a warning by umpire Gerry Armstrong for intimidating a lineswoman. Later, after he was docked a point for smashing a racket, McEnroe fired off a volley of vindictive language toward the official. Unaware that a new "three strikes you're out" rule had recently been inserted into the code of conduct, McEnroe was disqualified from further play, and the match was awarded to Pernfors.

Jeff Tarango vs. Alexander Mronz—Wimbledon, 1995: Talk about mixed doubles! During his third-round match against Alexander Mronz, tennis menace Jeff Tarango put on a legendary display of spoiled sportsmanship, childlike insolence, and all-round bad judgment. After chair umpire Bruno Rebeuh ruled against him on several close line calls, the feisty Tarango refused to continue the match, demanded that the accumulated throng watching the debacle "shut up," and accused the umpire of being "one of the most corrupt officials in the game." At least one denizen in the crowd supported Tarango's view of the proceedings. His wife, Benedictine, strolled up to the on-court official and delivered an overhand smash of her own. She slapped the official twice across the face before storming out of the arena with her husband, who became the first player in Wimbledon history to default a match because of a disagreement over an official's judgment. Tarango was fined a record $15,500 for his tirade.

Serena Williams vs. Jennifer Capriati—U.S. Open, 2004: When her cross-court backhand was ruled out by chair umpire Mariana Alves, Williams was stunned but certainly not silent. She unleashed a barrage of uncomplimentary comments and emphasized her perspective on the proceedings by putting a ball on the court, pointing at it, and pouting. Williams went on to lose the match, and Alves did not umpire again during the tournament.

Tim Cahill, Adrenaline Junkie

Some travel the world and write about it. Some dine on haute cuisine; others lunch on sago beetle grubs. Meet Tim Cahill.

✳ ✳ ✳ ✳

The Genre

ADVENTURE TRAVEL IS supposed to be interesting, but in recent years, Tim Cahill has taken it to the extreme. The Wisconsin native's travel and writing style has made his books, with titles like *Pecked to Death by Ducks* and *A Wolverine Is Eating My Leg*, simultaneously entertaining and weird.

The Guy

Chops help: Cahill swam competitively in college and is an advanced climber, caver, kayaker, diver, rider, and backcountry survivor. Guts help: Cahill will try just about anything. One might expect an ego the size of Madagascar, but Cahill's writing doesn't reflect this. He doesn't get out of everything unscathed, and some situations in which he finds himself are just uncomfortable, embarrassing, or terrifying.

The Deeds

Over the course of a long career, Cahill's exploits have included:

✳ With Canadian endurance driver Garry Sowerby, setting a new speed record for driving from Ushuaia (Argentina's southernmost town) to Deadhorse (Alaska's northernmost road-reachable town).

✳ Doing yoga in Negril, Jamaica, while doing his all to avoid enlightenment.

✳ Teaching American grade-school kids gorilla etiquette (which Cahill learned by doing, naturally).

✳ Learning the art of Neolithic spear throwing in east Idaho with a soft-spoken Mormon ex-Marine.

* Stalking the platypus by night in southern Australia.

* Tagging along with Tanzanian tribespeople as they negotiated a solution to recent donkey thefts.

* Riding around rural Mongolia with a packful of human hair and clacking cheese, fleeing from the yogurt riders.

* Kayaking in Glacier Bay while building-sized icebergs 'calved' from the glaciers.

* Drinking manioc beer among the jungle-dwelling Aguaruna of Peru while investigating the death of an idealistic young American.

* Hanging from a cliff in a diaper over the rapids of the Yellowstone River.

* Chowing on iguana eggs and meat in Honduras, then herding cattle from kayaks.

* Hobnobbing with New Guinea tribes where the men wear no clothes, but would feel naked without their penis gourds.

* Sea kayaking on wave-lashed California rocks with the Tsunami Rangers.

* Counting mounds of feces left by Iraqi troops in Kuwaiti buildings.

* Watching old movies with Marquesans who found Paul Newman's kissing hilarious.

* Looking for grizzlies in the Montana mountains—and finding them.

* Drinking *kava* (a mild intoxicant) with Tongans, while learning about giant clams and Tongan ways.

* Spelunking in a New Mexico cave where it snows gypsum.

* Taking a rubber boat onto Antarctica in five-foot swells, watching penguins bicker and bodysurf.

* Discovering witchcraft and getting drunk on pisco sours in southern Chile.

* Riding with low-rider enthusiasts and PCP users in East San José.

* Paragliding in Idaho, with an unerring ability to land in cow manure during training.

* Getting arrested in England along with the Dangerous Sports Club for watching them bungee-jump off a 245 foot high bridge.

* Lunching on baked turtle lung with Aboriginal Australians near the tip of the Cape York Peninsula, Queensland.

* Investigating Olive Ridley sea turtle egg poaching in southern Mexico.

* Flying into a hurricane's eye with the Air Force.

* Watching Chinese archaeologists grapple with the challenges of eating lutefisk.

And those are just the ones he wrote about in books!

A Winning Trade?

Yankee pitchers Fritz Petersen and Mike Kekich not only swapped wives, they swapped lives.

* * * *

Familiarity Breeds Desire

WHEN IT COMES to the art of the spousal swap, New York Yankees pitchers Fritz Petersen and Mike Kekich were far ahead of the curve. In sandlot terms, their exchange stood out as a grand slam of such trades. Not only did each have the temerity to swap wives, they also swapped families in what turned out to be a pennant win for one couple and a sacrifice fly for the other.

When Kekich joined the Yankees in 1969 he became roommates with Petersen. Since both men were pitchers, and lefthanders at that, they already had something in common. Since they were also married, lived in New Jersey, and had children of similar ages, their friendship was almost predestined.

Over the course of regular get-togethers, Kekich' wife Susanne and Petersen's wife Marilyn became close friends. But something unforeseen was also developing as the couples came to know each other better. Kekich, the more reserved of the pitching duo, became enamored of Marilyn, who enjoyed deep conversations as much as he did. Petersen, the livelier of the two men, was drawn by Kekich's wife Susanne, a bubbly former cheerleader and cross-country runner.

Over time and after much joking that they should swap partners, the foursome began to ponder if they had indeed married the wrong people. "By American standards, I had a good marriage," Kekich later said in explaining what occurred next. "But I wanted a great marriage. I was idealistic I guess."

Making the Swap

The couples took the plunge in the summer of 1972 when they threw caution to the wind and began affairs with each other's spouses. By October of that year, Kekich had moved in with Marilyn Petersen while Petersen paired off with Susanne Kekich. The strangest thing was that both men seemed to have no problem swapping out their children as part of the trade—a fact that would later find people scratching their heads in utter bewilderment.

Since Kekich and Petersen were high profile ballplayers, the improbable swap was carried out discreetly. But eventually both men realized that they'd have to come clean. During spring training of 1973 the pitchers called a press conference to set the record straight.

Winners and Losers

After explaining their new living arrangements to the gathered throng of sports writers, Petersen and Kekich admonished the press. "Don't make anything sordid out of this," Petersen said with conviction.

"Don't say this is wife-swapping, because it wasn't," added Kekich. "We didn't swap wives, we swapped lives."

To make things official, Fritz Petersen married Susanne Kekich in 1974. They had four children together and remain married to this day. Mike Kekich and Marilyn Petersen weren't quite as lucky. Their relationship fizzled after a couple of months and the pair split up.

Many years later Kekich described the swap in detail: "Marilyn and I thought we were perfectly suited, just like Fritz and Susanne. Marilyn was all for the swap in the beginning, but then she backed off. All four of us had agreed in the beginning that if anyone wasn't happy, the thing would be called off. But when Marilyn and I decided to call it off, the other couple already had gone off with each other."

From Diamonds to the Rough

You might be surprised to learn what interesting twists some players' lives took when their baseball careers ended.

❋ ❋ ❋ ❋

SOMETIMES, THE NAME suggests the destiny. Hi Jasper, an early 20th-century pitcher for the White Sox, Cardinals, and Indians, had the perfect first name to greet patrons in his second career as a bartender. Others, like Happy Finneran, might have considered a name change once their playing days were over. Finneran went from the pitcher's mound to the funeral home, where he worked as a funeral director and embalmer.

Joe Quinn: Undertaker

The first Australian to reach the major leagues played second base sporadically for 17 years, through 1901. He played on five championship teams but was also a player/manager with the 1899 Cleveland Spiders, whose 20–134 record remains the worst in history.

Having been involved with that club must have made Quinn's "other" job a little easier to bear. This colorful character spent his off-seasons and part of his post-playing career serving as an undertaker in St. Louis, Missouri.

Lu Blue: Chicken Farmer

A switch-hitting first baseman with a terrific eye at the plate, Blue spent most of his 13-year career with the Detroit Tigers. In 1929, he finished first in the American League in total times on base and finished second in the AL in walks four times in his career.

In 1941, he retired to a career as a chicken farmer in Virginia, dabbled in chinchilla farming, and later owned a chicken hatchery in Maryland. A World War I veteran, Blue is perhaps the best-known former big-leaguer buried in Arlington National Cemetery.

Grover Cleveland Alexander: Performer in a Flea Circus

One of the greatest pitchers of all time, Alexander won 373 career games, led St. Louis to a World Series title with the famous 1926 strikeout of Yankee Tony Lazzeri, and was enshrined in the Hall of Fame in 1938. Out of uniform, Alexander experienced many struggles in life, such as epilepsy, hearing loss, and double vision. Within a year of his induction to the Hall, Alexander could be found working for Hubert's Museum and Flea Circus on 42nd Street in Manhattan. For $100 a week, Alexander would stand on a small wooden platform and recount tales of his career at 30-minute intervals.

Rocky Colavito: Mushroom Farmer

Rocky Colavito was one of the most popular players—and people—in Cleveland early in his career. He was a skilled fielder and powerhouse hitter, with 41- and 42-homer seasons. In 1959, he hit home runs in four consecutive at-bats in a single game. He was traded to Detroit before the 1960 season for Harvey Kuenn, an act that Tribe fans blamed for putting a curse on their club.

Colavito finished his career with 374 home runs, a .266 batting average, 1,159 RBI, and one season with a perfect 1.000 fielding percentage. Then he slipped away into an unusual post-baseball job. Rocky went from big-slugging outfielder to mushroom farmer, a gig that kept him well out of the limelight that his sometimes tumultuous playing career had attracted.

A Staggering Spectacle

What event mixes hardcore disciplined athletes with hardcore disciplined drinkers? The Riverwest Beer Run! It should be no surprise that Milwaukee, Wisconsin, known as Beer City, is home to a race in which participants chug beer as they sprint, jog, walk . . . or stagger.

❋   ❋   ❋   ❋

A Long-Running (and Drinking) Event

SINCE 1977, MILWAUKEE's Riverwest neighborhood has hosted the Locust Street Festival of Music and Art. About 20,000 people from Wisconsin and beyond flock to this big street party each year. Along with live music and arts and crafts booths, the block party is known for its Beer Run. The biathlon (the two events being running and drinking) is a 1.8-mile weaving course, and runners pitch and weave their way through Riverwest streets. Considering that many participants wear costumes, it's not viewed as a highly competitive race, unless the competition is to see who can slam their beer the fastest.

The run starts at 11:30 A.M. sharp, and preregistration is strongly encouraged, as it usually reaches its 900-runner limit early. The combination of beer and moderate exercise must be quite appealing to health-conscious drinkers. That Lakefront Brewery pint for breakfast? Why, that's just warming up.

Beer has actually become a welcome fixture at plenty of other races—usually at the finish line. But the official Riverwest Run entry form takes the beer component seriously and states, "Includes four mandatory beer stops for beer provided at tables along the route. Non-drinkers are welcome, but ineligible for prizes." Indeed, there are prizes (a fresh six pack, perhaps?) for the top three winners in each gender and age bracket. All contestants go home with a t-shirt and possibly a buzz. So it's the rare race where everybody wins!

No Little Feat

Even the batting average for 3' 7" Eddie Gaedel in his only game is short: a solid .000. But while he was up at the plate waving his miniature bat, Gaedel was as big as Babe Ruth.

✳ ✳ ✳ ✳

Go For the Gimmick

ST. LOUIS BROWNS owner, Bill Veeck, loved a good show. Having a Little Person up at bat was Veeck's brainchild, as were exploding scoreboards, outlandish giveaways, and other promotions. (For more about Veeck, see page 440.)

The Browns provided Veeck with a great challenge. The team was the perennial sad sack of the American League, and was constantly outdrawn by the rival St. Louis Cardinals. As the public's interest waned for the losing team, Veeck tried every trick he could think of to boost attendance.

Double the Fun

For the August 19, 1951, doubleheader between the Browns and Detroit Tigers, Veeck promised team sponsor Falstaff

Brewery something "spectacular" in honor of Falstaff Brewery Day. The first game was routine, but in the bottom of the first inning of the second game, it was announced, "[Batting] for the Browns, number $1/8$, Eddie Gaedel." Armed with his miniature bat, 65-pound Gaedel was at the plate.

The park erupted in laughter, and photographers scrambled to get pictures. The Tiger's catcher got down on his knees to offer his pitcher a target. Veeck had worked with Gaedel on a crouch that made his strike zone $1^1/_2$ inches high, but the excited Gaedel stood straighter. No matter—the Tiger pitcher was laughing so hard, four straight throws whizzed over Gaedel's head. By the time Gaedel trotted to first base and was taken out for a pinch runner, he was a sensation.

Outraged, the American League immediately banned Gaedel from ever playing pro ball again. Veeck (with tongue firmly in cheek) threatened to investigate whether diminutive New York Yankee shortstop Phil Rizzuto was a short ballplayer or a tall Little Person. Eddie Gaedel, meanwhile, just enjoyed his 15 minutes of fame.

A Grand Gesture

In ancient Rome, gladiators fought each other in front of thousands of spectators, but the last thing the loser wanted to see from the crowd was a collective "thumbs-up."

✳   ✳   ✳   ✳

IN THE ROMAN empire of the first centuries A.D., gladiatorial games that pitted man against man or man against beast were the most popular form of public entertainment. With these games came an involved set of rules, including what a gladiator should do once he had his opponent defeated: Go for the kill, or show mercy. Historians have argued that this decision was often left up to the crowd. According to popular belief, a thumbs-down gesture meant instant slaughter, while spectators' thumbs turned up meant the loser would live. In fact, it worked the opposite way.

It is almost certain that the Roman crowds used some sort of thumb gesture to indicate the fate of the vanquished, but some historians believe "thumbs-down" actually indicated that the triumphant gladiator should lay down his weapon and spare his foe, while "thumbs-up" indicated that the victor should slash open his opponent's throat. Another theory posits that a "thumbs-sideways" motion symbolized a slash to the neck.

"I Can Pitch Forever"

When the Providence Grays lost one of their two pitchers to a rival franchise in 1884, Charley "Old Hoss" Radbourn literally took matters into his own hands.

✳ ✳ ✳ ✳

CHARLEY "OLD HOSS" Radbourn had a rubber arm and an iron will. When his team, the Providence Grays, found themselves without one of their pitchers in 1884, the gritty right-hander made a deal with team owners: He would pitch the rest of the season, he said, but if the Grays won the National League pennant, he would earn a bonus and the right to free agency.

So began one of baseball's most remarkable tales of endurance: When it was all over, the Grays were pennant winners, and Radbourn had logged 73 starts—including a stretch of 19 consecutive starts and wins—and 678 $^2/_3$ innings, just four outs short of Will White's all-time record of 680 innings, set in 1879. Radbourn's 59 victories that year are an all-time record and six more than his closest challenger. Radbourn then pitched three straight victories over American Association champion New York, sweeping the Mets in what some consider the first World Series. He collected a $2,000 bonus and then re-signed with Providence in 1885.

Radbourn's stamina was outstanding even in his day, an era when teams carried two pitchers, 30-win seasons weren't uncommon, and the concept of relief pitching was barely developed. Radbourn tried to conserve his achy arm using a variety of deliveries, but the strenuous workload took its toll nonetheless; the dependable Old Hoss reportedly had difficulty combing his hair before and after games.

The record feats of rubber-armed 19th-century hurlers such as Radbourn and White get safer every year. Bill Hutchison, who threw 622 innings in 1892, was the last pitcher to surpass 600—and 500—innings in a season. Ed Walsh in 1908 was the last 400-inning pitcher. And it's been more than a quarter-century since Steve Carlton in 1980 was the last player to throw more than 300 innings in one year.

Craig Breedlove and the Spirit of America

This driver made his claim on the title of the fastest human being in the world.

✳   ✳   ✳   ✳

CRAIG BREEDLOVE WAS an authentic American icon. Five-time holder of the world land-speed record and innovator in the design and engineering of rocket cars, he was born in Southern California on March 23, 1937. Growing up in the car-crazy 1950s, Breedlove obtained his first automobile at age 13. By 16, he was winning drag races with his souped-up 1934 Ford Coupe. Using an alcohol-based fuel, he pushed the vehicle to 154 miles per hour in the dry lake beds found in the Mojave Desert.

A job as a structural engineering technician at Douglas Aircraft gave Breedlove an education in designing his own high-speed cars, leading ultimately to the Spirit of America, a car designed with a surplus military jet engine as its propulsion system.

Affable and handsome, Breedlove became a major celebrity, earning the heroic nickname "Captain America." The Beach Boys even included a song about him on their hit album *Little Deuce Coupe*.

Is It a Rocket or a Car?

Breedlove built the first version of his Spirit of America rocket car in the early 1960s and tested it in Utah's Bonneville Salt Flats in 1962. His goal was to reclaim the world land-speed record for the United States, but poor handling led to failure. Undeterred, Breedlove tinkered with the design, adding a more easily steered front wheel and a new stabilizer, and tried again in 1963. This time the vehicle worked perfectly. On August 5, 1963, at Bonneville, the Spirit of America reached a speed of 407.45 mph to break the previous record of 394.2 mph, set by English driver John Cobb in 1947.

This new record was not without controversy. Some claimed that the vehicle, with its three-wheel design, was a motorcycle rather than a car. Others said the fact that the wheels were jet-driven meant it was neither car nor motorcycle. Regardless of how you pigeonhole the Spirit, however, no vehicle had ever traveled that fast on land.

Not So Fast

As it turned out, Breedlove's record was short-lived. In February 1964, fellow American Tom Green managed 413 mph at Bonneville. And just three months later, Art Arfons from Ohio hit 434 mph. After breaking Cobb's 16-year-old record, Breedlove saw his record fall to third place in less than a year. Not content to be outdone so quickly, he returned to Bonneville on October 13, 1964, and reclaimed the top spot with a 468 mph performance. For good measure, he tried again two days later and became the first person to go faster than 500 mph on Earth's surface, notching a mark of 526.28 mph. While the speed impressed the competition, not everything worked according to plan. Both drag chutes on the Spirit of

America were lost, as well as the wheel brakes. Because of these failures, Breedlove cut through a row of telephone poles at 400 mph and hit a brine pond while still going 200. Although the car would never drive again, Breedlove swam to shore unscathed.

Taking the Lead

In what was becoming a land-speed-record derby, Breedlove's record was broken again less than two weeks later, when Arfons managed 536 mph. Breedlove was already working on a new Spirit of America, but Arfons's mark stood for just longer than a year. Then the competition got fierce: On November 2, 1965, the Spirit of America Sonic 1 hit 555 mph at Bonneville. Just five days later, Arfons reached 576. Breedlove returned to Bonneville eight days after Arfons notched his mark to reclaim the record with a speed of 600, making him the first person to hit 600 mph in a land vehicle. This record would stand for almost five years. At the time of this writing, Andy Green holds the record, established in 1997: 736 mph.

8 Hours, 25 Minutes, and 33 Innings to History

A look at the longest professional game of all time.

✳   ✳   ✳   ✳

THE LONGEST GAME in professional baseball history took 33 innings and parts of three days to complete. While many of the players who suited up for the Class AAA epic between the Pawtucket Red Sox and Rochester Red Wings on April 18, 1981, later saw action in the majors, this is one minor-league contest they would never forget. Both starting third basemen are in the Hall of Fame, as is the scorecard.

The "PawSox"—Boston's top farm club, led by star third baseman Wade Boggs—played host for the game, which began on a cold and windy Rhode Island night before 1,740 fans at McCoy

Stadium. They watched the visitors (affiliates of the Baltimore Orioles) take a 1–0 lead in the seventh, but Pawtucket knotted the score in the ninth. And there the seemingly endless string of zeroes on the scoreboard began, altered only by a matching pair of "1s" when both teams scored in the 21st.

Conditions grew so frigid after midnight that pitchers broke up benches and lit fires in the bullpen. Umpires could not find a rule about International League curfews, so action continued until league president Harold Cooper was reached by phone. Play was suspended after 32 innings at 4:07 A.M. on Easter Sunday. At that time only 19 fans remained, and Red Wings third baseman Cal Ripken later remembered that it was the only time in his career that his post game meal was breakfast.

The 2–2 contest made national headlines, both in the days that followed and when it resumed on June 23. By then Major League Baseball players were on strike, so reporters descended 140 strong on Pawtucket. They were joined by a sellout crowd of 5,746, who waited just 18 minutes before Dave Koza singled in Marty Barrett to give Pawtucket a 3–2 victory in the bottom of the 33rd. All told, 41 players saw action over 8 hours, 25 minutes of play, but only one stat mattered to Pawtucket center fielder Dallas Williams: 0-for-13, the worst one-game batting line ever.

A Royal Flush

Every year at the end of January, rumors begin to swirl that the sewer systems in several major cities fail due to the number of toilets that are flushed during halftime of the Super Bowl.

✳ ✳ ✳ ✳

A Mad Dash

DURING SUPER BOWL XVIII in 1984, a water main in Salt Lake City ruptured, dampening the sporting spirit in that community. The next day, conversations around office water coolers were rife with rumors that toilet trauma, prompted by a flood of beverage-logged football fans all using the facilities at the same time, had caused the sewer systems of numerous cities to clog up. Such a myth would almost make sense if it were applied to the final of the World Cup of Soccer, where there is continuous action without stoppages of any kind until the half-time break. But anyone who has sat through the six-plus-hour spectacle known as the Super Bowl realizes that there is no merit to this tall tale. The North American brand of football—especially the game played on that particular Sunday—has numerous breaks, pauses, and lapses throughout. So to suggest there is a simultaneous dash to the latrine at any time during this all-day marathon is silly.

Golf Ball Diver

Remember the time you duck-hooked 3 consecutive tee shots into the lake before finally hitting a lousy 80 yards into deep rough? What happens to that layer of golf balls at the bottom of the lake? We're asking the question for you in an interview with someone who retrieves those golf balls professionally.

✳ ✳ ✳ ✳

Q: How many balls does a golf ball diver fish out of a water hazard in a day?

A: At a large course, probably 2,000 or more. That's assuming I don't die in the process. In many parts of the United States, golf ball diving is an extreme sport.

Q: Because you get hit with golf balls?

A: No, though it does happen. Because I can drown, or have an encounter with an alligator, or get bit by a water moccasin—I have lots of hazards of my own. Leeches attach to me. Turtles have tried to take off my fingers. Even some fish think I'm food.

Q: Come on. Most of these lakes are less than ten feet deep, and you're fully qualified in scuba and wearing scuba gear. How could you drown?

A: You'd be sad to see how easily a diver, especially one carrying a big netlike bag full of golf balls in a dark environment, can get hung up in weeds along the bottom of a lake. I could be down there struggling to get free, running out of oxygen, while ten yards away Joe Duffer is celebrating because he just hit the green in regulation for the first time in a week. If I panic, I'm dead. The only way I live through that is if I can remain calm and methodically get myself loose.

Q: Okay, but alligators and snakes? Don't most golf courses remove dangerous reptiles?

A: In Southern states, these critters are everywhere. I don't know of any gator that can read "no trespassing" signs. Usually, where there's water, there are alligators and snakes.

Q: Threatening animals aside, how do you manage to find balls in the dark water?

A: By feel. I can't wear gloves, which is dangerous. I curse the people who have thrown beer bottles into a water hazard to a life of four-putts, because I've been cut quite a bit. I also find a lot of other junk, and stuff that's not junk. I've recovered quite a few golf clubs, often really expensive ones.

Q: Do you make good money?

A: I can. You have to love to dive, and you have to be able to work alone, because unlike the usual dives, you aren't with a buddy. I get a few cents a ball, but that adds up. Sometimes I find specialty balls that sell for a lot more—souvenir balls, really expensive premium balls. One time I pulled out a ball with the presidential logo. If I can get paid to go diving, I don't mind the occasional leech bite.

Maalox Moments: Unexpected Upsets

Enjoy these moments of college football history when events ended up defying expectations.

✳   ✳   ✳   ✳

Notre Dame 35, Army 13—1913: Often regarded as the game that changed the face of football, the event occurred when the Irish attacked Army for the first time in the school's history and came away with an unlikely victory. With only 18 players on their roster and only enough cleats for 14 of them, Notre Dame used a secret weapon known as the forward pass and the combination of Gus Dorais and Knute Rockne to crush the Cadets.

Carnegie Tech 19, Notre Dame 0—1926: Irish sideline boss Knute Rockne was so confident his charges would trample the Tartans, he didn't even bother to attend the game, deciding instead to scout an Army–Navy match. While the Rock skipped, the Tech attacked, whipping the Irish with a 19–0 whitewashing.

Columbia 21, Army 20—1947: Undaunted by Army's pair of national titles and unfazed by the Cadets' 32-game unbeaten streak, Columbia rebounded from a 20–7 fourth quarter deficit to score a pair of unanswered touchdowns, including the infamous "shoestring" catch by Bill Swiacki, to squeeze past Army by a slim 21–20 score.

Miami 31, Nebraska 30—1984: In a hotly contested back-and-forth tundra tussle that many scribes describe as the most exciting college game ever played, the fifth-ranked Hurricanes shocked the top-ranked and undefeated Cornhuskers to win the Orange Bowl and claim the national championship. After Nebraska scored a last-second touchdown to pull within a single point, coach Tom Osborne decided to forgo the tie and attempt a two-point conversion. The Hurricanes held and climbed all the way to the title.

California 17, Stanford 11—1986: In the Bay area, the annual match-up between Stanford and California is known simply as "The Big Game." In most years, both schools are usually battling for Bowl positions, not bragging rights, but in 1986, the Cal team was in a state of disarray. They entered the contest with a 1–9 record, a lame duck coach who had already been fired, and an offense that hadn't been able to find the end zone in more than a month. That was then and this was now. The Bears combined a smothering sack attack that flattened Stanford pivot John Paye seven times with an opportunistic option end-around ramble by Mike Ford to send Stanford shamefaced to the sidelines.

Temple 28, Virginia Tech 24—1998: Entering the game as 35-point favorites, the 5–0 Virginia Tech Hokies learned an important lesson in the perils of overconfidence when the 0–5 Temple Owls shocked the football establishment by bouncing back from a 17–0 halftime deficit to embarrass the Hokies on their home turf. With freshman quarterback Devin Scott taking the snaps for the first time in his collegiate career and sneaking into the end zone late in the game, the Owls tutored Tech to register the biggest upset in school history.

Appalachian State 34, University of Michigan 32—2007: The game was dubbed "The Miracle in Michigan" when Appalachian State, a Division II school, motored onto Michigan's home turf and pulled off what many pundits hail as one of the biggest upsets in the history of American sports, much less college football. After a late field goal propelled the Mountaineers into a 34–32 lead, Michigan marched down the field, eventually setting up a seemingly simple 27-yard three-pointer for the win. However, Appalachian defender Corey Lynch blocked the kick to secure the Mountaineers' victory.

Rocky Marciano Retires Undefeated

This heavyweight boxing champ achieved a feat no one else had ever managed.

✳ ✳ ✳ ✳

BORN ON SEPTEMBER 1, 1923, in Brockton, Massachusetts, Rocco Francis Marchegiano was the heavyweight champion of the world from 1952 to 1956. To this day, with 43 knockouts to his credit, he remains the only heavyweight champion in boxing history to retire without a defeat or a draw.

Solid as a Rock

When he was a year old, Rocky Marciano survived a near-fatal bout of pneumonia. This was perhaps the first evidence of the strength and resilience that led him to spend his childhood and young adulthood wrestling and playing baseball and football. He worked out on homemade weight-lifting equipment, including a makeshift heavy bag formed from an old mailbag that hung from a tree in his backyard. He dropped out of high school in tenth grade and worked as a ditchdigger, sold shoes, and found employment at a coal company.

In 1943, Marciano was drafted into the army, where he spent two years ferrying supplies across the English Channel to Normandy. During his stint in the military, Marciano won the 1946 amateur armed forces boxing tournament. He ended his amateur year with an 11–3 record—the last time Marciano ever experienced a loss.

"Timmmberrr!"

In 1947, Marciano tried out for the Chicago Cubs baseball team, but he was cut three weeks later. Subsequently, he turned professional in the boxing ring. *Sports Illustrated* reported, "He was too short, too light, and had no reach … Rough and tough, but no finesse."

Marciano's hometown fans were believers, and they traveled in groups to watch his fights. When Rocky had an opponent ready to go down, they would yell, "Timmmberrr!" as they would for a falling tree, and the audience would go wild.

Rocky catapulted to stardom in 1951, when he was pitted against Joe Louis, his most formidable opponent and also his childhood idol. The match, which was the last of Louis's career, was aired on national television. Marciano KO'd Louis in the eighth round—and later sobbed in Louis's dressing room after the fight.

The KO Kid

Marciano's trainer, Charley Goldman, taught Rocky his trademark technique—a short, overhand right to the jaw. This move served Marciano well when, in the 13th round against the defending heavyweight champion, lagging behind in points and struggling offensively, he suddenly KO'd Jersey Joe Walcott. The year was 1952.

Firmly established as a "marquee" fighter, Marciano went on to defend his title six times, including a first-round knockout victory in a 1953 rematch with Walcott and another knockout win over Roland La Starza later that year. With a left and a quick right to the jaw, Marciano won a decision against Ezzard Charles in 1954. But fans had a moment of panic when, in a rematch later that year, Marciano nearly lost his title in the sixth round. Charles cut Marciano's nose so badly that his corner trainer couldn't stop the bleeding. When the ring doctor considered stopping the fight, Marciano erupted against Charles and knocked him out in the eighth round. Ding!

A year later, despite organized crime enticements to throw the fight, Rocky KO'd European champion Don Cockell in an exciting nine rounds. Marciano's last fight was in Yankee Stadium on September 21, 1955. He knocked out Archie Moore in the ninth round as more than 400,000 people watched over closed-circuit television.

The Rock

Marciano spent his retirement years working as a boxing show host and commentator and making personal appearances. He died at the age of 46 when a small private plane he was riding in crashed into a tree as it attempted to land in Newton, Iowa.

Inducted into the Boxing Hall of Fame in 1990, Rocky Marciano was honored in 1999 on a commemorative U.S. postage stamp. Marciano lives on through a myriad of books, films, and of course, in the minds and hearts of fans.

And although he may not rank among the top five boxers of all time, one sportswriter summed Marciano up accurately: "If all the heavyweight champions of all time were locked together in a room, Marciano would be the only one to walk out."

In It to Win It

The phrase, "running from the truth" was quite literal in this case of a marathon-running politician.

❋   ❋   ❋   ❋

ROBERTO MADRAZO, FORMER presidential candidate in Mexico, was proclaimed the winner of the 2007 Berlin marathon in the 55-and-older category. His time was 2:41:12. But upon closer examination, he appeared to have ran 15 kilometers (9.5 miles) in 21 minutes—faster than humanly possible.

Madrazo apparently forgot about the microchip he was wearing, which lost track of him at two checkpoints. He was disqualified two weeks later. The politician later said that he'd finished the race after the 21st kilometer and drove to the finish line to get some clothes he had left there. He didn't explain why he pumped his fists in apparent victory as he crossed the finish line or why he didn't immediately correct marathon officials when they named him the winner.

Dribbling Drivel

There are numerous rules on how to properly dribble a basketball, but bouncing the ball with such force that it bounds over the head of the ball handler is not illegal.

✳ ✳ ✳ ✳

A LTHOUGH THE STANDARD NBA game might be more fun if players drummed dribbles with the exaggerated effort of the Harlem Globetrotters the practice wouldn't do much to move the game along. And contrary to popular belief, there is no restriction on how high a player may bounce the ball, provided the ball does not come to rest in the player's hand.

Anyone who has dribbled a basketball can attest to the fact it takes a heave of some heft to give the globe enough momentum to lift itself even to eye-level height. Yet, the myth about dribbling does have some connection to reality. When Dr. James Naismith first drafted the rules for the game that eventually became known as basketball, the dribble wasn't an accepted method of moving the ball. In the game's infancy, the ball was advanced from teammate to teammate through passing. When a player was trapped by a defender, it was common practice for the ball carrier to slap the sphere over the head of his rival, cut around the befuddled opponent, reacquire possession of the ball, and then pass it up court. This innovation was known as the overhead dribble, and it was an accepted way to maneuver the ball until the early part of the 20th century. The art of "putting the ball on the floor" and bouncing it was used first as a defensive weapon to evade opposing players.

By the way, there is absolutely no credence to wry comments made by courtside pundits that the "above the head" rule was introduced because every dribble that former NBA point guard Muggsy Bogues took seemed to bounce beyond the upper reaches of his diminutive 5'3" frame.

Odd Things About the 1900 Olympics

The second modern Olympic Games were held in 1900 in Paris and were billed as part of the Exposition Universelle Internationale, the world's fair that featured the unveiling of the Eiffel Tower. It was the first Olympiad to be held outside of Greece, and there were plenty of other firsts to it as well.

* * * *

* Despite the fact that just less than a thousand athletes competed in the 1900 Olympics, spectator attendance was low. The press preferred to focus on the Paris Exposition and seldom referred to the games as actual Olympic events. Instead, they were reported variously as "International Championships," "Paris Championships," "World Championships," and even "Grand Prix of the Paris Exposition." The founder of the International Olympic Committee, Baron Pierre de Coubertin, later said: "It's a miracle that the Olympic movement survived that celebration."

* The Olympic status of the athletes was equally downplayed, to the extent that many competitors never actually knew they were participating in the Olympics. Margaret Ives Abbott, a student from Chicago who won the nine-hole women's golf tournament, died in 1955 without realizing she was America's first female Olympic champion.

* Because the Olympics were held in conjunction with the Paris Exhibition, the scheduling and locations of the sporting events were often absurd. The fencing competition, for instance, was held as a sort of sideshow in the exhibition's cutlery area, and swimmers were forced to battle the polluted waters and strong currents of the Seine.

* After preliminary rounds, Myer Prinstein (from Syracuse University) had a clear lead in the long-jump competition and seemed poised to win. But when the final jump was scheduled on a Sunday, the official in charge of U.S. athletes disapproved of their competing on the Christian Sabbath. The athletes gave their word not to participate; Prinstein, who was Jewish, reluctantly agreed as well. On Sunday, however, Prinstein's main rival, Alvin Kraenzlein (University of Pennsylvania), broke his promise and competed, beating Prinstein's qualifying jump by a centimeter and winning the gold. Allegedly, Prinstein was so angry that he punched Kraenzlein in the face.

✳ Alvin Kraenzlein also won the 110-meter hurdles, the 220-meter hurdles, and the 60-meter dash—all in three days. As of 2007, he was still the only track-and-field athlete to have won four gold medals in individual events at a single Olympics.

✳ Women made their first appearance in the 1900 Games, albeit in small numbers: Of the thousand or so athletes participating, only 22 were women. The first female Olympic champion was Charlotte Cooper of Great Britain, who won the tennis singles and the mixed doubles. Female athletes wore the ankle-length skirts and dresses typical of the time.

✳ Ray Ewry of Indiana won the gold in three championships—standing high jump, standing long jump, and standing triple jump—all on the same day. A remarkable feat for any man, these victories amounted to Olympic heroism for Ewry, who had spent his childhood confined to a wheelchair because of polio.

✳ After the French won both gold and silver medals in the marathon, three runners from the United States contested the results, accusing the winners of taking a short cut. As proof, they submitted their observation that the new champions were the only contestants not splattered with mud. Although the objection was not sustained, the celebratory spirit had been soured.

* The 1900 Olympics saw the Games' youngest champion. On August 26, two Dutch rowers suddenly needed a replacement coxswain and chose a French boy, undoubtedly because of his small size. The pair rowed to a close victory, and the boy joined them in the victory ceremony. He then disappeared, but a photograph taken of the boy and the rowers indicates that he could have been as young as ten years old.

The Most Eccentric Executives

Some baseball owners make a lot of noise and stir up controversy. Some are lovable, some despicable, and most a measure of both.

* * * *

Chris Von der Ahe was one of the first of the eccentric owners. Proprietor of a St. Louis saloon in the late 1870s, the heavily accented and profit-driven German immigrant took notice of the increase in sales on game days. Before long, he owned the Browns in the American Association and became a sensational (and wealthy) promoter, à la Bill Veeck, and a noisy meddler, à la George Steinbrenner, even though he never really understood the game. In 1895, he modified Sportsman's Park to include nightly horse races and shoot-the-chute rides. Four years later, he had to double its seating capacity. After every game, von der Ahe would roll a wheelbarrow full of that day's gate to the bank, sometimes stopping at the saloon to buy the fans a few rounds. But in 1898, part of the ballpark was destroyed in a fire, and von der Ahe, whose fortunes had dwindled, lost his team.

Born into a prosperous banking family in 1890, **Larry MacPhail** became a lawyer and then used his legal wits to finagle himself into baseball. For the Reds and then the Dodgers, he was an innovator, responsible for the proliferation of night baseball, radio broadcasting of games, airplane travel for teams, and the use of batting helmets. MacPhail's hot-tempered battles with manager Leo Durocher were both legendary and frequent. He fired Leo dozens of times, only to hire him right back. MacPhail left the Reds after the 1937 season and went on to work for the Dodgers and Yankees before hanging up his cap for good in 1947.

Self-made millionaire **Charlie Finley** bought the Kansas City A's in 1960. His slew of wacky promotions—such as using orange baseballs or having a mechanical rabbit hand balls to the umpire behind home plate—didn't help attendance (the team still stunk). So he moved them to Oakland. He hired good scouts because they were cheaper than good players and built a strong team—perhaps made even stronger because of their total unity in their hatred for him.

Finley was well known—and infamously disliked—for micromanaging the team and the management. He often demanded that players change their style of play, and he fired any manager who publicly disagreed with him. He paid bonuses to players who would grow mustaches; pitcher Rollie Fingers' handlebar mustache was the most famous result of this. He tried to institute a "designated runner," and he dressed his players in garish green and gold uniforms. But it was his poor business decisions that ultimately did him in, and he stepped away from baseball in 1980.

Marge Schott inherited her husband's Cincinnati business empire when he died in 1968. Under her guidance, the businesses flourished, and she used part of her earnings to become partial owner of the Cincinnati Reds, eventually taking control in 1985.

Not only was she a woman in a man's world, her abrasive personality and controversial statements made her even more of an outsider. Fined and suspended for her racial and ethnic slurs, Schott didn't seem upset at all. But she was essentially forced out of the game in 1999, selling her controlling interest in the Reds that year. She died in 2004 at the age of 75.

George Steinbrenner is the only major-league owner to be a character on a hit TV comedy show (though he was portrayed by an actor on Seinfeld). His personality is almost a cliché—the boisterous, bullying, infuriating meddler, as capricious as he is strong. His most famous quote came the day he, as leader of a limited partnership buying the Yankees, said, "I won't be active in day-to-day club operations at all." In fact, he did little else—berating his players, firing his managers (including Billy Martin on five occasions), and "apologizing" to the fans when his team lost the 1981 World Series. After Steinbrenner paid a small-time gambler $40,000 for "dirt" on Yankees outfielder Dave Winfield in 1990, baseball commissioner Fay Vincent banned him from baseball for life. Word of his exile began to spread during a game being played at Yankee Stadium, and the crowd erupted into applause and a standing ovation. Steinbrenner was reinstated three years later and helped lead the Yankees to the American League East championship in 1994 and World Series wins in 1998, '99, and 2000.

Nuttiest Fans

Love is strange . . . and noisy, too.

❊ ❊ ❊ ❊

SOME FANS SKIM through the daily game reports and nod at the stats. Some pore over articles and numbers from across the country. And then there are the ultimate devotees—the ones whose lives are intertwined with the success of their team.

Hilda Chester—Brooklyn Dodgers

Famous for ringing her cowbell from the center-field bleachers in Ebbets Field, Chester was the epitome of the raucous Dodger fan. She carried not just one cowbell but two, to ring out in celebration or in mourning. (One of the bells is now in Cooperstown.) She also carried a large sign that let everyone know "Hilda Is Here."

Wild Bill Hagy—Baltimore Orioles

In Section 34 of Baltimore's Memorial Stadium in the late 1970s rose up a large, long-haired, full-bearded, well-beered cab driver who spelled out O-R-I-O-L-E-S with his body, and the crowd went bonkers. One writer said Hagy had "a voice that sounds like a cement mixer in action." When told he was "amazing," Wild Bill responded, "There ain't nothing amazing about it. They could do the same thing if they drank a case of beer every night."

Lolly Hopkins—Boston Red Sox

Unlike other famous fans, Lolly was a Boston fan of the pre–World War II era who would never think of hollering. She used a megaphone. In polite New England style, she was perfectly willing to cheer for good play on the part of either team.

Bruce "Screech Owl" McAllister—Pittsburgh Pirates

It wasn't a pleasant sound, but it was memorable. When Bruce McAllister let go one of his patented screams back in the 1930s, no one sitting in Forbes Field could miss it. Of course, with KDKA beaming Pirate games all over the East and Midwest, Bruce would often be heard in Missouri and Connecticut, too.

Mike "'Nuf Ced" McGreevy—Boston Red Sox

The man's moniker came about because he was the ultimate authority on any sports question you threw at him. Bartender McGreevy headed the Royal Rooters, a raucous group of Boston fans who drove the Pirates wacky in the 1903 World Series with their pronounced singing of "Tessie" (words altered to hassle the Pirates players). In 1912, when a front-office blunder shut the Rooters out of Game 6 of the World Series, they just broke down the gates and marched around the field.

Mary Ott—St. Louis Cardinals

One writer called Ott's voice "a neigh known to cause stampedes in Kansas City stockyards." That's particularly impressive when you realize Mary lived in St. Louis! Ott's voice carried, but she testified to her love of what she called "scientific rooting," the art of getting the other team's goat with her scornful laugh. The "Horse Lady of St. Louis" first came to national attention when revered umpire Bill Klem threatened to throw her out of a game in 1926.

Patsy O'Toole—Detroit Tigers

In Detroit in the 1930s, the fan who made the most noise was Patsy, who rightfully earned his nickname as the "All-American earache." Opposing players got the full brunt of a Patsy attack, and he was especially tough on the hated Yankees.

Jack Pierce—Brooklyn Dodgers

Pierce's fandom bordered on obsession. He was sure that Dodger infielder Cookie Lavagetto was the greatest player ever. To honor his idol, Pierce showed up at Ebbets Field every day, bought ten seats, and—using the containers of gas he brought along—blew up dozens of balloons with "Cookie" on them and released them throughout the game. He even continued this ritual in 1942, when Cookie was in the Army, not in Brooklyn.

Domestic Daredevils

Extreme ironing: serious sport or tongue-in-cheek response to the "extreme" sports of the '90s?

✳   ✳   ✳   ✳

Board to be Wild

IN 1997, PHIL Shaw of Leicester, England, faced a quandary: Should he do chores or have some fun? Shaw chose both and took his ironing board outside.

A new sport was born. According to Shaw's Web site, extreme ironing is a "danger sport that combines the thrills of an extreme outdoor activity with the satisfaction of a well pressed shirt."

With a bit of bravery and tongue firmly in cheek, athletes are required to take an ironing board and iron to an extreme location, such as a mountain cliff or deep underwater, and press a few items of clothing.

Go, Crease Lightning!

Shaw, who calls himself Steam, has toured America, Fiji, New Zealand, Australia, and South Africa in a worldwide recruitment campaign. Enthusiasm for the sport spread, and the 2002 Extreme Ironing World Championship took place near Munich, Germany. Since then, enthusiasts have been setting extreme-ironing records, which require a board that's at least 1 meter long and 30 centimeters wide, a recognizable landmark, visual proof of your feat, and a garment that is at least the size of a tea towel.

Extreme ironers, who go by nicknames like Perfectly Pressed and Crease Lightning, have ironed in the back of taxi cabs; underwater off the coast of Dahab, Egypt; in the Antarctic tundra; and while suspended from a crane in a transparent box. While early practitioners used extension cords to power their irons, serious contenders use battery-powered gear to reach the most extreme locations.

Whether these domestic daredevils are serious or merely poking fun at the absurdity of extreme sports remains to be seen. For those interested in taking their ironing outside, however, the Extreme Ironing Bureau recommends simply starting in your own backyard.

Danger on the Golf Course

Most golfers have encountered some wildlife on the golf course. And many of us have heard stories about people being struck by lightning—or errant golf balls. But if these golf courses could talk, they'd have some really scary stories to tell. Players beware.

✳ ✳ ✳ ✳

Beachwood Golf Course, Natal, South Africa

AFTER HITTING HER way out of a bunker on this beautiful African course, Molly Whittaker didn't have time to revel in her success. A monkey scrambled out of some nearby bushes, jumped on the unsuspecting woman, and tried to strangle her. Fortunately, her caddie knew just which club would stop the monkeyshines.

Crane's Landing Golf Course at the Marriott Resort, Lake Villa, Illinois

While the name alone evokes the image of large and graceful birds gliding in for a smooth landing, golfers on this course were not prepared for what they saw touch down on a spring day in 2008. Out of nowhere, a 1949 Piper Clipper airplane landed in the middle of the golf course. A man and his son hopped out, explaining to the surprised and worried golfers that this wasn't an emergency landing. The son was simply late for his tennis lesson across the street and this seemed the best way to get him there fast. Really?

Merapi Golf Course, Indonesia

The scenery is nothing short of spectacular at this golf course in Indonesia. Surrounded by lush forests, rich farmland, and majestic mountains, it's positively breathtaking—until the mountain volcano comes to life. Yes, Mount Merapi is still an active volcano, having erupted three times since 1990. It's an exciting place to play—but if the emergency warning whistle goes off, don't ask questions. Just run.

Singapore Island Country Club, Singapore

When pro golfer Jim Stewart played this course in 1982, he was horrified when he was confronted by a ten-foot cobra. He used his golf club to kill the interloper—and then watched in shocked disbelief as another snake slithered out of the dead cobra's mouth.

Pelham Bay and Split Rock Golf Course, Bronx, New York

On *Law and Order* it seems like all the dead bodies turn up in dumpsters or the East River. But venture a little further, and you'll find another deadly dumping ground. Unfortunately, it's not where you'd want or expect a body to turn up—right in the middle of your Sunday golf game. Between 1986 and 1992 alone, more than 40 bodies were discovered on the grounds of Pelham Bay Park. Now there's an incentive to stay in the fairway.

Cape Kidnapper's Golf Course, Hawke's Bay, New Zealand

Afraid of heights? This course will take that phobia to a new level. A 550-foot drop to the sea borders six holes. And you thought the rough was bad.

Uummannaq Golf Course, Greenland

A golfer's paradise this course is not. It's more likely a destination for those interested in extreme sports or defying Mother Nature. Located in Greenland, the world's northernmost golf course is situated on the ice and snow of a glacier, making the play not only chilly, but dangerous. Golfers shoot orange golf balls (the better to be seen in the snow) and dress in layers upon layers of thermal snow pants and insulated jackets.

Oh yeah, and did we mention that golfers are required to sign a waiver relieving the owners of any liability in case of injuries or death caused by the extreme conditions?

Lundin Links, Fife, Scotland

Most golf courses are on the quiet side. Lundin Links is no exception—except for the train tracks that run along the 5th green. Unfortunately for golfer Harold Wallace, even this area is quiet most of the time—until a train comes barreling down the tracks. Mr. Wallace had the misfortune of getting hit while crossing the tracks on his way to the green.

Skukuza Golf Course, Kruger National Park, South Africa

Violent monkeys like the one that choked Molly Whittaker at Beachwood Golf Course are probably scarce on this course due to the abundance of other wildlife – lions, elephants, buffaloes, rhinos, and leopards. Wild animals are truly common here, and dangerous. There have been numerous deaths over the years, of both humans and animals. But don't worry—according to management, most of the attacks have been against staff rather than paying guests.

Prison View Golf Course, Angola, Louisiana

Called the bloodiest prison in the United States, Prison View decided to open a golf course on the premises to encourage employees to hang around on their days off. Now that it's open to the public, who wouldn't jump at the chance to play a round?

Just remember these simple rules: You'll need to allow at least 48 hours between making your tee time and actually hitting the links so they can conduct a complete background check. When you arrive, be prepared to undergo an airport-style security check and vehicle search. In case you were wondering, no alcohol or weapons are allowed on the premises. And if a big burly guard—or anyone wearing handcuffs—catches up with your foursome, you might want to let them play through.

Annbriar Golf Course, Waterloo, Illinois

In March 2013, golfer Mark Mihal found himself plummeting 18 feet into a sinkhole that opened beneath him. That's not the kind of hole in one you want!

Carded!

Between photographic fails, airheaded airbrushing, and prankster players, the right set of sports cards would make anyone laugh.

✳   ✳   ✳   ✳

Hank Aaron, 1956 Topps baseball #31—While the headshot is Hank in his Milwaukee Braves cap, the inset action picture shows Giants star Willie Mays starting his slide into home plate. Some cheesy airbrushing has given Willie a Braves cap and uniform colors, but no team logo or front number. Value in Near Mint: $400.

Hank Aaron, 1957 Topps baseball #20—Hammerin' Hank hit 755 home runs in one of baseball's storied careers—but none left-handed. The image is a reverse negative (card lingo for 'mirror image'), easily discerned by the backward uniform number. NM: $325.

Red Wilson, 1958 Topps baseball #213—The Detroit backstop presumably used to have a bat, a right forearm, and a left arm. All were airbrushed out. NM: $8.

Gino Cimoli, 1958 Topps baseball #286—Cimoli strikes a hitting pose…without a bat. An over-eager airbrusher erased nearly every trace of the war club, making Cimoli look ridiculous. NM: $8.

Bob Cerv, 1958 Topps baseball #329—This card is all kinds of wrong. The airbrush-created A's cap is cockeyed and misshapen, and Cerv's pose makes him look like he's clubbing himself in the back of the head with his bat—left-handed (Cerv hit right). NM: $8.

Whitey Ford, 1962 Post Canadian baseball #9—Text on the back calls the Yankee Hall of Famer a Los Angeles Dodger. NM: $80–120.

Don Landrum, 1963 Topps baseball #113—Pictured is future Cub Hall of Famer (then a youngster) Ron Santo. NM: $4.

Willie Mays, 1963 Topps baseball #300—Some of these were printed with the Whitey Herzog back (#302). Wrong bio, wrong stats, wrong everything. While Whitey had a good career, and became a successful manager, his 25 career home runs by 1962 fall short of Willie's by hundreds. NM: at least $160.

Phillies' 1964 Rookie Stars, Topps baseball #561—Describing young Dave Bennett, Topps tells us: "The 19-year-old righthanded curveballer is just 18 years old!" Thanks for that, Topps! NM: $9.

Dick Ellsworth, 1966 Topps baseball #447—One of the more regrettable errors, the card actually pictures a dead ballplayer. Ken Hubbs was a promising, modest, popular young Cubs infielder who died in a February 1964 plane crash. Topps somehow managed to replace Ellsworth's image with that of Hubbs. Major ouch. NM: $5.

Aurelio Rodríguez, 1969 Topps baseball #653—It's a great shot… of Angels batboy Leonard García. NM: $3.

Norm Cash, 1970 Topps baseball #611—Detroit's mainstay hitter has his first baseman's mitt all up in the camera lens, which distracts the viewer from noticing that Norm's fly is open. Whoops. NM: $8.

Billy Martin, 1972 Topps baseball #33—The fiery Tigers skipper stands calmly regarding the camera with strained patience. That's fine, except that he's flipping the camera off. His left middle finger extends down a bat handle. With some people, we'd figure this an accident; with Billy, not so much. NM: $2.50 to $4.

Rich Gossage, 1974 Topps baseball #542—Some issues of the famous fireballing "Goose's" 1974 card have the back of card #474—the stats for Game 3 of the '73 World Series (Gossage's White Sox weren't involved). NM: $0.75 to $3.

Duane Kuiper, 1983 Fleer baseball #263—The fancy-fielding, light-hitting second baseman poses in his Giants uniform with a bat. A broken bat, that is. He grasps it by the barrel, the splintery handle hanging down over his shoulder, perhaps an emblem of his single career home run. NM: $0.05.

Gary Pettis, 1985 Topps baseball #497—The Angel in the photo looks like a teenage boy, posed with his chin resting on his index finger. That's because it is a teenager: Gary's 16-year-old little brother Lynn. NM: $0.05.

Barry Bonds, 1987 Donruss baseball #361—In early versions, Bonds's card depicts Johnny Ray. The two men don't even much resemble each other. NM: $1100+.

Edgar Martínez, 1988 Donruss baseball #36—Wrong guy. Pictured is pitcher Edwin Nuñez, who looks nothing like Edgar, a famous designated hitter and one of the most loved Mariners in history. NM: $1.50.

Jerry Browne, 1988 Fleer baseball #462—Some cases of mistaken identity are understandable. When the real player is African American and the guy on the card is Caucasian, not so much. Actually pictured is Bob Brower. NM: $3.

Frank Thomas, 1990 Topps baseball #414—It's the future Big Hurt's rookie card, thus a big deal. It's made more so because, on early printings, Topps left his name banner blank on the front! NM: $500.

Alex Gordon, 2006 Topps baseball #297—A 2005 decision from the Major League Baseball Players Association ruled that rookies could only get baseball cards under certain circumstances. Alex Gordon didn't meet the criteria, but he got a card anyway. Topps quickly pulled the card, after reportedly producing fewer than 100. NM: $1200.

"I Kick a Touchdown!"

*European kickers first arrived in professional football in the 1960s.
Some, like Garo Yepremian, had steep learning curves…*

✳ ✳ ✳ ✳

It Beats Making Neckties

GARABED SARKO YEPREMIAN was born in 1944 to
Armenian parents on the eastern Mediterranean island of
Cyprus. Standing 5'7" and prematurely bald, he was making
neckties in London in 1966 while playing soccer on weekends.
His brother called from Indiana: He had been watching football on TV and believed that Garo could out-kick the place-
kickers he saw. Garo agreed to come.

Soccer-style specialists were new to American football in 1966.
Most kickers played other positions as well, and they kicked
straight-on with the toe. Barred from the NCAA for having
played semipro sports, Garo's only option was professional
football. The Yepremian brothers wangled Garo a tryout with
the NFL's Detroit Lions, and Garo boomed his kicks with
accuracy. Despite English that was as limited as his football
knowledge, he had a new career.

Welcome to the NFL (*crunch*)

Legends abound regarding Garo's rookie year. As Garo puts it,
he didn't know a chin strap from a jockstrap, much less how
to put on the uniform. During his first game, Coach Harry
Gilmer advised Garo that Detroit had lost the coin toss; Garo
ran to midfield to look for the coin.

He also faced prejudice, as many professional players disliked
both foreigners in football and placekicking specialists. On
kickoffs, every opposing Neanderthal wanted to knock Garo
silly. After a memorable Week 4, when he was leveled by famed
Packer linebacker Ray Nitschke, Garo began wearing a face bar
on his helmet.

In Week 6, Gilmer finally let Garo do some placekicking. He was 3 for 3 on extra points and 1 for 4 on field goals, a middling start. As famed Lions defensive lineman Alex Karras told, during one early losing effort, Garo kicked an extra point that didn't affect the outcome of the game and began to celebrate wildly. Karras asked Yepremian what he was celebrating. Garo answered: "I keek a touchdown!" Whether or not Karras jazzed up the story, it became part of the Garo legend. During the Colts' return visit to Detroit later that season, Garo booted a league-record six field goals, including four in one quarter.

After two years with Detroit, Garo joined the Army. When he got out, Detroit didn't need a kicker. He played semipro football in 1968 but sat out 1969. In 1970 the Miami Dolphins invited him to try out. Garo became a two-time Pro Bowler in Miami, a fan favorite, and their 1970s kicking mainstay.

Super Bowl VII

The Dolphins' perfect 1972 season pitted them against the Washington Redskins for the NFL title. If they won, they would finish 17–0—the greatest season in NFL history. With Miami up 14–0 late in the game, Coach Don Shula sent Garo out to kick a game-icing field goal. Redskin defensive tackle Bill Brundige blocked the kick, which bounced to Garo's right. Garo picked it up. With Brundige thundering in on him, Garo next attempted an impromptu forward pass. The ball went straight up. As it fell, Garo batted it—right to Washington defensive back Mike Bass, who dashed past Garo for a touchdown. The play went into the books as a fumble return. Miami held on to win, and Garo Yepremian's place in the history of NFL humor was forever secured.

The normally easygoing kicker was depressed after the game, but some encouragement from Coach Shula helped him overcome such a public embarrassment. Today Garo is a motivational speaker and cancer fundraiser who not only laughs at funny stories about his football days—he tells them himself!

Keeping Score and Hawking Dogs

You can thank 19th-century entrepeneur Harry M. Stevens for many of the staples found nationwide at ballparks today.

✳ ✳ ✳ ✳

I N 1885, OHIO entrepreneur Harry M. Stevens invented score-cards as a way to keep track of the players and the action (and to sell some advertising space). He sold them at various ballparks for five cents each. By the turn of the century he was also selling ice cream and sodas to baseball fans. When sales proved slow on cold, early-season days at New York's Polo Grounds, he sent out some of his salespeople to buy "dachshund" sausages and buns, then encouraged them to yell, "Get 'em while they're red hot!" Thus the term "hot dog" was popularized. Even today, when fans can find everything from nachos to sushi at the ballpark, people still line up for the staples that have been sold for more than a century, including bags of peanuts and soda drunk through a straw (both of which were also Stevens's ideas).

Prices for everything at the ballpark have increased by leaps and bounds through the years, but this has become especially true in the past two decades as the corporate culture has provided a base of customers willing to pay more for better seats and fancier eats. A brief history of a few of the staples:

Some selected ballpark prices from selected seasons (not adjusted for inflation):

	1920	1942	1962	1980	2006
Program/Scorecard	$.10	$.10	$.25	$.50	$4.00
Hot Dog	$.10	$.15	$.35	$1.00	$4.50
Soda	$.05	$.10	$.25	$.55	$4.75
Beer	Prohibition	$.25	$.45	$1.00	$6.50
Box Ticket	$1.00	$2.20	$3.50	$6.00	$41.00

Shake, Rattle & Play Ball!

The real drama at the 1989 World Series turned out to have nothing to do with baseball.

✳ ✳ ✳ ✳

IT MEASURED 6.9 ON the Richter Scale (7.1 surface-wave magnitude), claimed more than 60 lives, and injured thousands. Technically, the earthquake that rocked San Francisco at 5:04 P.M. on October 17, 1989, was the Loma Prieta Earthquake. But it's known as the World Series Earthquake.

The Oakland A's and San Francisco Giants, Bay Area neighbors, were squaring off for the ultimate prize, and the nation was watching. While people in the region were affected by the quake no matter what they were doing, the rest of the nation experienced the tragedy through the eyes of World Series television cameras. ABC Sports play-by-play man Al Michaels was reading taped highlights during the Game 3 pre-game show when millions across the country heard him utter the words, "I'll tell you what—we're having an earth— ..."

Screens went black. When backup power was restored, the images transmitted were powerful. Among them: chunks of concrete falling from an upper deck section of Candlestick Park; Commissioner Fay Vincent looking dazed after nearly being knocked out of his seat near the Giants' dugout; players from both teams leading their wives and children onto the field, away from the stadium's walls.

Though the old stadium shook, the walls held, and no one inside was seriously hurt. Some players clung to their families on the field, thankful for their safety. Others remained lighthearted, not knowing the severity of the damage outside the stadium. It was only on their way home that many people learned they had just survived the area's strongest quake since the 8.3 monster of 1906.

The Series resumed ten days later with a tribute to those who had lost their lives. A moment of silence was observed at 5:04 P.M., followed by the singing of "San Francisco," an unofficial city anthem. The ceremonial first pitch was thrown by representatives of public safety and volunteer organizations who responded to the disaster. Oakland then completed a bittersweet sweep on a stage that wound up being far more about life than baseball.

Quick Quotes

"When I broke in, they didn't keep track of things the way they do now. These days they have a stat for how many times a guy goes for a cup of coffee."

—MARK MCGWIRE ON THE HABIT OF SPORTSWRITERS CHARTING THE DISTANCE OF HIS HOME RUNS, *SPORTS ILLUSTRATED*, AUGUST 26, 1996

"Shall I get you a net, or do you want a basket?"

—RED SOX SHORTSTOP HEINIE WAGNER NEEDLING GIANTS SHORTSTOP ART FLETCHER DURING THE SECOND GAME OF THE 1912 WORLD SERIES; FLETCHER HAD MADE THREE ERRORS

"I know, but I had a better year than Hoover."

—BABE RUTH'S RESPONSE WHEN A REPORTER POINTED OUT THAT HIS 1930 SALARY DEMAND OF $80,000 TOPPED THE PRESIDENT'S $75,000 SALARY

"Show me a good loser, and I'll show you an idiot."

—LEO DUROCHER

"All I could think about was, 'We beat the Yankees! We beat the Yankees!' I was in a kind of daze."

—PIRATE BILL MAZEROSKI ON HIS THOUGHTS AS HE ROUNDED THE BASES FOLLOWING HIS WORLD SERIES–WINNING HOME RUN IN 1960, *CLOUT! THE TOP HOME RUNS IN BASEBALL HISTORY*

"You spend a good piece of your life gripping a baseball and in the end it turns out that it was the other way around all the time."

—JIM BOUTON, *BALL FOUR*

How Do People Swallow Swords?

Short answer: verrry carefully. Read on for the longer explanation.

✳ ✳ ✳ ✳

THERE ARE WAYS to fake it—such as using a trick sword with a plastic blade that collapses into the hilt—but authentic sword swallowing is no optical illusion. The blade isn't as sharp as that of a normal sword, but that doesn't change the fact that the swallower is pushing a hard metal shaft deep into his or her body.

Ironically, one of the essential skills of sword swallowing is not swallowing. When you stand and face upward, your upper gastrointestinal tract—the passageway that's made up of your throat, pharynx, esophagus, and stomach—is straight and flexible enough that a sword can pass through it. When you swallow, muscles contract and expand along the passageway in order to move food down to your stomach. Two sphincters along this tract—the upper esophageal sphincter between your pharynx and esophagus and the lower esophageal sphincter between your esophagus and stomach—are normally closed; they open involuntarily as food moves past. To keep the passageway clear, the swallower must learn deep relaxation techniques to resist the urge to swallow.

Sword swallowers also have to suppress their gag reflex, an automatic muscle contraction triggered when nerve endings in the back of the throat sense a foreign object. To deactivate the gag reflex, a sword swallower crams progressively larger objects into the back of the throat while trying not to gag. After hours of disgusting noises and periodic vomiting, the gag reflex is numbed and the aspiring swallower can get down to business.

As the sword slides down the gastrointestinal tract, it straightens the various curves of the tract. Some swallowers coat their swords with a lubricant, such as olive oil, to help them along.

This mind-over-matter feat is one of the oldest stunts there is. Historians believe that the practice originated in India around 2000 B.C., as a part of rituals designed to demonstrate powerful connections to the gods. The ancient Romans, Greeks, and Chinese picked up the practice, but generally viewed it as entertainment rather than religious observance. Sword swallowers at the 1893 World's Fair in Chicago sparked America's interest in the spectacle, and it soon became a staple of traveling sideshows.

Did we mention that you shouldn't try this trick at home? It goes without saying that sword swallowing is a dangerous and generally ill-advised endeavor. Even master swallowers sustain injuries—cram a sword, even a dull one, down your throat enough times, and you're likely to nick something important. If you must impress your friends, stick with more manageable sharp objects, such as Doritos.

Bill Veeck

Bill Veeck was the most colorful team owner in the history of baseball. Was he just a goofball party animal, or was he a genius ahead of his time? Read on and decide for yourself

✳ ✳ ✳ ✳

The Case for Goofball Party Animal

Personal life: Bill Veeck smoked like an Industrial Revolution chimney. Not only did he close down bars, he kept them in business. He barely maintained contact with his children by his first wife—irresponsible, most would say. He loved to use his wooden leg for gags: He'd suddenly stab it with an ice pick or use it as an ashtray. He sat shirtless in the stands, booing the umpires and chatting with the fans over beer. Any photograph of Veeck wearing a necktie is phonier than a refunded legal fee.

He simply didn't look or act like the important baseball executive he was.

Operations: He loved to annoy other owners, especially the Yankees', then managed to look shocked when they voted against him nearly every time. He brought 42-year-old Negro Leagues legend Satchel Paige into the American League, then sent telegrams to the disapproving, ultra-establishment *Sporting News* in which he proposed Paige as Rookie of the Year. He cheated like a riverboat cardshark at grounds maintenance: He watered the basepaths when the visiting team was faster, groomed the infield to help his side and irritate the opponents, and once set up an outfield fence that could be moved in and out between innings. Veeck was chaos theory applied to sports management.

Promotions: Not even the legendary Chris von der Ahe pulled stunts as goofy as Veeck's gags. Veeck used professional clowns to coach bases. He was always giving away bizarre door prizes, including kegs of nails, live pigeons, and blocks of ice. Traditionalists considered him a moneychanger in the game's venerated temple.

The Case for Foresighted Genius

Finance: Veeck rarely had anywhere near enough money to buy a baseball team, but he had few equals at lining up capital. He had studied accounting but kept that detail secret so that his competition would think he was a business buffoon. He bought several teams with relatively little of his own money, yet sold them for capital gains. In what universe is this buffoonery?

Winning/attendance: Veeck took the Cleveland Indians from 68–86 (1946) to 97–58 and a World Series title (1948). He didn't win with the St. Louis Browns on the diamond, but he got far more people to come watch the most consistently lousy team in baseball history than anyone imagined possible. When he took over the Chicago White Sox, they won their first pennant (1959) since 1919. He tended to shatter attendance records and win ball games, which is pretty much the point.

Promotions: Veeck generated buzz by reflex. He did everything possible to welcome women to his ballparks: decent restrooms, daycare, ladies'-day promotions. He invented the exploding scoreboard. He gave the fireworks contractor extra money and told him to "knock the joint down." He invited St. Louis fans to serve as grandstand managers while his trained pro sat in a recliner wearing a bathrobe and smoking a pipe—and the amateurs managed the team to victory!

The Verdict

How you evaluate Bill Veeck's career depends largely on how seriously you take baseball. If baseball was a sacred, dignified, deadly serious game for you, Veeck was likely an offensive travesty. But if you attended ball games for pure fun, no owner gave better value.

Houston's Astrodome

The first covered baseball and football stadium—nicknamed the "Eighth Wonder of the World"—is a tribute to American ingenuity.

✳   ✳   ✳   ✳

THE STORY OF the Astrodome began in 1962 when Major League Baseball expanded to include the Houston Colt .45s, owned by Houston Judge Roy Hofheinz. The city's subtropical weather made scheduling difficult—extreme heat and humidity were a challenge for players, and tropical downpours were always a risk.

What About a Roof?

However, after a trip to Rome's Colosseum, Judge Hofheinz had an idea. He'd learned that the original Colosseum had a retractable fabric canopy called a *velarium*. With more modern technology, Hofheinz speculated, a modern sports arena could be enclosed within a dome and air-conditioned.

In November 1964, his dream became a reality as the Harris County Domed Stadium was completed. Found about six miles from downtown Houston, it stood 18 stories tall and covered nearly ten acres of land. The ceiling was made of clear Lucite plastic; sunlight lit the interior well enough that the playing field could be natural Bermuda grass, bred for indoor use.

Around the world, Houston's domed stadium was acclaimed as an engineering miracle. Almost immediately, other cities launched plans to enclose their existing stadiums or build entirely new ones based on the Houston design.

The Space Age

Hofheinz soon renamed the stadium the Astrodome to highlight Houston's connection with the space industry. At the same time, the Houston Colt .45s became the Astros. During an exhibition game, Mickey Mantle hit the first home run in the Astrodome. Everything seemed perfect, until the first official games in the new dome. Players complained that they couldn't see fly balls due to glare from the Lucite panes that formed the ceiling.

Two sections of the panes were painted white, but the grass died when it couldn't get enough sunlight. For most of the 1965 season, teams played on dying grass and dirt that had been painted green.

Installing the Astroturf

Researchers at Monsanto invented artificial grass, which they called *ChemGrass*, that same year, but it wasn't in full production at the start of the 1966 baseball season. So, although most of the infield was covered with the ChemGrass—soon renamed *AstroTurf*—the outfield remained painted dirt until more AstroTurf arrived in July.

The stadium continued to adapt to challenges, and its popularity grew with fans and teams alike. In 1968, the Houston Oilers football team made the Astrodome their stadium, following the arrival of the annual Houston Livestock Show and Rodeo in 1966. Basketball games were also featured at the Astrodome, including the 1971 NCAA Final Four games and the 1989 NBA All-Star Game.

Declining Fortunes

However, by 1996, the age of the Astrodome became evident. The Oilers demanded a new stadium, but when Houston turned them down, owner Bud Adams moved the team to Tennessee. Next, the Astros insisted on a new ballpark or they'd leave the city as well. In 2000, a new park, now called Minute Maid Park, was built in downtown Houston. And this ballpark has a retractable roof.

In 2002, Reliant Stadium opened next to the Astrodome, as the home of Houston's new NFL team, the Texans. Like Minute Maid Park, it features a retractable roof.

The Astrodome became known as the "lonely landmark" due to the fact that so few events have been scheduled there since the new stadiums were built. The stadium did, however, serve one more noble act of kindness in 2005, when its doors were opened to welcome displaced survivors of Hurricane Katrina. For two weeks, more than 13,000 people found shelter inside the Astrodome, which once again became the focal point of world headlines and applause.

Byrd's First Antarctic Expedition

Richard Byrd introduced a new sort of Antarctic expedition.

✳   ✳   ✳   ✳

U.S. NAVY REAR Admiral Richard E. Byrd's 1928 Antarctic Expedition broke a rather long U.S. Antarctic exploration dry spell (88 years, since the last trip had been in 1840). Byrd was the first to integrate aerial photography, snowmobiles, and advanced radio communication into Antarctic study. With two ships, three airplanes, 83 assistants, lots of dogs, and a large heap of radio gear, Byrd set up a camp on the Ross Ice Shelf called Little America.

The expedition spent all of 1929 and January 1930 in Antarctica, making a flight over the South Pole and exploring Antarctic topography while recording a full year on the icy continent. Its tremendous success made Byrd famous.

The MVP of the Expedition

Norman Vaughan, Byrd's chief dog musher, dropped out of Harvard and became the first American to drive sled dogs in the Antarctic. Byrd gave him lasting credit by naming a 10,302-foot Antarctic mountain and a nearby glacier after him. (A few days before turning 89, Vaughan became Mount Vaughan's first ascender!)

At the 1932 Winter Olympics at Lake Placid, New York, Vaughan competed in dog mushing as a demonstration sport. Serving in the army in World War II, he became a colonel in charge of Greenland dogsled training and rescue. In one famed exploit, he rescued 26 downed airmen, then returned alone to recover the Norden bombsight, a top-secret device that was able to pinpoint targets using infrared radiation.

Born in 1905, Vaughan passed away on December 23, 2005, at age 100. He was the expedition's last living member.

The Art of Gurning

An untold number of mothers have warned their children, "If you keep twisting your face, it will stay that way permanently!" Little did Mom know that making ugly faces could be viewed as training for a gurning competition.

✳ ✳ ✳ ✳

GURNING IS A contest that pits challengers vying to contort their faces into unbelievable displays of anatomical distortions. The mother of all gurning contests is held each year at the Egremont Crab Fair in Cumbria, England. Contestants come from every corner of the globe to see who can pull the "world's ugliest face." But, unlike other natural advantages in life, being ugly to begin with doesn't necessarily mean that you'll win.

"Just because you're oogly doesn't mean to say that ya [gonna] win it," says gurning champion Peter Jackman in the book *True Brits*. "Because gurnin' means the art of pullin' faces, not oogliness."

Winning a gurning championship doesn't come easy. Champs like Gordon Mattinson practice day in and day out. The most successful gurners even come up with names for their faces. Mattinson perfected his "Quasimodo," while the late Ron Looney became famous for his "Popeye."

And, just in case you're thinking about stopping by Egremont on your next vacation to capture the prize, be advised that gurning is a sport for professionals. Amateurs rarely make it to the final round. "They don't really know what gurnin's about," says Jackman. The Egremont Gurning Championship is held every year during the third week of September.

Mighty Joe Rollino

A centenarian Coney Island strongman laughed at the odds and never gave in as time marched on.

✳   ✳   ✳   ✳

NEW YORK HAS had more than its fair share of colorful characters with unique stories, but few could outstrip the feats of The Great Joe Rollino. This Coney Island strongman once purportedly lifted 475 pounds with his teeth and 635 pounds with one finger.

Mighty Mite

Standing just five foot five and weighing between 125 and 150 pounds, Mighty Joe was, relative to his size, one of the most powerful men alive. Born on March 19, 1905, to Italian immigrants, Rollino spent his earliest years building his body and flexing his muscles while training with America's first great strongman, Warren Lincoln Travis. After touring the United States as a boxer, Rollino began showing off his strength as a

Coney Island performer, squashing nails with his gnashers and bending coins with his bare hands. He labored as a longshoreman, served as a bodyguard to film star Greta Garbo, and got to know Harry Houdini. While in the Pacific during World War II, he earned a Silver Star, a Bronze Star, and three Purple Hearts (he took shrapnel in his legs and rescued several soldiers on the field of battle by grabbing and transporting each of them under one arm).

The Colder, the Better

Aside from working out, part of Joe's secret was a healthy lifestyle that included yogurt and wheat germ long before they were popular. What's more, he took frequent swims in the Atlantic Ocean, regardless of whether it was lukewarm or freezing. As far as he was concerned, the colder, the better. During one winter in the 1950s, when the police didn't have the necessary protective gear to jump into icy waters, Joe retrieved the bodies of two people who had drowned in Prospect Park. A couple of decades later, in January 1974, a six-degree day saw the 68-year-old join a half dozen other members of the appropriately named Iceberg Athletic Club for a swim in the frigid waters off Coney Island.

A Marvel to the End

A longtime member of the not-for-profit, New York-based Association of Oldetime Barbell & Strongmen—which educates people about the hazards of drug use and the benefits of drug-free weightlifting and other sporting activities—Joe was handing out free advice to fellow "Iron Game" participants when celebrating his 103rd birthday at a Brooklyn restaurant. And he was still bending quarters with his teeth and regaling people with tales of his past achievements. A year later, the 104-year-old was struck by a car and died shortly thereafter. His friend Charlie Laird told the *New York Daily News*, "Father Time didn't stand a chance against Joe Rollino. It took all the speed and might of a minivan, and I'm shocked that *that* was even able to take him down."

Chapter 6

The Human Body

Lefty

What do you know about southpaws? Find out more with these fun facts!

✳   ✳   ✳   ✳

* There is no standard for what constitutes left-handedness, making research into handedness difficult.

* Left-handed adults find many workplaces inefficient or dangerous because they're designed for right-handed people.

* Around 10 percent of the population is left-handed.

* Famous lefties include Mark Twain, Whoopie Goldberg, Ronald Reagan, George H. W. Bush, Bill Clinton, Jay Leno, Julia Roberts, Oprah Winfrey, and Barack Obama.

* More men than women are left-handed.

* Left-handers are more likely to stutter, have dyslexia, and suffer from allergies.

* International Left-Handers Day is August 13, and was first celebrated in 1976.

* Lefties are three times more likely to become addicted to alcohol or other substances.

* Lefties might be better in hand-to-hand combat.

* The term *southpaw* was first used to refer to left-handers in the 1890s.

* At one time, teachers would force left-handed students to write with their right hands. Luckily, that bias is changing.

* Researchers at Oxford University have found a gene for left-handedness.

* Scientists have found that handedness develops *in utero*.

* The hair of right-handed people swirls clockwise on the top of their head, but the hair of left-handed people can swirl in any direction.

* Lefties tend to perform better on IQ tests.

How Did I Get My Birthmark?

In the old days, you would have gone to your mother with some questions. While pregnant with you, did she: spill wine on herself? Get an X-ray? Suffer a terrible fright? Eat excessive amounts of beets, watermelons, or strawberries? These days, we know those practices don't cause birthmarks. But what does?

❋ ❋ ❋ ❋

THE TRUTH IS, the causes of most birthmarks are unknown. We do, however, know how some kinds of birthmarks, including ones known as vascular birthmarks, physically form.

Vascular birthmarks—such as macular stains, port-wine stains, and hemangiomas—happen when blood vessels get bunched together, tangled, or just don't grow normally. Pigmented birthmarks—such as café-au-lait spots and congenital moles—form when an overgrowth of cells creates extra pigment on the skin.

Like we said, the experts insist that birthmarks are not caused by what your mother did, craved, ate, or wished for during her pregnancy. Furthermore, they can't be prevented. This earthshaking news affects a whole lot of people: Up to a third of newborns have some kind of colorful spot, mark, mole, blemish, or blotch. Think of them as nature's tattoos.

Whether brown, red, pink, black, blue, or purple, most birthmarks are harmless. Some will shrink on their own over time. Others can be removed with surgery or the zap of a laser. The rest are permanent fixtures.

If you have a birthmark, don't waste time worrying about it. Instead, you should consider yourself special. Depending on the old wife with whom you consult, it could well be the sign of an angel's kiss or even a battle wound from a previous life. How's that for a mark of honor?

The New "Normal"

The next time you anxiously await the readout on your thermometer, consider this: 98.2, 98.8—and even 99.9—are the new 98.6.

✳ ✳ ✳ ✳

NORMAL HUMAN BODY temperature used to be defined by just one number: 98.6 degrees Fahrenheit. But now medical experts say that a range of numbers can be considered normal body temperatures for healthy individuals.

Researchers have found that the new "normal" for adults can range from 98.2 degrees Fahrenheit (36.8 degrees Celsius) to 99.9 degrees Fahrenheit (37.7 degrees Celsius). That's good news for worrywarts and bad news for children hoping that a thermometer reading of 99 degrees will get them out of school.

What Is "Normal"?

Carl Wunderlich, a 19th-century German doctor, is responsible for designating 98.6 as normal temperature. He studied the body temperature of 25,000 adults, took 1 million temperature readings, and determined that body temperature averaged 98.6 among people in good health.

We now know that many factors can affect the number that shows up on a thermometer. Your temperature changes throughout the day: It's usually lower in the morning and higher in the evening. Eating, drinking, exercising, and taking a hot shower can all skew a body temperature reading if it's taken just after those activities. Women's body temperatures fluctuate during the menstrual cycle and ovulation. People who have a higher metabolic rate often will have a higher body temperature than those with "slower" metabolisms. And, like everything else in our bodies, our core temperature can change as we age. One study found that seniors have a lower average thermometer reading than younger adults.

Thermometer Barometer

How your temperature is measured and what kind of thermometer is used also can make a difference in the number that pops up. Most adults prefer to take their temperature orally, by putting a thermometer under the tongue for a few minutes. In the doctor's office, a tympanic ear probe is often the thermometer of choice. Temperature readings can also be taken by placing a thermometer under the arm (called an axillary reading) or in the rectum. Any of these methods can give an accurate measurement, but different body sites will yield different results. An axillary reading, for example, can be a full degree lower than a reading taken from the ear.

In the past, medical thermometers were made of glass and filled with mercury. Today, there are many more choices with better technology, such as digital electronic thermometers, mercury-free oral thermometers, and infrared ear thermometers.

Feeling Hot, Hot, Hot

Our body temperature is an important reading. It's one of the vital signs, along with pulse rate, breathing rate, and blood pressure, that give doctors an overview of how a patient is doing. If any one of those readings is off, it can be a signal that something is awry.

A fever can occur for many reasons, most commonly when the body is fighting an infection. A doctor should be consulted when a baby's temperature is above 100 degrees Fahrenheit (37.8 degrees Celsius). Most pediatricians want to see any child who seems to be under the weather and is running a fever. In adults, fevers usually are evaluated in the context of other symptoms, such as headache, sore throat, cough, or chills. If a fever persists, it's a good idea to call your doctor.

Living in Fear

Approximately 20 percent of people in the United States have an intense, irrational fear of common things or experiences, such as spiders, heights, or confined spaces. Sometimes they fear something more unusual, such as pine trees or public bathrooms.

✳ ✳ ✳ ✳

Acrophobia is the fear of heights. This fear is often very specific. A person may be able to ski the Alps with no problem but be overcome with panic on a fifth-floor balcony.

Astraphobia is a paralyzing fear of thunder and lightning. As with other phobias, the reaction often causes a rapid heartbeat or labored breathing. People, and even pets, often seek shelter in confined spaces such as closets and basements.

Cacophobia is the fear of ugliness. Sufferers aren't just repulsed by unattractive people or things; they actually have intense panic attacks around them. When they see someone or something they consider ugly, they often turn away and flee.

Coulrophobia is the fear of clowns. It is a basic survival instinct to react with suspicion to a "person" with a painted smile and unsmiling eyes, but people with this phobia are terror-stricken when they see this circus staple.

Dendrophobia is the fear of trees. A child on a camping trip may be afraid there will be bears wandering among the pines. A fear of bears is not unusual, but the child may subsequently develop a paralyzing fear of pine trees. People with dendrophobia usually have strange stories about why they are terrified of a particular type of tree.

Friggatriskaidekaphobia is the fear of Friday the 13th. This fear is more typical among people who are from England, Poland, Germany, Bulgaria, or Portugal—countries in which the number 13 is traditionally deemed unlucky.

Nyctophobia is an irrational fear of nighttime or the dark. Rationally, an adult (the fear is common among children) may understand that there is nothing to be afraid of, but he or she may still experience heightened anxiety when the lights go out.

Trypanophobia is an exaggerated fear of injection with a hypodermic needle. This phobia may have a history in genetic memory. Thousands of years ago, the people who avoided being stabbed in general were the most likely to survive.

Further Phobias

Alecktorophobia—a fear of chickens

Arachibutyrophobia—a fear of peanut butter sticking to the roof of the mouth

Basophobia—fear of standing, walking, or falling over

Catagelophobia—fear of being ridiculed

Chorophobia—fear of dancing

Didaskaleinophobia—fear of going to school

Doxophobia—fear of expressing opinions or of receiving praise

Elurophobia—fear of cats

Ergophobia—fear of work

Gamophobia—fear of marriage

Hexakosioihexekontahexaphobia—fear of the number 666

Hippopotomonstrosesquippedaliophobia—fear of long words

Iatrophobia—fear of doctors or going to the doctor

Linonophobia—fear of string

Nyctohylophobia—fear of dark wooded areas or of forests at night

Ochlophobia—fear of crowds or mobs

Paralipophobia—fear of neglecting duty or responsibility

Phengophobia—fear of daylight or sunshine

Soceraphobia—fear of parents-in-law

An Infectious Personality

Typhoid Mary was bad—but not as bad as most people think.

✳   ✳   ✳   ✳

Who Was Typhoid Mary?

MARY MALLON WAS an Irish cook who is often blamed for a multitude of deaths. She was feared and vilified, accused of consciously spreading typhoid fever. But contrary to legend, the feisty immigrant who earned the Typhoid Mary moniker likely infected just 47 people, only three of whom died.

Typhoid fever is rarely seen today in industrialized countries because of improvements in sanitation. The bacteria that cause it are carried in the bloodstream and intestinal tract, and they are deposited in food and water by people who are infected. Typhoid is contracted by eating or drinking something handled by a carrier who is not meticulously clean or from drinking contaminated water. Mary—a "healthy carrier" who had no symptoms herself—unwittingly made her victims sick.

Her condition was discovered in 1907 when New York public health officials linked her to an outbreak of typhoid in a family that had hired her as a cook. But Mary refused to believe that she was the cause. When a civil engineer experienced in typhoid outbreaks went to her workplace to ask for blood, stool, and urine samples, she ran him off with a carving fork!

What Became of Her?

Mary was eventually institutionalized and held in isolation to prevent her from spreading the disease further. She was freed three years later, after promising not to work as a cook again—a promise she didn't keep. A typhoid outbreak at Sloane Maternity Hospital in Manhattan five years after her release was traced to a cook named Mrs. Brown, who turned out to be Mary using a pseudonym. This time, public outrage forced authorities to send Mary away for good. She lived out the remaining 23 years of her life in the isolated community of North Brother Island.

Mary Mallon died on November 11, 1938—not from typhoid but from complications brought on by a stroke.

It's All in Your Mind

Mental health is as important as physical health and can be just as tricky to diagnose and treat. Our understanding of mental illness has changed over time and continues to develop.

✳ ✳ ✳ ✳

✳ In 1375, the Bethlem Royal Hospital in London became one of the first hospitals to take in "lunatics." The asylum became synonymous with chaos, so much so that Bethlem became the origin of the word "bedlam."

✳ In the 1600s, mental patients were a tourist attraction in London at Hospital of St. Mary. Anyone who paid a penny could observe and taunt the "lunatics" for their own amusement.

✳ Medical care of the mentally ill became more humane after the publication of Darwin's *Origin of the Species* in

1859, when people realized that insanity was hereditary. Previously, madness had been seen as demonic possession, loss of a soul, weakness of character, or a feminine trait.

* In Australia in the late 1940s, manic depression was the first mental illness to be successfully treated with lithium. In Scandinavia in the 1950s, Dr. Morgens Schou pursued the same course of treatment with beneficial results.

* The first recorded case of dream-induced amnesia occurred in 2004. After a man dreamed that his son had been killed, he woke up screaming , with no memory of the previous day.

* We now know that one of the greatest environmental risks for people with schizophrenia is living in an urban area. It is speculated that air and noise pollution, stress, fear, electromagnetic fields, and other factors either cause the condition to develop or make a latent condition active.

Stick Around

What happens if you swallow a stick of chewing gum? Will it stick around for seven years? Twist around your innards? Form a blockage in your digestive tract?

✳   ✳   ✳   ✳

IT'S CALLED CHEWING gum, not swallowing gum. But sometimes, accidentally or on purpose, a piece of gum ends up dropping down the gullet. When that happens, who hasn't wondered what the consequences will be?

No one knows how it got started, but the idea that swallowed chewing gum stays in the digestive system for seven years is a pervasive myth. It seems the misconception dates back thousands of years, as archaeologists have found evidence of ancient wads of chewing gum. Way back when, gum didn't come wrapped in paper and foil, but the concept was the same—it was something pleasant to chew on but not to swallow.

No matter how old the myth, you need not worry about swallowed gum taking up long-term residence in your stomach. Gastroenterologists say that inspections of the digestive tract, with exams such as colonoscopies and endoscopies, do not reveal clumps of petrified gum. When gum does show up on such scans, it is most often a recent arrival.

Although it's not intended to be ingested, chewing gum usually is not harmful if it ends up in your stomach instead of a trash bin (or under a desk). Some chewing gum additives, such as sweeteners and flavoring, are broken down by the body, but the bulk of gum is not digestible. Ingredients such as rubbery elastomers and resins remain intact during their slow voyage through the digestive tract. Eventually, the gum moves down and out.

In rare cases, an extremely large clump of swallowed gum could get stuck on its journey out of the body, causing a dangerous blockage. This potential problem can be avoided, however, if you chew just one stick at a time.

All Shook Up

Achy back? Sleepless nights? Simply bored in your motel room? Put Magic Fingers to work!

✳   ✳   ✳   ✳

IN THE 1960s, although motel rooms were cheap at $25 a night, independent motel owners still had to be mindful of the competition. After the Motel 6 chain started adding free color televisions, telephones, and coffee makers to its rooms, competitors were left scrambling for amenities to add value to their rooms. Enter the "Magic Fingers" machine.

Gently Shake You to Sleep

John Houghtaling invented Magic Fingers in 1958; initially it was sold as a device guaranteed to solve many of the medical problems that occur when traveling: back pain, stress, and sleeplessness. In reality, it was nothing more than an electric motor that, when fastened to the underside of a mattress, shook the guest until they fell asleep or were pitched off the bed. Originally selling for more than $200, the Magic Fingers included not only the vibrator but the mattress as well.

After months of dismal sales, Houghtaling realized that replacing the mattresses in each motel room was cost prohibitive for owners, so he retired to his basement "research facility" to develop a portable model. The earliest units were far too big and shook violently. He finally came up with a much smaller version that could be used with existing mattresses and were coin-operated at 15 minutes for a quarter.

New and Improved

Franchisers sold the new models to motels for $45. After installation, the franchisers collected 80 percent of the revenue, and motel owners got the remaining 20 percent. The average haul for a week was $2 per room. Houghtaling sold a lot of franchises, and the monthly sales exceeded $2 million.

Eventually, the novelty of the units wore off, and motel owners found that guests were prying open the coin boxes and stealing the proceeds. Magic Fingers machines were discontinued, but you can still buy a home version of the gadget online.

The Great Beyond

"In this world," Benjamin Franklin once observed, "nothing is certain but death and taxes." Both are equally mysterious to the average person. Read on for some interesting burial traditions.

❉ ❉ ❉ ❉

All About Embalming

EMBALMING IS CURRENTLY the most widely accepted method of preparing a body for viewing and burial. The idea of preserving bodies by pumping them full of chemicals gained acceptance during the Civil War, when soldiers who died in combat were sent home for burial—oftentimes many states away. The technique was improved in the years that followed, and today many of those who die in the United States are embalmed as a part of the funeral process.

Chemical embalming helps ward off the natural decomposition that begins almost immediately upon death. A variety of bacteria and enzymes start to break down the body once we leave this mortal coil, and without embalming we would very quickly be very unpleasant to be around. The chemicals used in the embalming process—specifically formaldehyde—help kill the bacteria and stop the enzymes from doing their job. Formaldehyde is also a good embalming fluid because it is an effective disinfectant, and it coagulates protein, which makes the body sturdier and easier to work with.

The big question, of course, is how long do the effects of embalming last? Many people believe that the process leaves the body looking pretty practically forever, but that's not true. No matter how talented the embalmer, sooner or later a body will begin to decompose. A variety of factors play a role in determining how long that might take, however. If embalming is done immediately after death, the embalmer does a thorough job, and the casket remains airtight, a body can remain in very good condition for many, many years. However, if the body is exposed to air in any way, decomposition will set in fairly quickly. In addition, bodies interred in aboveground mausoleums tend to break down faster than those in the ground.

Funereal Facts

Interestingly, certain ancient techniques, such as mummification, have proved very effective at body preservation, sometimes even more so than modern embalming. Back in the day, mummification involved removing the brain and internal organs (with the exception of the heart); treating the body with a variety of preservative compounds, including a natural salt called "natron;" then wrapping it in linen. This process was so efficient that mummies thousands of years old have been found in astoundingly good condition.

Burial ceremonies are as old as human civilization, and perhaps even older. Certain Neanderthal burial grounds dating back to 60,000 B.C. suggest that the prehistoric dead weren't simply stuck in the ground. Instead, they were sent on their way with meaningful rituals, which at times included placing animal antlers and flowers with the deceased.

Many of today's burial customs are actually based in pagan beliefs. Wakes stem from the ancient custom of keeping watch over a dead person in the hope that he or she might return to life. Wearing special clothes, such as black, harkens back to the custom of donning a disguise to confuse returning spirits.

Potty Talk

Studies show that you spend an average of 30 minutes a day in the bathroom. Seems to us you could stand to know a little more about bathroom-related topics.

✳ ✳ ✳ ✳

✳ Antacids have been around for more than 5,000 years. Ancient stomach remedies included chalk, which can still be found in some over-the-counter heartburn remedies today.

✳ Bathtubs, too, have been around for centuries, but earlier ones were made of clay, marble, and even wood. Claw-foot tubs were invented in Great Britain in the mid-1800s. In 1911, the bathtub as we know it was invented, in part because a claw-foot tub is difficult to clean under.

✳ Prior to World War II, the average American bathed just once a week.

✳ In Elizabethan times, the smell of sweat was considered to be an aphrodisiac, but about 100 years ago Americans decided otherwise. The first deodorant made its appearance in 1888, and the first antiperspirant was available in 1902. Yes, by the way, there is a difference between antiperspirants (which can be used on the feet and other body sites) and deodorants (used mostly on the underarms).

* Ancient people kept their toothsome smiles by chewing a stick shredded at one end. About 1,000 years ago, the Chinese plucked hog bristles and inserted them into a wooden handle to clean their teeth. While hog bristles worked well enough, most people preferred the softness of horsehair brushes (though the cleaning power wasn't as good) until soft nylon was invented in the 1950s.

* Cotton swabs were invented in the 1920s by an American father who had a "Eureka!" moment as he watched his wife wrap cotton around a toothpick to better clean their baby's ears, fingers, and toes.

* Over the centuries, many products have been used as shampoos, including vinegar, eggs, rainwater, lemon juice, and fermented beverages. Soft detergents (basically shampoo) were invented by the Germans during World War I. They were searching for an effective, cheap cleanser to get them through the war. In the process, they really got into our hair.

* Soap has been around for thousands of years. An old recipe, still used in some places, adds animal fat, ashes, and water to make lye soap, which cleans but is hard on the skin. In the mid-to-late 1800s, mass-produced (soft) soap replaced the caustic, homemade stuff in most homes.

* While nail decoration has been around for more than 3,000 years, modern women didn't really know what to make of liquid, synthetic polish when it first became available. By the 1920s, though, they were happy to dig their fingernails into the new, popular cosmetic. Red polish—so much a staple in many women's beauty routines even today—wasn't popular until a decade later.

* Did you know that you have the remains of an animal in your bathroom? If you've got a natural sponge, you do. Natural sponges are, basically, the skeletons of sea creatures.

* For centuries, doctors have believed that a lack of, um, elimination was the root of all ills. Ancient Egyptian physicians offered their patients a variety of laxatives, including goose fat, figs, and castor oil. Chinese medicine used gingerroot and licorice root, while other remedies included aloe vera, honey, and rhubarb. Though "modern" doctors preach colon health and seem at times to be obsessed with it, laxatives as we know them were created only 100 years ago.

Dem Bones

Do you think bones are only good for keeping vertebrates from being shapeless lumps of goo? Think again! Bones get pressed into use as art, medicine, weapons, and furniture. Bones tell tales dead men can't. Sometimes they even go bump in the night. Here are some fast facts about all things osseous.

✳ ✳ ✳ ✳

* At birth, human babies have more than 300 bones, but adults have only 206. Some bones fuse together as we grow.

* The human femur (thighbone) is stronger than concrete.

* In 2006, an Indian yogi was arrested for using ground-up human bone in his homemade impotence medicine.

* Although Westerners usually think of vampires as "bloodsuckers," in African cultures, vampires are believed to eat bones.

* Drink your milk! Ninety-nine percent of the calcium within the human body is contained in the bones.

* The entire human skeleton is replaced with new bone matter every 10 to 25 years.

* Like all other cells, your bones "breathe" by consuming oxygen and releasing carbon dioxide.

* Most mammals, including raccoons, horses, walruses, gorillas, and whales, have a *baculum*, or penis bone.

* In the Ozark Mountains, raccoon penis bones are used as love amulets and toothpicks.

* Bone china dishes are actually a type of porcelain that is made from powdered clay and stone mixed with bone ash. *Bon appétit!*

* The phrase "to make no bones about" means tackling a difficulty with little hesitation. It mostly derives from the ease of eating stew without bones.

* In parts of Africa, "throwing the bones" is a form of divination.

* The bones from more than 40,000 human skeletons have been turned into chandeliers, sculptures, religious vessels, and decorations at the Kostnice Ossuary in Sedlec in the Czech Republic.

* Human bones can be owned, bought, or sold legally in most parts of the United States, except Tennessee and Georgia.

* The easiest way to clean large quantities of bones is to employ a colony of flesh-eating dermestids, otherwise known as "museum beetles."

* Embedded in the ethmoid bone, located between the eyes, humans have a sliver of magnetite, which acts as a small compass.

* Measuring only one-tenth of an inch, the stapes, or stirrup bone located inside the inner ear, is the smallest bone in the human body.

Heads Up: The Study of Phrenology

Sure, someone may look like a nice enough guy, but a phrenologist might just diagnose the same fella as a potential axe murderer.

✳ ✳ ✳ ✳

He Had the Gall

THERE ARE BUMPS in the road and bumps in life. Then there are the bumps on our heads. In the last half of the 19th century, the bumps and lumps and shapes of the human skull became an area of scientific study known as *phrenology*.

Early in the century, an Austrian physicist named Franz Joseph Gall theorized that the shape of the head followed the shape of the brain. Moreover, he wrote, the skull's shape was determined by the development of the brain's various parts. He described 27 separate parts of the brain and attributed to each one specific personality traits.

Gall's phrenological theories reached the public at a time of widespread optimism in Europe and North America. New and startling inventions seemed to appear every week. No problem was insurmountable, no hope unattainable. And a belief in physical science prevailed.

By mid-century, Gall's theories had spread favorably throughout industrialized society. What was particularly attractive about phrenology was its value as both an indicator and predictor of psychological traits. If these traits could be identified—and phrenology presumably could do this—they could be re-engineered through "moral counseling" before they became entrenched as bad habits, which could result in socially unacceptable behavior. On the other hand, latent goodness, intellect, and rectitude could also be identified and nurtured.

As it grew in popularity, phrenology found its way into literature as diverse as the Brontë family's writings and those of Edgar Allen Poe. It also influenced the work of philosopher William James. Famed poet Walt Whitman was so proud of his phrenological chart that he published it five times. Thomas Edison was also a vocal supporter. "I never knew I had an inventive talent until phrenology told me so," he said. "I was a stranger to myself until then."

Criminal Minds

Early criminologists such as Cesare Lombroso and Èmile Durkheim (the latter considered to be the founder of the academic discipline of sociology) saw remarkable possibilities for phrenology's use in the study of criminal behavior. Indeed, according to one tale, the legendary Old West figure Bat Masterson invited a phrenologist to Dodge City to identify horse thieves and cattle rustlers. A lecture before an audience of gun-toting citizenry ended with the audience shooting out the lights and the lecturer hastily departing through the back exit.

In 1847, Orson Fowler, a leading American phrenologist, conducted an analysis of a Massachusetts wool trader and found him "to go the whole figure or nothing," a man who would "often find (his) motives are not understood." Sure enough, years later Fowler was proven to be on the money. The man was noted slavery abolitionist John Brown, and he definitely went the "whole figure."

Bumpology Booms

By the turn of the century, the famous and not so famous were flocking to have their skulls analyzed. Phrenology had become a fad and, like all fads, it attracted a number of charlatans. By the 1920s, the science had degenerated into a parlor game. Disrepute and discredit followed, but not before new expressions slipped into the language. Among these: "low brow" and "high brow" describe varying intellectual capacity, as well as the offhand remark, "You should have your head examined."

Odontologist

Talk to the expert! You may have heard the phrase, "The remains were identified from dental records." Behind the phrase is a forensic dentist, or odontologist. Here's some insight into the job.

Q: You could be doing root canals on live, squirming people. But you look at the teeth of the dead and tell us about their final hours.

A: True confession: In dental school, I learned that I loved dentistry but couldn't stand inflicting pain. I got physically ill if I felt I was hurting someone, but I still had a strong interest in the science of teeth.

Q: How long has forensic dentistry been around?

A: In 1849, a Viennese opera house went up in flames, and a number of people were incinerated beyond recognition. Teeth are incredibly durable; the fact that we have the power to break a healthy tooth with our bite proves just how strong our jaws are. The fire victims' teeth enabled families to obtain the correct remains to bury and have closure. Odontology has grown with advancements in dental science and record-keeping.

Q: This is a full-time job?

A: In larger cities it is. In smaller towns, most odontologists operate traditional dental practices and consult on the side as needed by local government. I like being near research universities, because my work also fits into archaeology.

Q: So you get to examine mummies?

A: Not quite. Bites leave patterns. What people eat and the way they chew suggests things about their diets. We can estimate age. All odontologic procedures begin with specific questions. In the case of a tooth from an ancient midden, they might include: "What species was this? From what period of time? How long did he or she live? What did this person usually eat?"

Take a Seat

When your mother told you to sit up straight, she was off by about 45 degrees.

✳ ✳ ✳ ✳

Mother Usually Knows Best

MOM WAS RIGHT when she admonished you not to slouch. But universal maternal advice about sitting perfectly straight can actually be harmful to your back's long-term health. That's right—when it comes to sitting up straight, you're advised not to listen to your mother.

Until recently, the long-standing conventional wisdom about sitting was that the back should be held ramrod straight, with thighs parallel to the floor. This posture was believed to protect the spine and cause the least amount of strain. New research appears to have pulled the chair out from under this theory. It turns out that sitting upright for long periods of time can actually trigger chronic back pain. Several studies have found that the once-recommended 90-degree sitting posture puts strain on the lower back. This position causes the disks between each vertebra to shift out of alignment. Over time, this can cause pain, deformity, and damage to the disks. And, as anyone who has tried to sit up straight for an extended period of time will tell you, it's just not very comfortable.

Experts now say it's best to sit with the chair back adjusted at a slight recline—a 135-degree angle—while your feet rest on the floor. This position reduces stress on the spine and causes the least amount of misalignment. Using this optimal position may help prevent back pain as well as treat it. Although modern life dictates that we spend a majority of our time seated, our bodies were not built to sit for long stretches. Research shows that getting up periodically and walking around during the day, along with adjusting chairs to the optimal recline, considerably helps reduce—and may even prevent—back strain.

Answers About Gas

Nope, we're not talking about the kind you put in your cars.

※　※　※　※

WHAT CAUSES FLATULENCE? High-fiber foods tend to cause intestinal gas, but beans seem to bear most of the blame, maybe because other world-class gas-promoters like cabbage and Brussels sprouts aren't as big a part of our diet.

The culprit in these foods is a natural family of hard-to-digest sugars called oligosaccharides. These molecules boogie their way through our small intestine largely unmolested. The merrymaking begins when they hit the large intestine. Bacteria living there strap on the feedbag, chomping away at this nutritional bounty, multiplying even. Our intestinal gas is the by-product of their digestive action.

Most of this gas is composed of odorless hydrogen, nitrogen, and carbon dioxide. In some humans—about 30 percent of the adult population—this process also produces methane.

Could this bodily function be useful? After all, hydrogen and methane are flammable gases. In fact, hydrogen is a player in the fuel-of-the-future derby and already powers experimental fuel-cell vehicles.

Alas, human flatulence simply doesn't contain hydrogen or methane in quantities sufficient to fuel anything more than a blue flame at a fraternity party. Even if we did generate enough of these gases to power a car, they'd have to be collected and carted around in high-pressure tanks to be effective as fuels.

Human biochemistry is a wonderful thing, but it isn't yet a backbone of the renewable-energy industry. For that, breathe a sigh of relief.

Cut the Cord!

People know that their belly button was once the place where their umbilical cord was attached. What else should you know about the umbilical cord?

✳ ✳ ✳ ✳

CHILDBIRTH IS ONE of life's greatest miracles—actually, it's a series of small miracles within that great miracle. Among them is the umbilical cord. A narrow tube of tissue that connects the fetus' navel with the placenta, the umbilical cord contains two umbilical arteries and one umbilical vein. The fetus' heart pumps blood to and from the placenta via the umbilical cord, drawing in nutrients and oxygen while sending away waste materials.

Once the baby is born, the umbilical cord is rendered unnecessary and needs to be cut. This is where the whole childbirth thing would logically take a sharp turn for the worse, but it doesn't. And for that, we can thank one of those small miracles: Wharton's jelly.

No, we're not talking about a breakfast spread that's handcrafted in a New England village. Wharton's jelly is the soft connective tissue in the umbilical cord. A key feature of Wharton's jelly is its lack of nerve endings—this means that when the umbilical cord is clamped and cut, neither the mother nor the baby feels a thing. The joyful moment can continue.

The Funny Bone

It might be the most misnamed bone in the human body.

✳ ✳ ✳ ✳

IT'S HAPPENED TO all of us. You're walking a bit too quickly around a corner, and *bam!* You smash your elbow on the corner of a table. And seemingly every time it happens, some stooge is standing right there and says with a chuckle, "Oh, did you hit your funny bone?"

As you're seized by a sensation akin to thousands of pins piercing your arm, it takes everything good inside of you not to scream, "No, I hit my '$#+! you' bone!"

The funny bone is the most misnamed part of the body—and not just because of "$#+! you" situations like the one just described. Truth is, the funny bone isn't even a bone; it's a nerve—one of three main nerves in the arm. Called the ulnar nerve, it passes under the collarbone and along the inside of the upper arm, through a tunnel of tissue at the elbow, under the muscles on the inside of the forearm, and into the palm of the hand on the side with the little finger.

The nerve goes around a bump at the elbow called the medial epicondyle. There's a slight groove in the bone where the nerve fits; since the groove is shallow, the nerve sits unusually close to the surface. With so little protection, it can easily be dinged.

Some say that the sensation associated with this ding is painful. Others call it prickly. Still others think that the feeling is funny in a peculiar sort of way—but that's not why it's called the funny bone.

What's so funny about it, then? Well, the elbow connects three bones: the radius, the ulna, and the humerus. That's right, humerus, as in "humorous." As in people think it's humorous that you smacked your funny bone on the corner of a table.

The ulnar nerve wasn't meant to be comic relief. In addition to providing feeling to the little finger and half of the ring finger, the ulnar nerve controls many of the muscles in the hand that aid with fine movements, as well as some of the bigger gripping muscles in the forearm.

Sound funny to you? We didn't think so.

Packing on the Pounds

Your metabolism gets way more blame than it should for that spare tire you call a stomach. The fact is, a slow metabolism is rarely the primary reason for excessive weight gain.

✻ ✻ ✻ ✻

BROADLY SPEAKING, YOUR metabolism comprises all the chemical processes your cells undertake to sustain life. But when people talk about a fast or slow metabolism, they generally mean the basal metabolic rate—the rate at which the body turns nutrients into energy (burning calories) when at rest.

While it's true that genetics plays a role in defining the baseline for this rate and that some people naturally burn more calories than others, very few folks have metabolic rates that are slow enough to single-handedly make them fat. The main culprit is almost always too many calories or too little exercise (or both).

The body's metabolic rate is highly flexible—it changes with your habits. For example, you can speed it up somewhat by adding more muscle; muscle burns more calories while you're at rest than fat does. On the other hand, you can slow your metabolism down through inactivity. And if your metabolism is naturally slow and you don't work out enough, you'll probably put on weight faster than somebody who has a quicker metabolism and doesn't exercise much.

Oh, and one more thing: In a cruel twist of fate, serious dieting tends to slow down the metabolism. If you cut back drastically on your caloric intake, the body typically enters "starvation mode"—it reacts to a perceived lack of available food by storing fat. If only you could explain to your body that you could have a cookie, you're just choosing not to...

How to Survive a Winter Night Alone in the Woods

You may not need to worry about lions and tigers and bears (well, maybe bears), but that's no reason to think you're home free. Cold weather can be just as deadly as wild animals. Here are some tips to help.

✳ ✳ ✳ ✳

Make a Shelter—The chief danger when you're stuck in the cold is hypothermia, a potentially deadly drop in your core body temperature. The most important factors in preventing hypothermia are staying dry and blocking the wind. To make a shelter, prop a large branch against a stump or rock, leaving enough room to lie underneath. Make a bed of sticks, leaves, and moss under the branch. This helps insulate you from the cold, wet ground. Prop smaller branches along each side of the large branch to make a simple tent. Fill the tent with leaves. The leaves will help retain your body heat, block the wind, and keep moisture away from your body.

Signal for Help—While you're in your shelter, tie a piece of clothing in a visible spot. When you're lost, periodically yell for help—but without expending so much energy that you wear yourself out.

Don't Eat Mysterious Plants—Only a fraction of the tens of thousands of North American plant species are edible. It's best not to take the chance, when you can survive for weeks without food.

Don't Drink Dirty Water—You need two to four quarts of water per day for optimum health, but drinking potentially contaminated water in rivers and streams can do more harm than good. If you don't have a way to purify water, like iodine tablets, it's safer not to drink anything, even if you're without water all night.

Stay Put—If you figure out you're lost and don't know how to get back to civilization, your best bet is to stay in one place. This will make it easier for rescuers to find you.

9 Particularly Germy Places in Hotel Rooms

If you want your hotel stay to be a healthy one, be ever vigilant. Nasty microscopic critters are present and waiting to pounce.

✳   ✳   ✳   ✳

1. **Bedspreads**—We've all heard that bedspreads at hotels are washed less frequently than sheets. Is it true? You bet your E. coli. Bottom line? Ditch the bedspread.

2. **Carpets**—With gravity acting as it does, some pretty nasty germs work their way into carpets. Wear proper footwear.

3. **Whirlpool Tubs**—A veritable breeding ground for germs, hotel whirlpools are rarely serviced with the same frequency as private baths. In one study, 100 percent of whirlpool water samples tested came up positive for agents that can cause urinary tract infections, rashes, and pneumonia.

4. **Shower**—Can you say athlete's foot? Shower floors are rife with the bacteria that cause this condition. Wear flip-flops.

5. **Mattress**—If germ-laden bodies never come in direct contact with a mattress, what's the risk? Bedbugs. To see if such nasties are present, aim a hair dryer at the mattress and observe closely. Bedbugs are attracted to heat and if present will likely make an appearance.

6. **Sink**—Common sense dictates that a basin used for frequent hand washing and tooth brushing contains an abundance of germs.

7. **Faucets**—Think of the number of people who touch these. Then wipe down accordingly.

8. Toilet Seat—This one is almost too obvious. The best defense is a complete wipe down with an antibacterial wipe.

9. Remote Control—Cold viruses and other nasty bugs can live on this surface for a day or more.

Munchie Mythology

Food: It's fodder for the best urban legends and old wives' tales. Myths range from complete nutritional nonsense to gluttonous celebrity gossip. Are you one of the gastronomically gullible?

✳   ✳   ✳   ✳

Bad Raps

MYTH: Chocolate causes acne.

TRUTH: No specific food has been scientifically proven to produce pimples—not chocolate, pizza, potato chips, or French fries. Acne's true cause is a buildup of dead skin cells within the pores. This can be triggered by hormones, environment, and heredity, but not by a Mr. Goodbar.

MYTH: Mayonnaise is the major cause of poisoning outbreaks from picnic foods.

TRUTH: Commercial mayonnaise is pasteurized and, thanks to ingredients like salt and lemon juice, has a high acid content that actually slows the growth of food-borne bacteria. Improperly handled meats and veggies in picnic salads and sandwiches are more likely to be your number one *Salmonella suspects*.

Brown Is Better than White

MYTH: Brown eggs are more nutritious than white eggs.

TRUTH: Brown eggs come from hens with red earlobes, and white eggs come from hens with white earlobes. Crack through the outer shell, and brown eggs offer no better nutritive value, taste, or quality. Why are they more expensive? Brown eggs are usually a smidge larger in size.

MYTH: Brown sugar is healthier than white sugar.

TRUTH: Brown sugar is simply ordinary white table sugar that's turned brown by the addition of molasses. While molasses does contain certain minerals (calcium, potassium, iron, and magnesium), they are only present in negligible amounts. The real difference between brown sugar and white is only apparent in the taste and texture of your baked goods.

A Lie Your Parents Told

MYTH: Coffee will stunt your growth.

TRUTH: Research does not support the notion that drinking caffeinated coffee will hinder your height. That doesn't mean coffee belongs in a child's diet, however. Some actual adverse effects include bellyaches, nervousness, headaches, rapid heartbeat, and insomnia—all of which make for one crabby kid.

Into the Water

MYTH: You must wait an hour after eating before swimming.

TRUTH: Though swimming strenuously on a full stomach could lead to cramps, the chance of that happening to a recreational swimmer is quite small. One study of drownings in the United States found that less than 1 percent happened after the victim had recently eaten a meal. What you really need to avoid: eating or chewing gum while in the water. According to the American Red Cross, both activities can lead to choking.

Celebrity Stories

MYTH: Caesar salad was named for Julius Caesar.

TRUTH: The famous salad has no connection with that particular Caesar, or with Rome at all for that matter. Its creation is most often credited to Caesar Cardini, owner and chef of Caesar's Place in Tijuana, Mexico. His original recipe (concocted around 1924) contained romaine lettuce, garlic, croutons, Parmesan cheese, eggs, olive oil, and Worcestershire sauce. No anchovies!

Do People Really Go Mad During a Full Moon?

The story goes that if you ask emergency-room workers or police officers, they'll tell you that the number of disturbed individuals who come to their attention rises dramatically during a full moon. What's the truth behind the story?

✳ ✳ ✳ ✳

I T'S A LONG-HELD belief that a lunar effect causes "lunacy" in susceptible people—resulting in an increase in homicides, traffic accidents, suicides, kidnappings, crisis calls to emergency services, admissions to psychiatric institutions, and all kinds of other things. The rationale: The earth is 80 percent water, and so is the human body. Theoretically, then, since the moon has such a dramatic effect on the tides, it could move the water in our bodies in some similar way, causing strange behavior.

Are the stories true? Most evidence says no.

In 1996, scientists Ivan Kelly, James Rotton, and Roger Culver did a thorough examination of more than one hundred studies of lunar effects. Perhaps surprisingly, they found no significant correlation between the state of the moon and people's mental and physical conditions. When all of the statistical wrinkles had been smoothed out, there was no evidence of a rise in violence, accidents, disasters, or any other kind of strange behavior.

A study by C. E. Climent and R. Plutchik, written for *Comprehensive Psychiatry*, showed that psychiatric admissions are lowest during a full moon, and an examination conducted at the University of Erlangen–Nuremberg in Germany indicated no connection between suicide rates and phases of the moon. So why the myths? Perhaps people just want to believe the spooky tales, and lunar effects are tossed into movies and literature simply because they're compelling drama. Who doesn't love a good werewolf tale?

The constant reinforcement of the "full moon" message makes it much more likely that the public will accept it as proven fact. Myths also tend to stay alive if you pick and choose the data to fit the story. One murder that occurs during a full moon creates a story that can be told over and over, yet the ten homicides that happen at any other time of the month just disappear into a pile of statistics.

Renowned UCLA astronomer George O. Abell consistently dismissed claims that the moon could have a strong enough effect on the water in a human body to cause any behavioral changes. Abell pointed out that a mosquito would exert more gravitational pull on a human arm than the moon ever might.

So, is that arm-biting mosquito spooked by the moon? That's not entirely a joke, because it seems animals actually are affected by lunar activity. It might be a bit scary to read a study in the *British Medical Journal* that appears to prove there's a significant increase in bites by cats, rats, horses, and dogs when the moon is full.

Suddenly, the image of a dog howling at the moon might give you a little shiver. But a man baying at the moon? Most likely he'd be someone who's goofy all month long.

Circus Artist

Talk to the expert! Find out more about the art of flying through the air from someone who does it for a living.

❋   ❋   ❋   ❋

Q: You prefer to be called a "circus artist," rather than a "trapeze artist," because you've done a little bit of everything.

A: I consider myself an "aerialist," because I've done trapeze and Spanish web and aerial fabrics—what they call "the silks." I used to be an acrobat, and I'd fly through the air and somersault.

Q: I can't resist: Did you fly through the air with the greatest of ease?

A: I would have to say that I did. When you do it as much as I did growing up—I started training when I was five—it actually becomes second nature. Like being a musician: Your muscles remember where the chords are; your body remembers how to do it.

Q: You grew up in a circus family, which is unusual.

A: Not to me! All of my friends grew up in a circus family. My dad joined the circus in his 20s and wanted his family to be a part of it. My mother was a second-generation circus family.

Q: You make it look so easy up there, but it really takes amazing strength. How do you achieve that?

A: What I tell my students is that if you keep doing it, you build up the strength for it. A lot of people come in and get really frustrated. They say, "I'm gonna go work out and come back stronger." But the strength that you develop is really specific for aerial. You can work out; you can do Pilates every day of your life. You still wouldn't have the skills or level of strength for these specific apparatuses.

Q: Is it true what they say about not looking down?

A: Yes! I've never really been scared of falling. I mean, everybody should be scared of falling, because that's natural. But if you focus on the fear, you're not going to do anything.

Time for a Recount?

Some people can bend themselves into mind-boggling positions. Others have one cool trick, such as wrapping their legs behind their neck or bending their thumbs backward. Talented? Maybe. Double-jointed? No.

✳ ✳ ✳ ✳

To explain such feats, people boast that they're "double-jointed," as though they either have more joints than the rest of us or have joints with twice the normal range of motion. Even if you can twist yourself into the shape of a pretzel, you are not, in fact, double-jointed.

Bend Me, Shape Me

Circus promoters often claim that their star contortionists have a little extra in their anatomy, but that's just to sell tickets. In fact, we all have the same number of joints. Those dramatic twists and turns are a combination of genetic flexibility—which allows for extra movement in the joints—and intense training. The technical term for extraordinary joint flexibility is *hypermobility*.

Hypermobility is most often seen in children. Most of the time, the condition doesn't cause any problems, but in some cases, it can be a sign of an underlying medical condition. When hypermobility causes dislocations and sprains, or pain and swelling in the joints, the diagnosis is Benign Hypermobility Syndrome. Also called "looseness of joints," this condition is characterized by loose and weak ligaments, which do a poor job of providing stability to the joints.

Experts do not know why some hypermobile individuals are pain free while others experience discomfort. Treatment varies but may include exercises to increase muscle strength and training to prevent hyperextension.

6 Unusual Beauty Pageants

Beauty may only be skin deep, but beauty pageants go a lot deeper, right to the heart of what makes us Americans. We don't just love the Miss America pageant, we love everything leading up to it, from Miss Ohio all the way down to Miss Drumsticks. Check out some of America's more unusual beauty pageants.

✳ ✳ ✳ ✳

1. **Miss Drumsticks:** Every October, Yellville, Arkansas, gets ready for Thanksgiving with two days worth of turkey-related fun and games, culminating with the selection of Miss Drumsticks. Contestants are judged on their legs only, with their faces and bodies hidden behind a picture of a turkey, so as not to influence the judges. And the prize is nothing to shake a tail feather at. Past winners have received trips to Los Angeles to compete on game shows and to New York for appearances on the *Late Show with David Letterman.*

2. **Miss Klingon Empire:** Beam me down, Scotty, there's a Miss Klingon Empire beauty pageant held every year in September at the Star Trek Convention at Dragon*Con in Atlanta. Contestants assume the persona of a female Klingon character from any Star Trek TV series or movie. The Klingon babes are judged on beauty, personality, and talent, which includes singing and dancing. (No planetary destruction is allowed.) Winners receive a trophy, a tiara, and a satin sash outlined in blue and green—the official colors of the Klingon Empire.

3. **Mr. or Ms. Mosquito Legs:** To become Miss America, contestants need good-looking legs, but to win the title of Mr. or Ms. Mosquito Legs, guys and gals need skinny legs. Clute, Texas, hosts the pageant as part of the Great Texas Mosquito Festival, held each July. Anyone attending the festival is eligible to strut their legs and take their chances.

4. Miss Sweet Corn Queen: It must be tough, buttering up judges who are buttering their sweet corn, but that's the task of competitors in the Miss Sweet Corn Queen pageant held each August in Mendota, Illinois. Local high-school girls compete for the coveted title and a place of honor in the parade, which is held at one of the largest harvest festivals in the Midwest.

5. Miss Exotic World: True practitioners of the dance form known as the striptease flock to the Exotic World Burlesque Museum and Striptease Hall of Fame in Las Vegas every Memorial Day weekend for the annual Miss Exotic World Pageant. Ranging in age from 18 to 80, these burlesque beauties flirt with the judges with smiles, winks, and teases. The winner of the Miss Exotic World pageant gets a trophy and the right to be called the Miss America of Burlesque.

6. The Armpit Queen: In Battle Mountain, Nevada, nobody raises a stink about the Armpit Beauty Pageant. After humorist Gene Weingarten of *The Washington Post* dubbed Battle Mountain "the armpit of America" for its "lack of character and charm," the small town's residents turned the joke into an annual celebration of all things smelly every August. Sweaty T-shirt contests, deodorant throws, and a "quick-draw" antiperspirant contest lead up to the selection of the Armpit Queen. The pageant and festival are sponsored by Old Spice deodorant and draw an estimated 3,500 visitors with signs along the highway proclaiming: "Make Battle Mountain Your Next Pit Stop."

Death—Isn't It Ironic?

No matter who you are, it's inevitable: Your time on this earth will end. But some people have a way of shuffling off this mortal coil with a bit more ironic poignancy.

✳ ✳ ✳ ✳

✳ In 1936, a picture of baby George Story was featured in the first issue of *Life* magazine. Story died in 2000 at age 63, just after the magazine announced it would be shutting down. *Life* carried an article about his death from heart failure in its final issue.

✳ In the early 1960s, Ken Hubbs was a Gold Glove second baseman for the Chicago Cubs. The young standout had a lifelong fear of flying, so to overcome it, he decided to take flying lessons. In 1964, shortly after earning his pilot's license, Hubbs was killed when his plane went down during a snowstorm.

✳ While defending an accused murderer in 1871, attorney Clement Vallandigham argued that the victim accidentally killed himself as he tried to draw his pistol. Demonstrating his theory for the court, the lawyer fatally shot himself in the process. The jury acquitted his client and Vallandigham won the case posthumously.

✳ Private detective Allan Pinkerton built his career on secrecy and his ability to keep his mouth shut. However, biting his tongue literally killed him when he tripped while out for a walk, severely cutting his tongue. The injury became infected and led to his death in 1884.

✳ When he appeared on *The Dick Cavett Show* in 1971, writer and healthy living advocate Jerome I. Rodale claimed, "I've decided to live to be a hundred," and "I never felt better in my life!" Moments later, still in his seat on stage, the 72-year-old Rodale died of a heart attack. The episode never aired.

* South Korean Lee Seung Seop loved playing video games more than anything. His obsession caused him to lose his job and his girlfriend and eventually took his life as well. In August 2005, after playing a video game at an Internet café for 50 consecutive hours, he died at age 28 from dehydration, exhaustion, and heart failure.

* Jim Fixx advocated running as a cure-all, helping develop the fitness craze of the late 20th century. However, in 1984, he died from a heart attack while jogging. Autopsy results showed he suffered from severely clogged arteries.

* Thomas Midgley Jr. was a brilliant engineer and inventor who held 170 patents. After contracting polio at age 51, he turned his attention to inventing a system of pulleys to help him move around in bed. In 1944, he was found dead, strangled by the pulley system that he had invented.

* At least two of the Marlboro Men—the chiseled icons of the cigarette culture—have died from lung cancer. David McLean developed emphysema in 1985 and died from lung cancer a decade later. Wayne McLaren portrayed the character in the 1970s, and although he was an antismoking advocate later in life, he still contracted cancer that spread from his lungs to his brain. He died in 1992.

* Author Olivia Goldsmith wrote *The First Wives Club*, a book that became an icon for older women whose husbands had tossed them aside for younger trophy wives. A generation of women embraced their wrinkles and weren't afraid to let the world know. Ironically, Goldsmith died while undergoing cosmetic surgery.

* Shortly before he died in a high-speed car crash, James Dean filmed a television spot promoting his new film *Giant*. The interviewer asked Dean if he had any advice for young people. "Take it easy driving," he replied. "The life you save might be mine."

Ten Years After

What would you look like if they dug you up after you'd been buried for a decade? The simple answer is: a skeleton. But we know what you really want—you're dying to know all of the gory details about bulging eyeballs and rancid smells.

✳ ✳ ✳ ✳

Putrefaction: It Ain't Pretty

HOLD ON TO your barf bag, gentle reader, because you're about to learn the finer points of putrefaction. First, though, let's clear up a common misconception: Worms don't dine on corpses. Unless a person is buried without a coffin, the main cause of decay is bacteria that are inside the body. These microorganisms exist when a person is living, but the immune system keeps them in check. However, once a person dies and the immune system shuts down, it's open season on the body.

Here's what will happen to your body when you leave it behind. About a week after your death, bacteria will be raging inside your body, and your red blood vessels will begin to rupture, releasing hemoglobin into you. Hemoglobin is the iron-rich element that gives your blood a red appearance. Once the hemoglobin is dispersed, your skin will have the same reddish hue. Eventually, the hemoglobin will break down, turning your skin various shades of green before it becomes dark purple.

A few weeks later, your body will start to ferment, much like alcohol. Fermentation occurs when the bacteria in your body start to break your tissue down into simpler chemical compounds, resulting in the production of gases such as carbon dioxide and methane. Naturally, your body will begin to bloat and take on a puffy appearance. Because the majority of bacteria are in the intestines, most of the swelling will take place in the abdomen. This is also when many of the rank smells associated with death will begin to emerge.

In the final stage of putrefaction, the tissues of your body will completely break down. Your organs will become all sorts of nasty colors and will eventually start to liquefy. Because lean tissue decomposes faster than muscular tissue, the eyes will go first, quickly followed by the stomach and intestines. Once all of the tissue has been destroyed, the skeleton will be all that remains of you. Normally, this process takes about ten years.

But Wait . . . You Can Avoid the Yucky Stuff

If you're embalmed, it'll be a completely different story. Fluids and gases will be drained from your body, and a disinfecting fluid will be introduced into it. The putrefaction process is much slower; in fact, sometimes the body can be preserved for quite a long time. Just look at Vladimir Lenin. He's holding up pretty well, considering he died in 1924.

15 Most Common Causes of Death in the United States

Where you live has a good deal to do with how you will die. In the United States, the top two causes of death (2011) are responsible for more than 50 percent of the annual death toll. In the world at large, there's a lot more variety in how you meet your Maker.

✳   ✳   ✳   ✳

1. Diseases of the heart

2. Malignant neoplasms

3. Chronic lower respiratory diseases

4. Cerebrovascular diseases

5. Accidents (unintentional injuries)

6. Alzheimer's disease

7. Diabetes mellitus

8. Influenza and pneumonia

9. Nephritis, nephrotic syndrome, and nephrosis

10. Suicide

11. Septicemia (blood poisoning)

12. Chronic liver disease and cirrhosis

13. Primary hypertension and hypertensive renal disease

14. Parkinson's disease

15. Pneumonitis due to solids and liquids

Under the Mistletoe

Christmas kisses are nothing to sneer at. When else do you get to grab and snog complete strangers because a plant sprig happens to be hanging from a well-placed nail? But what other uses are there for mistletoe?

✳ ✳ ✳ ✳

THAT CUSTOM, BY the way, is loosely based upon a Norse myth in which Frigg, goddess of love, restores her son to life and joyfully kisses everyone in sight. Combined with a bit of Victorian romanticism, kissing under the mistletoe became a popular pastime. But how else do humans interact with it?

American mistletoe is toxic, while the European variety can be used medicinally. Europe's mistletoe, *Viscum album*, is found in herbal teas and shampoos. It has potential as a cancer treatment, and some study groups are actually conducting clinical trials with mistletoe lectins. Traditionally, *Viscum album* was used by the Greeks, Celts, and other ancient folks to treat epilepsy and infertility, among other ailments. It was also considered just plain lucky.

If you get your mistletoe in North America, though, be careful! Deer and certain birds eat the berries, but they are poisonous to humans. The American mistletoe seen at Christmas is called

Phoradendron. At least thirteen hundred species of the plant exist, and many will do nasty things to your insides. While it makes a pretty holiday decoration, the plant is a parasitic pest that attaches itself to hardwood and fir trunks, digs in, and sucks water and sap from the host tree to stay alive.

What's So Charming About a Dimple?

Who knew that a minor birth defect could melt so many hearts?

✳ ✳ ✳ ✳

SHIRLEY TEMPLE. ROBERT Mitchum. Jay Leno. Jessica Simpson. Are these celebrities more famous for their talents or those darling divots on their cheeks and chins? Dimples, after all, are pretty darn hard to resist—especially when they're flashed alongside a smile from Brad Pitt. But technically, most dimples are actually "malformations." They're caused by shorter-than-normal facial muscles or indentations in the bone structure of the jaw. It just goes to show that some facial flaws are attractive. In fact, dimples seem to convey an endearing sense of vulnerability and innocence, which may be why we find them so appealing.

Ever notice how babies are often born with dimples? Lots of times, these dimples become less noticeable or disappear as the muscles in the face lengthen with age. Still, we can't help but associate those cute little craters with blamelessness and youth. Come on—who doesn't love a fully grown man with a pretty baby face?

Of course, from an aesthetic point of view, it doesn't hurt that dimples seem to perfectly accentuate and frame the face. Often, they only pop out when a person smiles. We already perceive smiling people to be more attractive and approachable, and if you add a dashing dimple to that toothy grin, you've got quite an attractive package.

Another plus: Dimples make perfect kissing targets. No wonder they're considered to be such a winning physical trait in so many cultures. In parts of Asia, these facial dips, dents, and hollows are even believed to bring good fortune, increased fertility, and better prospects for marriage.

If you aren't lucky enough to have been born with the facial deformity known as the dimple, here's some good news: Your local cosmetic surgeon will gladly give you one or two. Now, if you could only figure out a way to get Cindy Crawford's mole.

Can Coca-Cola Burn a Hole in Your Stomach?

The world's most famous soft drink has been the subject of seemingly countless urban legends. Let's examine the truth of one of them.

✳   ✳   ✳   ✳

ONE URBAN MYTH suggests that Coca-Cola can cause death from carbon dioxide poisoning, another says that it dissolves teeth, and still another posits that it makes an effective spermicide. The topic here is whether Coke can burn a hole in your stomach.

The answer is, quite simply, no. Your stomach is designed to withstand punishment—it's the Rocky Balboa of internal organs—and it can handle a lot worse than what little old Coca-Cola throws at it.

Your stomach takes every culinary delight that you consume and prepares it for the body to use as fuel. It breaks down food using hydrochloric acid—a substance that, in its industrial form, is used to process steel and leather, make household cleaning products, and even aid in oil drilling in the North Sea. Since this acid is highly corrosive, a mucus is secreted to protect the stomach lining.

The strength of an acid is measured on a pH scale that ranges from zero to fourteen. A pH level of seven is considered neutral; any substance with a pH level of less than seven is acidic. Where does your stomach's hydrochloric acid fall on the pH scale? Its pH level is one, meaning that it is among the most potent acids in existence. Coca-Cola contains phosphoric acid, a substance with a pH level of about 2.5. Phosphoric acid, then, is less potent than what is already inside you. In other words, Coca-Cola isn't going to burn a hole in your stomach.

Still, there are some reasons to hesitate before you take the pause that refreshes. Coca-Cola contains the stimulant caffeine. (There is a caffeine-free Coca-Cola, but we're talking about the original version.) The stomach reacts to stimulants by creating more acid, which isn't an issue when the stomach is working well. But when the stomach contains ulcer-causing bacteria called *Helicobacter pylori*, the production of extra acid can exacerbate the problem. Further, people with gastroesophageal reflux disease (GERD) should avoid caffeinated drinks. And finally, phosphoric acid has been linked to osteoporosis.

But under ordinary circumstances, a big swig of Coca-Cola isn't going to harm your stomach, or any other part of your body. Enjoy. Just don't pour any on raw pork. Apparently, that will cause worms to crawl out of the meat.

Strange Stats

✳ Each day, a healthy individual releases a minimum of 17 ounces of gas due to flatulence.

✳ A human can survive weeks without food but only about ten days without sleep.

✳ The left lung is smaller than the right lung in order to provide room for the heart.

✳ The average human body contains enough fat to create seven bars of soap and enough iron to form a three-inch-long nail.

On the Wagon

What does staying sober have to do with being on the wagon? Plenty, it turns out.

✳ ✳ ✳ ✳

THE PHRASE "ON the wagon" likely originated in America sometime in the late nineteenth century, a period of fervent campaigning for temperance and prohibition. With breweries and saloons popping up everywhere, organizations like the Woman's Christian Temperance Union, the Anti-Saloon League, and the Total Abstinence Society actively encouraged husbands and fathers to stay sober and out of trouble.

"I promise to abstain from all intoxicating drinks, except used medicinally and by order of a medical man, and to discountenance the cause and practice of intemperance," went the pledge of the Total Abstinence Society. Millions of people took it, and they were then considered to be "on the water cart."

Why, you ask? At that time, horse-drawn water carts were common sights in U.S. cities. They weren't used to distribute drinking water, but rather to wet down the dusty roads during hot, dry weather. So the metaphor "I'm on the water cart" really came from this sentiment: "Sure, I'm thirsty for a beer, but I'd rather take a drink from that old dusty water cart than break my solemn vow."

The earliest literary citation of "on the water cart" likely can be found in Alice Caldwell Hegan's 1901 comic novel *Mrs. Wiggs of the Cabbage Patch:* "I wanted to git him some whisky, but he shuck his head. 'I'm on the water-cart,' sez he." After that, the popular American idiom evolved into "on the water wagon" and then simply into "on the wagon." But regardless of whether it's a cart or a wagon, we all know just how easy it is to fall off.

Why Do Brits Lose Their Accents When They Sing?

Partly because they have to, but mostly because they want to.

✳ ✳ ✳ ✳

A S TO THE "have to," linguists say that in order to project your voice, you have to open your mouth a little wider, and this has the effect of neutralizing some of the vowel tones that are key to any accent. Thus, the voice is regularized in a way that isn't specifically American, but does eliminate some of the qualities that characterize an accent.

As to the "want to," consider that you can find many pop singers who "lose" their accents. It's because they want to sound more authentic to the styles of music that they're adopting. Folks say that U2's Bono, an Irishman, usually sounds quite American—maybe because he sometimes emulates Van Morrison, another Irishman, who often sounds American because his music draws so heavily from American blues and soul.

Sometimes the Beatles sound British, sometimes American. On *Abbey Road's* ditty "Her Majesty," Paul McCartney comes off as plenty British—he's claiming to be in love with the Queen. On *The White Album*, John Lennon sounds fairly American on the grungy blues tune "Yer Blues"—reportedly, he was mocking the British blues scene with its Yank pretensions.

Want more proof that singers can control their accents? The Proclaimers, a popular Scottish folk-rock duo from the late 1980s and 1990s, had brogues as thick as fog—no sounding American for them, because it would have diminished their fresh-faced, folksy appeal.

Pop diva Lily Allen purposely sounds every bit the Londoner on her tunes—and draws barbs from some who say it makes her seem trite.

The same type of criticism is aimed at Green Day, though in reverse. The members of this American pop-punk band have a vaguely British sound to their voices, probably in homage to— or simply in imitation of—the British groups that started the punk revolution. The upshot is that singers cop the inflections that seem to suit the genre they're in or even the individual tune they're performing. Be attuned to that, and you'll enjoy pop music even more, mate.

Who Decided Suntans Are Attractive?

Suntans have been in and out of fashion throughout history. In many primitive societies, the sun was revered as the center of the spiritual universe, and a perpetual tan was a sign of religious fidelity. In our own slightly less primitive time, sun worship is still common, but the purpose isn't religious.

* * * *

How DID SUNTANS become a fashion statement? In the nineteenth century, debutantes and socialites, the Paris Hiltons of their day, would have been praised for their paleness. To compare a lady's skin to alabaster—a hard, white mineral used in sculpture—was to offer a high compliment indeed. But toward the end of the nineteenth century, doctors began to realize that sunlight is necessary for good health, as it promotes vitamin formation in the body.

This didn't make suntans attractive overnight, but it helped dissolve the stigma against them. In the twentieth century, suntans grew more popular from aesthetic and social perspectives, even as evidence that linked sun exposure to skin cancer mounted.

If one person deserves credit for really sparking the current suntan rage, it's famed fashion designer Coco Chanel. She was sunburned while on vacation one summer in the 1920s, and her resulting tan became all the rage.

"The 1929 girl must be tanned," she would later say. "A golden tan is the index of chic." A pronouncement of this kind of out-and-out shallowness is perfectly suited to today's world, too, though it might translate to the current youth vernacular as something more like, "OMG tans rule!!!!" Coco was clearly on to something: As a society, we do think that tans are attractive.

Experts say that a suntan nowadays suggests someone who is rugged, athletic, and unafraid of things. It also suggests wealth, leisure, and the freedom to be outside while others are slaving away indoors. This represents a dramatic change from the nineteenth century, when tanned skin was more likely to indicate a life of manual labor in the fields—a sign of someone at the bottom of the social ladder rather than the top.

That's the sociological explanation. There's also a theory that centers on evolutionary psychology—it has to do with the "attractiveness of averageness." Studies have shown that when there is a heterogeneity (or range) of genes present in a person, the resulting face is more average—it is free of unusual quirks of size or shape. Over the millennia, humans have come to understand that such a person is also more robust physically, without the genetic weaknesses or flaws inherent in inbreeding.

When a fair-skinned person's face is tan, it appears to be closer to the overall human average, theoretical as this might be. If it seems far-fetched, consider that studies have shown that people of all skin colors tend to believe that the most attractive faces have hues that are between light and dark. In other words, the folks we find most alluring have suntans.

9 Strange Last Wills and Testaments

A will is supposed to help surviving family and friends dispose of your estate after you've passed away. Many people use it as an opportunity to send a message from beyond the grave, either by punishing potential heirs with nothing or perhaps by giving away something fun or unusual to remember them by. Where there's a will, there's a way, so make sure you have a good will before you go away for good.

✳ ✳ ✳ ✳

1. **Harry Houdini:** Harry Houdini, born in 1874, was considered the greatest magician and escape artist of his era, and possibly of all time. When he died in 1926 from a ruptured appendix, Houdini left his magician's equipment to his brother Theodore, his former partner who performed under the name Hardeen. His library of books on magic and the occult was offered to the American Society for Psychical Research on the condition that J. Malcolm Bird, research officer and editor of the *ASPR Journal*, resign. When Bird refused, the collection went instead to the Library of Congress. The rabbits he pulled out of his hat went to the children of friends. Houdini left his wife a secret code—ten words chosen at random—that he would use to contact her from the afterlife. His wife held annual séances on Halloween for ten years after his death, but Houdini never appeared.

2. **Marie Curie:** Born in Russian-occupied Poland in 1867, Marie Curie moved to Paris at age 24 to study science. As a physicist and chemist, Madame Curie was a pioneer in the early field of radioactivity, later becoming the first two-time Nobel laureate and the only person to win Nobel Prizes in two different fields of science—physics and chemistry. When she died in 1934, a gram of pure radium, originally

received as a gift from the women of America, was her only property of substantial worth. Her will stated: "The value of the element being too great to transfer to a personal heritage, I desire to will the gram of radium to the University of Paris on the condition that my daughter, Irene Curie, shall have entire liberty to use this gram . . . according to the conditions under which her scientific researches shall be pursued." Element 96, Curium (Cm), was named in honor of Marie and her husband, Pierre.

3. **William Randolph Hearst:** Multimillionaire newspaper magnate William Randolph Hearst was born in San Francisco in 1863. When he died in 1951, in accordance with his will, his $59.5 million estate was divided into three trusts—one each for his widow, sons, and the Hearst Foundation for Charitable Purposes. Challenging those who claimed he had children out of wedlock, Hearst willed anyone who could prove "that he or she is a child of mine . . . the sum of one dollar. I hereby declare that any such asserted claim . . . would be utterly false." No one claimed it. The book-length will included the disposition of his $30 million castle near San Simeon, California. The University of California could have had it but decided it was too expensive to maintain, so the state government took it, and it is now a state and national historic landmark open for public tours.

4. **Jonathan Jackson:** Animal lover Jonathan Jackson died around 1880. His will stipulated that: "It is man's duty as lord of animals to watch over and protect the lesser and feebler." So he left money for the creation of a cat house—a place where cats could enjoy comforts such as bedrooms, a dining hall, an auditorium to listen to live accordion music, an exercise room, and a specially designed roof for climbing without risking any of their nine lives.

5. **S. Sanborn:** When S. Sanborn, an American hatmaker, died in 1871, he left his body to science, bequeathing it to Oliver Wendell Holmes, Sr., (then a professor of anatomy at Harvard Medical School) and one of Holmes's colleagues. The will stipulated that two drums were to be made out of Sanborn's skin and given to a friend on the condition that every June 17 at dawn he would pound out the tune "Yankee Doodle" at Bunker Hill to commemorate the anniversary of the famous Revolutionary War battle. The rest of his body was "to be composted for a fertilizer to contribute to the growth of an American elm, to be planted in some rural thoroughfare."

6. **John Bowman:** Vermont tanner John Bowman believed that after his death, he, his dead wife, and two daughters would be reincarnated together. When he died in 1891, his will provided a $50,000 trust fund for the maintenance of his 21-room mansion and mausoleum. The will required servants to serve dinner every night just in case the Bowmans were hungry when they returned from the dead. This stipulation was carried out until 1950, when the trust money ran out.

7. **James Kidd:** James Kidd, an Arizona hermit and miner, disappeared in 1949 and was legally declared dead in 1956. His handwritten will was found in 1963 and stipulated that his $275,000 estate should "go in a research for some scientific proof of a soul of a human body which leaves at death." More than 100 petitions for the inheritance were dismissed by the court. In 1971, the money was awarded to the American Society for Psychical Research in New York City, although it failed to prove the soul's existence.

8. **Eleanor E. Ritchey:** Eleanor E. Ritchey, heiress to the Quaker State Refining Corporation, passed on her $4.5 million fortune to her 150 dogs when she died in Florida in 1968. The will was contested, and in 1973 the

dogs received $9 million. By the time the estate was finally settled its value had jumped to $14 million but only 73 of the dogs were still alive. When the last dog died in 1984, the remainder of the estate went to the Auburn University Research Foundation for research into animal diseases.

9. **Janis Joplin:** Janis Joplin was born in Texas in 1943. In her brief career as a rock and blues singer, she recorded four albums containing a number of rock classics, including "Piece of My Heart," "To Love Somebody," and "Me and Bobby McGee." Known for her heavy drinking and drug use, she died of an overdose on October 4, 1970. Janis made changes to her will just two days before her death. She set aside $2,500 to pay for a posthumous all-night party for 200 guests at her favorite pub in San Anselmo, California, "so my friends can get blasted after I'm gone." The bulk of her estate reportedly went to her parents.

Decapitation Doesn't Always Mark the End

A person can't remain conscious long enough after being beheaded to plan and exact revenge on the executioners, but it seems that a severed noggin can get in a final thought or two.

✳ ✳ ✳ ✳

A S HORRIFIC AS the possibility seems, it is biologically feasible to temporarily survive a decapitation. The brain can still function as long as it receives oxygen delivered via blood. While the trauma of the final cut and sudden drop in blood pressure would likely cause fainting, there still would be enough blood available to make consciousness possible. Exactly how much consciousness isn't clear, but the likely cap is about 15 seconds. The next logical question is, what might the beheaded be thinking in these final seconds?

Here's a possibility: "Ouch!"

Cracking the Case

Scare tactics can sometimes get people to give up annoying habits—and that may be the origin of the misconception that cracking one's knuckles will cause arthritis.

✳ ✳ ✳ ✳

Experts insist that there is no medical evidence that frequent knuckle-cracking leads to the development of arthritic hands, but that doesn't mean it's a good habit to have. Many people find those knuckle-cracking noises highly annoying—a lot like fingernails on a chalkboard.

That distinctive sound is created by a fairly complicated sequence of events. Our joints are covered by connective-tissue capsules. Inside them is a thick, clear substance called synovial fluid, which lubricates our joints and supplies nutrients to our bones. The fluid also contains gases, including carbon dixoide. When a knuckle-cracker goes into pre-pop mode and extends the fingers, the capsule around the knuckles gets stretched out and its volume increases. This, in turn, lowers the pressure of the fluid inside the joints and causes carbon dioxide bubbles to form, a process known as cavitation. The popping or cracking sound is created when the bubbles burst. It takes about half an hour before the gases are reabsorbed into the synovial fluid. Until that happens, the knuckles can't be cracked again.

Although knuckle-crackers are not at increased risk for arthritis, a long-term cracking habit can cause injury to the ligaments around the finger joints. One study found that habitual knuckle-crackers might also end up with decreased grip strength, swelling of the hands, and soft-tissue damage.

Many people who repeatedly crack their knuckles claim it relieves finger stiffness and gives them greater finger mobility, especially after typing on a keyboard. A better, if less noisy, solution is a simple stretch of the hands.

Where Does Weight Go?

When we lose weight, where do the pounds go?

✳   ✳   ✳   ✳

M ANY OF US carry a bit of extra weight. In fact, according to the National Center for Health Statistics, 69 percent of adult Americans were overweight or obese in 2009/2010, and the number is on the rise. Some people have started hitting the gym in order to lose weight. But where are those pounds going? There are no big piles of fat dotting the countryside (apologies for that gruesome image, but fat is gruesome stuff).

Most of us are vaguely aware that it's being "broken down." And that's the simple answer: Fat gets broken down by complicated processes into things like heat or energy, water, and carbon dioxide. Those things then leave your body in various ways.

The Weighty Details

But you're not satisfied with the simple answer, are you? Fine, here comes the complicated one, courtesy of *Scientific American*. All fats, you see, are triglycerides (scared yet?), which means they're made up of a glycerol molecule attached to three fatty-acid chains. They're generally oily fluids that sit around in our fat cells waiting to be used as a type of fuel. Sort of like a tank of gas, but way more gross. When we exercise, these triglycerides react by breaking down into their components: glycerol and fatty acids.

With us so far? These components then float along into the bloodstream to be made available for the rest of the body to use. Your liver is fond of glycerol, so it grabs most of that and some of the fatty acids as well. The rest is taken by your muscles. Inside the liver and muscles, the triglyceride components are modified until they change into something called acetyl-CoA. Acetyl-CoA combines with other compounds to set off a series of reactions that creates usable energy from all the bits.

As these reactions are doing their things, they release carbon dioxide, which we then breathe out; water, which we then pee out or sweat out; heat, which maintains our body temperature; and energy-carrying molecules called adenosine triphosphate, which powers your cells.

And that's what happens to weight when you lose it. So fear not—you're not in danger of stumbling over any fat piles on your next walk through the countryside.

Dying Laughing

Just a figure of speech? Not quite.

✳ ✳ ✳ ✳

SURELY YOU'RE FAMILIAR with this phrase: "I nearly died laughing." You've probably used it multiple times just while reading this book—you may have even said it right now. Gosh, when you think about it, it's really sort of a miracle that you've made it this far. That's because dying from laughter isn't just a figure of speech—people really have keeled over due to cases of the giggles.

The phrase "dying from laughter" dates back to the sixteenth century, and its endurance in the language may have to do with the disturbing number of deaths, both recorded and anecdotal, that have been connected to laughing fits.

Cause of Death: Too Many Jokes?

One of the first to succumb to giddiness was the Stoic Greek philosopher Chrysippus in 207 or 206 BC. The story goes something like this: Chrysippus fed his donkey some wine. (We're not sure why he would do this, but Greek philosophers were known to have some unusual tastes.) A drunk donkey is funny enough, but here's the "killer": The donkey then tried to eat some figs! Evidently, the sight of a donkey eating figs was just too much for a Stoic to bear, and Chrysippus keeled over mid-chortle.

Over the ensuing two thousand years, a number of other deaths reportedly have been caused by laughter. The casualties have included a British bricklayer who was watching a sitcom called *The Goodies* (it is unclear whether this man died from laughter or stupidity) and a Danish physician who was watching one of John Cleese's scenes in *A Fish Called Wanda*.

It isn't entirely clear if laughter actually caused these deaths or if it merely acted as a catalyst for other conditions. For example, studies have shown that cataplexy (a condition in narcoleptics that causes seizures) can be triggered by strong emotional responses such as laughter, while other research has suggested that laughter may cause heart attacks in people who are already susceptible to them.

However, there is one documented disease in which laughter is a primary symptom. Kuru—a.k.a. "the laughing disease"—plagued the indigenous people of New Guinea during the turn of the twentieth century. This degenerative viral disease is largely spread through ritual cannibalism, however, so most of us don't need to worry about contracting it.

On the Other Hand

Many health experts believe that laughter is more apt to help than harm you. Some research indicates that laughter may play a role in increasing amounts of the antibody immunoglobin A, which fights bacterial and viral infections. So there's no need to worry—reading this book isn't going to kill you.

It might even make you healthier.

Maybe She's Born With It...

T. L. Williams boosted his sister's love life and revolutionized the cosmetics industry in the process.

✳ ✳ ✳ ✳

I T WAS 1913, and as the story goes, Mabel Williams had man trouble: Another woman had caught the eye of her beau, Chet, and poor Mabel didn't know what to do. Her brother T. L. Williams, a chemist by trade, set his sights on a solution to the problem. The answer? More dramatic eyelashes, of course! He came up with a concoction of Vaseline-brand petroleum jelly and coal dust to darken and thicken Mabel's eyelashes. What man could resist? Apparently not Chet—he and Mabel married the following year.

Into the Industry

Mr. Williams realized that what worked for Mabel would work for any woman. To market his new mascara, he formed a company called Maybelline—named after his sister and Vaseline, one of the lash darkener's principal ingredients—and took the cosmetics industry by storm.

Of course, T. L. Williams was not the first person to come up with this kind of beauty aid. The earliest known eye darkener, kohl, was an ancient Egyptian mixture that came in a variety of formulas based on minerals such as malachite, lead, or manganese. The upper classes of many later cultures also had their own methods of accentuating eyelashes. But Williams's invention was both affordable and convenient to use. He sold it via mail order in cake form, with a small brush that would be wetted, rubbed in the mascara, and then dabbed on the lashes. He also enjoyed the benefit of excellent timing, as prudish Victorian attitudes about "painted ladies" were fading and the dark-eyed vamps of Hollywood silent films, such as Theda Bera, were just coming onto the scene.

Soon Maybelline mascara was a must-have item on every woman's vanity, and by the 1930s, it was commonly available in retail drug stores across the nation. And just in case you're wondering, Maybelline and all other cosmetics companies long ago abandoned the use of coal-based ingredients in their products, having found safer and more effective coloring agents.

"Will You Starve That They Be Better Fed?"

In 1944–45, 36 U.S. conscientious objectors volunteered to starve, in hope that lessons learned would save many lives.

❋ ❋ ❋ ❋

WAS IT NEWS that starving people lost weight and had health problems? Surely not. During World War II, millions died of starvation; many others suffered greatly from it. Famines had long been endemic in Southern Asia, and the Soviet Union had known them in 1921 and 1932–33. Yet no one had studied the mechanics of starvation in a controlled, scientific environment.

Starving for Science

You need two things, evidently: a major war and a proven track record in nutritional science with the military. Ancel Keys, a professor at the University of Minnesota, was a pioneer in nutritional studies. Early in the war, the U.S. Army contacted him to design a lightweight ration for airborne troops. The K-Ration, named for Keys, proved so compact and nutritious the army ordered well over 100 million throughout the war.

Who Volunteered?

For religious or idealistic reasons, some draftable men were conscientious objectors (COs): They refused to bear arms. Some COs became medics, but for others, even that was too militaristic. With much work to be done, putting these men in jail would have been wasteful. Instead, the COs became part of the Civilian Public Service (CPS), an organization at the disposal of the U.S. Army. One accusation leveled against COs was that they were cowards. While some CPS jobs were make-work, many required courage and dedication. CPS men fought fires as smoke jumpers, worked in insane asylums, manufactured items for the war, and assisted with farming and forestry. They also volunteered for medical experiments: vitamin effects, severe cold, severe heat, extended bed rest, lice infestation, even malaria. Most CPS volunteers believed there was a difference between pacifism and cowardice, and they intended to prove it.

Even so, these experiments sound rather unpleasant. One obvious question was whether anyone was forced into participating. The answer is no. Keys sent out a brochure depicting hungry children that read, "Will you starve that they be better fed?" Four hundred people volunteered—many times more than he needed. Thirty-six were selected, and they actually cheered at the outset of the experiment. This was the heart and soul of their refusal to drop bombs, carry submachine guns, or point battleship cannons: They believed it was better to endure suffering than to kill.

The Doctor

Keys didn't enjoy watching anyone suffer, nor did he make the process worse than necessary—and he did believe it necessary. He doubted anyone could teach starving people democracy; starvation had to be addressed. Though the law imposed few constraints on him, his academic and professional principles governed his actions. During the experiment, he often asked himself, "What am I doing to these men?"

The Methods

Perhaps no one ever starved so scientifically. The doctors first examined and tested nearly every aspect of the subjects' physical and mental health, then regularized their diets on bland but filling fare. On November 19, 1944, the first phase began with a normal, 3,200 calorie-per-day diet. After three months, the starvation phase began: the ration was halved to 1,570 calories per day. The subjects had to walk 22 miles per week, and endured batteries of psychological and medical tests. This phase of starvation lasted six months.

Keys based meals on typical European famine fare. A sample starvation-phase dinner included 36g of beans, peas, and ham in a soup, 255g of macaroni and cheese, 40g of rutabagas, 100g of potatoes, and 100g of lettuce salad—about 1.17 pounds of food. The men got all the black coffee, water, chewing gum, and cigarettes they wanted. On this diet, they grew weaker, testier, and more apathetic by the day. When they heard that Germany surrendered and Hitler had died, they barely cared.

While the men had some freedom to move about, they were forbidden to cheat by eating outside food. No man was allowed to go out without a buddy. Four men were prematurely discharged from the test: one for ill health, two for cheating, and one for suspected cheating. In a moment of temporary derangement and frustration, one man cut off three of his fingers with an ax, but begged to remain in the experiment.

The Results

Imagine clean, well-dressed concentration camp survivors. By the end of the starvation phase, the average subject weighed about 115 pounds, down from an average starting weight of 153 pounds. Many had retained water and had bloated shins or ankles. The only man who showed a serious medical side effect (blood in the urine) was discharged for ill health, and he soon recovered.

The Recovery Period

During recovery, the men kept losing weight at first, as they shed the retained water. Shortly after near-normal rations resumed, the staff psychologist brought Dr. Keys a manifesto from the volunteers, demanding an end to the buddy system. Keys scowled at the psychologist's unseemly amusement.

"Don't you see?" answered the psychologist. "It is the ultimate validation of your theories. Hungry people mindlessly follow orders. You feed them enough and right away they demand self-government." Keys gave in.

The primary experiment ended October 20, 1945, not long after Japan's surrender. Twelve volunteers stayed for a fourth phase of "unrestricted recovery." Even on 5,219 calories per day, the men reported many psychological effects: fear that food might be taken away, a tendency to gorge, and feeling hungry even when stuffed.

What We Learned

While the immediate postwar European relief effort took place without Keys's data, the results later supplied a much better understanding of starvation. In 1950, Keys published his 1385-page magnum opus, *The Biology of Human Starvation*. It remains the main reference on the subject because it would be very difficult to duplicate. It proved that neither protein nor vitamin supplements, for example, accelerated recovery from starvation. Recovery was proportionate to the number of calories consumed. Psychologists learned valuable lessons from Keys. Without this experiment, relief efforts today would be less effective. And perhaps that's why, when interviewed many years later, most of the volunteers said the same thing: They would do it again.

Chapter 7

Wars and Conflicts

Were Chariots Used in Battles or Just for Racing?

Battles, definitely. But since their role in combat peaked more than three thousand years ago, it's hardly surprising that most people don't realize that chariots were once used as transports during times of war.

✳ ✳ ✳ ✳

THE EARLIEST CHARIOTS can be traced to around 2000 B.C., and their original purpose may have been for racing. Before chariots came into the picture, wheels on carts were built out of solid wood and were prohibitively heavy. Chariot wheels had spokes, which helped make them about one-tenth the weight of the cart wheels. The chariot itself was constructed from the lightest woods available and sometimes had a leather platform. Clearly, speed was the primary objective.

Chariots proved to be effective for warfare. When battle chariots raced out, one man held the reins and steered the horses, while a second man fought. Sometimes this soldier threw spears, but most often he was an archer.

During the Bronze Age, warriors used chariots to pursue enemies in places like Troy and Crete. In Egypt, they took on a larger role. In the fifteenth century B.C., Pharaoh Thutmose III used two thousand chariots against the Canaanites in the

Battle of Megiddo. The mighty Pharaoh Ramesses II helped to wage what might have been the biggest chariot confrontation in history—the Battle of Kadesh, during which at least five thousand chariots were deployed between the Egyptians and the Hittites.

By 1200 B.C., warriors on horseback had replaced the chariot in most warfare, although chariots maintained a ceremonial status and never completely went out of style—especially when it came to racing. Tracks called hippodromes and circuses were built throughout the Roman Empire, where these races were hot tickets. (Think of chariot racing as a Roman version of NASCAR.) Even after the Western Empire fell, chariot races continued in the East in Constantinople (present-day Istanbul), right up until the Middle Ages.

Today, chariots live on in our memories—thanks in large part to a toga-wearing Charlton Heston in *Ben-Hur*.

The Hundred Years' War— in Five Minutes

Although the name would suggest otherwise, the Hundred Years' War was not actually one drawn-out, century-long fight. Rather, it was a period of time containing multiple episodes of conflict.

✳   ✳   ✳   ✳

BEGINNING IN 1337 and ending in 1453, the ongoing trouble between England and France persisted through 116 years with unsuccessful attempts at truces, treaties, and peace between battles. Only in hindsight did historians combine these events under the descriptive title of the Hundred Years' War.

More than 400 years before the start of the Hundred Years' War, the region of France now known as Normandy welcomed a handful of Scandinavians. A century and a half later, with offspring of those feisty Vikings in tow, the Normans seized control of England and made it their own. Although settled comfortably into England, the Normans would maintain control over regions of France; however, with nationals from each region intermingling across country lines, ownership of and control over various regions became hazy. The question of who could claim rights to the different areas soon led to fierce bickering. These battles between France and England revved up and eventually turned into the Hundred Years' War.

First Things First

The first phase of the Hundred Years' War, often called the Edwardian War (1337–60), was instigated by a saga comparable to the Shakespearean struggle between the Montagues and Capulets: The son of King Edward I of England married the daughter of King Philip IV of France, and their mixed-breed child was in line to claim the French throne. But nobles of the land would not hear of someone they considered a mutt running their country, so they required that the royal ancestral lineage be paternal. All the while, control of France's Gascony and Calais regions was in dispute, and this monarchal twist only added to the tension. Ultimately, the English were the victors. The nobles of France, in a tizzy over their questionable leadership in the crown, couldn't unify their vast resources and relinquished control of huge swaths of land. The French became awash in national disenchantment.

Take Two

Although a peace treaty had been agreed upon, the two countries still couldn't get along. They were ready to fight again, so the second phase of the Hundred Years' War, called the Caroline War (1369–89), began. Spies aided France in learning England's fighting methods. Armed with this knowledge, the French soldiers were better mobilized with the hand-to-hand combat tools that had brought England victory in the first phase of the Hundred Years' War. This time, the win went to France. Once again, a truce was signed.

At It Again

The truce didn't last, and the Lancastrian War (1415–29) broke the peace as England attacked. Outnumbered, the English engaged their previous tactics and caught France off guard. The French succumbed to defeat. They refused to accept terms, however, so the truce was left up in the air. The Lancastrian War dragged on until Joan of Arc came forward to claim that she was destined to lead France to triumph over England. She did, in fact, win many a great victory, but her efforts didn't end the fighting, and she suffered execution at the hands of the English.

All's Well That Ends Well?

Although it had appeared England would be the final victor in this series of wars, at the last minute, Philip the Good of Burgundy pulled his troops from England and turned things around for France. Additionally, France finally one-upped England's weaponry advantage with its heavy artillery and mobile cannons. Although England had dominated 100 years earlier with longbows, the new technology made them seem crude by comparison. In the end, France earned back the majority of the land it had lost, with England retaining the city of Calais for roughly another century. During the final stretch of their century-long fight, their differences were settled with another, more lasting, treaty.

The Chain Is in the Mail

Sticks and stones may break bones, but in the Middle Ages, an infected wound was the real scare. Chain mail armor was a warrior's only line of defense on the battlefield.

✳   ✳   ✳   ✳

WHEN YOU THINK of knights, you probably picture suits of highly polished armor. This is a common misconception. Throughout much of the Medieval era, a different type of armor—chain mail—was far more common.

Constructed of interconnected metal rings linked together to form a type of flexible mesh, chain mail was effective against blades and even arrows. In an age where broken bones could be set but even the slightest of cuts could result in deadly infections, chain mail armor saved many lives on the battlefield.

The actual process of creating mail armor began much earlier than the Middle Ages, likely in the first millennium B.C. when Celtic tribesman in Gaul (what is modern-day France, Belgium, and Northern Italy) invented a crude form of mail by interconnecting loops of iron to form flexible defensive clothing. It's likely that the Roman Legions of the Republic first came into contact with this form of mail in Gaul and adopted it as their own. Refined versions were used throughout the Imperial Roman era, and mail survived even the Empire's fall. It lasted until the Renaissance, when gunpowder weapons finally rendered it obsolete.

A similar type of mail armor developed independently in the Far East and was used to a limited degree in China and more notably by the Samurai armies of Japan. Instead of serving as full shirts or even suits of armor, the mail of Japan was used to connect plates of armor and provide protection at key joints.

Interestingly enough, the term *chain mail* is actually fairly modern, dating to the 17th century—after its use had already become obsolete.

To War Over…Chocolate?

In the 16th century, one of the treasures that Spanish conquistadors found was far more delicious than gold.

✳   ✳   ✳   ✳

I T'S HARD TO believe now, with candy bars sold at nearly every store, but at one time, the cacao plant (used to make chocolate) was so valuable that the beans were used as currency. In the Americas, 100 cacao beans could buy a turkey hen or a slave; one bean could buy a tamale. The Spanish wrote that after the Aztecs conquered the tropical lowland areas of Central America in the 1400s, tribute was often paid in cacao beans. In fact, the Aztecs invaded the region of Xoconochco in part because of its production of high-quality cacao. Thereafter, local leaders had to pay tribute to the Aztec empire in precious items such as jaguar skins, the brilliant blue feathers of a cotinga bird, and hundreds of loads of cacao beans.

Not for Everyone

Aztec society was extremely stratified. Only the elite were allowed to drink *xocoatl* or "bitter water," a hot beverage made from cacao beans that had been ground into a paste and flavored with chilies, herbs, or honey. Franciscan missionary Fray Bernardino de Sahagún listed the different chocolate drinks served to the emperor: "green cacao-pods, honeyed chocolate, flowered chocolate, flavored with green vanilla, bright red chocolate, huitztecolli-flower chocolate, black chocolate, [and] white chocolate." This hot chocolate was hardly the stuff of Swiss Miss. Once mixed, the chocolate was poured from container to container to produce the stiff head of foam that was an important element of the drink.

A descendent of the ancient Aztec beverage remains popular in the form of Mexican hot chocolate, a frothy drink flavored with cinnamon, almonds, vanilla extract, and even chili powder.

Pride and….Öööps!

Ask the Swedes: For wounded national dignity, it's hard to surpass having your state-of-the-art warship sink in sight of shore—on its maiden voyage!

❋   ❋   ❋   ❋

From Kingdom to Empire

S WEDEN WASN'T ALWAYS famous for neutrality. The early 1600s saw the rise of Sweden, under the leadership of

King Gustav II Adolf Vasa, as the strongest Baltic power, with Poland as the primary challenger. In 1625, deploring recent storm losses and damage to the Royal Swedish Navy, His Majesty ordered four new ships of the line. Shipwrights began work on the first, HMS *Vasa*, in late 1625.

Pride and Joy

Vasa took nearly two years to build. No expense was spared. Over a thousand mature oaks went into her construction, with sixty-four bronze cannons. Her masts rose over fifty yards high. Six of the cannons were 'assault guns' meant to fire lethal blasts of scrap metal and grapeshot at close range. She could throw one of the heaviest broadsides of her day.

Vasa was designed not only to usher in a new era of Swedish maritime power, but as an artistic showcase. Her figurehead and stern were intricately carven artworks, painted in bright colors and trimmed with gold leaf. While the royal ego played a part, the baroque display was also intended to awe the opposition with evidence of wealth and power, while inspiring Swedes to patriotic pride.

The King meddled with the design, demanding changes mid-project to the original keel size and armament, all the while badgering the builders to hurry up and finish *Vasa*. The Swedish crown's powers are very limited today, but in 1627 Gustav's word was law. The shipwrights wisely obeyed.

In hindsight, His Majesty should have let his shipwrights do the job their way.

Physics Always Wins

On August 10, 1628, HMS *Vasa* was finally ready to move from the shipyard to its naval base. Only 100 sailors and soldiers were aboard, roughly one quarter of the wartime complement. Some had brought families aboard for the adventure. Crowds lined the docks of Stockholm to watch this symbol of Swedish imperial might make her maiden voyage.

All was fine as the shore crews towed *Vasa* to her sailing point. Guns roared in salute, crowds cheered, and the crew made sail. The costly new battleship caught her first gust of wind, rocked uneasily to port, and then steadied. The second gust heeled her over far enough to submerge her gunports. *Vasa* swiftly sank in only 100 feet of water, settling with her maintop visible barely a hundred yards offshore. Her maiden voyage spanned less than a mile. Those who could do so took to boats or flotsam, and numerous boats rushed out to rescue the passengers and crew, but some forty people drowned.

We Are Not Amused

King Gustav wasn't in attendance. When he heard the news, he was furious and demanded an inquest, jailing the captain. Of course, everyone blamed someone else. In the end, the inquest attributed the sinking to God, who received no punishment.

We now know that *Vasa* didn't have enough ballast in the hold to keep her stable, given her high upper gun deck (a mid-construction modification by Gustav). The captain had run a stability test before sailing, showing that rapid weight shifts might capsize her. The shipwright supervising the latter phase of construction had lacked experience with warship design, and the King, no naval architect, had altered the original plans.

In 1961, a team of experts succeeded in raising *Vasa*. Thanks to diligent modern restoration work, she has been preserved for future generations. Since 1990, *Vasa* has resided in her own museum in Stockholm, open to the public.

Stars & Stripes Seamstress

Schoolchildren are taught numerous things about the American Revolution that aren't necessarily supported by history. Among the debated stories is the "fact" that Betsy Ross stitched the first American flag.

✳   ✳   ✳   ✳

ELIZABETH (BETSY) GRISCOM was born in 1752 to a Quaker family, the eighth of 17 children. When she turned 21 in 1773, she eloped with an Episcopalian named John Ross, and because of their union she was expelled from her congregation. Before they met, John and Betsy had both worked as apprentice upholsterers, so they decided to start their own business. Sadly, John died in January 1776 while serving with the Pennsylvania militia. The patriotic seamstress continued to run the business, and she soon expanded her efforts, making and mending gear for the Continental Army (a receipt exists that shows she made flags for the Pennsylvania State Navy in 1777).

So she could have sewn the first flag, but there's no proof that she actually did. In 1870, at a meeting of the Historical Society of Pennsylvania, Betsy's grandson, William Canby, insisted that George Washington had sought out Betsy and asked her to design and create a flag for the new country. Other Canby relatives swore out affidavits in agreement. The claim, however, came long after the supposed fact. Betsy Ross died in 1836, yet her family waited 34 years to announce her accomplishment. It could be that the family legend embellishes a grain of truth. Betsy Ross did make flags for the war effort—she may have even believed herself that she made the first American flag.

Ethan Allen

In the spring of 1775, when Ethan Allen and Benedict Arnold seized strategic Fort Ticonderoga at the start of the Revolutionary War, it's said that Allen claimed to have done so "in the name of the Great Jehovah and the Continental Congress."

✳ ✳ ✳ ✳

THAT'S THE EXPLANATION Allen later alleged he gave British lieutenant Jocelyn Feltham, who challenged Allen's authority to enter Fort Ticonderoga. It sounds so red-white-and-blue: The homespun citizen-soldier cites God and Country as his authorities, and the rebellious redcoat backs off.

There is, alas, good reason to believe Allen's words were cruder. By all accounts, Allen was often crude—because he had to be. No mild-mannered dilettante could possibly have controlled Allen's Vermont militia, the Green Mountain Boys, who despised New York and the British alike. It is unlikely Allen would have invoked the Continental Congress, because he hardly respected its authority; it is far more likely he would have heaped scorn upon said Congress.

Another problem with the quote is its source—Ethan Allen himself. Lieutenant Feltham and one of Allen's junior officers agree, nearly to the word, that Allen actually yelled, "Come out of there, you damned old rat!"

How Old Is Old Ironsides?

It is the oldest warship in the U.S. Navy—and it's still in service. But the 44-gun frigate USS Constitution, *the hero of the War of 1812, has survived only through numerous restoration efforts and a lot of patriotic passion.*

✳ ✳ ✳ ✳

The Legend's Service Record

COMMISSIONED IN 1797, this salty warrior made its name in an 1812 duel with Britain's HMS *Guerriere* off Nova Scotia. As *Guerriere* fought for its life, a U.S. sailor watched a British cannonball glance off *Constitution* and crowed, "Its sides are made of iron!" The name ennobled a legend. A few months after *Guerriere* settled beneath the Atlantic waves, *Constitution* wrecked the speedy HMS *Java* off Brazil. Later, Old Ironsides would pummel two smaller vessels, HMS *Cyane* and HMS *Levant*, taking *Cyane* into U.S. service as a prize.

Old Ironsides actively served until 1855. The ship sat out the Civil War in New England after a quick escape from Annapolis. When the war ended, the Navy meant to tow it back, but Old Ironsides returned under its own power ten hours ahead of the steam tug. However, things were about to get ugly for the brave old frigate. By 1871, its sea legs were failing, so the Navy sent it to Philadelphia for repairs.

A Humiliated Hulk

Even given five years' lead time, no one managed to get *Constitution* shipshape for the 1876 Centennial. The job was completed a year late, with questionable workmanship and materials. On its last foreign cruise in 1879, Old Ironsides ran aground off Dover, England, then endured its worst indignity to date: It had to be hauled to safety by a British tug. The Navy sent it to Portsmouth, New Hampshire, and built barnlike barracks on its deck to house new recruits, much like Noah's Ark.

National Change of Heart

By 1900, some felt it was time to use Old Ironsides for target practice, but Congress realized that a national treasure was going to waste. Work finally started in 1906, and the deeper the crews dug, the worse decay they found—especially in the original timbers. A national campaign raised one-fourth of the million dollars needed to gut and restore the ship, which took until 1930. It spent the next four years showing the flag from Puget Sound to Bar Harbor, visited and loved by millions.

Later Restorations

Old Ironsides's home port is Boston, and there it spends most of its time as a beloved monument to the days of a young Republic. It underwent major renovations in the mid-1950s, early 1970s, and early 1990s, and by now even its original cannons have been replaced. Though only the keel and some ribs remain of the proud frigate that watched HMS *Guerriere's* masts fall, Old Ironsides gets better care entering its third century of service than it ever has. After far too much abuse, it finally has the dignity it is due.

Constitution is used today mainly for tours and education, but it still has an active-duty crew.

Laura Secord: "The Yanks are coming! The Yanks are coming!"

Even those of you who have eaten Laura Secord candy probably don't know her story; now you will. Was she truly a Canadian Pauline Revere?

✳ ✳ ✳ ✳

Who was she? Laura Ingersoll Secord was a homestead wife in Upper Canada (now Ontario) during the early 1800s. Modern Canadians count her among the greats of Canada for her courage during the U.S. invasion in the War of 1812. And yes, there is a brand of sweets bearing her name, which is kind of like Ethan Allen furniture or Revereware; you don't really think of the historical figure when you think of the consumer commodity.

The United States invaded Canada? For the second time, as a matter of fact. Remember the Colonial complaint about British troops quartered in people's houses? It chapped their cheeks so much that the new U.S. Constitution explicitly outlawed it. When the troops were American and the soil was foreign, that was somehow different. Laura and her husband, James, lived at Queenston, Upper Canada (near Niagara Falls), during the U.S. invasion. American officers ordered them to house and feed troops. Direct resistance would have been suicidal even had James been healthy (his leg had been shot beyond use in an earlier battle).

What did Laura supposedly do? Though it's cheap and easy to force the enemy's innocent civilians to feed and house your troops, you then can't talk about your plans over dinner. Laura overheard that U.S. troops were planning a surprise attack at Beaver Dams.

According to the legend's variations, she left in slippers and walked barefoot part of the way; she took along a cow so that she would appear less suspicious; she cooked up a cover story about a sick relative; she risked accidental gunshot by an eager sentry; and she spent hours climbing treacherous cliffs. In all variations, she met up with Mohawk warriors friendly to the British/Canadian cause. They escorted her to Lieutenant FitzGibbon, the British officer in command, and she told what she knew. Native and Anglo-Canadian forces used the information to ambush the U.S. invaders, taking most of them prisoner. This turned back the Niagara frontier offensive into Upper Canada, thus affecting the strategic overall course of the war.

What's true? Here we have a true story with minor embellishments that should not diminish its veracity. It is possible the Mohawks also figured out the U.S. plans, but we have FitzGibbon's testimony that Laura had warned him. He recounted it many years later, well removed from the heat of battle. We also have FitzGibbon's account of a conversation with his captured U.S. counterpart, confirming that Laura's information had been correct. FitzGibbon, a credible man, went on to a distinguished military and civil career. He certainly took good advantage of what he learned. Most of the troops on the British side were First Peoples, so they deserve credit for carrying out such a great ambush.

Was she rewarded? Not right away, though she did try hard to milk her deed for all it was worth. For much of her life, she and James pressured the British government for some form of official recognition, perhaps a comfortable civil service job. Finally, when she was in her 80s, she got official praise and a pension. She lived just long enough to see Canada become a Dominion.

How can she compare to the great Paul Revere? Laura walked, instead of riding, about 20 miles through dangerous, difficult country. Any way you examine the evidence, Laura Secord was a brave, loyal Canadian who answered the bell when her country needed her, despite great risk and hardship. Her act made a real difference in the outcome. Revere was only one of several riders, and he got caught; Laura won through.

The Toledo War

The city of Toledo, by all accounts, is a lovely place. And no doubt it is; how else to explain why in 1835 and '36 Ohio and Michigan waged war—sort of—for the privilege to call Toledo their own.

✳ ✳ ✳ ✳

A S AMERICA BEGAN expanding westward, Congress passed the Northwest Ordinance in 1787, creating the Northwest Territory and establishing the north-south border between the future states of Michigan, Indiana, and Ohio. Michigan's southern border was to be a straight east-west line running from the southernmost point of Lake Michigan to the shore of Lake Erie. But the seeds of one of America's kookiest armed conflicts had already been planted when the border was drawn on a map charted in 1755 by John Mitchell.

Borderline Fraud

The Michigan-Ohio border drawn on the Mitchell Map (regarded as the most accurate map of eastern North America at that time and used extensively to determine international and state borders) intersected Lake Erie just north of the Maumee River. This placed the river mouth—and site of the future port settlement of Toledo—in Ohio. However, when Congress passed the Enabling Act of 1802, allowing Ohio to begin the process of becoming a state, the language was more ambiguous when it came to the state's borders.

The situation got sticky in that year, when a fur trapper alerted Ohio delegates drafting a state constitution that Lake Michigan was actually farther south than on the Mitchell Map. Fearful of losing territory, the delegates engaged in some creative border drawing, slightly angling the boundary with Michigan to ensure the Maumee River basin remained Ohio property. The U.S. Congress never formally acted on Ohio's claim either way. The Ohio-drawn boundary remained unchallenged as Ohio gained statehood in 1803.

In 1805, the Michigan Territory was created, and its border with Ohio was determined by the provisions of the Northwest Ordinance (which predated the Mitchell Map). By then, cartographers had figured out where Lake Michigan really was, and Michiganders, armed with updated maps, contested Ohio's claim by declaring ownership of the Maumee River basin.

Settlers moving into the area, unsure if they were now Michiganders or Ohioans, petitioned for a resolution to the competing claims but were sidelined with the coming of the War of 1812.

The Toledo Strip

In 1817, U.S. Surveyor General and former Ohio governor Edward Tiffin moved to settle the issue by ordering William Harris to survey the border as drawn in the Ohio constitution. Miffed at Tiffin's blatant partiality, Michigan Territory governor Lewis Cass commissioned John Fulton in 1819 to survey the line as defined by the Northwest Ordinance. The resulting Harris and Fulton Lines created a narrow stretch of no-man's-land five miles wide at the Indiana border and eight miles wide at Lake Erie. Dubbed the Toledo Strip, the 468-square-mile area contained decent farmland in its western half, but swampland mostly surrounded the backwater port settlement of Toledo. Not much worth feuding about, it may have seemed, but feud the two sides did. For the next 15 years, Michigan assumed de facto jurisdiction over the strip, including Toledo, while Ohio refused to cede its claim to the territory.

The dispute came to a head in 1835 during Michigan's bid for statehood—the final obstacle being the continued squabble over the Toledo strip. Michigan Territory governor Stevens Mason proposed negotiations to settle the issue in January. Uninterested, Ohio governor Robert Lucas established a county government in the strip. Enraged, Mason enacted legislation making it illegal for Ohioans to conduct government activity in the strip. Undaunted, Lucas dispatched 300 Ohio militia to claim the land. Unimpressed, Mason marched a force of 250 Michigan militia to stop them. Michigan and Ohio were suddenly at war.

It's War! (Sort Of)

For a week in April, the two armies slogged through the Maumee swamps unable to find each other. Instead of battling it out, the two sides settled for hurling profanities at each other from opposite banks of the Maumee. Then came the farcically named Battle of Phillips Corners on April 26, in which a band of Michigan militia set upon a group of camping Ohio surveyors. Ohio accused the Michiganders of unleashing a barrage of gunfire at the surveyors; Michigan claimed its soldiers had fired a few rounds skyward as the Ohioans scrambled to the woods. No one was injured in the skirmish, which either confirmed Michigan's version of events or exposed them as awful shots.

Warfare consisted primarily of sheriff's posses from both sides bullying civil servants and local residents. In one incident in July, Michigan sheriff Joseph Wood arrested Ohioan Benjamin Stickney. Stickney's son Two (the elder Stickney preferred to number his sons rather than name them) attacked Wood and stabbed him in the thigh with a penknife, thus making Wood the war's lone casualty (he survived). The only real fighting of the war occurred between drunken Buckeyes and Wolverines in Toledo's brawl-infested saloons.

Who Really Won?

By summer's end, President Andrew Jackson grew weary of the backwoods brouhaha. After failed attempts to mediate a solution, Jackson chose a side to end the conflict—and with an election coming up, he sided with Ohio. Jackson sacked Mason in August and offered Michigan the western three-quarters of the Upper Peninsula in return for giving the Toledo Strip to Ohio. Michigan refused.

Jackson denied Michigan statehood until it ceded the strip. In December of the next year, facing bankruptcy and desperate for a share of federal cash earmarked for the states, Michigan finally signed the so-called Frostbitten Convention, accepting the federal government's offer and ending the Toledo War.

Having secured Toledo, which many thought would become a great gateway to the American West with the building of the Erie Canal, Ohio was deemed the victor. But Michigan arguably fared better, growing wealthy from the bountiful timber, copper, and iron reserves in the Upper Peninsula territory that was once considered the booby prize for losing the war. Though no lives were lost, both sides gave up a little dignity in this farcical bureaucratic conflict.

The Death of Davy Crockett

You can start fights in Texas suggesting that the Alamo fighters— Davy Crockett was prominent among them—didn't die fighting to the last man. But do we really know that they did?

✳   ✳   ✳   ✳

First, the orthodox version: Davy Crockett grew up rough and ready in Tennessee, wrestling bears and otherwise demonstrating his machismo. He went into politics, lost an election, and moved to Texas. His homespun, informal braggadocio went over just fine in what would soon become the self-proclaimed Republic of Texas. Mexico, of course, didn't grant that Texas had the right to secede. General Antonio López de Santa Anna invaded the Republic and cornered one group of its defenders in Alamo Mission, San Antonio de Béxar (now just San Antonio). Shortly before independence, Crockett had signed on to fight for Texas, and he was one of the men who died fighting in its defense.

Why question that? Most of the questions stem from the memoir of a Mexican officer who fought there, Jóse Enrique de la Peña. De la Peña says that seven captives, including Crockett, were brought before Santa Anna and murdered in cold blood after the battle. He also says that Crockett took refuge in the

Alamo as a neutral foreigner rather than as a volunteer militiaman. That poses authenticity problems, because there was no logical reason for Crockett to be at the Alamo unless he planned to fight in its defense.

It's worth noting that de la Peña says he found the execution appalling. However, the Mexican officer also tells an implausible version of the death of Colonel William Travis, commander in charge of the siege of the Alamo: He claims to have seen it occur, but there's little chance de la Peña could have positively identified Travis at a distance. This was, after all, a battle with thick black-powder smoke, hand-to-hand combat, and concealment.

What evidence supports the orthodox version? Travis's slave, Joe, survived the battle and says Travis died defending the north wall (not where de la Peña has him). Joe also says he saw Crockett's body surrounded by dead Mexican soldiers, and an officer's wife who survived also testifies that Crockett died in battle. Santa Anna himself didn't say anything about executing Crockett in his after-action report; he did say that Crockett's body was found along with those of other leaders.

Why is it contentious? The memory of the Alamo is a Texan cultural rallying point. Opposing this view is a revisionist stance that seems so ready to dismiss tales of military valor that it dumps the orthodox account as too simple and perfect to be true. Either side has generally drawn a conclusion and seeks evidence to support it.

Do we know? So much happened at Alamo Mission between February 23 and March 6, 1836, that we will never know. It is plausible that some wounded survivors, possibly dying, were executed after the battle; that doesn't negate anyone's heroism. What's lacking is compelling, credible evidence to contradict the eyewitnesses who report no such thing. Absent that evidence, and with de la Peña's writing a questionable account well after the fact, the weight of documentation suggests that Davy Crockett went down fighting.

The Pig Standoff

It began with a dead pig in America's remotest corner. It nearly became a shooting war.

✳ ✳ ✳ ✳

Keep Your Potatoes out of My Pig!

BY 1858, AMERICAN settlers and the British Hudson's Bay Company both had a presence on disputed San Juan Island, Washington Territory (or Canada, depending on your perspective). Tensions mounted until June 15, 1859, when American Lyman Cutlar shot a Company boar that was ravaging his potatoes. The pig's manager, Englishman Charles Griffin, demanded $100 in compensation—or he would have Cutlar arrested.

Not So Fast, John Bull and Uncle Sam

Cutlar and his fellow settlers sent for help, and U.S. military governor William Harney sent an infantry regiment. The Royal Navy responded with a flotilla of warships under Admiral Baynes, who decided to act as an adult on the scene. In his view, two great nations ought not to wage war over swine and potatoes. Both sides beefed (porked?) up their forces but gave orders not to fire the first shot.

Calm heads prevailed, but the United States and Britian left token forces in place. Both nations' settlers kept the peace thereafter, but the underlying sovereignty issue went unresolved until well after the Civil War. In 1872, the parties asked Kaiser Wilhelm I of Germany to arbitrate. Wilhelm awarded San Juan Island to the United States, averting any future swine wars.

Lest the incident seem insignificant, remember the timing. The Union and Confederacy drew sabers in 1861. Imagine that the Union had already gone to war with England in 1859. History might have been very different. All because of a pig, and pig-headed frontiersmen.

Myths and Misconceptions

There's a certain romance to the tales that have circulated in the almost 150 years since the Civil War. Many are true, but many others are laced with falsehoods.

✳ ✳ ✳ ✳

AT THE RISK of bursting some American history bubbles, here are some of the myths swirling around the Civil War.

Myth: The Civil War was America's first disagreement over slavery.

The founders of the United States had been concerned with the ownership of slaves, particularly as it played out in the issue of states' rights, since the Articles of Confederation were ratified in 1781. A confederation, by definition, is a loose alignment of states, each with the power to self-regulate. The Southern states favored slavery, and every time the issue of states' rights emerged on the national front, the South would threaten to secede.

Other landmark Congressional acts and court judgments that influenced slavery in America before the Civil War include the Three-Fifths Compromise in the Constitution, the Missouri Compromise of 1820, the Compromise of 1850, the Kansas-Nebraska Act, and the Dred Scott Decision.

Myth: The Emancipation Proclamation freed all the slaves in America.

Lincoln wrote the edict in September 1862, and it went into effect on January 1, 1863. The language of the document was clear: Any slave that was still held in the states that had seceded from the Union was "forever free" as of January 1, 1863.

Significantly, this edict did not include border states in which slaves were still held, such as Kentucky or Missouri, because Lincoln didn't want to stoke rebellion there. As one might expect, the Southern states paid hardly any attention to the announcement by the Union president. They'd already turned their backs on him and his nation, and as far as they were concerned, the Union president held no power over them.

Myth: The Union soldiers firmly believed in the cause of freeing the slaves.

For the most part, Union soldiers had little, if any, opinion on slavery. Especially at the beginning, many young men enlisted in the Union army as a romantic adventure. Early opinion estimated that the war would end within a few months, and many decided they could afford that much time away from their work, school, or family life.

Myth: The South's secession was the first time in American history a state tried to leave the Union.

During the War of 1812, New England almost seceded in order to protect its trade with Great Britain. In the 1850s, President James Buchanan, who held office immediately before Abraham Lincoln, stated the federal government would not resort to force in order to prevent secession. In 1869, four years after the end of the war, the Supreme Court declared the act of state secession to be unconstitutional.

Myth: The Confederate attack on Fort Sumter was the first act of Southern aggression against Northern targets.

The attack on Fort Sumter was preceded by attacks on other forts and military installations in Confederate territory. On January 9, 1861, Mississippi followed South Carolina to become the second state to secede from the Union. Within a week, Mississippi's governor ordered an armed battery placed on the bluff above the wharf at Vicksburg. His declared intention was to force Union vessels to stop to be searched—after all, it was rumored that a cannon had been sent to a Baton Rouge arsenal. Intentions aside, the fact is the battery actually fired on a number of vessels in order to make them come about, including the *Gladiator*, the *Imperial*, and the *A. O. Tyler*.

Prior to this incident, the Confederate Congress had approved the creation of a volunteer army of 100,000 soldiers—far larger than any military force that was intended strictly for keeping the peace would presumably need to be.

Myth: Abraham Lincoln wrote his Gettysburg Address on the back of an envelope while riding the train on his way to make the speech.

Lincoln would never have waited until the last minute to write such an important oration, which was part of the consecration of the Gettysburg Cemetery in November 1863. But even if he had, the train ride itself would have prevented legible writing. The 1860s-period train cars bounced, swayed, and made horseback riding seem smooth by comparison. Several drafts of the Gettysburg Address (including what is referred to as the "reading draft") have been archived at the Library of Congress and other academic institutions. They are written—very legibly—on lined paper and Executive Mansion stationery.

Myth: The "Taps" bugle call was first used by Union Captain Robert Ellicombe after Ellicombe discovered his son dead on the battlefield wearing a Confederate uniform. The son had been a music student, and the music for "Taps" was found in the boy's pocket. Captain Ellicombe had it played as tribute during his son's funeral.

There is no proof that Captain Robert Ellicombe even existed at all, and certainly there is no record of any captain by that name in the Union army during the Civil War. "Taps" actually came from Union General Daniel Butterfield, although it is not certain whether Butterfield composed the tune or adapted it from an earlier piece of music. Not happy with the existing bugle call for lights out, which the general thought was too formal, he presented his bugler, Oliver Norton, with the replacement during the summer of 1862. Although it was soon used by both Union and Confederate armies as a funeral call, it did not become an official bugle call until after the war.

They Marched, Too

Men and boys weren't the only recruits brought into the army—animal mascots made life in camp better for soldiers.

✻ ✻ ✻ ✻

JACK WAS A model soldier. A member of the 102nd Pennsylvania Infantry, he always responded quickly to bugle calls and obeyed his superiors. He served heroically in the Wilderness Campaign, the Battle of Spotsylvania, and the Siege of Petersburg. He had a big heart, and he hovered around the dead and wounded after battles. He himself was wounded at Malvern Hill and twice was taken prisoner. Nevertheless, some members of his regiment called him a dog. But he didn't mind, because he was a dog. Jack was a brown-and-white bull terrier and the regiment's mascot. He entertained the troops of the 102nd until he was sadly dognapped and never seen again.

Many regimental mascots such as Jack existed throughout the war. Dogs were most common, but some regiments adopted other animals, including raccoons, a black bear cub, a badger, and chickens. The 2nd Rhode Island took a sheep into battle, until hunger forced them to sell it for $5 to buy food. One of the most unusual mascots was a camel that trundled into battle with the 43rd Mississippi Infantry until it was killed during the Siege of Vicksburg.

Perhaps the most famous regimental mascot was Old Abe, an eagle carried into battle by Company C, 8th Regiment of the Wisconsin Volunteers. A Wisconsin family gave Old Abe—named after Abraham Lincoln, of course—to the regiment as the soldiers marched off to war. When they went into battle, Old Abe flew over the fighting and screeched at the enemy. Confederates tried to kill or capture the eagle but failed—it survived an astounding 81 battles and skirmishes. Old Abe was retired on September 28, 1864, and was given to the state of Wisconsin. It lived at the state Capitol until it died in 1881.

No Time for R & R

Civil War soldiers had to be ready to fight at any moment—no matter what else they were doing!

✳   ✳   ✳   ✳

THE CONFEDERATE VOLUNTEER 24th North Carolina Company B had been ordered on July 28, 1963, to Weldon, North Carolina, to defend a railroad bridge. The Confederate and Union forces in the region had fought each other on and off since early July with neither side gaining an advantage.

In a way, Company B, raised and first mustered at Weldon, was returning home. As the soldiers moved along the road to their positions at the Weldon railroad bridge, they passed the old gristmill and pond at Boone's Mill. The mill was likely well known to many in Company B. They probably remembered its cool, secluded pond as a refuge in the Carolina summer heat.

A Nice, Relaxing Swim

Experiencing a lull in the fighting, the company commander let the troops relax and indulge themselves with a rare wartime treat, a leisurely bath in a pond. Soldiers eagerly stripped off their uniforms, discarded their weapons, and entered the water.

While the group was enjoying the pond, a Union cavalry unit headed along the road to capture—and possibly destroy—the vital Confederate railroad bridge. So the Confederates faced a few immediate problems. They were stark naked, and their weapons and gear were scattered along the pond's edge. The Union cavalry, bearing down on the pond, were ready to engage. When the two groups met, both sides likely had to overcome quite a surprise.

A brief but savage battle erupted. Once the Confederates recovered their wits and enough of their equipment, they delivered a fierce resistance to the larger Union force. The Union cavalry were driven off, and the Weldon bridge was preserved.

Up, Up, and Away

As the war continued, the armies were desperately in need of military innovation. One man helped them look to the skies for possible answers.

✳ ✳ ✳ ✳

O NLY EIGHT DAYS after the Confederate assault on Fort Sumter and the beginning of fighting in the Civil War, a strange object appeared in the sky above Unionville, South Carolina. Within minutes, the apparition began to descend, and its sole occupant was captured near the town and jailed on the suspicion of being a Union spy.

The man who fell from the sky was Thaddeus Lowe, a balloonist from Cincinnati, Ohio. He had been on one of several practice runs that he hoped would eventually lead to an attempt to cross the Atlantic Ocean by balloon. On this excursion, he set a distance record for traveling 900 miles from Cincinnati in nine hours. But with war now underway, he was also suddenly a prisoner. Once the South Carolina authorities determined that Lowe presented no threat to them, they released him and allowed him to return north by train.

An Idea Is Launched

Once he arrived back in Cincinnati, Lowe got together with an influential supporter who also happened to be the editor of the *Cincinnati Daily Commercial*, Murat Halstead. Lowe wanted Halstead's help in approaching the government with a lofty idea: using balloons to observe the position and movements of enemy troops. Utilizing balloons in warfare was certainly not a new concept by any means—observation balloons had been used by the French for military reconnaissance during the Battle of Fleurus in 1794. Observers in balloons could rise above the landscape and gather valuable information. Halstead contacted Secretary of the Treasury Salmon Chase, who arranged a meeting between Lowe and President Lincoln.

Upward Bound

The balloon Enterprise was launched on the first of several flights from the Columbian Armory in Washington, D.C., on June 18, 1861. For one launch, telegraph equipment was set up between the balloon and the ground, and Lowe telegraphed to Lincoln the very first message sent from a balloon. The demonstration was a success. Within months, the President called for the creation of a Balloon Corps and placed it under the Bureau of Topographical Engineers. It was to be manned by civilians under Lowe's direct supervision. Lincoln also authorized funds to purchase equipment and hire personnel. Lowe used that funding to construct five observation balloons of varying sizes, the smaller ones intended to accommodate inclement weather.

Lowe finished constructing his first military balloon, made from the "best India silk," on August 28, with an initial test run scheduled for September 24 outside of Arlington, Virginia. As he reached approximately 1,000 feet on that test flight, Lowe telegraphed the position of Confederate troops near Falls Church, Virginia, to his assistants below. Coordinates were then passed to the artillery, which began firing on the Confederates' position. It was the first time in history that artillery successfully hit an enemy target the gunners couldn't see.

Not All Smooth Sailing

Lowe was not without his detractors and competitors, however. Contrary to Lowe's wishes, John Wise of Pennsylvania and John La Mountain of New York, both experienced aeronauts, were considered by the Bureau of Topographical Engineers and the War Department to serve as vendors of balloons and, more annoyingly for Lowe, his assistants. In the end, however, Lowe's wishes prevailed due to the intervention of General George McClellan. Lowe and his balloonists joined the general's Virginia Peninsula Campaign to participate in the federal advance on Richmond. During that campaign, Lowe made hundreds of trips to survey Confederate positions.

In addition to his flights over land, Lowe also experimented with flights tethered to a boat. In these instances, a barge was converted into an "aircraft carrier" by replacing its deck with a wooden platform from which several flights were launched. One of the launched flights carried a balloon piloted by Lowe for approximately 13 miles at a height of about 1,000 feet.

Diminishing Returns

After roughly four months of surveying Confederate positions, Lowe contracted malaria, which caused the activities of the Balloon Corps to be suspended. When his health was restored, Lowe provided reconnaissance during the Fredericksburg and the Chancellorsville campaigns, but a disagreement with his supervisor over funding eventually led to his resignation from the Balloon Corps. He was replaced by two of his assistants, brothers James and Ezra Allen. They also ran into conflicts with military authorities, and the corps was finally disbanded in August 1863.

The experiment with the Balloon Corps ended with mixed results. On one hand, Lowe's observations certainly helped the Federals during the Peninsula Campaign. Using the balloons, he discovered that the Confederates had abandoned Yorktown, and his observations during the Battle of Fair Oaks played an important role in the Union victory.

On the other hand, there had been some problems with the quality and interpretation of some of Lowe's reports. McClellan's approach to battle was already turtle-like, but Lowe's ambiguous sightings of enemy troops only heightened the general's anxiety. Ultimately, the sightings contributed to McClellan's decision to shift his army from a position of offense to a defensive posture around Harrison's Landing, Virginia. While Generals Ambrose Burnside and Joseph Hooker requested Lowe's assistance, they placed little value on his observations. That lack of trust contributed to the end of the Balloon Corps.

Experiments in the Southern Skies

Once the Federals revealed their balloon project, the Confederate government began examining the merits of the concept. In early 1862, Captain John Randolph Bryan was directed to build an observation balloon. Northern balloons had been inflated with gas. The Confederates, however, did not have the ability to produce gas in the field, so their balloon was filled with hot air. Bryan's initial flight went well, but on his second trip, someone got tangled in the balloon's tether. When the tether was cut to free the person, the balloon moved away in free flight. Thinking it was a Union balloon, Confederate troops used it for target practice before Bryan safely brought it in for a landing. A second Confederate balloon that used gas was constructed, but the balloon ran aground and was captured by Union troops. A third Confederate balloon was ripped from its mooring by high wind and also fell into the hands of the enemy. This was enough to make the Confederates end their balloon experimentation.

Ultimately, the idea of observation balloons was uncomfortable to both Union and Confederate commanders. Each side abandoned its respective program because neither side grasped the worth of the information relayed from the pilots. The real value of flight in military operations would not be recognized for several more decades.

Getting the Glory

The most famous black regiment in the Civil War overcame incredible struggles to emerge as an indispensable link in the Union's success.

✳ ✳ ✳ ✳

THE 54TH MASSACHUSETTS Infantry wasn't the first black regiment of the Civil War, and it certainly wouldn't be the last. But this regiment became the most celebrated, its fame enduring for more than a century after the last shots were fired.

Former slaves had been enlisted in military units in South Carolina, Louisiana, and Kansas before the 54th was organized, but Massachusetts Governor John Andrew fought for a different approach. Receiving permission from the War Department in early 1863, he asked fiery abolitionists such as Frederick Douglass and Sojourner Truth to recruit free Northern blacks into a showcase fighting unit. They took the charge seriously, recruiting two of Douglass's sons and Truth's grandson. The 54th Massachusetts Infantry was soon born.

Fighting More than Just the Enemy

The first foe these soldiers faced was racism. Though well trained, the thousand-strong regiment was taunted and paid less money than were white soldiers. The 54th's white commander, Colonel Robert Gould Shaw, believed in his men, but many other people did not. In the North, there was prevailing doubt blacks could prove their mettle on the battlefield. In the South, meanwhile, politicians and commanders vowed that they wouldn't treat captured blacks as legitimate prisoners.

The 54th undertook its first significant military action on July 18—a frontal assault of Fort Wagner, the heavily defended sand fort at the mouth of South Carolina's Charleston Harbor. Running down a narrow causeway of sand right into a blitz of fire from Confederate guns, the troops seized the Wagner parapet and held it for an hour before being brutally pushed back.

A Moral Victory

The poorly conceived mission—ordered by white generals—was a complete disaster. The 54th lost more than a third of its troops, including Colonel Shaw. Ironically, this military defeat ended up being a tremendous political victory for the regiment. The press and public sympathized with its heavy losses and recognized its daring heroism in what was essentially a suicide attack. The *New York Tribune* wrote that the battle "made Fort Wagner such a name to the colored race as Bunker Hill had been for ninety years to the white Yankees."

The Northern public, recognizing the courage of the 54th's valiant effort in the face of overwhelming odds, came to view the idea of black soldiers in a more positive light and appeared to show greater support for emancipation in general. Moreover, the acclaim given the 54th may have played a role in sparking widespread black enlistment in the Union army. By the following year, there would be almost 200,000 black troops, a number that became a crucial part of the Northern war effort.

The 54th's military exploits didn't end in the Carolina sand. In 1864, it covered retreating Union forces in the Battle of Olustee, Florida. Had the 54th faltered, the Federals could have been decimated.

The regiment was remembered—and honored—for years afterward. In 1900, 54th veteran Sergeant William H. Carney was awarded a Medal of Honor for his courageous act of keeping the Union flag aloft during the firestorm at Fort Wagner. Eighty-nine years later, Hollywood produced *Glory*, a major motion picture that profiled the 54th and portrayed the heartbreaking and heroic battles it fought and survived.

She Had the President's Ear

Ambition turned into pestering and disappointment for one woman of the Civil War era.

❊   ❊   ❊   ❊

To HEAR HER tell it, Anna Ella Carroll—pamphleteer, feminist, and gadfly—saved the Union. She had the ear of Abraham Lincoln himself, and she formulated the strategy that was to cut the Confederacy in two. To hear her tell it.

Carroll came from a blue-blooded, slaveholding Maryland family of great economic and political power. Her father, Thomas King Carroll, had been the governor of Maryland when she was a teenager. Anna Carroll had an active mind, did not lack for ambition, and was not content to sit at home in luxury. At an early age, she threw herself into controversial politics, becoming a propagandist for the American party, or as it was more commonly known, the Know-Nothing Party. Then Republican Abraham Lincoln was elected president.

Despite coming from a slave state, Carroll became a Union apostle. She freed her own slaves and began writing pamphlets in support of the Lincoln administration. The President appreciated this and wrote to her about one of her pamphlets, "Like everything else that comes from you I have read ... [it] with a great deal of pleasure and interest." Anna Carroll seemed to be rising in the world.

By the 19th century, women were just beginning to find their power in society. Florence Nightingale had revolutionized the medical treatment of soldiers in Europe, and Harriet Beecher Stowe's *Uncle Tom's Cabin* had likely turned many more people against slavery than any speech ever had. Tapping into this sense of possibility, Carroll aspired to her own role on the political stage. She first proposed that Lincoln send her to Europe to carry out a U.S. propaganda campaign, which she predicted would cost the Union $50,000—a colossal sum in those days. Not surprisingly, the President decided against it.

Carroll continued writing pamphlets about the Union cause and bombarding the White House with offers of her services. Finally, perhaps to get her away from Washington for a while, Lincoln sent her westward with an army escort to record her observations about any strategic opportunities ready to be exploited. Well, that's how she told it later.

While traveling in the West, she had a revelation: The Union should attack the Confederacy along the twin gateways of the Cumberland and the Tennessee Rivers. Such a strategy would guard the flank of the military thrust down the Mississippi River and effectively split the Confederacy in two. This, of course, is precisely what the Union did, and Anna Carroll wrote a letter to the President claiming credit for the idea.

Judging from previous behavior, she may even have sent a bill for services rendered.

The Lincoln administration resisted her claim. One argument against it is the fact that both the Union and the Confederacy were well aware of the possibilities of such a strategy. The Union navy had been sending gunboats up those rivers since the beginning of the war to keep an eye on the fortifications Confederates were building at Fort Henry and Fort Donelson. Anyone with a map could see that the rivers were highways of advance and supply into the South. Further, by the time Carroll wrote her letter, planning for the Union Tennessee Campaign that involved this strategy had been underway for months.

The war ended in 1865, but Carroll kept pressing her case for years afterward. As late as 1890, she was still suing Congress for what she believed was her just compensation—and she was still getting turned down. Although early feminist writers took up her cause, her claims have never been validated. Few if any of today's serious historians believe that Anna Ella Carroll's assertions about her contribution to the war effort were rooted in anything but her own self-aggrandizement.

After the War Was Over...

Life didn't end when the Civil War was over. A number of soldiers from both sides went on to find fame—or infamy—in other pursuits after the war.

✳ ✳ ✳ ✳

Lived To Tell

SOME YOUNG VETERANS turned their war experience into literary careers. General Lew Wallace, for instance, saw action under General Grant at the Battle of Shiloh. After serving on the military commission that tried the Lincoln assassination conspirators, he gained worldwide acclaim for penning the novel *Ben-Hur*.

Ambrose Bierce began the war as a battlefield cartographer, serving bravely under fire until he was sidelined with a head wound at Kennesaw Mountain. Today, he's best known for penning the short story "An Occurrence at Owl Creek Bridge."

Missourian Mark Twain served in a Confederate militia under his real name of Samuel Langhorne Clemens for a few uneventful weeks before heading west and beginning his literary career.

Wild Subjects

Some notables gained their notoriety after the war in the American Wild West. Chief among them was George Armstrong Custer, who proved himself at Antietam, Brandy Station, and Gettysburg. Unfortunately, his military career had a less than heroic end at Little Big Horn in 1876.

James "Wild Bill" Hickok was a Nebraska constable when the war began, and he served as a scout for the Union. His skills with a gun and a rather nonchalant disposition toward killing would eventually catch up with him during a poker game in Deadwood in the Dakota Territory.

Another Union scout was William Cody, who began the war in the employ of the Pony Express. Afterward, his prowess as a buffalo hunter working for the railroad earned him a name, a reputation, and a subsequent career as the showman "Buffalo Bill." His "Wild West Show" helped establish many myths of the West.

Among the infamous Confederate guerrilla fighters known as Quantrill's Raiders were Frank and Jesse James. After the war they continued some of their guerrilla exploits, robbing banks, stagecoaches, and trains.

And Last But Not Least...

Erroneously credited with inventing baseball, Captain Abner Doubleday does have one legitimate claim to fame. He fired the first return shot of the war at Fort Sumter.

Maass-ively Brave

Today the name Clara Maass is not well known. But at the turn of the century, at the time of the Spanish-American War, practically everyone in the United States knew her as the nurse who risked her own life to help defeat the dreaded yellow fever epidemic.

✳ ✳ ✳ ✳

Young Girl Grows Up

CLARA LOUISE MAASS was born in East Orange, New Jersey, on June 28, 1876, the daugher of German immigrants who quickly discovered upon their arrival in America that the streets were not paved with gold. The family was just barely getting by. Clara began working while she was still in grammar school. At around age 16, she enrolled in nursing school at Newark German Hospital in Newark, New Jersey. Graduating from the rigorous course in 1895, she continued working hard; by 1898, she was the head nurse at Newark German.

Yellow Jack War

The Spanish-American War began on February 15, 1898. As wars go, the war was more period than paragraph, lasting just four short months. However, there was something more deadly to American troops than Spanish bullets: yellow fever.

Since its arrival in America in the summer of 1693, yellow fever had ravaged the country. For two centuries, "Yellow Jack" killed randomly and indiscriminately. The disease would devastate some households, while those next door would go untouched. One in ten people were killed by yellow fever in Philadelphia in 1793. The disease caused the federal government (Philadelphia was then the U.S. capital) to flee the city. In 1802, Yellow Jack killed 23,000 French troops in Haiti, causing Napoleon to abandon the New World and eventually agree to the Louisiana Purchase. An 1878 outbreak in Memphis killed 5,000 people there, and 20,000 total died in the Mississippi Delta. No one knew what caused yellow fever or how to stop it.

The Experiments

In April 1898, Maass applied to become a contract nurse during the Spanish-American War; in Santiago, Cuba, she saw her first cases of yellow fever. The next year she battled the disease in Manila, as it ravaged the American troops there. No one knew why Maass kept going to these danger zones when she could have remained safely at home nurturing her burgeoning nursing career. Yet when Havana was hit by a severe yellow fever epidemic in 1900, Maass once again answered a call for nurses to tend the sick.

In Havana, a team of doctors led by Walter Reed was trying to find the cause of yellow fever. They had reason to support a controversial theory that mosquitoes were the disease carrier, but they needed concrete proof. Desperate, they asked for human volunteers, offering to pay them $100—and another $100 if they became ill. Maass volunteered for the tests, though no one is sure why she put herself up to it. Possibly she hoped that contracting a mild case of the disease would give her immunity to it and allow her to better treat patients.

On August 14, 1901, after a previous mosquito bite had produced just a mild case of sickness, a willing Maass was bitten once again by an *Aedes aegypti* mosquito loaded with infectious blood. This time the vicious disease tore through her body. She wrote a feverish last letter home to her family: "You know I am the man of the family but pray for me . . ."

On August 24, Maass died. Her death ended the controversial practice of using humans as test subjects for experiments. But it also proved, beyond a doubt, that the *Aedes aegypti* mosquito was the disease carrier—the key to unlocking the sickness that scientists had been seeking for centuries. Yellow fever could finally be conquered, in part because of Maass's brave sacrifice.

The next day, a writer for the *New York Journal* wrote, "No soldier in the late war placed his life in peril for better reasons than those which prompted this faithful nurse to risk hers."

The Paris Peace Conference

In 1919, in the aftermath of the First World War, leaders of countries gathered to forge a treaty.

✳ ✳ ✳ ✳

IN 1914, ARCHDUKE Franz Ferdinand of the Austro-Hungarian Empire was assassinated in a Serbian plot, pushing a long-simmering feud in the Balkans to all-out war. Unfortunately for the rest of Europe, a network of treaties and alliances between the combatants and their neighbors drew virtually all other major powers on the continent into the conflict. World War I had begun.

The conflict involved the greatest mobilization of soldiers and war machinery the world had yet seen, but the next several years were spent fighting to a draw at the cost of millions of lives. Both the Allied Powers and Central Powers struggled to win the support of other nations. Italy and the United States were eventually lured into the conflict on the side of Britain, France, and the other Allies, sealing the fate of Germany, Austria-Hungary, and the Central Powers.

The tide clearly turned in 1918, and during 1919, leaders of the Allied nations spent months at the palace of Versailles in France planning their new vision for war-ravaged Europe. Given their great economic and military power, the "Big Four" countries—the United States, France, Great Britain, and Italy—dominated the discussions.

American President Woodrow Wilson pushed hard for measures that would ensure stability in Europe, including a new body called the League of Nations that would endeavor to resolve international disputes in a peaceful fashion.

Bowing to popular pressure at home for some benefit to come from the terrible war, the other leaders focused more on financial and territorial gains for their nations. Italy's prime minister,

Vittorio Orlando (1860–1952), stormed out of the conference after his bid for control of Balkan lands was rejected by the other leaders. Eventually, however, the meetings produced the Treaty of Versailles and brought an official end to the war.

Orlando resigned as prime minister of Italy before the treaty was signed. He occasionally reemerged as a significant figure in Italian politics during the next 25 years and helped establish democracy in his country in the years following World War II. He died in 1952, the last of the Versailles Treaty's "Big Four" leaders to do so.

The other major participants in the Versailles Treaty at the end of World War I were Woodrow Wilson (1856–1924), U.S. president; Georges Clemenceau (1841–1929), French premier; and David Lloyd George (1863–1945), British prime minister.

In the Year…1939

The peace established in 1919 did not last; World War II came quickly. In September 1939, Germany invaded Poland, marking the beginning of the war in Europe. What else was happening in the world at that time?

✳ ✳ ✳ ✳

✳ The January 2 cover of *Time* magazine features Adolph Hitler as "Man of the Year."

✳ Nazis seize all enterprises of German Jews.

✳ *Gone with the Wind* premieres in Atlanta.

✳ *The Wizard of Oz* premieres in New York City.

✳ Marian Anderson, celebrated contralto of American opera, is refused a performance at Constitution Hall in Washington, D.C., by the Daughters of the American Revolution.

✳ Hewlett-Packard opens for business.

* A massive earthquake hits Chile, obliterating a surface area of 50,000 miles and killing approximately 30,000 people.

* The Borley Rectory, long reputed to be England's most haunted house, burns to the ground.

* The Spanish Civil War ends.

* Faisal II becomes King of Iraq.

* *The Grapes of Wrath* by John Steinbeck is published.

* More than 900 Jewish refugees on the SS *St. Louis* are denied entry to the United States after being rejected by Cuba, resulting in their forced return to Europe. Most later died in Nazi concentration camps.

* The National Baseball Hall of Fame and Museum opens in Cooperstown, New York.

* The country of Siam becomes Thailand, a name that translates as "Free Land."

* The New York Yankees' Lou Gehrig, whose ill health is attributed to amyotrophic lateral sclerosis (ALS), gives his last public address, which includes the famous line, "Today, I consider myself the luckiest man on the face of the earth."

* Al Capone gets out of the joint (Alcatraz).

Going to War in Style

Millions of Allied troops got to experience something they likely wouldn't have as ordinary civilians—an ocean voyage on a luxury passenger liner.

* * * *

DURING WORLD WAR II, scores of luxury passenger liners were pressed into service as troop-transport ships. Symbols of grandeur, privilege, and national prestige, these magnificent vessels were stripped of their finery, refitted, repainted, and recommissioned into decidedly more utilitarian craft that were indispensable to the Allied war effort.

The first large-scale troop transport involving luxury passenger ships left Halifax on December 10, 1939. Five camouflaged luxury liners—*Empress of Britain, Duchess of Bedford, Monarch of Bermuda, Aquitania*, and *Empress of Australia*—carried 7,400 soldiers of the Canadian Army 1st Division for deployment in Britain.

By war's end, millions of Allied soldiers had sailed aboard converted ocean liners to and from North America, Europe, Africa, Asia, and Australia. Here are looks at some of the more notable luxury ships that carried them to war in style.

Queen Mary

The jewel of the Cunard-White Star Line fleet, the *Queen Mary* stood alone among the classic ocean liners of its era, both as a peacetime luxury liner and as a wartime troopship.

It began its wartime service in May 1940. Painted gray while laid up in New York and fitted as a troopship in Sydney, the *Queen Mary* initially transported Australian troops to Scotland and Africa. In mid-1943, it was transferred to service in the Atlantic Ocean.

The *Queen Mary* was fast—at the outbreak of the war it was the undisputed holder of the shipping industry's Blue Riband award for the fastest trans-Atlantic liner. With a cruising speed of 28.5 knots, it often sailed unescorted, as German subs could not catch or keep up with it. The *Queen Mary* was also huge. It was eventually fitted for a capacity of 15,000 troops—equivalent to a whole division—and in July 1943, it established a record for the most people on a single voyage when it set sail with 16,683 soldiers and crew on board.

In all, the *Queen Mary* sailed 569,429 miles and carried a total of 765,429 military personnel during the war, surviving both a collision with a British light cruiser and a $250,000 bounty placed by Adolf Hitler. It returned to civilian service in 1946, but not before making 11 voyages bringing war brides to the United States and Canada.

America (USS West Point)

The queen of the United States Line fleet, the *America* was launched on August 31, 1939, and entered into service in 1940. Within a year, the 33,560-ton liner was commissioned as an AP (armored personnel) ship by the U.S. Navy, renamed the USS *West Point*, and in only 11 days, refitted and put into service as the navy's largest troopship.

Nicknamed the "Gray Ghost" because of its wartime, dull gray makeover, the *West Point* could carry up to 8,175 troops at average speeds of approximately 25 knots. Through the course of the war, it would log distances equivalent to 16 circumnavigations of the globe while enduring several perilous encounters with the enemy. Off of Singapore in January 1942, Japanese bombers attacked the *West Point* and came within 50 yards of scoring a direct hit. The ship also faced air attacks in the Red Sea, off Australia, and at Port Suez. It also had close calls with submarines, including one that fired torpedoes across its bow off Brazil.

The *West Point* was decommissioned in early 1946 after having transported more than 350,000 troops to ports of call all around the world.

Manhattan (USS Wakefield)

Another ship of the United States Line fleet, the *Manhattan* was chartered by the U.S. government in 1940 to bring American citizens home from warring Europe. It was later commissioned by the U.S. Navy in May 1941 for use as a troop carrier and renamed the USS *Wakefield*.

Capable of carrying up to 6,000 passengers, the *Wakefield* often traveled as a "lone wolf," unescorted and fast enough to outrace German subs. Despite this, the *Wakefield* had a rough go of it early in its commission. It was traveling with the *West Point* off Singapore when alert Japanese bombers attacked the *Wakefield*, scoring a direct hit that resulted in five fatalities.

In September 1942, the *Wakefield* caught fire in the North Atlantic and was towed while still burning to Halifax, where it was almost capsized by a torrential storm.

The *Wakefield* was eventually repaired and recommissioned in February 1944 to continue serving as a troop transport. It finished out the war sailing primarily in the Atlantic Ocean, carrying 217,237 troops and passengers before being decommissioned in June 1946. Unlike the *Queen Mary* and the *America*, however, the *Wakefield* never returned to its former glory as a luxury liner. It remained in the navy's possession, in reserve and out of commission, until released in 1959 and scrapped five years later.

A Wing and a Prayer

Thousands of World War II's aviators spent their days in small wooden boxes, didn't use parachutes, and couldn't fire a gun— yet managed to save hundreds of lives.

✳ ✳ ✳ ✳

BY 1939, THE era of the homing pigeon was mostly history. Radio technology had improved over the Great War era, when war pigeons were in their heyday, making the winged messengers a thing of the past. But for men on a hot battlefield or partisans operating behind enemy lines, sometimes getting a message back to headquarters wasn't so simple. On such occasions, a humble carrier pigeon was a unit's best friend.

Allied Birds

Great Britain used carrier pigeons, also known as homing pigeons, more than any other military. An estimated quarter million of His Majesty's feathered subjects flew in service from 1939 to 1945.

The U.K.'s Royal Air Force (RAF), Civil Defense, and Home Guard made good use of pigeons, and even the home front did its part to support England's littlest wingmen: Pigeon racing was prohibited, birds of prey were hunted along the English coasts, and pigeon corn was rationed.

Homing pigeons were employed in a variety of jobs. RAF bombers and reconnaissance aircraft were equipped with pigeons so that if a plane had made an emergency landing, the birds could alert headquarters and a rescue could be launched. They were also extremely useful for sending secret messages to London. In occupied France, for example, resistance fighters regularly sent homing pigeons from the French coast to London with messages describing the dispositions of German units stationed along potential Allied landing zones.

The U.S. Pigeon Service, a branch of the Signal Corps, assigned more than 3,100 officers and men to manage some 54,000 pigeons during World War II. About a dozen pigeon companies were activated, and most were deployed overseas in all theaters.

Axis Birds

Germany had used carrier pigeons for many years. According to MI5, Britain's secret service agency, SS Führer Heinrich Himmler, a pigeon aficionado, made a "pet" project of air-dropping carrier pigeons to German spies stationed in England. One declassified MI5 report noted that two clandestine German birds had been captured, commenting wryly, "Both birds are now prisoners of war working hard at breeding English pigeons."

High-Flying Heroes

One British pigeon, named Scotch-Lass, was dropped into the Netherlands with a secret agent and arrived, wounded, back in London bearing 38 microfilm images. Another, a hen named Mary, was wounded several times during her five-year career before being killed in action. The pigeon White Vision flew more than 60 miles across churning waters near Scotland to deliver a distress message from a downed PBY (patrol bomber) flying boat in October 1943.

One Italian campaign veteran, a cock named G.I. Joe, flew 20 miles from the town of Colvi Vecchia, which British troops had occupied ahead of schedule, to U.S. bomber headquarters. The bird arrived in time to halt a planned bombing run on the city that would have brought down friendly fire on the Brits. The 5th Army's commander, Lieutenant General Mark Clark, estimated that G.I. Joe saved the lives of as many as 1,000 men. The bird was awarded the U.K.'s highest honor for a war animal, the Dickin Medal of Gallantry, nicknamed the "Animal's Victoria Cross."

Of course, pigeons were susceptible to the kinds of hazards every bird faces. For example, pigeon "10601" of the Royal Canadian Air Force, deployed from Allied submarines, accomplished many missions but was eventually brought down by a bird of prey. To neutralize the German spy threat, MI5 actually set up a falcon program to catch eastbound pigeons in one high-threat area. But through winds, hostile fire, and even the occasional enemy barn owl, these feathered messengers made contributions to the war efforts on both sides.

Boyington's Black Sheep

The men of VMF-214 had a reputation as the black sheep of the U.S. Air Corps. However, the tactics and skill of the pilots and their commanding officer, "Pappy" Boyington, made them heroes.

✳ ✳ ✳ ✳

IT WAS AUGUST 4, 1941, and Marine Corps aviator Gregory Boyington had reached rock bottom. Stationed in Pensacola, Florida, he was broke, his wife and children had left him, and his reputation for brawling and drinking had eliminated his chances of promotion despite his talent as a pilot.

That night in Florida, he knew that a representative of the Central Air Manufacturing Company was in a nearby hotel recruiting pilots for a volunteer mission in China. Tired of the Marines and lured by the promise of money, Boyington stopped at the bar for a few drinks and signed up.

He trained with the American Volunteer Group (AVG) in China, also known as the Flying Tigers. Led by Claire L. Chennault, the notorious group learned tactics to combat Japan's best pilots. Boyington remained a drinker and brawler, but with six kills, he earned another sort of reputation as a formidable combat pilot. However, Chennault had a maverick personality, and his views frequently clashed with Boyington, who eventually left the AVG and rejoined the Marine Corps. He was recommissioned as a major and sent to New Caledonia in the South Pacific, where he mastered one of the service's newest planes, the bent-wing F4U Corsair.

A New Unit

While on convalescence following a leg injury, Boyington learned that the Marines badly needed to form new Corsair squadrons, and he organized an ad hoc unit comprising pilots and Corsairs dispersed by other units. The pilots' levels of experience ranged from combat veterans with several victories under their belts to new replacement pilots from the United States. Many of the pilots that Boyington pooled to form VMF-214 were known as misfits with reputations for discipline problems. The group quickly earned the nickname "the Black Sheep." Boyington once famously quipped, "Just name a hero and I'll prove he's a bum." A discipline problem himself, Boyington understood these pilots and trained them using tactics he'd learned as a Flying Tiger. It worked—in 84 days the Black Sheep destroyed or damaged 197 enemy planes.

His men called their leader "Gramps" because, though only in his early thirties, Boyington was ten years older than most of them. The press dubbed him "Pappy," and the name stuck as his reputation grew even larger. Between August and September 1943, Pappy had added 22 confirmed kills and was on his way to eclipsing Eddie Rickenbacker's World War I record of 26 downed planes.

On January 3, 1944, however, Boyington was shot down and believed to be dead. In fact, he was taken prisoner by the Japanese, who, knowing his identity, tortured him and refused to report his status to the International Committee of the Red Cross. His fate was not known until 18 months later, when Boyington emerged from a POW camp. Though the numbers are disputed by some historians, Boyington is officially credited with 28 kills, making him the leading Marine ace of the war. He was awarded the Medal of Honor.

Lady Killer

Lyudmila Pavlichenko was the first Soviet citizen ever to be received at the White House. She killed 309 Axis soldiers to gain the honor.

✳ ✳ ✳ ✳

HER SOVIET COMRADES knew her as the "Death Sniper." German soldiers on the eastern front just knew she was deadly. She is now known as the greatest woman sniper of all time. Lyudmila Pavlichenko earned that title by killing 309 German and Romanian soldiers in less than a year while fighting in the Crimean Peninsula.

A Sharp-Eyed Beauty

Born in 1916 in the Ukrainian village of Belaya Tserkov, Pavlichenko moved with her parents to Kiev after completing ninth grade. There she joined a shooting club and honed her sharpshooter prowess. After Germany invaded the Soviet Union in June 1941, she left her studies at the University of Kiev to join the fight against the Nazis. When Pavlichenko told her recruiter that she wanted to join the infantry and carry a rifle, he laughed and asked what she knew about rifles. Pavlichenko coolly responded by showing him her marksmanship certificate. Astounded but not convinced, the recruiter tried to persuade the dark-haired beauty to become a field nurse. But Pavlichenko persisted and eventually joined the 25th Infantry Division, becoming one of 2,000 Soviet women who fought in the war as snipers.

Pavlichenko entered action near Odessa, where in August 1941 she recorded her first two kills while helping to defend a key hill. Over the next two and a half months, using a Mosin-Nagant Russian five-shot, bolt-action rifle, she would record 187 kills.

After the Germans captured Odessa, her unit was sent to Sevastopol. In May 1942, now-Lieutenant Pavlichenko was cited by the Southern Red Army Council for killing 257 German soldiers. Among her eventual confirmed total of 309 kills were 36 Nazi snipers, including one whose kill logbook listed more than 500 victims. Pavlichenko's combat duty ended in June 1942 after she was wounded by mortar fire. By then, she was a hero in her homeland.

A Star Is Born

Recognizing her value to the propaganda effort, the Soviets sent Pavlichenko on a speaking tour of North America in 1942. She became the first Soviet citizen to be received at the White House and enjoyed a hero's welcome when she appeared before the International Student Assembly in Washington, D.C. She later made appearances in various American and Canadian cities, proudly relating her wartime experiences to enthralled audiences. Her American admirers presented her with a Colt semiautomatic pistol, while Canadian fans gave her a Winchester rifle, which is now on display at the Central Museum of the Armed Forces in Moscow. Her celebrity status was cemented when legendary American songwriter Woody Guthrie penned a song about her exploits.

After returning to the Soviet Union, Pavlichenko was kept from action but became a sniper instructor. In 1943, she was awarded the Hero of the Soviet Union, her nation's highest honor. After the war, she remained active in Soviet military circles as a research assistant of the chief headquarters of the Soviet Navy and as a member of the Soviet Committee of the Veterans of War. She died in 1974 at the age of 58.

Rollin' With the Big Boys

The story of the Allied war effort in World War II is too often told solely from the perspective of the "Big Three." But eventually 55 countries throughout the world, including many small and less prominent nations, joined the Allied cause—earning the right to share in the victory with the great powers.

❋　❋　❋　❋

MANY HISTORICAL ACCOUNTS tend to downplay or even ignore the contribution of smaller or less powerful countries to the Allied cause, focusing on the major Allied players: the United States, Great Britain, and the Soviet Union. The fact is, 55 countries of assorted sizes and strengths contributed to the Allied war effort to varying degrees, ranging from providing significant quantities of fighting men and war materiel to merely offering political support. In the end, these contributions all added up to victory.

Here's a brief look at the how some of the smaller Allied countries factored in the win.

New Zealand

New Zealand declared war on Germany on September 4, 1939, making it one of the original Allied countries along with Britain, France, Poland, and Australia. Over the course of the war, 140,000 men and women from New Zealand served in army, navy, air force, and auxiliary units in North Africa, Italy, Southeast Asia, and the south Pacific.

Upright British officers were irked by the New Zealanders' disdain for proper military protocol, but couldn't help but respect the Kiwis' tenacious fighting spirit.

Thousands of Kiwis served in British or New Zealand naval and air force units. The vast majority, however, fought in infantry units as part of the Second New Zealand Expeditionary Force (2NZEF). Some 104,000 New Zealander soldiers fought in some of the war's toughest battles, including Crete, El Alamein, Cassino, Singapore, and Bougainville. By war's end, New Zealand counted 11,625 killed in action, giving it the grim distinction of having the highest ratio of fatal casualties per capita among all the Commonwealth nations.

New Zealand itself experienced an armed invasion of sorts. More than 100,000 U.S. servicemen were stationed in the country, as it became a prime jump-off point for American operations in the Pacific.

Morocco

Morocco's fierce Goumier mountain fighters, known as Goums, were used as a spearhead raiding force against German alpine defenses in Tunisia and Italy. The Goums were tough, nomadic indigenous people who were highly skilled in traversing nearly impassible mountain terrain. They wore ankle-length striped robes called *djellabas* rather than regulation uniforms and sported long beards and pigtails, which they said provided Allah with handles to carry them to heaven when their time came. They preferred fighting at night and in close quarters using knives, which they wielded with deadly skill. The Goums had a reputation as bloodthirsty fighters, particularly for their tendency to cut off the ears or heads of enemy soldiers. A French officer once asked a Goum going out on patrol to bring him back a German wristwatch—he was later handed the severed forearm of a German soldier with a watch still attached.

Some 12,000 Goums fought in Italy as part of the French Expeditionary Force. Their defining moment came in May

1944 when they unraveled German strongholds in the imposing Aurunci and Lepini mountains that blocked the southern approach to Rome. Their actions forced the Germans to abandon the ranges and opened the way to Rome through the Liri Valley. The Goums pursued the Germans northward through the Italian mountains to Siena before being transferred with the French Expeditionary Force for the invasion of southern France. The Goums continued to fight with effectiveness through the French Alps and into southern Germany.

Mexico

Mexico's most notable contribution to the Allied war effort was the Mexican Expeditionary Air Force. Three squadrons of Mexican fighter pilots were trained in the United States, but only one squadron, the 201st Fighter Squadron, saw combat duty. Indeed, it was the only Mexican military unit to see action outside Mexico during the war.

The 201st was commissioned in February 1945 and transferred to the Philippines in April as part of the U.S. Air Force's 58th Fighter Group. Flying P-47 Thunderbolt fighters, the 201st carried out 96 combat missions, primarily in support of American ground troops in Luzon in June and July 1945.

Nepal

Some of the most fearsome soldiers to fight on the side of the Allies came from Nepal. The famed Gurkha warriors of the Himalayan highlands had served in the British Indian Army since the 1850s and eagerly answered the call again during World War II. More than 112,000 Gurkha soldiers in 40 battalions fought alongside British and Commonwealth troops in far-flung locations ranging from Italy, North Africa, and the Middle East to Burma, Malaya, and Singapore. British officers commanding the best of the Gurkha battalions considered their units superior to most in the regular British Army.

The Gurkhas earned a reputation among their fellow Allied soldiers for being tough, brave, and extremely likable.

They excelled in solo attacks against enemy bunkers and machine-gun nests and seldom lost in hand-to-hand fights. In close encounters, a Gurkha traded his rifle for his kukri, a boomerang-shape machete with a razor-sharp inner blade. (An unsheathed kukri was announced by the battle cry, "Aayo bir Gorkhali!"—"The Gurkhas are upon you!") Allied soldiers asking to see the exotic knives would gape in bewilderment when their Gurkha comrades nicked their own fingers with the blade before returning it to its casing: Gurkha tradition dictated that a kukri could not be unsheathed without drawing blood.

The Philippines

At the time of the Japanese invasion of the Philippines in December 1941, the regular Philippine Army boasted 100,000 troops. But the vast majority of them were raw recruits who were insufficiently trained, badly under-equipped, and poorly led. Approximately 65,000 Filipino soldiers were taken prisoner by the Japanese during the battle for the Philippines. But most remaining units of the Philippine Army didn't give up the fight. Instead, they melted into the jungles and mountains and formed the backbone of a hardy guerrilla force that incessantly harassed the Japanese during their three-year occupation of the islands.

By the time of MacArthur's return to the Philippines in October 1944, approximately 250,000 Filipino guerillas were actively fighting the Japanese. They provided invaluable reconnaissance and fighting support to American forces throughout the campaign to liberate the Philippines. They also played a major role in one of the most dramatic operations of the campaign—the liberation of the Cabanatuan POW camp.

The Cabanatuan raid was led by the U.S. Army 6th Ranger Battalion, which carried out the main assault against the camp and freed the POWs. But it's very unlikely that the raid would have succeeded without the vital contribution of several hundred Filipino guerrillas led by former Philippine Army captains

Eduardo Joson and Juan Pajota. The guerillas provided key pre-raid intelligence to the rangers and mobilized support from the local civilians for food and transportation to evacuate sick and wounded POWs. Most importantly, the guerrillas sealed off all routes to the camp and fought off 800 Japanese troops attempting to abort the raid and subsequent evacuation.

Audie Murphy's Awards

Audie Murphy was the most decorated U.S. soldier during World War II. He received 23 awards, including 5 awards from France and Belgium, and every decoration of valor that the United States offered. After the war, he pursued a successful movie career, starring in films such as The Red Badge of Courage, The Unforgiven, *and* To Hell and Back, *based on his autobiography. Murphy won each of the following 23 awards—some of them more than once.*

✳ ✳ ✳ ✳

1. Medal of Honor

2. Distinguished Service Cross

3. Silver Star with First Oak Leaf Cluster

4. Legion of Merit

5. Bronze Star with V Device and First Oak Leaf Cluster

6. Purple Heart with Second Oak Leaf Cluster

7. U.S. Army Outstanding Civilian Service Medal

8. Good Conduct Medal

9. Distinguished Unit Emblem with First Oak Leaf Cluster

10. American Campaign Medal

11. European-African-Middle Eastern Campaign Medal

12. World War II Victory Medal

13. Army of Occupation with Germany Clasp

14. Armed Forces Reserve Medal

15. Combat Infantry Badge

16. Marksman Badge with Rifle Bar

17. Expert Badge with Bayonet Bar

18. French Fourragere

19. French Legion of Honor, Grade of Chevalier

20. French Croix de Guerre with Silver Star

21. French Croix de Guerre with Palm

22. Medal of Liberated France

23. Belgian Croix de Guerre 1940 Palm

Beyond the Blast: Hiroshima's Trees

On August 6, 1945, American forces dropped an atomic bomb on the Japanese city of Hiroshima. Buildings were decimated, and between 70,000 and 100,000 people died from the bombing. But throughout the city, there are trees that somehow survived the blast and now rank among the most sacred and beloved of Japan's treasures.

* * * *

"Nothing Will Grow"

THE ATOMIC BOMB was the outcome of an undertaking known as the Manhattan Project. Two days after the blast, one of its scientists, Dr. Harold Jacobsen, deemed Hiroshima contaminated with radiation and barren of life. Manhattan Project leader Dr. Robert Oppenheimer, however, contradicted Jacobsen's claim.

Nevertheless, American armed forces in Japan issued the following statement: "Hiroshima will be barren of human and animal life for 75 years. Any scientists who go there to survey the damage will be committing suicide."

Professor Masao Tsuzuki, leader of the Hiroshima Disaster Survey Team, also disagreed with Jacobsen. Beginning on August 30, he conducted a survey of the city. "The rumor about 75 years is completely mistaken," Tsuzuki wrote. "In the ruins of Hiroshima's Gokoku Shrine, sprouts have already grown to 15 centimeters." Today Gokoku Shrine is one of the city's most treasured places.

Rising from the Ashes

Many of the trees that survived the atomic blast were sheltered by buildings or natural declivities. However, a surviving cluster of Chinese parasol trees (or phoenix trees) grouped nearly one mile from the blast center stood exposed. That anything of them remained at all following the explosion was unbelievable; that they should continue to grow is something of a miracle. Yet, stripped of their branches, their trunks hollowed out and badly burned, the Chinese parasols sprouted new leaves the following spring. Today, they serve as symbols of the city's rebirth.

Prehistory vs. the Atomic Age

Having survived for about 200 million years, ginkgo trees are among the oldest living seed plants. They are exceptionally hardy—individual trees can live for thousands of years. The resilience of these prehistoric trees was demonstrated by the six ginkgos that stood within 1.24 miles of the Hiroshima atomic blast hypocenter. They include four trees shielded by temples (that were later rebuilt around the surviving trees), a tree in the Shukkeien Sunken Garden whose trunk collapsed but now flourishes, and a tree next to the Senda Elementary School that was stripped of limbs and foliage but began to bud soon after a school was re-established on the site. Today the ginkgo tree is regarded as the "bearer of hope" throughout Japan.

Instead, Let's Blow Up Some Trees

If Special Assistant to the Secretary of the Navy Lewis Strauss had had his way, many more Japanese trees would be dead (although perhaps many fewer civilians). Strauss recommended that the United States demonstrate the power of its awesome new weapon by dropping the first bomb over an easily observed area where Japanese officials could fully appreciate its destructive power. To this end, he suggested a forest of *cryptomeria* trees (a type of conifer) near Tokyo, reasoning that a high-altitude blast would splay the trees in a radial pattern and create a firestorm at the center. Such a sight, he felt, would convince the Japanese government to surrender immediately. As history shows, the U.S. government didn't use Strauss's idea.

A Different Sort of Tree

In December 1945, a woman living in Hiroshima erected a small metal-and-plastic Christmas tree in her family's ruined home. There wasn't much to celebrate: She had lost one of her young sons to the atomic blast, and the city was a smoldering wasteland. But she kept the Christmas tree tradition alive as she had every year since 1937 when her husband had purchased the tree in Hawaii. Even during the war, when possession of a Christmas tree was grounds for arrest, the Iwatake family displayed the small tree in a back room away from windows. The same tiny tree remains an Iwatake family tradition, displayed in their home as a remembrance of those who died during the war.

Beyond the Law

After World War II, the victorious Allies brought quite a few Nazi war criminals to justice. Through careful planning, dumb luck, or Allied oversight, quite a few also escaped due justice.

✳   ✳   ✳   ✳

Milivoj Ašner, Croatian police chief: Affiliated with the brutal *Ustaše* (Croatian SS-equivalent), he organized the deportation of many Serbs, Roma, and Jews to concentration camps. He avoided capture and became an Austrian citizen after the war, then moved back to Croatia, where life was comfortable until a researcher found him. Ašner bailed for Austria, which refused to extradite him for trial in Croatia. He died of dementia in 2011.

Alois Brunner, Austrian SS *Hauptsturmführer*: Assistant to the infamous Adolf Eichmann, he was responsible for deporting well over 100,000 people to their deaths. His name resembled that of captured (and executed) fellow war criminal Anton Brunner, making the search less intense. Alois escaped to Syria under a fake name. His status is unknown but he is presumed dead.

Anton Burger, Austrian SS *Sturmbannführer*: First a bureau-crat coordinating the deportation of French, Belgian, Dutch, and Greek Jews to concentration camps, he then became commandant of Theresienstadt concentration camp. He escaped first from an internment camp, then from postwar Austrian custody, and lived anonymously in West Germany until his 1991 death.

Mikhail Gorshkow, Russian-Estonian Gestapo interpreter: He stands accused of involvement in the murder of several thousand Jews in the Slutsk ghetto of Minsk, Belarus (then the U.S.S.R.). He evaded capture and emigrated to the U.S., becoming naturalized in 1963. After his history surfaced, the U.S. stripped him of citizenship for lying on his application. Gorshkow fled to Estonia, where a war crimes investigation proved inconclusive.

Dr. Aribert Heim, Austrian SS *Hauptsturmführer*: The 'Dr. Death' of Mauthausen concentration camp, he specialized in killing by injecting toxin into the heart, as well as dissecting live prisoners without anesthesia. Somehow overlooked by his American captors, he practiced medicine in West Germany until the heat was on, then fled to Egypt and converted to Islam. He died in Cairo in 1992.

Dr. Josef Mengele, German SS *Hauptsturmführer* (captain): One of the most infamous men of World War II, he practiced well-documented war crimes both in selecting victims for gas chambers, and in experimentation: live dissections of pregnant women, sewing twins together, and other monstrosities. Mengele fooled his American captors with a fake name, then escaped to Argentina. He looked over his shoulder until his 1979 drowning in São Paulo, Brazil.

Walter Rauff, German SS *Sturmbannführer* (colonel): The designer of the gas vans, trucks set up to pump the exhaust into the bed, killing the passengers (Jews and the disabled) with carbon monoxide poisoning. He devised this solution because simply shooting prisoners was doing emotional harm to the shooters. He snuck out of an American internment camp in Italy and escaped to Chile, where he died in 1984.

Doin' the Duck and Cover

Growing up as an American child during the 1950s and '60s with the Cold War and the threat of Soviet attack looming made for an interesting, and often surreal, childhood.

✳ ✳ ✳ ✳

Only a Sunburn

IF YOU CAN remember hiding under your school desk with your hands over your head, then you are most likely a "Cold War survivor." For those who grew up in America during the 1950s, this "Duck and Cover" drill would have been part of their education. Intended to teach kids what they should do in the event of a nuclear blast, the drill even had its own mascot, Bert, an astute turtle who happened to carry his shelter on his back. Newsreels featuring Bert the Turtle warned children that the explosion of a nuclear bomb could "knock you down hard." But, if you only managed to "duck and cover" under a table or desk, you would be safely protected from the "sunburn" caused by the explosion.

Head in the Sand

These films were created by the Federal Civil Defense Administration, which had been given the responsibility of educating and protecting American citizens in the event of nuclear war. In effect, they were responsible for much of the American Cold War propaganda produced during this time. One of their newsreels assured Americans that they would fare much better than the Japanese had in Hiroshima.

After all, they reasoned, unlike the Japanese, Americans were being given the information they needed to survive: If they just remembered to "clean under their fingernails, and wash their hair thoroughly," Americans were sure to be spared the effects of radiation.

A Culture of Fear

Fear had enormous impact on those growing up during the '50s and '60s. Many mid-century suburban towns had been built, in part, with the fear of Soviet attack in mind. Since it was expected that cities would be obliterated from falling bombs, the government encouraged suburban development as a way to scatter the population. Did you share a room with your brothers or sisters? During the Cold War, large families were encouraged as a way to fight the virus of communism—what better way to fight Soviet domination than to arm the country with a bursting population of wholesome capitalist American children? Birthrates soared to the highest levels of the century, with 29 million "baby boomers" born during the '50s.

The Cold War paranoia escalated after October 4, 1957, the day the Soviets launched *Sputnik I*, the world's first satellite. Suddenly, the nuclear threat emanating from Russia felt tangible. U.S. leaders decided the nation's best weapon against it was the youth of America, and so money was poured into schools and universities. No longer eggheads, scientists and engineers suddenly became the new elite.

Americans' response to the very real danger of nuclear war was sometimes surreal. In 1959, *LIFE* magazine ran a story featuring a couple planning to spend their honeymoon in a bomb shelter. The young couple was pictured surrounded by tin can provisions, which they took with them into their concrete "hotel." Children played with Sputnik toys and dressed as rockets for Halloween. Teenagers sported the latest swimsuit fashion, the bikini, named for the Bikini Island H-Bomb test site because its daring style was equally "dangerous."

On the Other Side

Since the fall of the Soviet Union it has been possible to learn how these years were experienced behind the Iron Curtain. Many Soviet people did not fear impending nuclear war nearly as much as Americans did. For a child in the Soviet Union, *Sputnik's* flight was a celebration of scientific progress, and America was the source of pop songs—not total destruction.

Mutiny or Mistake?

Military casualties aren't always the result of combat. A commander's own men can turn against him, too, whether by accident or by design.

✳ ✳ ✳ ✳

B EING A MILITARY commander sometimes means becoming a target, whether by the enemy or their own troops. Here are some commanders who found themselves dead at the hands of the men serving directly beneath them.

Nadir Shah

Cause of death: mutiny

Persian leader Nadir Shah ruled his empire during the 1700s, leading his army to victory over the Mongols, Turks, and other rivals. His career came to a sudden stop when his military-appointed bodyguard murdered him. Since Shah was said to be cruel, the other troops weren't too torn up about his death.

Colonel David Marcus

Cause of death: mistake

In the late 1940s, U.S. Army Colonel David Marcus decided to join Israel's army, as the nation was in the midst of a tense war. Marcus was helping build a road from Tel Aviv to Jerusalem. One night, he couldn't sleep. He got up to go for a walk and an Israeli Army guard opened fire and killed him. Apparently, the guard saw a bed sheet wrapped around Marcus and thought he was an Arab fighter. His story was made into the 1966 film, *Cast a Giant Shadow*, starring Kirk Douglas.

Colonel John Finnis

Cause of death: mutiny

This one may not be a shock: Colonel John Finnis was slaughtered while lecturing his troops about insubordination. In 1857, the British Indian Army commander went to address his men after learning they were moving toward mutiny. Unfortunately, his message didn't carry much weight—the troops killed him mid-speech.

General Thomas "Stonewall" Jackson

Cause of death: mistake

On May 2, 1863, famed Civil War Confederate General "Stonewall" Jackson went out with a small crew to scout out his team's upcoming path. When he came back to camp, a group of Confederate fighters thought he was a Yankee and shot him. He died eight days later.

Captain Pedro de Urzúa

Cause of death: mutiny

In the mid-1500s, Spanish Captain Pedro de Urzúa found himself on the wrong side of his troops while leading soldiers on a mission across the Andes. De Urzúa's men rallied together and decided to take their leader's life, pledging their allegiance instead to another uniting figure. The story was later told in the 1972 movie, *Aguirre, the Wrath of God.*

Captain Yevgeny Golikov

Cause of death: mutiny

In 1905, Captain Yevgeny Golikov died over a dispute about meat. His crew, apparently upset over the low quality of meat available onboard, grabbed Golikov and tossed him into the sea. The story was the inspiration for the 1925 silent film, *Battleship Potemkin.*

Armor: Outstanding and Interesting Tanks

The 20th century saw the armored fighting vehicle (AFV) supplant heavy cavalry as a swift, hard-hitting arm of war. Some tanks have been a cut above their contemporaries, while others were funny looking, or failures, or both. Let's start with the great ones.

✳ ✳ ✳ ✳

The Great

FT-17 (France, 1917; 37mm or machine gun): Unlike most elephantine World War I armor, the small FT-17 had a 360-degree rotating gun turret, and it crossed trenches with the help of extended rear rockers rather than oversized, diamond-shaped treads. It was the first World War I tank that looked like World War II tanks, and it was the only one to see significant World War II service.

Matilda II (U.K., 1937; 40mm): If you want to stop the enemy in its tracks, bring a tank that can barely be harmed. Mattie's crews could laugh at German tank cannons until 1942, when most Soviet Matildas were phased out in favor of faster, more powerful tanks. Although the relatively small Matilda waltzed slowly, her bulldog presence commanded respect.

KV-1 (U.S.S.R., 1939; 76mm): This hulking brute owes its fame partly to timing. When Germany invaded the Soviet Union, the KV was a monster only the Stuka dive-bomber or 88mm flak gun could slay. Outside Leningrad, one KV-1 withstood 135 German cannon hits.

T-34 (U.S.S.R., 1941; 76mm, then 85mm): Looking for credibility around World War II zealots? Call this the best tank of the war. Its amazing speed, sloped armor, and strong gunnery enabled aggressive tank tactics, perfectly suited to Eastern Front warfare and deadly to Germany. The 1944 T-34 (85) model was still serving in some armies in 2000.

Panzerkampfwagen V Panther (Germany, 1943; 75mm): Remember the guys who sneered when you heaped praise on the T-34? They have nothing on Panther advocates. Speedy and well armored up front, the Panther's hard-hitting long gun could engage at ranges that enabled few enemies to harm it.

M-60 Patton (U.S., 1960; 105mm): For two decades, this reliable tank was NATO's mainstay—and perhaps the finest tank of the 1960s. Its variants formed the backbone of Israeli armor during the Yom Kippur War, and the U.S. Marines drove some into battle during the 1991 Gulf War. The trustworthy M-60s were routinely updated until the end of the Cold War.

T-72 (U.S.S.R., 1971; 125mm): Any tank this prolific rates mention. When introduced, the T-72's 125mm cannon raised the gunnery bar above the common 105mm. It proved fast and reliable, while delivering a lot of bang for the ruble, and in 2002 it was still the world's most widely deployed tank.

The Odd

A7V (Germany, 1917; 57mm): This clunker looked like a railroad caboose covered with a big steel drop cloth, and it fought about as well. It couldn't cross trenches, which was disappointing, because the goal of tanks was to break up trench warfare stalemates. If you romanticize German tanks, try not to look too hard at pictures of this armored banana slug.

Fiat 2000 (Italy, 1917; 65mm): While heavily armored and bristling with seven machine guns, the slow F-2000 could barely outrun a briskly marching infantryman. Fortunately for its crews, it never had to try; it only served in peacetime.

M13/40 (Italy, 1940; 47mm): Lousy armor, weak gun, underpowered and unreliable engine, prone to stalling or catching fire when hit—what a combination. This bowser was the mainstay of Italian armor in North Africa. With equipment like this, who can blame Italian crews for bailing out of their tanks and surrendering?

Elefant tank destroyer (Germany, 1943; 88mm): A perennial candidate for Dumbest World War II Armor Design, the glacially slow Elefant mounted the famous 88mm cannon and looked like today's self-propelled howitzers. It had no machine guns of its own, so enemy infantry were welcome to spray tags on it or use its massive front housing as a latrine.

Churchill Crocodile (U.K., 1944; 75mm, flamethrower): Most World War II powers developed flamethrowing tanks; this was one of the best designs. The Crocodile pulled a trailer of modified gasoline "ammo" yet still mounted a standard tank cannon. Hosing flaming gas the length of a football field, the Croc was hell for dug-in defenders.

Sherman DD (U.S./U.K., 1944; 75mm): Tanks don't swim well, which is an issue when you're planning a D-Day. Allied engineers invented a watertight skirting for the Sherman so that it could float, and then added a little propeller for instant buoyancy—at least enough for the tank to reach the beach. Ten Sherman DD battalions, the equivalent of a full division, waded ashore this way on June 6, 1944. A number swamped and sank, but on that day any Allied tank on shore was very welcome.

Zap! Boeing's Flying Laser Cannon

Just when you thought the military has already come up with every conceivable way to wreak havoc on its adversaries, in 2008 the Pentagon announced that it had developed a new device that was so accurate, it could melt a hole through objects as small as a soda can from over five miles away.

✳ ✳ ✳ ✳

Reach Out and Fry Somebody

ALTHOUGH THE CONCEPT behind Boeing's Advanced Tactical Laser (ATL) began several years prior, the first ATL was tested in 2008. Weighing more than 40,000 pounds, the ATL was mounted in the belly of a C-130 Hercules turbo-prop cargo plane.

The ATL is related to the Airborne Laser, a smaller weapon still under development that would use a modified 747 with a focus on ballistic missiles. In addition to making Swiss cheese out of soda cans, the ATL is designed to fry trucks, tanks, ammunition dumps, and communication stations from a safe distance without the fallibilities of missiles and rockets that can be shot down and destroyed before they reach their targets.

The Three-Second Blast

Here's how it works: At the heart of the device are storage tanks that contain chlorine gas and hydrogen peroxide. When mixed together, a chemical reaction creates high-energy oxygen molecules that are sent through a mist of iodine. The resulting energy is converted into an intense form of light, or laser beam.

Stay with us here. After resonating through a series of mirrors, the laser beam travels through a long pipe and is adjusted for the external movements of the airplane and weather conditions. Just before the beam is delivered to its target through a revolving turret, it is "widened" to approximately 20 inches, condensed, and then focused on its target.

A series of onboard computers help to make microscopic adjustments in its path before delivering a burst of a few seconds of energy to the target. Each laser-equipped aircraft is capable of delivering up to 100 laser blasts before it needs to return to its home base for further refueling.

Hot Stuff

Similar to lasers used in the medical field, the ATL itself isn't hot, but it is capable of heating its target to more than several thousand degrees. If the target is a solid substance (such as an al-Qaeda jeep or a metal building), the laser is capable of melting it like ice cream on a hot summer sidewalk. While ATL technology is fascinating, its power is also disturbing: If the target is made from combustible material such as wood or paper, it will literally burst into flames.

A Safer Tool of Destruction

What makes the ATL such an effective weapon is that the laser beam can be delivered from a safe distance from the target, enabling the chance of an attack without having to actually be on location. The weapon can also send a number of lethal light beams to targets in different locations—all within a few seconds. Plus, unlike a gun or other arms, lasers are silent and invisible, enabling more covert operations.

But there are definitely some downsides to having such a complex weapon. For one, the ATL will toast anything in its path, such as people or a bird that has wandered into its trajectory. Another is that the laser's operation and accuracy depends largely on factors such as altitude, weather, and variables regarding geographic location—for instance, in the Middle East, visibility is limited due to blowing sand.

But, all things considered, experts feel that the ATL is a much "safer" tool of destruction because it reduces the collateral damage that is typical even with smart bombs.

Although the ATL completed its critical design review in 2004, it is still considered under development. The weapon is currently being tested by the Department of Defense. There are also plans to develop smaller, more streamlined versions that can be mounted on surface vehicles such as tanks and trucks.

Arlington National Cemetery

Arlington is much more than just a cemetery—it's a tribute to those who fought for freedom. Here are nine intriguing facts you probably didn't know.

1. The land was once owned by George Washington Parke Custis, who was the adopted grandson of President George Washington. The land, and the mansion built on it, passed via inheritance and marriage to Confederate General Robert E. Lee.

2. The property was confiscated by the U.S. government during the Civil War. The 200-acre tract was officially designated a military cemetery on June 15, 1864, by Secretary of War Edwin Stanton.

3. More than 300,000 people are buried there. They represent all of the nation's wars, from the Revolutionary War to the wars in Iraq and Afghanistan.

4. Those who died before the Civil War were reinterred after 1900.

5. Arlington National Cemetery boasts the second largest number of burials (for a national cemetery in the United States), after Calverton National Cemetery near Riverhead, New York.

6. An average of 28 funerals per day are conducted at Arlington National Cemetery. The flags on the cemetery grounds are flown at half-mast from a half-hour before the first funeral of the day until a half-hour after the final funeral ends. Funerals are not usually held on weekends.

7. The remains of an unknown serviceman from the Vietnam War, interred in 1984, were disinterred in 1998 after being positively identified as Air Force 1st Lt. Michael J. Blassie.

8. The Tomb of the Unknowns is guarded 24 hours a day by members of the 3rd U.S. Infantry, also known as "The Old Guard." They began guarding the tomb on April 6, 1948.

9. Among the famous people buried in Arlington National Cemetery are presidents William Howard Taft and John F. Kennedy, civil rights activist Medgar Evers, mystery writer Dashiell Hammett, Supreme Court justice Thurgood Marshall, arctic explorers Robert Peary and Matthew Henson, and band leader Glenn Miller. The resting places of some of the people mentioned in this book, such as Gregory "Pappy" Boyington (page 528) and Audie Murphy (page 557), can be found there as well.

Chapter 8

Law and Disorder

Odd Ordinances

✳ It's illegal for horses to eat fire hydrants in Marshalltown, Iowa.

✳ Presumably, it's all right to drink beer from a bucket in St. Louis. Just don't do it while sitting on the curb—that's against city law.

✳ Better wear shoes if you're getting behind the wheel in Alabama. Driving barefoot or in slippers is illegal.

✳ Youngstown, Ohio, has made it a crime to run out of gas.

✳ In Memphis, a law was passed to prohibit women from driving unless they have a man walking in front of the car while waving a red flag.

✳ You aren't allowed to ride public transportation in Atlanta if you have bad body odor.

✳ Putting salt on a railroad track could get you the death penalty in Alabama.

✳ Having an unusual haircut is against the law in Mesquite, Texas.

✳ The state of Washington has made it illegal to pretend your parents are rich.

✳ Don't give a baby coffee in Lynn, Massachusetts—it's illegal.

✳ No one other than a baby is allowed to ride in a baby carriage in Roderfield, West Virginia.

✳ Playing Scrabble in the moments before a politician's speech is against the law in Atwoodville, Connecticut.

True Tales of the Counterfeit House

On a hill overlooking the Ohio River in Monroe Township, Adams County, sat a house that wasn't what it seemed. Its modest size and quiet exterior hid countless architectural and historical secrets that earned it the nickname "The Counterfeit House."

✳ ✳ ✳ ✳

IN 1850, OLIVER Ezra Tompkins and his sister, Ann E. Lovejoy, purchased 118 acres and built a rather peculiar house to suit the needs of their successful home-based business. Tompkins and Lovejoy were counterfeiters who specialized in making fake 50-cent coins and $500 bills. They needed a house that could keep their secrets. Although passersby could see smoke escaping from the house's seven chimneys, only two of those chimneys were connected to working fireplaces; the others were fed by ductwork and filled with secret compartments. The front door featured a trick lock and a hidden slot for the exchange of money and products, and the gabled attic window housed a signal light.

The counterfeiting room was a windowless, doorless room in the rear of the house, accessible only through a series of trapdoors. A trapdoor in the floor led to a sizeable tunnel (big enough to fit a horse) that provided an escape route through the bedrock of the surrounding hills to a cliff. Although no records exist to support the imagined use of these features, local historians believe the reports to be true.

Visitors Not Welcome

While Lovejoy was in Cincinnati spending some of her counterfeit money, she was noticed by the police. A Pinkerton agent followed her home and watched as she opened the trick lock on the front door. He waited until she was inside, then followed her inside.

Immediately past the door, in a 10-foot by 45-foot hallway, Tompkins was waiting—and he beat the agent to death. To this day, bloodstains are still visible on the walls and floor. Tompkins and Lovejoy buried the agent's body in one of the nearby hills, and Tompkins used the hidden tunnel to escape to a friendly riverboat, collapsing the tunnel with explosives as he went. Lovejoy held a mock funeral for Tompkins and thus inherited his estate, although shortly after she went into debt and moved away.

Keeping Up the Counterfeit House

Although Tompkins never returned to the house, both his ghost and that of the agent were said to haunt it. Tourists reported seeing a man's shape in the front doorway and claimed that they felt unexplained cold spots and an unfamiliar "presence."

In 1896, a great-great uncle of Jo Lynn Spires, the last owner, purchased the property. It passed to Spires's grandparents in the 1930s, and Spires and her parents lived in the house with her grandfather. Although privately owned, the house was a tourist attraction, and Spires regularly kept the house clean, repaired, and ready for the stream of visitors that would trickle in each weekend. Unable to keep up with the repairs on the house, however, Spires moved into a trailer on the property in 1986. She continued to welcome approximately 1,000 tourists each summer.

In February 2008, windstorms caused severe damage to the house. One of the false chimneys blew apart, and the roof ripped off. Eventually, the house was demolished, and only its eerie memory lives on.

Strange Justice

Lawsuits can be very, very strange. The three stories included here are just the tip of the iceberg.

✳ ✳ ✳ ✳

He Ought to Get Some Credit for Trying

URING THE 1990S, a prisoner doing time in Virginia for breaking and entering and grand larceny came up with a novel way of getting someone else to pay for his troubles. Noting that his civil rights had been abused, he sued himself for violating his own religious beliefs by getting drunk. Because of excessive drinking, he maintained, he had failed to exercise good judgment and had committed the acts that led to his incarceration. The prisoner believed he was owed five million dollars for all this: three million for his wife and children for pain and suffering, and two million to make up for the salary he'd fail to earn during his 23-year sentence. Since he was behind bars, however, he had no money to pay in case the judgment went against (or would that be for?) him. He had a solution, though: As a prisoner, he was a "ward of the state," so the government should be responsible for his debts. Alas, he neither won nor lost, as the judge threw the case out of court.

Fear of Flying

An airline was found liable when a flight was too bumpy. Flying into a thunderstorm in 1995, a pilot for a large commercial jet failed to turn on the "fasten seat belt" signs, and passengers were caught by surprise in what they claimed was extremely violent turbulence. Some of the passengers not wearing seat belts were thrown from their seats, and many thought the plane was going down and that they were all going to die. Particularly traumatized, the suit claimed, were the children aboard the plane. In part, the lawsuit argued that the flight crew and those on the ground could have used radar to detect and avoid the storm. At the very least, the seat belt sign could have served as a warning. A jury granted the 13 passengers who sued a total of two million dollars for their emotional distress.

His Reputation Was at "Steak"

Who doesn't like a nice steak now and then? One man went to his local steak house, ordered a thick and juicy slab, and asked for the senior-citizen discount. There was one problem—he was only 31 years old, so the discount didn't apply. He sued the restaurant chain for age discrimination. Not only did the judge throw the claim out like a spoiled sirloin—he fined the man more than $8,500 for abusing the legal system.

DUI Nonsense

People drink and people drive, and then there are those who mix the two. Because that's against the law, the act of disguising the deed has become an art. But putting a penny under your tongue to pass a breath-analysis test will get you nowhere.

✳ ✳ ✳ ✳

DESPITE THE FACT that some people put an amazing amount of effort into it, there is no successful way to beat the breath alcohol testing devices that police officers use in field sobriety tests. Still, some genius at some point in time decided that placing a penny under the tongue would do the trick. Supposedly, when the copper in the penny combines with saliva, it sets off a chemical reaction powerful enough to disguise the smell of alcohol. But this preposterous proposition doesn't even have potential. The modern U.S. one-cent piece is composed of 97.5 percent zinc and only 2.5 percent copper. And zinc doesn't mask stink.

Some equally ineffective methods include mixing a tablespoon of mustard in some milk and drinking it (you'd have to be booze-addled to drive around with a supply of mustard and milk) and chewing on a wad of cotton (worse than nails on a chalkboard!) to absorb the offending "mouth alcohol."

John Myatt, Master Forger

When people hear the word forgery, they usually think of money. But legal currency isn't the only thing that can be faked.

❋ ❋ ❋ ❋

J OHN MYATT'S HUMOROUS lament, "Monet, Monet, Monet. Sometimes I get truly fed up doing Monet. Bloody haystacks," sounds curiously Monty Pythonesque, until you realize that he can do Monet—and Chagall, Klee, Le Corbusier, Ben Nicholson, and almost any other painter you can name, great or obscure. Myatt, an artist of some ability, was probably the world's greatest art forger. He took part in an eight-year forgery scam in the 1980s and '90s that shook the foundations of the art world.

Despite what one might expect, art forgery is not a victimless crime. Many of Myatt's paintings—bought in good faith as the work of renowned masters—went for extremely high sums. One "Giacometti" sold at auction in New York for $300,000, and as many as 120 of his counterfeits are still out there, confusing and distressing the art world. But Myatt never set out to break the law. Initially, Myatt would paint an unknown work in the style of one of the cubist, surrealist, or impressionist masters, and he seriously duplicated both style and subject. For a time, he gave them to friends or sold them as acknowledged fakes. Then he ran afoul of John Drewe.

The Scheme Begins

Drewe was a London-based collector who had bought a dozen of Myatt's fakes over two years. Personable and charming, he ingratiated himself with Myatt by posing as a rich aristocrat. But one day he called and told Myatt that a cubist work the artist had done in the style of Albert Gleizes had just sold at Christies for £25,000 ($40,000)—as a genuine Gleizes. Drewe offered half of that money to Myatt.

The struggling artist was poor and taking care of his two children. The lure of the money was irresistible. So the scheme developed that he would paint a "newly discovered" work by a famous painter and pass it to Drewe, who would sell it and then pay Myatt his cut—usually about 10 percent. It would take Myatt two or three months to turn out a fake, and he was only making about £13,000 a year (roughly $21,000)—hardly worthy of a master criminal.

One of the amazing things about this scam was Myatt's materials. Most art forgers take great pains to duplicate the exact pigments used by the original artists, but Myatt mixed cheap emulsion house paint with a lubricating gel to get the colors he needed. One benefit is that his mix dried faster than oil paints.

The Inside Man

Drewe was just as much of a master forger, himself. The consummate con man, he inveigled his way into the art world through donations, talking his way into the archives of the Tate Gallery and learning every trick of *provenance*, the authentication of artwork. He faked letters from experts and, on one occasion, even inserted a phony catalog into the archives with pictures of Myatt's latest fakes as genuine.

But as the years went by, Myatt became increasingly worried about getting caught and going to prison, so at last he told Drewe he wanted out. Drewe refused to let him leave, and Myatt realized that his partner wasn't just in it for the money. He loved to con people.

The Jig Is Up

The scam was not to last, of course. Drewe's ex-wife went to the police with incriminating documents, and when the trail led to Myatt's cottage in Staffordshire, he confessed.

Myatt served four months of a yearlong sentence, and when he came out of prison, Detective Superintendent Jonathan Searle of the Metropolitan Police was waiting for him. Searle suggested that since Myatt was now infamous, many people would love to own a real John Myatt fake. As a result, Myatt and his second wife Rosemary set up a tidy business out of their cottage. His paintings regularly sell for as much as £45,000 ($72,000), and Hollywood has shown interest in a movie—about the real John Myatt.

Subway Vigilante!

Bernhard Goetz shot four young men he said tried to rob him. The result was a national debate on vigilantism that still rages today.

✳   ✳   ✳   ✳

IT WAS LIKE a scene out of the Charles Bronson thriller *Death Wish*. Three days before Christmas in 1984, Bernhard Goetz, a white, mild-mannered electronics expert, shot four youths he claimed tried to rob him on a crowded Manhattan subway car. He then fled the scene, eventually turning himself into police in New Hampshire. The incident was headline news for weeks. Some hailed Goetz as a hero and commended him for standing up to thugs; others considered him just as bad as the young men he said tried to rob him.

Instinct or Malice?

According to accounts, it all went down quickly. The youths— Barry Allen, 18; Troy Canty, 19; James Ramseur, 19; and Darrell Cabey, 19—told police they were just panhandling money to play video games. Goetz, who had been mugged previously, claimed he felt threatened and believed the youths, all of whom were black, were going to rob him. When Canty demanded five dollars, Goetz rose, pulled a gun from beneath his windbreaker, and quickly fired five shots, striking each of his alleged assailants. All survived, though Cabey was left paralyzed and brain damaged when a bullet severed his spinal cord.

In the aftermath of the shooting, Goetz found himself a public figure. He gave only one interview, to the *New York Post*, in which he said, "I'm amazed at this celebrity status. I want to remain anonymous." But that was not to be.

In 1987, Goetz was acquitted of attempted murder and assault but found guilty of criminal possession of an unlicensed weapon. He spent 250 days in jail. Nine years later, Cabey and his family won a $43 million civil-court judgment against Goetz, who declared bankruptcy.

Lizzie Borden Did What?

Despite the famous playground verse that leaves little doubt about her guilt, Lizzie Borden was never convicted of murdering her father and stepmother.

❋　❋　❋　❋

THE SENSATIONAL CRIME captured the public imagination of late-19th-century America. On the morning of August 4, 1892, in Fall River, Massachusetts, the bodies of Andrew Borden and his second wife, Abby, were found slaughtered in the home they shared with an Irish maid and Andrew's 32-year-old daughter, Lizzie. A second daughter, Emma, was away from home at the time.

Rumors and Rhyme

Although Lizzie was a devout, church-going Sunday school teacher, she was charged with the horrific murders and was immortalized in this popular rhyme: "Lizzie Borden took an ax and gave her mother 40 whacks. When she saw what she had done, she gave her father 41." In reality, her stepmother was struck 19 times, killed in an upstairs bedroom with the same ax that crushed her husband's skull while he slept on a couch downstairs. In that gruesome attack, his face took 11 blows. One cut his eye in two. Another that severed his nose.

Andrew was one of the wealthiest men in Fall River. By reputation, he was also one of the meanest. The prosecution alleged that Lizzie's motivation for the murders was financial: She had hoped to inherit her father's estate. Despite the large quantity of blood at the crime scene, the police were unable to find any blood-soaked clothing worn by Lizzie when she allegedly committed the crimes.

Ultimately Innocent

Lizzie's defense counsel successfully had their client's contradictory inquest testimony ruled inadmissible, along with all evidence relating to her earlier attempts to purchase poison from a local drugstore. On June 19, 1893, the jury in the case returned its verdict of not guilty.

Fumbling Felons

All of us have probably had days where we wished we hadn't gotten out of bed. Criminals are no exception.

✳ ✳ ✳ ✳

Choose Your Designated Driver Carefully

MANY PEOPLE DRINK alcoholic beverages responsibly. If they do have a little too much, most designate a capable driver. In November 2007, however, a 41-year-old man in Clio, Michigan, made a few key mistakes in his choice. Despite the fact that the man selected his son as his designated driver, the two ended up stuck in the mud where police arrested them both—because his son was only 13 years old and also drunk.

He Was Only Reporting a Robbery

A man in south Texas called police to report a theft in 2007. Nothing unusual about that, right? Yet, the man told police that two masked gunmen had kicked in his door and stole 150 pounds of marijuana. He then explained to police that he was wrapping the drugs for shipment when the gunmen arrived. When police investigated the "crime," they found 15 pounds of the stuff lying on the man's floor. Not only did police charge the man with felony possession of marijuana, but he also turned out to be an illegal immigrant.

Half-Baked

After robbing two convenience stores in an hour, a man went for a third caper just a few hours later on September 30, 2007, in Delaware. The thief used a note that read, "Give me your money I'll shoot you." It was the same note used in the previous robberies. This time, however, the 25-year-old robber left his demand behind, and it just so happened to be written on the pay stub from his job at a local bakery. Along with fingerprints, the stub included the thief's full name.

Funny Money

In Gary, Indiana, a cafeteria worker broke up a money-counterfeiting scheme when she was handed a fake $20 bill. The culprit: a ten-year-old boy. He aroused her suspicion when he paid for lunch with the large bill, so she turned it in. Police say the boy enlisted the help of two of his friends and created the money on his home computer. In December 2005, the children faced charges of forgery and theft. The boys are the youngest counterfeiters the FBI has ever come across. Reportedly, the counterfeits were even pretty good.

Paper or Plastic?

Disguises can be tricky things—sure, they're great if they work, but every little detail has to be taken into account for that to happen. Especially details like, say, breathing. An Arkansas thief found this out when he broke into an electronics store. He had forgotten his disguise, so he grabbed the first thing he could find—an opaque plastic bag. Not only did the bag prevent him from seeing where he was going, it also didn't allow in any air. The robber spent several minutes stumbling and tripping through the store, then finally collapsed and crawled away.

Not willing to throw in the towel, the hardy crook was back a few minutes later with yet another plastic-bag disguise. This time, he had cut two eyeholes into the bag, which presumably let in some air as well. Fortified by fresh air, the crook managed to grab thousands of dollars worth of electronic equipment.

When the cops reviewed the surveillance footage, they found that in his haste, the thief had neglected to remove the nametag from his clothing—a security guard's uniform from the mall where the store was located. The cops quickly corralled the crook, and took him to a place where he was issued a number to go with his name.

Criminal Quickies

A police department in Ottawa, Canada, had to expel a cadet from its officer training school when they discovered he'd stolen a car to get to class on time.

In Benecia, California, two armed robbers stuck up a credit union only to discover it was one of many "cashless" credit unions in the state. It would've paid to do some research first.

When Long Beach, California, armed robber James Elliot's revolver misfired, he peered down the barrel to check out the problem. He didn't survive.

Jack the Ripper

Between 1888 and 1891, he brutally murdered at least five women in London's East End. Was there really a connection between Jack the Ripper and the British royal family?

✳ ✳ ✳ ✳

THE SERIAL KILLER known as Jack the Ripper is one of history's most famous murderers. He breathed terror into the gas-lit streets and foggy back alleys of the Whitechapel area of London and became renowned the world over. Despite the countless books and movies detailing his story, however, his identity and motives remain shrouded in mystery.

One of the most popular theories, espoused by the 2001 movie *From Hell* (starring Johnny Depp), even links the killer to the British royal family.

The Crimes

Five murders are definitively attributed to Jack the Ripper, and he has variously been connected to at least six other unsolved slayings in the London area. The body of the first victim, 43-year-old Mary Ann Nichols, was discovered on the morning of August 31, 1888. Nichols's throat had been cut and her abdomen mutilated. The subsequent murders, which took place over a three-year period, grew in brutality. The killer removed the uterus of his second victim, Annie Chapman; part of the womb and left kidney of Catherine Eddowes; and the heart of Mary Kelly. All of his victims were prostitutes.

The Name

A man claiming to be the murderer sent a letter (dated September 25, 1888) to the Central News Agency, which passed it along to the Metropolitan Police. The letter included the line, "I am down on whores and I shant quit ripping them till I do get buckled." It was signed, "Yours truly, Jack the Ripper." A later postcard included the same sign-off. When police went public with details of the letters, the name "Jack the Ripper" stuck.

The Suspects

Officers from the Metropolitan Police and Scotland Yard had four main suspects: a poor Polish resident of Whitechapel by the name of Kosminski, a barrister who committed suicide in December 1888, a Russian-born thief, and an American doctor who fled to the States in November 1888 while on bail for gross indecency. Since there was little or no evidence against any of these men, the case spawned many conspiracy theories, the most popular of which links the killings to the royal family.

The Royal Conspiracy

The heir to the British throne was Prince Albert Victor, grandson of Queen Victoria and son of the man who would later become King Edward VII. The prince, popularly known as Eddy, had a penchant for hanging around in the East End, and rumors abounded that he had a daughter, Alice, out of wedlock with a shop girl named Annie Crook. To prevent major embarrassment to the Crown, Eddy sought assistance from Queen Victoria's physician, Dr. William Gull, who institutionalized Annie to keep her quiet. However, her friends, including Mary Kelly, also knew the identity of Alice's father, so Dr. Gull created the persona of Jack the Ripper and brutally silenced them one by one. A variation on this theory has Dr. Gull acting without the knowledge of the prince, instead driven by madness resulting from a stroke he suffered in 1887.

Royal involvement would certainly explain why the police were unable to uncover the identity of the Ripper or to even settle on a prime suspect. There *was* a shop girl named Annie Crook who had an illegitimate daughter named Alice, but there is nothing to connect her to either the prince or the murdered prostitutes. In fact, there is no evidence to suggest that the murdered women knew one another. Until the identity of Jack the Ripper is settled beyond doubt, these and other conspiracy theories will likely persist.

The Eerie Austin Connection

Speaking of Jack the Ripper, here's another theory

✳   ✳   ✳   ✳

BEFORE JACK THE Ripper made his bloody trail through London, Austin experienced a similar murder spree. The Ripper-like murders began on New Year's Eve, 1884. Someone killed Mollie Smith, a servant girl, and put a large hole in her head. Two more women were butchered in similar attacks a few months later.

A Trail of Blood

The killings weren't limited to servants. As the Austin murder spree continued, victims became more upscale. Each death was a little more gory. The final murders recorded occurred on

Christmas Eve, 1885, almost a full year after they had begun. The victims included Mrs. Eula Phillips, a wealthy woman who, for amusement, worked as a prostitute. To stop the binge of killing, Austin police began questioning men on the streets after dark. The city erected "moonlight towers" to illuminate the streets. (Seventeen of those towers still light downtown Austin and are listed in the National Register of Historic Places.) The city's efforts were apparently successful, as the slaughter ended.

The Whitechapel Murders

The Ripper's physical description, style of killing, and victims seemed eerily similar to the Austin murders. Possible killers included a man called "the Malay Cook," who left Austin late in January 1886 and was interviewed in London in 1888. According to that interview, he said he'd been robbed by a woman "of bad character." Unless he recovered his money, he planned to murder and mutilate women in London's Whitechapel area.

Smooth Criminals? Not These Folks

If you're a law-abiding citizen, it's probably a comfort to realize that not all criminals are competent. Some are quite the opposite.

✳ ✳ ✳ ✳

Her Number Was Up

FORGERY IS ONE of those criminal techniques that takes considerable skill. It also helps to have an iota of common sense. For one Oregon woman, the time to try her hand at forgery had come. Standing in a convenience store with a state lottery ticket in her hand, she knew her ticket was a loser—just one number away from winning $20—but she didn't care. She wanted that money. The woman slipped to the back of the store, where she furtively altered the wrong number on the ticket into the winning one with a ballpoint pen.

The alert store clerk immediately spotted the forgery and called the police. The woman was arrested and charged with fraud. But then the arresting officer looked closer at the forged ticket. Squinting, he could just make out the original number underneath the pen mark. When he looked up at the chart of winning lottery numbers, he discovered that the original ticket had, in fact, been a winner—of $5,000.

(Try to) Drive My Car

At least the crook in this story had the right idea—getaway cars are for getaways. Of course, it's ideal if the car can actually be entered before the getaway takes place. At a Honolulu mall, a shoplifter grabbed several expensive ladies' handbags. He sprinted out of the store and headed for his car in the parking lot. Alerted by the store clerk, security guards gave chase.

For a moment, it seemed like the story had all the classic elements: a crime, a chase, and a getaway car ready for action. But when the thief dashed to his car, he stopped short. Seconds later, the guards caught up to him. Baffled, they asked why he had stopped when it seemed as if he was going to beat them to his car. The crook pointed inside the car: Dangling in the ignition were the thief's car keys. He had locked himself out.

Odd Laws in Ohio

Here kitty, kitty... In Canton, people are required to notify authorities within one hour of losing their pet tiger or any other dangerous animal.

Put away the chicken paint... It is against the law to sell any rabbit or baby poultry, including, but not limited to, chicks and ducklings, that have been colored with dye.

But it's better than a window seat... In Youngstown, it is illegal to ride on the roof of a taxi cab.

Don't try this at home... In Marion, it is against the law to eat a doughnut and walk backwards on a city street.

Hey, I'm talking here... Anyone can be nailed for a $25 fine in Ohio if they blatantly ignore a public speaker on Decoration Day by playing croquet or pitching horseshoes within one mile of the speaker's stand.

It sounds a little fishy to me... It is illegal in Ohio to fish for whales on a Sunday. It is also illegal to get a fish drunk, no matter what day of the week it is.

It's no reflection on you, ma'am... The wearing of patent leather shoes in public by women is prohibited in Cleveland in order to prevent men from using the reflection as a way to peer up a woman's skirt.

What about thumb wrestling?... It is forbidden for anyone to hold office in Ohio who has participated in a duel.

Clamping down on extreme cruising... In Oxford, it is against the law to drive around the town square more than 100 times in a single session.

You Don't Need Help With That

The creation of 911 as an emergency response number has been an unqualified success. Fires are put out, people are rescued and lives are saved every minute of every day. But then there are those people who make calls that leave dispatchers—and everyone else—just scratching their heads.

❊   ❊   ❊   ❊

"My son won't clean his room." A father of a 28-year-old (yes, 28 year-old!!) called 911 to report that his son wouldn't clean his room. Police responded and took a hard line with the offender who burst into tears and promised to shape up.

"My husband is watching porn!" When a teary female called 911 to report an emergency, officers hurried to her home expecting a domestic dispute. They found her husband watching porn. Questionable judgment perhaps, but no real grounds to arrest him. They referred her to a therapist.

"Burger King won't give it to me 'my way!!'" When a woman called 911 to report that Burger King wasn't living up to their ad slogan, the dispatcher was unsympathetic, refusing to send officers to the scene. It was a whopper of a disagreement, but the restaurant chain committed no actual crime.

"They're out of McNuggets." In another restaurant emergency, police responded after a woman called 911 three times to report that McDonald's was out of Chicken McNuggets and the cashier didn't want to give her a refund. The distraught woman was promptly arrested for misuse of the 911 system and taken to jail with no dinner at all.

"I'm locked in my car!!" This sounds like a legitimate concern and even a danger in Florida's summer heat. So what's the problem? The able-bodied woman hadn't thought to pull up the door lock – a simple fix that freed her within seconds.

"I just don't get this math!" When a little boy called 911 because he didn't understand a math problem, an understanding – and math-savvy officer – not only responded but helped the young student. That's going beyond the call of duty! Thanks, officer.

"My drug dealer changed my product!" When a woman's drug dealer started adding hallucinogens to her crack, she called 911 to complain. While fixing that problem was not within the realm of a 911 response, officers were definitely interested in chatting with them both.

"Those young kids damaged my car!" When an older gentleman called 911 to report that a couple of girls had damaged the paint on his car, officers determined that the white substance found on his vehicle actually came from a couple of fowls, rather than foul play.

"It's a blizzard!" A Canadian driver called 911 in January to complain that the local radio station had forecast flurries when the precipitation coming down was clearly a snowstorm. Wow.

"Talk to me, please." An unemployed man who called 911 because the calls were "free" is now facing a $1,000 fine or six months in jail. The man, who said he was lonely, called 911 more than 27,000 times. Some days he placed several hundred calls to emergency responders, often disguising his voice and making strange noises. Police found him by tracing his cell phone signal. Right back atcha.

Wedding Police Blotter

In these real-life examples of weddings-gone-wild, there's plenty of fodder for front page headlines. When police arrived at these nuptials, they encountered all sorts of disturbances, from fistfights to shouting matches.

✳ ✳ ✳ ✳

Crowbar Crasher: When Lisa Coker showed up at her ex-boyfriend's wedding reception, she didn't come empty-handed. Coker brought a crowbar and a razor blade to the Tampa, Florida, affair. After fighting with the mother of the groom, who then required 16 stitches, Coker was arrested.

Groom vs. Fashion Police: John Lucas, age 53, was arrested during his own wedding reception when a police officer working the event attempted to enforce the venue's dress code. Apparently, Lucas's nephew appeared at the Kenner, Louisiana, reception dressed in sagging pants. A police officer asked the teenager to pull up his pants, and he refused. Before long, the groom entered the fray and was arrested for disturbing the peace.

Outspoken Ex-Girlfriend: When Marie Salomon attended the Bridgeport, Connecticut, wedding ceremony of her ex-boyfriend, the minister uttered the weighted phrase: "Speak now or forever hold your peace." Salomon stood and yelled her objections in the middle of the ceremony. Eventually, police were called to the scene, and Salomon was charged with breaching the peace and trespassing.

Attack of the Bride's Sister: Annmarie Bricker wasn't invited to her sister's Hebron, Indiana, wedding reception, but she went anyway. Bricker wanted to talk out a few family problems, and by the time police arrived, the 23-year-old had wrestled the bride to the ground and pulled out clumps of the woman's hair. Bricker was arrested on a misdemeanor battery charge and later resigned from her job as a 911 dispatcher.

Newlyweds Cash In: Brian Dykes and Mindy McGhee wed at a quaint chapel in Sevierville, Tennessee, then promptly robbed the place. After the wedding, the couple waited until the cover of darkness and then stole a cash-filled lockbox from the chapel. They were later found at a local restaurant where they confessed to the $500 theft and were jailed on $10,000 bonds.

Right in the Kisser: How can a prenuptial party go wrong? When the groom kisses the bride's friend, for starters. The bride's 12-year-old son reported that her fiancé had smooched one of the female attendees. The bride-to-be tackled the groom, punched him in the face, threw his watch in the bushes, and broke his glasses. The Poulsbo, Washington, woman was jailed on assault charges.

Bride and Groom Brawl: Pittsburgh, Pennsylvania, newlyweds David and Christa Wielechowski spent the night in jail after duking it out in a hotel hallway. The couple insisted they were joking when the groom kicked his vociferous bride squarely in the rear. When hotel guests came to the bride's rescue and restrained the groom, the bride attacked them. The brawl then moved into an elevator and to the hotel lobby, drawing more guests to the fracas. The groom—a local dentist—was booked into the county jail with a black eye and only one shoe. His bride, still wearing her wedding gown, was in a separate holding cell.

Nancy Drew and the Hardy Boys: The Mystery of the Ghostwriters

Nancy Drew and the Hardy Boys may be aces at uncovering secrets, but the real secret lies in the origins of these teen detective novels. The credited authors—Carolyn Keene and Franklin W. Dixon—are as fictitious as the teen sleuths themselves. And all are the brainchildren of early 20th-century children's literature magnate Edward Stratemeyer.

✳ ✳ ✳ ✳

Fiction Factory

EDWARD STRATEMEYER WAS a successful juvenile fiction writer—so successful that he didn't have time to finish all of the books assigned to him. So he assembled a group of ghostwriters to help, and around 1904–1906 (sources vary), Stratemeyer Syndicate was born.

The process functioned like an assembly line: Stratemeyer developed the outlines and character descriptions, farmed them to ghostwriters who worked under the pseudonym assigned to each series, and then edited each story to ensure consistency across the series. The ghostwriters received a meager $75 to $150 and gave up "all right, title and interest" as well as "use [of] such pen name in any manner whatsoever."

Mystery Makers

Following the syndicate's first successful ventures—the Bobbsey Twins and Tom Swift—Stratemeyer masterminded what would become his greatest legacies. In 1927, mystery-solving teen brothers Frank and Joe Hardy, aka the Hardy Boys, debuted, authored primarily by Canadian writer Leslie McFarlane under the pseudonym Franklin W. Dixon. Two years later, all-American girl sleuth Nancy Drew hit the scene, written mostly by Mildred Wirt under the pen name Carolyn Keene. Fun fact: Stratemeyer first wanted to name his heroine

Stella Strong, with alternate suggestions of Diana Drew, Diana Dare, Nan Nelson, Nan Drew, and Helen Hale. Publishers Grosset & Dunlap were the ones who chose Nan Drew and lengthened it to Nancy.

Unfortunately, Stratemeyer would not live to see the success of Nancy Drew; he died just two weeks after the first books, *The Secret of the Old Clock*, *The Hidden Staircase*, and *The Bungalow Mystery*, hit stands in April 1930.

Initially, Stratemeyer's daughters, Edna and Harriet, hoped to sell the syndicate, but it was the height of the Great Depression, and buyers were scarce. So the two sisters took over the business. They managed the ghostwriters and, above all, endeavored to keep their authors' identities secret.

Ghostbusters

In 1958, Grossett & Dunlap, requested an update of the books for contemporary audiences. (For example, Nancy's car was updated in 1959 from a roadster to a convertible. Today she drives a hybrid.) Harriet, who had severed the syndicate's ties with Mildred Wirt five years earlier, assumed the rewriting of Nancy Drew herself and even added new titles to the series. Suddenly, despite her previous reticence, Harriet began claiming publicly that she was the real Carolyn Keene and always had been.

In 1980, Harriet sold the Nancy Drew series to Simon & Schuster, who made national fanfare over the series' 50th anniversary, touting Harriet as the originator. Wirt, along with Grossett & Dunlap, promptly sued—and promptly lost. The media had a field day with the "real" Carolyn Keene.

Simon & Schuster subsumed the entire syndicate after Harriet's death in 1982. Despite evidence to the contrary, her obituary lamented the passing of the real Carolyn Keene.

Twenty years later, Mildred Wirt's did the same.

More Fumbling Felons

These folks should have considered another line of work.

✳ ✳ ✳ ✳

Better to Use OnStar

THERE MUST BE a lesson here. If you drive a stolen car, don't ask police for roadside assistance. In 2007, Dean Gangl of Richmond, Minnesota, did just that. After the vehicle he stole went into a ditch, he flagged a passerby for help. Unfortunately for Gangl, the motorist passing by just happened to be an off-duty deputy sheriff. The officer recognized the car as one that had been reported stolen in St. Cloud a few hours earlier. Then during the routine arrest for auto theft, the deputy discovered Gangl was also in possession of a white crystal substance—methamphetamine.

This Crime Doesn't Add Up

The would-be robber who walked into a Fairfield, Connecticut, Dunkin' Donuts should have waited for a response from the cashier before acting on his own. The perp handed the clerk a note threatening that he had a bomb and a gun, and that he'd use both if he didn't get money right away. But apparently he got antsy, and without waiting for a reply, he grabbed what he thought was the cash register and ran from the store. Alas, no cash for him—the man took off with an adding machine.

Overdrawn Check

A Texan named Charles Fuller said he planned to start a record company when he tried to cash a personal check for $360 billion at a Fort Worth Bank. He said his girlfriend's mother had given him the check. She denied it. Guess who police believed?

Not For Sale

Have you ever gone to a garage sale and thought to yourself, "Oh, I have one of these I could sell"? Well, that happened to a woman in Severn, Maryland—literally. When she attended a yard sale three doors down from her home, she found almost $25,000 worth of stuff that previously had been stolen from her. She immediately called the police. When they arrived, they arrested David Perticone, who admitted that he had taken the items. His excuse: He needed money to purchase cocaine and heroine with his girlfriend. Oh, and he thought the house was abandoned, and that he may as well clear it out before the stuff was thrown in the dump. See? He was just trying to help!

That's a Crime Too

✳ In Alabama, you can't play dominos on Sunday.

✳ In Kansas, you can't sell cherry pie with ice cream on a Sunday.

✳ Providence, Rhode Island, doesn't allow stores to sell toothpaste on Sunday.

✳ Columbus, Ohio, made it illegal to sell corn flakes on a Sunday.

✳ You can't even cross the street on Sunday in Marblehead, Massachusetts.

✳ Selling suntan oil after noon on Sunday is a crime in Provincetown, Massachusetts.

✳ Humming on the street on Sunday is illegal in Cicero, Illinois.

✳ Hunting is illegal in Virginia on Sundays. That is, except for raccoons—you can hunt them until 2 A.M.

✳ Kissing your wife is a Sunday no-no in Hartford, Connecticut.

✳ In Houston, it's illegal to sell Limburger cheese on Sundays.

Stars Behind Bars!

Most actors have done their time working their way up the ladder through roles in B-movies, television, or theater. But a surprising number of actors have literally done time—as in prison time. Here's a sample:

✳ ✳ ✳ ✳

Lillo Brancato

BRANCATO PLAYED ROBERT De Niro's son in *A Bronx Tale* (1993) and a bumbling mobster on *The Sopranos*. But drug addiction took its toll on his career. In December 2005, Brancato and a friend broke into an apartment looking for drugs. In the process, an off-duty policeman was shot and killed. Brancato was charged with second-degree murder and attempted burglary. He was acquitted on the murder charges in 2008 but served time for attempted burglary.

Errol Flynn

One of the most popular leading men in Hollywood history, Errol Flynn frequently found himself in trouble with the law. His various stints behind bars included two weeks in a New Guinea jail for hitting an Asian man who addressed him without the prefix "Mr." and several days in lock-up for striking a customs officer in the tiny African country of Djibouti.

Stacy Keach

In the mid-1980s, the star of the acclaimed Western *The Long Riders* (1980) served six months in prison for smuggling cocaine into England.

Paul Kelly

Paul Kelly played lead roles in many B-films, mostly crime melodramas. In the late 1920s, he killed his best friend, actor Ray Raymond, in a fistfight over Raymond's wife, actress Dorothy MacKaye. He served two years for manslaughter, then went on to a successful film and stage career.

Robert Mitchum

As a teenager in the 1930s, Mitchum was arrested for vagrancy in Georgia and was sentenced to a week's work on a chain gang, but he escaped the first chance he got. In California, in 1948, the movie tough guy served 50 days in jail for marijuana possession.

Tommy Rettig

As a child actor, Rettig gained lasting fame as Lassie's master in the popular 1950s TV series. But in 1972, he was arrested for growing marijuana, and in the mid-1970s, he was sentenced to five and a half years in prison for smuggling cocaine into the U.S. The charges were dropped after an appeal, as was another drug charge five years later.

O. J. Simpson

A football Hall of Famer whose movies include *Capricorn One* (1978) and *The Naked Gun* (1988), Simpson was acquitted of the murder of his ex-wife, Nicole Brown, in 1995. In December 2008, the football superstar was handed a sentence of 9 to 33 years in prison for armed robbery and kidnapping as a result of a botched attempt to get back items Simpson claimed a sports memorabilia dealer had stolen from him.

Christian Slater

In 1989, Slater was involved in a drunken car chase that ended when he crashed into a telephone pole and kicked a policeman while trying to escape. He was charged with evading police, driving under the influence, assault with a deadly weapon (his boots), and driving with a suspended license. In 1994, Slater was arrested for trying to bring a gun onto a plane. In 1997, he was sentenced to 90 days in jail for cocaine abuse, battery, and assault with a deadly weapon.

Mae West

In 1926, Mae West, one of Hollywood's most iconic sex symbols, was sentenced to ten days in jail when her Broadway show, *Sex*, was declared obscene.

Show-and-Tell Hell

What did you take to show-and-tell when you were in preschool and kindergarten? Well, things have gotten a lot wilder since then. If nothing else, this list should convince you that it's a good idea to check your child's backpack before sending him or her off to school!

✳   ✳   ✳   ✳

CRACK COCAINE DOESN'T really belong in a backpack. Believe it or not, a first grader from Louisiana brought the narcotic as his show-and-tell item, prompting officials to arrest the boy's mother for improper child supervision.

Continuing in that same vein, a six-year-old brought **marijuana** to school for show-and-tell, along with a pipe so he could demonstrate the drug's use for his classmates. Needless to say, his teacher wasn't chill with it, and the boy's father was arrested for child endangerment.

A second grader from Texas looking for an explosive show-and-tell item hit the mark when he brought a **hand grenade** into school, prompting a school-wide evacuation. The grenade later turned out to be inactive, but it sure looked real! No word on whether or not the second-grade teacher had the courage to continue with show-and-tell after that incident.

Not to be outdone, a student in Des Moines, Iowa, brought in an entire bag of **shell casings**, which she had taken as souvenirs during a trip to a South Dakota ranch. The casings had the word "blank" imprinted on them, but the 12-year-old was suspended anyway for violation of the school's weapons policy. Needless to say, her parents were not pleased.

That's a Crime Too

* In Chicago, serving whiskey to a dog is against the law.

* Fishing tackle isn't allowed in cemeteries in Muncie, Indiana.

* Shooting rabbits from motorboats is illegal in Kansas.

* You can't take your French poodle to the opera in Chicago.

* Hartford, Connecticut, has made it illegal for dogs to go to school.

* Cats and dogs can't fight in the town of Barber, North Carolina.

* A dentist who pulls the wrong tooth from a patient in South Foster, Rhode Island, can be required to have the same tooth removed from his own mouth by a blacksmith.

* Mannequins can only be dressed behind closed shades in Atlanta.

* Any woman weighing 200 pounds or more is forbidden from riding a horse while wearing shorts in the town of Gurnee, Illinois.

* Putting a skunk in a boss's desk is a crime in Michigan.

* It's illegal to fall asleep during a haircut in Erie, Pennsylvania.

* In Florida, snoozing under the hair dryer is prohibited.

* Sleeping in the fridge is illegal in Pittsburgh.

* Any man shaving his chest is breaking the law in Omaha, Nebraska.

* Mispronouncing the city name is illegal in Joliet, Illinois.

* Snoring so loudly that your neighbors can hear you is illegal in Dunn, North Carolina.

* Throwing a knife at anyone wearing a striped suit is illegal in Natoma, Kansas.

* Oxford and Cleveland, Ohio, made it illegal for women to wear leather shoes at voting polls.

If It Exists, It Can Be Stolen

Turns out the five-finger discount can net an enterprising criminal some truly memorable merchandise.

✳ ✳ ✳ ✳

ALMOST ANYONE COULD steal a candy bar. And many a shoplifter has gotten away with food, clothing, and DVDs. Cell phones and jewelry? Pretty easy. Famous paintings and valuables kept under lock and key get a little harder. But the following items really take the cake!

6,000 Pounds of Cheesecake Near Orlando

Now that's really taking the cake. It happened when Gary LaSalle left the cooling unit running on his refrigerated rig for the night with 6,000 pounds of unattended, chilling cheesecake. When he came back the next day, he found his $50,000 truck, $120,000 trailer, and all those cheesecakes, missing. Whoever ate them isn't talking.

The Kia Gorilla from Simi Valley, California

King Kong he is not, but this 350-pound inflatable primate would be just as identifiable for anyone trying to sell him. The gorilla, who was perched on the roof of an auto showroom, sometimes deflated in the wind, so owners assumed that's what had occurred—until they climbed up there and found he was long gone. Due to his size, it would probably have taken two or three thieves to free the gorilla, but residents have been warned to be on the lookout in case he's still on the loose.

Tons of Sand in Jamaica

This was not the the work of a pickpocket. In fact, investigators estimate that hundreds of truckloads of sand were hauled from a Jamaican beach. The resort hotel industry is under suspicion since sandy beaches are a must to attract tourists. Insiders believe a police cover-up may have contributed to the success of this heavy heist.

Hulk Hogan's Toilet Seat in Florida

This theft is no mystery, but that doesn't make it any less bizarre. When Hulk Hogan separated from his wife Linda, she ignored court orders and walked away with a variety of items that were supposed to remain as part of the house sale. These included a bathtub, tanning bed, chandelier, and yes, the Hulk's antique wooden toilet seat. She claims to be using it as a picture frame.

A 400-Pound Bronze Elephant in Texas

Bon Bon Babar was almost like a family pet, except that he wasn't real. The 400-pound bronze statue graced the front yard of the Darnell family in Garland, Texas. The elephant, a gift from wife to husband, disappeared in broad daylight, leaving the couple heartbroken. They offered $500 for Bon Bon's safe return, but so far no one has trumpeted his whereabouts.

A 38-Foot Steel Bridge in Russia

Workers planning to cross a Russian river at the usual spot were in for a surprise when they arrived to find the 200-ton bridge gone. Apparently thieves dismantled the bridge in the dead of night in order to sell the scrap metal on the black market. The replacement bridge will be concrete.

300 Manhole Covers Throughout Los Angeles

In another scrap metal heist, two manhole bandits single-handedly stole more than 300 manhole covers around Los Angeles. They were either very strong or very stupid or both. The covers, weighing 300 pounds each, fetched the thieves a mere $6.00 apiece for their trouble.

A Live, Full-Grown Shark Near Hampshire, UK

Unknown thieves climbed a ladder and stole a mama shark from an aquarium. The two-foot-long brown shark was discovered missing when its owner found the shed door open, the lights on—and the aquarium empty. The missing shark, worth roughly $5,000, had recently given birth to six babies. What do you do with a stolen shark? We suggest those thieves beware.

Ludicrous Laws in the Lone Star State

✳ Public buildings in El Paso, such as stores, banks, hotels, railroad and bus depots, and churches, are required to supply spittoons for those who chew tobacco (or don't but just need to spit anyway).

✳ It's against the law in Dallas to throw anything out the window or door of a tall building.

✳ The Texas Supreme Court allows public funds to pay for utilities and ice for the governor's mansion but not for groceries and personal items.

✳ Although the law specifically states that "no religious test shall ever be required as qualification to any office," politicians must acknowledge a supreme being to hold public office in the state of Texas. No particular supreme being is identified, however, so all those followers of Zeus, Apollo, Poseidon, and the rest of the Greek pantheon can step right up.

✳ Elevators must be odor-free in Abilene.

✳ There can be no late-night parties or Irish wakes in the city cemeteries of Brownsville, as the consumption or possession of alcohol is illegal there. It is, however, legal to bury a bottle of whiskey with the deceased.

✳ City ordinances in El Paso prohibit "a person from playing ball, shinny [a form of ice hockey] or any other games or skating on or along any street in the city."

✳ Parking lot owners in Grapevine can be fined for endangering public health and safety and charged with a misdemeanor offense if their lots emit dust, sand, or dirt.

✳ It's against the law for someone to drive a horse and buggy through the town square of Temple. But if that same person wants to unhook the buggy and saddle up the horse, it's perfectly legal there to ride that horse into the saloon.

✳ Keep your hands to yourself when it comes to the livestock! It's illegal to milk someone else's cow.

You're Suing Me For What?

The law can protect us, but it can also subject us to strange lawsuits that seem custom-written for late-night monologues. Here are seven of the oddest and most amusing lawsuits.

✳   ✳   ✳   ✳

Thongs of Pain: They may not be the most comfortable things, but it turns out thongs can also injure you—at least, according to a 2008 lawsuit filed against Victoria's Secret. A woman claimed her thong snapped while she was putting it on and ended up hitting her in the eye. The underwear apparently had metal links holding a jewel in place on its waistband, which, upon contact caused her "excruciating pain."

Bathroom Explosion: A bank president sued a construction company after the toilet in his executive bathroom flooded. The water "came blasting up out of the toilet with such force it stood him right up," the man claimed, and the resulting media coverage wiped away his good reputation. A judge didn't buy it.

Reality Show Regurgitation: Sure, bad reality TV is painful to watch, but is it bad enough to warrant a $2.5 million lawsuit? In 2005, Austin Aitken sued NBC over its *Fear Factor* program. The man said the show's disgusting displays caused him to become lightheaded, then vomit and run into a doorway. The courtroom tribunal voted him off the stand, and he didn't get a dime of NBC's dough.

Beer Disappointment: Getting a buzz wasn't enough for one Michigan beer drinker. In 1991, he decided to sue Anheuser-Busch for $10,000, saying the company's Bud Light commercials provided false and misleading advertising. His beef? The ads depicted regular guys having a grand time with beautiful women while drinking the beer, and no matter how many cold ones he pounded back, this kind of "unrestricted merriment" just wasn't occurring. It's probably no surprise that this lawsuit fell flat.

Killer Whale Confusion: The killer whale really needs to make its intentions more clear. In 1999, a man snuck past security guards at SeaWorld Orlando to take a late-night swim. He was later found naked and dead in a killer whale's tank. His parents sued the park, saying there was no kind of "public warning" that the animal known as the killer whale might be inclined to, well, kill someone. SeaWorld described the lawsuit as being "as crazy as they come."

Mistaken Celebrity: Most people would love to be mistaken for a successful celebrity. But in 2006, Allen Heckard from Oregon found the fact that he looked like Michael Jordan insulting—so much so that he sued both Jordan and Nike, the shoe company he blamed for making Jordan a household name. Heckard said he'd experienced emotional pain and suffering from people noticing his resemblance to the NBA star. He asked for $832 million, leading one news agency to say the case was "so outrageous that it actually [gave] frivolous lawsuits a bad name."

Bathroom Bother: What does a guy have to do to use the bathroom in peace? A man attending a 1995 Billy Joel and Elton John concert in San Diego claimed to have seen women in every restroom he tried to use at the stadium. The fellow said the sightings caused him emotional distress, and he sued the stadium and city for $5.4 million. Probably even more distressing to him: He lost.

Murder at the Garden

The world was fascinated when a skirt-chasing Gilded Age architect died atop the landmark he designed.

✳ ✳ ✳ ✳

CONCERTS BY SUPERSTARS the likes of Jimi Hendrix, Elvis Presley, John Lennon, Michael Jackson, Frank Sinatra, and Barbra Streisand; legendary boxing matches featuring Joe Louis, Rocky Marciano, Sugar Ray Robinson, Joe Frazier, and Muhammad Ali; home games of basketball's New York Knicks and ice hockey's New York Rangers. These are just some of the events that have taken place at Madison Square Garden since the first of its four incarnations was constructed in 1879. Yet, perhaps the most notorious Garden event was the cold-blooded murder of the man who designed the second Garden, located like its predecessor at 26th Street and Madison Avenue.

That man's name was Stanford White, and his 1906 Garden shooting in front of a high-society audience led to the "Trial of the Century." (A somewhat premature title? It would subsequently be shared with court cases starring, among others, Leopold and Loeb, John Scopes, Gloria Vanderbilt, the Nazis at Nuremberg and O. J. Simpson). Indeed, the aforementioned witnesses were not only elevated in terms of their social status but also in terms of their location, since the crime took place at the venue's rooftop theater during the premiere of the saucy musical *Mam'zelle Champagne*. Soon, the general public was abuzz with gossip about the sex and jealousy that gave rise to the murder.

Mirrors and a Swing

Stanford White was not only the esteemed architect of numerous neoclassical New York City public buildings and private mansions, he was also a notorious (and married) womanizer who enjoyed assignations at a downtown loft apartment where he had installed a red velvet swing so that his girls could "entertain" him. A standout among them was Evelyn Nesbit, a beautiful artists' model and chorus girl who had met "Stanny" shortly after relocating from Pittsburgh to New York in 1901. At the time, she was 16; he was 47. As Nesbit would later recall, it was during their second rendezvous at the apartment on West 24th Street, where some walls and ceilings were covered in mirrors, that the redhead "entered that room as a virgin" and emerged with a little more experience.

Thereafter, while White continued treating nubile girls to his swing and mirrors, Nesbit embarked on a relationship with—and was twice impregnated by—young actor John Barrymore. Yet, it was the details of her affair with White that tormented Harry Kendall Thaw, the man whom Nesbit married in 1905. The son of a Pittsburgh coal and railroad tycoon, Thaw was a violent, drug-addicted ne'er-do-well who also had a taste for chorus girls. When he met Nesbit, the stage was set for a tragic showdown.

White's first bad move was to make less-than-complimentary remarks about Thaw to some ladies they both were pursuing. When Thaw learned about these cracks, he wasn't exactly delighted. His annoyance turned to jealous rage when, after he somehow turned on the charm to woo Nesbit, she admitted that she kept declining his proposals of marriage because "Stanny" had taken her virginity. This only made Thaw more determined, and after he forced his marriage proposals—and himself—on the social-climbing Nesbit, the chorus beauty finally relented.

A Pistol in His Pocket

According to Nesbit, she was continually brutalized by Thaw, and his preoccupation with her deflowering at the hands of "The Beast" finally exploded in violence on the night of June 25, 1906. It was on that evening that the Thaws happened to dine at the Café Martin where White, his son, and a friend were also eating. Like White, the Thaws were planning to attend the play's premiere at the Madison Square Roof Garden, and at some point Harry must have learned about this. After dropping Evelyn off at their hotel so that he could arm himself, he reappeared in a black overcoat (despite the summer heat), whisked his young wife off to the show, and paced nervously up and down between the dinner-theater tables before White arrived at around 10:50 P.M. Thaw continued to hover for the next 15 minutes, until an onstage rendition of a song unfortunately titled "I Could Love a Million Girls" inspired him to approach the seated architect and shoot him three times from point-blank range.

One bullet entered White's left eye, killing him instantly; the other two grazed his shoulders as he fell off his chair. However, since two stage performers had just engaged in a dueling dialogue, most audience members thought the shooting was all part of the fun—until several witnesses screamed. At that point, according to the following day's *Times*, the theater manager leapt onto a table and demanded that the show must go on. Yet, when "the musicians made a feeble effort at gathering their wits" and "the girls who romped on the stage were paralyzed with horror," the manager informed his audience that an accident had occurred and they should leave quietly.

Arrested near the venue's elevators, Thaw asserted that White "deserved it . . . I can prove it. He ruined my life and then deserted the girl." However, according to another witness quoted in the *Times*, Thaw claimed that "Stanny" had ruined his *wife*, not his life.

Either way, after the jury at this first "Trial of the Century" was deadlocked, Thaw's plea of insanity at the second resulted in his imprisonment at a state hospital for the criminally insane. Released in 1913 and judged sane in 1915—the year he granted Evelyn a divorce—he was again judged insane and sentenced to an asylum two years later for assaulting and horsewhipping a teenage boy.

In the Aftermath

The 1955 movie *The Girl in the Red Velvet Swing*, starring Joan Collins as Evelyn Nesbit, Ray Milland as Stanford White, and Farley Granger as Harry Kendall Thaw, recounts the love-triangle murder. An even more fictionalized account was provided in James Cagney's final feature film, *Ragtime* (1981) with Norman Mailer as White and Elizabeth McGovern as Nesbit.

Following the first two incarnations of the Garden that were constructed at 26th Street and Madison Avenue in 1879 and 1890, Madison Square Garden III opened at 50th Street and Eighth Avenue in 1925. The current version of the indoor arena, located at 8th Avenue and 33rd Street, opened in 1968.

Interesting Animal Laws

* In Alaska, you can't look at a moose from an airplane.

* In Corpus Christi, Texas, you can't raise alligators in your home.

* It's illegal to imitate an animal in Miami.

* Ohioans need a license to keep a bear.

* Utah drivers must beware: Birds have the right of way on all public highways.

* Oftentimes, a homeowner's insurance premiums will increase if they decide to adopt an exotic or unusual pet.

* In Madison, Wisconsin, divorcing couples must be aware that joint custody is not allowed for family pets. Custody is awarded to the party who is in possession of the animal at the time of the divorce.

* Choose your exotic pets well: Zoos will usually refuse to accept pets, and in most places it's against the law to release animals into the wild. Now *what* are you going to do with that pet panther?

* In French Lick Springs, Indiana, there was once a law that required black cats to wear bells around their necks on Friday the 13th.

- In most villages, towns, and cities, it's illegal to take in a wild animal as a pet.
- In Oregon, you can be fined up to $6,250 and face up to a year in jail if you adopt an endangered animal.
- In most jurisdictions, keeping a deer in your backyard is illegal.
- Many states, including Minnesota, Wyoming, Georgia, California, and Kentucky, ban the private ownership of primates as pets.
- In Florida, it is illegal to have sexual relations with a porcupine.
- Tying a giraffe to a telephone pole is against the law in Atlanta.
- In Arizona, you can't shoot a camel.
- Blindfolding cows on highways in Arkansas is illegal.
- Punching a bull in the nose is illegal in Washington, D.C.
- It's a crime to swim with a deer in water higher than its knees in North Carolina.
- Giving booze to fish is illegal in Oklahoma.
- Giving a lit cigar to a pet is against the law in Zion, Illinois.
- Bothering a butterfly will result in a $500 fine in California.

Northern Justice: Canada's Weird Laws

Canada is one of the world's most peaceful and underpopulated countries, so naturally one would think it would be easy to keep the citizens in line. So then why are all these strange laws still on the books?

✳ ✳ ✳ ✳

Scamming the Queen

CANADA IS STILL technically a constitutional monarchy, so when Her Royal Highness visits, you'd best show some respect! For instance, it's a severe offense to sell the queen shoddy or defective merchandise.

Slaying Sasquatch

Some folks outside of Canada call it Bigfoot, but no matter what the name, it's against the law to hunt or shoot the fabled man-beast, rumored to live in the forests of British Columbia. Since the creature is presumably a human ancestor, plugging the 'Squatch gets the hunter dangerously close to a murder rap. Sasquatch is reportedly timid, but if it charges, you'd better hope that your interspecies negotiation skills are in top order.

No Fake Witches

Canada has complete freedom of religion, so if you're claiming to be a witch, you better be the real thing. Genuine witches, or wiccans, are considered fine, but should you grab a broom and a pointy hat and pretend to be a witch, you are violating the Criminal Code of Canada. Those who "pretend to exercise or use any kind of witchcraft, sorcery, enchantment, or conjuration" can be punished. Makes you wonder whether the jails are filled to capacity on Halloween.

Penny Pummeling

When Canadian kids leave coins on the railway tracks to be flattened by trains, they could be facing a year in juvenile jail or a $250 (that is, a 25,000-penny) fine. This is because they are defacing the currency of the country and the law clearly states that it is illegal to "melt down" or "break up" money.

11 Stupid Legal Warnings

✳ Child-size Superman and Batman costumes come with this warning label: "Wearing of this garment does not enable you to fly."

✳ A Powerpuff Girls costume discourages: "You cannot save the world!"

✳ A clothes iron comes with this caution: "Warning: Never iron clothes on the body." Ouch!

✳ The instructions for a medical thermometer advise: "Do not use orally after using rectally."

* The side of a Slush Puppy cup warns: "This ice may be cold." The only thing dumber than this would be a disclaimer stating: "No puppies were harmed in the making of this product."

* The box of a 500-piece puzzle reads: "Some assembly required."

* A box of PMS relief tablets has this advice: "Warning: Do not use if you have prostate problems."

* Cans of Easy Cheese contain this instruction: "For best results, remove cap."

* A warning label on a nighttime sleep aid reads: "Warning: May cause drowsiness."

* Cans of self-defense pepper spray caution: "May irritate eyes."

* Boys and girls should read the label on the Harry Potter toy broom: "This broom does not actually fly."

The Mad Bomber

Sure, he wanted revenge, but he also wanted to protect New Yorkers from their utility company.

✳ ✳ ✳ ✳

NINETY MILES NORTH of New York City, George Metesky, an amiable-looking middle-aged man in a business suit, drove his car 80 feet from his driveway to the garage workshop at his family's house. He changed into coveralls and used gunpowder extracted from rifle bullets to craft what he called "units." He wanted New Yorkers to know that he had been wronged. When he meticulously packed away his tools at the end of the day, Metesky's bomb was ready.

The man who became the Mad Bomber nursed a grudge against his former employer, Consolidated Edison (Con Ed), New York's utility company. While working for Con Ed in 1931, Metesky suffered an accident and came to believe that he had been gassed and contracted tuberculosis as a result. Two things were indisputable: The illness left him unable to work, and Con Ed denied him workman's compensation.

A Little Attention, Please

More than 900 letters sent by Metesky to elected officials and newspapers failed to bring Con Ed to account. Frustrated, he devised an alternative plan. In November 1940, he left a pipe bomb outside a Con Ed plant on Manhattan's Upper West Side. A note read, "CON EDISON CROOKS, THIS IS FOR YOU." He signed it, "F.P." The bomb didn't go off, but Con Ed—and New York—had been warned.

The following September, an unexploded pipe bomb wrapped in a sock with a note signed "F.P." was discovered near Con Ed's head-quarters. However, before Metesky could scare the city a third time, the nation entered World War II. New York City police received a letter from "F.P." outlining his patriotic claims: "I WILL Make no more BOmB UNITS for the Duration of the WAR ... Later I WILl bring The con EDiSON to JUSTICE—THEy will pay for their dastaRdLy deeds."

New York saw no more bombs from "F.P." for nearly ten years, although the threatening letters continued. Then, in March 1950, an intact bomb was found in Grand Central Station. "F.P." was back.

Clues

Metesky rapidly escalated his Con Ed war. A bomb blew up in the New York Public Library in April 1951, and another hit Grand Central. Between 1951 and 1956, Metesky placed at least 30 bombs. Although 15 people were injured by 22 that exploded, no one was killed.

The lead detective turned to a criminal psychiatrist. Dr. James Brussel studied the case and concluded that the "Mad Bomber" was of Slavic descent, Catholic, and was burdened with an Oedipal complex. Detectives could find him outside the city living with a female relative. The NYPD was dubious. Dr. Brussel even told them that when they found "F.P.," he wouldn't come along until donning a buttoned double-breasted suit.

To trap "F.P.," the *New York Journal-American* encouraged him to submit his story. Metesky bit, and the story was printed. A Con Ed clerk had previously sifted through files of "troublesome" former employees and discovered Metesky. All this information added up to an identification. In January 1957, the cops drove to Waterbury, Connecticut, where Polish Catholic Metesky lived with his sisters. He opened the door in his pajamas and cheerfully admitted to being "F.P.," explaining that the initials stood for "Fair Play." Before he was arrested, he changed into a doubled-breasted suit.

Just What Is Insanity, Anyway?

Metesky grinned throughout his arraignment. He was sent to Bellevue Hospital for evaluation and ruled insane. He was committed to Matteawan State Hospital for the Criminally Insane without trial. On his release in 1973, Metesky told the *New York Times* that he wished he had stood trial. "I don't think I was insane," he said. "Sometimes . . . I wondered if there was something wrong with me, because of the extreme effort I was making." He reminded reporters that he was trying to help others. "If I caused enough trouble, they'd have to be careful about the way they treat other people." George "Fair Play" Metesky died in Waterbury in 1994 at age 90.

Whatever Happened to D. B. Cooper?

A parachute, a load of money, and a disappearing criminal combine in this strange tale.

✳   ✳   ✳   ✳

ON THE DAY before Thanksgiving, 1971, in Portland, Oregon, a man in his mid-forties who called himself Dan Cooper (news reports would later misidentify him as "D. B.") boarded a Northwest Orient Airlines 727 that was bound for Seattle. Dressed in a suit and tie and carrying a briefcase,

Cooper was calm and polite when he handed a note to a flight attendant. The note said that his briefcase contained a bomb; he was hijacking the plane. Cooper told the crew that upon landing in Seattle, he wanted four parachutes and two hundred thousand dollars in twenty-dollar bills.

His demands were met, and Cooper released the other passengers. He ordered the pilots to fly to Mexico, but he gave specific instructions to keep the plane under ten thousand feet with the wing flaps at fifteen degrees, restricting the aircraft's speed. That night, in a cold rainstorm somewhere over southwest Washington, Cooper donned the parachutes, and with the money packed in knapsacks that were tied to his body, he jumped from the 727's rear stairs.

Unanswered Questions

For several months afterward, the FBI conducted an extensive manhunt of the rugged forest terrain, but the agents were unable to find even a shred of evidence. In 1972, a copycat hijacker named Richard McCoy successfully jumped from a flight over Utah with five hundred thousand dollars and was arrested days later. At first the FBI thought McCoy was Cooper, but he didn't match the description provided by the crew of Cooper's flight. Other suspects surfaced over the years, including a Florida antiques dealer with a shady past who confessed to his wife on his deathbed that he was Cooper—though he was later discredited by DNA testing.

Cooper hadn't hurt anybody, and he had no apparent political agenda. He became a folk hero of sorts—he was immortalized in books, in song, in television documentaries, and in a movie, *The Pursuit of D.B. Cooper*. In 1980, solid evidence surfaced: An eight-year-old boy found $5,800 in rotting twenty-dollar bills along the Columbia River, and the serial numbers matched those on the cash that was given to Cooper. But while many leads have been investigated over the years, the case remains the only unsolved hijacking in U.S. history.

Convicted Conspirators in President Lincoln's Assassination

Most of us learned in school that on April 14, 1865, President Abraham Lincoln was shot by John Wilkes Booth. What you may not have known was that Booth did not act alone, and that the plot wasn't limited to killing Lincoln.

✳ ✳ ✳ ✳

John Wilkes Booth, mastermind of Lincoln's assassination, was shot to death by Union soldier Boston Corbett while attempting to escape on April 26, 1865.

Lewis Powell stabbed U.S. Secretary of State William H. Seward, but Seward recovered. (The assassinations of Seward and Vice President Johnson were part of the conspiracy, but these assassination attempts were unsuccessful.) Convicted of conspiracy to commit murder and treason, Powell was hanged July 7, 1865.

George A. Atzerodt was assigned to kill Vice President Andrew Johnson, but he never got very close to the vice president; most historians believe he merely wimped out. His second thoughts didn't save him, and he was convicted of conspiracy to assassinate the president. Atzerodt was hanged July 7, 1865.

David E. Herold guided Lewis Powell to Seward's home. Convicted of conspiracy to commit murder and treason, Herold was hanged July 7, 1865.

Mary E. Surratt owned the boardinghouse where the conspirators met. Convicted of conspiracy to assassinate the president, Surratt was hanged July 7, 1865.

During early conspiracy plans, **Michael O'Laughlen**, a boyhood friend of Booth's, was assigned to help kidnap Lincoln. Convicted of conspiracy, O'Laughlin received a life sentence. He died of yellow fever in prison in 1867.

Edman Spangler held Booth's horse during the assassination. Charged with conspiracy to assassinate the president, Spangler was sentenced to six years. Pardoned by President Andrew Johnson due to lack of evidence in March 1869, Spangler eventually died in 1875.

Dr. Samuel A. Mudd harbored Booth and Herold during their escape attempt. Mudd was charged with conspiracy and sentenced to life in prison, but he was pardoned by President Johnson in March 1869 for his lifesaving efforts at Fort Jefferson during a yellow fever outbreak in 1867. Mudd resumed his medical practice. He died of pneumonia in 1883.

Samuel Arnold was involved in the early plans to kidnap President Lincoln. He was convicted of conspiracy and sentenced to life in prison. President Johnson pardoned Arnold in March 1869 because of his minimal role and early attempt to break from the conspirators. Arnold died of tuberculosis in 1906.

John Surratt also participated in the early plans to kidnap President Lincoln. He remained a fugitive until November 27, 1866, when he was apprehended in Alexandria, Egypt. He was charged with conspiracy, but a deadlocked jury resulted in Surratt's release in 1868. Surratt died of pneumonia on April 21, 1916. He was the last living convicted conspirator in the assassination of President Abraham Lincoln.

Further Fumbling Felons

Sometimes criminals work against their own interests.

✳   ✳   ✳   ✳

When Honesty Is the Worst Policy

A CLERK AT A New Zealand food store was describing to police the man who had just robbed the store at gunpoint. Since the clerk had said that the man wasn't wearing a mask, the cop asked him to describe whatever he remembered to a police sketch artist. As the clerk worked with the artist, it was clear that he had an amazing eye for detail. He noted specific features of the robber's face—a remarkable feat, especially for someone who had been held at gunpoint.

At last the artist finished and handed the picture to the investigating officer. The officer did an immediate double take. The clerk had described himself! When confronted with the fact, the clerk confessed that it was indeed he who had robbed the store. When the cop asked him why he had so accurately described himself to the sketch artist, the clerk responded: "I was just being honest!"

Wedding Bell Blues

An Alabama female police officer had previously worked prostitution stings, and she had seen a lot of odd things in her time. So she didn't think much of it when, while she was working undercover, a man dressed in a tuxedo pulled up in a car alongside her and propositioned her. The officer played along, and soon the man found himself under arrest. Then the cop discovered why her "john" was dressed so nice: It was his wedding day. He had gotten married just a few hours before and had dashed out from the reception to buy more beer. But once out he apparently decided that booze wasn't enough to quench his thirst.

It's a good bet that her husband's arrest warrant was the one "gift" the bride didn't expect to receive on her wedding day!

No Sale

Sometimes you have to know when to walk away. A man from South Carolina bought substandard cocaine from his dealer. But instead of just feeling burned, he indignantly stormed into a police station. Throwing the bag of drugs disdainfully onto an officer's desk, the man demanded that the police arrest the dealer who had sold him the mediocre coke.

A Pirate's Life for Me

Time travelers from the Golden Age of Piracy (1650–1725) would be dismayed at the way pirates are portrayed today—as drunken, bloodthirsty, torturous derelicts who talked funny. On behalf of pirates everywhere, we'll address the myths.

✳ ✳ ✳ ✳

Pirates were just drunken debauchers. Yes, these guys tended toward drunkenness and debauchery; it's the "just" part that's inaccurate. They were also violent, womanizing scoundrels—but for the most part, they restricted these unseemly behaviors to shore. Rules governing their conduct often stipulated a lifestyle better suited to Boy Scouts than to bloodthirsty thieves. To avoid shipboard violence among the crew, captains frequently banned women and gambling, forbade drunkenness while on duty, and strictly enforced early "lights out."

Pirates made their prisoners walk the plank. Pirates had a number of unpleasant punishments for prisoners and rule break- ers, including twisting cords around an offender's head until his eyes popped out, forcing him to eat his own ears, or tying him to a mast and throwing glass at him or burning him with matches. What pirates didn't do was make prisoners walk the plank (how nice of them). Only one reputable, first-hand account of plank walking exists, and it took place 100 years after the peak of piracy. The idea that this was a common practice comes primarily from J. M. Barrie's play *Peter Pan* and old Hollywood movies in which walking the plank was one of the few forms of torture that would get past the censors.

All pirates talked the same way. If for a period in the 1950s it seemed like every movie pirate had the same accent, it's because they did, or rather, they shared an accent with Robert Newton, the actor who portrayed both Blackbeard and Long John Silver several times on big and small screens. Newton was born in Dorset, England (as were many famous pirates), and his rough accent and trilled "r" fit the public's image of pirates nicely. But pirate ships were melting pots, pulling sailors in from all over Europe, the Caribbean, and the Americas, so there was no "typical" pirate accent. What's more, Ol' Chumbucket and Cap'n Slappy, the aspiring-pirate masterminds behind International Talk Like a Pirate Day, would like to point out that no pirates—fictional or otherwise—ever said, "Arrrgh," though they might have said, "Arrr."

Pirates were lawless criminals. Who says there's no honor among thieves? Pirates had few qualms about liberating a treasure-laden merchant ship of its burden, but they operated under strict codes of conduct on their own ships. Called Articles of Agreement, these pirate codes varied from ship to ship and governed elections and management, division of booty, disability compensation, shipboard safety, ethics, and responsibilities. Each pirate was required to sign the agreement before embarking on a voyage, and those who violated the rules found themselves marooned—that is, left on a remote island with as little as a flask of water and a weapon. Here are a few of the provisions in the Articles of Agreement drawn up by Captain John Phillips for the crew aboard his ship *Revenge:*

* If any Man shall steal any Thing in the Company, or game, to the Value of a Piece of Eight, he shall be maroon'd or shot.

* That Man that shall strike another whilst those Articles are in force shall receive Moses's Law (that is 40 Stripes lacking one) on the bare Back.

* If at any time you meet with a Prudent woman, that Man that offers to meddle with her, without her Consent, shall suffer present Death.

Tripped Up by Technology

Enjoy these stories of criminals who might have been more sucessfully in a low-tech world.

✳ ✳ ✳ ✳

Printer Theft Leads to Sentence

SOMETIMES PEOPLE AREN'T entitled to tech support on their electronics. Perhaps they didn't buy the warranty or register the equipment. Or in the case of Timothy Scott Short, maybe he stole the machine. Shortly after a printer that was used to make driver's licenses was stolen from the Missouri Department of Revenue in 2007, Short called the printer company's tech support wondering whether it was possible to buy a new part for it. A voice message and the suspect's phone number led police back to Short, who was charged with the felony of possessing document-making implements and theft.

No Dancing Matter

It all began on Andrew Singh's 2009 wedding day in Preston, Lancashire, England. A coach bus from Manchester was hired to transport three loads of wedding guests to the ceremony. On the way there, a car swerved into the bus causing a small collision. Oddly, the groom decided this was the perfect opportunity to come away with a bit of cash. He and his family sued the motor coach company, claiming that they had suffered injuries such as bruising and whiplash. But the case had no legs: It was soon discovered that Andrew and his father were not actually passengers on the bus during the accident. A judge threw out their claim, and a police investigation was launched. The final straw was a video taken at the wedding reception, showing Andrew, his family, and festive wedding guests dancing, clapping, and cheering—and not looking very injured at all. The groom and his parents were convicted of conspiracy to defraud and perjury, and they were sentenced to a year in jail. Wisely, the bride ditched them all. Who's dancing now?

A Developing Crime

Two boys from Louisville, Kentucky, stole a woman's Polaroid camera as she strolled through the park. Alerted by the woman's screams, a police officer gave chase, but the two thieves already had a head start.

Fortunately for the cop, the two boys had stopped and were taking pictures of one another. But much to their chagrin, the pictures that emerged from the Polaroid were all black, which, as many people know, is simply how Polaroid pictures look before they develop. Muttering about broken cameras, the boys continued on their way, occasionally stopping to take a photo. Each time a picture emerged from the camera all black, the thieves discarded it. All the pursuing cop had to do was follow the trail of rapidly developing photographs to find the technology-challenged crooks.

Who Ya Gonna Call?

With all of the informational resources available today, such as the Yellow Pages and the Internet, it's surprising that some people still have trouble finding the right person to contact for a particular task.

This was certainly the case for an Arizona woman who decided that she just couldn't stand her husband anymore. But instead of taking the obvious road and asking for a divorce, she contacted a company called "Guns for Hire" that staged mock gunfights for Wild West theme parks and the like. The woman asked them if they could kill her husband for her.

Now, while advertising is supposedly a key to a successful business, it's unlikely that a hired killer would go about broadcasting his or her services. After all, it tends to make the whole anonymity thing a bit difficult. On the plus side, however, at least the woman's prison sentence gave her a years-long vacation from her husband.

A Love Eternal

Carl Tanzler couldn't have his dream girl in life, so he bided his time. When she passed away from natural causes, the door to romance—creepy, morbid, romance—suddenly sprang open.

✳ ✳ ✳ ✳

GERMAN IMMIGRANT CARL Tanzler (AKA Count Carl Von Cosel, 1877–1952) loved to tell tall tales. While working as an X-ray technician at the U.S. Marine Hospital in Key West during the Depression years, Tanzler claimed to be an electrical inventor, the holder of multiple university degrees, even a submarine captain. None of it was true. In reality Tanzler was a lonely, conflicted man caught up in a fantasy world of his own design. But this profound sense of loneliness ebbed the instant that he met hospital patient Elena Hoyos, a fetching 22-year-old Cuban woman suffering from tuberculosis. He believed that it was his destiny to be with her.

Snake Oil Therapy

Try though he might, Tanzler was mostly rebuffed by his new-found object of affection. Undeterred by her rejection, Tanzler set his sights on working to cure her and tried his best to win the approval of her family. His efforts were in vain.

After reviewing Hoyos's X-rays, Tanzler realized that she wasn't long for the world. Nevertheless, he convinced her that he could cure her with a combo of X-rays and daily doses of his special tonic, a bizarre mixture comprised of gold and water. Not surprisingly his "cure" failed as badly as his attempts at winning her hand, and Hoyos succumbed to her illness.

A Love Realized

After Hoyos's passing, Tanzler was devastated but strangely optimistic about their future together. This was a man with a plan—a depraved and twisted plan to be sure—but a plan nonetheless. By hook or by crook Hoyos would soon be his.

Hoyos was buried in a common grave. Unhappy with this arrangement Tanzler asked Hoyos's family for permission to rebury her in a stone mausoleum. After getting the go-ahead, Tanzler discovered that Elena's body hadn't been embalmed. He hired a mortician to do the job, and her body was moved to its new home. Now Hoyos would ride out eternity with the dignity that Tanzler felt she deserved. Now, too, he could make unauthorized visits to her remains compliments of a solitary key that her parents knew nothing about.

Proving that obsessive love knows neither bounds nor boundaries, Tanzler brought her flowers and gifts each night and counted the hours in between their visits. It was said that he even installed a telephone in her tomb in hopes that she'd communicate with him. After a two year "courtship," Tanzler removed Elena's body from the tomb and relocated it to an abandoned airplane fuselage behind the hospital.

Quality Time

Using wax, plaster of Paris and glass eyes, Tanzler restored "life" to his beloved. A shocker came when Tanzler learned that the military had plans to move the old airplane. With loving concern, Tanzler relocated Hoyos once again—this time to his house, where no one could interfere. As a sign of his commitment, Tanzler dressed Hoyos in a wedding gown and slept with her each evening. He anointed his lady with body oils, chemicals and perfumes—all the better to keep the putrid smell of decomposition at bay.

Rigor Mortis Interruptus

Tanzler made regular trips into town to obtain supplies, and that's where his troubles began. People became curious when they saw Tanzler purchasing women's clothing and perfumes, especially after a paper boy claimed to have seen him dancing with a big doll through a window at his home. Before long, rumors began to circulate. Could Tanzler be spending time with the corpse of Elena Hoyos?

Elena's sister Nana asked Tanzler if there was any truth to the macabre assertions. Not wanting to disgrace himself any further, he came clean. He led Nana to his house to show her how beautifully he'd arranged Elena. There, propped up in a chair, was Nana's dead sister, looking much the worse for wear after nine long years. Nana, disbelieving, summoned the police.

Ghoul's Luck

Tanzler was arrested and charged with grave robbing and abusing a corpse. He was ultimately convicted of grave robbery, but got off on a technicality. The statute of limitations had expired and Tanzler received no jail time for his offense.

Hopeless Romantic

The case drew great publicity. For this reason, authorities decided to put Elena's corpse on public display at a funeral home. After the viewing, her remains were placed in a metal box and buried in a secret location.

Despite the setbacks, Tanzler's obsession with Elena continued. For the rest of his years he carried his beloved close to his heart—exceedingly close. When authorities discovered Tanzler dead at his house in 1952, he was clutching a life-sized doll with a face that looked uncannily like Elena's.

Unthinking Thieves

Something catching and convicting criminals is almost too easy. Almost.

✳   ✳   ✳   ✳

Hands Up! This Is a Confession!

SOMETIMES IT JUST doesn't pay to volunteer—just ask the two crooks who were on trial for armed robbery and assault. In the courtroom, the female victim took the stand, and in a quavering voice, proceeded to tell her story. Then the prosecutor asked her the jackpot question: "Are the two men who committed this horrible crime in the courtroom today?"

Before she could say anything, the two defendants helpfully raised their hands. Even the judge cracked up at the sight of the two crooks aiding their own conviction.

It's Always Something

An Ohio crook walked into a local café, waved a gun, and demanded money from the proprietors. The waitress filled a paper bag with cash. But as the thief was escaping across the parking lot toward his pick-up truck, the bag ripped open, and the money spilled out onto the concrete. The crook grabbed as much money as he could with his hands. Then, fists stuffed with greenbacks, he got to his pick-up, fished his keys out of his pocket, and thrust them into the door lock.

The key broke off in the lock.

Not wanting to admit defeat, the criminal still tried desperately to open the door. He twisted, jiggled, and rattled the lock, but to no avail. However, his gyrations did accomplish something. He shot himself in the foot with his gun.

Finally realizing that this wasn't his day, the thief gave up and limped from the parking lot. But when he hobbled into a hospital emergency room a few minutes later, the staff notified police, who took him to the station without further mishap.

Old Enough to Drink

A man walked into the corner store intending to rob it, and he started by asking for all the money in the register. It doesn't sound particularly strenuous, but the effort must have made him thirsty, because he added a bottle of scotch to his order. The clerk refused, saying she didn't think he was over 21, the legal drinking age.

The robber swore that he was and pulled out his driver's license to prove it. She looked it over thoroughly and gave the man a bag filled with the cash and the liquor. As soon as he left the store, the clerk called the police with the robber's name and address. He was arrested two hours later.

The Wrong Bar

An 18-year-old Janesville, Wisconsin, man got into trouble at a local bar—but it wasn't for underage drinking. In August 2009 at 11:00 P.M., he burst into Quotes Bar and Grill with a bandana covering his face. Although he didn't actually have a weapon, he had his hand placed in his pants pocket as though he was armed.

But the teen picked the wrong night and the wrong bar: The Wisconsin Professional Police Officers Association was in town for their annual golf outing, and Quotes was full of cops from around the state. On the bright side, police responded so quickly to the robbery that the man didn't have time to demand money. He claimed he wasn't planning to rob the bar, but that he sported the mask so no one would recognize him. He was charged with disorderly conduct.

Quotables

"The foundation of justice is good faith."

—MARCUS TULLIUS CICERO

"He reminds me of the man who murdered both his parents, and then when sentence was about to be pronounced pleaded for mercy on the grounds that he was an orphan."

— ABRAHAM LINCOLN

"It's a proven fact that capital punishment is a detergent for crime."

—CARROLL O'CONNER AS ARCHIE BUNKER IN *ALL IN THE FAMILY*

Chapter 9

Beyond Natural

Cryptozoological Creatures

Cryptozoology is the study of creatures that are rumored to exist. But for true believers and alleged eyewitnesses, these "cryptids" are alive and well and lurking among us.

✳ ✳ ✳ ✳

Marozi: With a maned lion's face fronting a jaguarlike body, the Marozi (also known as the spotted lion) was reported several times in the 1930s in Kenya's mountains but hasn't been mentioned much since. The Natural History Museum in Great Britain is said to be in possession of the spotted skin of a marozi, but many experts think the specimen represents a jaguar that bred with common spotless plains lions.

Kamchatka Giant Bear: Swedish zoologist Sten Bergman, working in Russia's Kamchatka Peninsula in the 1920s, discovered a paw print that measured a full square foot, suggesting a bear of remarkable size. Similar sightings tell of an ursine almost twice the size of a typical North American grizzly bear, measuring six feet at the shoulder. Some Russian biologists believe there is a small group of Kamchatka Giant Bears that survived the most recent ice age.

Skunk Ape: Bigfoot's smelly Southern cousin has been reported a number of times in Florida's swamps, most convincingly in 2000 by a couple who took an excellent snapshot of what looked to be a six-foot-six orangutan. The picture didn't capture its scent, of course, but the couple attested to its horror.

Lizard Man: This scaly green hominid, the resident mysterious beast of Escape Ore Swamp in South Carolina, has long been at the center of local lore. While many consider the creature a hoax, others swear they've encountered it face to face. Lizard Man has had several brushes with fame: A local radio station once offered $1 million for a live capture, and in 1988, a South Carolina Republican leader labeled Lizard Man a staunch Democrat.

Jersey Devil: According to most reports, New Jersey's crypto-zoological curiosity has wings, a horse's face, a pig's hooves, and a kangaroo's body. The legend of the Jersey Devil was born in the 1700s—based on a tale of a cursed baby-turned-demon that flew off into the night—and boomed in the early 1900s, with supposed sightings all over the state. To this day, people report Devil sightings, mostly in the spooky Pine Barrens of southern New Jersey. While some locals think the creature is truly a supernatural beast, others say it's probably a misidentified sandhill crane.

El Chupacabra: Puerto Rico's legendary "goat sucker" is a fanged and clawed beast that performs vampirism on livestock. The first accounts of its victims—often goats, chickens, horses, and cows—were reported in the 1950s by farmers who found animals drained of blood, with several large puncture marks. Some who have allegedly sighted the creature describe it as a short, kangaroolike monster with oversize teeth and an oval head, but others liken it to a large reptile or bat.

Tessie: Deep in Lake Tahoe on the California–Nevada border lurks a storied sea creature that's the Sierra Nevada cousin of the Loch Ness Monster. It's alleged that after a submarine expedition, undersea explorer Jacques Cousteau said, "The world isn't ready for what's down there." (He could, of course, have been referring to anything odd.) Popular descriptions portray Tessie as either a freshwater relative of a whale or a 20-foot sea serpent with a humped back.

Champ: Like Tessie, Champ is named for the body of water in which it purportedly lurks, in this case New York's Lake Champlain. Several hundred recorded sightings typically describe the beast as an angular black sea monster measuring about 50 feet in length. One investigative group believes the often-sighted Champ is actually a surviving plesiosaur, a dinosaur that died off 60 million years ago.

Deadly Bling?: The Curse of the Hope Diamond

Diamonds are a girl's best friend, a jeweler's meal ticket, and serious status symbols for those who can afford them. But there's one famous diamond whose brilliant color comes with a cloudy history. The Hope Diamond is one of the world's most beautiful gemstones—and one that some say causes death and suffering to those who possess it. So is the Hope Diamond really cursed? Evidence says "no," but there have been strange coincidences.

✳ ✳ ✳ ✳

The Origin of Hope

IT'S BELIEVED THAT this shockingly large, blue-hued diamond came from India several centuries ago. At the time, the exceptional diamond was slightly more than 112 carats, which is enormous. (On average, a diamond in an engagement ring ranges from a quarter to a full carat.) According to legend, a thief stole the diamond from the eye of a Hindu statue, but scholars don't think the shape would have been right to sit in the face of a statue. Nevertheless, the story states that the young thief was torn apart by wild dogs soon after he sold the diamond, making this the first life claimed by the jewel.

Courts, Carats, and Carnage

In the mid-1600s, a French jeweler, Tavernier, purchased the diamond in India and kept it for several years without incident before selling it to King Louis XIV in 1668, along with several other jewels. The king recut the diamond in 1673, taking it down to 67 carats. This new cut emphasized the jewel's clarity, and Louis liked to wear the "Blue Diamond of the Crown" around his neck on special occasions. He, too, owned the gemstone without much trouble.

More than a hundred years later, France's King Louis XVI possessed the stone. In 1791, when the royal family tried to flee the country, the crown jewels were hidden for safekeeping, but they were stolen the following year. Some were eventually returned, but the blue diamond was not.

King Louis XVI and his wife Marie Antoinette died by guillotine in 1793. Those who believe in the curse are eager to include these two romantic figures in the list of cursed owners, but their deaths probably had more to do with the angry mobs of the French Revolution than a piece of jewelry.

Right This Way, Mr. Hope

It is unknown what happened to the big blue diamond from the time it was stolen in France until it appeared in England nearly 50 years later. When the diamond reappeared, it wasn't the same size as before—it was now only about 45 carats. Had it been cut again to disguise its identity? Or was this a new diamond altogether? Because the blue diamond was so unique in color and size, it was believed to be the diamond in question.

In the 1830s, wealthy banker Henry Philip Hope purchased the diamond, henceforth known as the Hope Diamond. When he died (of natural causes) in 1839, he bequeathed the gem to his oldest nephew, and it eventually ended up with the nephew's grandson, Francis Hope.

Francis Hope is the next person supposedly cursed by the diamond. Francis was a notorious gambler and was generally bad with money. Though he owned the diamond, he was not allowed to sell it without his family's permission, which he finally got in 1901 when he announced he was bankrupt.

It's doubtful that the diamond had anything to do with Francis's bad luck, though that's what some believers suggest.

Coming to America

Joseph Frankel and Sons of New York purchased the diamond from Francis, and by 1909, after a few trades between the world's most notable jewelers, the Hope Diamond found itself in the hands of famous French jeweler Pierre Cartier. That's where rumors of a curse may have actually originated.

Allegedly, Cartier came up with the curse concept in order to sell the diamond to Evalyn Walsh McLean, a rich socialite who claimed that bad luck charms always turned into good luck charms in her hands. Cartier may have embellished the terrible things that had befallen previous owners of his special diamond so that McLean would purchase it—which she did. Cartier even inserted a clause in the sales contract, which stated that if any fatality occurred in the family within six months, the Hope Diamond could be exchanged for jewelry valued at the $180,000 McLean paid for the stone. Nevertheless, McLean wore the diamond on a chain around her neck constantly, and the spookiness surrounding the gem started picking up steam.

Whether or not anything can be blamed on the jewel, it certainly can't be denied that McLean had a pretty miserable life starting around the time she purchased the diamond. Her eldest son died at age nine in a fiery car crash. Years later, her 25-year-old daughter killed herself. Not long after that, her husband was declared insane and was committed to a mental institution for the rest of his life. With rumors swirling about the Hope Diamond's curse, everyone pointed to the necklace when these terrible events took place.

In 1947, when McLean died (while wearing the diamond) at age 60, the Hope Diamond and most of her other treasures were sold to pay off debts. American jeweler Harry Winston forked over the $1 million asking price for McLean's entire jewelry collection.

Hope on Display

If Harry Winston was scared of the alleged curse, he didn't show it. Winston had long wanted to start a collection of gemstones to display for the general public, so in 1958, when the Smithsonian Institute started one in Washington, D.C., he sent the Hope Diamond to them as a centerpiece. These days, it's kept under glass as a central figure for the National Gem Collection at the National Museum of Natural History. So far, no one's dropped dead from checking it out.

E. T. Phone . . . Canada?

Do extraterrestrials prefer Canada? The nation ranks first in UFO sightings per capita, with 1,981 reported in 2012 and 10 percent of Canadians claiming to have encountered one.

✳ ✳ ✳ ✳

What's That?

THOUGH RECORDED INSTANCES of UFO sightings on Canadian soil date back to the 1950s, extraterrestrial encounters emerged most prominently on the global radar in 1967 with two startling occurrences. The first happened when a quartz prospector near a mine at Falcon Lake in Manitoba was allegedly burned by a UFO.

The second followed in October of that year at Shag Harbour, Nova Scotia, when several witnesses—including residents, the Royal Canadian Mounted Police, and an Air Canada pilot—reported strange lights hovering above the water and then submerging. A search of the site revealed only odd yellow foam, suggesting something had indeed gone underwater, but whether it was a UFO remains a mystery.

A Growing Phenomenon

Since then, the number of sightings in Canada has increased nearly every year. Most take place in sparsely populated regions—the rationale being that "urban glow" obscures the lights of spaceships and that country folk spend more time outdoors and thus have better opportunities to glimpse UFOs. It may also be that rural areas are simply more conducive to extraterrestrial activity. (We've heard of crop circles, but parking garage circles? Not so much.)

Most sightings reported are of the "strange light" and "weird flying vessel" variety, and indeed most have rather banal explanations (stars, airplanes, towers). Still, each year between 1 and 10 percent of sightings remain a mystery.

Ghost Lights

The legends are similar, no matter the locale. It's whispered that mysterious lights that blink and wink in the night are the spirits of long-dead railroad workers, jilted lovers, or lost children.

✳   ✳   ✳   ✳

THEY GO BY many names: marsh lights, ghost lights, will-o'-the-wisp, feu follet, earth lights, and even, to the skeptical, swamp gas. They occur in remote areas, often near old railway tracks or power transmitters.

Some are thought to issue from the geomagnetic fields of certain kinds of rock. But tales of lights that change color, follow people, foil electrical systems, or perform acrobatic stunts are harder to explain.

Mysterious Marfa Lights

The famed Marfa Lights of Marfa, Texas, have become almost synonymous with the term ghost lights. Since 1883, they have been spotted in an area southwest of the Chisos Mountains, some 200 miles south of El Paso. The lights appear almost playful in their gyrations, skimming over the fields, bobbing like a yo-yo, or chasing visitors. One woman reportedly witnessed a white ball of light three feet in diameter that bounced in slow motion alongside her car as she drove through the Chisos one night.

Some of the lights have been attributed to auto headlights miles away across the desert, but the Marfa Lights were witnessed long before automobiles came to the area.

The Peculiar Paulding Light

According to legend, an old railway brakeman was killed near the Choate Branch Railroad tracks that used to run near Paulding, Michigan, along the northern Wisconsin–Michigan border. People have observed strange lights near the tracks for decades, and it is said that they're from the railman's ghostly lantern swinging as he walks his old beat. Others, armed with telescopes and binoculars, believe that the famed Paulding Light is actually caused by headlights shining from a highway a few miles away.

Still, many claim that the lights behave like anything but distant reflections. The lights are said to change from red to green, zoom up close as if peering into people's cars, chase people, flash through automobiles either cutting off all electric power or turning radios off and on, and zigzag through the nearby woods. Crowds flock to the Robins Wood Road site off Highway 45 to see the phenomenon for themselves, and a wooden sign has been erected complete with a drawing of a ghost swinging a lantern.

The Fiery Feu Follet

During the mid-18th century, when Detroit was being settled by the French, aristocrats and working folks feared the *feu follet*, spirit lights of the marshy river area.

One local legend tells of a rich landowner who nearly drowned one stormy night when the brilliant lights lured him into a swamp. Luckily, two guests staying at his house heard his terrified cries and managed to rescue him. At the time, the prevailing theory of the marsh lights was that windows had to be closed when the *feu follet* were near or they would enter the house, snake their way into the windpipes of those present, and choke them to death.

Baffling Brown Mountain Lights

Although scoffed at as nothing more than reflected train lights, the multicolored light show in the foothills of North Carolina's Blue Ridge Mountains has fascinated humans since an early explorer reported it in 1771, and even earlier according to Native American legend. Several centuries ago, many people were killed during a battle between the Cherokee and the Catawba tribes. Legend has it that the Brown Mountain Lights are the spirits of those lost warriors.

Another tale states that a plantation owner got lost hunting on Brown Mountain and that one of his slaves came looking for him, swinging a lantern to light his way. The slave never found his owner but still walks the mountainside with his eternal lantern. Still another legend claims the lights come from the spirit of a woman murdered on the mountain by her husband in 1850.

Whatever the source of the colorful lights, they come in many shapes, from glowing orbs to trailing bursts to still, white areas. Crowds flock to at least three locations to view the lights, but one of the most popular is the Brown Mountain overlook on Highway 181, 20 miles north of Morganton.

Glowing in Great Britain

The Lincolnshire region was notorious in the mid-1960s as the site of unexplained balls of colored light. On August 10, 1965, a woman named Rachel Atwill woke up just before 4:00 A.M. to see a reddish light over some nearby hills. The light persisted for almost a half hour, and Atwill reported that the experience gave her a headache. The same light was seen about an hour later by a truck driver, but he had a more harrowing experience as the light hovered only 50 yards from his truck. The situation grew worse when the light zoomed right up to his windshield and sat there, lighting up the inside of the truck and waking his sleeping wife and daughter. Luckily, it soon lifted back into the atmosphere and disappeared.

Werewolves in Wisconsin?

Do you believe in werewolves? If you head out to southeastern Wisconsin, you might just meet one face-to-fang.

❋ ❋ ❋ ❋

Meeting the Beast

THE FIRST RECORDED sighting of the Beast came in 1936, long before it even had a name. Security guard Mark Schackelman was walking the grounds of a convent near Jefferson shortly before midnight when he saw a strange creature digging on top of a Native American burial mound. As Schackelman got closer, the creature ran off into the darkness. The scene repeated itself the following night, but this time, the creature stood up on its hind legs, growled at the shocked security guard, and simply walked away.

Encounters like this have continued through the years. Most people describe the creature as six to eight feet tall. It gets around on all fours but can also walk on two feet. Its entire body is covered with fur (similar to Bigfoot), but this Beast also has clawed hands, the head of a wolf, and bright yellow eyes. With a description like that, it's easy to see why some people believe that the creature is a werewolf. But several people have seen the Beast in broad daylight.

The Beast Gets a Name

In the early 1990s, an outbreak of Beast sightings in the southeastern part of Wisconsin—specifically, along an isolated stretch of Bray Road, just outside the town of Elkhorn—led a local reporter to dub the creature "The Beast of Bray Road."

Today, the Beast continues to linger around southeastern Wisconsin, but it's seldom seen on Bray Road anymore. It was, however, spotted in Madison in 2004. So if you're ever driving through the area, keep an eye out for what might be lurking around the bend.

Can Dogs See Spirits?

It's late at night and you're lying in bed watching TV with your faithful pooch snoring softly at your feet. Suddenly and without warning, your dog bolts upright and looks into the darkened hallway, growling while the hair on the back of his or her neck stands up. Cautiously you investigate, but you find nothing, which leads you to wonder, "Did my dog just see a ghost?"

✳ ✳ ✳ ✳

What Are You Looking At?

IN ORDER TO ascertain if dogs can see spirits, we must first determine what a ghost looks like. By most accounts, spirits appear as dark shadows or white, misty shapes, often only briefly visible out of the corner of one's eye. Sometimes, people report ghosts as balls of glowing light that move or dart about. In most cases, they are reported in low-light conditions, which is why many ghost hunters use infrared extenders when they shoot video or take photographs. So to sum up, if dogs are able to see ghosts, they would need to be able to see:

✳ Dark shadows or white, misty shapes

✳ Moving balls of light

✳ In low light

How a Dog Sees

Just like a human's eye, a dog's eye is made up of rods and cones. Rods function well in low light and are also helpful in detecting movement. Cones help to define colors. Unlike a human eye, the center of a dog's eye is made up mainly of rods, so dogs can't see colors very well. But because apparitions are usually described as dark shadows or white shapes, dogs should be able to see them just fine.

The rods in dogs' eyes allow them not only to detect motion but also to see phenomena such as flickering lights better than humans can. So if ghosts appear as flitting lights that move quickly, dogs should be able to see them.

Finally, the additional rods in the centers of dogs' eyes make it possible for dogs to see much better than humans in low-light situations. So while humans scramble for flashlights and infra-red extenders to try to see ghosts, dogs would only have to use their eyes.

A Dog's-Eye View

Another factor to consider is the location from which dogs view the world. Most adult humans spend the majority of their time viewing the world from a standing position—in general, more than five feet off the ground. Dogs, however, spend most of their lives looking up at things from two feet or so off the ground. That doesn't sound like a big difference, but it is. Just lie on the floor at night and look up at some objects; it really gives you a unique perspective. Perhaps that different vantage point is what's needed to see spirits.

Refusing to Conform

Finally, consider the idea that, despite what most ghost-hunting shows would like you to think, the majority of people do not believe that ghosts exist. Maybe that's exactly why dogs can theoretically see them: Because modern society cannot force dogs to conform to its beliefs.

In other words, dogs don't know that they're not supposed to see ghosts because they allegedly don't exist. Therefore, it would stand to reason that a dog, upon seeing an apparition, simply acknowledges it as being a living, breathing person, unlike many skeptical humans who would immediately try to convince themselves that they did not just have a paranormal encounter.

"A ghost is someone who hasn't made it—in other words, who died, and they don't know they're dead. So they keep walking around and thinking that you're inhabiting their—let's say, their domain. So they're aggravated with you."

—Psychic Sylvia Browne

Fort Worth Stockyards

The spirits haunting the Fort Worth Stockyards are well aware they are in Texas, because they have made their hauntings as prominent as possible—exactly as state custom requires!

❋ ❋ ❋ ❋

What, All Hat and No Cattle?

WELL, THE STOCKYARDS used to have quite a few head of beef, but now they mostly have tourists. Today the Fort Worth Stockyards are a historic district (or a tourist trap, depending on perspective) like Vancouver's Gastown or Wichita's Cowtown. Fort Worthians revel in the ghosty spice that seasons the Stockyards' history. For a slight fee, some will take you on a tour. Here are some of the highlights.

Good Golly...

One of the Stockyards' most famous haunted spots is Miss Molly's Hotel, formerly a boardinghouse, speakeasy and bordello. Seven themed and named rooms are lush with all the all the attendant décor you'd expect. The Cattleman's and Cowboy's rooms are notorious for ghost sightings. Most commonly, the apparitions look like young women, perhaps the spirits of past 'soiled doves' who too often came to grief in the old West. One modern housekeeper quit after extra coins kept appearing after she'd already collected her tips!

Cantina Cadillac

This hopping night spot is so haunted that it always has at least two staffers at night. Tills are often short or over, with the shortage or overage made up the next day. This could just be human error, except that it happens here suspiciously more often than in most establishments. One day, while closing out downstairs, the Cantina crew heard noise topside. They went up to find all the furniture shoved into the middle of the dance floor. Clever prank or ghost? We don't know.

Cattlemen's Steakhouse

Would you like some spirits with your enormous medium rare rib eye? Can do, if you can get staff to take you downstairs at the Cattlemen's—they go in pairs. Disembodied voices call their names, doors open and close unattended, and stuff gets moved around at random. Ghost hunters have bagged some nice orb photos here, and an actual ghost photo adorns the upstairs wall—an odd face behind a bolo-hat-wearing mortal.

Maverick Building

It has seen many uses, including its current incarnation as a western apparel store. Of old, the Maverick was a saloon. The ghost upstairs is believed to be female, probably hailing from the brothel days of the early 20th century. Even when the Stockyards mostly smelled of cattle, and what goes into and comes out of them, one could smell roses upstairs. Years back, someone experimented by leaving a bouquet of roses upstairs. She came back later to find them tastefully distributed throughout the rooms.

White Elephant Saloon

In the old days, this was one of the rougher drunkeries, and was in a different location. When that old structure crumbled, owners moved all the memorabilia here with the name. It seems that the unseen inhabitants came along, or were perhaps already in residence. Three violent deaths have occurred in the basement of the current building, leaving it with a creepy sensation. As with many hauntings, the staff describe glasses and implements mysteriously moving to new locations.

Knife Alley…

…is an alley no more, since people roofed and walled it. Today you can buy some of the finest blades in Texas in this shop. You can also watch the power go out, which the local utility finds very suspicious, considering that they have replaced the transformer several times. Ghost hunters reckon that paranormal activity might be to blame.

Haunted Leap

They call it Ireland's most haunted castle, which says much in a country where the authorities must route new roads around fairy trees and mounds because they cannot find workers willing to disturb them.

✳ ✳ ✳ ✳

A Violent History

Leap (rhymes with 'step') Castle is located in southern Co. Offaly, in the middle of the Republic of Ireland. It dates back to 1250. Legend says that the site was originally a druidic worship area. The Gaelic O'Carroll clan located their new stronghold with keen strategic eyes, commanding a pass leading to the province of Munster in southwestern Ireland. With a large tower and walls nine feet thick, besiegers would find Leap Castle a formidable target.

After 1532, the O'Carrolls entered a period of division, internal scheming, and backstabbing. In this weakened state, Leap was ripe for an English seizure. With a covert romance and a quick thrust of the sword—in the chapel during Mass, no less—the castle became Darby family property in 1659. They held it until 1922, when Irish rebels drove out the last Darbys with explosives and fire, leaving much of the castle in ruin.

Sordid Secrets Revealed…Somewhat

Around 1900, the Darbys hired workmen to clean out a windowless oubliette (dungeon pit). It contained hundreds of skeletons, evidently centuries old. Evidence indicated that prisoners were pushed through a hole into the oubliette, where they might die of immediate impalement on vertical spikes; those with less luck would miss the spikes and succumb to thirst in a lightless hole atop a pile of bones and rotting bodies. No one was sure whose bones they were, but Leap's past lords had clearly committed great cruelty and murder at the castle. Workers also found a mid-1800s pocket watch among the bones, raising suspicion that the oubliette had seen use in living memory. A nearby field called Hangman's Acre turned up iron hooks that suggested hangings by crueler means than the rope.

Then-châtelaine Mildred Darby was a devotee of the early 1900s occultism fad, and wrote of encounters with an inhuman elemental that looked and smelled like a decomposing corpse. Ghost hunters visiting the castle have reported similar sights and smells. Those who have seen the oubliette describe it as radiating profound evil, even with all remains removed.

In Recent Years

Leap lay vacant for some fifty years, boarded up and mostly avoided, though passersby sometimes reported seeing lights in the top windows. An Australian purchased the property in the 1970s, and brought a *bruja blanca* (white witch) from Mexico to cleanse all vileness from the castle. After getting plenty of exorcise, so to speak, the witch explained that the remaining spirits had no more ill intent, and wished to remain.

In the 1990s, the Ryan family purchased the property and started renovations. Soon after these began, Mr. Ryan broke his kneecap in one freak accident. A year later, after his recovery, the ladder he was working from somehow tilted away from the wall—forcing him to jump, which broke his ankle.

Not easily cowed by spirits and happenstances, the Ryans have continued restoration while living in Leap Castle, christening their baby daughter in the old chapel where such great malice was done long ago.

Today, visits to Leap are by prior appointment only, respecting that parts are inaccessible and that all is private property. A courteous phone call might obtain you an appointment. We recommend inquiring in nearby Roscrea—at the Heritage Centre in season, or if you prefer to do it Irish style, over pints at a local pub.

The Grey Ghost of Fort LaTour

Born of a 400-year-old Acadian Civil War atrocity, Fort LaTour's haunting history underlines its place in Canadian heritage.

✳   ✳   ✳   ✳

The Deed

IN 1631, A presumptuous Frenchman named Charles LaTour decided to appoint himself governor of Acadia (today, the southern part of Canada's Maritime Provinces). Near modern Saint John, New Brunswick, LaTour built a fort for fur trading, naming it for himself. Rival governor Charles d'Aulnay disputed the self-promotion by force of arms, resulting in the Acadian Civil War (1640–1645).

In 1645, while LaTour was away in Boston, d'Aulnay assaulted the fort. Despite an able defense led by LaTour's wife, Françoise Marie Jacquelin, d'Aulnay captured the fort in five days by bribing a defender to let him in. Mme. Jacquelin surrendered, accepting d'Aulnay's promise to spare her men.

D'Aulnay lied. Forcing Mme. Jacquelin to watch with a rope about her own neck, he hanged the surviving defenders one by one. We aren't sure whether the brave woman was poisoned by d'Aulnay, or died of grief, but die Mme. Jacquelin did, her resting place still unknown.

The Spirit

The old fort's wreckage decayed, and locals forgot its location—but not its story. Many have reported seeing a spectral woman strolling along the bay. Some suppose that she waits for people to find her bones and bury them with proper dignity; a number of women's unmarked graves have been unearthed nearby, but none are proven to belong to Mme. Jacquelin. There are no reports of harassment or pranks, as with many ghostly interactions. Using special equipment, ghost hunters have picked up a voice telling them to keep walking.

Is it Mme. Jacquelin? No one knows for sure. But if ever a woman's spirit had reason to haunt a place, it would be the ghost of Françoise Marie Jacquelin.

The Black Dog of Moeraki

Moeraki, New Zealand is home to the frightening Maori legend of the Black Dog.

✳ ✳ ✳ ✳

Long Ago

BEFORE EUROPEANS CAME to New Zealand's South Island, seafaring Maori were its sole human residents. One tribal group lived on the Moeraki peninsula in the modern Otago Region, noted for its round granite boulders and wave-bashed coast. The Maori kept dogs, mostly for guard purposes.

Maori legend tells that the Kuia (wisewoman) of Moeraki loved her huge, fierce black dog. One night, the chief tripped over her dog in the dark, injuring his leg and getting a nasty bite from the startled canine. Enraged, the chief ordered the Kuia's dog served for dinner without telling her. At mealtime, seeking to share some scraps with her dog, she asked the chief where Rover was. He told her: "You're eating him." She pronounced a curse on the chief, and a ban on harming black dogs. The story goes that he choked on a bone and died that night. From that day forward, the Maori of Moeraki considered large black dogs to be ill omens.

The Legend Today

Europeans came to Moeraki in 1836 and built a whaling village. Many intermarried with the Maori, who probably taught the newcomers the Black Dog legend. Locals and visitors have reported seeing the animal, which has two reported behavior patterns: one benign, one not.

Some persons lost in the dark have reported the dog walking a straight path, leading them safely home; this version of the

Black Dog was calm and helpful. In other cases, the story grows more sinister, with the dog taking an irregular and disturbed path while barking and growling. Those attempting to follow it have reported stumbling and falling, with the dog agitated by something they couldn't discern.

If the Black Dog doesn't go straight, don't follow it!

Hilarious Human Hoaxes?

Cereology is the study of crop circles. It's not a new endeavor, but there is plenty of disagreement over who or what creates these odd-looking formations.

✳ ✳ ✳ ✳

The History

AN ENGLISH WOODCUT from 1678 describes the "Mowing-Devil of Hertfordshire," history's first known crop circle. Those were simpler days, when one could blame any weird events on Satan. The demonic hordes seem to have taken a two-century break, as the next recorded mention dates to 1880, in Surrey, England. No one understood what or who made these crop circles, but blame was again directed downward.

In the 1970s, crop circles made a big comeback in the English countryside and soon began showing up all over the world. At first, people thought aliens had landed (some still do). The basic disc shape of yore gave way to intricate designs that could be described as crop spirograms, crop mandalas, and even crop snowflakes. Whatever they were called, they were obviously manmade, and paranormal explanations became a tough sell.

The Hullabaloo

Suppose your wheat-farming friend Bob calls about a big circular patch of crushed wheat in his field. Because Bob keeps screaming about crop damage as opposed to alien intrusion, you figure this isn't his attempt at a rural practical joke. There are no tractor tracks or boot prints, except where Bob obviously clod-hopped through the site. The wheat is crushed and matted, not cut. You and Bob put your minds to what might have possibly caused it. A cyclone? It would have had to be a mighty precise one, not to mention stealthy. An alien starship? Maybe one that wasn't big enough to torch the entire wheat field. A sign from spirits? Looks like their alphabet only has one letter. Secret intelligence projects? An intelligence agency that drew such attention to a secret project would be a stupidity agency. You can see why such mysteries created controversy.

When the patterns went beyond discs, someone was obviously just doing crop art. In September 1991, two merry Englishmen, Dave Chorley and Doug Bower, finally admitted that they had created many crop circles. Their method made a perfect circle: Dave stood in the middle and held a rope attached to a board, while Doug stomped the board down in a fixed radius. Or vice versa. Cereologists were embarrassed and felt they'd been played. Meanwhile, Farmer Bob learned that he could charge the curious a nice fee to view the damaged crops, so he stopped cussing and paid off his tractor loan with the proceeds.

But not all crop circles have been positively identified as hoaxes, and some have been quite complex.

The Hypotheses

The fact is that no one has a definitive explanation for the crop circles that can't be traced to hoaxers. Does that point back to space creatures? If alien ships made the crop circles, you'd think someone would have a credible photo of one, or that they'd show up on air-defense radar. Then again, some people report having seen precisely these things. Compared to aliens who could make the trip here, we on Earth would just be technological Neanderthals. Surely, such advanced beings could manage to sculpt away at some crops without Bob shooing them away with a shotgun or jet fighters intercepting them. But why in the world would aliens even want to doodle in our dirt? That's a harder question to answer.

The Curse of King Tut

Many people still believe that anyone associated with the excavation and unsealing of King Tutankhamen's tomb suffered an untimely death. Here's the truth.

❋ ❋ ❋ ❋

Myth: Lord Carnarvon died because of his association with King Tut's tomb.

Fact: Medical records say he succumbed to pneumonia, but when Lord Carnarvon—the financial backer of the Tutankhamen excavation—died on April 5, 1923, people genuinely believed he was the victim of a curse from King Tut's tomb.

The idea of a curse was already afoot before Lord Carnarvon died. As soon as archaeologist Howard Carter discovered Tutankhamen's tomb, people started predicting that terrible things would happen to anyone who entered it. The public's fears were realized when there was report of a cobra that devoured Carter's pet canary the very day he entered the secret sanctuary. In Egyptian lore, cobras were the protectors of the pharaohs.

Things got even more sensational when Lord Carnarvon died. The thrill of the curse soon matched the obsession over the glorious treasure Carter found in the young pharaoh's tomb. Newspapers of the day feasted on it, and so did the public. Even Sir Arthur Conan Doyle, the creator of Sherlock Holmes, believed in the curse, postulating that Egyptian priests frequently placed deadly spores in tombs to punish grave robbers. The frenzy over Carnarvon's curse-caused death escalated despite the knowledge that the lord had been in poor health for at least 20 years before he set foot inside Tutankhamen's tomb.

Myth: Everyone associated with Tut's tomb met untimely deaths

Fact: The existence of a curse would be more believable if many people had died soon after their association with the tomb. In reality, only a handful of individuals died in the decade after. Howard Carter lived 17 more years—after working in the tomb for almost 10 years. Richard Adamson, a guard who slept in the tomb, died in 1982 at the age of 81. And the daughter of Lord Carnarvon, Lady Evelyn Herbert, entered the tomb with her father, but she died in 1980 at the age of 78. Despite these facts, tales of the curse of King Tut live on.

Monumental Myths

Historians and conspiracy theorists have long debated the true meaning and origin of Stonehenge, the prehistoric series of stone monoliths located in England. Were they erected as an altar to aliens, a calendar for cosmic calculations, or a health spa?

❊   ❊   ❊   ❊

No one really knows who built Stonehenge, because it was erected at a time before written language as we know it existed and word of mouth was, at best, unreliable. The ancient rumor mill claims that the Druids—a sect of Celtic priests—built the structures as a site for ceremonial sacrifices. This theory was posited by a couple of 16th-century Stonehenge antiquarians, John Aubrey and William Stukeley. But later archaeologists determined that the monuments pre-date the Druids by a thousand years, and it's also been noted that the sect worshipped in wooded areas, not stony enclaves.

Skyward Speculations

Because the entire structure has an out-of-this-world mystique, some imaginative analysts suggest it was built as a shrine to extraterrestrials, or that aliens themselves assembled the monuments. As evidence, these believers point to the fact that crop circles have repeatedly formed near the site. Still others are convinced that the monuments were created to act as a cosmic timepiece, and that the stones are precisely situated so the shadows they cast move like the hands of a clock.

Healing Among the Rocks?

Evidence of an ancient village on the outskirts of the site suggests the area was a place for the living, and that Stonehenge was a cemetery and memorial. Some researchers believe Stonehenge was a haven for wellness. The first stones moved to the site originally came from a bluestone quarry in west Wales that was used as a healing retreat. Archaeologists maintain that these stones were believed to have medicinal powers and were brought to Stonehenge for that purpose.

A Bump in the Light: America's Haunted Lighthouses

More than 60 lighthouses in the United States are believed to be haunted. Whether they stick around because of tragedy, love, or some other reason, these spectral visitors add an otherworldly element to already-fascinating places.

✳ ✳ ✳ ✳

St. Simons Island Lighthouse, Georgia

THIS LIGHTHOUSE MAY have been cursed from the start. Originally constructed in 1811, the first building was destroyed by Confederate soldiers. While the lighthouse was being rebuilt, the architect fell ill and died of yellow fever. Then, on a stormy night in 1880, a dispute between the lighthouse keeper and his assistant resulted in gunshots. The keeper died after days of suffering from his wounds, though the assistant was never charged with the crime. The new keeper maintained he could hear strange footsteps on the spiral staircase to the tower. To this day, subsequent lighthouse keepers, their families, and visitors have also heard the same slow tread on the tower's 129 steps.

Minots Ledge Lighthouse, Massachusetts

Despite the sweet nickname, the ghosts of the "I Love You" lighthouse tell a tragic story. The first Minots Ledge Lighthouse began operating in 1850, and being its keeper was arguably the most frightening assignment around. Built directly in the rough waters around the Cohasset Reefs, the spidery metal skeleton of the lighthouse swayed and buckled in the wind and waves. On April 17, 1851, a sudden nor'easter stranded the keeper on the mainland; he could only watch as the storm slowly destroyed the lighthouse, with his two assistants inside. Their bodies were found after the storm cleared.

A new storm-proof stone tower was built, and the spirits of those who perished in the first lighthouse seem to reside in the new building. Subsequent keepers have heard them working, and sailors see them waving from the external ladder. On stormy nights the light blinks "1–4–3," which locals say is code for "I love you." They believe this is the assistants' message to their loved ones, passing ships, and anyone caught in a storm.

Yaquina Bay Lighthouse, Oregon

In 1899, Lischen M. Miller wrote a story for *Pacific Monthly* about a girl who disappeared at the Yaquina Bay Lighthouse. The girl, a captain's daughter, was left with a caretaker while her father was at sea. One day she and her friends went to explore the abandoned lighthouse. When she got separated from her friends, they heard her shriek. They searched for her but only found some blood and her handkerchief. A door that had been open only moments before was locked. Although many maintain that this story is pure fiction, the spectral figure of a girl has been seen around the tower.

St. Augustine Lighthouse, Florida

St. Augustine is often called America's most haunted city, and the lighthouse there might claim its own "most haunted" title. So many different spirits are rumored to haunt this light that it's probably a bit crowded. Visitors report seeing a young girl with a bow in her hair. She is thought to be the ghost of a girl who died during the tower's construction. A tall man is often seen in the basement of the keeper's house, and doors unlock mysteriously, footsteps follow visitors, and cold spots move around the buildings. The spirits seem mostly harmless, but construction workers have complained of foreboding feelings and freak accidents.

Owls Head Lighthouse, Maine

An older woman dubbed "Little Lady" is frequently seen in the kitchen of this lighthouse. Although most spirits tend to bring cold spots or unease, this one reportedly causes a feeling of calm and warmth. No one is sure who she is, but it is possible that she's keeping the other Owls Head ghost company. Believed to be a previous keeper known for his frugal nature and attention to his post, this ghost makes himself known by turning thermostats down, polishing the brass, leaving footprints in the snow, and occasionally appearing in the tower. He seems to be training his replacement: A resident's young daughter announced one day that fog was coming in and that they should turn on the beacon, something she claimed to have learned from her "imaginary friend."

Fairport Harbor Light, Ohio

This lighthouse is rumored to have two rather playful ghosts. The first is of a keeper's young son who died. The second appears to be a charming gray kitten that routinely seeks out museum staff and visitors to play. Its spectral nature becomes apparent when visitors realize the kitten has no feet—it simply hovers above the ground. Although a former keeper's wife had a beloved kitten while she lived in the lighthouse, the "ghost cat" story was dismissed as silly until workers found the body of a cat in a crawl space there.

Old Presque Isle Lighthouse, Michigan

This lighthouse was decommissioned in 1870 and became a museum. In 1977, when George and Lorraine Parris were hired as caretakers, they ran the light regularly until the Coast Guard warned that running a decommissioned light was hazardous and illegal. To ensure it wouldn't happen again, the machinery that rotated the light was removed. But since George's death in 1992, the lighthouse has frequently glowed at night—not so brightly as to cause harm but bright enough to be seen by passing ships and across the bay. Although the Coast Guard has classified it as an "unidentified" light, Lorraine believes that it is George, still happily working in his lighthouse.

The Most Haunted House in Ohio

Secret passageways. Ghostly women in black. Mass murder in the basement. A curse that's lasted about 130 years. Simply put, if anything's ever been said about something spooky going on inside a house, chances are someone's said it happened in Cleveland's Franklin Castle.

✳ ✳ ✳ ✳

HANNES TIEDEMANN, A successful banker and businessman, planned and built what would become Franklin Castle in 1865. Once completed, the four-story building on Franklin Boulevard did indeed look like a castle, right down to the turrets and gargoyles. The house had close to 30 rooms, including a grand ballroom.

But after the Tiedemann family had made the castle home for 16 years, a string of misfortunes hit them in 1881. Both Hannes Tiedemann's mother and his 15-year-old daughter, Emma, passed away. Emma's death hit Tiedemann's wife, Luise, exceptionally hard, and she was said to be inconsolable. As a way to cheer Luise up, Tiedemann began construction on the many secret rooms and passageways supposedly hidden inside the castle. Luise passed away from liver disease in 1895, and Hannes sold the castle and moved out shortly thereafter.

Murderous Tales and a Cursed Castle

According to legend, Tiedemann was an angry man prone to violent outbursts. Rumors started that while Emma Tiedemann's cause of death was officially listed as diabetes, in reality, her father murdered her. What's more, Tiedemann was rumored to have murdered several other people inside the castle, including a niece and a castle employee. That, the whispers said, was the real reason Tiedemann created the secret rooms and passageways—to carry out his crimes undetected. Some say that his wife found out and that Hannes murdered her to keep her quiet.

The result of all this? The castle became cursed, destined to bring misfortune to all who own it. More than a few ghosts have been reported to haunt the building. The most often sighted today is Tiedemann's daughter, Emma. She is said to be seen throughout the house but especially in the attic, where she was allegedly murdered. Emma shares the attic with another ghost, a young girl dressed all in black, believed to be another unnamed victim of Tiedemann's murderous rampage.

More Owners, More Mystery

The National Socialist German Workers' Party owned the castle from 1913 until the 1960s. Rumors from this period ran wild: secret Nazi meetings, 20 people being gunned down in the castle's basement, or mysterious boarders that included an unnamed doctor conducting experiments on human subjects in the castle's hidden areas.

In 1968, the castle was sold to the family of James Romano. Almost immediately after the Romanos moved in, they began to experience strange things they could not explain. Perhaps most disturbing was that the Romano children would often talk about one of their friends, a young girl that only they could see who lived in the attic. Eventually, Romano's wife came to believe that the ghost of Luise Tiedemann was also haunting the castle and was warning the Romanos of bad things coming if they stayed there. The Romanos put the castle up for sale.

The Romanos sold the castle to Sam Muscatello in 1974. And Sam Muscatello made sure the stories didn't die. He opened up the castle for guided tours and was always willing to talk about the latest ghost sighting. It was also Muscatello who found human skeletal remains inside a secret room in the attic. The bones were never positively identified, and while some believe they were the remains of one of Tiedemann's victims, other people thought Muscatello planted them as a publicity stunt. Muscatello once even invited local news reporters to the house for a live broadcast from a "real haunted house." It was during this broadcast that Cleveland radio host John Webster reported having his tape recorder yanked from him by an unknown force and thrown down the main staircase.

Haunted House, or Money Pit?

By the time Muscatello had his fill of Franklin Castle, the years had not been kind to the property. Muscatello eventually found buyers, but they didn't stay long. This started a pattern over the years of someone buying the house, investing large sums of money to fix it up, and eventually selling it—all lending more credence to the castle's curse. Michelle Heimburger, a former Cleveland resident, purchased the building in April 1999 solely to remodel it. Less than six months after the purchase, the castle fell victim to arson, and the fire destroyed almost the entire fourth floor.

The Franklin Castle Club

For years after the fire, the castle had the appearance of an abandoned building set for demolition. Then, in late 2005, a sign appeared on its front door heralding the arrival of the Franklin Castle Club. Shortly thereafter, e-mails were issued from the Castle Club's Web site, proclaiming a members-only dinner club that was accepting members at the low, low price of $5,000 annually. As with most things associated with Franklin Castle, all was not as it seemed. Even though the club's Web site claims it is currently holding events inside Franklin Castle, a drive past the building proves otherwise:Doors and windows remain boarded up, and the only light in the castle comes from drop lights hanging from bare ceilings. The only thing lurking inside is the long, storied legend of Franklin Castle itself.

Lincoln's Ghost Train

Abraham Lincoln's funeral train appears to have been much like the president himself: uncommonly determined and larger-than-life.

✳ ✳ ✳ ✳

Final Journey

WHEN PRESIDENT LINCOLN was assassinated in April 1865, the nation was understandably plunged into a state of mourning. Swept away was the "Great Emancipator," who had not only put an end to slavery but also preserved a fractured American union. For everything that he had done for the nation, it was decided that Lincoln's funeral procession should be as great as the man himself. In order to bring the president close to the citizens who loved and mourned him, his funeral train would trace the same route—in reverse—that Lincoln had traveled when he went to Washington, D.C., four years earlier as president-elect. Covering a vast 1,654 miles, the procession left Washington on April 21, 1865, and finally pulled into Springfield, Illinois, on May 3. Officially, this was Lincoln's last ride—but unofficially, some say that Abe and his funeral train have never stopped chugging along.

First Phantom

In April 1866, one year after Lincoln's assassination, the first report of the ghost train surfaced. The sighting occurred along a stretch of railway in New York's Hudson Valley. Witnesses told a fantastic tale of a spectral train that whooshed by them without making a sound. They identified it as Lincoln's funeral train after they observed the president's flag-draped coffin on board. Surrounded by black crepe, the casket was identical to the original but with one notable difference: This time, a *skeletal* honor guard stood at attention beside it. Witnesses also recalled an equally skeletal band playing what must have been a dreary funeral dirge; that no sounds were emitted from their musical instruments also seemed bizarre. A strange bluish light surrounded the train as it chugged silently northward. Witnesses recalled that a blast of warm air could be felt and that clocks inexplicably stopped for six minutes as the train slowly passed by. Over time, this vision would be reported surprisingly often along much of the original train's route.

Mass Hysteria?

With a tragedy of such immensity seizing the national psyche, it was almost a given that sightings of Lincoln's ghost would occur. Psychologists attribute such phenomena to denial—the subconscious act of refusing to let go. Lincoln had saved the union and restored peace to a nation whose future had hung precariously in the balance. It seemed extremely unfair, even unbelievable, that he should be taken away in such a brutal fashion. And yet, he had been.

Still, what can be said of a phantom train that appears to numerous people along so vast a route? While shock and denial might account for individual sightings of a spectral president, it seems doubtful that an entire funeral train could be hallucinated by scores of people at precisely the same time. And how could the details of such sightings match so closely from person to person and region to region?

Just Passing Through

If witnesses are to be believed, Lincoln's ghost train still chugs along on its seemingly endless journey. Sightings of it generally occur in April (the month in which the original funeral train began its trek), and details of eyewitness accounts are surprisingly similar to each other. But a few differences in these sightings have been documented. Some people say that the spectral train contains several cars that are all draped in black; others say that it only consists of an engine and one flatbed car that holds the dead president's coffin. And every so often, someone claims to hear a shrieking whistle coming from the phantom locomotive.

The Dark Side of the White House

From the East Wing to the West Wing, our presidential palace is reportedly one of the most haunted government buildings anywhere, which is hardly surprising given the rich history that has transpired within its walls.

✳   ✳   ✳   ✳

The White House's First Ghost

THE GHOST OF David Burns may be the first spirit that haunted the White House. In life, Burns donated the land on which the structure was built. One day, Franklin Roosevelt heard his name being called, and when he replied, the voice said that it was "Mr. Burns."

Roosevelt's valet, Cesar Carrera, told a similar story: Carrera was in the Yellow Oval Room when he heard a soft, distant voice say, "I'm Mr. Burns." When Carrera looked around, no one was there.

During the Truman years, a guard at the White House also heard a soft voice announce itself as Mr. Burns. The guard expected to see James Byrnes, Truman's secretary of state, but no one appeared. When the guard checked the roster, he learned that Byrnes hadn't been in the building at all that day.

William Henry Harrison Feels a Little Blue

William Henry Harrison was the first American president to die in office. While giving his inauguration address in icy, windy weather on March 4, 1841, Harrison caught a cold that quickly turned into pneumonia. Stories abound about Harrison wandering the corridors of the White House, half-conscious with fever, looking for a quiet room in which to rest. Unfortunately, there was no escape from the doctors, whose treatments may have killed him. While Harrison's lungs filled with fluid and fever wracked his body, his doctors bled him and then treated him with such remedies as mustard, laxatives, ipecac, rhubarb, and mercury. It is speculated that the president died not from the "ordinary winter cold" that he'd contracted, but from the care of his doctors. Harrison passed away on April 4, 1841, just one month after taking office.

Harrison's translucent ghost is seen throughout the White House, but it is most often spotted in the residential areas. His skin is pale blue and his breathing makes an ominous rattling noise. He appears to be looking for something and walks through closed doors. Some believe that he's looking for rest or a cure for his illness; others say he's searching for his office so that he can complete his term as president.

Andrew Jackson Likes the Ladies

If you'd prefer to see a happier ghost, look for the specter of Andrew Jackson; he's often seen in the Queen's Bedroom, where his bed is on display. But Jackson may not necessarily be looking for his old bed; in life, "Old Hickory" was quite the ladies' man, and today, the Queen's Bedroom is reserved for female guests of honor.

Visitors sometimes simply sense Jackson's presence in the Queen's Bedroom or feel a bone-chilling breeze when they're around his bed. Some have reported that Jackson's ghost climbs under the covers, sending guests shrieking out of the room.

Mary Todd Lincoln frequently complained about the ghost of Andrew Jackson cursing and stomping in the corridors of the White House. After she left the presidential estate, Jackson stopped fussing.

Oh Séance Can You See?

Séances at the White House have been nearly as numerous as the phantoms that inhabit its hallways. It has been well documented that in the early 1860s, President Lincoln and his wife contacted the spirit of Daniel Webster while attempting to reach their dearly departed son Willie during a séance. According to witnesses, the former secretary of state implored the president to continue his efforts to end slavery. Some years later, relatives of President Ulysses S. Grant held another séance at the White House, during which they reputedly spoke with young Willie Lincoln.

In 1995, with the help of medium Jean Houston, First Lady Hillary Rodham Clinton reportedly established contact with Eleanor Roosevelt and Mahatma Gandhi. It seems some séances yield better results than others. Describing her fascination with White House spirits, Clinton said, "There is something about the house at night that you just feel like you are summoning up the spirits of all the people who have lived there and worked there and walked through the halls there."

Ghosts of Presidents' Families and Foes

Abigail Adams used to hang laundry on clotheslines in the White House's East Room; her ghost appears there regularly in a cap and wrapped in a shawl. She's usually carrying laundry or checking to see if her laundry is dry.

The spirit of Dorothea "Dolley" Madison defends the Rose Garden that she designed and planted. When Woodrow Wilson's wife Edith ordered staff members to dig up the garden to plant new flowers, Dolley's apparition appeared and allegedly insisted that no one was going to touch her roses. The landscaping ceased.

One very out-of-place spirit appears to be that of a British soldier from around 1814, when the White House was besieged and burned. The uniformed specter looks lost and holds a torch. When he realizes that he's been spotted, he becomes alarmed and vanishes.

"Now about those ghosts. I'm sure they're here and I'm not half so alarmed at meeting up with any of them as I am at having to meet the live nuts I have to see every day."

—First Lady Bess Truman

Under a Raging Moon

Does a full moon really influence people's behavior?

✳ ✳ ✳ ✳

EVERYONE KNOWS THAT crazy things happen during a full moon. Or do they? Folklore regarding the connection has long, deep roots. In fact, the word lunatic derives from the Latin *luna*, or "moon." Recently, studies have been performed to establish a tie between human behavior and the phases of the moon. These tests have focused on such things as homicides, common crimes, even post-surgical crises during lunar phases. Like the full moon itself, the results have proved illuminating.

In one prominent study, University of Miami psychologist Arnold Lieber zeroed in on homicides. During a 15-year period, his team collected murder data from Dade County, Florida. The researchers found that of the 1,887 recorded murders during the period, the incident rate uncannily rose and fell based upon phases of the moon. As a full moon or a new moon approached, murders rose sharply. Homicides dropped off significantly during the moon's first and last quarters.

A study performed by the American Institute of Medical Climatology had similar findings. That test revealed a correlation between the full moon and peaks in psychotically oriented crimes such as arson and murder. But criminal impulses aren't the only things mirroring phases of the moon. A study of 1,000 tonsillectomies listed in the *Journal of the Florida Medical Association* revealed that 82 percent of postoperative bleeding crises occurred nearest the full moon, even though fewer tonsillectomies were performed during that period.

While such findings certainly sound definitive, scientists are reluctant to pronounce a direct connection until a physical model becomes accepted. As for theories that explain *why* the moon might have an influence over human behavior, Dr.

Lieber speculates that a human being's water composition may undergo a "biological tide" that wreaks havoc with emotions and body processes. But the fact is that no one can say for certain if the human/lunar connection is real or just so much howling at the moon. Stay tuned.

Nessie: Shock in the Loch

The legend of Nessie, the purported inhabitant of Scotland's Loch Ness, dates back to the year 565 when a roving Christian missionary named St. Columba is said to have rebuked a huge water monster to save the life of a swimmer. Rumors persisted from that time on.

✳   ✳   ✳   ✳

Monster Ahoy

IN 1933, ONE witness said he saw the creature three times; that same year, a vacationing couple claimed they saw a large creature with flippers and a long neck slither across the road and then heard it splash into the lake. These incidents made news around the world, and the hunt for Nessie was on.

Sightings multiplied and became more and more difficult to explain away. In 1971, a priest named Father Gregory Brusey saw a speedy long-necked creature cruising through the loch. One investigator estimates that more than 3,000 people have seen Nessie. The witnesses come from every walk of life.

Monster Media Madness

As technology has advanced, Nessie has been hunted with more sophisticated equipment, often with disappointing results. In 1934, a doctor snapped the famous "Surgeon's Photo," which showed a dinosaurlike head atop a long neck sticking out of the water. It has since been proven a hoax and what was thought to be Nessie was actually a picture of a toy submarine. Many other photos have been taken, but all are inconclusive.

Since 1934, numerous expeditions have been mounted in search of Nessie. Scuba divers and even submarines have scoured the lake to no avail because the amount of peat in the water makes visibility extremely poor.

In 2003, the British Broadcasting Corporation undertook a massive satellite-assisted sonar sweep of the entire lake, but again with no results. And in 2007, cameras were given to 50,000 people attending a concert on the lake's shore in hopes that someone might get lucky and snap a shot of Nessie. But apparently she doesn't like rock music—Nessie was a no-show. In 2011, two local residents spotted what they believe to be Nessie; she stuck around for four to five minutes.

The Ness-essary Debate

Theories about Nessie's true nature abound. One of the most popular ideas, thanks to the oft-reported long neck, flippers, and bulbous body, is that Nessie is a surviving plesiosaur—a marine reptile thought to have gone extinct 65 million years ago. Critics insist that even if a cold-blooded reptile could exist in the lake's frigid waters, Loch Ness is not large enough to support a breeding population of them. Other theories suggest that Nessie is a giant eel, a string of seals or otters swimming in formation, floating logs, a porpoise, or a huge sturgeon.

Locals have hinted that the creature is actually a demon. Stories of devil worship and mysterious rituals in the area have gone hand in hand with rumors of bodies found floating in the loch. In the early 1900s, famed occultist Aleister Crowley owned a home on the lake's southern shore where he held "black masses" and conducted other ceremonies that may have aimed to "raise" monsters. And for centuries, Scots have repeated folktales of the kelpie, or water horse, a creature that can shape-shift in order to lure the unwary into the water.

Whatever the truth about Nessie, she has made quite a splash. Every year thousands of people try their luck at spotting—and recording—the world's most famous monster.

Mermaids: Real or Fish-ction?

The idea that mermaids actually exist is, well, a bit fishy. But anyone who has ever watched The Little Mermaid *or* Splash, *knows that there's a magic surrounding mermaids that is irresistible. And now a Discovery Channel documentary has stunned viewers with their suggestion that the answer is "maybe."*

✳   ✳   ✳   ✳

THE EARLIEST IMAGE of a mermaid comes from 1000 B.C. in Syria, when the goddess Atargatis tried to take on the form of a fish by diving into the sea. She was not allowed to give up her great beauty, however, and the result was half fish and half human—a goddess of the sea with a beautiful face, long flowing hair and the sleek glimmering tale of a fish.

Homer's work *The Odyssey* expanded on that idea by creating half human sea creatures called "sirens." Beautiful? Yes. But a little evil as well. These mermaids sang harmonious tunes, luring sailors to their death in the sea.

Stories of their existence have been told and retold for a couple thousand years. And artists have depicted the mythical creatures in their artwork for just as long. Almost every country and culture has tales of mermaids and many people claim to have seen one. It begs the question: before mass communication as we know it today, how did all these separate cultures come up with the same imaginary creature with so many of the same characteristics?

Could They Be Real?

The answer is maybe. The Discovery Channel program follows the scientific investigation of two former National Oceanic Atmospheric Administration (NOAA) scientists who started out to learn more about the beaching of whales in 2007. What they discovered were some mysterious underwater sounds—like nothing they had ever heard before.

Underwater singing? There must be mermaids! Well, it wasn't quite that simple, but the team did feel that the noises merited additional investigation—especially since they were convinced that this mysterious creature was attempting to communicate with them.

When another whale-beaching occurred along the coast of South Africa, the scientists traveled there and found that African scientists had recorded similar underwater communications. Further investigation revealed the remains of this sea creature in the belly of a great white shark—and it was definitely a marine animal. And a human. In short, it appeared to be a mermaid.

This creature was not a Disney princess by any means. But it did appear to possess the tail of a fish along with the clearly defined hands associated with the human body. If nothing else, this unusual creature supported an old "aquatic ape" theory about ancient mammals that lived on both land and sea. But alas, the government took possession of these remains, leaving the scientists with nothing but their recording of an unusual sea-sound.

As is often the case with government actions, their decision to confiscate the remains only convinced the scientists, and everyone hearing the story, that they were on to something. They tracked down a local teenager who claimed to have seen the body of a mermaid on the beach along with the whales. And surprise—he had taken a video with his cell phone.

Unfortunately the video wasn't clear and the government denies any discovery or cover-up of mermaids. The NOAA has also issued a statement saying there's no evidence that "aquatic humanoids" have ever been found. And the Discovery Channel admits that their show was meant to entertain—while it shows how mermaids could be real, it was as much science fiction as science. So are there mermaids? Maybe.

The Wreck of the *Titan*

A book that eerily foreshadowed the Titanic *tragedy fourteen years before it occurred? You bet your iceberg!*

✳ ✳ ✳ ✳

Doomed Voyage

As THE WORLD'S greatest steamship moved across the North Atlantic darkness, an unseen foe lay in wait. The ship dubbed "virtually unsinkable" by its creators would suffer a fatal collision with an iceberg spotted too late. The staggering loss of life associated with the craft's sinking would deliver a blow to man's hubris and act as a cautionary tale never to underestimate the forces of nature.

The story of the RMS *Titanic* has become the stuff of legend. But this isn't that story.

Life Imitates Art

This is the story of another ship, the imaginary creation of author Morgan Robertson. Robertson had a great love for the sea. He wrote many tales of adventure on the ocean and his stories were regarded as some of the most accurate and vivid of his day. He told of the ill-fated passage of his fictional ship, the implausibly named *Titan*, in the book, *Futility, or the Wreck of the Titan*. Had this tome been written after the 1912 sinking of the *Titanic*, some might have accused Robertson of sensationalism and cashing in after the fact. As it happened, however, this was far from the case. Robertson wrote his sixty-nine page novella in 1898, fourteen years before the *Titanic* slipped beneath the waves. Its similarities to that tragedy run the gamut from uncanny to eerie.

Titan vs. Titanic

How uncanny? The fictional *Titan* and the very real *Titanic* both sank in April in the icy North Atlantic. Both vessels used three propellers for propulsion and were traveling at over

22 knots per hour. Even the ships' dimensions were close, with the *Titan* stretching out to 800 feet and the *Titanic* to 882 feet.

Both ships met their end around midnight compliments of the aforementioned icebergs, after taking a hit on the starboard side. The *Titan* was described as "practically unsinkable" in the book, while the *Titanic* was described in newspaper articles as "virtually unsinkable."

Each vessel was the largest afloat for its day, and each operated with an insufficient number of lifeboats, an oversight that would result in an appalling loss of life in both instances.

That last factoid is where things get really interesting. The *Titan* carried 24 lifeboats, less than half needed for her 3,000 passenger capacity. Likewise, the *Titanic* carried 20 lifeboats, less than half needed for her 3,000 passenger limit. Both ships satisfied the legal requirements in this area, but only just. When the *Titan* went down, more than half of her 2,500 passengers died as a result. More than 1,500 perished when the *Titanic* sank, more than half of the 2,200 passengers onboard!

Explaining the Inexplicable

Many of Robertson's contemporaries felt that he had a sixth sense. Since Robertson was known to have an interest in the occult, parapsychologists believed that the writer had experienced a paranormal vision. Others, grounded in religion, believed that the Robertson had been granted a gift of prophecy and used as a conduit. Naysayers, however, felt that the similarities between the *Titan* and the *Titanic* could be chalked up to little more than a grand coincidence.

But Robertson's story gets better still. In 1914 he released a book titled *Beyond the Spectrum*. The book told of a Japanese sneak attack on American ships docked in Hawaii. The aggressive action leads to a war between Japan and the United States. Coincidence? Precognition? Divine intervention?

You be the judge.

Predictions, Premonitions, and Precognition

Some believe strongly in precognition, while others aren't so sure, but when it arrives it's mighty hard to explain. Here are some freakishly accurate premonitions that might just stand your hair on end.

✳ ✳ ✳ ✳

Cayce at Bat

EDGAR CAYCE (1877–1945) is to prophets what ballplayer Derek Jeter is to the Yankees. As one of the most reliable seers, Cayce, like Jeter, got the job done much of the time. Fittingly referred to as "The Sleeping Prophet," Cayce would enter a trancelike state before issuing his readings. While in this state, Cayce predicted the stock market crash of 1929 six months before it occurred; the beginning of both world wars; the death of President Franklin D. Roosevelt; and the assassination of President John F. Kennedy.

Hoy Foresees Tragedy

On April 19, 1995, during a live radio program in Fayetteville, N.C., clairvoyant Tana Hoy hit prophecy pay dirt when he told the interviewer that there would be a deadly terrorist attack on a building in an American city beginning with the letter "O." He added that the tragedy would occur before the first of May. Just ninety minutes later, the Alfred P. Murrah Federal Building in Oklahoma City was blown up by Timothy McVeigh and other radicals in what was, up to that point, the worst terrorist attack on U.S. soil.

Twain to See

Writer Mark Twain (Samuel Clemons) eerily predicted the deaths of both his brother and himself. In a prophetic dream, Twain saw his brother laid out in a coffin resting between two folding chairs in his sister's parlor.

A few weeks after the unsettling vision, Twain's brother was killed in a boating accident. When Twain entered his sister's living room to pay his last respects to his sibling, his eyes were confronted by a startling sight. Before him lay his brother in a coffin stretched across two folding chairs—precisely as he had envisioned the scene during his dream.

Twain was born in 1835, the year that Halley's Comet was visible. He believed that his life force would be extinguished when Halley's Comet came back for its encore. In 1910, Halley's Comet came back into view. And Mark Twain exited the mortal world. Coincidence?

Rockin' Out in the Afterlife

Twain certainly wasn't alone in predicting his own death. Reports that President Abraham Lincoln witnessed his own assassination in a dream have long made the rounds, but the premonition lacks substantiation and is considered dubious.

Harder to discount is the vision that bassist Mikey Welsh had on September 26, 2011. A former member of the rock band Weezer, Welsh logged onto his Twitter account and issued the following statement: "Dreamt I died in Chicago next weekend (heart attack in my sleep). Need to write my will today."

Then, before signing off Welsh added this: "Correction—the weekend after next."

Two weeks later Welsh travelled to Chicago for Riotfest—an annual rock music festival that was featuring his former band. Unfortunately, he never made it to the show. Staff at the Raffaello Hotel found Welsh's body in his room on October, 8, 2011, one day before the scheduled concert.

His death came as the result of an apparent drug overdose that in turn led to a heart attack. The time of his passing meshed precisely with his prediction.

The Catacombs of Paris

Six million souls are buried beneath the "City of Lights." According to reports, some aren't happy with the arrangement.

✳ ✳ ✳ ✳

For the Poor No More

INDIGENCE AND INDIGNITY seem to go hand in hand. In Paris during the twelfth century, financially-strapped souls were buried in mass burial grounds, an unenviable fate worlds removed from the dignified private plots and ceremonies available to the rich.

During the late eighteenth century, however, the poor would have the last ghoulish laugh, when Parisian cemeteries were filled to overflowing and all deceased people, regardless of their station in life, were committed to a common grave. *Touché!*

An abandoned network of underground stone quarries beneath Paris was chosen for this macabre purpose. The Catacombs of Paris offered a way to sidestep the problem of decaying flesh leaching into the ground, a bona fide health concern for a society that drew its drinking water from underground wells. Over time, more than six million people were committed to the 'combs. Here, they would sleep away eternity.

Or would they?

Rest in Pieces

Piled up in a 180-mile stretch of tunnels, the dead bodies of the Catacombs are anything but ordinary. The remaining skulls and bones have been stacked in orderly if bizarre fashion to create grisly monuments and walls, and the dank, dark setting is conducive to frights both real and imagined.

This spooky underground netherworld currently operates as the Catacombs Museum. For a fee, visitors can walk through a section of the tunnels and commune with the dead.

Contrary to popular belief, visits to this no-man's-land of death and decay is anything but new. Tours of the Catacombs have taken place since 1867. Members of the French Resistance used the network of tunnels to hide out from the Germans during World War II, and the Germans used a portion of the Catacombs as a bunker during the same world-shaping conflict.

Rude Awakenings

If visitors to the Catacombs should forget where they are, a sign reading *"Arrête! C'est ici l'empire de la mort"* (Stop! This is the Empire of Death) gives fair warning about what they will soon encounter. When six million corpses are crammed together, there are bound to be a few spirits that grow restless. The Catacombs are deemed one of the most haunted places on earth by travel journals, and reports of ghostly sightings and other paranormal encounters seem as numerous as the bodies themselves.

Unfriendly Ghosts

Based on the accounts of startled witnesses, those who expect to find friendly ghosts in the Catacombs will be terrified by the ones that they do encounter. Some visitors claim that they were "touched by unseen hands." Others tell of an uncanny feeling of being watched as they walked through the underground labyrinth. Several people tell of an ominous group of shadows that followed them step for step as they moved through the tunnels. Photos of apparitions snapped by visitors are plentiful and varied. Creepy cold spots and inexplicable photographic orbs have also been detected. Some even claim to have been choked with great might by a frightening invisible force.

Frightful Fun

Tours have occasionally been cut short when visitors grew hysterical due to such ghostly pranks, but the popularity of the Catacombs as a haven for visitors has remained strong throughout the years. In fact, more than one million visitors make the subterranean journey each year.

Real Vampires

Can corpses prey on people from beyond the grave? In the cases outlined below, someone clearly thought they could.

✳ ✳ ✳ ✳

IN 1857, THE *Wooster Republican* featured an article entitled "An Extraordinary Superstition: A corpse exhumed." According to the article, residents of Euphrata, Pennsylvania, had been shocked to hear that the body of one Sophia Bauman had been exhumed, nine years after her death, so that the body could be destroyed in order to save the lives of her surviving family members. Residents suspected that her body was "feeding" on living flesh from beyond the grave.

A Misunderstood Disease

Consumption—as tuberculosis was known in those days—was the single most common cause of death in the 19th century, and one of the least understood diseases of them all. When someone contracted it, it did look as though the life was slowly being sucked out of them. That the life was being sucked away by a person already dead was not exactly "superstition" so much as a form of folk medicine; in those days before contagious disease was really understood, the idea that a dead body could "feed" from the living seemed reasonable enough, and when entire families were dying of the disease, survivors became desperate. Sometimes it seemed that stopping a corpse from "feeding" on the living was the only way to halt the spread of the disease before it claimed an entire family. Two of Sophia Bauman's sisters had died of consumption, along with her mother and two of her bothers, and the family was getting desperate for a treatment.

It was believed, or at least suggested, that if the "winding sheet" got into a corpse's mouth, the dead body might "suck" on it and the "continual suction" from beneath the ground could draw life out of the living by causing consumption. Evidently someone wondered if perhaps that had happened to Sophia, and so, one sunday morning, her coffin was exhumed from the cold ground. However, no winding sheet was in the skeleton's mouth—any such sheet would have long ago disintegrated after nine years in the grave.

Suspicions and Remedies

Around the time of Sophia's death, a similar case occurred elsewhere in New England in which a physician opened the graves of two people whose family had been ravaged by consumption. In the coffins, he found that mysterious snow white vines had grown all over the corpses, and seemed still to be growing. While the physician stated that he had no faith in an old superstition which held that plucking such a vine off the corpse would truly cure consumption in a family, he chose to cut away the vines anyway.

The belief that dead people could suck the life out of the living was not a new one at the time; it appears to have been going around for centuries, following European immigrants into the New World. But in some cases, simply removing a vine or winding sheet wasn't thought to be enough. In some, perhaps more common, versions of the practice, the method said to arrest the spread of the disease actually involved mutilating or destroying the corpse altogether.

A Grisly Discovery

In 1990, a group of children playing in Connecticut stumbled onto a long abandoned burial ground near a gravel mine. Police initially believed it was a serial killer's dumping grounds, but further inspection found that the graves were actually part of a colonial cemetery in which residents had been buried in simple wood coffins, unadorned by jewelry, with their arms at their sides or across their chest.

But two of the coffins were in stone crypts, and one of them was in a red coffin with the letters J.B. spelled out in tacks on the outside. The bones inside had been rearranged inside of the coffin, with the skull and thigh bones set into a perfect skull and crossbones pattern. Analysis later showed that the body had been beheaded, and the bones moved around, some five years after "JB" had died. It seemed that someone had suspected JB of infecting the living from inside of his coffin.

Perhaps the exhumation was done quietly, but for these things to happen in large public ceremonies was not unknown. In 1793, hundreds of people went to a blacksmith's forge in Machester, Vermont, to watch the heart of a suspected "vampire" be burned up in attempt to cure the dead man's wife's illness. That the whole town came out to see JB's bones be rearranged is not impossible.

The Case of Mercy Brown

Though JB's is the only such body to be studied firsthand by modern scientists, written testimonies and reports suggest that simply burning the heart and lungs seems to have been the most common way to "cure" a corpse that was thought to be feeding off the living, and this seems to have been the case with the most famous, and probably most recent "vampire," Mercy Lena Brown of Exeter, Rhode Island.

Mercy died of consumption in 1892, a year when the disease was devastating the families who had remained in Exeter, a community whose population had been cut in half over the course of a couple of generations.

By then, it was known in the medical community that consumption was caused by bacteria, not by the dead, but such scientific news spread only slowly to isolated rural towns. By the time Mercy died, two of her family members had already succumbed to the disease, and her brother was battling it too.

Desperate to save Mercy's brother when he took a turn for the worse, their father agreed to have Mercy's corpse exhumed a few months after her death to see if there was fresh blood in the heart, which was said to be a sure sign that the body was still being kept alive by feeding on living tissue. Mercy's mother and sister, who had also died of consumption, were exhumed first, though they were merely skeletons by then. The winter weather, though, had kept Mercy's own body from decomposing too much. When blood was found in her heart, it was burned on a nearby rock, and the ashes were fed to her brother.

The "cure" didn't work; Mercy's brother was dead within two months. News of the event circulated through the national press, and other cases were reported. A 1893 *Chicago Tribune* article referred to it as a "grewsome (sic) superstition" that still survived in Pennsylvania, though there's some evidence of it having occurred in Chicago itself a couple of decades before.

Mercy, though, is the last known person to have been suspected of "vampirism," but it's generally believed that only a tiny fraction of cases are still known today, as most were never written down or reported at all. There may have been hundreds more. New stories are being found in old newspapers, ancient diaries, and faded letters all the time.

5 Ways to Get Rid of a Ghost

Something strange in your neighborhood? Something weird and it don't look good? Here's a do-it-yourself guide to ghost-busting. But please note: In the world of ghost-busting, there are no guarantees, so proceed at your own risk.

❋   ❋   ❋   ❋

1. **Give it a good talking-to:** The first tactic is simply to ask your ghost, politely but firmly, to leave. If you think the ghost is hanging around the physical world because of fear of punishment in the spirit world, tell it that it will be treated with love and forgiveness. Try not to show anger (which may give a negative spirit more power) or fear (since it's unlikely that a spirit will be able to harm you, especially in your own home).

2. **Clean and serene:** If tough talking doesn't work, the next step is a spiritual cleansing or "smudging." Open a window in each room of your home, then light a bundle of dry sage and walk around with it (have something handy to catch the ashes), allowing the smoke to circulate while you intone the words: "This sage is cleansing out all negative energies and spirits. All negative energies and spirits must leave now through the windows and not return." Do this until you sense that the negative energy has left the building (and before you set fire to the house), and then say, "In the name of God, this room is now cleansed."

3. **Bless this house:** If smudging doesn't do the trick, it may be time to call in the professionals. Ask a local priest or minister to come to your home and bless it. There is usually no charge for this service, but you might be expected to make a small donation to the church.

4. **The Exorcist:** Exorcism is usually carried out by clergy using prayers and religious items to invoke a supernatural power that will cast out the spirit. Roman Catholic exorcism involves a priest reciting prayers and invocations, often in Latin. The priest displays a crucifix and sprinkles holy water over the place, person, or object believed to be possessed. Exorcism has been sensationally depicted in movies but it's no laughing matter—in the past, people who would now be diagnosed as physically or mentally ill have undergone exorcism, sometimes dying in the process.

5. **What not to do:** Don't be tempted to use Ouija boards, tarot cards, or séances, as these may "open the door" to let in other unwanted spirits. Also be very suspicious of anyone offering a commercial ghost-busting service, including any medium or spiritual adviser who offers to rid your home of a spirit in return for payment. They're almost certain to be charlatans, and you're unlikely to get your money back if their services don't work.

Eerie Haunted Objects

Many ghost hunters believe that solid objects, such as buildings, furnishings, and decorative items, retain psychic energy. People who come into contact with these objects may sense stored emotions, as though they're revisiting the original events that surround the items. Usually these "flashbacks" are associated with past tragedies and death. Others objects appear to channel actual spirits. Either way, they're just plain creepy.

✳ ✳ ✳ ✳

Robert, the Haunted Doll

F EW DOLLS ARE as haunted as "Robert," a straw doll once owned by Florida artist Robert "Gene" Otto. During Otto's lifetime (he died in 1974), the doll was often heard walking, humming, and singing in the attic. Some witnesses even claim they saw the doll staring out the window at them. Today, the doll resides in the Fort East Martello Museum in Key West, where he continues to frighten visitors. As ghost hunter David Sloan said after investigating Robert, "Be careful of the objects you possess, or one day they may end up possessing you."

A Haunted Painting

A disturbing—and apparently haunted—painting entitled *Hands Resist Him* became famous on eBay in February 2000. The painting portrayed a little boy standing in front of a window next to a girl with jointed, doll-like arms.

Artist Bill Stoneham painted the picture in 1972. Within a year of the art's first showing, both the gallery owner and the Los Angeles critic who reviewed it were dead. No one is certain what happened after the painting's original owner, actor John Marley, died on May 22, 1984, but years later, the art was found behind a brewery.

People continue to report strange events after merely viewing photos of the painting online. (An Internet search for "haunted painting" will lead you to such photos.) One person heard an eerie, disembodied voice when viewing the artwork. Others talk about fainting as soon as they look at it. Some say that they have been visited by spirits from the painting.

Comte LeFleur's Ghostly Portrait

If you dine at Brennan's Restaurant in New Orleans, be sure to visit the Red Room upstairs and watch the portrait of Comte LeFleur for several minutes. Many guests watch his smile change to an expression far more sinister.

Wealthy Comte LeFleur was well liked in colonial New Orleans. One day, he cheerfully went around town making funeral and burial arrangements for three people. Then he returned home and killed his wife and his college-age son. The count then hanged himself from the sturdy gas chandelier overlooking the corpses of his family.

Today, the LeFleur residence is home to Brennan's Restaurant. Like the ghosts of the count and his family, the chandelier is still there. But it is the painting of Comte LeFleur that catches the eye of most visitors. Those who spend a few minutes watching the killer's image understand why it is one of America's most frightening portraits. LeFleur's head tilts slightly, and his expression changes from a mild smile to an evil grin until you blink or glance away.

An Especially Spooky Ouija Board

Many people avoid Ouija boards because they may connect us with "the other side" or with evil entities. This certainly seemed to be the case with the board Abner Williams loaned to a group of El Paso "Goths."

In mid-2000, after the board was returned to him, Williams complained of scratching noises coming from the board, along with a man's voice addressing him, followed by the sound of children chanting nursery rhymes at his window. When Williams tried to throw the board in the trash, it reappeared in his house. A paranormal investigator borrowed the board, and a hooded figure appeared from nowhere and growled at his son.

When a paranormal research team investigated the Ouija board, they found spots of blood on the front of it and a coating of blood on the back. They measured several cold spots over areas of the board, and photos revealed a strange ectoplasm rising from it. The board was eventually sent to a new owner, who did not want it to be cleared of negative energy. That person has remained silent about any recent activity surrounding the Ouija board.

Although this is an unusually well-documented haunted Ouija board, this is not an uncommon tale. Many psychics warn that, if you ask a spirit to communicate with you through a Ouija board, it's like opening a door between the worlds. You never know what kind of spirits—good or evil—will use that Ouija board to visit you. In general, it's wise to be cautious with "spirit boards" of any kind.

Nathaniel Hawthorne and the Haunted Chair

You may have seen a creepy old chair or two, but when author Nathaniel Hawthorne encountered one that was actually haunted, he wrote a short story about it. Hawthorne's "true family legend," which he titled "The Ghost of Dr. Harris," wasn't published until 30 years after the author's death.

According to Hawthorne, Dr. Harris used to sit and read the newspaper in the same chair at the Boston Athenaeum each morning. When the old man died, his ghost continued to visit, and Hawthorne, who was researching at the library, saw it daily until he had the courage to look him in the eye. There, the author reported a "melancholy look of helplessness" that lingered for several seconds. Then the ghost vanished.

So if you visit the Boston Athenaeum, be careful where you sit. Dr. Harris may be in that "empty" chair.

Dream Weaver

As an aeronautical engineer and author of books about paranormal phenomena, John William Dunne (1875–1949) questioned much in life, but nothing more keenly than human dreams and their meanings. His obsession with the twilight world was sparked by an odd event that he couldn't explain. How had Dunne been able to "see" one of the world's greatest tragedies while he was sleeping? And how could this have occurred before the event took place?

✳ ✳ ✳ ✳

JOHN WILLIAM DUNNE is best known for the invention of the first practical and stable tailless airplane. But in addition to his aeronautic accomplishments, Dunne offered compelling theories about the very structure of time in his book *An Experiment with Time*. Dunne's interest in this area was prompted by his uncanny knack for forecasting events through his dreams. Of these, one proved particularly mind-boggling.

On the chance that there might be something to his nocturnal visions, Dunne recorded each dream in writing. In early May 1902, while working as an engineer for the British military in South Africa, Dunne had a dream in which he found himself on the island of Martinique. In his vision, the French territory exploded and some 30,000 people perished as a result. Waking up in a cold sweat, Dunne weighed his options. Should he warn the French authorities? Or would his amazing claim fall upon deaf ears? Dunne chose to alert the powers that be, but he was unable to persuade what he later called "incredulous French authorities" to evacuate the island.

A few days after he had his vision, Dunne received a newspaper at his outpost. To his absolute horror, he discovered that his chilling dream had become a reality: Mount Pelée, located on the island of Martinique, had erupted with unbelievable force. In its wake, around 30,000 people lay dead.

Had Dunne foreseen the future, or are the past, present, and future simply illusive human perceptions? The question would preoccupy Dunne for the rest of his waking days—and many of his sleep-filled nights, too.

Fireball in the Sky

What happened on the night of September 12, 1952? Was it a meteor or a UFO? A robot or an alien monster? A hoax or the simple truth? Read the account and decide for yourself.

✳ ✳ ✳ ✳

WHILE PLAYING FOOTBALL on the afternoon of September 12, 1952, a group of boys in Flatwoods, West Virginia, saw a large fireball fly over their heads. The object seemed to stop near the hillside property of Bailey Fisher. Some thought the object was a UFO, but others said it was just a meteor. They decided to investigate.

Darkness was falling as the boys made their way toward the hill, so they stopped at the home of Kathleen May to borrow a flashlight. Seeing how excited the boys were, May, her two sons, and their friend, Eugene Lemon, decided to join them. The group set off to find out exactly what had landed on the hill.

Walking Through the Darkness

As they neared the top of the hill, the group smelled a strange odor that reminded them of burning metal. Continuing on, some members of the group thought they saw an object that resembled a spaceship. Shining their flashlights in front of them, the group was startled when something not of this world moved out from behind a nearby tree.

The Encounter

The description of what is now known as the Flatwoods Monster is almost beyond belief. It stood around 12 feet tall and had a round, reddish face from which two large holes were visible. Looming up from behind the creature's head was a large pointed hood. The creature, which appeared to be made of a dark metal, had no arms or legs and seemed to float through the air. Looking back, the witnesses believe what they saw was a protective suit or perhaps a robot rather than a monster.

When a flashlight beam hit the creature, its "eyes" lit up and it began floating toward the group while making a strange hissing noise. The horrible stench was now overpowering and some in the group immediately felt nauseous. Because she was at the head of the group, Kathleen May had the best view of the monster. She later stated that as the creature was moving toward her, it squirted or dripped a strange fluid on her that resembled oil but had an unusual odor to it.

Terrified beyond belief, the group fled down the hillside and back to the May house, where they telephoned Sheriff Robert Carr, who responded with his deputy, Burnell Long. After talking with the group, they gathered some men and went to the Fisher property to investigate. But they only found a gummy residue and what appeared to be skid marks on the ground. There was no monster and no spaceship. However, the group did report that the heavy stench of what smelled like burning metal was still in the air.

The Aftermath

A. Lee Stewart, a member of the of the search party and copublisher of the *Braxton Democrat,* knew a good story when he saw one, so he sent the tale over the news wire, and almost immediately, people were asking Kathleen May for interviews. On September 19, 1952, May and Stewart discussed the Flatwoods Monster on the TV show *We the People.* For the show, an artist sketched the creature based on May's description, but he took some liberties. The resulting sketch was so outrageous that people started saying the whole thing must be nothing more than a hoax.

Slowly, though, others came forward to admit that they too had seen a strange craft flying through the sky near Flatwoods on

September 12. One witness described it as roughly the size of a single-car garage. He said that he lost sight of the craft when it appeared to land on a nearby hill.

Since that night in 1952, the Flatwoods Monster has never been seen again, leaving many people to wonder what exactly those people encountered. A monster? An alien from another world? Or perhaps nothing more than a giant owl? One thing is for sure: There were far too many witnesses to deny that they stumbled upon something strange that night.

America From Ghost-to-Ghost

Although Americans have been chasing ghosts for centuries, today there is a glut of books, movies, television shows, and paranormal research societies that offer plenty of insight into the unknown. Here are some of the best stories and legends.

✳   ✳   ✳   ✳

NO MATTER WHERE people are in the United States, chances are good that they'll find a number of legends attached to their hometown. The trappings of the tales may be different, but you can find something of interest throughout the country.

The East Coast

Take New York City, for instance. The city is world-renowned for Broadway and the theater. Not as well known are the stories of ghosts treading the boards.

At the Belasco Theatre on 44th Street, there's at least one person who's no longer on the program but still shows up for every curtain call. This theater has reportedly been haunted for decades by the ghost of former owner David Belasco, who had the neo-Georgian playhouse built in 1907. Originally known as the Stuyvesant, Belasco renamed the theater three years after it opened. Once one of the most important men on Broadway, Belasco was so passionate about the theater that, undeterred by death, he has continued to attend opening night performances since his death in 1931. Sometimes, his spirit is accompanied by that of a woman known simply as the "Blue Lady."

The New Amsterdam Theater on West 42nd Street is said to be haunted by the ghost of a *Ziegfeld Follies* chorus singer. Despondent over her bad marriage, Olive Thomas apparently committed suicide in the place where she was happiest. Dressed in her green beaded stage costume and headpiece, she wanders through the building after the final curtain call, carrying a blue glass bottle of pills.

The internationally known Palace Theatre on Broadway is said to be home to more than 100 spirits, including singer Judy Garland, who apparently still hovers by the stage door—perhaps waiting for her fans. However, there's one ghost that no one wants to encounter: the acrobat who broke his neck onstage. The story goes that anyone who has the misfortue to see him will die soon afterward.

The West Coast

Travel west to California and you'll find a haunted site that is open to the public and annually attracts more than a million visitors. Alcatraz, the forbidding facility that sits on a barren, rocky island, became known as America's most famous—or infamous—maximum-security prison between 1934 and 1963. During that time, it served as the home of notorious criminals, such as Al Capone and George "Machine Gun" Kelly. Maybe a few of them still haven't left.

Visitors have reported the presence of cold spots as they enter the cell house through double steel doors. A metal door in C Block, which had been welded shut, leads to a utility corridor that is reportedly haunted by three convicts who were killed during a 1946 escape attempt. Over the years, prison guards allegedly reported eerie sounds, including crying and moaning from empty cells. Phantom figures were seen walking the corridors late at night.

One of the most psychically disturbed areas at Alcatraz is "the Hole," the place where prisoners who broke the rules were punished. Cell 14D, one of the underground four-foot-by-eight-foot cells, is noticeably colder than the others. A supernatural presence is believed to have existed there since the 1940s—ever since the night an inmate screamed that a ghost with glowing eyes was locked inside the cell with him. While the guards had always joked about a phantom haunting that part of the jail, no one was laughing when they opened the cell the next morning to find the inmate dead, with hand marks on his neck.

Although the cause of death was listed as strangulation, no earthly or unearthly source was ever discovered that could have caused the inmate's death. What happened the following day was equally upsetting. During roll call, the guards discovered that one extra convict kept appearing in line—the same man who had died the night before. As the guards and the other inmates watched, he vanished before their eyes. Like the evil that may have murdered him that fatal night, his ghost is reportedly still imprisoned in the Hole.

Down South

But if there is one spot that can be considered the capital of America's supernatural world, it's New Orleans, Louisiana. Even skeptics change their minds after a visit to the fascinating world of the French Quarter.

What lurks there, aside from the beautiful centuries-old buildings, the music, and the nightlife? Take a "ghost tour" of this part of the city and find out. First settled by the French in the early 18th century, the Quarter has been home to a host of memorable characters who apparently refuse to leave even after death. Marie Laveau, the voodoo priestess who captivated the city in the early 19th century, is reportedly buried in St. Louis Cemetery No. 2, but her spirit is said to linger close by. Many people believe that Laveau will answer the prayers of anyone who leaves an offering at her grave.

At the heart of the French Quarter stands the elegant three-story mansion that once belonged to Louis and Delphine LaLaurie, an attractive, popular couple who lived there in the 1830s. They enjoyed hosting lavish parties, but one night a fire broke out, and guests were shocked to discover a number of terrified slaves chained in a secret room. It seemed that the LaLauries also enjoyed torturing and conducting medical experiments on their servants, who in some cases had been held captive for years. Infuriated local residents were ready to lynch the couple when they learned of the abuse, but Louis and Delphine managed to slip away. The ghosts of their victims are said to still wander the house—reenacting the most terrible moments of their lives.

If the thought of coming face-to-face with a few ghosts isn't too alarming, then visit some of these locations and others like them, some of which may be found close to home. Just remember, people can shut off the television or put down the scary book—it's not quite that easy to walk away from the real thing.

Spotting Sasquatch

Throughout the world, it's called Alma, Yeti, Sasquatch, the Abominable Snowman, Wildman, and Bigfoot. Whatever the name, people agree that it's tall, hairy, doesn't smell good, and has a habit of showing up in locations around the globe, most especially in North America.

✳ ✳ ✳ ✳

Jasper, Alberta, Canada (1811)

THIS WAS THE first known Bigfoot evidence found in North America. An explorer named David Thompson found 14-inch footprints in the snow, each toe topped by a short claw. He and his party didn't follow the tracks, fearing their guns would be useless against such a large animal. In his journal Thompson wrote that he couldn't bring himself to believe such a creature existed.

British Columbia, Canada (1924)

In 1957, prospector Albert Ostman was finally able to come forward about a chilling event that had happened to him more than 30 years prior. While camping at the head of Toba Inlet near Vancouver Island, Ostman was snatched up, still in his sleeping bag, and taken to a small valley where several Bigfoot were living. Held captive for several days, Ostman was only able to escape when one of the larger creatures tried to eat his snuff and chaos ensued.

Wanoga Butte, Oregon (1957)

After a long, uneventful morning hunting, Gary Joanis and Jim Newall were ecstatic when Joanis felled a deer with a single shot. But when a hairy creature "not less than nine feet tall" emerged from the woods, threw the deer over its shoulder, and lumbered off, the two men were left speechless.

Monroe, Michigan (1965)

On August 13, Christine Van Acker and her mother were driving when a large, hairy creature came out of the nearby woods. Frightened by the creature, the mother lost control of the car and grazed the beast. The car stalled and while the mother struggled to start it, the creature put its arm through the window, struck Christine in the face and slammed her mother's head against the car door, leaving both women with black eyes, photos of which were widely circulated in the press.

Bluff Creek, California (1967)

The famous sighting by Roger Patterson and Bob Gimlin yielded the first home-movie footage of Bigfoot. Although critics said it was obviously a man in a gorilla suit, Patterson denied the hoax allegations until his death in 1972. As of 2008, Gimlin still contends that the footage wasn't faked.

Spearfish, South Dakota (1977)

Betty Johnson and her three daughters saw two Bigfoot in a cornfield. The larger of the two was eight-feet tall. They both appeared to be eating corn and making a whistling sound.

Paris Township, Ohio (1978)

Herbert and Evelyn Cayton reported that a seven-foot-tall, 300-pound, fur-covered creature appeared at their house so frequently that their daughter thought it was a pet.

Jackson, Wyoming (1980)

On June 17, Glenn Towner and Robert Goodrich went into the woods on Snow King Mountain to check out a lean-to built by a friend of theirs. After hearing moaning and growling, the pair was chased out of the woods by a 12-foot-tall creature covered in hair. The creature followed them back to civilization, where it was last spotted standing briefly beneath a streetlight before vanishing back into the woods.

Crescent City, California (1995)

A TV crew was driving in their RV, filming the scenery in Jedediah Smith Redwoods State Park, when an eight-foot-tall hairy giant crossed their path and was caught on tape.

Cotton Island, Louisiana (2000)

Bigfoot surprised lumberjacks Earl Whitstine and Carl Dubois while they were clearing timber. The hairy figure returned a few days later, leaving behind footprints and hair samples.

Selma, Oregon (2000)

While hiking with his family near the Oregon Caves National Monument on July 1, 2001, psychologist Matthew Johnson smelled a strange musky odor. Hearing odd grunting noises coming from behind some trees, Johnson went to investigate and saw something very tall and hairy walking away. When asked to describe it, Johnson said that it could be "nothing else but a Sasquatch."

Granton, Wisconsin (2000)

As James Hughes was delivering newspapers early one morning, he saw a shaggy figure, about eight feet tall, carrying a goat. However, sheriffs called to the scene couldn't find any footprints or missing goats.

Mt. St. Helens, Washington (2002)

Jerry Kelso made his wife and two-year-old child wait in the car, while he chased what he thought was a man in a gorilla suit. When he was about 100 feet away, he realized that it wasn't a gorilla suit and that the seven-foot-tall creature was carrying a club.

Liberty Country, Florida (2013)

On his way to the town of Bristol, a motorist saw a bipedal creature covered with black hair on the road.

Monster on the Chesapeake

Scotland has the famous Loch Ness Monster, but Nessie isn't the only sea monster lurking in the deeps. People who live on America's East Coast may be surprised to know that there's reportedly one close to home.

✳ ✳ ✳ ✳

CHESAPEAKE BAY, A 200-mile intrusion of the Atlantic Ocean into Virginia and Maryland, is 12 miles wide at its mouth, allowing plenty of room for strange saltwater creatures to slither on in. Encounters with giant, serpentine beasts up and down the Eastern seaboard were reported during the 1800s, but sightings of Chessie, a huge, snakelike creature with a football-shape head and flippers began to escalate in the 1960s. Former CIA employee Donald Kyker and some neighbors saw not one, but four unidentified water creatures swimming near shore in 1978.

Then, in 1980, the creature was spotted just off Love Point, sparking a media frenzy. Two years later, Maryland resident Robert Frew was entertaining dinner guests with his wife, Karen, when the whole party noticed a giant water creature about 200 yards from shore swimming toward a group of people frolicking nearby in the surf. They watched the creature, which they estimated to be about 30 feet in length, as it dove underneath the unsuspecting humans, emerged on the other side, and swam away.

Frew recorded several minutes of the creature's antics, and the Smithsonian Museum of Natural History reviewed his film. Although they could not identify the animal, they did concede that it was "animate," or living.

The Chessie Challenge

Some believe Chessie is a manatee, but they usually swim in much warmer waters and are only about ten feet long. Also, the fact that Chessie is often seen with several "humps" breaking the water behind its head leads other investigators to conclude that it could be either a giant sea snake or a large seal.

One Maryland resident has compiled a list of 78 different sightings over the years. And a tour boat operator offers sea-monster tours in hopes of repeating the events of 1980 when 25 passengers on several charter boats all spotted Chessie cavorting in the waves.

Phantom Ships and Ghostly Crews

Ghost ships come in a variety of shapes and sizes, but they all seem to have the ability to slip back and forth between the watery veil of this world and the next, often making appearances that foretell of impending doom. Come with us now as we set sail in search of the most famous ghost ships in maritime history.

❋ ❋ ❋ ❋

The *Palatine*

ACCORDING TO LEGEND, shortly after Christmas 1738, the *Princess Augusta* ran aground and broke into pieces off the coast of Block Island, Rhode Island. Roughly 130 years later, poet John Greenleaf Whittier renamed the European vessel and told his version of the shipwreck in his poem *The Palatine*, which was published in the *Atlantic Monthly*. Today, strange lights, said to be the fiery ghost ship, are still reported in the waters surrounding Block Island, especially on the Saturday between Christmas and New Year's Day.

Mary Celeste

The Amazon was cursed from the beginning. During her maiden voyage, the *Amazon*'s captain died. After being salvaged by an American company that renamed her the *Mary Celeste*, the ship left New York on November 7, 1872, bound for Genoa, Italy. Onboard were Captain Benjamin Briggs, his family, and a crew of seven.

Nearly a month later, on December 4, the crew of another ship, the *Dei Gratia*, found the abandoned ship. There was plenty of food and water onboard the *Mary Celeste*, but the only living soul on the ship was a cat. The crew and the captain's family were missing, and no clues remained as to where they went. The last entry in the captain's logbook was dated almost two weeks prior to the ship's discovery, meaning it had somehow piloted itself all that time.

To this day, the fate of the members of the *Mary Celeste* remains unknown, as does how the ship piloted its way across the ocean non-crewed for weeks. Many believe it was piloted by a ghostly crew that kept it safe until it was found.

Iron Mountain

A ship disappearing on the high seas is one thing, but on a river? That's exactly what happened to the *Iron Mountain*. In June 1872, the 180-foot-long ship left New Orleans heading for Pittsburgh via the Mississippi River with a crew of more than 50 men. A day after picking up additional cargo, which was towed behind the ship in barges, the *Iron Mountain* steamed its way north and promptly vanished. Later that day, the barges were recovered floating in the river, but the *Iron Mountain* and its entire crew were never seen nor heard from again. For years after it disappeared, ship captains would whisper to each other about how the *Iron Mountain* was simply sucked up into another dimension through a ghostly portal.

Edmund Fitzgerald

When it comes to ghost ships, the *Edmund Fitzgerald* is the biggest—literally. At more than 720 feet long, the freighter shuttled iron ore across the Great Lakes beginning in the late 1950s. On November 9, 1975, Captain Ernest M. McSorley and his crew pulled the *Edmund Fitzgerald* out of dock at Superior, Wisconsin, with a load of iron ore to be delivered to a steel mill near Detroit. The following day, "The Fitz" sank during a violent storm without ever issuing a distress signal. All 29 members of the crew were presumed dead, but their bodies were never found.

Almost ten years to the day after it sank, a strange, dark ship was seen riding along the waves of Lake Superior. One look at the monstrous ship was all witnesses needed to recognize it as the *Edmund Fitzgerald*.

Flying Dutchman

Easily the world's most famous ghost ship, the *Flying Dutchman* has a story that's legendary. Stories say that during the 1800s, a Dutch ship captained by Hendrick Vanderdecken was attempting to sail around the Cape of Good Hope when a violent storm came up. Rather than pull into port, the *Dutchman's* stubborn captain claimed he would navigate around the Cape even if it took him all of eternity to do so. The ship and all of the crew were lost in the storm, and as foreshadowed by Vanderdecken, they were, indeed, condemned to sail the high seas for all eternity.

Almost immediately, people from all over the world began spotting the Dutch ship moving through the ocean, often cast in an eerie glow. Because of the legend associated with Captain Vanderdecken, sightings of the *Flying Dutchman* are thought to be signs of bad things to come. Case in point: The most recent sighting of the vessel occurred off the coast of North Carolina's Outer Banks prior to Hurricane Isabel in 2003.

Time Travelers

Hold on to your hat—you're in for a wild, mind-blowing ride back and forth through the realms of time!

* * * *

IN 2013, MANY people didn't believe President Obama when he claimed that he often fired guns on the skeet shooting range at Camp David. But others believed that Obama had actually come close to revealing the "real" truth: that he has been working for the CIA for more than 30 years, and that he had personally used the CIA's top secret "jump room" to visit Mars on several occasions as a young man.

This is probably not the wildest conspiracy theory about a president that's ever circulated, but it's certainly in the top tier.

A Witness to Events?

However, there's at least one witness who claims to have known the future president in his Mars-hopping days: a Seattle attorney named Andrew Basiago, who also only claims to have been to Mars himself as an Earth ambassador to a Martian civilization in the early 1980s.

But by then, Basiago says, he was an old hand with the CIA: some years before, when he was only 12, he was a participant in a top secret initiative called "Project Pegasus," an elite force that used "radiant energy" principles discovered in the papers of inventor Nikola Tesla to travel through time.

Basiago claims that he traveled through time using eight different technologies as a boy, but mainly using a teleporter that consisted of two "elliptical booms" that stood eight feet tall, positioned about ten feet apart and separated by a curtain of "radiant energy." Participants would jump through the curtain and enter a "vortal tunnel" that took them through time and space. By jumping though, Basiago claims to have attended Ford's Theatre on the night Abraham Lincoln was shot more than once—often enough that on a few occasions, he saw himself, on other trips, among the crowd. Oddly, though this would imply that each "jump" took him to the same "timeline," he says that every time he attended the theatre, the events of the night came off slightly differently, as though he were going to different "timelines" on each trip.

But Lincoln's assassination wasn't the only historic event Basiago claims to have attended. In 1972, he says, he used a "plasma confinement chamber" in East Hanover, New Jersey, to travel back to 1863 to see the Gettysburg Address. Basiago even claims that photographic evidence of this exists; In the foreground of the one photograph of Lincoln at Gettysburg that exists stands a young boy in oversized men's clothes, standing casually outside of the crowd in the background. Basiago says that the boy is him.

Information From the Future?

Basiago told his story over the course of several appearances on Coast to Coast AM, a radio program where conspiracies, UFOs, hauntings and other strange phenomena are discussed during late night broadcasts. The online forums on which listeners discuss the topics spoken about on the show once brought forth the story of another alleged time traveler: the story of John Titor, who began posting on the forum in 2000 and claimed to be a time traveler from 2036. Physicists tried to drill him on the mathematics and theories behind time travel, and he seemed to pass every test.

Titor claimed that he was a soldier based in Tampa who was visiting year 2000 for personal reasons—perhaps to collect old family photos that had been destroyed by his time. He even posted schematics showing the devices he used to travel in time, and many people at the time became convinced that he was telling the truth.

However, the stories he told about the future of the United States failed to come to pass. In 2001, he claimed that unrest in America surrounding the 2004 presidential election would gradually build up until it became a full-on Civil War, broadly defined as a war between urban and rural parts of the country, eventually splitting the United States into five regions. In 2011, he claimed, he was a young teenage soldier for a group called The Fighting Diamondbacks fighting for the rural armies. But the war, he said, would end in 2015 when Russia launched a nuclear assault destroying most American cities, killing as many as half of the people in the country and creating a "new" America in which Omaha, Nebraska served as the nation's capital. Titor said there was an upside to this: in many ways, he said, the world was better with half of the people gone.

Titor's odd story found a lot of supporters when it was first posted, and the events of September 11, 2001 convinced many people that World War III was, in fact, at hand. However, the 2004 election came and went without anything happening in the United States that could ever reasonably be called a civil war breaking out. There was still no such war going in 2008, either, by which time Titor claimed that the war would be fully raging and undeniable.

Not All Trips Are Planned

Fans of Coast to Coast AM are certainly not the only people who claim to have traveled through time, though, and some of the supposed time travelers have far more bona fide military credentials than Titor, who eventually disappeared from the forums. In 1935, Sir Victor Goddard, an air marshall in the Royal Air Force, claimed that he flew into a strange storm while flying his plane above an airfield in Scotland. The turbulence was so bad that he nearly crashed, and he emerged from the storm to find that the landscape beneath him now contained strange-looking aircraft in hangars that weren't there before, all attended by officers wearing blue uniforms instead of the brown ones the RAF normally used. Four years later, the RAF officially changed the uniforms from brown to blue and began using planes like the ones he had seen after the "storm."

This wasn't Goddard's only brush with the unknown. A decade later, he overheard an officer telling of a dream he'd had in which Air Marshall Goddard had died in a wreck when the plane he was flying in iced over and crashed on a beach. That night, Goddard's plane did, indeed, ice over, and an emergency landing was forced on a beach. Though the dream had ended with Goddard dead, Goddard, having had a sort of early warning, kept his cool and brought the plane safely down. The dream he overheard may very well have saved his life.

A Condemned Man Leaves His Mark

Does the ghostly handprint of a coal miner convicted of and executed for murder still proclaim his innocence?

✳ ✳ ✳ ✳

IN 1877, CARBON County Prison inmate Alexander Campbell spent long, agonizing days awaiting sentencing. Campbell, a coal miner from northeastern Pennsylvania, had been charged with the murder of mine superintendent John P. Jones. Authorities believed that Campbell was part of the Molly Maguires labor group, a secret organization looking to even the score with mine owners. Although evidence shows that he was indeed part of the Mollies, and he admitted that he'd been present at the murder scene, Campbell professed his innocence and swore repeatedly that he was not the shooter.

The Sentence

Convicted largely on evidence collected by James McParlan, a Pinkerton detective hired by mine owners to infiltrate the underground labor union, Campbell was sentenced to hang. When the prisoner's day of reckoning arrived, he rubbed his hand on his sooty cell floor then slapped it on the wall proclaiming, "I am innocent, and let this be my testimony!" With that statement, Alexander Campbell was unceremoniously dragged from cell number 17 and committed, whether rightly or wrongly, to eternity.

The Hand of Fate

The Carbon County Prison of present-day is not too different from the torture chamber that it was back in Campbell's day. Although it is now a museum, the jail still imparts the horrors of man's inhumanity to man. Visitors move through its claustrophobically small cells and dank dungeon rooms with mouths agape. When they reach cell number 17, many visitors feel a cold chill rise up their spine, as they notice that Alexander Campbell's handprint is still there!

"There's no logical explanation for it," says James Starrs, a forensic scientist from George Washington University who investigated the mark. Starrs is not the first to scratch his head in disbelief. In 1930, a local sheriff aimed to rid the jail of its ominous mark. He had the wall torn down and replaced with a new one. But when he awoke the following morning and stepped into the cell, the handprint had reappeared on the newly constructed wall! Many years later Sheriff Charles Neast took his best shot at the wall, this time with green latex paint. The mark inexplicably returned. Was Campbell truly innocent as his ghostly handprint seems to suggest? No one can say with certainty, but the legend lives on.

Snakes Alive!

Residents of the town of Peninsula reported seeing a giant snake in several different places over a series of months in 1944. But was the "Peninsula Python" a real-life monster or just a hoax?

✳ ✳ ✳ ✳

GIANT SNAKES ARE no fantasy. Pythons ten feet or more in length are commonly found in South America. Closer to home, South Florida is seeing more than its share of sensationally large serpents as owners cast unwanted pets into the wild.

Unlike Florida, Ohio isn't famous for its weird flora and fauna. However, one of the state's most enduring legends is the so-called "Peninsula Python," a snake of frightening proportions that terrorized the town of Peninsula in the mid-1940s, and whose offspring, some believe, still inhabit the region's forests and marshes.

No Ordinary Snake

The Peninsula Python first made headlines in June 1944, when a farmer named Clarence Mitchell reported seeing it slithering across his cornfield. According to Mitchell, what he witnessed was no ordinary corn snake—it was at least 18 feet long, and so big around that its trail was the width of a tire track.

Two days later, the snake appeared again, this time leaving its huge track across Paul and John Szalay's fields. Two days after that, Mrs. Roy Vaughn called the fire department to report that some sort of giant reptile had climbed a fence, entered her henhouse, and devoured one of her chickens.

By then, the residents of Ohio had accepted the snake as real, and both the Cleveland and Columbus zoos offered a reward for its live capture. To calm fears, the Peninsula mayor's office formed a posse to hunt down the snake and bring it in—dead or alive.

Python Fever

Because giant pythons aren't indigenous to Ohio, people speculated as to where the snake may have come from. The most popular theory was that it had escaped from a crashed carnival truck, a common explanation for unusual animal sightings.

The town of Peninsula quickly became "snake happy" as sightings of the Peninsula Python continued. On June 25, sirens alerted the posse to a sighting near Kelly Hill, but after searching through the prickly brush for a while, they were told it was a false alarm. Then, on June 27, Mrs. Pauline Hopko told authorities that the giant snake had leaped from a willow tree, frightening her, her dogs, and her milk cows, which broke their harnesses and hightailed it for fields afar. On the same day, a group of boys playing also reported seeing the snake.

Sightings became almost commonplace over the next few days. Mrs. Ralph Griffin said the snake reared up in the middle of her backyard, and Mrs. Katherine Boroutick alleged the behemoth fell from her butternut tree while she was getting rid of some trash down by the river. But every time the mayor's posse arrived at the scene of a reported sighting, the snake was nowhere to be found.

Myth or Real Creature?

The Peninsula Python continued to terrorize the residents of Peninsula through the summer and into the fall, when reports suddenly ceased. It was assumed that the bitter Ohio winter ultimately did the snake in, but no evidence of its remains was ever discovered.

Was the Python real? Many residents believe so, but others suspect that the whole thing was just a hoax perpetrated by writer Robert Bordner, a local resident whose account of the snake's mysterious appearance was published in the November 1945 issue of the *Atlantic Monthly*.

Regardless, the town of Peninsula has heartily embraced the snake, and now celebrates the legend with an annual Peninsula Python Day. The celebration includes food, fun, and festivities such as a Python Scavenger Hunt, face painting, and a display of live snakes from the Akron Zoo—all of normal size.

Guest Ghosts Are the Norm at Austin's Driskill Hotel

Southern hospitality abounds at the Driskill Hotel in downtown Austin, Texas. Built in 1886 by local cattle baron Colonel Jesse Lincoln Driskill, this lodging is hardly short on amenities. As a member of Historic Hotels of America and Associated Luxury Hotels International, the Driskill offers every comfort imaginable: From fancy linens to complimentary shoeshines, this Austin institution has it all—including a few resident ghosts.

Since it opened, the Driskill has been a magnet for the rich and famous: Lyndon and Lady Bird Johnson had their first date at the hotel's restaurant, and Amelia Earhart, Louis Armstrong, and Richard Nixon have all sought respite there. The upscale clientele mixes with the invisible guests that reside there full-time.

✳ ✳ ✳ ✳

Meet the Ghosts

CONSIDERED ONE OF the most haunted hotels in the United States, the Driskill is the eternal home of many spirits. First and foremost would have to be the ghost of Colonel Driskill himself. He makes his presence known by entering random guest rooms and smoking the cigars that he once loved so dearly. Driskill is also said to play with the lights in bathrooms, turning them on and off for fun.

Hotel guests and employees have seen water faucets turn on and off by themselves; some have even reported hearing the sound of noisy guests coming from an empty elevator. Others have felt as if they were being pushed out of bed, and some wake in the morning to find that their room's furniture has been rearranged during the night.

When singer Annie Lennox stayed at the Driskill Hotel in the 1980s while performing in Austin, she laid out two dresses to consider after she got out of the shower. When she emerged from the bathroom, only one dress was still on the bed; the other was once again hanging in the closet.

A ghost dressed in Victorian-era clothing has been seen at night where the front desk used to stand, and guests have detected the scent of roses in the area. This is believed to be the spirit of Mrs. Bridges, who worked at the Driskill as a front-desk clerk in the early 1900s.

The spirit of a young girl haunts the lobby on the first floor; she is believed to have been the daughter of a senator. In 1887, she was chasing a ball on the grand staircase when she tripped and fell to her death. Today, her ghost is often heard laughing and bouncing a ball up and down those same stairs.

The spirit of Peter J. Lawless might still be residing in Room 419, where he lived from 1886 until 1916 or 1917. Although the housekeeping crew cleans and vacuums that room like all the others, they often report finding rumpled bedclothes, open dresser drawers, and footprints in the bathroom—after they've already cleaned the room. Lawless is typically blamed for this mischievous behavior, and his specter is also often spotted near the elevators on the fifth floor. He pauses to check his watch when the doors open, then promptly disappears.

In the Spirit of Things

A modern ghost that hangs around the Driskill is the "Houston Bride." When her fiancé called off their wedding plans in the 1990s, the young woman did what many other jilted brides would be tempted to do: She stole his credit cards and went shopping! She was last seen on the hotel elevator, loaded down with her packages. She was found dead a few days later, the victim of a gunshot wound. Some guests have seen her apparition with her arms full of packages; others have spotted her in her wedding gown. It seems to be those guests who are at the hotel for weddings or bachelorette parties that are most likely to see her. Oddly, some brides even consider it good luck to see the "Houston Bride." Maybe she's their "something blue."

Haunted eBay

Many people drive hours to reach haunted destinations, but a new trend might save you some gas money: bringing the ghost into your own home instead! All you need is a computer, the money, and some luck when it comes to bidding.

✳ ✳ ✳ ✳

Since the early days of eBay, people have offered all sorts of "haunted" items for sale on the online auction site, and some of the objects have sold for thousands of dollars. These days, eBay even offers a Guide to Buying Haunted Items on its website. So what sorts of haunted objects can be found on eBay? Read on to find out.

Haunted Cane

After Mary Anderson's father passed away in 2004, her five-year-old son was convinced that his ghost was haunting the house. Specifically, the boy felt that it had taken up residence in an old cane. In an effort to convince her son that the spirit was gone, Anderson put the "haunted" cane up for sale on eBay. Following a bidding war that resulted in 132 bids, website GoldenPalace.com shelled out a mind-boggling $65,000 for the haunted cane, making it the most expensive haunted item sold on eBay to date.

Haunted iPhone

In 2008, people lined up for the chance to buy their very own iPhone, and it was at around this same time that someone offered up a haunted iPhone on eBay. Not only did this iPhone act strangely and make odd noises (like laughing out loud), but the ghostly image of what appeared to be Apple founder Steve Jobs (who was still very much alive then) also seemed to be "burned" onto the iPhone's screen. With a starting price of more than $8 million, the haunted iPhone seemed unlikely to sell. Several days after it was posted, the auction was taken down without receiving a single bid.

Ghost in a Bottle

"Supernatural or novelty? You decide!" That was the tagline for the Ghost in a Bottle when it appeared on eBay in 2008 for $20 a pop. The seller wouldn't guarantee what would happen if a customer decided to open one of these bottles and release the ghost inside, but that didn't stop people from buying them. The creator of the "original" Ghost in a Bottle no longer sells them on eBay, but similar items occasionally go up for auction starting at around $29.

Spooky Dolls A-Plenty

By far, the most popular "haunted" items on eBay are dolls. On any given day, hundreds of listings promise to deliver a haunted doll to your door. Most haunted dolls sell for around $25, but some go for $100 or more, especially if they look very creepy.

Human Soul

Some people believe that ghosts are the restless souls of the deceased. Perhaps that's why there was so much interest when college student Adam Burtle put his soul up for auction in 2001. Believe it or not, eBay policy dictates that souls fall under the site's "no body parts" policy, so it traditionally shuts down such auctions. However, this one slipped through. Burtle's ex-girlfriend bid $6.66, and it appeared that she might win the auction, but then a bidding war erupted in the final hour of the sale. When the dust settled, the soul sold for $400 to an anonymous bidder from Des Moines, Iowa. As of this writing, the winner has yet to try and collect her prize. As for Burtle, eBay suspended his account.

Haunted Antique Hat Pin

The seller of an antique hat pin claimed to be a paranormal researcher with more than 45 years of experience. The pin was supposedly found inside a secret room of a haunted mansion. The seller stated that he'd seen a "blue, glowing streak that swirls" around the item. It also purportedly moved on its own, including "spinning wildly." The auction's sole bidder paid $15.

14 Mythical Creatures

1. **Basilisk:** a serpent, lizard, or dragon said to kill by breathing on or looking at its victims

2. **Centaur:** half human, half horse

3. **Cerberus:** a dog with many heads that guards the entrance to the underworld

4. **Chimera:** part serpent, lion, and goat

5. **Faun:** half man, half goat

6. **Gorgons:** winged and snake-haired sisters

7. **Griffin:** half eagle, half lion

8. **Harpy:** a creature with the head of a woman and the body, wings, and claws of a bird

9. **Hippocampus:** a creature with the tail of a dolphin and the head and forequarters of a horse

10. **Hippogriff:** a creature with the wings, head, and claws of a griffin but the hindquarters of a horse

11. **Pegasus:** a winged horse with the ability to fly

12. **Siren:** half bird, half woman

13. **Unicorn:** a horse with a horn

14. **Wyvern:** a winged dragon with a serpent's tail